BACK FROM THE BRINK:
The Greenspan Years

STEVEN K. BECKNER

John Wiley & Sons, Inc.

New York • Chichester • Brisbane • Toronto • Singapore • Weinheim

This text is printed on acid-free paper.

Copyright © 1996 by Steven K. Beckner.
Published by John Wiley & Sons, Inc.

All rights reserved. Published simultaneously in Canada.

This publication is designed to provide accurate and authoritative information in regard to the subject matter covered. It is sold with the understanding that the publisher is not engaged in rendering legal, accounting, or other professional services. If legal advice or other expert assistance is required, the services of a competent professional person should be sought.

Library of Congress Cataloging in Publication Data:
Beckner, Steven K., 1951–
    Back from the brink : the Greenspan years / by Steven K. Beckner.
        p.   cm.
    Includes index.
    ISBN 0-471-16127-6 (cloth : alk. paper)
        1. Greenspan, Alan, 1926–   .   2. Government economists—United
    States—Biography.   3. Board of Governors of the Federal Reserve
    System (U.S.).   4. Monetary policy—United States.   I. Title.
    HB119.G74B43   1997
    332.1'1'092—dc20
    [B]   96-36171

Printed in the United States of America

10 9 8 7 6 5 4 3 2 1

Lovingly dedicated to my wife Janice,
and my four children,
Erica, Stefanie, Douglas, and Craig

Contents

Preface

My first encounter with Alan Greenspan was literary, not personal. I had come to Virginia's Bridgewater College as a freshman in 1969 with a mild interest in economics and public policy (my first love being theater). In an effort to further my education beyond the classroom, a favorite uncle provided me with a list of suggested readings, one of which was an anthology of essays by Ayn Rand and her associates. I was soon immersed and found myself particularly intrigued by the writings of a young economist by the name of Greenspan, who propounded the virtues of laissez-faire economics and the gold standard. I could not have imagined that this radical libertarian would someday become the most accomplished central banker in history and, indeed, one of the most powerful men in the world. Nor could I have imagined I would someday get to know him and write a book about his reign as chairman of the Federal Reserve system.

Greenspan's essays, written a few years earlier, piqued my interest in economics, particularly monetary policy. After flirting with acting, I decided my real interest lay in studying the interaction of government and the marketplace. Ultimately, after soaking up all the economics I could, first at Bridgewater and then at Duke University, I decided I would starve to death a little more slowly if I traded applause for a byline and bumbled my way into journalism. After working for a couple of daily newspapers in Virginia, I moved to Washington in the fall of 1975. It wasn't long before I crossed paths with Greenspan, who, to my surprise, had become a rising star in the Ford administration. I followed Greenspan's career as chairman of the Council of Economic Advisors and later talked to him from time to time when he had returned to the private sector as an economic consultant.

While Greenspan was analyzing and commenting on the economy in New York City in the late seventies, the Fed was going through some dark years, battling double-digit inflation and a near collapse of the U.S. dollar in world currency markets. A literally towering figure named Paul Volcker came to the rescue, quashing inflation and restoring confidence in the U.S. currency. For those of us who covered Volcker, it was difficult to imagine anyone else as Fed chairman. Then, suddenly, the reins were turned over to Greenspan. No one knew quite what to expect from this long-time Republican Party activist.

Shortly after he had assumed the chairmanship in August 1987, the Fed arranged a reception in its ornate boardroom so reporters could meet the new headman. Somewhat sheepishly, I told him I had once been inspired by his essays. "That was a long time ago," he replied wistfully. Later, he told me he was glad somebody had gotten something out of his writings.

A lot has changed since I first read Greenspan's monographs. The federal government has grown bigger, more intrusive, and, of course, more expensive, making the task of the Federal Reserve much more complicated than it was in the sixties. Though still a libertarian at heart, who believes along with Thomas Jefferson that "that government is best which governs least," he has reluctantly learned to live with a larger government role. He has become more of a mainstream conservative who would settle for something short of pure laissez-faire if only the government would trim its sails. After 21 years in Washington, I have become less idealistic about what can be expected from our politicians and the huge bureaucracy they have empowered. However, one thing that has changed for the better is the respect that I and many others have developed for the Federal Reserve system—that darkly mysterious, vaguely conspiratorial, and not-always-successful institution created in 1913, the same year the income tax was instituted. That automatically made it suspect to many people, and they were in good company. Since the days of Andrew Jackson, Americans have distrusted central banks and their paper money machinations. In 1978, I wrote a book premised on the then widely held belief that double-digit inflation would continue and worsen. I was dead wrong, as were a lot of other people who just could not believe the Fed would summon up the guts to defeat inflation or that, if it did, Congress and the White House would stand still for it. Yet, that is just what the Fed has done, first under Volcker, then under Greenspan. To use the vernacular, who would've thunk it?

The fruit of the Fed's long and harrowing battle is the environment of low inflation, low interest rates, and low unemployment we have today. The fact that conventional mortgage rates have fallen to around 7 percent, compared to more than 16½ percent in 1981, is a tribute to the credibility the Fed has earned. What makes it all the more amazing is that it was accomplished in spite of massive federal budget deficits. The Fed is often criticized by politicians for holding down economic growth. They should be asked instead how conducive to growth their own taxing, spending, and regulatory policies are. The Greenspan Fed's policies have not been flawless, as the reader will discover in the following pages. However, he has compiled a remarkable record considering the obstacle course he had to run. Two months after taking office, Greenspan had to cope with a stock market crash that exceeded the ferocity of 1929. And as terrifying as that was, it was easy lifting compared to the unprecedented debt burdens, the burgeoning budget and trade deficits, the banking problems, the tumultuous shake-up of the corporate sector, the wild swings in exchange rates, the severe credit crunch, and other crises with which he next had to grapple. The title of this book suggests just how bad it might have been if Greenspan and his crew had made different decisions on this and other occasions. Yet the Fed remains largely unappreciated.

The Greenspan years, 1987 through the present, have probably been the most difficult time to make monetary policy in the Fed's 83-year history. But the story of how the Fed got the United States successfully through this period has never been fully told. Upon returning from vacation in the summer of 1995, I was sifting through the enormous piles of clips and documents that usually obscure my desk in Market News Service's bureau in the National Press Building and straightening up my voluminous files. Just thinking out loud, I told my bureau chief, Denny Gulino, "You know, I ought to write a book on the Fed." Offhandedly, he responded, "Why don't you?" "Maybe I will," I replied. Denny probably kicked himself for his suggestion later, for it wasn't long before I had tackled the project with fervor, which meant our financial wire service got less than my full attention. The truth is Denny has been very supportive of the labor of love that this book project became, as have my other Market News Service colleagues. The product you have before you is more than just a segment of monetary history. It is a fresh look at one of our most powerful institutions: its goals, its methods, and the vital role it has come to play. Having covered the Fed day by day, blow by blow for 21 years, the last 11 of them for Market News Service, I felt I owed it to myself and to the Fed to tell the story of the Greenspan years. People deserved to know just how close to the precipice they came during that period and how fortunate they were to have had a person of Greenspan's caliber running U.S. monetary policy. Reflecting on the Fed's successes of the eighties and nineties, Richmond Federal Reserve Bank president Alfred Broaddus says this country was just plain "lucky" to have had the right cast of characters at the Fed. One does not have to go too far back to find Fed chairmen who were clearly not up to the responsibility entrusted to them. Nor is it hard to imagine a future president appointing an unqualified political hack to head the central bank at some critical juncture. House Banking Committee chairman James Leach correctly argues a president's choice of nominees to the Federal Reserve Board should be treated with as much importance as those he appoints to the Supreme Court.

There was another reason for writing this book: Despite the fact that the Fed affects all of us, few people understand it, although there is a higher level of awareness than there once was. As full of arcana as it is, monetary policy has great impact on everyone from the most savvy bond trader to the average citizen. No one can afford to ignore the Fed, and the best way to learn about it is to study its recent history. If you are a financial professional, I hope you will gain a clearer understanding of the Fed's thinking and tactics and derive clues for anticipating policy shifts. If you're an average investor, I hope you will not only learn how the central bank works, but will emerge with a grasp of why interest-rate and exchange-rate changes occur which can have a dramatic impact on your finances. Hopefully, you will even learn how to read economic omens, forecast the likely Fed response, and adjust your finances accordingly.

Most important is the message this book is intended to convey to the average citizen. The issue of just how independent the central bank should be to pursue its monetary policy objectives free from political pressure is a perennial issue that will long outlast the Greenspan Fed. Concerned citizens must ask themselves whether future Fed chairmen, faced with the need to finance a massive national debt and the seemingly insatiable Washington appetite for deficit spending, will uphold Greenspan's anti-inflationary legacy, whether they will be able to resist the temptation and the pressures to debauch our currency. If this book has a philosophy, it is this: Commendable as the Fed's work has been, it is a very bad sign when our central bank has come to occupy a spot of such central importance, when the name Greenspan has become a household word. It should not be that way. Over the past decade and a half, it has been truly said monetary policy is "the only game in town," because fiscal policy (the taxing and spending habits of the federal government) has been completely out of control. We as a nation must get a grip on our finances and stop putting the onus on the Fed to manage our economy and stave off financial disaster—or financial disaster we shall surely have.

Steven K. Beckner

Acknowledgments

As you can imagine, this book is a result of countless interviews with policymakers and their advisers, but in a broader sense it has grown out of three decades of educational and career experiences and reflects many influences. Along the way, there have been innumerable people who have made both direct and indirect contributions to the production of this book. I hardly know where to begin.

I trace my interest in what used to be called political economics to my uncle, Dr. Phillip Stone, now president of Bridgewater College of Virginia. Going forward, I am grateful to Dr. William Yohe, the Duke University economics professor who sparked my interest in the Federal Reserve and monetary policy, and to the late Dr. Joseph Spengler, who awakened my interest in economic history at Duke.

One can hardly undertake a project of this scope and ambition without the support and encouragement of one's family. In this I have been fortunate. I am indebted to my wife Janice, who put up with me as I went through the agonizing process of writing this book out of my home office while continuing to feed the Market News Service financial wire and do spots for National Public Radio. Her parents Jean and Allen Stuhl were a great help as we concurrently endeavored to raise two small boys, Douglas and Craig, who must have wondered what on earth Daddy was doing all those months. My own mother and father instilled in me a strong work ethic and intellectual curiosity without which this book would never have been conceived or carried to completion.

I also could not have undertaken the project without the support of my colleagues at Market News Service. My bureau chief Denny Gulino, my managing editor Tony Mace, and the president of Market News Service Mike Connor both encouraged me and granted me the necessary flexibility in fulfilling my routine reportial duties to enable me to write the manuscript. Other Market News Service reporters, including budget reporter John Shaw and economic data czar David Sherrill, provided invaluable input. Nancy Proyect lent technical assistance. I would also like to recognize and pay high tribute to the creator and principal shareholder of Market News Service, Bob Jones, one of the pioneers of Fed watching, who has been a source of inspiration in my coverage of the Fed for years.

It was a pleasure working with my diligent and unfailingly cheerful agent Alice Martell, to whom I was steered by Lee Connor and Kathy Samon.

Thanks as well go to my editor at John Wiley & Sons, Jacque Urinyi, publisher Myles Thompson, his assistant Jennifer Pincott, and managing editor Michael Detweiler. My friend Dick Schmidt recommended that I publish my book with John Wiley & Sons, putting me in touch with its president Charles Ellis, and I am grateful for the introduction. Christina Palaia's copyediting was also indispensable. Others who provided aid and comfort included National Press Club librarian Barbara Vandegrift, authors James Srodes, Paul Dickson, and Michael Lewis, and literary agent Kristin Lindstrom.

I would also like to thank the many money market economists who provided helpful information and suggestions, including David Jones, Mickey Levy, Charles Lieberman, Maria Fiorini-Ramirez, Robert Brusca, and numerous others. One of my most admired academic economists, Professor Alan Meltzer of Carnegie-Mellon University, head of the Shadow Open Market Committee, stimulated me in my decision to go forward with this project.

I am grateful, above all, for the cooperation of Alan Greenspan, his fellow members of the Federal Reserve Board of Governors, and many other Federal Reserve policymakers, former policymakers, and Fed staffers. In particular I would like to thank Joe Coyne, the Fed's chief spokesman, and Peter Bakstansky, chief spokesman for the Federal Reserve Bank of New York, for their assistance.

Thanks, likewise, to officials and staffers at foreign central banks and finance ministries who helped in the research and writing of the book, notably including Manfred Koerber of the Deutsche Bundesbank and Juliette Healey of the Bank of England.

There were many members of the Reagan, Bush, and Clinton administrations, most of whom cannot be named, who contributed material from the political side of the sometimes adversarial relationship between the Fed and the White House/Treasury Department. Likewise, my thanks to those at the House and Senate Banking Committees and others on Capitol Hill for their unique perspective on the Fed.

Those I interviewed are far too numerous to mention, and many cannot be identified. I thank them all and hope that I have faithfully and fairly rendered their comments.

Introduction

A Nightmare That Almost Happened. . . .

When the stock market crashed on October 19, 1987, it was just the beginning of America's long slide into chaos.

When the Dow Jones Industrial Average plunged 508.32 points that day, after having fallen more than 235 points the previous week, panic ensued both on Wall Street and in Washington. No one seemed to know what to do, and so nothing effective was done. The collapse of share values spilled over into the financial system generally, causing massive bank failures, the bankruptcy of the major securities houses, and a flood of misery that swept inexorably across the nation and the world. It wasn't just stock investors who suffered, of course. The meltdown of the interdependent financial system meant that the credit which had lubricated the gears of commerce stopped flowing. Soon companies were announcing massive layoffs with no prospect for rehiring. Average Americans lost their savings, their homes, and, in many cases, their lives. Riots broke out in many cities, as desperate citizens fought over dwindling supplies of food and fuel. In Los Angeles, among other places, armed gangs descended on more prosperous neighborhoods. In some places the anarchy took on an ugly racial tinge, and there was much bloodshed.

It was the Great Depression all over again—only worse.

The United States had been a more cohesive nation in the 1930s. It was the rare family that wasn't together then. Churches, synagogues, and other institutions held greater sway. People had more confidence in a government that had yet to abuse their trust and waste their tax dollars. Even though the civil rights movement was years in the future, the races were on better terms. What's more, we were a more rural nation, and a greater proportion of the population was self-sufficient. This time around, things really came unglued—and not just in the United States. Because of the expansion of international trade and the accompanying globalization of money markets that had taken place, the whole world sank into depression, despair—depravity. This sort of thing wasn't supposed to happen again. After all, hadn't the federal government promised us that the Federal Deposit Insurance Corporation (FDIC) and other "safety net" features made such debacles impossible?

It's hard to say just how it all got started and got out of control. Oh, everyone knew that a stock market correction was overdue. Since the start of 1987, the Dow Jones Industrial Average had broken through the 2000 barrier for the first time and soared nearly 45 percent to an all-time high of 2746.65 on August 25—on top of the 122 percent surge the Dow had enjoyed in the previous five years. Share prices had gotten wildly overpriced relative to earnings. Risky stock investments made increasingly less sense as rising interest rates made things like bank certificates of deposit and U.S. Treasury securities more attractive. Plus, there was all that international squabbling over the weak dollar and concern that the Federal Reserve was going to have to jack interest rates sky high to protect it. Overhanging it all was a huge burden of debt. But few of the experts thought the correction would turn into catastrophe that Monday—that "Black Monday." Like the ominous approach of a distant tidal wave, the cascade of selling began in Tokyo and rolled on through London trading hours before hitting the stock exchanges of New York and the stock index futures pits of Chicago full force. Individuals and institutions rushed to liquidate their holdings at any price, and traders could barely keep up. Yet, for all of the unprecedented stock selling, which was putting tremendous strain on the ability of firms and exchanges to clear and settle transactions, there was realistic hope that the damage could be confined to Wall Street. After all, if Treasury secretary James Baker could be believed, the economy was "fundamentally sound." Surely cooler heads would prevail and keep the contagion of fear from spreading to the larger financial system.

It was not to be.

People are still arguing over what triggered the larger calamity. Maybe the trigger was pulled Tuesday morning, when David Ruder, chairman of the Securities and Exchange Commission (SEC), and New York Stock Exchange president John Phelan—panicked by the continuing avalanche on Wall Street—succeeded in convincing President Reagan to invoke his executive authority and close the stock market. That only accelerated the rush to unload stocks while there was still time. Or maybe it was when the president declared a bank holiday, which backfired by spurring the most violent bank runs in history, quickly exhausting the banking industry's supplies of ready cash.

But perhaps the most critical event, or nonevent, was the strange silence of "the Fed," as the late central bank was—not always affectionately—known. Market participants were clamoring for a statement of support from the Fed— some indication that it would play its "lender of last resort" role to the hilt and provide banks and brokers with ample credit. It was not forthcoming. Next, predictably enough in retrospect, came the refusal of a major New York bank to extend credit to securities firms. Unwilling to bear the risks alone, other banks followed suit, and soon banks were not only refusing to provide new credit but calling existing loans. The financial markets ran on credit and were underpinned by a highly sophisticated but vulnerable payments system designed to speedily debit and credit millions of accounts in thousands of banks soon after securities and other transactions took place. Even in normal times, to span the gap between the time an asset was sold and the time payment was received, securities firms depended on lines of credit from the commercial banks. Standing behind it all was the Fed. When the banks stopped lending, the entire system seized up, and the Fed did little to help, preferring instead to stick to its tight money stance, just as it had in 1929.

Disaster struck. Stock and bond transactions could not be cleared and settled. Margin calls went unmet. Defaults proliferated, as companies and investors awaiting payment could not, in turn, meet obligations to yet other parties. Like a nuclear chain reaction, the financial damage mushroomed explosively. One major securities firm after another closed its doors, and soon the bankruptcies spread into the larger corporate world. Whatever the cause, money and credit dried up and with it economic activity. The huge loss of stock values precipitated a collapse of values generally. The price of land, homes, everything dropped like a stone, but very few had the cash to take advantage of these "bargains." By the time the FDIC could seize shuttered banks and dole out freshly printed greenbacks to their insured depositors, the financial system had imploded. All those inflated paper values, all those book entries had evaporated, and a valueless American society couldn't cope.

In Washington, the government was reduced to muttering impotence, as the economy quickly disintegrated around it, while the politicians engaged in pathetic shouting matches. The Federal Reserve system itself was abolished in a fit of righteous populist fury. Democracy itself became imperilled, and a bellicose Texas billionaire went on national television offering to assume command. . . .

No, that's not what happened, of course. But it could have, and perhaps still could. Why didn't it? Because the Federal Reserve, under the new command of Alan Greenspan, did not let it happen.

Hard as it may be to believe in hindsight, when the long reign of Paul Volcker gave way to the era of Greenspan just two months before the crash, the financial markets and the Democratic Congress shuddered at the thought of President Reagan appointing a right-wing Republican to head the world's most powerful central bank. Now, the prospect of the Fed being led by anyone else sends shivers up Wall Street spines.

Greenspan gives Volcker tremendous credit for defusing what had been a very real threat of U.S. hyperinflation in the early years of his 1979–1987 tenure. When he arrived at the Fed in August of 1987, "the big job had been done." Volcker had confronted "a very dangerous situation" in which inflation was ratcheting ever higher in the late seventies, and he "did enough to break the back of inflation." When Volcker presented Greenspan with the Concord Coalition's Economic Patriot Award in New York City the night of November 2, 1995, Greenspan responded with a tribute to his predecessor. "I don't think there are many people who understand what Paul contributed to this country as much as I do. . . . The economy we see today is to a substantial extent a result of what Paul and his colleagues were able to do with that extraordinary inflationary acceleration, which, had it not been reined in, the issue we would be talking about today would not be the deficit, which is a relatively civilized concept, but we'd be talking about the stability of our society."

It would be hard to overstate the importance of what Greenspan was saying. At the double-digit rate that prices were rising in the late seventies, Americans' savings were being rapidly eaten away. As people lost trust in the purchasing power of paper money, a speculative, spendthrift instinct developed. Americans fled from traditional investments whose interest and dividends no longer kept up with inflation, and there were huge run-ups in the prices of precious metals, real estate, and other physical assets. At one point on January 31, 1979, inflation hysteria drove the price of gold as high as $875 an ounce—25 times its official price of just eight years earlier—and investment advisors were predicting prices of $3,000 per ounce. The international value and status of the dollar crumbled, and hot money flowed into the Swiss franc and other *hard currencies*. Only with great difficulty (and even greater optimism) could businesses and households make financial plans and investment decisions.

The roots of the inflation problem went back many years. When the dollar was placed at the center of the post–World War II Bretton Woods system, the U.S. currency was literally "good as gold." The dollar was officially backed by gold at $35 per ounce, and other currencies were linked to the dollar at fixed exchange rates. Foreign central banks could present excess dollar reserves to the U.S. Treasury in exchange for gold at the official price. But, while U.S. finances were relatively responsible by today's standards, the dollar's soundness began to erode, slowly and imperceptibly at first. Taking advantage of fixed exchange rates, more and more dollars were created, enabling the United States to buy up foreign goods and assets at, in effect, subsidized rates. By 1959, America's external dollar liabilities exceeded the official dollar value of its gold holdings for the first time. No one took much notice at the time. The United States was the most powerful country on earth, both economically and militarily, and there was a tremendous reservoir of confidence in the U.S. currency. But as the tumultuous 1960s wore on, more chinks in the dollar's golden armor began to appear. This was reflected in a rising market price for gold. France began presenting dollars and demanding gold at the official price from the U.S. Treasury. To keep the price from going above $35 per ounce, U.S. authorities persuaded other Western governments to join in a "gold pool," and during a five-month period in late 1966 and early 1967, the United States and its partners dumped millions of ounces of gold on the market to hold down its price. It was a futile effort, and as the gold pool collapsed, the U.S. government abolished the statutory gold backing of domestic banknotes.

The expansion of the supply of U.S. dollars and the dollar's proliferation throughout the world accelerated as the United States tried to fight a "War on Poverty" and the Vietnam War at the same time. In 1971, the United States officially ended the convertibility of foreign central banks' dollars into gold, simultaneously devaluing the dollar by raising the now-superfluous official gold price to $38 per ounce. Two years later, President Nixon declared the fixed exchange rate system a dead letter and set the dollar free to float to whatever level the currency markets determined. As the dollar depreciated, the OPEC oil cartel, spurred on by anger at U.S. aid to Israel, began a process of tripling the price of oil, reflecting the lower value of the dollars it was receiving for each barrel. The oil shocks of 1973 and 1979 hit the U.S. economy hard but need not have been inflationary if the Fed had not bowed to political pressure and inflated the money supply. Given a certain quantity of money and a certain quantity of goods, an increase in the price of one of those goods, to the extent that people are willing to pay the higher price, lessens the amount of money available to spend on other goods, so that the prices of other goods tend to fall. There need be no rise in prices overall. But allowing prices to adjust in this fashion can be a painful process, and the Fed increased the money supply to minimize the pain.

Under Arthur Burns, who chaired the Fed from 1970 to 1978, and under G. William Miller, who was chairman from January 1978 to August 1979, the Fed provided the monetary fuel for an inflation that began as a flicker and grew into a fearsome blaze. In fairness, the Fed had had very little experience with inflation. Prices had been relatively stable throughout the fifties and most of the sixties. Even in 1971, when Nixon imposed wage-price controls, inflation was a relatively mild 4.3 percent. There was little appreciation of how inflation could become ingrained in public and market psychology and begin to feed on itself as business and labor demanded ever higher prices and wages, and lenders and investors demanded ever higher interest rates in fear of escalating price increases. There was also a great deal of skepticism, not to say ignorance, on the part of many Fed officials about the key role of money. Some simply did not recognize that, over time, expansion of the money supply tends to push up prices and wages. Some viewed inflation as largely a result of demand and cost pressures. There was also a feeling among some officials that a little inflation could be a good thing, helping to lubricate the economy's gears and create jobs.

If Nixon appointee Burns lit the fire, Miller poured gasoline on it during the administration of President Jimmy Carter. Without question the most partisan and least respected chairman in the Fed's history, this former Textron executive worked in tandem with fellow Carter appointee, Treasury Secretary W. Michael Blumenthal, in pursuit of monetary policies that were expansionist domestically and devaluationist internationally. The goals were to spur employment and exports, with little thought to the dollar's value. By early 1980, inflation was running at 14 percent. Before the Carter administration announced a desperate dollar rescue plan in November 1978, which included emergency sales from the U.S. gold stock, borrowing from the International Monetary Fund (IMF), and auctions of Treasury securities denominated in foreign currencies, the dollar had fallen nearly 34 percent against the German mark and almost 42 percent against the Japanese yen in under two years. So determined was Miller to gun the economy's engine at all costs that he holds the dubious distinction of having been outvoted by his own Board of Governors when he tried to prevent a long overdue increase in the discount rate, at which the Fed lends to banks. Finally, in August 1979, Carter put Volcker in charge.

The autocratic Volcker gave the sick economy strong medicine. In a stunning announcement on Saturday, October 6, 1979, Volcker abandoned the Fed's policy of targeting the benchmark federal funds rate, at which banks borrow reserves from each other overnight. Henceforth the Fed would concentrate on controlling the explosive growth of bank reserves themselves. Instead of controlling the price of money, he would control its supply. The implication of this momentous change was that interest rates would be allowed to rise as high as supply and demand in the money market carried them as the Fed brought down the double-digit growth of money that was fueling the price spiral. Rise they did, to unheard of levels. The federal funds rate, which had been held below 6 percent in 1977 and below 8 percent in 1978, zoomed to more than 19 percent by early 1981. The prime rate charged by banks to their preferred customers soared to more than 21 percent. The dollar began a steep upward climb, while gold plummeted. So did economic activity. Inevitably, rooting out inflation from an economy in which it has become imbedded is disruptive. Consumers, businesses, as well as the government itself, had made many decisions in the expectation of never-ending price hikes. It was a rude shock to many when the Fed began altering those assumptions. Unemployment climbed as high as 10.7 percent in 1982, as the iron-willed Volcker Fed pounded inflation. The medicine worked. By 1986, inflation was less than two percent. Unfortunately, it did not stay down. Greenspan inherited an economy still infected with the inflation virus and suffering from a variety of other ailments.

Modestly, Greenspan says he "could scarcely argue that the kind of problem that I confronted when I came in here was of the order of magnitude that Volcker confronted. He had a real tough problem." But the truth is the Greenspan Fed faced many difficulties: reckless fiscal policies, which led to a breathtakingly costly expansion of government debt, accompanied by soaring corporate and household debt; a chronically weak dollar often encouraged by myopic Treasury policies; political pressure from both ends of Pennsylvania Avenue, including threats to its independence; the worst banking crisis since the 1930s; large-scale corporate restructurings and downsizings; military base closings; and the impact of the Persian Gulf War and related oil price shock. For what seemed like an interminable period, the economy went through a series of rolling recessions, with one sector or region after another taking its place in the doldrums. Recovery was beset by recurring bouts of weakness. At times the economy seemed impervious to efforts to stimulate it, mired as it was in a "credit crunch" caused by banks' inability or reluctance to lend and unwillingness to borrow. Dealing with it all was a tall order, and a misstep here or there could have proven disastrous. We will examine how a remarkable group of men and women tiptoed along the precipice and avoided losing their balance.

As this was written in early 1996, inflation had averaged 3 percent or less for five consecutive years. Long-term interest rates, the ones that most matter for the economy, had been brought to their lowest level in decades, and the unemployment rate was holding around 5½ percent, validating Greenspan's contention that price stability is the best, indeed only, foundation for sustainable prosperity. What makes this success all the more remarkable is that, until recently, the Fed has received little help from fiscal policy. As E. Gerald Corrigan, colorful former president of the New York Federal Reserve Bank, put it at an October 3, 1989, meeting of the Fed's policymaking Federal Open Market Committee (FOMC), "We have an absolutely lousy policy mix in this country." While the Fed fought for credibility against inflation, it had one hand tied behind its back because the government's budgetary practices were anything but credible. While the Fed worked to defeat inflationary expectations, Congress outstripped rising government revenues by authorizing even higher expenditures. In every year but one (the recession year of 1983), revenues rose dramatically—going from $517.1 billion in 1980 to $1.351 trillion in 1995. But spending went from $590.9 billion to $1.514 trillion, swelled by the soaring interest on the national debt. While revenues as a percent of gross domestic product (GDP) stayed relatively steady in the range of 18 to 19 percent throughout the period, outlays rose to 23.5 percent of GDP during the Bush years. Spending remains near 21 percent of GDP. Politicians have had the nerve to blame the Fed for the shortcomings of the economy while they perpetuated a fiscal nightmare. As credible as the Fed's commitment to maintaining the dollar's purchasing power may be, deficit spending foments fear in the minds of lenders and investors that someday the Fed will effectively default on the accumulated debt by monetizing it and inflating it away. Inevitably, they demand higher rates of return to compensate for this potential default risk. The Fed has had to battle these costly perceptions.

The Fed also had to battle perceptions that the U.S. Treasury wanted a weak dollar during much of the 1987 to 1996 period. Before the markets finally became convinced of the Fed's determination to protect its purchasing power, the dollar fell 26 percent against the German mark and 44 percent against the Japanese yen from August 1987 to its low point in the spring of 1995. While the dollar's depreciation was generally accepted (even cheered on) by both Republican and Democratic administrations, it ran counter to the Fed's effort to contain inflation. Politicians of both parties have preferred the lowest possible interest rates along with a "competitive" dollar to stimulate economic activity. While the politically independent Fed also wanted growth, it wanted to keep it within the economy's long-run, noninflationary potential. In raising interest rates to slow growth and contain inflation, the Fed has sometimes given the dollar more strength than the politicians desired. Policies and wills clashed, making for pyrotechnics between Fed and Treasury, as well as among the Group of Seven (G-7) industrial nations.

Fed officials regularly maintain they do not base monetary policy on exchange rates, but as former Assistant Treasury Secretary Charles Dallara says, "The Fed is pretty good about keeping half an eye on the exchange rate at just about all times. The notion that the Fed is a purist on these issues is simply, in my view, not a realistic description." The dollar has figured more importantly in monetary policy than the Fed is willing to admit. After all, as former Bank of Canada governor John Crow says, "An exchange rate is the ratio of monies, and central banks are about money." When the dollar *depreciates* (when it takes more dollars to buy a foreign currency unit) import prices tend to rise and push up domestic prices. A weaker dollar also makes U.S. products cheaper abroad (since foreign currencies will buy more dollars), tending to stimulate demand for U.S. exports. That's good, but if plants are operating near capacity, increased foreign demand can strain available productive resources of labor and capital and put upward pressure on wages and prices. Moreover, a falling dollar can undermine foreign investor confidence in dollar-denominated assets. That is something the United States can no longer afford. From 1980 through 1994, foreign holdings of U.S. securities rose more than 11-fold (19 percent per year), to the point that at the end of 1994, 22 percent of all Treasury securities outstanding were held by foreigners. When foreign investors lose confidence in the greenback, they bid up yields to cover the risk that they will be repaid in cheaper dollars. The result is that not just the government, but everyone, pays more to borrow. Ironically, inflationary policies and dollar depreciation lead to slower growth, not prosperity, but politicians during the Greenspan years seldom saw beyond the time horizon of the next election.

Traditionally, the United States' large internal market has made it less dependent on foreign trade and hence less concerned about exchange rates than, say, the United Kingdom. But this is changing. The Greenspan years have coincided with a great globalization of markets, forcing the Fed to become more attuned to international concerns. Exports and imports amounted to 22.8 percent of GDP at the end of 1994. The United States imports roughly half its oil, up from 20 percent in 1960, and in 1994, it imported 45 percent of producers' durable equipment, compared to 7 percent in 1970. Even in the United States, therefore, a weaker dollar can lead to imported inflation. With openness to trade has come exposure to fickle foreign capital flows, and what flows in can quickly flow out in capricious and disruptive ways. All the more reason for the Fed to desire stable prices and stable exchange rates, but that is something Greenspan and his colleagues have sometimes found it difficult to get their Treasury counterparts to understand. Whether the Fed was consciously seeking to support the dollar, the tight money policies needed to fight inflation lent support to the dollar. From the latter years of the Reagan administration to the Clinton administration, the White House and Treasury had different aims: lower interest rates to stimulate growth, jobs, and reelection of the party in power. During much of his chairmanship, Greenspan has had to contend not just with inflation, but with pressures from three different administrations to hold interest rates as low as possible—and the dollar be damned.

In addition to having presidents, Treasury secretaries, and congressional committees breathing down his neck and calling for his scalp, Greenspan sometimes had to contend with dissension within his own ranks. Present and former Fed officials have marvelled at his musician's talent for orchestrating agreements among the so-called "hawks" and "doves" (in terms of their willingness to tighten credit) on key votes over the years. I don't mean to suggest the Greenspan Fed could do no wrong. Mistakes were clearly made. The Fed could have done more to head off the banking problems of the late eighties and early nineties. It could have recognized the credit crunch and other economic "headwinds" earlier than it did. It could have eased credit more aggressively during the 1989 to 1992 period. On the whole, though, as Bush's economic adviser John Taylor says, the Fed "got it about right."

CHAPTER ONE

The Makings of a Central Banker

People used to say Paul Volcker was born to be a central banker. One does not hear that said quite as much about Alan Greenspan, although no one would deny his preeminence among central bankers. As unlike Volcker as he could be, Greenspan lacks the élan and commanding presence of his predecessor. Unlike Volcker, who came up through the ranks of the Treasury Department and the Fed, he took a considerably more unorthodox path to leadership of the world's most important central bank. A clarinet player who fell in love with economics, an economist who fell in love with politics, he is something of an enigma.

By nature quiet, contemplative, almost shy, he is nevertheless a man of great ambition and calm self-confidence, comfortable sitting down with presidents, testifying before Congress, or schmoozing with the movers and shakers of Washington, New York, and foreign capitals. A conservative Republican, he has built across-the-aisle friendships with prominent Democrats. Modest, even self-effacing, he is nevertheless a man of strongly held ideas and dogged determination both mentally and physically. Relatively slight in build and given to fainting spells over his adulthood, he has nevertheless driven himself to become an accomplished tennis player and golfer. His mental toughness goes without saying, given the treacherous Washington waters he has navigated. Unlike policymakers of lesser prominence that I can think of, Greenspan has not allowed his brilliance or his accomplishments to make him arrogant. Whether responding to a representative's stupid question or talking to a reporter, he is rarely condescending or impatient and always puts those around him at ease.

It should not be assumed, however, that Greenspan is devoid of temper or combativeness. During the Bush administration, when Undersecretary of Treasury Robert Glauber recruited one of Greenspan's most trusted lieutenants, William Taylor, head of the Fed's Division of Banking Supervision and Regulation, to run the Resolution Trust Corporation's S&L clean-up operations, he neglected to clear it with him. An angry Fed chief complained vociferously to Treasury Secretary Nicholas Brady, and Glauber had to go hat in hand and ask Greenspan's forgiveness. Later, when the Clinton administration tried to take away the Fed's bank regulatory responsibilities he fought back fiercely.

His grim countenance conceals a dry sense of humor. In fact, he is a man of considerable wit. At a dinner which he and long-time companion NBC correspondent Andrea Mitchell hosted at the latter's house in Georgetown, attended by the upper crust of Washington society, a newcomer asked Greenspan, "Where are all the real people in Washington?" Without looking up from his plate of veal, the Fed chairman replied drolly, "There aren't any." At a December 19, 1989, meeting of the Fed's policymaking Federal Open Market Committee (FOMC), Richmond Federal Reserve Bank president Robert Black sought to illustrate consumer resistance to price increases. "I refuse to pay list on anything," the Kentuckian drawled. "Somebody accused me the other day of shopping three places before I'd buy an ice cream cone. I haven't gotten quite that bad!" Greenspan jumped in to ask, "Do you buy the ice cream at a different place than you buy the cone?"

No one is ever really born to be chairman of the Fed. One thing is for sure. No one gets there by accident. The mantle does not fall on the shoulders of one who waits quietly, laboring in the vineyards of econometric forecasting or academic research. One has to want the job and campaign for it, but not too overtly. Like others before him, Greenspan worked assiduously to make sure he was in the right place at the right time. To become chairman of the Fed, one has to be more than a respected economist, more than a market savant. One has to make the requisite career moves, get to know the right people along the way, and position oneself to get the nod when an opening appears. Once having become Fed chairman, there is no guarantee one will be effective or command respect among one's fellow policymakers, advisers, foreign peers, and market players, as G. William Miller proved. "The reason the Fed chairman is so powerful is not because you're chairman," observes a Fed staffer. "The Fed chairman has power because he has the Rolodex, because he knows people"—on Wall street, in government, overseas, so that when a crisis arises and a rescue package needs to be arranged, or policy coordination is needed, or some regulation or law needs to be waived, the chairman can act swiftly and authoritatively. "You have to have the force of personality and the connections so it will happen. You have to be able to say, 'Okay guys, this is the way it's going to be. We'll work out the details later, but this is what we're going to do.' " That is why it is so important for the president not "to appoint someone who's never presented his calling card to Wall Street."

For Greenspan, it all started in New York City, where he was born on March 6, 1926, the only child of stockbroker Herbert Greenspan and his wife, Rose. His parents divorced, and he was raised in Washington Heights by his mother, who died in the summer of 1995. He stayed in New York throughout his education and early business career. After graduating from George Washington High School in Manhattan, Henry Kissinger's alma mater, Greenspan set out to become a musician, not a professional economist. For two years, he studied at the prestigious Juilliard School, learning to play the clarinet and the saxophone with sufficient expertise to tour professionally with the Henry

Jerome swing band. Portentously, the band included Leonard Garment, who would later become a top aide to President Nixon. But a different muse began to bewitch Greenspan, and he decided to study economics. "I was a pretty good amateur musician, but I was average as a professional, and I was aware of that because you learn pretty quickly how good some professional musicians are," he says. "I realized it's innate. You either have it or you don't. . . . So I decided that, if that was as far as I could go, I was in the wrong profession." Dance bands in those days were on for 20 minutes and off for 20 minutes, and during breaks Greenspan devoured books he had gotten from public libraries wherever the band happened to be playing. More and more he found himself immersed in finance and economics tomes. "I found the stuff fascinating." After a year on the road, he quit the band and enrolled at New York University (NYU) to study business finance. That meant taking prerequisite economics classes, which led him into more advanced economics courses and econometrics. He was hooked for life.

After graduating summa cum laude with a bachelor of science degree in economics from NYU in 1948, he went on to earn his masters degree and his doctorate in economics from the same institution. The doctorate did not come until 1977, long after he had become a renowned economic consultant and presidential adviser. After earning his masters in 1950, he began advanced graduate studies at Columbia University. It was there he met his first great mentor, Professor Arthur Burns. Already a prominent economist, known for his business cycle research, Burns was going places. He would soon become chairman of President Eisenhower's Council of Economic Advisors and later Nixon's choice to chair the Federal Reserve. He and Greenspan established a lifelong friendship that was to prove influential in fulfilling the younger man's destiny. Greenspan was so close to the late Burns that, when Burns came to Washington in 1970 to take over the Fed from William McChesney Martin, Greenspan held the first mortgage on his house, because Burns preferred going to a friend, rather than a bank. He learned a lot from Burns about the workings of the Fed.

In the meantime, Greenspan came in contact with a woman who became an even more important mentor: Ayn Rand, the iconoclastic Russian-born novelist and philosopher. She had achieved fame with a best-seller titled *The Fountainhead*, about a lone-wolf architect's refusal to compromise his individualistic principles. The hero dynamites a building he has designed after city authorities alter it without his authorization. The book, which features a lengthy courtroom monologue by the protagonist in defense of his actions rivaling any testimony Greenspan ever gave before the Senate Banking Committee, was made into a film starring Gary Cooper and Patricia Neal. By the early fifties, Rand had become the center of her own movement, Objectivism, and she regularly held forth on her philosophy of rational selfishness at salons in her midtown Manhattan apartment to a tight-knit group of fiercely devoted followers. Into this coterie, which included psychologist Nathaniel Branden and others, came Greenspan quite by accident. Still a student at Columbia, Greenspan was introduced to Rand in 1952 by his then wife, Joan Mitchell. He was immediately captivated by Rand's unabashed defense of laissez-faire capitalism, mixed though it was with heavy doses of atheism, dogmatic rationalism, and not a little idolatry. Admitted to Rand's inner circle, he began to lecture, along with Rand and her other disciples, on the principles of free market economics at a series of courses which Branden sponsored.

Objectivism had its quirks. In his hilarious send-up, *It Usually Begins with Ayn Rand*, Jerome Tuccille describes sessions with Rand as a cross between a gathering of "capitalistic Jehovah's Witnesses" and an Alcoholics Anonymous meeting. He tells of Rand's followers being pressured to smoke cigarettes like their leader, who considered smoking pro-capitalist and pro-life, and being purged from the inner circle if they did not lead the correctly rational life. But for a budding economist with political leanings, Rand's salons had a powerful, codifying influence on his belief in the ability of free people acting in free markets to accomplish great things. Greenspan emerged with his belief in the evils of government intervention in the economy reinforced. As he told the *New York Times* in 1974, "When I met Ayn Rand, I was a free enterpriser in the Adam Smith sense—impressed with the theoretical structure and efficiency of markets. What she did—through long discussions and lots of arguments into the night—was to make me think why capitalism is not only efficient and practical, but also moral." Above all, under Rand's tutelage, he developed an almost visceral aversion to inflation. As his fame as an economic consultant soared, Greenspan continued his devotion to Rand and her movement. He wrote occasional essays for Rand's journal, *The Objectivist*. In a July 1966 piece entitled, "Gold and Economic Freedom," he argued that "gold and economic freedom are inseparable." The gold standard was a free society's bulwark against overreaching government programs financed by inflationary deficit spending. Since welfare state advocates could not win public support to fund their redistributionist policies through taxation, they resorted to government borrowing, but since the gold standard limited deficit financing, they destroyed it. "The abandonment of the gold standard made it possible for the welfare statists to use the banking system as a means to an unlimited expansion of credit." The result, he predicted, would be inflation.

A year after meeting Rand, the 27-year-old Greenspan got divorced, suspended his doctoral studies at Columbia, and began to put his economics training to work. Now a confirmed bachelor, in 1954, he and an older bond trader named William Townsend established the New York–based consulting firm Townsend-Greenspan & Company, with Townsend as president and Greenspan as vice president. Townsend imparted to his partner the lessons he had learned in the bond markets, including how inflationary expectations could depress bond prices and increase long-term interest rates. When Townsend died in 1958, Greenspan took over the firm and built it into a highly profitable boutique consulting company, providing services to some of the nation's biggest banks and manufacturing companies. Economic consulting and forecasting not only made Greenspan a millionaire, it gave him an intimate knowledge of the U.S. economy at all levels. Fascinated and gifted with numbers since he was a child, Greenspan became an economic numbers cruncher par excellence. He devoured the minutiae of business inventories, shipments, delivery lead times, and hundreds of other aspects of business activity on an industry-by-industry basis. Everything from overtime hours in the auto industry to scrap metal prices became grist for his mill. Getting close enough to corporate America to take its pulse and know the economy's inner sinews and synapses proved to be excellent preparation for the future Fed chief.

Among other things, he learned not to take the numbers or his econometric models too seriously. Joshing and reminiscing with members of the National Association of Business Economists at a Fed reception in February 1995, a relaxed Greenspan joked about the foibles of forecasting. He recalled how proud he was in the sixties when Townsend-Greenspan got a new state-of-the-art computer which filled a good-sized room, yet had a memory of just 16K. After programming the computer to forecast economic trends, "we thought we could really pin down the business cycle," he recounted, but the economy did not cooperate. "It moved. . . . It wigged when it should have wagged." Since those days, both computers and econometric models have become vastly more sophisticated, but "our ability to forecast has not improved" because "that crazy economy out there doesn't stand still long enough for us to get a fix on it. It continually changes too rapidly for us to apply our techniques." If anything, economic change is accelerating so that "our computer models are running at an accelerating pace, but the economy manages to keep that much ahead of us. . . ." To demonstrate how fast things are moving in the real world and how difficult it is for forecasters to keep pace, Greenspan employed a bit of economic gallows humor by noting that a 28-year-old trader for Barings PLC had just managed to quickly lose an estimated $1 billion through stock index futures trading and bankrupt the centuries-old British investment house. And little more than a year earlier, Mexico had been trying to figure out how to keep the peso from rising, rather than worrying about its 40 percent devaluation. These examples were "extraordinarily disturbing to anyone who wants to forecast," and showed that "no matter how much our techniques improve [economic events] are just going to be a little bit ahead of us." He said there was an economic law of nature to explain this phenomenon: "You can't get there from here."

In 1968, with Rand's encouragement, Greenspan made a fateful decision. He entered the political arena, becoming the director of domestic policy research for Nixon's presidential campaign. Although Garment, Nixon's law partner, was active in the Nixon campaign, Greenspan credits fellow Rand follower Martin Anderson for getting him involved after arranging a luncheon with Garment and a pair of Nixon speechwriters, Raymond Price and Patrick J. Buchanan. When Nixon beat Hubert Humphrey the next fall, Greenspan stayed in Washington to serve on Nixon's transition team on budgetary and trade issues. Nixon offered him a spot in his administration, but Greenspan declined, returning to private consulting after the inauguration. But Greenspan had been bitten by Potomac fever, and from then on would never be far outside the Washington ambit. He became an informal Nixon adviser and served on a variety of Nixon-era task forces and advisory boards.[1] Greenspan found he liked political life and was good at it. He made countless valuable contacts in the nation's capital.

When Herbert Stein retired as chairman of the Council of Economic Advisors (CEA) in 1974, during Nixon's second term, Greenspan was offered the nomination. Initially reluctant, he accepted in July after Burns urged him to take the job and use it as a platform to combat inflation. By the time the Senate took up his nomination in late August of that year, Nixon had been forced to resign and Greenspan soon found himself the top economic advisor to President Gerald Ford. Ford, whom Greenspan had already gotten to know during his previous sojourns in Washington, affirmed the nomination on the recommendation of L. William Seidman, Ford's economic policy coordinator, and Greenspan took office on the first of September. Now he had really arrived, and he made the most of his new position so close to the commander in chief. "Greenspan has an unbeatable way of getting next to the guys in power and getting their attention, and he certainly did that with Ford," Seidman recalls. "So, he became an advisor not only on economics, but politics and everything else. In fact, I'm not sure he didn't spend as much time on politics as he did on economics." Not content just being a member of Seidman's Economic Policy Board, which included secretary of the Treasury William Simon and other cabinet officers, Greenspan developed a close relationship with the president directly, even attending football games with him. "He spent a lot of time with Ford," Seidman says. "Ford was, as almost all these guys are, very impressed with him, and Greenspan has about as good a 'bedside manner' with people in power as anybody I've ever seen, one of the reasons being he's very smart. But he also speaks in ways that sound profound even if you don't understand what the hell he's talking about." Greenspan not only advised Ford on economic legislation, but told Ford how he could best sell it to the press and the public and get it through Congress.

The White House tennis court, then as now, was the venue for power games, a place for cementing political alliances and heightening one's influence. Greenspan was not much of a tennis player when he came to Washington, but he remedied that with a vengeance. One of his tennis partners in the Ford days was Seidman, who recalls Greenspan "didn't know which end of the racket to use, and he saw that tennis was quite a great thing among people in the administration, and when he came back and became chairman of the Fed, somebody lined up a tennis game. It was Baker, Bush, Greenspan and I or something like that. And I said, 'My God! Look at these guys! This is the tennis-playing group! What's Greenspan doing out here with this group?' Well, apparently, over the eight- or nine-year period there he had taken lessons and worked and become a tennis player in his later days."

The story illustrates Greenspan's deceptive tenacity, which he sometimes jokes about. "I've been tracing the quality of my tennis since I actually started playing at an elderly age on the White House tennis courts in 1974, and I've improved year-by-year," Greenspan said at the Concord Coalition award dinner. "As economists are prone to do, I've been extrapolating, and I've concluded that I'll join the professional tennis tour at age 104." He had been introduced by Pete Peterson, Nixon-era crony and tennis partner, who said Greenspan plays left-handed, but "at a decisive moment in the game he'll suddenly shift to his right hand in a totally unexpected move that totally disorients his opponent, and he wins that decisive point. If you play golf with him, his central banker personality comes out in different ways. . . . On the first hole, if you have a 12-inch putt, he will say, 'Of course, Pete, take it, take it as a give-me.' However, should the same situation occur on the eighteenth hole, in which the stakes are much higher, he waits just until the moment when you're about to pick it up and will say something like, 'I think it's better if you putt this one, Pete.' So that element of Greenspan psychological surprise keeps his skilled opponents off guard. . . ." Peterson was being semiapochryphal, but those who have seen Greenspan at play describe him as extremely competitive, contesting line calls and going for the kill.

The 1974 to 1976 period was not an easy time to be CEA chairman, and it would turn out to be an ideal testing ground. Inflation, which had been artificially suppressed by Nixon's wage-price controls, was running nearly 12 percent in 1974, boosted by the OPEC cartel's oil embargo and the Fed's past overly expansive monetary policy. Greenspan was determined to do as Burns had urged and persuade Ford to focus on fighting inflation, although he does not deserve dubious credit for the administration's short-lived WIN (Whip Inflation Now) button campaign, which was practically laughed out of town. But the administration's anti-inflation fervor cooled when the economy went into recession in late 1974, in reaction to the tripling of oil prices and the Fed's belated effort to stifle inflation. A heated debate ensued among Ford's advisers and congressional Republicans. Greenspan says he advised cutting taxes while at the same time cutting government spending, to prevent a ballooning of the deficit. But others advocated a combination of tax cuts, increased government spending, and stimulative monetary policy. Outside economists with Democratic Party connections, such as Walter Heller and Charles Schultze, who Seidman had brought in to advise the president, were also recommending some old-fashioned Keynesian pump priming. Greenspan, according to Seidman, "thought that was a disaster." Ford was even getting unsolicited advice from overseas. Seidman tells the story of a meeting at Blair House across Pennsylvania Avenue from the White House, where German chancellor Helmut Schmidt urged stimulative spending. "Apparently Greenspan's blood pressure went through the roof." Afterward, walking back to the White House, he collapsed in the middle of the street, and Seidman says he picked Greenspan up, threw him over his shoulder, and carried him to his office in the Old Executive Office Building.

In his book, *A Time For Truth*, Simon credits Greenspan and Burns for helping him convince Ford "not to follow this destructive formula" of tax cuts unbalanced by spending reductions. Too late to prevent a Republican debacle in the 1974 congressional elections, a temporary income tax cut was introduced and passed in early 1975, which helped revive the economy, though not enough to assure Ford's reelection the following year. Greenspan's vociferous opposition to deficit spending, together with that of Simon and Burns, influenced Ford to veto no less than 45 spending bills passed by the Democratic Congress in the remainder of his term. Ford had proposed a budget with an unprecedented peacetime deficit of $51.9 billion in 1975. The actual deficit rose to $53.2 billion in fiscal year 1975 and $73.7 billion in fiscal 1976, but without the spending restraints which Greenspan helped spearhead, the deficit could have gone much higher. By the end of the Ford administration, inflation had been reduced to less than 5 percent with the help of tighter money and, of course, the recession.

Greenspan returned to New York and Townsend-Greenspan in January 1977, enriched, not financially, but politically. In the Ford administration, he had built close working relationships with men who would become important allies and associates when the Republicans were returned to power: men such as James Baker III. Seidman would serve as chairman of the Federal Deposit Insurance Corporation while Greenspan ran the Fed, sharing responsibility for overseeing the nation's banking system during one of its rockiest periods. Back in New York, Greenspan continued to build his expertise, his resume, and his rolodex. He was never far out of the public eye, hitting the social scene like a whirlwind, usually in the company of Barbara Walters of ABC News, and the lecture circuit. I covered a speech he made to the National Press Club in February 1978, in which he attacked Carter administration policies for sending prices soaring again and the dollar tumbling. The country was "on a track of inflationary deficits," he warned, and if "not reversed, they will lead this nation into an economic crisis." With little chance spending would be held in check or the budget balanced, "the Federal Reserve will inevitably start to balloon money growth." When I reminded Greenspan of his endorsement of the gold standard, he replied, "Structurally, it is very difficult to improve on the workings of the international gold standard." However, "it presupposes that governments are willing to abide by the exchange rate impact on their domestic policies. If you have a number of countries who are unwilling to abide by fixed exchange rates then you can't impose a gold standard." A gold standard had to be "the end result of international economic stability—not the cause of it."

Greenspan sounded much like the retiring Burns, who the month before had told the Press Club that the country was on a disastrous "path of enormous budget deficits and rapid inflation." Prophetically, he added, "I have no doubt that the will to get on energetically with the job of unwinding the inflation will be forged someday. I only hope this will come through a growth of understanding, not from a demonstration that inflation is the mortal enemy of economic progress and our political freedom." Burns had no way of knowing that two years later Volcker would begin that unwinding, or that ten years later his former student would build on Volcker's legacy. Greenspan let it be known he had the will and the understanding to be an inflation fighter. He did not see it as just a matter of preserving the dollar's domestic purchasing power. Because of the "huge proliferation" of U.S. dollars abroad—so-called *Euro-dollars*, which by then had amassed to some $400 billion—the dollar would come under ever greater downward pressure internationally. If the United States expected foreigners to hold dollars and buy its debt, it would either have to stabilize the dollar's value by reducing inflation or pay ever higher interest rates.

Though ready to take on the challenge, Greenspan's time had not yet come. By the time a Republican was returned to the White House, Carter had put a very able Democrat in charge of the Fed, where he would be ensconced for eight years. In the meantime, Greenspan had to content himself with political odd jobs, not to minimize their importance. After evenhandedly advising both Bush and Ronald Reagan, as well as other candidates for the 1980 Republican presidential nomination, Greenspan served as Reagan's economic adviser in his successful campaign to unseat Carter. He seemed to be a logical choice as Treasury secretary, but was never seriously considered for that position, possibly because his well-known emphasis on balancing the budget did not sit well with some of Reagan's more ardent "supply-side" supporters, who believed stimulative tax cuts would generate so much revenue that deficits would not be a problem. (They did not reckon on Congress's propensity to spend money or on the administration's unwillingness to resist excessive spending.) Greenspan was approached to once again chair the Council of Economic Advisors, but the job went to Harvard economist Martin Feldstein. Instead, President Reagan put Greenspan in charge of his National Commission on Social Security Reform which worked from 1981 to 1983 to produce recommendations, mostly enacted, to restore the financial integrity of the troubled Social Security system for the next quarter century. He also served as a member of Reagan's Economic Advisory Board (EAB). During these years, Greenspan served on the boards of directors of Aluminum Company of America (Alcoa), Automatic Data Processing, Capital Cities/ABC, General Foods, J.P. Morgan & Company, Morgan Guaranty Trust Company, Mobil Corporation, and the Pittston Company.

When it came time for Volcker to be reappointed or replaced in August 1987, the job was Volcker's for the asking, but he did not ask, according to former administration and Fed sources. Reagan was not about to push the nomination on him, and Volcker was not about to beg. Baker, then Treasury secretary, says "quite a bit" of consideration was given to reappointing Volcker to a third term, "but Volcker indicated that he didn't want to be reappointed, that he had had the job for a long time and was pretty well ready to go into the private sector." In truth, many in the administration were anxious to have the opportunity to replace a man they considered difficult and unreliable.

There was little doubt who Reagan would choose. Friends from the Ford days who had risen to new prominence in the Reagan administration, like Baker, urged that Greenspan be appointed. He had traveled with Baker on Ford's campaign plane when Baker ran Ford's failed reelection effort and later helped George Bush's campaign for the 1980 Republican nomination, which Baker also ran. The two were good friends, and Baker pushed for Greenspan's nomination. "He was well regarded in the field of markets and finance, well regarded in the business community and on Wall Street, and he was the one person whose name kept cropping up as being the only alternative to Paul Volcker who was acceptable to the markets," Baker recalls. "So all those things combined, I think, led us toward the choice of Greenspan, and I don't remember a lot of debate about it within the administration. I think it was a rather general consensus." James Baker's recommendation carried the heaviest weight, but he was backed up by former Tennessee senator Howard Baker, then White House chief of staff. Greenspan visited James Baker at his home on posh Fauxhall Road in Northwest Washington to discuss the nomination. If it were offered, would Greenspan accept? Greenspan did not hesitate to say he would.

Upon assuming leadership of the War Cabinet during World War II, Winston Churchill is said to have remarked, "I've been preparing for this job my whole life." Greenspan might have said the same thing. Although he never consciously set the Fed chairmanship as his goal, thinking it involved more regulatory responsibility than was his cup of tea, there was never a man better poised for a position—at least as prepared as a person can be to run an institution that prides itself on its cloak-and-dagger style of operations. His friendship with Burns had given him entrée to the Fed, and he knew more than most about how the Fed works, although he had much to learn about the Fed's culture and operations. He felt he already had most of the tools. He felt confident he was well equipped to assume responsibility for U.S. monetary policy, having developed an extraordinarily well-detailed understanding of how the American economy works. His economic consulting had gotten him deeply involved in the numbers of different companies and industries, giving him intimate knowledge of the U.S. economic system. He also felt he had a good understanding of how the political system works.

Five weeks after he took office on August 11, 1987, Greenspan elicited laughter when he told an audience, "Since I've become a central banker I've learned to mumble with great incoherence. If I seem unduly clear to you, you must have misunderstood what I said." On another occasion, he remarked, "I know you believe you understand what you think I said, but I am not sure you realize that what you heard is not what I meant." Central bankers have long been notorious for their obfuscatory language. Two of his more notable predecessors, pipe-fancier Burns and cigar-chomping Volcker, had literally blown smoke when grilled by congressional committees on where they intended to steer monetary policy. But for all of his joking about continuing this tradition, Greenspan turned out to be far more clear and forthright than his predecessors, at least to those who knew what to listen for.

A big part of being a successful Fed chairman is winning over the other members of the Federal Reserve Board of Governors and the Federal Reserve Bank presidents and the Fed's influential staff of professional economists. He wasted no time in winning their respect and loyalty, not so much by overawing them with his intellect but by loosening up some of the stiffness that he inherited from the Volcker era, which in fact had existed at least since the Burns regime. He went out of his way to take an interest in other policymakers and staffers, soliciting their views, encouraging their research, getting down in the trenches with the professional economists and comparing notes. He infected the Board staff with his love of numbers. He found himself in an economist's fantasyland where undreamed of amounts of economic information could be collected and analyzed. It wasn't just statistics that captivated him. "He looks a lot at anecdotes—stories coming out of the business sector, like whether their order books are doing well," says former Fed Board vice chairman Alan Blinder. "He has a way of thinking about the role of primary metals and telling you things about inventories and what's happening in durable goods sectors that he tracks routinely," marvels Governor Janet Yellen. "He understands that inventories are very important to business cycles, and he has his own personal system he's developed that he's gotten the staff to work with. . . . It involves calculations and computations that most of the rest of us do not understand and are certainly not part of the normal forecasting process that our staff uses." Like a bee in clover, he was free to indulge his passion for data. His already well-developed grasp of the intricacies of the economy and his ability to carry enormous amounts of statistical information in his head became legendary throughout international central banking circles.

"One of the things that we used to nearly tease him about was that when he was describing the state of the U.S. economy he would say that 'The information that I have from the vacuum cleaner industry in the state of Iowa indicates that the economy is moving up or down or sideways' or something like that," recalls former governor of the Bank of England Robin Leigh-Pemberton. "I mean he had the most detailed knowledge of what was going on in the real economy." On one occasion several years ago, while in London, Greenspan and Leigh-Pemberton were invited to visit with then prime minister Margaret Thatcher at Chequers, her weekend house. After lunch, they spent Saturday afternoon talking, and in his unassuming way Greenspan regaled Thatcher with a detailed analysis of the U.S. economic condition and outlook. He then spent the night at Leigh-Pemberton's country home. A few days later, Leigh-Pemberton (now Lord Kingsdown) recalls, Thatcher told him, "That man knows everything about what's going on in the United States of America. Why don't you know so much about what's going on in the U.K.?"

So notorious is Greenspan's penchant for gathering economic information that, at the 1996 White House Correspondents Dinner, President Clinton joked that, when Greenspan arrived with Andrea Mitchell, he paid the coat-room fee of $1 and remarked that the previous year it had been 75¢.

As immersed as he is in economic minutiae, Greenspan also delights in the big picture. He is fascinated by economic history and likes to extrapolate trends into the future. "He is a visionary," says Hugh Brown, chairman of the board of directors of the Federal Reserve Bank of Atlanta. "He sees far ahead of the next 10 [policy] moves. He understands the inter-relatedness of trends that to others seem to have no connection." Leigh-Pemberton's successor as governor of the Bank of England Eddie George recalls Greenspan being invited to make some remarks at "the Old Lady of Threadneedle Street," as the world's oldest central bank is known, and choosing to talk about *miniaturization* in the world economy in the broadest terms—not just the physical fact that high technology has made modern computers and other machines smaller and more efficient, but the fact that the financial system has evolved to permit financial institutions and markets to break down risk into its component parts. Greenspan often muses that technological progress may increase growth of productivity, in turn speeding the pace at which the economy can grow without developing wage-price pressures. At the same time he has warned of the need to enhance education so that vast portions of the population are not left behind.

Unlike Volcker, Greenspan had had relatively little experience in the international arena, but he moved quickly to remedy this. Part of being Fed chairman is joining the fraternity of central bankers known as the Group of Ten, which actually has eleven members: the Group of Seven's United States, Germany, Japan, France, Great Britain, Italy, and Canada plus Belgium, the Netherlands, Sweden, and Switzerland. They meet monthly in Basel, Switzerland, under the auspices of the Bank for International Settlements (BIS), the central banker's bank. These meetings, as well as the thrice-yearly meetings of G-7 central bankers and finance ministers, gave Greenspan a chance to form close bonds with his foreign counterparts, and they all speak highly of him. In one of a series of get-to-know-you meetings, Greenspan invited Leigh-Pemberton to breakfast in Basel soon after becoming chairman and immediately impressed him with his "tremendous perception and analytical powers" conveyed with a "most agreeable modesty." Greenspan also visited early with Bundesbank president Karl Otto Poehl at the Bundesbank's fortresslike headquarters on the edge of Frankfurt. The dinner meeting of the world's top two central bankers was "a bit stiff," with each man taking a "very cautious" approach to the other, recalls Gerd Häusler, then Poehl's top assistant, now a Bundesbank council member. "They had a very intellectual conversation." Greenspan would later develop friendly relations with the Bundesbank, particularly with current president Hans Tietmeyer. But at that first meeting, Greenspan was "more like a European. He's not a typical American who shakes your hand and says, 'Hi, my name is Bill.' He's more detached."

George calls Greenspan "an extremely thoughtful, subtle kind of chap" gifted not only at technical analysis but with "immense skill in managing Congress and managing his relationship with the Treasury and the White House." Tietmeyer compliments Greenspan's combination of theoretical and practical economic knowledge mixed with an appreciation of "the political institutional problems and limitations. A lot of people understand economics, but they don't understand the policy area, how it works, and this is a very good background for a central banker—economic knowledge, political knowledge and a third element: He is a man who is not simplistic or crude in his conclusions. He balances the argument, and he is never willing to propose a too simple solution." Tietmeyer says he has always had "a very positive understanding" with Greenspan because he is "market oriented and stability oriented, not short-term, anti-cyclical" oriented. Greenspan's language is low-key, "But you should not underestimate his sentences. It's sophisticated. You have to follow him very closely to understand precisely when he is sending a message. He has this very subtle language. . . . It is sometimes useful for a central banker to be a little bit mysterious and not be too outspoken." Crow says he "can never remember a heated discussion [in Basel] when Alan was there." Greenspan is "always steadfastly courteous and quiet and makes his point extremely carefully." Jean Claude Trichet, head of the Bank of France praises his "special gift to profoundly analyze the situation, to remain calm, I would say, in all circumstances. And always he has an elegant way of assessing the situation, even the most acute and the most difficult situations, and then he has a special gift to produce consensus."

Present and former Fed colleagues say the hallmark of Greenspan's chairmanship has been his collegiality and, related to that, his remarkable ability to meld a consensus out of disparate views among the 12 voting members of the Fed's policymaking Federal Open Market Committee (FOMC). The FOMC consists of the seven members of the Washington-based Board of Governors plus, on a rotating basis, five of the twelve district Federal Reserve bank presidents, with the other seven participating but not voting. The committee meets behind closed doors eight times a year to review the state of the economy and decide whether to change interest rates. As a rule, those who have served on the committee speak of him not just with respect but with affection. "I'm one of his great admirers," says former Richmond Federal Reserve bank president Robert Black. "If I'd have given my proxy to anyone around that table he would have gotten my proxy." Loyalty to Greenspan spans political affiliations, which mean surprisingly little once a new official has matriculated in the Federal Reserve system. The day President Clinton belatedly announced his intention to reappoint Greenspan to a third term, February 22, 1996, Clinton appointee Yellen described herself as "thrilled. He has an enviable record, and I've enjoyed working with him enormously. He's a very wise leader. . . ."

By all accounts, the second floor of the Fed's art deco headquarters, along which the seven members of the Board of Governors have their offices, became a more open channel for the exchange of ideas when Greenspan arrived. He would visit other governors to seek their opinions and opened his door to them. He is a study in contrasts with Volcker, who did not suffer fools (or anyone foolish enough to disagree with him) gladly. Volcker was known to browbeat members of Congress and fellow Fed officials and even explode in anger if he could not have his way, as when Reagan appointees threatened to outvote him in favor of easier credit in 1986. On another occasion, he lashed out at Vice Chairman Preston Martin, who made no secret of his partisan views or his ambition to replace Volcker. It would be wrong to paint Volcker as a bully, however. He began the process of democratizing the Fed. After they led a policy rebellion against him, Volcker began taking Martin successor Manuel Johnson and Governor Wayne Angell into his confidence on monetary policy issues. Greenspan introduced more openness, although he did not completely dismantle the Fed's stiff, hierarchical traditions. "Board members were already being heard [by the chairman] before Alan came in," Angell says, but adds, "Alan's consensus talents were particularly well suited for working with the Board."

Volcker protégé Corrigan, the former New York Fed president, says the biggest difference between the two men was that Volcker had a stronger "financial orientation" than Greenspan, who was more devoted to "devouring information" on the real economy. "In terms of the way that they ran the committee meetings, the big contrast isn't between Volcker and Greenspan; it's between Volcker and Greenspan, and Burns," says Corrigan. "A lot of people don't see it this way, but both Volcker and Greenspan to me were both extremely democratic and both, in their own ways, really did have a large measure of success in terms of generating meaningful discussion, wide range of opinion, point of view, and both encouraged that. The contrast was Burns, who didn't want to know about that!"

Republican and Democratic administration officials, who did not always see eye to eye with Greenspan when in office, generally give him high marks in retrospect. Michael Boskin, President Bush's Council of Economic Advisors chairman during one of the most trying times of Greenspan's tenure, says he could quibble with the timing of the Fed's interest rate cuts during the 1989 to 1992 period, but gives him "straight As" for engineering a second round of disinflation instead of allowing inflation in the 4 to 5 percent range to become a "floor" for future increases. "Greenspan will go down in history as highly regarded unless something happens in the meantime." Robert Glauber, Treasury undersecretary in the Bush years, acknowledges the high level of "frustration" that marked Treasury secretary Nicholas Brady's dealings with the Fed, but says, "Being Fed chairman is one of the world's hardest jobs, and he's done it year-in and year-out. He's both an extraordinarily sophisticated scholar and an extraordinarily sophisticated politician. He's a man of remarkable talents." Clinton's first Treasury secretary Lloyd Bentsen, another Greenspan tennis partner who enjoyed more favorable economic circumstances than Brady, says he "had an excellent relationship with him, both officially and personally. He's a man certainly of high integrity. He is careful about the commitments he makes, and he keeps them."

Notwithstanding his reputation as an inflation giant killer—or, perhaps more aptly, given his six-foot-seven height, a giant inflation killer—Volcker did not bequeath lasting price stability to his successor. On the contrary, by the end of the Volcker era, inflation pressures and expectations were once again on the rise. Greenspan has nothing but praise for the job Volcker did, but he faced a different sort of problem. A virulent strain of inflation had been brought under control. But it had not been killed, and like a dormant virus it had reactivated and was again coursing through the nation's bloodstream. This cannot be blamed entirely on Volcker. The long-running eighties' expansion, sparked by tax cuts, had pushed the economy near full employment, and Volcker's hand had been stayed in combatting the resulting wage-price pressures by the Reagan appointees.

Volcker had been humiliatingly forced into cutting interest rates when Johnson and Angell confronted him in late February and threatened, along with two other Reagan appointees, to outvote him on the board. Angry but not wanting to be publicly embarrassed, Volcker agreed, after a rancorous meeting, to go along if the cut was delayed until he could persuade his counterparts at Germany's Bundesbank and the Bank of Japan to cut their rates too. On March 7, 1986, the Fed cut the discount rate, at which it lends to banks, from 7½ to 7 percent, its lowest level since July 1978. After being reluctant to start cutting the discount rate, Volcker turned to easing with the fervor of a convert. The Fed cut the discount rate three more times in 1986, bringing it to 5½ percent by August. The federal funds rate—a key determinant of banks' cost of funds and loan rates—was brought below 6 percent by the end of the year. "Paul came around to that point of view, and after Manley and I worked to get him into a compromise mode to do the first 50 basis points, Paul himself was the leading force in the other three," recalls Angell, who says the final half percent rate cut in August was taken "because we were going on vacation and we thought it was our last chance to act." Only four of the seven board members were on hand for the August vote, and they all supported the rate cut. Angell says he soon "knew we were wrong" because "the price of platinum took off and the price of gold and silver went with it."

"Paul Volcker and I both agreed that we went too far in '86," says Angell. On August 11, 1987, a year after the final discount rate cut, Volcker and the entire Fed Board were at the White House for Greenspan's swearing in ceremony. While Reagan and Bush were talking with Greenspan and various Fed governors by the fireplace in the Red Room, Angell and Volcker were off in a corner. "Wayne, I want you to know that you were right when you said that the Fed generally does one discount rate cut too many," Angell says Volcker told him. "What Paul meant by our 'overdoing it' was we then had to move rates back up, and it was very difficult for the Fed, in '87, to get corrected what had happened to us in '86." With rates falling and demand for money rising, the broad money supply, known as $M2$ (cash in circulation, checking and savings accounts, money market funds, and small time deposits) grew 10 percent in 1986. Narrow money ($M1$) grew more than 18 percent. The money supply grew much more slowly in 1987, but the economy was feeling the effects of the previous year's monetary stimulus with a lag. Inevitably, the consumer price index's rate of increase, which had been painstakingly reduced to just 1.9 percent in 1986, was on its way back up. The consumer price index (CPI) rose 3.6 percent in 1987 and in subsequent years retail price inflation got as high as 6 percent.

The Fed began gradually and half-heartedly nudging up the funds rate on April 30, 1987, but by the time Greenspan took office, the Fed had retraced relatively little of the 1986 rate cuts and the economy was racing on high-test fuel. The discount rate was still at 5½ percent, and the federal funds rate was trading in a range of 6½ to 6¾ percent. Passing judgment that monetary policy was too loose, the markets sent the dollar and bond prices plummeting in the spring and once again in late summer, and, since a bond's yield moves inversely to its price, that meant soaring long-term interest rates on mortgages and other loans—hardly what the economy needed. Moreover, the dual drop of the dollar and bond prices was an unsettling influence on the otherwise ebullient stock market.

A relatively easy credit stance in the face of resurgent inflation was not the only dubious legacy of "Tall Paul," as the financial press affectionately called Volcker. Sometimes reluctantly, sometimes enthusiastically, he had played ball with Treasury Secretary Baker in manipulating the dollar exchange rate. From September 1985, when the Group of Five finance ministers and central bank governors (from the United States, Germany, Japan, France, and the United Kingdom) met at New York's Plaza Hotel and decided the dollar was overvalued, until February 1987, when the same G-5 plus Canada met at the Louvre in Paris and decided the dollar was getting too weak, the Fed had collaborated with the Treasury Department in encouraging a steady depreciation of the dollar relative to other major currencies. This meant, among other things, keeping U.S. interest rates lower longer than they should have been for purely domestic purposes in 1986. By early 1987, the dollar had become so weak the Treasury and Fed—under considerable pressure from America's major trading partners—did an about-face.

At the Louvre, on February 22, 1987, the finance ministers and central bankers issued a fateful communiqué in which they pledged to "cooperate closely to foster stability of exchange rates around current levels," which at that time consisted of 153.60 yen per dollar and 1.82 marks per dollar—down from 238.85 yen and 2.839 marks at the time of the September 22, 1985, Plaza Accord. There was a vague agreement—differently understood by different parties—that exchange rates were going to be kept within a range of plus or minus 2.5 to 5 percent around the February 22 rates, although when the monetary authorities failed to keep the dollar from sliding to 142 yen per dollar by the time the G-7 met in Washington in mid-April, they sheepishly restated the Louvre Accord language of keeping the dollar "around current levels." From the beginning, a German policymaker says, his country regarded these exchange rate targets as "unrealistic." Although the Louvre and son-of-Louvre pacts were primarily intended to prop up the dollar via foreign exchange intervention (central bank dollar purchases in the currency markets), in the minds of many, U.S. monetary policy had also now been hitched to a policy of bolstering the buck, and to a large extent the Fed behaved as if it was. There was a great deal of troublesome misunderstanding on this point. Whether the Fed was too tight or too loose with money in 1987 is still a matter of debate, but there is one thing with which few would disagree: Perceptions of what the Fed would or would not do to support the dollar became a source of considerable problems for Greenspan and his colleagues in late 1987.

The dollar exchange rate was no mere trader's or economist's toy; it was a political hot potato. Backtracking a bit, the dollar had reached what nearly everyone agreed was a ridiculously high level in 1985 (a peak of 3.477 marks and 263.65 yen per dollar in February) as a direct result of Volcker's anti-inflationary policies of the early eighties, which had made interest yields on U.S. assets so attractive that foreign capital flooded into this country. All that foreign money helped fuel economic expansion and made it easier to run growing budget deficits, but in the process the dollar became so overvalued many companies became uncompetitive. Since a German had to pay many more marks or a Japanese many more yen to buy dollars, U.S. exports were priced out of overseas markets. Meanwhile, imports surged because the dollar suddenly had much greater purchasing power. The trade deficit, which had been just $25.5 billion in 1980, rose to $122 billion in 1985, and even after the dollar had fallen considerably, continued to mount to $145 billion in 1986 and $159.5 billion in 1987, as a delayed reaction to the earlier dollar strength. Politicians like Missouri Democratic congressman Richard Gephardt called for punitive surcharges on imports from countries which were running trade surpluses with the United States. Keeping the dollar at a competitive level to defuse protectionism without letting the dollar depreciate to the point that it caused inflation or undermined foreign investor confidence would be a treacherous balancing act for Greenspan and Baker.

Greenspan would have other crosses to bear as well. While the Fed worked to reduce the fear of escalating prices which made investors and lenders demand higher interest rates, the government continued to run such large deficits that markets understandably built an inflation premium into yields on the vast quantities of government securities that were flooding the market. The federal deficit was reduced from more than $221 billion in fiscal 1986 to less than $150 billion in 1987, but then headed back up. This, in turn, meant higher mortgage and other interest rates. And while the federal government was going deeper and deeper into debt, American households and businesses were also becoming debt-ridden. Since there were insufficient savings in this country, increasingly it was foreigners who held the claims on much of all this debt. By the time Greenspan took office, America's financial institutions found themselves in trouble because their borrowers could not bear up under this debt burden. After decades of minimal bank problems, bank and thrift failures and insolvencies soared in the mid-eighties. In the two years before Greenspan's arrival, 118 banks failed in 1985 and another 144 went under in 1986. In 1987, the number of bank failures leaped to 201. Meanwhile the number of thrifts that were insolvent and unprofitable rose from 387 with assets of $119 billion in 1985 to 509 with assets of $215 billion at the end of 1987, and the numbers kept getting worse as Congress dawdled on providing additional capital so that the Federal Savings & Loan Insurance Corporation (FSLIC) could shut sick thrifts down and pay off their depositors. Less than a month after Greenspan took office, Houston-based First City Bank Corporation became just the first of a series of major Texas banks to fail due to bad energy and real estate loans at a cost to the FDIC of $1 billion.

So, it was no cushy job Greenspan was taking over. Volcker probably did not make it any easier for him when, on July 21, 1987, in his final Humphrey-Hawkins report to Congress (a semiannual exercise in which the Fed chairman must present the Fed's economic forecasts and monetary goals), Volcker suggested only modest credit tightening was needed. Since the late-April rate hike had served to "calm concerns about the future course of the dollar and inflation," the Fed's credit stance "has not changed," he told the House Banking Committee. The Fed had tentatively reduced its target for how much M2 growth it wanted by a half percent to a range of 5 to 8 percent per year, but not until 1988—hardly an indication of bold action against inflation. The best thing Congress could do to ward off inflation, the departing chairman said, was to reduce deficit spending and keep the Fed independent of politics. "I don't know anything more important than that." Greenspan had more ambitious plans. He was determined to return to 1950s style price stability. It would not be an easy task.

CHAPTER TWO

Hitting the Ground Running

Filling the shoes of a man who had come to epitomize the ultimate central banker was not going to be easy, and not just because Volcker was a hard act to follow. There was also a little matter of perception. The same day Volcker was presenting his final Humphrey-Hawkins report, Greenspan was on the opposite side of the Capitol being grilled by the Senate Banking Committee. He had been identified with Republican politics for two decades, so his independence was suspect in the mind of committee chairman Senator William Proxmire. The first thing the Wisconsin Democrat wanted to know was, "Are you the man who can say 'no' to the president and the Congress?" He and others feared Greenspan would turn the Fed into an arm of the administration.

Greenspan aced his July 21, 1987, confirmation hearing, winning over Proxmire and his committee. Greenspan's unruffled reply to Proxmire's skeptical query was, "Certainly. I will be taking an oath of office, and I take that very seriously." Besides, it would not be "credible" to adopt a monetary stance other than that indicated by economic and financial market conditions. Any change in monetary policy "certainly would not be on the basis of politics rather than economics." He vowed to do "everything" he could to assure that the Fed "maintains its independence." In what would become his familiar refrain, Greenspan told the committee he saw no conflict between the goals of economic growth and low inflation. "It is absolutely essential that our central focus be on restraining inflation" because "if that fails we have very little opportunity for sustained economic growth." Proxmire, who had voted against Greenspan's nomination to chair the Council of Economic Advisors in 1974, admitted he had "made a mistake." Though bothered that the Fed Board was filling up with Reagan "clones," Proxmire pushed Greenspan's nomination through the committee, and on August 3, he was confirmed by the full Senate on a 91 to 2 vote.[1]

While Proxmire suspected Greenspan might keep credit too easy to please the president who appointed him, nervous aides to Reagan and his friends in the business community were afraid he would "out-Volcker Volcker." The latter proved much closer to the mark. It was clear Greenspan was not going to let fear of recession keep him from battling inflation from the way he responded to a question by Senator James Sasser. The Tennessee Democrat, a frequent Fed critic, had charged Volcker's draconian tightening of credit in the late seventies and early eighties with pushing the economy into recession by driving interest rates to 20 percent. Greenspan told him the lesson he learned from Volcker was not that high interest rates must be avoided but that the country must not "get into a set of policies that are unfocused and that lead us into an environment where that is the only thing that stands between the economy and catastrophe." Greenspan dropped some heavy hints of the credit tightening he had in mind. As a private economist he had stated on March 20 that the economy was in its "final surge" and that recession would arrive by late 1988 or early 1989. But now he had revised his forecast and saw "no evidences of recession" and even compared the eighties to the roaring twenties—a comment laden with ironic foreshadowing since that earlier boom time ended abruptly in October 1929 with the Great Crash and the Great Depression, which he called a "one in twenty occurrence." A few short months later, he was to go through his own, even bigger October stock market collapse, and it would take all his wits to prevent another depression.

There was one danger signal in Greenspan's testimony. He hinted he would continue to base monetary policy partially on the exchange rate commitments Baker and Volcker had made at the Louvre. Asked by Michigan Democratic senator Donald Riegle about the consequences of the dollar falling to 130 yen, Greenspan said, "I would hope we don't get down there, and I see no reason why we will." It was an indication that, in the first months of his chairmanship, Greenspan would raise interest rates in part to fix the dollar exchange rate, not for its own sake but to calm investor fears and stabilize U.S. financial markets. A perception that U.S. interest rates were wedded to exchange rates was to become a source of major disruption for the financial markets.

At the swearing-in ceremony, Reagan praised Greenspan as "an economist's economist" who would "bring all his skill to bear to the task of promoting continued economic growth while keeping inflation low." He added that "low inflation and economic growth can and must go hand in hand." Greenspan deflected the president's implication that the Fed would not fight inflation too aggressively with a bit of humor. The next four years, he joshed, would be a period of "inflation, which always stays put; the stock market, which is always a bull; the dollar, which is always stable; interest rates, which always stay low, and employment, which stays high." He added a word of thanks to "those who have the capability of repealing the laws of arithmetic." Greenspan had fairly high regard for President Reagan in his handling of relations with the Fed. He feels Reagan was genuinely interested in sound money and was generally supportive of his anti-inflation policies, as he had been of Volcker's. It helped that Greenspan had a close relationship with James Baker. But, as we shall see, while Reagan himself abstained from criticizing the Fed, that was not always true of his advisers.

A week after he was sworn in, Greenspan convened his first FOMC meeting. At each meeting this powerful policymaking body issues a *directive* to the open market trading desk of the Federal Reserve Bank of New York, which acts as agent for the entire Fed system in adjusting the availability of bank reserves. Through purchases or sales of government securities, the New York Fed regulates the level of reserves—sometimes known as *high-powered money* because for every dollar of reserves a bank could then make roughly $8 of loans. When it buys securities it creates money by giving banks a credit at their reserve account at the Fed and expands banks' ability to lend. When the Fed wants to tighten credit, it drains reserves by selling government securities, which reduces banks' reserves. By the time Greenspan became chairman, the Fed had stopped targeting the growth of reserves and money and returned to targeting the price of money, the federal funds rate. Throughout the Greenspan years, the Fed has essentially supplied as much reserves as are demanded at any given funds rate. When it wants to slow the economy it pushes up banks' cost of funds, making it less profitable for them to make loans and/or forcing banks to increase their loan rates, making it more costly to borrow money to finance consumer spending, business investment, and so forth. In Greenspan's early years, the Fed was targeting how much reserves it wanted to induce banks to borrow from the discount window, but this was largely just another means to the end of setting the funds rate.[2]

It was crucial for Greenspan to gain the confidence of the other FOMC members at that initial meeting if he was to take command and get started on his mission of squeezing the remaining life out of the inflation monster. Oil prices had virtually collapsed in 1986 to just $10 per barrel, wreaking such havoc in the southwestern United States that Bush had flown to Saudi Arabia to appeal to the OPEC oil cartel leaders to stabilize prices, but by August 1987 oil prices had rebounded to as high as $22 per barrel. Greenspan was afraid a bounceback of inflation would follow. If the Fed did not resist price pressures, he was convinced inflation would retrace half of the decline the Fed had succeeded in bringing about since 1979. It nearly did over the next few years, despite the Fed's efforts.

It was not going to be a slam dunk for Greenspan to advance his anti-inflation agenda, though. The new chairman was ready to push the federal funds rate higher, but not yet ready or able to convince his colleagues to go along with him. While the Fed presidents, for the most part, supported Greenspan's desire to take another step to head off inflation, he met with opposition primarily from other Reagan appointees—particularly Johnson, a 39-year-old former Reagan Treasury official. The Board's vice chairman and a man of strong views, this former Green Beret from Alabama harbored ambitions of perhaps becoming chairman himself some day. He did not always see eye to eye with newcomer Greenspan. In an interview just four days before Greenspan took office, Johnson said the Fed had done enough credit tightening. With the economy doing "fine" and inflation "decelerating," monetary policy was "appropriate" and could stay on "a stable track," he told me. "There doesn't seem to be any further need for tightening at this point, but nor does there seem to be any case for easing. . . . Once you've had the economy expanding for five years, you've got to be closer to the inflationary threshold than when you started, but if we can continue these productivity gains we can continue to sustain growth without inflation and we can avoid tightening monetary policy."

Johnson was a keen observer of the *yield curve*—the closely watched curve you get when you plot the rates on money market instruments of different maturities on a graph, with the vertical axis representing yield and the horizontal axis years to maturity. The yield curve shows the ever changing differential among rates on securities ranging from 3-month Treasury bills all the way up to 30-year bonds and everything in between. When the curve is flat or sloped gently upward, that is, when rates on longer-term instruments are not much higher than on short-term money, it usually indicates the markets do not have high inflationary expectations. It can also simply mean the market is expecting a soft economy. Sometimes the yield curve can even become inverted, with short rates higher than long rates, usually signifying that the economy is headed for recession.

In 1987, the yield curve was steepening much of the time; rates on longer maturities were steadily rising relative to short-term rates, due not just to domestic price pressures but also to investor fear of a weakening dollar. That meant, among other things, higher mortgage rates. The cost of servicing the federal debt soared, swelling the budget deficit. It was this phenomenon that had led the Fed to raise interest rates on April 30. At that time, the yield on the bellwether Treasury long bond had gone as high as 9¼ percent, compared to a three-month bill rate below 6 percent. That action temporarily calmed inflation fears in the market and lent support to the dollar, with the result that the long bond yield came down to as low as 8.4 percent. But in the first week of August, it had spiked up above 9 percent before settling back to around 8.9. Johnson's view in early August was that, while the Fed would "have to watch carefully" and be prepared to tighten credit to take upward pressure off long-term rates, there was no need to act yet. By the time of the August 18 FOMC meeting, the yield curve had flattened a bit as a bond market rally pushed the 30-year bond yield down to 8.8 percent. The dollar had also been strengthening for three months. This strengthened the hand of Johnson and like-minded FOMC members who opposed raising rates.

Setting his pattern of behavior for many subsequent meetings, Greenspan quietly but firmly voiced his concerns and desires. Although money supply growth had slowed to just 5 percent, "we could very well be running into trouble at these monetary aggregate levels" because the robust pace of economic activity was increasing the "*velocity*" of money (basically how many times a dollar is spent each year). "I think there is more of a potential on the inflation side . . . at fairly low credit and monetary aggregate expansion than I think we're willing to admit." He warned of inflationary impulses stemming from dollar depreciation and from the strains continued growth would put on the country's limited resources. "Basically, my own view is that the risk of snuffing out this expansion at this stage with mild tightening is extraordinarily small." In another bit of foreshadowing of the coming crash, after listening to one official after another talk about every conceivable aspect of the economy, Greenspan observed, "We spent all morning, and no one even mentioned the stock market, which I find quite interesting in itself." It was already becoming apparent the stock market was getting overpriced relative to the bond market. Yields on risk-free government securities were far outpacing yields on much riskier common stocks, yet the Dow Jones Industrial Average kept climbing.

Greenspan got strong backing from Corrigan, who would become a valuable lieutenant and ally of the new chairman. He saw the risks as "strongly asymmetrical on the side of the economy being stronger and the inflation rate being higher." Corrigan, whose voice has a unique undulating quality going from a low rumble to a high-pitched screech, warned inflation could easily get up to 5 or 6 percent, and, "if we get to that point, then we are looking at a situation that inevitably carries with it the risks of highly destabilizing consequences for the real economy here and around the world. . . . The lessons of the past are clear: if you wait to see that kind of problem staring you in the face, the costs of unwinding it are going to be exponentially greater than the costs of checking it in the first place." San Francisco Fed president Robert Parry, who as chief economist of now-defunct Security Pacific National Bank had hired Greenspan as a consultant in the seventies, agreed that "the economy and inflationary pressures are picking up" and urged even stronger credit tightening measures than Corrigan. Minneapolis Fed president Gary Stern said the economy was "approaching a critical point when it comes to inflationary pressures." St. Louis Fed president Thomas Melzer leaned toward "worrying about inflation as opposed to the recovery. If we lost control of the dollar on the downside, we could kick off that whole cycle that we dealt with just a couple of months ago," when a falling dollar sent bond prices sprawling.

Other Fed presidents were inclined to agree rates had to go higher, but were not ready to raise them yet—in part because the dollar had strengthened about 6 percent against the currencies of other industrialized nations since May. In fact, the Fed had actually sold dollars against foreign currencies in the first two weeks of August to prevent it from strengthening too much after having earlier in the year done just the opposite—to the annoyance of officials who felt the Fed should refrain from intervention and let the market set exchange rates. The New York Fed routinely "sterilized" purchases or sales of dollars by taking offsetting open market operations to avoid any unintended contraction or expansion of the money supply, but that didn't assuage the concerns of people like Angell. Even as the FOMC met, the dollar was taking a dramatic turn for the worse, but it had no way of knowing the downtrend would continue. There was a certain schizophrenia to the Fed's dollar policy, due in good part to Jim Baker's influence, but also to the desire of some Fed officials to play the intervention game with the Treasury. The staff had built into its economic forecast an assumption the dollar would need to depreciate to boost exports and reduce the yawning U.S. trade deficit, even though it would tend to increase inflation. What was seen as excessive dollar strength was countered by dollar sales. Yet, at the same time, the Fed felt bound by the Louvre Accord to buy dollars and even raise interest rates when the dollar was weak. When the Treasury asked it to intervene, it invariably complied. As Kansas City Fed president Roger Guffey put it, "Monetary policy has to act against a depreciation in the dollar that becomes fast no matter what the cause." To some, there appeared to be no rhyme or reason other than an artificial but rather ambiguous target range for exchange rates imposed by the G-7.

At the August meeting the dollar still seemed strong enough to prevent Greenspan from getting the immediate credit tightening he wanted. The "doves" on inflation held sway for the time being. Pointing to the dollar's deceptive strength, Johnson questioned where any inflationary pressures were going to come from. Certainly, money supply growth of only 5 percent wasn't going to cause wages and prices to shoot up dramatically, since that amount of money growth also had to fuel a certain amount of real growth (nominal GNP being the sum of real output plus inflation). Governor Robert Heller didn't see how the Fed staff could justify warning about inflation in the 4 to 5 percent range. "What does that mean for the real economy if you want to make that equation square?" he asked. "I certainly disagree with the view of the world that we're having zero growth." So the most Greenspan was able to get agreement on was an "asymmetrical directive"—one that leaned toward credit tightening between the August and September meetings. For the moment the funds rate would stay in a range of 6½ to 6¾ percent. It was not a very satisfactory outcome for the new chairman, but the stage had been set for real action. It wasn't long in coming.

Selling pressure on the dollar soon resumed in earnest. It all started with a dismal and disappointing report on the deteriorating U.S. balance of trade. The dollar's depreciation since 1985 was supposed to be reducing the trade deficit by making American goods cheaper for foreigners to buy while making foreign goods more expensive for Americans to buy, but a day after FOMC met, the Commerce Department announced the deficit had widened from $14.04 billion in May to $15.71 billion in June (an annual rate of $188.5 billion per year). Currency traders jumped quickly to the conclusion that the United States would have to let its currency decline much further if it was to reduce the deficit and rushed to sell greenbacks. In the days following the meeting, the dollar plunged from roughly 150 to 141 yen and from 1.88 to 1.81 marks. In seven days, the dollar lost 7 percent of its value, nearly reaching its May lows.

Just as Melzer had warned, the dollar drop triggered a sell-off in the stock and bond markets, which gained momentum in early September when the dollar fell through the psychologically important 1.80 mark level. As it would turn out, the Dow peaked at a then record 2746.65 during trading on August 25, culminating a five-year, 122 percent upsurge. From there it was downhill at an accelerating pace. The New York Fed's foreign exchange trading desk, which just weeks before had been selling dollars to prevent what it considered undue strength, was forced to frantically buy dollars. The triple dip of the dollar, stocks, and bonds was what Greenspan needed to galvanize the FOMC into action, but he didn't wait for its next meeting—still several weeks off. Notwithstanding the Fed's own forecast for a 10 percent dollar drop, the New York Fed acted to increase pressure on reserves with the result that the funds rate rose from around 6⅝ percent to a range of 6¾ to 6⅞ percent by September 3. The next day, before the Labor Day weekend, with only three other governors on hand, Greenspan persuaded the Board to increase the discount rate from 5½ to 6 percent, which had the further effect of raising the funds rate to 7 to 7¼ percent. Banks raised their prime lending rate a half percent to 8¾ percent.

Many on Wall Street saw the Friday, September 4, discount rate hike as totally inadequate and long overdue. "It's about as exciting as 'No-Doze,' " cracked Robert Brusca, chief economist for Nikko Securities International. The Dow fell more than 38 points to 2561.38. Greenspan still had a lot to prove but had to be cautious how he proved it. For once (and maybe for the last time), the White House was more supportive of the Fed action than Wall Street. Reagan spokesman Marlin Fitzwater said the discount rate hike "should be helpful" in sustaining noninflationary economic growth, a sentiment echoed by a Treasury spokesman. Although it did not end the run on the dollar, the discount rate hike staunched the bleeding. As Sam Cross, head of the New York Fed's foreign exchange desk, later explained, traders thought, "The administration faces a dilemma—if they should pursue a strategy of allowing the dollar to decline further to deflect protectionism, it would risk further substantial rises in U.S. interest rates, given the bond market's recent sensitivity to movements in the exchange rate, as well as add to inflation concerns."

In the minds of many, the discount rate hike signaled the Fed would raise rates to protect the dollar. It was a valid perception, though not one readily admitted by Fed officials then. Corrigan now says concern about the weak dollar was a "not inconsequential" factor in the Fed's decision making, because "the exchange market and the bond market were kind of feeding on themselves. . . . The concern that I had was that renewed or intensified weakness of the dollar was going to show itself through in the first instance in the bond market, which in turn raised the spectre of renewed pressure in the stock market. . . . That was the line of thinking that was very much in my mind, rather than any suggestion of being enamored with a specific exchange rate. . . ." Baker says Greenspan was fully on board, as had been Volcker, with the Treasury's effort to support the dollar at Louvre levels, and not just through foreign exchange intervention. "Alan signed onto that Louvre agreement, and that agreement was to basically take action jointly to maintain exchange rates at or near their then current levels, then current being February of '87. And when we put stuff like that in the communiqué we didn't mean intervention solely. . . . We recognized all along . . . that you cannot stabilize exchange rates by picking a target and intervening in exchange markets. It just doesn't work. You have to coordinate the underlying economic fundamentals, and I think Alan signed onto that, as best I can recall. I don't recall any problems at all." Reagan's CEA chairman Beryl Sprinkel is even more emphatic in saying Greenspan was raising rates to support the dollar. The FOMC was divided over the role exchange rates should play in setting interest rates. Just coming into office as new president of the Federal Reserve Bank of Cleveland was a firebrand named W. Lee Hoskins, who believed the dollar would have to depreciate by 5 percent per year and saw no reason for the Fed to slow its descent. "Monetary policy shouldn't focus solely on the dollar," he told me. "Market forces basically determine the value of the dollar as they determine everything else."

Registering the markets' concern about the dollar and inflation, the yield on 30-year bonds went as high as 9¾ percent after the Fed raised short-term interest rates, before settling back to around 9.60 percent. Meanwhile, the dividend-to-price ratio on the New York Stock Exchange (NYSE) was averaging just 2.78 percent in September. It was not a sustainable situation, and stock prices were already undergoing a correction. From its close on the peak day of August 25 through September 4, the Dow had fallen more than 161 points. By the time the FOMC convened again on September 22, the Dow had fallen almost another 158 points. The Fed could only hope the long overdue correction in the overpriced market proceeded in an orderly manner. What baffled and worried officials was the behavior of bond yields. "I must say I've been surprised at the extent of the reaction," said Parry. If the trade deficit continued at a $16 billion monthly clip, the Fed might have to raise rates further to prevent another round of falling dollar, bond, and stock prices. Two days later, the Commerce Department announced the trade deficit had been $16.5 billion in July. Despite a mild wholesale price report, the dollar weakened anew, falling below 1.80 marks.

Meanwhile, some in the administration were becoming alarmed. Though publicly upbeat, Sprinkel was privately fuming over the Fed's credit tightening. So was Michael Darby, who had succeeded Johnson as assistant Treasury secretary for economic policy. After the Fed raised rates in early September, the two paid Greenspan a visit and told him they thought the Fed was "going too far" with its restrictive policy. While they agreed with the goal of reducing and ultimately eliminating inflation, they told him he was going about it too rapidly. They were not upset so much about the interest rate level as about the slow growth of money, which by then was expanding at an annual rate of less than 4 percent. Both men were "monetarist" disciples of Nobel Prize–winning economist Milton Friedman, who popularized the doctrine that the quantity of money provided by the central bank ultimately governs the level of economic activity and prices. They warned the Fed chairman he was risking "a classical monetary shock situation," where tight money precipitates recession or financial crisis. Greenspan thought Sprinkel and Darby were "overly concerned" and that the Fed could continue tightening credit without difficulty, according to a source.

Sprinkel, who as undersecretary of Treasury for monetary affairs in the first Reagan term had opposed almost any foreign exchange intervention as Volcker's policies launched the dollar to the stratosphere, was a small, barrel-chested Missourian. Affable but bombastic, he had a booming baritone voice and a penchant for using it to broadcast his views. When I interviewed him on September 18, 1987, after he had announced his intention to retire, he struck a positive pose, defending the discount rate hike as "in line with the market" and saying the Fed was committed to "sustaining economic growth without inflation. . . . I would not expect them to get off their basic course, which is to sustain growth." But privately, he was convinced the Fed was on the wrong track. About that same time he went to see new White House chief of staff Howard Baker. "I told him that I thought serious troubles were brewing and that it could lead to a very severe break in the market and probably a recession if it wasn't handled properly, and that made no sense in terms of our interests, either ending up the Reagan administration or beginning the new administration, and I said, furthermore, it will be coming on your watch." Sprinkel recalls, "Of course, I did that on purpose because that's the way you get his attention or anybody's attention. And I explained to him what I thought the problem was and still believe the problem was, namely that Jim Baker had, ever since I'd left the Treasury, been piddling around with the idea that he knew better about the level of the dollar than the markets did." After getting the Volcker Fed to ease in 1985 to depress the dollar's value, Baker in 1987 was coaxing first Volcker and now Greenspan to raise rates to support the dollar, he says.

Sprinkel, who had hoped to succeed Volcker but got thumbs down from James Baker, says Greenspan's total record "has been outstanding," but initially "under the influence of Jim Baker I think he had a misguided policy which did a lot of damage." Darby says, "It's an overstatement to say the Fed was working with Baker," although "the Fed got pulled along" on Baker's G-7 initiatives. Darby has less invidious recollections of Baker's alleged Svengali influence on Greenspan and maintains Baker never committed U.S. monetary policy to pegging the dollar, but agrees Greenspan was pursuing an overly restrictive policy. "There was concern, not only with myself but among a number of the administration and outside economists that the Fed was tightening faster than we would want in terms of risking a recession and a potential financial crisis. . . . I think that was, in fact, ultimately one of the primary factors leading to the crash, that monetary policy was not supportive of the kind of growth that was built into stock prices."

At any rate, Howard Baker was impressed enough by Sprinkel's rather terrifying presentation to ask him to write a memo formally outlining his arguments, and that in turn led to the White House chief of staff asking for a meeting among the president, the two Bakers, Greenspan, and Sprinkel. But by the time everyone could be brought together it was practically the eve of Black Monday. Some Fed officials were also concerned about the impact tight money might have on unstable financial markets. By mid-September, Johnson had coauthored with Darby a proposal to set up a crisis contingency planning group that would involve the Fed, Treasury, Securities and Exchange Commission, and Commodity Futures Trading Commission (CFTC) in preparing for a possible stock market collapse. Their premise, in Darby's words, was that "given the monetary conditions and whatever else, the stock market still had a ways to fall, and it was going to fall gradually or suddenly." They presented their proposal to Greenspan and Undersecretary of Treasury George Gould and got a mixed reception. "Greenspan, I don't think, agreed with our concern," says Darby. "I don't think Greenspan thought that there was as high a probability of a crisis as Manley Johnson and I were concerned about."

Deservedly, Greenspan has been credited with being prepared to cope with the crisis when it came, but back in September, when Darby and Johnson were seeking authorization for the crisis group, the former says, "Manley and I pushed it and George Gould and Alan Greenspan thought we were a bit of nervous nellies, but at any rate, he thought there was enough reason there to spend the resources and said, 'Go ahead.' And I think they deserve credit for that."

Greenspan says he came into office aware the stock market was in an elevated state and soon ordered internal Fed committees to begin studying how the Fed could best respond to various exigencies, including a sharp market correction. "It helped us when the market broke," he recalls. "It's not as though it broke in the way we expected it would break precisely, or that the views we had as to what we would do were the ones that we eventually did, but it forced us to think out what type of problems might emerge, and indeed those were similar to what actually did occur. But the problem is, in an event like that you can never fully pre-plan how you'll react. It's like a war; the strategy in a war never goes the way you plan it. Nevertheless, having a strategy gives you a conceptual basis to think through the issues. . . ."

Administration concerns that monetary policy was dangerously tight do not seem to have swayed Greenspan's thinking at the September 22 FOMC meeting. Transcripts show Greenspan and senior Fed staffers felt there was no alternative but to maintain, if not increase, a tight credit posture in the face of weakness in the dollar and bond prices. But there was no consensus for aggressively raising rates so soon after the early September actions. Technically, the committee left pressure on bank reserves unchanged by keeping its target for bank discount window borrowings at $600 million, where it had been since early September, but the practical effect was to increase the funds rate to around 7½ percent because banks had been borrowing less than that amount before the meeting, and now the New York Fed tightened reserve pressures to force banks to borrow more.

Despite the Fed's concern about the dollar, its staff forecast was counting on further dollar depreciation. "We continue to anticipate that a considerable further depreciation of the dollar will be needed eventually to achieve acceptable external adjustment [trade deficit reduction] in the face of at best moderate growth of aggregate demand abroad," Michael Prell, director of the Fed's Division of Research and Statistics, told the FOMC. "Thus, we have built into the forecast a decline in the dollar of roughly 10 percent at an annual rate." Prell's dollar assumption was made in the context of a forecast that real GNP would slow from 3 percent in 1987 to 2¼ percent in 1988, with much of the growth coming from net exports, fueled by a cheaper dollar and faster growth by foreign economies. However, the tendency for dollar weakness to pull down bond prices and drive up medium- and long-term interest rates, dictated that the Fed moderate the dollar's decline by raising short-term rates. Before the meeting, the long bond yield had zoomed toward 10 percent before retreating to around 9.6 percent, and Peter Sternlight, who ran the New York Fed's open market desk, told the committee the market was "uneasy." Cross advised that the dollar "remains vulnerable to downward pressure." In light of those circumstances, Donald Kohn, director of the Fed Board's Division of Monetary Affairs, recommended a policy "in which dollar declines are partly resisted with interest rate increases in order to contain inflation pressures." Otherwise, there could be "a sudden drop in demands for dollar assets, perhaps associated with a loss in confidence in the future purchasing power of the dollar. . . ." Prell envisioned a federal funds rate in the 8 to 8½ percent range by the following spring, compared to 7 to 7¼ percent at the time.

The staff's assumption that a 10 percent dollar drop would fuel export-led growth while higher interest rates would cool domestic spending and reduce the trade deficit was greeted with skepticism. Philadelphia Fed president Edward Boehne questioned whether the trade deficit could be brought down significantly without a recession. History suggested "the U.S. is going to have to go through kind of a wringer" to suppress domestic demand for imported goods. Fed governor Martha Seger thought it was a mistake to rely on exports to produce at least half the economy's growth. Melzer warned a 10 percent dollar drop would be inflationary. Angell blasted "the development of an exchange rate policy that no one thought out that carefully ahead of time." He felt the Louvre Accord had committed the Fed to set exchange rates. "It's unfortunate that there can't be some median ground between recognizing that monetary policy needs to be adjusted to take into consideration foreign exchange developments and trying to pinpoint and draw lines in the sand in regard to foreign exchange rates. If we had been willing to make monetary policy adjustments before we drew the lines in the sand, we probably would have avoided some of the difficulties we are now in." Now that the line had been drawn it was going to be "very difficult to unhitch during a period in which inflation expectations are on the increase" because the markets expected the Fed to raise rates to support the dollar.

The market's palpable shakiness caused a tense atmosphere around the huge conference table at the Federal Reserve Board, over which hangs the world's most threatening-looking chandelier like a scene from Edgar Allan Poe's *The Pit and the Pendulum*. Heller said, "It would be a mistake to hold up the dollar with further tightening of monetary policy, because we would be inviting a slowdown in those sectors that, at the moment, are really carrying the economy: real estate would be further depressed, and the capital sector would slow down." Johnson also opposed raising rates and, like the proverbial optimistic child searching for the pony in the manure, found encouragement that inflation fears had been overcome in an ephemeral "flattening in the yield curve." He argued the markets had gotten carried away with their inflation fears and would "eventually settle down." Seger blamed the run-up in long-term rates on Wall Street "gunslingers" who were trading bonds on the basis of dollar movements and causing a "transmission from the exchange market into the bond market with the speed of light almost." But Corrigan saw the need to raise rates not just to help the dollar but because he feared price-wage pressures with "actual GNP brushing up against potential GNP" and labor markets "near the danger zone."

Corrigan's comment typified how the Fed looked at the world. Key to the Fed's thinking on controlling inflation is its concept of noninflationary growth potential. The Fed believed the economy can grow no more than 2½ percent in real terms over the long-run without causing wage-price pressures to accelerate. That potential growth estimate is based on the growth rate of the population and productivity. A related concept is the "nonaccelerating inflation rate of unemployment" (NAIRU), also known as the "natural rate of unemployment." The Fed has no fixed idea of where NAIRU lies, but whenever unemployment gets much below 6 percent, officials' palms start to sweat on the premise that labor shortages will spur higher wage demands, higher production costs, bigger price hikes, and so on. This is sometimes known as the *Phillips Curve* analysis, which postulates an inverse relationship between inflation and unemployment. If NAIRU were to fall from 6 percent to 5½ percent, as some think it has, Fed doctrine holds the economy would be able to grow above its potential or *trend* rate until unemployment is reduced to 5½ percent, but then growth would have to be restrained to no more than potential to prevent inflation. The Fed staff is guided by its *"output gap"* model, which essentially tries to project where actual growth is headed relative to the economy's potential. The staff forecasts where GDP or at that time GNP (gross national product, or the total output of goods and services) will be a year ahead, compares it to what it thinks potential GDP should be at that point, and on the basis of the output gap (the extent to which actual GDP falls short of or exceeds potential), forecasts what inflation will do a year beyond that. If it appears GDP is on a trajectory that will exceed potential, the staff projects rising inflation and recommends credit tightening to slow the pace of actual growth. If actual GDP seems destined to come in below potential, the staff recommends stimulative policies to spur growth.[3]

Greenspan split the difference at the September 22 meeting and crafted a compromise for "maintaining" the prevailing degree of reserve pressures, knowing this would mean a higher funds rate. Describing himself as "about in the middle," Greenspan said the economy was "clearly quite strong" but also "fairly well balanced." While "we do not yet have any evidence of actual inflation," the Fed was "tight and likely to get tighter." Oddly enough, not knowing that the Fed had taken another step up in interest rates, the stock market mounted a rally the day of the meeting, with the Dow rising more than 75 points. The rate hike further convinced elements of the administration that monetary policy was being skewed by external considerations. The Fed was "focusing more on the dollar than on the state of the economy," a Reagan adviser complained. "The problem with that kind of approach is that when a monetary slowdown affects the economy, by the time you see the signs of it it's too late. You tend to get a false sense of security, and you can end up stabilizing the dollar by running the economy into the toilet. The probability of that occurring is getting larger the longer we have this relatively restrictive policy stance." Just because other G-7 countries "want to try to stabilize the dollar . . . it need not be in our interest to stabilize it." In fact, the dollar needed to come down to lower the trade deficit, and the Fed had no cause to raise interest rates to control inflation because "the economy is not that strong to generate inflationary pressures."

Instead of a united front to settle nervous global markets, there was open bickering among the major industrial nations even before their finance ministers and central bankers met Saturday, September 26, during the annual IMF–World Bank meetings in Washington—Greenspan's first G-7 meeting. They issued a communiqué papering over their differences, recommitting themselves to "cooperate closely to foster the stability of exchange rates around current levels." But deep divisions were not far below the surface. Before the meeting James Baker let it be known he intended to pressure Germany to stimulate its economy, which was falling far short of the 2½ percent real growth pace it had projected earlier in the year. Baker leaned on Germany to pursue an easier monetary policy and cut taxes and pressed Japan to stimulate its economy, even though it was growing at a 3½ percent rate. Japan countered that the United States should reduce its budget deficit.

Japanese money market rates were already on the rise, and Deputy Finance Minister Toyoo Gyoten hinted at yet higher rates due to inflation pressures. After the G-7 meeting, Bank of Japan governor Satoshi Sumita, who largely did the Ministry of Finance's bidding, said, "For the time being we have no intention of raising the discount rate in Japan." When I asked Greenspan about Sumita's comment, his skeptical reply was, "Does he mean because the markets are closed for the weekend?" Despite rapid money growth and rising inflation, Japan bowed to U.S. pressure and did not tighten monetary policy; indeed, it would soon turn to an easier policy, leading to a stock and real estate bubble, followed by recession and severe banking problems. Germany chose a different course, refusing to give in to U.S. demands that it hold interest rates down to keep the mark from rising against the dollar. Feelings still run high. Tietmeyer, at the time Germany's deputy finance minister, says, "There were no formally agreed Louvre exchange rate targets, at least not ones that Germany would have supported, and it would have been even worse if the Bundesbank, at this time, would have done the same thing the Japanese did. We would be in a [mess]. . . . The Japanese gave in, not on their fiscal policy, but they gave in on their monetary policy. They created the big bubble, with all the consequences we see today." Like Japan, Germany was "under pressure" from Baker to run looser policies, but "the German side didn't give in to the pressure."

A day after the G-7 met, tensions surfaced among the world's top finance ministers at a meeting of the IMF's policymaking Interim Committee. Taking another thinly veiled shot at Germany, Baker declared "slow growth in Europe is a matter of concern, particularly in the largest countries. It will be difficult to sustain strong export-led growth in the developing world if Europe does not participate in the process of strengthening growth now underway in other countries." No doubt Baker was serious about wanting less developed countries, or LDCs, to grow so they could service their debts to American banks, but his subtext was promoting export-led growth in the United States, and he expected Germany and Japan to do their part by stimulating demand. Neither

German finance minister Gerhard Stoltenberg nor Bundesbank president Poehl gave Baker much satisfaction. The former said he had no intention of proposing any further tax cuts, while the latter defended German rate hikes. Summing up the German attitude, a Stoltenberg aide told me, "We're doing our best. Our total demand is increasing, the contribution to growth of exports is decreasing, and we're planning tax reform for next year, so I'd say we are on the right way." Baker said the G-7 had achieved "greater stability of exchange rates," but "further progress" was needed. The dollar had indeed "stabilized" at around 142 yen and 1.82 marks, but at the price of higher U.S. interest rates, and as usually happens, European and Japanese rates were feeling the tug from U.S. rates. Baker expected Germany and Japan to stimulate their economies to reduce their trade surpluses, but they had been forced to raise rates. British chancellor of the exchequer Nigel Lawson said he did not want a weak dollar, but it did "not necessarily follow" that the United States had to raise interest rates and put upward pressure on rates around the world. Dutch finance minister and interim committee chairman Onno Ruding warned, "The world would be on the wrong track if both surplus and deficit countries raised their interest rates." The stage was set for the next even nastier round as world financial markets grew increasingly uneasy.

In the meantime, fiscal policy briefly took center stage. After endless wrangling with the Democratic Congress, President Reagan on September 29 reluctantly signed a bill increasing the national debt limit to $2.8 trillion and amending the 1985 Gramm-Rudman-Hollings balanced budget act. The legislation relaxed the deficit reduction requirements for fiscal year (FY) 1988, which began October 1, 1987, and extended the supposed deadline for a balanced budget two years until 1993. In place of a deficit target of $108 billion for FY 1988, Congress had now given itself a $144 billion target, with a maximum $23 billion automatic cut. The president was forced to sign it or close down the government and default on the national debt. The budget package was not well received by the financial markets. On top of inflation and dollar fears, dealers and investors now had the prospect of larger-than-planned amounts of government paper coming to market to drive down prices and drive up yields. As it would turn out, 1987 was the low ebb for the deficit—$149.8 billion.

On Friday, October 2, a strong employment report that sent the unemployment rate down to 5.8 percent overall renewed speculation the Fed would raise rates further to counter economic "overheating." Greenspan tried to dampen such talk. Taking the unusual step of appearing on ABC-TV's *This Week With David Brinkley* on Sunday, October 4, he said longer-term interest rates embodied an unjustified "inflation premium," which the Fed had been trying to counter by nudging up short-term rates. He didn't rule out further rate hikes "if we can calibrate a small rise" that would reduce that premium in long rates, but he "hoped" to avoid raising the discount rate again. If the Fed's past rate moves were successful, "we might see interest rates starting down." Voicing his frustration with market psychology, Greenspan said that even though "there are just no signs that inflation is picking up," the public was afraid that "now that we've gotten inflation under control the next step is to get it out of control again. . . . If everyone gets it into his head that inflation is inevitable, they'll start taking steps that will make it inevitable."[4] Instead of the hoped-for calming effect, Greenspan's hints of no further rate hikes helped renew downward pressure on the dollar and in turn bond and stock prices. In the ensuing week, the yield on 30-year Treasuries soared to within a hair's breadth of 10 percent, and intermediate and long-term interest rates throughout the world followed. Banks raised their prime lending rate a half percent from 8¾ to 9¼ percent on October 7. Economists were critical of Greenspan's performance. "He's not establishing much credibility," said one Fed watcher. "He hasn't made a consistent view known. What I can't understand is why he's saying that there is no danger of inflation, then talks down the dollar." Another analyst said Greenspan "sounded more like a Fed watcher than the chairman of the Federal Reserve." It was Greenspan's last TV show.

After rising nearly 73 points since the FOMC meeting, the Dow fell almost 159 points in the week after Greenspan's television debut, including its largest ever one-day decline to date—a 91.55 point plunge on October 6. It was just the beginning of a weeks-long nightmare. The following week, the Dow broke more records, falling cumulatively almost 225 points, culminating with the 108.35-point fall on Friday, October 16. Then came Black Monday, October 19. Many technical explanations have been offered, many scapegoats sought, but the fundamentals were obvious: Soaring interest rates (1) dimmed prospects for the economy, (2) raised business borrowing costs and narrowed prospective profit margins, and (3) made stocks less attractive to investors. With the dollar weak and the Fed talking about inflation, the outlook was for yet higher interest rates. Why hold stocks? Very similar fundamentals, minus the weak currency element, were at work in other nations. Those fundamentals did not guarantee a stock market collapse as large or as sudden as what occurred, however. For that a trigger was needed. Some blame evil speculators and high-tech arbitrageurs using sophisticated computerized trading strategies. Some blame Japanese investors for pulling out of the bond market. Some blame congressional tax talk. Some blame the Fed. Another frequently cited catalyst is Baker's rhetoric about interest and exchange rates.

Looking back at the week of October 16, the only wonder is that the stock market did not fare worse. On Tuesday, the thirteenth, came news that House Ways and Means Committee chairman Representative Dan Rostenkowski and his troops were pushing a $12 billion package that would have eliminated the tax benefits associated with corporate leveraged buyouts and raised taxes on profits made by so-called corporate raiders. A flurry of statements by Fed officials left the markets bewildered. Greenspan, Angell, and Heller all spoke about the strength of the economy, but downplayed inflation and suggested the rise in long-term interest rates had been unjustified. Heller emphasized the Fed's role was to "maintain constancy in the dollar," thereby confirming suspicions the Fed was raising rates to support it. On Wednesday, came word of a $15.7 billion August trade deficit, $2 billion more than expected, causing the dollar to plunge and the yield on the Treasury long bond to approach 10 percent. Although the Fed had probably suspended credit tightening, many were convinced the Fed would raise the discount rate from 6 to 6½ percent, and fear of rising rates caused the Dow to close down a new record 95.46 points.

On Thursday, October 15, the yield on 30-year Treasury bonds went through the 10 percent barrier and kept right on going—up to nearly 10.4 percent. Banks raised the prime another half percent to 9¾. Once again, Fed officials were out and about making not always consistent statements that did little to clarify where policy might be headed and kept discount rate hike talk going. Volcker, whose thoughts still carried weight, said the Fed should not relax its fight against inflation. Meanwhile, Baker went to the White House and, after a meeting with the president, visited the press room to give reporters an earful. Sounding ominously like Herbert Hoover, he declared rising interest rates were not justified by a "fundamentally sound" economy and railed against the bond market's "overblown" inflation fears. Worst of all, at a time when the markets were already jittery about the dollar, Baker lambasted the Bundesbank for raising rates. In truth, German short-term interest rates, the only rates under direct Bundesbank control, had risen modestly.[5] Nevertheless, he charged Germany's rate hikes were "not in accord with the spirit" of G-7 agreements. Baker's comments left the impression that G-7 cooperation to keep the dollar stable was breaking down. Already that morning, the Fed had injected reserves into the banking system to hold short-term interest rates down, thereby signaling it was not about to raise the discount rate again despite the dollar's woes. Just for good measure, the administration cast doubt on its ability to meet the Gramm-Rudman deficit target for 1988. Most of the Dow's 57.61 point loss on October 15 occurred in the final half hour of trading after Baker spoke.

On Friday, October 16, to make things even more interesting, Iran attacked a U.S.-flagged oil tanker an hour and a half before the opening bell on the New York Stock Exchange, adding to the general sense things were coming unglued. By late morning, the rout was underway, as so-called *program selling* of large blocks of shares commenced. At one point, I called a contact at the Treasury to get his reaction. "It's down 130 points? Jesus!" he yelped. By the time trading had mercifully ended for the week, with the Dow off more than 100 points for the first time ever on volume of 338 million shares, it was obvious this was more than your ordinary stock market correction. Since October 1, the Dow had fallen 392 points, 15 percent of its value; since the August 25 peak, 475 points or 17½ percent. Stock sales by just four trading institutions totalled over $600 million. There was a feeling it was not going to get any better.

That day, the meeting Sprinkel had requested weeks before was finally convened in Reagan's quarters on the top floor of the White House. Present, besides Reagan and Sprinkel, were both Bakers and Greenspan. First to speak was James Baker, who "explained to the President that everything was going just fine—no difficulty, a little rise in interest rates, nothing to be concerned about," Sprinkel recalls. "And then it was passed to Alan Greenspan, and he went through the same song and dance." Baker and Greenspan appear to have "compared their notes before they came in." Sprinkel had tendered his resignation as CEA chairman and was retiring from government to care for his sickly wife. He felt free to say what was on his mind after Greenspan had finished, and he didn't hold back. "I told the President that Alan Greenspan and I had been good friends for many years—25 or 30 years—and that we usually agreed on most economic policy issues. I used to be on the board of economists of *Time* magazine with Alan, so I knew him, and I knew him quite well, and I said, 'We usually agree, but in this case I want to tell you why he's dead wrong.' Of course, that didn't sit very well with either Jim Baker or Alan Greenspan. And I explained why I thought the problem developed." Once again, Sprinkel accused Baker of inducing Greenspan to raise rates to peg the dollar. After considerable bickering, the meeting broke with nothing resolved.

Baker scoffs when reminded of Sprinkel's arguments. "There wasn't a substantial increase in interest rates, and that wasn't the way we operated anyway. I mean, the fact of the matter is there were many more important factors than U.S. interest rates in terms of how the markets viewed the dollar. The trade deficit was the primary factor, but also the presumed intentions of policymakers like the Treasury and the administration. Did you want the dollar to stay where it was? Did you want it to go higher? Did you want it to go lower? That's basically what people, what market people acted on. They didn't act on whether or not the federal funds rate was up a little bit or not. The truth of the matter is Beryl was one of these guys who felt that you never did anything to coordinate economic policy. I mean, he was the foremost proponent of benign neglect that led to a situation that helped create . . . the structural imbalances that we were trying to address in the Plaza. Look where the dollar was [in 1985]—3.50 marks and 250 yen! . . . And also, that view totally overlooks the importance of staving off what were then some significant protectionist pressures in the Democratic Congress. . . . And the one thing that got them off of it, frankly, was the fact that we were willing to try to coordinate policies in a way to reduce the [trade] imbalances . . . And Beryl just didn't like it. It wasn't his policy, he didn't know anything about it when we changed it, so he didn't like it."

Sprinkel was not alone, however. Fairly or unfairly, there was a widespread view on Wall Street that Greenspan and the Fed had gotten themselves into a box on exchange rates and had lost their grip on the economy and the financial markets.

Over the weekend, the world's financial leaders and policymakers waited in dread for what might happen Monday morning when trading opened on the Tokyo Stock Exchange, then swept relentlessly westward with the hands of the clock to London and on to New York. They would not be disappointed. Baker made sure of that. On Sunday, October 18, he went on NBC's *Meet The Press*. After blaming the Democrats for "making business extremely nervous" and spooking Wall Street by talking higher taxes, he did a little spooking of his own. He blasted German monetary policy with even greater ferocity than before and came even closer to implying the United States would let the dollar fall rather than raise its own rates. "We will not sit back in this country and watch the surplus countries jack up interest rates and squeeze growth world-wide on the expectation that the United States somehow will follow."

Trichet, then director of the Treasury in the French Finance Ministry, is too polite to mention Baker by name, but says, "It seems to me that it's obvious that quarrels triggered [the crash]. . . . The world was in a very unstable situation, particularly because of the decoupling [of stock and bond prices] . . . and, of course, in this uncertain world, the fact that the G-7 could be obviously and openly and visibly divided created a sentiment, a fantastic sentiment, of uneasiness. . . . To embark on open quarreling is always a very, very bad influence, in a world which is marked by psychology as well as by realities." Crow says Baker's incitement "was pretty evident." As for Baker's contentions that Germany had not lived up to its Louvre commitments, Crow says, "It could be, of course, that their commitments weren't as clear as Mr. Baker thought they were. . . ." Tietmeyer recalls, "Stocks were very high; everybody was over-optimistic, and then the triggering point was, of course, the criticism by Baker to the Bundesbank." "Tight-meyer," as Baker jokingly calls him, says the crash grew out of "a misinterpretation" of the Louvre Accord on exchange rates and what it implied for the monetary policies of the G-7 countries. Baker and his deputy at the time, Richard Darman, "followed a policy of establishing a sort of target zone [for exchange rates] with precise rules for intervention and with pressure . . . to orient the policy of the countries simply to the exchange rate agreement . . . ," says Tietmeyer, who adds Baker was demanding more fiscal and monetary stimulus than Germany could prudently do. "The Bundesbank didn't give in more than it could do for looking at the internal stability. . . ."

Angell says the Fed had failed to take adequate steps to arrest inflation expectations during 1986 to 1987, "and then having Jimmy Baker be involved as he was in regard to sort of playing the dollar card with Germany and Japan, we ended up with that stock market crash." Baker did not singlehandedly cause the crash but was "the straw that broke the camel's back." Even the so-called Brady Report on the crash, prepared under the direction of the Treasury secretary's hand-picked task force chairman and eventual successor, Nicholas Brady, finds Baker culpable: "He appeared to warn the Bundesbank that if monetary easing in Germany was not forthcoming, the U.S. could feel less inclined to support the dollar in the foreign currency markets. Reacting to press accounts, Japanese and European investors would sell the dollar in early Monday trading." Baker dismisses allegations he precipitated the crash, calling his role "at most de minimis."

Darby says it was "a fundamental misunderstanding" that Baker had committed the Fed to support the dollar at the Louvre. "Jim Baker was quite clear that at the Louvre he never put U.S. monetary policy on the table, that not objecting to the mark or the yen being pegged to the dollar was far different from our agreeing to put U.S. monetary policy on the table. If the Bundesbank or the Bank of Japan (BOJ) wanted to adjust their monetary policy in order to do so, to in effect go back to the good old days of Bretton Woods, that was acceptable to the U.S., [but Baker only agreed] to cooperate with minor amounts of support of sterilized interventions. But there was a misperception out that the Fed would have to tighten to maintain the value of the dollar, and then it came as a shock when the Secretary said that the Federal Reserve's monetary policy is not constrained by the exchange rate." Fed governor Edward Kelley, an old friend of Baker who joined the Fed that May, calls it "absurd to say that [Baker's rhetoric] was a major cause or even a minor cause of that market crash. What happened in that crash was that the market, and all the pros in it, had been expecting a decline of about the magnitude that, in fact, occurred, for a long time! But what happened was that the mechanics of the market, how the market actually works, internally, just broke down under the pressures that began to emerge, and those pressures fed on themselves as a result. And you got what would have been, under more normal circumstances, a decline that might have taken three to six months to play out, you got it in two trading sessions."

Whatever the cause, people awoke Monday morning to find global markets in disarray. After spending a nerve-wracking weekend, Sprinkel came in before the regular 7 A.M. staff meeting to check overseas markets and found "things were coming apart around the world. And all the guessing was that there was going to be a resumed sharp break in the [U.S.] market that day, and we had meetings in the White House as to what we should do about it." It all started in Tokyo, where the Nikkei index, the Dow Jones of Japan, fell 2½ percent. The selling accelerated on the London Stock Exchange, which had been closed Friday due to a devastating gale, which uprooted trees and kept people at home. By midday, the market was off 10 percent before closing down 10.84 percent. A number of firms unloaded U.S. stocks listed in London to get a jump on New York trading. One mutual fund complex sold $95 million of its equity portfolio there. Unlike Friday, a torrent of selling started the moment trading began on the New York Stock Exchange at 9:30 A.M.

Unlike 1929, there were not a lot of investors who had borrowed from their brokers and bought stock on margin, but 1987 had something which 1929 did not. Equities markets were now closely interlocked with the commodity exchanges of Chicago, which had only five years earlier innovated trading in stock index futures. These contracts enabled individuals and institutions to take a leveraged position on the entire stock market, either for speculative or hedging purposes.[6] Leading the way were the Chicago Mercantile Exchange (CME) with its S&P 500 index contract, and the Chicago Board of Trade (CBT) with its Major Market Index (MMI), a contract based on the share values of 20 leading companies. One could also buy options (*puts* and *calls*) on the stock indices. The real stock market was connected to the futures and options markets via *DOT*, an automated transaction system operated by the New York Stock Exchange, which was about to be strained to the limit, along with the exchanges' clearing and settlement systems.

Stock index futures had created a whole new playground for Wall Street whizkids—and a whole new type of market player: the *index arbitrageur*, who sought to profit from disparities between the futures contract and the underlying component stocks. Whenever futures appeared undervalued relative to stocks, the arbitrageur could buy futures and sells stocks or vice versa. A variation was *index substitution*, where an institutional investor might substitute positions in index futures for actual stock holdings if it appeared the futures were selling at a discount to shares. Not merely speculative, these *derivative products* had created valuable risk hedging opportunities for pension funds and mutual funds, to whom Americans had entrusted billions of dollars worth of savings. By buying and selling derivatives, portfolio managers could limit the risk of loss on their cash securities holdings. The advent of index futures and options had revolutionized the practice of *portfolio insurance*. Investment managers could now use an array of techniques to buy and sell stocks and/or futures whenever the market had moved a predetermined amount. As much as $90 billion in assets were being managed with portfolio insurance at the time of the crash. There was nothing inherently wrong with these new products or strategies, but in an overpriced and unstable market, they likely sped up the inevitable.

On Friday, October 16, program trading models, not to mention common sense, were telling institutional investors it was time to sell, and sell they did. There was massive unloading of stocks, but at the end of the session the bears' appetite was not sated. "The market's decline created a huge overhang of selling pressure—enough to crush the equity markets in the following week," according to the Brady Report. "The portfolio insurers had sold fewer futures contracts than their models had dictated." One portfolio insurance client was told over the weekend it needed to sell 70 percent of its remaining shares on Monday to conform to the parameters of the insurance model. The CFTC said in a January 1988 report "There was, as a result of stock price declines the previous week, a significant overhang of portfolio insurance sell programs, which were likely to be implemented in the stock or futures market that Monday."

Before the New York and American exchanges opened Monday, investors were venting their bearish wrath in the futures market. Both the MMI and S&P 500 futures contracts opened down sharply, as portfolio insurers sold futures equivalent to nearly $400 million worth of stocks in the first half hour of trading on the CBT and CME. This selling, on top of what had gone on Friday, left the index futures trading at a gaping discount to the value of the underlying indices, and this in turn induced index arbitrageurs to sell actual shares when trading opened on the Big Board. At the opening bell, "specialist" firms that made a market in individual stocks "faced large order imbalances," says the Brady Report. In the DOT system alone, roughly $500 million of sell orders were awaiting the start of trading, half of them from index arbitrageurs seeing an apparent chance to make a killing on the futures discount. That discount grew in the first hour or so, making it seem even more attractive to sell stocks, but it was an illusion, reflecting stale stock price quotes caused by delays in the start-up of trading in some stocks and trading halts in others as specialists frantically tried to deal with the onslaught of selling. "During the first hour, the reported levels of the S&P and Dow indices reflected out-of-date Friday closing prices for the large number of stocks which had not yet been opened for trading," says the Brady Report. "Based on this apparent discount, index arbitrageurs entered sell-at-market orders through DOT, planning to cover by later purchases of futures at lower prices." The CFTC concurs: "Since a substantial number of the component stocks of the indices were not trading, their current values were not reflected in the indices . . . it became very difficult or impossible to execute index arbitrage or other stock trades on that Monday afternoon because no one could be sure whether stock sale orders would be executed and, if executed, what the transaction prices of the individual stocks in the arbitrage portfolios would be."

A large mutual fund group sold 25.8 million shares of stock on the NYSE, nearly 17.5 million of them in the first half hour of trading. By 10 A.M., as the weight of selling pressure became obvious, the exchange's chairman John Phelan was already rattled enough to call a special meeting of the heads of the largest member firms to assess the situation and consider whether to take the unprecedented step of halting trading. By 10:30 A.M., the Dow was off 104 points, and by 11 A.M. another 104. Spurring the selling binge, the fixed income market continued its parallel implosion. The yield on the Treasury long bond rose to 10½ percent in the early going. Strangely, when it became apparent shortly before 11 A.M. that the discount on futures was indeed an illusion, a rally began in futures which carried over into equities.

Greenspan had been closely monitoring the markets all morning and had convened the joint agency crisis contingency planning group which he had authorized. He had turned his office into a command post, a nerve center for hotline communications with top officials at the New York and other Federal Reserve banks, foreign central banks, and the major stock and commodities exchanges. Here, he and his key lieutenants took scores of frantic calls about overloaded trading systems, precariously situated major market players, and strained financial institutions. But now, with the market seemingly coming back, and not wanting to appear panicked, Greenspan decided to keep an engagement in Dallas, Texas, where he was to make a major speech the next morning to 6,000 delegates to the American Bankers Association convention. Leaving the crisis management in the capable hands of Corrigan in New York and Johnson at the Board, he took a flight around midday. Little did he know the market was about to take a dramatic turn for the worse.

The late morning rally was soon broken by wave after wave of selling by portfolio insurers. One firm made 13 sales of $100 million blocks of stock. Amplifying the rush to sell early that afternoon was SEC chairman David Ruder's statement that he was considering closing the market. Ruder had talked about imposing a trading halt two weeks earlier in a speech. Now, asked by reporters whether he had discussed halting trading, Ruder replied, "Anything is possible. . . . There is some point, and I don't know what that point is, that I would be interested in talking to the NYSE about a temporary, very temporary halt in trading." The top securities regulator's uncircumspect musings made people even more panicky to sell while they had the chance, knowing that whenever the market reopened stocks would start trading well below where they were when the market closed. Between 1:30 and 2 P.M., portfolio insurers, index arbitrageurs, and others sold hundreds of millions of dollars worth of stock. Sixteen minutes after Ruder had made the comment, the SEC put out a statement saying it was not considering closing the market. As he was besieged by calls, Ruder denied he ever said it. At the Treasury, absent traveling James Baker, Gould and Darby were on a conference call with Ruder. "We were trying to figure out what was going on, and we were assuring [Ruder] on the phone that we never ever told anyone that he might close the markets," recalls Darby, "and Gould asked him, 'You know, there are reports that you're contemplating closing the market,' and Ruder told him, 'No.' And CNN was, at that moment, playing the videotape. So that caused a few guffaws." Darby says "Ruder probably didn't realize what he was saying and how that might scare people, lead them to try to get to the door before it was too late." Corrigan advised, "The problem is if you close this thing you've got to figure out how you're going to open it."

At the White House, Reagan's advisers were madly scurrying around trying to decide what to do as the news from Wall Street got more and more scary. Some were urging the president to use emergency authority to close the financial markets and declare a bank holiday. "It was just chaos that day, honestly it was just chaos," a former official recalls. "There was real panic in that building that afternoon." Sprinkel says, "People had crazy ideas. A member of the White House staff wanted to shut down the market, which I thought was preposterous. I convinced Howard Baker that would be foolish, that we ought to keep the markets open." With both Baker and Greenspan out of pocket, Howard Baker urged Sprinkel to maintain communication with the markets in New York and Chicago and keep them open and functioning.

Two blocks to the east, at Treasury, Gould turned his office into a war room. Deploying Darby and Assistant Secretary for Domestic Finance Charles Sethness to ride herd on the futures and cash markets, Gould coordinated with the Fed, SEC, and CFTC to stay abreast of developments and make sure no major financial institutions failed. Gould, a well-connected former investment banker, was concerned whether otherwise sound securities firms could meet their commitments in such a crazed climate, where banks might be reluctant to extend their usual credits. Market players needed the proceeds of sales in New York to pay for purchases in Chicago and vice versa. Firms had hedged securities positions, and rumors were flying that firms' cash flows would be insufficient to meet margin calls on losing futures positions. If enough of that went on, exchange clearinghouses might not be able to deliver funds to other market participants. "At times these houses had to pay a billion or two on one leg that they were making on the other leg of a hedge," says Darby. "Those uncoordinated payments, the inability at the time to use a big position in one part of the hedge to offset a big negative position on the other part, were the cause of a lot of unfounded fears. . . . If we could just fix that, that would solve a lot of the potential risks from people being afraid to live up to commitments where there was no real change in net worth."

The Treasury's international team also sprang into action, fearing the crash would set off secondary shock waves in currency and bond markets. Charles

Dallara, then deputy assistant secretary for international finance, arrived in Dakar, Senegal, "dead-tired," after a long trip via Paris, and was immediately told by a U.S. Embassy official he had been summoned back to Washington by Assistant Treasury Secretary for International Affairs David Mulford. "I said, 'you've got to be kidding! I'm not doing anything but getting some rest.' He said the stock market dropped 500 points, and I thought he was joking. Then I went to bed, and the phone rang a few hours later, and Mulford called and, sure enough, they were very anxious." Within 24 hours he was back in Washington manning phone lines to Frankfurt, Tokyo, and elsewhere.

On the front lines in New York, Corrigan played the most critical role of all. "Corrigan was crucial to the whole operation," says Greenspan. "To the extent that he was dealing with the larger banks that the Federal Reserve Bank of New York supervised, Corrigan was the key player as far as I was concerned. Without his skills, it would have been much more difficult for us." The Fed's main troubleshooter since his days as Volcker's top assistant, Corrigan had long ago concluded the stock market's "overbought" condition relative to bonds was "trouble looking for a place to happen." He and his New York Fed colleagues had "done a lot of brainstorming" about the linkages between the stock futures and cash markets and the "flash points" that might arise in the financial system. He had developed a sixth sense about where the vulnerabilities lay, and he turned his extensive experience and contacts to making sure that, no matter how bad the bloodletting on Wall Street became, the underlying structure would stand. Above all, these billions of dollars in transactions among countless market participants had to be swiftly cleared and settled so that a chain reaction of defaults and failures did not occur among financial institutions. Corrigan knew it was a time of severe testing for the nation's sophisticated but largely untried electronic payments system.

After a final rally which brought the Dow back up 50 points between 2:00 and 2:30 P.M., selling became even more furious than before. As the January 1988 Brady Report succinctly puts it, "The rest of Monday afternoon was disastrous." The SEC, in the report it issued a month later, talks of "near panic selling by the end of the trading session." The CFTC, which interviewed scores of arbitrage traders and investment managers for its report, says, "It became very difficult or impossible to execute index arbitrage or other stock trades on that Monday afternoon because no one could be sure whether stock sale orders would be executed and, if executed, what the transaction prices of the individual stocks in the arbitrage portfolios would be. . . . Some said it was days before they learned whether stock orders entered on October 19 had been filled." Many index arbitrageurs just stopped trading, thereby denying buying support to the futures market, which plunged to a deep 20-point discount. Such a large discount on futures seemed to be saying stocks were still overvalued, making people even more reluctant to buy shares. In the final hour of trading, the Dow plunged 300 points.

No one had ever seen anything remotely like it. As news of the mounting losses on Wall Street came in to the White House, a usually sane senior administration official was seen running down the corridors of the Old Executive Office Building shouting, "It's in free fall!" with what a source describes as "an alarming degree of panic in his voice. I mean it was just your worst nightmare. We had this paper version of AP [the Associated Press], and it was just shooting out bulletin after bulletin: 'It's down 150, it's down 200, it's down 250,' and he was just running down the hall waving these things. It's comical now, but at the time it was actually quite serious, because we didn't know how much further it was going to go, and it did seem just like the bottom had fallen out of the whole market." Talk mounted that Reagan should close the markets and the banks. A close observer recalls a feeling of helplessness. "There was a perception that something dramatic had to be done, that this wasn't a problem that you could just start again in the morning and, 'Ah well, we'll work it out bit by bit' . . . that the action needed to be symbolic as well as effective, and officials were very aware of the need to send a calming signal to the markets and to the country, and to international partners. . . ." Yet no one knew quite what to do other than keep their fingers on the pulse of the markets.

Finally, the market was literally saved by the bell that ended trading at 4 P.M. The 508-point drop in the Dow to 1738.74 constituted a single-day loss of value of 22.6 percent, dwarfing the 11.7 percent decline registered on Black Tuesday, back in 1929. To put this in perspective, from the record highs reached in February 1996, it would take a drop of more than 1267 points to equal the October 19, 1987, crash in proportional terms. Declining issues outnumbered gainers 50 to 1. The AMEX composite index fell 12.7 percent, and the NASDAQ index of over-the-counter shares fell 11.35 percent. Index futures fell even more.[7] Phelan called it "the worst market I've ever seen" and "as close to a financial meltdown as I'd ever want to see." Money stampeded out of stocks into bank deposits, Treasury bills, and gold, which closed up $10.50 an ounce that day. On the Big Board, a record 604 million shares had traded, overwhelming data processing and communications systems. Stock trades were executed as much as an hour late. The DOT computer link with Chicago had broken down due to inadequate capacity, causing orders for 112 million shares to go unexecuted. Because of lengthy trading delays and communications breakdowns, investors did not know if their orders had been executed. The options market had also been overloaded, and when investors could not hedge their holdings in the options market, they sold the underlying stock, thereby increasing selling pressure. It did not bode well for Tuesday's trading session.

While the Monday massacre was occurring, both James Baker and Greenspan were winging their way in opposite directions. Greenspan had left for Dallas before the worst of the selling frenzy. Baker had taken a much earlier flight to Stockholm for what he expected to be a relaxed hunting trip with the king of Sweden. ("It was the first boondoggle I was going to take in seven years," he chuckles.) Never one to miss a chance to play Henry Kissinger, though, Baker stopped en route for an unannounced meeting in Frankfurt with Stoltenberg and Poehl to discuss their differences. The meeting gave rise to a joint statement by the three, pledging cooperation to "foster exchange rate stability around current levels," but in a new twist on the Louvre Accord they now declared the currency pact "flexible." This hasty effort by the top U.S. and German economic policymakers to undo the damage caused by their earlier spat was far too little too late to help the by now berserk markets. The country's two top money men were in for a shock when they landed. "When I got off the airplane the Swedish Finance Minister said that the market was down five," Baker recalls. "I thought, 'Well, that's great, the market's down five.' I thought he was talking about five points," not 500 points. Greenspan had a similar experience. He was met at the airport by a representative of the Dallas Fed who informed him the market had closed down "five-O-eight." Greenspan, thinking he had meant 5.08, was relieved the market had rallied, until he was told, "No, five hundred and eight points."

I was in Dallas covering the ABA convention, anxiously awaiting Greenspan. It was an odd scene. Even before the crash, the once lavish and uproarious annual bankers gathering had a distinctly subdued, if not somber atmosphere, aptly enough since the site of that year's convention was the hub of the banking industry's worst problems. Dozens of extravagant and empty office towers stood witness to Texas banks' lunatic real estate lending spree. Already that year, 40 of the proud state's banks had failed, and others had merged or been acquired by out-of-state institutions. Now a national disaster loomed over the financiers and government officials thronging the convention center. After first dismissing the crash as just a long overdue "correction," they were walking around slack-jawed by the end of the day. Dallas Fed president Robert Boykin did not seem worried when I visited him at his office. He had "no explanation" for what he euphemistically called "the volatility we see right now in the markets," but drawled, "In terms of the economy generally, I think we remain fairly optimistic about the national economy." The accent was Texan but the words were pure Fedspeak when he said the Fed would "watch very carefully." As it happened, Margaret Thatcher was in Dallas to visit her son Mark, and a party was given in her honor featuring top business leaders. Thatcher made some informal remarks, telling the party-goers, "You don't have to worry about this; the markets are essentially sound."

Greenspan was not present to hear Thatcher's words of cheer. He had gone straight to his hotel room, ordered in room service, and spent hours on the telephone. Seidman remembers telling Greenspan, "Make sure the banks don't cut off all their borrowers of short-term credit." Oddly enough, Greenspan recalls he slumbered peacefully that night, getting his usual five hours of sleep, and thankfully so, for the next 48 hours would require the full use of his faculties. Baker, meanwhile, had forgotten about hunting. "What I did was spend the entire night on the phone at the guest house that they have there in Stockholm for visiting dignitaries, and I talked at length with Stoltenberg particularly, but also some with Lawson."

It was a critical time. The wrong decision could have compounded the collapse. "We were in a situation which was really extremely grave with, I would say in some respects, a certain hesitation of minds," says Trichet. "There were really lost people at that time, lost minds. They did not understand what was happening and there was a tendency to make enormous mistakes, enormous mistakes. . . ." Back at the White House, everyone was frantic, desperate. After watching the market lose a quarter of its value in a single session, the feeling among Reagan's advisors was one of shock and fear. "You didn't know at that point where it was going," recalls a former administration official. "I mean, it went 508 points, and you didn't know what was going to happen the next day." Reagan kept his head. "He was the least uptight person that I saw around there at the time, and he was arguing 'the market has overdone it, but it will come back,' " Sprinkel recalls. "He was quite optimistic that this was 'not the end of the world,' and that we should continue doing what we were doing." Comforting words, but no substitute for action, and there was only one man with the power and expertise to give words real meaning. The call went up for Greenspan. "Everybody turned to the Fed, mentally turned to the Fed, and said, 'What are they going to do?' " a Reagan aide says. "And he took, obviously, the right actions. Even by the next day his reputation within the White House had gone up tremendously." Greenspan "had certain savior-like qualities in the view of some of the weaker White House staff members."

"We got hold of Alan Greenspan . . . and urged him to come home," says Sprinkel, who reiterated what he had told him before: "For God's sake, ease up. Put some money in the system." The White House dispatched an Air Force Gulf Stream jet to Dallas. Canceling his ABA speech, the Fed chairman flew back Tuesday morning, arriving at Andrews Air Force Base between noon and 1 P.M. Baker, meanwhile, had flown from Stockholm to London and boarded the Concorde for Washington. On board was Brady, former Dillon-Read executive, U.S. senator, and Bush buddy, whom Baker enlisted in the cause. Greenspan met at Baker's office in the afternoon, then went to the White House for further talks.

After carefully considering what to do overnight, Greenspan made perhaps the most important decision of his life. He ordered the Fed to issue a one-sentence statement, which crossed the wires roughly 50 minutes before the start of trading Tuesday: "The Federal Reserve, consistent with its responsibilities as the nation's central bank affirmed today its readiness to serve as a source of liquidity to support the economic and financial system." Elegant in its simplicity, the statement meant the Fed was going to abandon, for the time being, its tight money policies, and infuse the system with all the reserves it needed so banks could lend freely to securities firms and others desperately in need of credit. The policy was discussed by the FOMC in one of a series of short, daily telephone conferences that were to last through the end of the month. When Angell brought up the question of whether the Fed should stick to its precrash policy of forcing banks to borrow an average $600 million per day from the discount window, Johnson said banks were unwilling to borrow from the Fed and "trying to force the borrowing target in that environment could result in an unbelievable funds rate." Corrigan stressed, "We've got to have maximum flexibility, at least for the days ahead." It was agreed the $600 million borrowings target would be temporarily scrapped.

There was little hesitancy about what had to be done. Greenspan knew the Fed had to loosen credit until the crisis was past. "People think that was a tough decision," he says, but "anyone who knows anything about economic history knows that when you get a 500-point, 20 percent drop in the stock market you will have a major problem in the economy. There wasn't a question of whether you would open up the taps or not open up the taps. It was merely how you would do it, not if. That was one of the easiest decisions to make." "There wasn't much discussion about the need to lower rates a little bit to show that we're providing some liquidity," Hoskins agrees. "There was some discussion about 'How long should we do this? And we must get back on our track at some point,' but I don't think there was a very heavy debate about what we did." There was more doubt about whether to put out a statement and what kind. Fed legal counsel Michael Bradfield had drafted a lengthy statement, which he wanted to put out. Corrigan nixed that. "The lawyers came up with this very fancy formal statement," Corrigan recalls. ". . . Very long drafts, 'consistent with section so and so,' and I said, 'Come on!' There was no room for legalese at that point. It was pour the money out and ask questions later."

The strategy was simple: to openly provide ample credit to a system faced with a severe liquidity crisis. Even in the best of times the markets run on credit. To finance their inventories, cover cash flows required by hedged positions, provide margin loans and other reasons, securities firms rely on a steady stream of credit from commercial banks and other sources. Broker-dealers, in the process of buying and selling securities for their own account and for customers, end up with positions in excess of their capital, which they must finance, either by borrowing directly from banks or, more likely, by entering into *repurchase agreements* (*repos*), in which they sell securities to other financial institutions for a short period, often overnight, with the promise to buy it back at a higher price. (The difference between the price at which the dealer sold and the price at which he bought the security back is the rate of interest or repo rate it pays.) Institutional investors, as well as broker-dealers hedge their exposure to price movements in stocks and bonds by taking offsetting positions in futures and options. Investors worried that the value of their stocks will decline can sell (go *short*) the S&P 500 index futures contract, so that if stock prices do indeed fall, they will be able to recoup all or most of the loss by buying out their futures contract at a lower price than they initially sold. Inevitably time gaps arise between when hedgers exit their cash and futures positions, giving rise to credit needs. Or margin calls may arise in the futures market if the market moves adversely. There again credit needs arise.

This complex system usually runs like a top, but in October 1987, "the financial system came close to gridlock," says the Brady Report. The inability of the interlocking stock, futures, and options markets to absorb selling "pushed the country to the brink of the financial system's limits." Market participants need proceeds from sales in the futures market to pay for purchases in the cash market and vice versa, but this became dicey on October 19, as clearinghouse and other problems caused late payments.[8] As the exchanges' clearing and settlement systems became overloaded, fear spread that a Chicago clearinghouse might be unable to deliver funds owed to investors in New York or vice versa. On October 19 alone, the NYSE's massive volume of trading generated 68,000 questioned trades that brought into question some securities firms' financial condition. In Chicago, problems with settlement on futures and options created similar solvency issues. The Chicago Mercantile Exchange (CME) clearinghouse and the Options Clearing Corporation (OCC) required members with net losing positions to pony up a total of $3 billion in so-called variation margin, but the "winning" firms would not be paid until the next day. Major cash flow problems ensued for companies, as the Brady Report explains: "Because clearinghouse members are required to meet these calls even before any compensating deposits are received either from customers or clearinghouses, the clearing members were compelled to increase their reliance on intraday credit from their commercial bankers. However, the bankers in question were already concerned about potential losses that their clearing member customers might have suffered in other lines of activity such as risk arbitrage, block trading or foreign exchange trading. Bankers were also concerned that the clearinghouses would be unable to collect all their margin calls and would be unable to pay in full the balances owed to their clearinghouse members. These concerns apparently resulted in the withdrawal of uncommitted lines of credit to some market participants, restrictions on new loans to some clearinghouse members and a general concern on the part of bankers over extending credit to cover Tuesday morning margin calls."

To prevent these kinds of credit problems from spreading throughout the system, Greenspan and Corrigan acted boldly as another wild day of trading got underway Tuesday morning. Japan's Nikkei index plunged 13.2 percent. London was off 14 percent. It was obvious New York was in for another rocky day of trading—one that could produce destructive economic reverberations if not handled right. Step one was issuing the statement about providing liquidity. Step two was actually providing the liquidity by visibly pumping reserves into the system through aggressive purchases of government securities, which gave banks new credits at the Federal Reserve banks. But it was not good enough simply for the Fed to provide banks with the wherewithal. They had to actually lend. Announcing the Fed would provide liquidity was a "necessary but not sufficient" condition for holding the system together as panic selling resumed Tuesday morning, says Corrigan.

After conferring with Greenspan and other top central bankers overnight, Corrigan had come to a stark realization

> Even before we got into the trading day on Tuesday morning, and even before I knew what was going to happen in the foreign markets overnight, it seemed to me right from the outset that one of the critical difficulties on Tuesday was going to be the potential for gridlock in the system and, of course, by that I mean that even if there was an ample amount of liquidity there, getting that liquidity moved around and effectively utilized is quite another matter than simply making sure that it's there. . . . When you have a big market shock like that, the first thing most market participants and others say to themselves is, "Is there a risk that there are some big credit losses out there in the system?" In other words, by

virtue of the sharp fall in asset prices has some institution or have some institutions gotten themselves deeply into trouble, from a creditworthiness point of view? And of course, you don't need the reality of that; all you need is the fear of it. And that, of course, is what starts to influence behavior. And in those circumstances it just follows automatically that people are going to start to get defensive. And by defensive, I mean they will hold back on making a payment until the other side of the payment gets to them. They will not release securities out of collateral accounts until they get the money in hand, et cetera.

Fortunately, Corrigan had assiduously cultivated relationships with key people at leading banks, securities firms, and exchanges. They knew him and respected him. He also had the full support of Greenspan, who he says, "displayed a very large confidence in my judgment and never, ever, ever second guessed me on a single thing. Never." Corrigan had developed an instinct for where trouble was apt to arise. The "freezing up of securities lending" was "a no-brainer. . . . I knew people were going to be scared to death. It's perfectly natural." Corrigan was also behind the Fed's lesser-known but important decision to liberalize the rules under which it would lend government securities to financial institutions faced with the need to cover short positions with very specific issues. "As it turned out, it was hardly used, but it was just another step taken in the direction of making sure that we didn't get that freeze up of markets." He also suspected the hitherto obscure OCC would be "a point of vulnerability."

As trading volume swelled on October 19, the OCC had difficulty obtaining and verifying option prices. It was receiving late payments from members with net losses on options trades, causing the OCC in turn to delay its own payments to members. The deteriorating price situation forced the OCC to issue four successive margin calls, which came so fast and furious that, no sooner had one set of debit instructions gone out to clearing banks then another and another went out, with the result that margin payments to the OCC were delayed. On the twentieth, according to the SEC, "at least three clearing banks delayed settlement confirmations for two and a half hours apparently for credit reasons." After one options dealer defaulted on its obligations, the OCC had to liquidate its open positions, and assess the resulting $8.5 million loss to other member firms on a pro rata basis. In three other cases, firms came close to sizable defaults and forced liquidations. Of further concern to the Fed, over 50 retail or "introducing brokers" failed when their customers did not meet margin calls or pay settlement obligations, creating a potential domino effect. If customers cannot meet their obligation, it falls to their introducing broker. If it fails, the obligation passes to the broker which executed the trade. If it fails, the clearinghouse itself is left holding the bag. "Potentially, one or more clearing members could fail . . . creating enough momentum to jeopardize the clearing agency and all its members," the SEC found.

The Fed's larger concern was safeguarding the world's payments system—the electronic network that links the world's banks and their customers. In the

United States, the Fed's own Fedwire and the privately run Clearing House Interbank Payments System (CHIPS), see to it that not just buyers and sellers of securities but parties to all kinds of transactions swiftly have their bank accounts debited and credited through high-speed bookkeeping entries. Aside from processing billions of paper checks, the Fed in 1987 facilitated the movement of over $1 trillion per day in large dollar payments via wire transfers by adjusting the reserve accounts that America's thousands of depository institutions maintain at their district Federal Reserve banks. On Fedwire, throughout the day, the bank receiving payment is given immediate credit for the funds transferred by the sending bank, what is known as *final settlement*. During the course of an average day, banks make and receive billions of dollars in payments over Fedwire and are allowed to overdraw their accounts at the Fed until the end of the day. This gives rise to so-called *daylight overdrafts*, which in 1987 were running between $100 and $150 billion per day.

CHIPS, which was then handling more than $600 billion per day in transactions, many of them international, does not make final settlement until the end of the day, when it nets out each bank's debits and credits with the clearinghouse and presents a settlement sheet to the New York Fed, which then transfers reserve account balances to banks in a net credit position as soon as the Fed receives funds from banks in a net debit position. Other payments systems operated by foreign central banks interface with Fedwire and CHIPS. The concern in October 1987 was that large customer losses would cause banks in a net debit position to default on their payment obligations to other banks, leading to a chain reaction of defaults and failures. Since the ability of each bank to pay its obligations depends on receiving credit for payments owed to it by other banks, it was not inconceivable the failure of one or more large institutions could have caused the entire payments system to unravel, rendering it difficult to carry on ordinary commerce. Such a crisis had actually occurred on a small scale in 1974, when Germany's Herstatt Bank failed and defaulted on sizable payment obligations arising out of foreign exchange transactions, causing ripple effects throughout the European banking system. Ever since then, central bankers had worried about *Herstatt Risk* (the risk that one leg of a transaction will be settled with finality but that there will be a default on the other leg). The stock market crash threatened to become the mother of all Herstatts.

So, Corrigan began calling every major bank to, as he puts it, "remind them of the big picture." Ensconced in his paneled office atop the Fed's lower Manhattan building, Corrigan had nine phone lines ringing simultaenously. His terse message to one and all was simple and direct: Keep funds flowing. The emphasis was on solidarity. "I think there's a code for all this," he says. "You have to make it clear to them that they have to make their own credit decisions, but as they contemplate those credit decisions they have to keep in mind the larger picture and the interests of the well-being of the system. And I felt that, particularly since I felt I had pretty good relationships with all these people, they understood what I was saying. You know them all, at least I did quite well, so you know that in one case or another you might have to be a little bit more or less diplomatic in making the point." Some banks were teetering on the edge of denying vital credit lines to securities firms, and if one had broken rank, others would surely follow, causing the whole system to crumble like a house of cards. "Banker's Trust was being very cautious, if I can put it that way," Corrigan says, but ultimately "they did what had to be done." Contrary to rampant rumors to this effect at the time, one thing the Fed did not do was guarantee any bank or securitiies firm against loss.

Similar steps were being taken by other G-7 central banks in concert with the Fed. The Bundesbank took minimal measures, temporarily moving some government funds to accounts in commercial banks to enhance their liquidity and lowering money market rates ever so slightly. An official told me the Bundesbank was "looking forward to cooperating with the United States and the Federal Reserve in particular," but said further efforts by Baker to "talk down the dollar . . . would not be welcomed." Other central banks were more aggressive.

One of the many Corrigan spoke to that morning was the Bank of Canada's Crow. He called Corrigan before 7:30 A.M. to tell him he had decided to "push quite a lot of liquidity" into the six large Canadian banks, which were financing the Canadian securities business. "I said, 'I just want you to know that this is our analysis and this is what we're going to do,' " says Crow. "He didn't tell me what they were going to do, but he clearly didn't think that we'd gotten it wrong, and he made it clear that he understood the issue as we saw it." Corrigan hinted the Fed would also be "addressing the situation." The Bank of Canada did not issue a statement, but Crow called each Canadian bank to tell them, " 'We've put a lot of cash in the system. You make decisons on credit, but you can't make your decisions on the grounds that there isn't much liquidity in the system, because there's a lot.' What I tried to get across is, 'We won't take responsibility for your credit decisions. That's your business. But there is a lot of liquidity.' " With stock values having plummeted, Crow's concern was "what would happen to security settlements? The concern was that people might not follow through on what they had agreed to transact. Then the question is 'Who gets stuck with what?' The problem you get into is that people stop and sit on what they have, and they do not give up anything. So the system seizes up. People drop credit lines. When one person protects himself, he's making the situation more difficult somewhere else." The central banks' task was to "assure people that, 'If you trade you won't be giving it away, without having someone else trade as well. If you extend credit, you should find that people will pay you.' The fear factor can rise very quickly in this environment. And spread very fast. So you can have a financial panic. That in turn will affect production and employment."

Corrigan also spoke to Eddie George, then a Bank of England executive director. "The problem was that everybody could see that a lot of people had lost quite a bit of money, and nobody knew who and nobody knew how much," says George. "Now if, in those circumstances, somebody had actually not been able to meet a liability then that could have directly affected the firm that it owed the money to, but more generally, in that sort of situation of nervousness, it could have made people feel that, well, if one firm had been affected by this, then there could be a number of others, and so it was a situation in which there could have very rapidly been contagion, and so the provision of liquidity and the encouragement of others to leave lines in place rather than simply to pull lines and run for cover was important." George had been collaborating with Corrigan since early Monday on the need to provide emergency liquidity and comparing notes on the condition of financial institutions. "What we were seeking to identify were businesses that were at risk and businesses that faced liquidity difficulties and businesses that might have needed to be helped in terms of being able to meet obligations in securities terms," George recalls. "There were particular firms, particularly internationally operating firms that were looking like they might need help."

As luck would have it, the Thatcher government had chosen this time to come to market with a huge public stock offering to complete the privatization of British Petroleum (BP). The roughly $12 billion BP sale was to have been the crowning achievement of her plan to privatize state-owned enterprises and boost government revenues. The week before the crash, the international consortium of investment banks put together to underwrite the offering had agreed to pay the British government 330 pence per share. Based on where extant BP shares had been trading, that seemed to guarantee them a tidy profit when they resold the shares to the public, but on Monday and Tuesday, the price plunged to less than 290. Suddenly firms like Goldman Sachs & Company were faced with huge losses, further fueling rumors of defaults and failures. "During that period we had the BP issue underwritten, but not actually subscribed, and of course that meant that some firms were looking at very large exposures," says George. "They had undertaken to subscribe to BP shares and that was pretty concentrated, so I was very involved with what we were going to do about that." Ultimately, the situation was resolved the following Wednesday when the Bank of England itself offered to buy back the BP shares below the underwriting price. "It turned out it didn't have to because the markets had stabilized," recalls Corrigan, "but had the markets tanked again in effect they would have." The Bank of England's offer "limited the pressure that that particular issue was having on the stock market," says George.

With nerves frazzled and systems strained beyond capacity, the market set off on another roller-coaster ride Tuesday. In the first hour of trading, a rally in futures and cash markets carried the Dow up 197 points, but then selling swamped buying support, and by 12:30 P.M., the Dow was 28 points below where it started. In just an hour it had fallen 225 points. It was beginning to look like Black Monday all over again. Talk of closing the market resurfaced. With the DOT system being denied to index arbitrageurs, futures became wildly out of whack with the underlying indices, and some were down the equivalent of a 500 points on the Dow. Though there was little index arbitrage actually going on, the mere existence of such a large discount on futures fueled fears of heavy selling in the spot market, and those fears became self-fulfilling, prompting investors to unload stocks. But Greenspan, who had been taking cat naps in his office command post to keep his strength up and his mind sharp during the crisis management marathon, never lost his nerve. In a telephone conference call with FOMC members, some of whom were in Dallas hobnobbing with bankers at the ABA convention, Hoskins recalls Greenspan was lighthearted enough to joke that "since I was the new boy on the FOMC, the markets weren't receiving me very well." As the afternoon wore on, a degree of confidence was restored. Numerous corporations took the opportunity to buy their shares back from investors at low prices. Pension funds and others joined in the bargain hunting. The Dow, which had closed Monday at 1738.74, rose as high as 1919, before closing at 1841.01—a net gain for the day of 102.27. The tide had turned. The crisis had passed.

On Wednesday, the Dow closed up nearly 187 points, before falling back more than 77 Thursday. The markets remained jittery for a couple of weeks, but calm was gradually restored. Bond yields, source of much of the problem, fell from nearly 10½ percent on Monday to below 9 percent, before settling in around 9¼. As the Fed flooded the banking system with reserves, short-term interest rates fell sharply. The Fed allowed the funds rate to drop from 7½ percent before the crash to near 6 percent, before bouncing back to 6½ and then 6¾. Rates on three-month bills (a haven in times of distress) plunged from 7.3 percent to below 5 percent before rebounding to above 5½. Banks even lowered their prime rate a quarter percent, some by more. Lower rates would soon resume downward pressure on the dollar, but, while worrisome, that was a problem Greenspan was prepared to accept for the time being as the price for saving the financial system.

Though Corrigan had the more hands-on role, Greenspan's leadership and overall coordination had been instrumental. "First, I think, he did the very chairman-like thing of assuring the markets that the Fed's there and the liquidity's there, so don't panic," says Hoskins, "and I think he did that in a very timely and forthright way. . . . Then his job was carefully monitoring and trying to understand what was going on and making sure that the Fed was there to do what needed to be done."

While the central banks had been rescuing the financial system, the U.S. Treasury was working with other finance ministries to salvage the G-7 process. The dollar recovered from 141 to 144 yen and from 1.77 to 1.82 marks, but this proved temporary, and dollar weakness soon became a focus of G-7 concern lasting through year's end. Chastened by the crash, G-7 officials intensified their cooperation for a while. "It was a sobering experience," says Dallara. "There was a sense all around the world, at that point, in the G-5 and G-7 circles, that we really had to get serious about how we dealt with some of the fundamental problems, and I think we learned from some of the mistakes of the Louvre process, and I think that probably we were more effective in intervention for a period after that." Baker had publicly smoothed things over with the Germans, but privately was unrepentant. Responding to German and Japanese criticism of Baker's precrash condemnation of their rising interest rates, a Baker aide told me, "We're not going to respond to that stuff. He knew exactly what he was saying. The Germans are being ridiculous [in refusing to stimulate their economy] with their zero inflation rate and low growth." Ironically, Baker claims the G-7 policy coordination process he crafted saved the day after the crash "because we were constantly in touch and we were taking coordinated action to inject liquidity in the worldwide markets, and the exchange rates were remarkably stable during that entire period."

The fall-out of the crash was relatively light. Despite dire predictions about the fate of the United States and world economy, "lo and behold it didn't go into a tailspin at all," says Crow, although the situation could have gotten "very bad because you can have the shock multiplying through the financial sector." In contrast to 1929, notes Seidman, "banks suddenly got very liquid" as frightened stock investors parked their money there. No major securities firms in the United States failed, although a weakened E.F. Hutton would later be absorbed by Shearson Lehman, one of the BP underwriters. A number of smaller fry did go under, including firms which had survived the Great Crash of 1929. In the immediate aftermath of the crash, it was by no means certain the economy would shake off its effects. In Dallas, Chase Manhattan Bank president Thomas Labrecque said, "The economic activity apparent today should carry us well into 1988. If monetary policy isn't tightened, capital spending could go on. The real question is what is going to be the net psychological impact on the consumer." But H. Ross Perot said the crash proved that those who thought the economy was "fundamentally sound" had "not done their homework." Foreign investors were "propping up" the economy and "the biggest thing coming out of New York's port is trash and steel scrap." The crash was "a warning light flashing on an aircraft." Ten days after the crash, Allen Sinai, respected chief economist for Shearson Lehman Brothers, warned that, if Congress did not reduce the budget and trade deficits and the Fed did not cut interest rates 2 to 3 percent, the effects of the crash could "cascade to a recession or something worse."

From the hinterlands, a surprisingly positive picture was emerging. On the Thursday after the crash, Corrigan met as scheduled with a Fed advisory board made up of farmers and small businessmen. He had thought about canceling the meeting given the press of dealing with the crash aftermath, but decided to "project business as usual." When the crash came up, "they didn't have any reactions," Corrigan recalls. "They thought, 'it's the fat cats on Wall Street getting beat up. That's what they get paid for.' " They told Corrigan the crash would not affect their spending plans, and this "had a very profound effect" on Corrigan's thinking. Similar reports were coming in from other Fed presidents, who Greenspan credits with playing an important role during the crash and its aftermath. Kelley says the crash proved the worth of the Fed's district information gathering apparatus, which provides the Fed with anecdotal reports from all sectors and regions of the economy. "Almost immediately after that crash we were beginning to get reports back that it was no big deal in the economy, that this was a Wall Street phenomenon, it was limited to the stock market and the people that worked there, and it was not affecting the mainstream. That came through very clearly and very quickly, and it was an enormous help in giving us confidence and helping us to maintain our balance as we were striving to create policy in the immediate aftermath of what looked like a real financial train wreck. We did ease policy and we did provide liquidity, but we were never in a panic mode about it, and because we got such good, accurate analysis from 'main street' across the country, we were able to get back on track very quickly. . . ."

Seidman, who was getting similar findings from an FDIC survey of banks, says the crash might have spread beyond Wall Street if the Fed had behaved differently. "If the Fed had said, 'You dumb guys made these loans' and 'we're not going to lend to anybody,' " and "if enough banks had panicked and closed down and put some of the major investment banks into trouble, it might have moved out" into the country. The Fed got high marks from nearly everyone, not just for its immediate reaction to the crash, but for its subsequent conduct. Leigh-Pemberton, who was in Bucharest of all places when the crash hit, shudders to think what might have happened if the Fed and the other central banks had not infused reserves into the system. "There was a considerable anxiety that we might see the repetition of 1929–1931—a serious lack of confidence in financial markets, a lot of people not being able to meet their obligations and, of course, the banks had played a very cautious role [in 1929], not coming to people's assistance, but rather doing the opposite. . . . We avoided all that and saw people through that crisis very quickly and with remarkably few losses too." But "there might have been" a large-scale, "systemic failure" if the central banks had not responded as they did. "How bad could it have gotten?" asks his successor George. "You could have had one or two firms fail because they were illiquid, not because they were insolvent. . . . There could have been a significant panic." Trichet says "Alan remained, all the time, extremely calm and quiet. He developed his own analysis of the situation, assessed the gravity and the acuteness of the situation with great, great skill, and taking his responsibility when it was needed."

Fed officials still shudder to think what could have happened if the Fed had acted differently. "When things start going badly, if they can be contained early on, then you don't have very much damage, but once things begin to get away, then who knows how far it can go, once that happens?" says one FOMC member. "And it becomes increasingly difficult to stop, once you start the snowball going down the hill. All I do know is that the snowball was stopped before it started getting a real strong amount of momentum going, and I think that that enabled the episode to play itself out fairly quickly, without ever really affecting the economy itself, directly, very much at all."

In its postmortem, the House Banking Committee said, "The actions taken by the Federal Reserve were instrumental in limiting the extent of the damage in the financial sector and confining the problems so that they did not spread throughout the financial system and to the economy at large." But it also found "the joint Federal Reserve–administration policy of exchange rate targeting may have postponed necessary adjustments in the exchange rate and have led to a sizable and abrupt ultimate correction of market prices to reflect underlying fundamentals. The policy may also have led to undesirably restrictive monetary policy which was used to defend the agreement. . . . If the Federal Reserve can be faulted, it is for not pursuing a policy that was more independent of the administration and which put less emphasis on the goal of exchange rate targeting."

Sprinkel still thinks the Fed provoked the crash by tightening monetary policy too much, then not easing credit on Friday, the 16, but has only praise for Greenspan's actions following Black Monday. Another former Reagan administration official is more effusive. "Just as a citizen, looking at the signal that he personally sent out to the American people by having an absolutely solid hand on the tiller, I mean, Jim Baker can be sitting at the Treasury having 15 meetings, but at the end of the day what people make a judgement on is how Greenspan handled it and the Fed handled it." Baker agrees. "You had a Fed chairman who quickly realized the importance of injecting liquidity and not biting his fingernails about a likely inflationary impact of that." As a result, "the crash was a major event, but it didn't leave any major scars; I mean any lasting scars. A lot of people lost some money, but you can just as easily argue that they were asking for it by buying into an overpriced market."

In Washington's favorite pastime of picking winners and losers, Sprinkel appeared to emerge a winner, Baker a loser. Not only had he predicted Baker's exchange rate policies would cause market turmoil, he had been on duty to deal with it while Baker was out of town. "Sprinkel had been warning about the consequences of a tight money policy to boost the dollar for months, and Baker was pooh-poohing it," a White House official confided. "When the shit hit the fan, all of a sudden Sprinkel looked prescient. In those critical hours, Sprinkel was there, and he knew the right things to say and do when it was needed." Baker's enemies alleged he had continued to lean on advice from Darman after he left the Treasury in early April to work for Shearson, and that Darman and others had steered him down the garden path of sacrificing economic growth to the goal of international cooperation and exchange rate stability in the months leading up to October. They sought to capitalize on the crash to reduce the Treasury secretary's influence. Sprinkel was prevailed upon to withdraw his resignation and was given full Cabinet rank, unprecedented for a CEA chairman. "It's not escaping the attention of a lot of us that Baker has been the prime advocate and implementer of policies that deal with the value of the dollar that are now proving disastrous," an administration official told me. "I can't believe he's going to get off scot free in all of this."

Greenspan had little patience for allegations that Fed policies, however motivated, caused the crash. In his February 24, 1988, Humphrey-Hawkins testimony before the Senate Banking Committee, he observed long-term interest rates were rising throughout the world during the late summer of 1987 and "the Fed could have done very little" to reverse that trend. "Even if that last surge in long-term rates had not occurred, the market would have topped out and come down anyway, and I find it difficult to perceive how actions of the Federal Reserve were material factors in the market."

The combined stock losses of October 1987 produced a $1 trillion reduction in share values out of roughly $3.2 trillion in stock wealth beforehand. Despite those apalling losses, the economy lost little momentum. Soon the

Fed faced the dilemma of wanting to keep rates low enough to avoid recession, but not so low as to provoke an inflationary dollar decline. It made for a lively discussion at the November 3 FOMC meeting. Fed officials were still far too concerned about market instability to pat themselves on the back for avoiding catastrophe. Foreign investor confidence in the United States was shaky. They would sell a net $6.5 billion in U.S. stocks in November—four times as much as the next largest monthly decline—and put most of the proceeds in safe T-bills. The dollar had fallen steadily since the crash, as the Fed lowered interest rates, to about 1.70 marks and a record low 136.15 yen per dollar, notwithstanding central bank dollar buying. If ever Baker had been guilty of coaxing the Fed into raising interest rates to support the dollar, he was not guilty of it now. He was urging rates be kept down to support the economy.

Describing Baker's new attitude to the FOMC, Greenspan said, "He would like to see the markets stabilize on their own without any actions on our part, whether through monetary or intervention policies. Should that not occur, his willingness to commit U.S. resources is limited. And the general impression that I get . . . is that if the market moves us down gradually without any secondary consequences until we reach a market equilibrium, that would suit Treasury just fine." Baker was aware dollar weakness could cause "a lot of dangerous, secondary problems," but "it is the Secretary's view—maybe I should use the word 'hope' because that is more relevant—that that will not materialize." Greenspan was not concerned about exchange rates for their own sake, but for the unsettling influence a continued dollar decline might have on still-nervous markets. "It is not that it is falling per se, but that whatever it is doing creates a judgment in the market that it will continue to do that." While a dollar "free fall" was unlikely, "the trouble is that even if the probabilities have diminished, the consequences of that event are extremely dangerous." Therefore, the Fed must "keep up its guard," and that meant not lowering rates as much as some, both in the administration and the Fed, would have liked. The usually hawkish Fed staff was predicting short-term rates would need to drop one percent within six months.

Greenspan painted a nightmare scenario for his FOMC colleagues, some of whom were not inclined to worry about the dollar, of what could happen if the Fed did not maintain the appropriate level of interest rates to stabilize currency and bond markets. There could be "a flight from the future. At the moment, there is investment going on in the longer term of this country. In other words, people are buying longer term bonds; they are still buying stocks, and yields are not all that bad; the exchange rate is soft, but it's not falling on its face." However, "it is not all that difficult to imagine a less developed country scenario where what we had would have led to a dramatic collapse in the exchange rate, a huge rise in long-term bond rates or the effective disappearance of the long-term bond market. . . . The stock market would fall away and everything would implode into the short run. And the bill rate would collapse, and we would have all these crazy, horrible events that none of us thinks can happen until we see them." In that event, the Fed would be forced to raise the discount rate two or three percent, "and then we would get into the types of problems that a historic monetary collapse always creates. We are far apart from that at this stage, but I suspect a lot nearer than we would like to believe. . . . We could very readily see a major endeavor to shift portfolios out of the dollar-denominated securities into those denominated in other currencies. . . ."

Johnson contended the real risk in "the new world we are in" was that the Fed would send the economy into "a tailspin" by trying to prop up the dollar. He was brought up short by Corrigan. "Manley, when you're talking about a brave new world, the thing that is most new and most brave about this world right now is that we have no policies. We have no fiscal policies; we have no exchange rate policies." There were "very real risks of a further substantial depreciation in the value of the dollar," which would "add to inflationary pressures at home" and would push up interest rates. Rolling the dice, the FOMC left the funds rate at 6¾ percent and hoped for the best.

Much as the Fed likes to claim that its policy decisions are made strictly according to domestic considerations and that exchange rates have only a minor influence, transcripts show clearly the dollar was a major factor in the decision to leave rates unchanged again at the December 16 meeting. "One could argue . . . that we should be easing from here," Greenspan told the FOMC, "but if we ease from here in the context of still soft exchange rates, I'm fearful that the system will crack, with the huge holdings of dollar-denominated assets in the world. . . . If we ever had private holders starting to try to liquidate, I think the effect would be a real free fall that could bring the stock market down and that would crash us. So, between Scylla and Charybdis, I sort of come out for [leaving rates unchanged]." Greenspan was "surprised at the strength of the economy," but did not "think we're out of the woods yet." Corrigan was even more anxious that a weak dollar not upset the markets again. "Were it not for the proximity to October 19th, I would actually favor tightening policy right now on the grounds that I regard the current exchange market situation as perilous. I recognize that there are risks on both sides. The exchange market could trigger a blowout in the stock market; or, the other way around, a blowout in the stock market could trigger a blowout in the exchange market." But he, too, settled for leaving rates unchanged.

Dallara says, "Both the Treasury and the Fed recognized that we needed to see some depreciation of the dollar that Fall and that it needed to be in an orderly fashion. . . . After all, there was a clear sense that one of the factors contributing to the crash was the effort to hold the dollar up over the course of the summer and early Fall of '87." However, the Fed did not want to risk a destabilizing dollar free fall. The dollar came under continuous downward pressure in the fourth quarter of 1987. By the time the G-7 held an emergency meeting via international telephone hook-up on Tuesday, December 22, 1987, the dollar had fallen to 126.30 yen and 1.6270 marks per dollar, compared to 142.40 Japanese yen and 1.8210 German marks at the September 26 G-7. And it didn't stop there, despite a lengthy G-7 communiqué—dubbed "the phone accord"—designed to stem the dollar's slide.

In a typical example of the cryptic mumbo jumbo G-7 officials spent end-less hours crafting and debating, the lengthy communiqué stated: "The minis-ters and governors agreed that either excessive fluctuation of exchange rates, a further decline of the dollar, or a rise in the dollar to an extent that becomes destabilizing to the adjustment process, could be counterproductive by dam-aging growth prospects in the world economy. They reemphasized their com-mon interest in more stable exchange rates among their currencies and agreed to continue to cooperate closely in monitoring and implementing policies to strengthen underlying economic fundamentals to foster stability of exchange rates. In addition, they agreed to cooperate closely on exchange markets." More than just an effort to stabilize the dollar, the communiqué represented an ambitious and sincere effort by the seven to "intensify their economic pol-icy coordination efforts." The phone accord was probably the high-water mark of G-7 coordination, as well as the peak of cooperation between the Fed and Treasury. "It was a very intense time of consultation among the G-7 mem-bers because everyone, I think, was aware that the crash had really been a wakeup call to the need not only for more urgent action on the U.S. budget front but more generally for more urgent policy coordination," says Dallara. "It struck me as a bit unusual because it was a sense of real commitment to the process which one didn't always see." Greenspan played an active role both in advance preparations and in the actual conference call that was arranged after logistical problems prevented a face-to-face meeting, participating in numer-ous meetings in Baker's large conference room to coordinate U.S. fiscal and monetary policy and agree on a U.S. position in talks with Germany, Japan, and the others. "It was very much a team effort," says Dallara. "I clearly recall a sense around the room of people genuinely trying to think through 'how can we deal with this? How can we provide a framework that's more convincing to the markets?' "

The result was an agreement that sought not only to stabilize exchange rates but to correct the underlying imbalances thought to be undermining the dollar. To reduce the large U.S. external deficit, the United States pledged anew to reduce its budget deficit, thereby reducing the need for foreign capi-tal. Japan pledged to stimulate demand in its economy through public works expenditures. Germany promised to expand previously announced tax cuts without offsetting spending cuts. And it was agreed G-7 monetary policies would be aimed at "providing adequate monetary conditions to achieve strong economic growth in the context of price stability as well as to foster financial market stability." Baker used the agreement as leverage to battle for budget concessions and fend off protectionist pressures in Congress. But it would take more than a paper agreement to convince the markets. They were not impressed. "Market participants appeared to be disappointed by the absence of new measures in the statement," a Fed staff document said later. The result was that the dollar sank to all-time lows of 120 yen and 1.57 marks per dollar by the end of 1987. It didn't help when Sprinkel asserted the G-7 communiqué contained "no statement about maintaining the dollar around current levels" and no U.S. commitment to raise interest rates to support the dollar. It continued to fall, hitting 120.45 yen and 1.5700 marks by year-end.

If Sprinkel and the administration were not particularly concerned about the dollar's fall, Greenspan saw it as a direct threat not only to financial market stability but to his ability to control inflation. By January 4, the first business day of 1988, the dollar had fallen 5 percent since the Fed's last meeting, and Greenspan and his foreign counterparts decided to call a halt. The Fed's concern about the dollar—shared by other G-7 monetary authorities—demanded action of some sort. "The concern I had was that renewed or intensified weakness of the dollar would show itself through in the first instance to the bond market," Corrigan says, and that in turn could have put "renewed pressure on the stock market." Since the Fed was not yet prepared to raise rates, it settled for heavy coordinated foreign exchange intervention with other central banks: a "bear trap" for speculators who were selling the dollar short. After extensive telephone conversations between Washington, New York, Frankfurt, Tokyo, and so on, the trap was sprung on January 5. It was one of the most successful, concerted intervention efforts ever undertaken. Working with the central banks of Japan, Germany, France, Britain, and others, the Fed sold foreign currencies and bought dollars to push the greenback up to nearly 128 yen and nearly 1.63 marks. The next day it climbed to as high as 131 yen and 1.66 marks.

As Cross later told the FOMC, "The central banks intervened in concert aggressively, visibly and noisily. The market had been looking for a signal, especially from the U.S., and these operations convinced many market participants that the G-7 countries were indeed now committed to halting the dollar's decline. The December G-7 accord was given new weight." The Fed alone bought almost $1.4 billion against the mark and nearly $1.1 billion against the yen, while foreign central banks bought another $9 billion. The intervention, along with widespread expectations the Fed would soon be raising interest rates, did not end the dollar's problems, but it helped set the tone for a firmer dollar throughout most of 1988. Even so, it was a tricky moment for the Fed because, while it wanted to give the dollar a boost, it did not want its dollar purchases to tighten domestic money and credit conditions and raise U.S. interest rates just yet. So quietly, it replaced the dollar reserves it had drained through its foreign exchange intervention by adding reserves through its domestic open market operations. By purchasing securities from banks it gave the banks credits at the Fed, which added to their reserves and offset, or *sterilized*, the dollars it had drained from the currency market.

Perhaps it is true that, as Laurence Sterne once wrote, "God tempereth the wind to the shorn lamb." The dollar soon stabilized, fears of recession diminished, and the Fed found itself back in the position of having to raise rates to cool an "overheating economy," much to the administration's dismay.

CHAPTER THREE

"Deep Root Canal Surgery"

Through Herculean effort, Greenspan and his colleagues had turned back the threat of financial collapse and economic depression. Now, strangely, they faced a very different test—one with not quite as much immediacy as Black Monday perhaps, but fearsome nonetheless: preventing a revitalized economy from generating escalating inflation. It was a moment of truth.

Greenspan knew all too well how the essentially monetary phenomenon of inflation—too much money chasing too few goods—could start out small, with prices rising three or four percent a year, then escalate until they rose hundreds, even thousands of percent. As a student of economic history, he knew how hyperinflation could completely destroy the political, economic, and social structures of nations. The ultimate example, of course, was Weimar, Germany. But even in the eighties, it was occurring in a host of countries in Latin America, the Middle East, and elsewhere. People never seemed to learn, and with the United States running budget deficits approaching $200 billion per year, who was to say it couldn't happen here? Inflation had never reached those runaway proportions in the United States, but at 13.3 percent in 1979, it had gotten close enough to getting out of hand to scare the hell out of the Fed. Volcker had squelched inflation by 1986, but then it had made a comeback not even the crash could derail. The question was whether the Fed was going to hold onto the gains it had made against inflation or give them back. Greenspan had the answer. From March 30, 1988, to February 23, 1989, the Fed put all thoughts of the crash behind it and—defying the wishes of the administration that appointed him—hiked the funds rate from less than 6½ percent to nearly 10 percent. "It was monetary policy's finest hour," says Corrigan, "because even as it was, we came a little closer than I would like to come to in terms of letting that inflation thing get away from us. . . ." Angell recalls 1988 as "the year in which we kind of put most of it back together," after the Fed had lulled itself into complacency in 1986 and 1987 and allowed wage-price pressures to revive.

The administration and Congress did not stand on the sidelines cheering. The administration wanted to combat inflation, but not at the cost of slowing growth. "The main players in the administration were all concerned that we were eliminating inflation in two years instead of four years," says Darby. "The cost of that would be an unnecessary recession. . . . Alan had plenty of time to eliminate inflation and he should start doing it. I don't think there was any disagreement over that." It was just that the administration wanted a "slow, gradual" approach to reducing inflation. The Fed saw that approach as the sure way to failure. "They were tightening too much," Sprinkel still alleges. "To try to throttle it that quickly could have led to a recession." Recession did come but not until August 1990, by which time the Fed had been lowering interest rates for more than a year.

It was a seminal time for the Greenspan Fed and taught it some valuable lessons. Then, as in the mid-nineties, the Fed was striving to achieve "a soft landing"—bring economic activity down from a growth pace it considered too fast to cool wage-price pressures without causing recession. It was a time of testing for Greenspan who, despite his heroics of the previous October, still had his doubters—among the other Fed officials and among that breed of Wall Street economists known as *Fed watchers*. There were those who questioned Greenspan's political independence and willingness to make the tough choices needed to build on Volcker's legacy. When it was over, Greenspan had won his spurs as an inflation fighter, along with some lasting enmity from friends of Reagan and Bush. Having been a loyal Republican, and having been rewarded with his life's ambition, Greenspan was no doubt expected to play ball. The administration and its supporters were startled to find Greenspan intended to be his own man. I particularly remember a conversation I had with an embittered Richard Rahn, who as chief economist of the U.S. Chamber of Commerce spoke for thousands of businesses and informally advised the White House and Treasury. As the Fed relentlessly raised rates, the black–eye patched Rahn fulminated that Greenspan was subjecting the economy to "deep root canal surgery." Rahn had plenty of company in the administration, and they made no secret of their displeasure. Greenspan cleverly turned administration pressure tactics to his advantage. The administration unwittingly helped cement Greenspan's standing with the public and his colleagues by furnishing him a foil against whom he could play.

To accomplish its mission, the Fed had to act preemptively. As Greenspan says, "If you wait to see the whites of the eyes of inflation, then it's too late." Fed officials talk about managing the supply of money and credit as if they were driving a car: You have to concentrate on what's on the road ahead, they say, not keep looking in the rear view mirror. It's also a bit like ice hockey. As Wayne Gretzky said, "You've always got to be moving to where the puck is going, not where it's been." Because of the lag between when the Fed changes interest rates and when that action begins to affect household and business behavior, the Fed must anticipate where the economy is headed a year or more into the future and adjust its credit settings to achieve its goal of noninflationary growth. There have been times in its history when the Fed has played like a hockey player on speed or on valium, getting to the spot either before or after the puck. The Fed has been known to gun the economy's engines too fast or for too long, leading to inflation. At other times, it has been known to slam on the brakes and throw the economy through the windshield. The quest for a happy medium—a "soft landing"—has been the Fed's holy grail. The Fed learned from its experience of the late eighties that it is vital to contain the inflation process before it gets started, for despite the dramatic rate hikes during the 1988 to 1989 period, inflation went as high as 6 percent in 1990, before retreating. In its most recent effort to head off inflation—the doubling of the federal funds rate from 3 to 6 percent between February 1994 and February 1995—the Fed was "more anticipatory" than during the 1988 to 1989 period, says William McDonough, who succeeded Corrigan as New York Fed president in July 1993. As a result inflation was restrained to about 3 percent.

Administration suspicions that the Fed was courting recession were not far wrong. If it had been known at the time, it would have been a scandal, but recently released FOMC transcripts reveal the Fed was consciously flirting with recession. It was a price some Fed officials thought was worth paying to kill inflation once and for all. Greenspan was determined to build on the slightly shaky foundation he inherited. "What I thought was required was basically a follow-on to the fundamental thrust that Volcker put in place, to make certain we kept leaning against the process until we wore it out," Greenspan says. To those who say the Fed overdid its credit tightening, he retorts, "I don't think so. The real danger you have in a period like that is that you don't do enough. We were still dealing with an unstable inflationary environment, and it was very easy to make a mistake on the side of ease and find that, all of a sudden, we had lost two percentage points of inflation on the upside."

Not everyone at the Fed agreed with Greenspan. As the Fed got closer to resuming credit tightening in early 1988, so did dissension among hawks and doves on the FOMC. In a January 7 speech, Johnson said the Fed would need to "moderate domestic demand" both to contain inflation and to limit imports and reduce the trade deficit. Privately, Johnson's views were closer to those of the administration, but his speech reflected the view of chairman and other Fed officials. By contrast, a few days later Seger told me the economy was "sluggish" with "borderline anemia in the consumer area." As for restricting demand to lower the trade deficit, "The consumers out there are calling the shots, and they don't always cooperate. What if consumers are cutting back not on imports, but on purchases of domestically produced products so the import flow continues? Given that they've got consumer sovereignty, if people still want to buy French wine and Swiss watches and German cars they can do it. So here's the import flood continuing, and the cut comes out of American goods and services."

The Fed was in a strange transition period as 1988 began. No longer was it pushing reserves into the banking system to prevent a financial and economic crisis, but it was not fully back to "normal operations" either, and it was not ready to resume raising rates. To further complicate matters, the dollar was under serious assault in part because the Fed had been lowering rates, in part because of a perception the administration did not want a strong dollar. This prompted a worried Corrigan to warn another financial crisis could be provoked if foreign investors decided to desert dollar-denominated assets. The

Fed was simultaneously allowing accommodative reserve conditions to reduce the funds rate while contemplating raising rates. Fed officials' contradictory comments created considerable confusion.

Greenspan and the Fed's senior staff knew it was just a matter of time before the Fed would have to go back on the offensive against inflation, but others were not prepared to move in that direction. Johnson warned his colleagues in February against "macho chest beating" over inflation that risked the Fed falling "asleep at the switch" and allowing "negative psychology" to cause "a plunge in real spending." Clearly, it would not be easy even for Greenspan to build a consensus among the fractious policymakers, but economic statistics were on his side. By late February it would be clear to most that the economy was not headed for recession and that the Fed would have to resume raising rates to avoid accelerating inflation, but the actual rate hikes would not come until the end of March. First, a major selling job had to be done on Congress, the White House, and the American people, who after all had been facing the specter of depression a few months earlier.

The supposition of many in the administration and elsewhere was that the huge stock losses individuals and institutions had sustained—what economists call negative *wealth effects*—would create a drag on the economy. As it turned out there had been few such wealth effects, but at the time inflation seemed like the last thing anyone should have to worry about. The administration considered it a slain dragon and was not pleased with the anti-inflationary saber rattling Greenspan and other Fed officials were doing to soften up the public for their eventual credit tightening. Though the administration had been generally supportive of the Fed's inflation fight throughout most of the eighties, the idea of jacking up rates so soon after Black Monday struck it as inexplicable. Ideology also played a big role in the looming showdown with the Fed. The Reaganite supply-side revolution was in decline by then, but still had its proponents in the administration and among GOP activists.

More important, there was a strong strain of *monetarism* at the White House and the Treasury. Reagan's monetarist advisors never tired of reminding Greenspan about the sluggish growth of the money supply. M1 growth had slowed from 18.1 percent in 1986 to less than 2 percent at an annual rate by the end of 1987. Broader M2 had grown 3.3 percent in 1987, well below the lower end of the Fed's 5½ to 8½ percent target range. So how could there be any inflation danger? Johnson and other Fed officials also fretted about weak money growth. But most policymakers sided with the Fed staff, which regarded the monetary aggregates as unreliable predictors of economic activity and prices, except perhaps over the long-run. They focused more on the level of aggregate demand in the economy relative to how much strain or slack there was in the labor market and in industry's capacity to produce. Conflict was inevitable.

As late as the December 15–16, 1987, FOMC meeting, the administration's emphasis on sustaining growth over containing inflation had been largely shared by the Fed staff. Despite upbeat reports from the 12 Fed districts, the staff was still assuming the crash would dampen growth and credit would need to be eased. "Basically, we have both long and short rates declining between a half and one percentage point by the middle of the year," said Prell. "While the recession-now scenario seems unduly pessimistic, any reasonable confidence interval around our forecast certainly would encompass the possibility of a modest downturn in activity." That view was soon to alter drastically. Although the full magnitude was not known at the time, real GNP had grown 6.1 percent in the fourth quarter of 1987, even faster than in the third quarter. By the time of the February 9–10 FOMC meeting, the Fed staff had shaken off its recession worries and was projecting that, after a dip to 1 percent in the first quarter, GNP growth would rebound to 3 percent. (In fact, the economy was to grow 3.4 percent in the first quarter of 1988, then taper off.) Total unemployment in December 1987 was just 5.7 percent (5.8 percent civilian) and was on a downward trajectory, reaching 5.2 percent by June of 1988. Industry was using a relatively high 82.1 percent of capacity in December 1987 and would hit 84.2 percent by November 1988.

Whenever the economy is going full tilt like that, the Fed's inflation feelers instinctively go "sproinggggg!" Even if the CPI is registering little or no inflation, the Fed begins anticipating wage-price pressures. In fact, as the lagged effects of the Volcker Fed's easier policies of the mid-eighties took hold, the CPI pace had nearly doubled from 1.9 percent in 1986 to 3.6 percent in 1987, en route to year-over-year increases of 4.1 percent in 1988, 4.9 percent in 1989, and 5.4 percent in 1990. By the end of 1990, inflation was running at 6.1 percent, at which rate prices double in less than a dozen years. With all the key economic indicators pointing upward, it became obvious the Fed would have to resume the preemptive rate hikes it had begun before the crash. In early January, before the Fed had even finished easing, Fed watchers were widely anticipating a return to tightening. Because of the approach of the November 1988 presidential election, some thought the Fed's political window of opportunity to raise rates was the first quarter. One prescient administration official had no such illusions. "The idea that the Fed is not going to do anything to hurt Republican chances is wrong. Greenspan is more likely to torpedo [the GOP] to prove his manhood."

The Fed chairman probably had less insecurity about his manhood than his critics. He certainly had the courage of his conviction that if the Fed did not take action, past gains against inflation would be lost. Leigh-Pemberton only wishes the Bank of England had followed his example. "What we learned afterwards was the fact that this [crash] had no effect on the real economy of the industrialized countries at all and that relaxation of interest rates proved to be excessive, certainly in the United Kingdom, and was the starting point of the excessive boom that we had toward the end of '88 and the bubble in 89. Hindsight told us we didn't tighten enough, early enough. Without a doubt . . . [the Fed] was more effective than we were on this." At the time, however, it was neither obvious nor easy for Greenspan—still less than six months on the job—to persuade other FOMC members with longer tenure to resume tightening, never mind Congress and the White House. Greenspan had all the support he needed from the Fed's eager beaver professional staff, who were delighted he meant business about preventing a reawakening of inflation. By the time of the February FOMC meeting, the staff had begun formulating a secret strategy that envisioned pushing the federal funds rate to near 10 percent by the spring of 1989 in a conscious effort to hold the economic growth rate below its potential.

Price stability was the Fed's main stated goal, and to get there, the Fed felt it had to discourage consumer spending. Since the economy had already approached what the staff considered full employment and full capacity in 1988, Kohn and Prell determined it was necessary to hold real GNP growth to no more than 2 percent and preferrably less. In fact, the staff was prepared to risk recession to defeat inflation. Describing one potential policy scenario at the February 9 meeting, Edwin M. ("Ted") Truman, head of the Fed Board's international division, told the FOMC, "We assumed that the federal funds rate would increase by 300 basis point [3 percent] over the next four quarters relative to the rates already embedded in the staff forecast." He said pursuing this course would cut the staff's forecast for growth "by more than half" in 1988. "In 1989, the effects are strong enough to push the economy into recession." Though the staff was not yet assuming a rate hike of that magnitude, it soon would become the staff's preferred path and the one chosen less than two months later and followed until the following February.

Before each FOMC meeting, with little or no input from the policymakers themselves, the Fed Board's staff economists prepare two highly confidential documents known as the *greenbook* and the *bluebook*. The greenbook, which the Fed governors and presidents receive five or six days before the meeting, contains a detailed economic forecast for the coming year and the year beyond. A critical assumption which the staff builds into the forecast is the projected path of the federal funds rate. In 1988 and until relatively recently, the staff conditioned its forecast on one rate path. The bluebook, which is usually delivered to each policymaker's home over the weekend prior to the Tuesday FOMC meeting, presents a set of short-term policy alternatives for how the Fed can best pursue its objectives in the roughly six-week interval between meetings. But while the bluebook is held even more closely than the greenbook, the latter arguably carries greater weight. The two documents form the basis for FOMC debate. Board members get the benefit of a staff briefing each Monday morning but are virtually prohibited from participating in the preparation of the forecasts. Fed presidents, who have their own economists, are even more out of the loop. The presidents often use the two books as fodder for mock FOMC meetings to prepare themselves for the actual event.

Although the staff does not formally make recommendations, and although the FOMC can choose to totally disregard its implicit advice, there is a strong presumption that the greenbook forecast and the rate path it embodies will form the basis of policy over the forecast period. "I certainly do interpret it as advice," one senior Fed official asserts. In the absence of strong argumentation to the contrary, there is a tendency for the FOMC to follow the course laid out by the staff. This, at any rate, was the case in 1988. The greenbook prepared for the February 1988 FOMC meeting assumed rates would be unchanged or even a bit lower through mid-year, then "trend upward gradually," rising three-quarters of one percent, but as Truman's statement indicates, the staff was already considering much more dramatic rate hikes. Soon it would be building an assumption that the funds rate would need to rise at least 3 percent into its forecast, and the FOMC would follow suit.

Beating inflation to a pulp was not the only reason the Fed wanted to slow demand. There was also an important international trade motive. By discouraging domestic consumption, the Fed hoped to give industry greater resources and capacity to produce for export—precisely the kind of export-oriented policies the United States has long criticized Japan for pursuing. How to reduce the huge U.S. current account deficit, which had bulged to $153.9 billion in 1987, and quash calls for protectionism had been discussed at the December FOMC meeting. To reduce the deficit to a manageable size without further unacceptable depreciation of the dollar, the United States might not have to have a recession, Corrigan said, but there would have to be "a long period of subpar growth in domestic demand in the U.S. economy and by implication a slower rise in the standard of living than we've been used to. . . . [D]omestic spending . . . is going to have to be restrained. . . ." "I hate to admit this," a like-minded Greenspan rejoined, "but I find the scenario the Vice Chairman has been outlining more benevolent than any of them that I've been contemplating." Boehne chimed in to say that reducing the trade deficit would likely necessitate a "shift from consuming more than we produce to producing more than we consume."

The other alternatives for reducing the current account deficit were either not viable or were out of the Fed's control. The Fed had been begging Congress for years to slash the budget deficit to reduce the drain on the country's limited pool of savings and lower the dependence on foreign capital which had been associated with increased importation of foreign goods. But no amount of pleading or shaming had succeeded in persuading Congress or the White House to stop deficit spending, and whenever taxes had been raised, Congress had outspent the increased revenues. James Baker had tried two other tacks: letting the dollar depreciate and pushing U.S. trading partners to buy more U.S. products. But both of those approaches had been miserable failures, helping to cause the stock market crash.

Before it could turn to fighting inflation, the Fed had first to extricate itself from the crisis mode in which it had been operating. In a January 5 conference call, Greenspan proposed that the FOMC move back to a "normal approach to open market operations," but he and others did not want to give the impression the Fed was moving immediately toward a tighter credit posture. Hoskins was doubly anxious for it not to appear the Fed was again "evolving policy in order to support the dollar." Greenspan assured him, "I think that we can make it fairly clear that that is not the case. . . . I think that that would be a very important misinterpretation of policy. I think we would work to avoid that becoming the market's perception."

As the effects of the crash wore off, Greenspan and Corrigan were anxious to get the Fed back to setting a target for how much banks borrow from the Fed's discount window as a means of regulating banks' ability to expand credit and keeping the funds rate in a certain fairly narrow range, instead of directly manipulating the funds rate, as it had been doing since the crash. Before the crash, the Fed had been tightening reserve pressures and raising the funds rate by targeting a higher level of discount window borrowings. After the crash it pushed reserves into the system so aggressively, through purchases of government securities, that banks' borrowings from the discount window fell dramatically, even though the Fed had encouraged banks to borrow as much as they wanted. As borrowings fell, so did the funds rate. From $700 million per day before the crash, seasonal plus adjustment borrowings fell to $300 million per day after the crash and later to just $200 million or less. The funds rate was allowed to fall to roughly 6¾ percent from 7½ percent before the crash, and the Fed essentially abandoned its borrowing target procedure and conducted open market operations to fix the funds rate at 6¾ percent. By the time of the December FOMC meeting, borrowings were averaging between $100 million and $150 million below where the New York Fed's open market desk calculated they should be to be consistent with a funds rate of 6¾ percent, but as Sternlight, who supervised the daily purchases and sales of government securities, told the committee, "No effort was made to push borrowing up to that [$400 million] level as it became clear that doing so would entail appreciably higher funds rates."

So, to the great annoyance of Corrigan, the desk found itself conducting open market operations on a day-to-day basis to keep the funds rate fixed precisely at 6¾ percent. At the December FOMC meeting the New York Fed president told his colleagues he had not expected to be "resisting even one-eighth of a percentage point wiggles in the federal funds rate. . . . That approach to policy, even on a very short-term basis, is one that I find very, very troubling." Even before the crash, the Fed had been targeting the funds rate much more than it cared to admit, but it had allowed some volatility. Although it was not, in those days, specifically targeting the federal funds rate, the Fed had in mind a fairly narrow funds rate range for any given level of borrowing, but now it was getting ridiculous. "I have been rather struck that in the last two or three days the funds rate all of a sudden has been locked," Greenspan told the FOMC. "It's an extraordinary thing to watch the screen and see high: 6¾ percent; low: 6¾ percent; last: 6¾ percent."

The Fed was sensitive politically to any appearance that it was fixing the funds rate and preferred the appearance of merely affecting reserve levels while the market set short-term interest rates. What's more, the funds rate pegging procedure had bad historical connotations. Burns had used the procedure in the mid-seventies, and the rap on funds rate pegging was that the Fed tended not to raise it fast enough to prevent inflation. Targeting borrowed reserves also gave the Fed a sense of greater flexibility. It was easier, in the minds of policymakers, to adjust banks' discount window borrowings than to take a highly visible direct action to change the funds rate. As Black said at the

December meeting, "There is inertia when operating under a federal funds target. The committee, just because it doesn't know where the funds rate ought to go, is less apt to move. There is also some substance, I think, to the political argument that it gives us a certain degree of protection if we can say we really don't control the federal funds rate, we control borrowed reserves." Outside of a few naifs on Capitol Hill it is doubtful Fed policymakers were fooling many people with their monetary version of "plausible deniability." In practical terms, they were talking about a distinction without much of a difference; one way or another they were aiming for a certain funds rate level. The FOMC had spent an enormous amount of time in December talking furtively about how it would make the transition from targeting the funds rate level back to targeting banks' borrowings from the Fed, and Greenspan, among others, talked about using the usual year-end volatility in the federal funds rate as "cover" for doing so. Hoskins lost patience: "We're sitting here looking for year-end cover and all that kind of thing; it seems to me we can get where we want to be very quickly with less misinformation or miscues by making an announcement."

The upshot of the January 5 conference call was a small, but significant change in the policy directive issued at its December meeting. At that time, the FOMC had instructed the desk that "still sensitive conditions in financial markets and uncertainties in the economic outlook may continue to call for a special degree of flexibility in open market operations." Now it was changed to say, "The passing of the year-end should permit further progress toward restoring a normal approach to open market operations, although still sensitive conditions in financial markets and uncertainties in the economic outlook may continue to call for some flexibility in operations." More than mere semantics, the change marked a step away from preoccupation with the crash. It was the beginning of the end of easy money. For the moment, the Fed was trying to bring the funds rate back down to around 6¾ percent following the usual year-end spike in the funds rate.

The Fed was to ease credit slightly on two more occasions. The first came a few weeks later, aided by a strengthening dollar. Angell, who did not think any easing was needed, knew it was coming but didn't like it. One day in mid-January, he went looking for Johnson and was told he was with Greenspan. Strolling down the hall, he wandered into Greenspan's office. "Have you already decided what you're going to do?" Angell asked them. "Yes, we have," Greenspan replied. "Well then, there's no use telling you my point of view," Angell told them. Greenspan and Johnson knew Angell was opposed to easing. Against Greenspan's wishes, he had gone on the Evans and Novak television show the Saturday after the crash to predict it would have no negative effects and that the economy would come back strong. On January 28, less than two weeks before the FOMC was to hold a two-day meeting in Washington, Greenspan took it on his own authority to order the New York Fed to cut the funds rate from the range of 6¾ to 6⅞ percent which had prevailed since December to roughly 6½ to 6⅝ percent by lowering its borrowing target $50 million to $250 million. The Commerce Department had just estimated GNP had grown strongly in the fourth quarter, but Greenspan had his doubts. Explaining his actions to a not-altogether-pleased FOMC on February 10, Greenspan said, "There was increasing evidence from the initial [unemployment insurance] claims figures that the economy was slowing down very dramatically. And this was subsequently confirmed by the January unemployment data. Secondly, and of considerable significance, was increasing evidence that the exchange rate was being stabilized."

After the January 5 bear trap, the dollar had gotten a further boost on January 13, when the crafty Baker had arranged for President Reagan and Japan's visiting new Prime Minister Noburu Takeshita to issue an unusual joint statement in which the two nations undertook to support the dollar by giving the U.S. Treasury and Fed expanded access to yen reserves, as needed, to sell if the dollar resumed its fall. Included in the arrangement was a provision for the United States to exchange Special Drawing Rights (allocated to it by the IMF) for yen. Even more oddly, the statement contained a pledge by Takeshita to have his central bank push down Japanese interest rates. The Fed must have cringed at the mere thought of an American president making such pledges on its behalf. It was bad enough that Baker, who had sat across the G-7 table from Takeshita when he was Japan's finance minister, told the Japanese leader a recession in the United States must "be avoided by all means." His comment seemed intended for Greenspan's ears. Two days later, the dollar got more help when the Commerce Department reported that the trade deficit had fallen from $16.7 billion to $13.2 billion. An administration official said the stronger dollar should keep the Fed from raising interest rates.

Such comments were part of a rising crescendo of public and private pressure on the Fed to hold the line on interest rates and preferably lower them. Leading the charge for the administration was Sprinkel. He argued the money supply had been growing too slowly to justify any concern about inflation. If the CPI was on the rise now, that was because the Fed had allowed the money supply to grow too fast in 1986, but now the Fed was swinging too far in the other direction. Taking the same view was Darby, who on January 21 fired off a letter to all the Fed governors and presidents which was to become a cause célèbre when it eventually became public. "The latest decline in real money has been taking place for about one year," he wrote. "If past relationships hold, this implies that economic weakness, if it is to occur, probably will begin sometime during the first quarter of 1988." Attached were charts on the behavior of the monetary aggregates.

In retrospect, the Darby letter seems pretty innocuous. "I didn't give it a second thought," says Corrigan. Darby focused singlemindedly on slow M2 growth, but neither he nor Sprinkel had made any secret of their views. Angell recalls having "mock debates" with Darby at meetings of the Public Securities Association around that time. There was "nothing new" in the Darby letter, said Johnson, who had not been shy about expressing his opinion of monetary policy when he held Darby's job. Nevertheless, the letter proved a godsend for Greenspan, the lion of October, who was about to be bearded in his own den by some of the Fed presidents, who were not pleased when the new chairman had cut interest rates on January 28 without consulting them.

Administration officials were keeping up a steady drumbeat of pressure on the Fed. On a routine basis, Darby and Sprinkel were telling the Fed governors, all of whom were Reagan appointees, that the Fed was too tight. Some sympathized. The presidents as a group were skeptical the economy was in any need of easier money. I conducted a district-by-district survey, interviewing Parry, Boykin, Boehne, and Boston Fed president Frank Morris, among others, and all were upbeat on economic conditions and prospects. By the time the FOMC gathered for its February 9 meeting, some of the presidents were spoiling for a fight. Aside from the Darby letter, they were aware of all the other political pressure that was being brought to bear on Greenspan and the Board, and it looked suspiciously like Greenspan had succumbed. In one of the few times Greenspan's authority was ever challenged, Guffey told Greenspan his January 28 rate cut, taken without FOMC consultation, was unjustified by economic evidence and "outside the confines of the directive" previously agreed on. Tweaking his sensitivity to allegations the move had been prompted by political pressure, Guffey told Greenspan, "It's particularly important, given the background of the political pressure that had come from the Treasury people . . . and so forth, that such a decision be a broader-based decision." Stung by the insinuation he had misused his discretion for political reasons, Greenspan responded vociferously. "I must tell you that I resented those calls that were being made by the Treasury, and I told them," he asserted. "And I must tell you that the Secretary of the Treasury was very upset when he heard about them and did not like them. I communicated in a manner which I hope will shut that nuisance off, because I thought it was most inappropriate. I can't believe the insensitivity of the people involved in doing what they were doing. That's the reason I asked you earlier on, by all means, to let me know if we failed to shut the valve down." If that "valve" through which pressure on the Fed had been flowing was not shut off, Greenspan vowed, "I'll just have to use a sledge hammer." In effect, he did just that.

It was a contentious meeting. At one point, after listening to Corrigan, Johnson, and Angell debate back and forth for several minutes whether the Fed could hit its funds rate target, Greenspan interrupted to exclaim, "Heavens, I haven't heard this conversation since Economics 101!" At another, when Johnson interrupted him, Greenspan ordered, "Quiet." Meekly, Johnson asked, "May I say one little word on this?" "One," Greenspan shot back. The FOMC finally agreed to ratify the easier credit market conditions that had prevailed in the days leading up to the meeting. To the annoyance of Angell and others, who saw themselves presented with another fait accompli, the open market desk had allowed credit conditions to relax prior to the meeting, and borrowings had fallen to $200 million. "What we end up doing . . . is never voting for a policy change in this committee," Seger complained. Although the published record suggested the FOMC had left policy unchanged, in practice it had eased again. Incredibly, the vote was unanimous, and as the raucous meeting concluded, Boehne turned to Greenspan and said wryly, "My congratulations to you, Mr. Chairman. You have performed a miracle." Greenspan replied, "I don't know where it came from." There was confusion about whether the Fed eased when strong retail sales and whole-sale price reports put upward pressure on rates, but the Fed made a roughly quarter-point reduction in the funds rate to a range of 6¼ to 6⅜ percent.

Greenspan conceded he had mixed feelings about this last easing move. On one hand, he said, "It's very difficult to find" signs of an "inventory recession" in which factories cut production to work off excess stocks of unsold goods, but he was worried about the nation's finances. "We had a major shock in October, and we seem to have temporarily come out of it. But the stock market, by anybody's measure, is not low. While a lot of the yield spread ab-normalities have come down, it is still a very unstable situation. What's con-cerning me is that there is a vulnerability out there which is continuing to heal but is not healed yet. . . . If we were to indicate that we were tightening, the shock to the markets I think would break the stock market and create some real problems." It would prove to be the Fed's final gesture of concern about the uncertainties growing out of Black Monday. From then on the Fed ruth-lessly raised rates until it saw the economy slowing down a year later. Little did the administration know the Fed was about to start tightening. One official said a further $1 billion drop in the trade deficit reported February 12 should give the Fed "more latitude" to ease by strengthening the dollar.

In a February 16 speech, Greenspan was still talking about the "the linger-ing impact" of the crash and other factors inhibiting growth, but hinted at the coming policy shift by observing, "Financial variables seem to be in equilib-rium. . . . I suspect we'll stay there." The administration could read the warn-ing signs of an impending swing toward credit tightening and turned up the heat. On February 17, the Economic Report of the President, a document produced each year by the CEA, which backhandedly credited the Fed for responding "promptly and unequivocally" to the crash but charged "rising interest rates certainly were a factor in the stock market's decline." Sprinkel contended, "There is room for further reduction in the unemployment rate without risking heating up inflation." He said he was "happy with their current stance," but said the Fed had to meet its money growth target if the adminis-tration was to realize its forecast of 2.4 percent real GNP growth for 1988, much less its goal of 3.3 percent growth in the following four years. However, the Fed viewed the prevailing 5.8 percent unemployment rate as perilously close to "full employment" for an economy that still seemed to have a full head of steam and regarded the projection of 3.3 percent growth during the 1989 to 1993 period as excessive and unacceptable. The same day, the administration released its fiscal 1989 budget message, which informed the Fed there was "no need, at present, for restrictive monetary measures."

Meanwhile, the Darby letter had been made public and, to its author's embarrassment, was gaining more notoriety than it had initially. Much was made of the letter's timing—19 days before the FOMC met to set its money growth targets and economic objectives for the year and prepare for the

Humphrey-Hawkins report to Congress. Democrats had a field day condemn-ing the administration for trying to "tamper" with the Fed's independence. "It is both deplorable and counterproductive for the Reagan administration to pressure you as much as they have in recent months," Proxmire told Greenspan on February 24, as he made his first Humphrey-Hawkins report. "The incumbent administration often has a desire to ease money more than would be good for the economy just before the presidential election. . . . You and your fellow governors are entrusted with resisting political pressure and implementing good economic policy." Ironically, administration pressure could "make it harder for you to ease monetary policy than would be the case if they were silent. Even if you have eased money for sound technical reasons, you will certainly be accused of bending to poltical pressure. . . . The adminis-tration's haranguing unnecessarily raises the cost to the Fed of making good policy." Proxmire's were some of the kinder words said about Darby by the Democrats, who had never been known for their scrupulous respect for the Fed's independence or for their reluctance to criticize the central bank. With-out missing a beat, Proxmire criticized the Fed for not targeting M1 and for widening its M2 growth range, while reducing it from 5½ to 8½ to 4 to 8 per-cent. He accused the Fed of "keeping the public in the dark."

Darby is still bemused by the pyrotechnics his letter set off, particularly since, he claims, it was Greenspan himself who requested it. "The letter was prompted by a lunch I had with Wayne Angell and Alan Greenspan," he recalls. "Alan asked me to write up some thoughts about it, so I copied every-body on the FOMC. I shouldn't have, but that's what happened." Unapolo-getic, he says, "The administration, outside economists, everybody is always giving their advice to the Fed, and the Fed is empowered to decide what to do. It would have been improper if we made some threat, but I am sure that nobody was doing that." Sprinkel says he "never believed that the Federal Reserve should be subject to an administration, that they should be submis-sive. . . . On the other hand, it didn't seem to me that, recognizing that the Fed should make up its own mind, you should sit there and do nothing if you thought they were doing something improperly. . . ." Darby jokes that his tiff with the Fed chairman "turned out pretty good. Greenspan ended up standing up to an assistant secretary, and his griping gave him credibility with the bank presidents. . . ." But he has some bitterness. "I think it was a little silly making it into a morality play. . . . Once things had gone on long enough and the let-ter was finally released to a congressional committee, everybody wondered, 'Why was Alan complaining about that?' I mean, everybody is always giving their opinion. . . . What pressure is there? The guys have 14-year terms, and Alan was appointed past the administration's life. I mean, you know, gee!"

Greenspan made hay with the Darby letter. Although he had taken charge impressively the previous fall, he was still an unknown quantity going into 1988. Wall Street wondered if he was up to making the hard choices to contain inflation. The Darby letter allowed him to show his independence. An atypi-cally animated Greenspan told Proxmire he had complained to Baker about Darby's letter and had extracted a promise that no further such letters would be written. "I objected quite strongly. I am reasonably sure such actions will not reoccur in the future." Darby disputes Greenspan's contention that Baker slapped his wrist. "I don't think I was doing anything out of line, and I don't think he [Baker] thought I was doing anything out of line. I certainly was not made aware of it." Darby said Greenspan was hearing the same thing from Sprinkel and from Baker himself. Baker chuckles in recalling the whole brouhaha. "I remember that; he sent copies to every member of the FOMC. I probably spoke to Mike and said, 'Mike that's not the best way to get something done on that. If we want something done on that there's a better way to approach it, and that's up at the top level.' "

Proxmire had a point about administration pressure being counterproductive. Greenspan himself hinted in his testimony that the Fed might dig in its heels due to administration pressure just to prove its independence: "The only thing that I hope does not happen is that the concern of our responding to political pressure gets so extraordinary that we will feel a necessity to do precisely the opposite, and we could very well be taking actions which would be counter to our best judgment. That is the type of problem which concerns me more than my concern that the current administration will pressure us into doing things that we don't think are appropriate for monetary policy for this country." Robert McTeer, then head of the Baltimore branch of the Richmond Fed, says political pressure has the opposite effect. "You might get a little stubborn if it puts you in the position of looking like you're reacting to political pressure. . . ."

There was something in Greenspan's February 23–24 Humphrey-Hawkins testimony for everybody, whether they were looking for the Fed to continue easing or begin tightening. Confirming the Fed had made a "further small easing step a few weeks ago," he said the Fed had "returned some way towards our earlier focus on reserve positions in the day-to-day implementation of policy," but that "markets still are exhibiting a certain edginess, and we can't be sure yet that normal market functioning has been fully restored." He told the House Banking Committee the dangers of inflation and recession were "about equal." Although the Fed had lowered its M2 growth range, he promised to achieve faster actual growth after M2's subpar performance in 1987. At the same time, he made light of Sprinkel's single-minded focus on the money supply in judging Fed policy, saying he "evaluates monetary policy differently" than the CEA chairman. He said the only reason M2 had been sluggish in 1987 was because rising interest rates available on such things as T-bills had caused people to pull money out of bank deposits. Since the beginning of 1988, M2 had picked up, but this was attributable to the fact that interest rates had come back down, making it more attractive for people to hold money in bank accounts again.

Greenspan's listeners could perhaps be pardoned for not realizing the Fed had turned its back on easy credit. Sprinkel was encouraged by Greenspan's commitment to faster money growth, little realizing Greenspan was about to turn off the credit spigots. What should have been the dead giveaway of Greenspan's true intent was his assertion the economy "does not exhibit the geriatric characteristics of the late stages of an expansion. We cannot be complacent about the potential for higher inflation; by the time an acceleration of costs and price pressures were to become evident, the inflation process would already be well-entrenched." The Fed would have to be "very careful" about inflation, because "once it starts, it can run away from you."

Nevertheless, the administration moderated somewhat its pressure on the Fed, at least publicly. "We are quite supportive of current monetary policy and the Fed's plans for this year, contrary to what you may have heard," Sprinkel told the National Association of Business Economists on March 1, although he couldn't resist adding that "moderate and stable money growth is a condition for continued economic growth." Fellow monetarist Lee Hoskins introduced Sprinkel with the comment that he "has criticized the Fed for 20 years or so and I don't see why he should cease doing so now." Sprinkel boomed back good-naturedly, "I hope you won't report me for having a very pleasant luncheon with the president of the Cleveland Fed." In a further show of good feeling, Baker told the Senate Budget Committee on March 4 he was "in fundamental agreement with the conduct of monetary policy presently being pursued by the Federal Reserve. . . . There really is no difference of opinion or difference of view between the administration and the Federal Reserve regarding the current conduct of monetary policy." Offering an olive branch from the Fed's side, Johnson said the Fed was "always seeking information and truth about what we need to do. We actually welcome the debate and we welcome different views." But the Fed "has to be independent in its determination of policy."

Between the Humphrey-Hawkins testimony and the rate-hiking March 29 FOMC meeting, Fed officials embarked on a publicity campaign to convince everyone the Fed might have to start raising rates, but that, like a kindly dentist, it would do so as painlessly as possible. Thus, in late February, Angell said the Fed would like to "get inflation down to zero" while being "conscious of the fact that we do not become disruptive to economic activity." Johnson said "Sharp unanticipated changes in monetary policy can be disruptive to the economy. Accordingly, the pursuit of price stabiity should also seek to minimize short-term disruptions to economic activity." On March 2, Greenspan told the Senate Budget Committee he foresaw "strong but not spectacular growth the rest of the year."

Meanwhile, the dollar was becoming a problem again. It had fallen from a mid-February peak of more than 131 yen and more than 1.71 marks per dollar to 126 yen and 1.66 marks on March 8. Johnson blamed falling oil prices, which tended to lessen demand for greenbacks since oil is priced in dollars. But others worried that the Fed's rate cuts had reduced the interest premium on dollar assets and made them less attractive to foreign investors. "With interest rates coming down, other things being equal, it has to imply some downward pressure on the dollar," said a Fed staffer, who hoped "the improvement in the current account could offset it." Others saw that as unlikely. The dollar's weakness was being driven by a "reassessment on the part of foreign investors of the strength of demand in the U.S. economy," an official told me. Job and consumer credit gains were suggesting "consumer demand is still quite strong, that demand for imports will be high and that therefore we're not going to see as much improvement in the current account deficit." Another Fed official said, "Clearly a decline of our interest rates—real interest rates vis à vis foreign interest rates—is bound to cause some decline in the dollar . . . [and] as long as we still have a deficit we're going to have pressure on the dollar." The Fed did not want to appear to base monetary policy on exchange rates, but its concern about the dollar gave it another reason to tighten. "We don't look at exchange rate stability as being desirable in its own right," an official said, but "if the dollar is falling too fast and putting upward pressure on inflation we might react."

Sensing the Fed was edging toward a tighter policy, the administration tried to counter the Fed's concerns. The dollar's slide was "not a nasty trend we have to get too concerned about," a Reagan adviser told me. "I don't think the Fed would have to respond at all at this point." However, if there was any doubt about the Fed's anxiety over the dollar's weakness, it was removed March 10 when Greenspan said, "Further declines in the exchange value of the dollar add to the general uncertainty regarding the prospects for inflation." He feared past dollar depreciation, while favorable to American exports, could cause inflation via two channels: (1) "export growth could place stronger demands on a domestic resource base that already is operating at high levels of utilization in some areas," and (2) it would tend to increase prices of imports and comparable U.S.-made goods. "We cannot allow the price level adjustments associated with the restoration of external balance to set off a renewed inflation process," he declared. Rising commodity prices were another factor threatening to aggravate inflation. What's more, most economic indicators were "pointing to further expansion this year." Seldom does a Fed chairman give such a clear indication of where he intends to take policy. "The road ahead could be bumpy at times," Greenspan warned presciently. He might have added, paraphrasing Bette Davis in the movie "All About Eve": Fasten your seat belts, it's going to be a long year.

On March 15, Greenspan gave more signals of the impending rate hikes. "Monetary policy needs to remain supportive of the expansion but also alert to the possibility of a reemergence of inflation," he told the Congressional Joint Economic Committee. "The cost of temporizing in the face of accumulating price pressures would be a far more serious and painful adjustment down the road." He saw little room for growth or for lower unemployment with the rate then at 5.7 percent and warned that the same forces that were reducing the trade deficit could lead to inflation. "Bottlenecks are not a serious problem at the present time," but "export growth could place stronger demands on a domestic resource base that already is operating at high levels of utilization in some areas. . . ." Therefore, the Fed must be "cautious about thinking that this adjustment [to greater production for export] can be accomplished without some upward pressure on prices." It was another way of saying the Fed intended to smother domestic consumption.

Seger scoffed at Greenspan's concerns about factories' rising rates of capacity utilization, which she called "a meaningless statistic." The Fed had recently announced that its measure of how much of their capacity factories, mines, and utilities were using had risen further in January to 82.1 percent, but Seger thought the Fed should stop publishing it. "Some of the comments I hear about capacity utilization are inconsistent with the way the world works," she told me. "Right now some industries are running at a very good clip, using a high percentage of their capacity, but that isn't saying all companies are running flat out." Besides, capacity "is not a hard and fast number that if you bump up against it the world falls apart. You have some give. You can put an extra shift on. You can work Saturday and Sunday." But Seger was a voice in the wilderness; most of her colleagues saw rising capacity utilization as inflationary.[1]

Greenspan's worst fears were soon confirmed. The Fed relies not just on statistics but on anecdotal information gathered from business, banking, and other contacts throughout the country. Two weeks prior to each FOMC meeting, this information is compiled into a document called the *beige book*, because of its putrid color. The beige book prepared for the March 29 meeting found continued economic expansion had created "tight labor markets" and a high pace of operation by factories. "Many producers are using all available capacity, causing higher prices in some areas." But such news didn't dissuade the doves. Eight days before the FOMC was to meet, Johnson held a soiree for representatives of major government securities dealers at the Federal Reserve which was closed to the press. According to a participant, the Fed Board's second in command said he did "not see any near-term danger of increased inflation stemming from the high rate of capacity utilization in American industry" and said "the current pace of the economy is neither too slow nor too fast to generate tremendous concern at the Fed. . . ." As the pivotal FOMC meeting drew even closer, Heller asked me, "Where do you see inflation? I've seen no hard statistics that show a resurgence of inflation." He added that "the risks are pretty evenly balanced right now. We can't neglect one or the other." Given such comments from Fed officials, it is not surprising that four days before the March 29 FOMC meeting, a poll of Fed watchers yielded a consensus for no change in policy. At most, some said, the Fed would adopt an "asymmetrical" directive with a bias toward tighter credit conditions.

On the eve of the FOMC meeting, administration officials downplayed Fed concerns about the weakness of the dollar, which at that point had fallen below 124 yen and 1.66 marks in wake of another bad trade report. Sprinkel said, "Near stability [of the dollar] is good enough" and said the administration wanted merely to prevent "major volatility." Treasury Secretary Baker, I was told, felt "a further decline of the dollar could be counteproductive" but was unwilling to authorize major dollar support operations. Baker "is not saying that if the dollar declines at all, we're going to jump in to prevent it from declining," said a Treasury official. "What kind of range he's willing to let the dollar fluctuate within depends on the strength of the economy. If the slowdown [in economic activity] is moderate and the dollar is weak we would be more willing to provide resources to support the dollar than if the slowdown is bad and the dollar is weak." Such talk was not very comforting for Fed officials who saw dollar depreciation as one of the most inflationary threats on their radar screen. Not only was the dollar weakening, it was taking bond prices with it, pushing up long-term interest rates. From 8.35 percent just prior to the FOMC's February meeting, the yield on the bellwether Treasury 30-year bond had risen above 8.80 percent. It was the same dread combination that had occurred prior to Black Monday.

Around the FOMC table on March 29 there was a sense of grim purpose as one member after another weighed the economic and financial evidence and came to the conclusion, sometimes reluctantly, that the Fed had stayed its hand against inflation long enough. "It was a tough call," as Corrigan recollects. Because of the residue of concern which committee members had about the stability of the financial system and doubts about the economy's strength, "It was a very, very difficult period. It was one of the most important, courageous moves we ever made." Even Johnson, who had led those wanting to hold the line on interest rates, gave in and voted to tighten credit after minimizing inflation and warning about the unsettling effect a rate hike might have on the stock market. Corrigan was most adamant, asserting, "The amount of room on the upside is just about zero. In other words, any acceleration of growth from these forecasts [2.5 to 2.75 percent real GNP growth from the Fed staff] carries with it rapidly escalating risks that the inflation problem will begin to show through again." What's more, there was "a clear risk on the side of a further depreciation of the dollar and I see very little to be gained by a further depreciation of the dollar." Corrigan also feared a "return of the wild, wild West to the financial scene"—a reference to the increasingly leveraged condition of financial markets associated with real estate speculation and the heavy issuance of junk bonds to finance corporate takeovers.

One-time rate-cutting rebel Angell was now among the most hawkish. He feared "the dollar could come under serious attack," but also pointed to the double-digit rates of money growth that had been registered in the first three months of 1988 and rising commodity prices. "In the past, I felt that we have been overpredicting the rate of inflation a little. Yet it seems to me that we are now at a crucial point where price rises could become rampant and could explode." Fueling these concerns, the staff argued that a likely 10 percent dollar fall would push up prices through the two channels Greenspan had cited. "We already have seen price pressures in some industries that we think are a function not just of the dollar decline but of actual pressures on capacity, with a backlog in orders that has built up," said Prell. "You could well get severe [inflation] pressures in particular industries," Truman added. Kohn raised the gory specter of October 19, noting the tandem decline in the dollar and bond prices that had occurred. "The recoupling in recent days of the dollar and the bond market certainly is reminscent of the pattern of the first three quarters of 1987 when concerns about inflation tended to dominate market reactions." The argument for higher rates had been clinched. The committee issued a directive stating it wanted to "increase slightly the degree of pressure on reserve positions"—Fed jargon for an immediate quarter percent increase in the funds rate to a 6½ to 6¾ percent range. It gave no indication it was inclined to tighten again before the next meeting on May 17.[2] This implied neutrality did not prevent Greenspan from tightening between meetings.

Corrigan and Greenspan now dismiss the dollar as a significant factor motivating the resumption of credit tightening. The former calls it "marginal," but the transcripts and sources suggest concern about the weak dollar was a major factor. "We didn't know what the long-term impact might be," but the hope was that "immediately it might have an important impact on exchange markets," one policymaker said.

In those days the Fed did not announce policy changes after FOMC meetings as it has since 1994, after years of congressional pressure, and the Fed's tightening on March 30 was not readily evident for several days because of uncertainties about the level of borrowings and the Fed's open market operations. Greenspan played coy in a visit to the Senate Banking Committee on March 31, not saying a word about the FOMC's policy shift. He said there were "lingering effects" of the crash. For instance, corporations had not returned to equity markets to raise capital, but the economy "has not fallen into recession as some had predicted. Indeed, it has shown considerable resilience." Three days after the meeting, it was still not widely assumed the Fed had tightened. After a large gain in nonfarm payrolls was announced, an administration official worried, "It's going to put pressure on the Fed to tighten. They're already skittish about bottlenecks and price pressures." It did not become clear the Fed had tightened until April 4, when the Fed failed to add reserves as expected, causing the funds rate to edge up close to 6¾ percent. Even then, the administration was holding out hope the Fed had not tightened. Perhaps problems with First Republic Bank of Dallas were "messing up forecasters' ability to project reserve demand," said a Treasury official. But by April 5, after two days of letting the funds rate trade up to 6¾ percent or higher without adding reserves in a "rate protest," it finally became obvious the Fed had swung from easing to tightening. It was this kind of pointless guessing game that raised the ire of Congress and finally forced the Fed to begin announcing rate changes right away.

When it became clear what the Fed had done, the reaction on Wall Street was enthusiastic. "I thought they wouldn't do anything until they actually saw inflation picking up," said Kasriel. "It shows some courage." "Having recently become accommodative they came to the conclusion that they acted prematurely in becoming more accommodative, and the fact that they reversed it shows they're willing to admit a mistake," said Charles Lieberman, then director of financial market research for Manufacturers Hanover Trust Company. The administration, having taken heat for pressuring the Fed, initially refrained from criticism. But knowing one rate hike would likely lead to another, it soon resumed carping. "I don't know where they see inflation," a senior Reagan advisor declared April 11. "There's no evidence of a sharp increase on the inflation front." Noting that only four industries (steel, paper, chemicals, and textiles) were operating near 90 percent capacity, he said, "A high rate of capacity utilization is not a general phenomenon. In fact, it's a very limited phenomenon. Plus we're coming into the higher rate of capacity utilization at a lower [economic] growth rate. They're overdoing the inflation scare." Sprinkel saw "no evidence that we're on the threshold of a sharp acceleration in inflation" and urged the Fed to continue "moderate growth of the money supply."

But policymakers signaled the Fed had only begun to tighten after it was announced the CPI had risen at a 6 percent annual rate in March. For the prior 12 months consumer prices had risen 3.9 percent, but even that was "unsatisfactory," Angell said in an April 20 interview. "We will either have a monetary policy consistent with improvement in the consumer price index and the producer price index, or we'll run the risk of having inflation accelerate." The administration expressed ironic relief when the Commerce Department on April 26 estimated GNP had grown just 2.3 percent in the first quarter. The data should keep the Fed in "neutral," an administration official said. Sprinkel turned up in the White House press room to remind the Fed of the need to keep M2 money growth in the middle of its target range (about 6 percent). The administration drew vain hope that the Fed might hold the line on rate hikes from the reaction some Fed officials had to the GNP report. "That's a good result," said Black, a voting FOMC member that year. "We ought to be able to maintain that rate without overheating." Angell said, "Those numbers don't look too bad" but cautioned they were "preliminary" and subject to "aberrations."

On April 28, the Fed got some support for its anti-inflation crusade from an unexpected quarter—Congress. The House Banking Subcommittee on Domestic Monetary Policy, chaired by monetarist-oriented North Carolina Democratic congressman Steve Neal, issued a report saying that "there is no ground for complacency" about inflation and warning "further declines in the dollar will bring higher import prices, which might warrant some tightening in monetary policy if they threaten to touch off compensatory increases in domestic prices and wages." On May 3, Angell and Kelley both testified before Neal's subcommittee and told him the Fed's long-run goal was "zero inflation." Seemingly not convinced, Neal told the two Reagan appointees, "You must not reinflate the economy for any reason, no matter how politically appealing." Neal need not have worried.

In early May, the Fed's tightening inclinations were reinforced by fears of foreign rate hikes. German officials had been hinting at the need to tighten German monetary policy because of the overshooting of the Bundesbank's money supply targets, and there was talk Japanese rates might also be raised—all of which would tend to depress the dollar. Speculation was heightened when Poehl, in Tokyo for the opening of a representative office there on May 2, met with Bank of Japan governor Sumita. Two days later, a U.S. monetary source said the possibility of rate hikes by the Bundesbank was putting additional pressure on the Fed to raise rates itself to avoid weakening the dollar. The dollar had recovered from its recent lows, but if the Fed did not keep up with higher German and Japanese rates the dollar would slide again and undermine its anti-inflation efforts. "If they tighten and there isn't a matching increase in interest rates here, given our external imbalances, it seems reasonable to expect that there would be some downward pressure on the dollar," the official said. Foreign rate hikes were delayed, but fear of what they might do to the dollar was all part of the witches' brew of factors drawing the Fed closer to another rate hike. There was a more general concern about inflationary pressures stemming from export-led reductions in the trade deficit. With domestic demand stronger than expected and with U.S. industry booming, many at the Fed were sure price and wage pressures couldn't be far behind. The Fed had hoped for some serious reduction in the budget deficit that year, which would tend to restrain demand, but as usual negotiations between the White House and Congress were deadlocked, and the deficit for fiscal year 1988 (ending September 30) was headed for $155.1 billion ($5.4 billion higher than in 1987) and for $153.4 billion in fiscal 1989. "There is a concern about what further substantial external stimulus would do to the economy when we're making only slow progress on the fiscal front," a Fed official said.

Greenspan continued to stress that if the trade deficit was to be brought down via increased exports, domestic demand would have to be restrained so foreign demand did not overstrain production capability and push up inflation. In an April 28 letter to Proxmire, he wrote that past dollar depreciation had led to a switch of resources to production to meet increased export demand. "In the context of an economy near full employment, this means that domestic absorption has to be restrained by macroeconomic policy to make room for the increase in export demand if we are not to incur an acceleration of inflation." He added a warning that further depreciation of the dollar would prove inflationary and wrote that "achieving a better external balance without increasing inflationary pressures will require a restrained pace of expansion of domestic demands."

In an odd speech he gave in Rio de Janeiro on May 5, Johnson seemed less onboard with Greenspan's strong dollar approach than with Baker's attitude as he talked about how the U.S. trade deficit could be reduced. Ruling out trade barriers, he said the other alternatives were for the "surplus countries" (Germany and Japan) to stimulate their economies, thereby increasing demand for U.S. exports, or the dollar would have to fall. Venturing over the line that usually restrains central bankers from publicly advising other nations' central banks, Johnson declared, "There is scope in some of these economies for a non-inflationary expansion of domestic demand, particularly in light of the expected continued easing in U.S. demand for their products." In the absence of such foreign stimulus, "another method for switching expenditures toward U.S. products is, of course, by means of a real depreciation of the dollar. . . ." While not directly advocating dollar depreciation, he suggested there were ways of achieving a cheaper dollar without bringing on adverse consequences for the U.S. economy. For instance, "an increase in U.S. domestic saving relative to domestic investment would avoid U.S. dependence on foreign capital and allow U.S. interest rates and the dollar's exchange rate to adjust without inflation risks." Johnson's remarks were in such peculiar contrast to Greenspan's that there was open astonishment in some quarters, but the vice chairman's international views reflected a more basic disagreement with the chairman on the direction monetary policy should take. Johnson had gone along with the March 30 rate hike, but he was not anxious to continue raising rates—to aid the dollar or for any other reason.

Unfortunately for Johnson, the weight of economic evidence was moving mostly in Greenspan's direction. Although the beige book survey prepared for the May 17 FOMC meeting found only "moderate growth," the Labor Department announced unemployment had fallen from 5.6 to 5.4 percent in April. "This can't help but revive fears of inflation whether it's real or not," said an administration official. There was still a good deal of doubt whether the Republican-dominated Fed would have the guts to tighten credit in an election year, but the Fed wasted no time proving those suspicions wrong. On Monday morning, May 9, eight days before the FOMC was scheduled to meet, Greenspan again acted on his own discretion to order the New York Fed to push the funds rate up a quarter percent to around 7 percent (with a further $100 million increase in the borrowing target to $400 million). William McChesney Martin, who chaired the Fed from the early fifties through 1970, once said a central banker's duty is to "take away the punch bowl just when the party gets going." Greenspan was proving he could beat the FOMC to the punch bowl. The May 9 rate move calmed inflation fears on Wall Street, bolstering sagging bond prices and the dollar. The Treasury long bond yield, which had risen to 9.17 percent before the move, fell to around 9.10, still well above where it had started the year. With the market building an "inflation premium" into long-term rates, even Seger said it was "very important that people know that we at the Fed are going to keep inflation under control." For the time being, Angell said the Fed had "succeeded in achieving a soft landing for the U.S. dollar and [had] stabilized commodity prices," but henceforth it had "an awesome responsibility—to make sure there is confidence in our currency." The Fed was in effect "the central bank of the world," and "our first priority at the Fed is to make sure that the purchasing power of the dollar remains constant over a period of years in terms of commodity prices."

For the most part, the Fed had the administration's grudging support at this point. The economy was still doing well, and the Fed was raising rates slowly. Reacting to the May 9 rate hike, Sprinkel said he was "not pleased that interest rates are going up, but it seems to me they are conducting their policy very sensibly. It's increasingly clear that we're not going to have a recession." For reasons not strictly related to Fed intentions, the money supply was growing at a good clip, which went a long way toward explaining the old monetarist's sanguinity. James Baker, appearing on ABC's *This Week With David Brinkley* two days before the May 17 FOMC meeting, was "convinced and confident that the Fed is committed to the idea of preventing any future inflation and at the same time preserving economic growth." He foresaw nothing more than a "modest" rise in inflation that year. The day of the meeting, Darby said there was no reason for the Fed to worry about inflation. The Fed saw it differently. Wholesale prices had risen at a 5 percent annual rate in April, and the bond and currency markets were signalling the pace would pick up.

The May 17 meeting was less contentious than the March one. Although there were still shades of opinion about how aggressive the Fed should be, there was much greater unanimity on the need for higher rates. As Greenspan put it, "I don't think there is any question that the next move that we have to make is on the upside. . . . The only question, basically, is whether we do it now or we do it before the next FOMC meeting on the basis of certain contingencies." He warned that "if we move too fast, we can get signficantly ahead of the curve," hurting consumer confidence and causing the stock market to "get pretty shabby." On the other hand, "We should not under any conditions allow ourselves to get behind the power curve. . . ." That morning, the Commerce Department announced a dramatic drop in the U.S. trade deficit from $13.83 billion to $9.75 billion in March, as a surge in exports swamped imports. The dollar rallied. But what seemed like good news to the administration bothered some Fed officials. The rise in imports was seen implying surging domestic demand, while the rise in exports was seen straining domestic capacity.

People like Johnson were still reluctant to raise rates right away, and Seger was reluctant to move at all, partially because, as she pointed out, the thrift industry was becoming "a disaster area." Higher interest rates would raise the S&Ls' cost of funds and further squeeze their puny net worth. True, Corrigan retorted, but unless the Fed began to exercise some restraint the problems of financial institutions "would be all the more difficult and all the more damaging." Boykin, whose Texas banking industry was in shambles, was also concerned about the impact of higher rates but was willing to support a rate hike anyway. Corrigan wanted an immediate rate hike plus authorization for Greenspan to raise rates again before the June FOMC meeting. Aside from the fact that the economy was growing "at a rate that simply won't work," he had "a nagging fear . . . that because of these highly mobile money and capital markets on a worldwide basis that it may take a higher level of interest rates to achieve a given degree of restraint in the real world." Morris saw "a head of steam building in the manufacturing sector" and argued that the funds rate needed to be pushed up a half percent. Parry said the 2 quarter-point rate hikes the Fed had made up until then "just don't do too much" and urged raising rates a further quarter point immediately and another quarter point soon. "If we delay in taking action, we're going to pay a price later . . . in terms of having to move even more aggressively."

There was also talk of raising the discount rate—a decision for the Board, not the full FOMC, but one based on requests from the Fed banks. The Fed's lending rate had been at 6 percent since the previous September, and some thought it was time to "ring the gong," as the "announcement effect" on market and public psychology has been described. But the committee agreed with Corrigan that the Fed should "keep our powder dry" until a discount rate hike was needed to make an impact. The meeting ended with an understanding that the Fed would raise rates within a couple of weeks and that Greenspan would have the prerogative of moving further after that. There were two dissents—

this time by hawks Hoskins and Parry, who wanted immediate credit tightening. The May 17 meeting marked another milestone: The FOMC finally dropped the reference to "sensitive conditions in financial markets" and the call for "continuing flexibility in the conduct of open market operations," which had been in its directive since the crash. After they had voted on policy, the FOMC members had a special discussion of the virtues of targeting short-term interest rates versus targeting a monetary aggregate or other variable. Some longed for a "monetary rule" that would essentially put the Fed on automatic pilot. After much inconclusive debate, Black had an apt summation: "Even if you could find a perfect rule, I doubt the committee would vote for it, because it's so much more fun making ad hoc decisions every time."

The Fed's inflation fears were validated three days after the FOMC meeting when the Labor Department announced the CPI had risen at a 5 percent rate. "I don't think I can get a lot of cold comfort out of a four-tenths rise of the CPI," an official confided. "Even after you net out food and energy, you still get four-tenths. . . . People around here would regard that as unsatisfactory. I don't see it as a full-blown disaster, but it's not good news."

Although the FOMC "maintained the existing degree of pressure" on reserves, its way of saying it was leaving policy unchanged for the moment, the FOMC issued a directive stating it expected "a slight increase in the degree of pressure on reserve positions would be appropriate in the weeks ahead." Greenspan did not wait long to use the leeway that had been given him. The move came May 25, when he ordered the funds rate taken up another quarter percent to around 7¼ percent by increasing borrowings another $100 million to $500 million. In fact, by mid-June, the funds rate was trading closer to 7⅜ to 7½ percent due to a combination of market expectations and seasonal pressures. Greenspan still had another rate hike in his pocket. The Fed was proceeding with caution—caution lest inflation get out of control, but also caution lest the Fed disrupt the financial markets in an election year. More than seven months after the crash, the Fed had largely put aside fears of recession, but many policymakers remained reluctant to take aggressive credit-tightening steps. The result was an ad hoc, finger-to-the-wind approach that some observers characterized as *fine-tuning*. The Fed's hope was that, by making incremental rate adjustments, it could assuage money market worries about inflation and flatten the yield curve without killing growth. It was loathe to take the politically provocative step of raising the discount rate.

Although the Fed was tiptoeing toward tighter credit and, indeed, had not even gotten back to the rate levels that prevailed prior to the crash, the administration was dissatisfied. Sprinkel could not resist needling the Fed in a June 1 interview. A mild rise in the April index of leading economic indicators had just been reported, and he said, "That puts another nail in the coffin of the inflation extremists." He was unhappy M2 had "dropped back a little" from the upper end of the target range, but said "they're not tempting fate at the moment." Likewise, he said a 0.2 percent rise in May unemployment to 5.6 percent proved there was "no sign of overheating," even though it also showed a substantial rise in nonfarm payroll and a sharp rise in hourly earnings.

Another administration official hoped the rise in unemployment would give the Fed "some breathing room" on tightening. "All these concerns about inflation are crazy anyway."

Presaging the kind of relationship his administration would have with the Fed, Bush, on a late May campaign swing through Maine, warned the Fed against credit tightening. "I have a lot of confidence" in Greenspan, he told reporters, but "as a word of caution, I wouldn't want to see them step over some [line] that would ratchet down, tighten down on economic growth. So I think there is more room for the economy to grow without unacceptable increases in inflation. . . . Watching for signs of inflation is fine," but the Fed is "at the lower end in terms of growth of the money supply." James Baker, already gearing up to run Bush's campaign, later tried to defuse the vice president's comments on CBS's *Face the Nation*. Bush was "not really" criticizing or warning the Fed. Bush "recognized the importance of guarding against inflation, but at the same time it's very important to make sure that we preserve growth, and to be very honest about it, I think that's exactly the policy that the Federal Reserve is following." Baker said Fed policy was then "very satisfactory." But within a couple weeks, Baker was downplaying the Fed's inflation worries and seizing on a one-month's drop in imports as evidence that the Fed did not need to slow consumption. Echoing Baker in mid-June, Heller said falling imports and weak retail sales showed "domestic demand is slowing down, making room for a more rapid expansion of our exports. It's all part of the overall strategy to move from consumption-led growth to export-led growth. It's exactly according to our game plan. . . ." He said the Fed's three small rate hikes had "blunted some of those inflationary expectations."

But June also brought news that wholesale prices were rising at a 6.2 percent rate, and Greenspan was worried. Although *lead times* (the amount of time it takes a factory to fill an order) were telling him the economy was not "yet experiencing any major supply-side constraints" that would push up prices, Greenspan still felt consumer spending had to be restrained to reduce the trade deficit. Failure to do so could itself lead to higher interest rates, he warned in a June 14 speech. When the United States runs a trade deficit, dollars flow out of the country, and are in turn reinvested in the United States in Treasury securities and other dollar assets. If the deficit kept growing, "foreign investors may require additional incentives to accumulate the increased supply of these [dollar] assets. A failure to achieve a substantial reduction in our current account deficit risks changes in market incentives—higher interest yields and/or a cheaper foreign currency price for the assets." Investor confidence "could be shaken by a variety of factors," including "increased concern about the future purchasing power of the dollar. Should investors lose confidence in the dollar for any reason, the inevitable consequence would be an attempted shedding of dollar assets and a corresponding drop in the value of the dollar and an increase in interest rates on dollar-denominated assets."

On June 22, seven days before the next FOMC meeting, Greenspan took it on his own authority to tighten credit further, raising the borrowings target to $550 million and pushing the funds rate target to around 7½ percent. The funds rate was now back to where it was prior to the crash, and the Fed had only begun to tighten. But tricky external factors now came into play. G-7 authorities were seeking through intervention to undo the dollar's new found strength which the Fed's credit tightening policies had inevitably provoked. The Fed, following the Treasury's directions, found itself trying to prevent the dollar from rising while simultaneously raising rates to prevent inflation—a near impossible task. In contrast to earlier in the year when dollar weakness helped prompt rate hikes, the FOMC record from mid-year on suggests the Fed may have pulled its punches in raising rates out of concern with the rising dollar. By the time of the June 29–30 FOMC meeting, the exchange rate pendulum had swung dramatically from concern about dollar weakness to dollar strength. By the eve of the FOMC meeting, the dollar had soared to more than 1.82 marks, compared to 1.57 marks in early January. It had risen less against the yen, but had gone as high as 133 yen per dollar, compared to roughly 120 at the start of the year. A stronger dollar was the kind of problem the Fed liked to have, but it did not suit the Treasury.

A few days before the FOMC gathered, an administration official warned that if the dollar went much higher it would "jeopardize external adjustment. When it got to 138 [yen per dollar] people would start taking notice of that. I don't think the Bank of Japan or the Bundesbank would tolerate that. They've got beaucoup dollar reserves and they would say 'let's liquidate some of our dollar reserves and get our portfolio in a little better shape for the next time we have to defend the dollar.' " At the Fed, far from the dollar's appreciation being a problem, "We're at a stage where it sort of gives you breathing room," an official said. "We're no longer bouncing along on the floor in a sense. It's absence of pressure." The Fed's biggest concern was the pressure being brought on it to hold the dollar down, and not just from Treasury. The Fed's fellow central banks did not like their currencies falling against the dollar because it made their imports of oil and other commodities more expensive. As much as the Fed might like to base monetary policy on domestic considerations alone, its fellow central banks could not because their economies were more trade-oriented. After fretting for several years about the depreciating dollar, the Bundesbank now found itself worrying about a depreciating mark— a major political no-no in Germany. In fact, it had begun selling dollars in early May to support the German currency, and by the time the G-7 nations held their annual Economic Summit in Toronto on June 21, it had sold roughly $5.5 billion. On June 30, before the FOMC began its second day of midyear Humphrey-Hawkins preparations, the Bundesbank decided intervention alone wasn't enough and raised its discount rate a half percent to 3 percent.

It was just the beginning of a pattern that was to last until the Fed stopped raising rates, in which the major central banks moved rates up in tandem, more competitively than cooperatively. Rate hikes in the United States prompted European and Japanese central banks to raise their rates as each new interest rate differential negatively impacted their currencies, leading to further rate hikes and so on. Poehl was prepared to do whatever was necessary, in terms of both intervention and rate moves, to support the mark against the dollar, and other European central banks had little choice but to follow suit. (The Bundesbank went on to raise its Lombard rate from 4½ to 5 percent on July 28, its discount rate from 3 to 3½ percent on August 25, its Lombard rate from 5 to 5½ percent on December 15, and its discount and Lombard rates again to 4 percent and 6 percent respectively on January 19.) Meanwhile, the Bank of Japan (BOJ) was slowly pushing up Japanese rates. Greenspan worried about U.S. rate hikes setting off a global interest rate race among the industrialized nations. "One thing we have to avoid is an international ratcheting game between the United States, the Germans and the Japanese," he told the FOMC. "We are in continuing consultation with them and we are all trying to avoid that sequence." A Fed discount rate hike would cause a plunge in the mark and the yen which would "almost automatically require the Bundesbank to match it because they are under severe political pressure with the exchange rate weakening for them. So . . . we have to be very careful not to trigger an international competitive spiral. . . ."

The Treasury was more concerned than the Fed. Baker's mantra had been that it was up to other countries to reduce the U.S. trade deficit by stimulating their economies, and if Germany and Japan were forced to raise rates to keep their currencies from falling against the dollar it would be anything but stimulative. A Baker assistant told me the Fed should consider how the Bundesbank and BOJ might react before continuing to raise rates. Though he and Baker were old friends, Greenspan made clear the Fed would call the shots on monetary policy. Dallara says that, for the most part, Greenspan and the Fed "resisted quite strongly, and quite successfully, the use of monetary policy or interest rates to accomplish international objectives which were not at all consistent with what they thought they had to do domestically."

The Fed was cooperating with the Treasury to restrain the dollar's rise by buying foreign currencies and "sterilizing" the intervention. Cross said his intervention had been "aimed not at trying to drive the dollar down; no one wants to do that. But equally, it seems to me, we do not have an interest in seeing the dollar move up to unsustainable levels and then see it fall again." Besides, the New York Fed was happy to be buying up these foreign currencies and storing them away because "those currencies could become very useful in future months when we could very well be needing them in order to help support the dollar." His foresight was to prove all too correct. Citing the old Scottish golfer's prayer—"Give me the strength to hit easy"—Cross said his desk, in selling dollars for marks and other currencies, had been "trying to operate so as not to give an impression that we are capping the dollar, and we have been urging the Europeans to operate in a way which would not give an impression that we were putting caps on the dollar at a particular level." The Japanese, who were well suited to a depreciating yen because it made their exports cheaper for Americans to buy, were being less than cooperative, Greenspan hinted. He revealed that the Fed would have been accumulating more Japanese yen "if the [Japanese] Minister of Finance were favorably disposed to our doing that." Baker says, "The Japanese, generally speaking, were fairly cooperative on exchange rate matters," but not always.

Concerned as he was about the global interest and exchange rate constellation, Greenspan could not let it unduly sway his primary concern: the U.S. economy and its growing inflationary impulses. He told the FOMC he wanted the markets to perceive "no ambiguity" about the fact that the Fed was gradually tightening credit. If the dollar rose, so be it, except insofar as currency intervention could slow it. That suited Angell, whose attitude was "whatever was right policy domestically would also be right policy internationally." In the Angell view, domestic and international monetary policy are two sides of the same coin, and "you really can't get in a situation where you have a huge mistake internationally and an opposite mistake domestically. . . . Any central banker worth his salt knows that you have a monetary policy problem if you have a weak currency." If the Fed was going to get inflation down it would have to settle for a stronger dollar and there was not a lot of point in trying to camouflage it with sterilized intervention in the currency market. It was an attitude that would eventually bring the Fed and Treasury to blows.

The economic picture that emerged at the June FOMC meeting as the district Fed presidents gave their usual reports on regional economic conditions did not lend itself to the lack of ambiguity Greenspan was hoping for, as he sought a consensus for higher rates. It seemed to frustrate the usually unflappable chairman. There was increasing concern about fragilities among financial institutions. Banks in the Southwest were in trouble. Morris said he was doing his best to discourage banks in New England from getting themselves in the same kind of predicament through speculative real estate lending. And S&Ls, with their much less diversified asset portfolios, were becoming insolvent nationwide as their funding costs rose and their loans went sour. There were those who contended inflation was not really a threat and opposed aggressive tightening. Predicting higher interest rates abroad would "damp foreign demand," Johnson warned against dampening domestic demand. He and Heller argued there were no wage pressures and that surging commodity prices were just transitory effects of that year's drought. "I think we are already on slowing trends," Heller argued. "We see the results of the tightness of policies that we instituted last year and in the early part of this year. And I would expect that inflationary expectations are on a downward trend."

But Greenspan felt it was too early to declare victory against inflation, fears of which were still built into market interest rates. True, rates had come down, but the Fed had "gone through the torture of the damned" since the late seventies "to get inflation expectations out of long-term bonds, and it hasn't fully succeeded." He said the "extraordinary rise in the [dollar] is something of a surprise and has to be part of anything we are considering relative to what we are going to do with respect to policy," but still favored continuing the credit tightening process. He got his biggest support from the presidents, who were chomping at the bit to raise rates. Some of the Fed banks had had requests in to the Board to raise the discount rate since spring, and by the time of the June meeting virtually all had discount rate hike requests on the table. "This was one of those points in time when the stuff coming out of the grassroots turned out to be right," Corrigan now says. The presidents tended to agree with Morris that "we're at a point now where the economy really can't sustain a growth rate of more than 2 percent without generating inflationary pressures." Atlanta Fed President Robert Forrestal disliked the "small bites" of tightening the Fed was taking in response to economic data. "We need to be more forward-looking and not seem to be reacting to individual pieces of information." Hoskins said "this tit-for-tat kind of following market rates up may not get us out in front of inflation. It's like trying to nibble it to death. . . ."

Toward the end of two days of debate, Greenspan grew frustrated with those who wanted to go slow. "I think we have been ahead of the power curve. We have been surprisingly, successfully ahead of what is an emerging inflationary process. In fact, I think it is very difficult to find a period such as this in which Fed policy has done as much as it has. The one thing I just absolutely find unacceptable is that we throw away any of the gains that we have made. And the notion that we are moving into a period where the economy is still quite strong, and we decide to wait and see, strikes me as risking at this point the loss of what we've accomplished since we started to tighten." At the end of the meeting there was a seemingly endless discussion of the policy significance and market perception of raising the borrowing target from $550 to $600 million, mostly driven by the didactically argumentative Angell. Back and forth they went, with Angell seriously suggesting moving the target to $565 million—"splitting hairs," said Kohn. Exasperated, Greenspan threw up his hands and declared, "We are getting a little silly, gentlemen." Johnson chirped, "We are arguing about angels on the head of a pin here."

Halfheartedly, the FOMC voted to "increase slightly" the degree of pressure on reserves by increasing the borrowing target $50 million, a relatively inconsequential "snugging" that implied not much more than keeping the funds rate around 7½ percent with perhaps an eighth of a point to spare. There were an unusually high three dissents. Kelley and Seger were simply against further tightening at that time. Angell's was a little more complicated. In the first place, he saw no point in tightening domestic credit conditions while at the same time selling dollars to keep the dollar from rising, then "sterilizing" those dollar sales to keep them from easing reserve conditions. "He wanted to call attention to the cross purposes of these actions." But Angell also felt economic and financial uncertainties "called for a pause in the process of continuous tightening in order to gain additional insight regarding the effects of previous actions." Today, Angell insists his "vote was misinterpreted as being opposed to raising interest rates, and I meant it to be opposed to intervening on the dollar while we were raising interest rates." The FOMC provisionally lowered its M2 growth range from 4 to 8 percent to 3 to 7 percent for 1989 to signify its intention to gradually retard the flame under inflation. Greenspan had to bide his time for something meaningful.

Two weeks after the Fed had nudged the funds rate to the 7½ to 7⅞ percent range, Greenspan gave his second Humphrey-Hawkins report to the Senate Banking Committee, where the same Senator Proxmire who had castigated the administration for daring to give the Fed policy advice in February now had plenty of his own. Warning about the impact of further tightening, he averred, "Huge accumulations of debt make our financial system quite fragile. Business debt, government debt and consumer debt have all soared in recent years. The debt accumulation, the crisis in the savings and loan industry, problems of debt service in Latin America and the agricultural crisis combine to raise the costs associated with a further significant rise in interest rates." Proxmire was also worried about the impact further tightening would have on the dollar and trade. Yet, having said all that, he said his "fear is that the overhang of problems in our economy and the presidential election, when all six members of the Federal Reserve Board are Republican Reagan appointees, will lead the Fed to be insufficiently strong in fighting inflation." When Greenspan's head had finished spinning, he defended the Fed's rate hikes as needed not just to cool inflation pressures but to reduce the current account deficit by reducing demand. He appealed for budget deficit reduction to help dampen demand and free up savings for investment in productive capacity. In the absence of fiscal restraint, "higher interest rates would become the only channel for damping domestic demands if they were becoming excessive."[3]

Greenspan left little doubt where the Fed was headed in the months to come. The Fed "at this juncture might be well advised to err more on the side of restrictiveness rather than of stimulus." After worrying behind the FOMC's closed doors about a global "ratcheting" up of interest rates, Greenspan disavowed any such concern to Proxmire's panel. "I'm not necessarily subscribing to the idea that rates are rising internationally," he said. "I know of no actions of my counterparts that would necessitate that." But in a July 19 FOMC telephone conference, Greenspan was again expressing the very concern he had just denied having. "As I see the outlook, I find it difficult not to envisage our having to tighten further as we move into the summer months. But it strikes me that with the continued strength in the dollar, if we were to do so at this stage, we would probably accelerate the dollar's strength and initiate some fairly broad increases in interest rates amongst our trading partners, which could create some international instability. I would be inclined at this stage to hold off [further tightening] until we get the dollar stabilized before we take another shot at it." Greenspan's reluctance to raise rates for fear of pushing up the dollar and spurring defensive rate hikes abroad did not sit well with some. "I don't think we ought to gear policy to [the dollar] even for a short period," said Hoskins, who wanted an immediate rate hike to 8 percent. Boykin and Melzer were also for tightening right away. The time was past for "following the market with modest moves," said the latter. Corrigan sympathized but said the dollar was a "fly in the ointment." Taking action that would push the dollar up further would be "a high risk strategy." The meeting ended on a desultory and frustrating note, particularly since technical reserve conditions were tending to soften the funds rate—exactly the opposite of what the Fed wanted.

The Fed's dilemma was deepened on August 5, when a strong employment report caused another jump in the dollar, as currency traders presumed it would force the Fed to raise rates. A Fed source left little doubt how the dilemma would be resolved: "The number one concern is going to be prospects for inflation. . . . That would take precedence over the possibility of further strength of the dollar, especially with the trade balance moving in the right direction. . . . Much as we'd like to see the dollar stabilize and not rise, that is not the number one concern." Black called the two-month 815,000 job gain "very, very high. Unless we're getting greater increases in physical capacity than I think we are, the economy can't continue to grow at the rate it has been without hitting bottlenecks." He conceded inflation was "not going to blow up right away. General Motors may have to pay more to its workers, but that doesn't mean it's going to fetch more for its cars." Nevertheless, he said, it was just a matter of time until shortages of labor and other resources pushed up wages and prices.

The handwriting was on the wall in glowing phosphorescent letters, but the administration did not want to read it, hoping against hope the Fed would somehow hold the line on interest rates and help it hold down the dollar. Sprinkel told me that, while he agreed with the Fed on the need to "avoid a resurgence of inflation," he saw no such danger. The economy "continues to taper at a sustainable long-term growth rate. There is no evidence of demand pressures that will reignite inflation. . . . I do not see any sudden lurch either toward tightness or toward ease." Sprinkel need not have given a second thought to ease. Clearly the next rate move was going to be up, and it came August 9, when the Fed Board jacked its discount rate from 6 to 6½ percent— its first discount rate increase in nearly a year, and Greenspan's second. Stocks and bonds plunged, while the dollar surged. In unanimously raising the discount rate a half percent, the Fed raised the funds rate from 7⅝ to between 8 and 8¼ percent. It had now raised the funds rate roughly 1½ percent since March. The Fed knew its industrial production index would show a sharp rise, accompanied by a surge in capacity utilization to 83.5 percent. Further validation of the Fed's action came three days later when the Labor Department said the July producer price index had risen 0.5 percent. Excluding volatile food and energy, the so-called *core* PPI rose 0.6 percent (7.2 percent annually). The CPI was only slightly better at 0.4 percent. Seeking to head off further rate hikes, Fitzwater declared that, notwithstanding the worrisome price numbers, inflation was "low and under control." Yet more justification for the Fed came when the Commerce Department revised its estimate of second-quarter GNP from 3.1 to 3.3 percent and revised its inflation yardstick (the GNP deflator) from 4.1 to 5.1 percent. The long bond yield went to 9½ percent.

Fed officials were eager to trumpet the action as a show of their determination. "There had been some criticism that the Board hasn't been leading the way," said one. "Maybe that will stop now." Parry said, "I hope it's interpreted as an indication of the resolve of the Fed to resist inflationary pressures." Wall Street economists were startled but pleased with the rate hikes. "Until now [the Fed was] showing a lack of backbone," said Charles Lieberman. "The conduct of the Fed until today was one of enormous restraint in the face of the economic data, but the rise in the discount rate reflects an effort to correct that and say they're cognizant of the risks out there." But a few blocks northeast of the Federal Reserve Board, the U.S. Chamber of Commerce issued a caustic statement by Richard Rahn accusing the Fed of "going around in circles. First they adopt the misguided theory that economic growth creates inflation. Based on this myth, they force up interest rates. Then they notice—surprise, surprise—the value of the dollar is rising. What do they do? Sell dollars, of course, to lower the foreign exchange value of the dollar. Then this increase in the supply of dollars world-wide are attracted back into the U.S. by the high interest rates engineered by the Fed. Holy smokes, this puts downward pressure on interest rates and the Fed finds it has to tighten even more. If the Fed keeps running in these circles long enough, it will succeed in aborting our economic expansion in its tracks. . . ."

The August 9 rate hike came at an awkward time to say the least for the Republicans, who were about to hold their convention in New Orleans. Both the Reagan administration and the Bush campaign organization were caught unawares. Just the previous Sunday, on NBC's *Meet The Press*, James Baker said he had no indication the Fed was going to raise rates. Baker was about to leave Treasury to run the Bush campaign, to be replaced by Nick Brady, already awaiting Senate confirmation. What's more, the Fed bombshell hit in the middle of a quarterly refunding operation, when the Treasury was auctioning massive amounts of three- and ten-year notes and thirty-year bonds. The public White House response was moderate. Though "disappointed . . . we understand there's a sound reason for it," Fitzwater said. "The Federal Reserve has the task of trying to balance resistance to inflationary pressures with maintenance of real growth in the economy. . . . We think the Federal Reserve has been doing a good job in balancing these interests." Privately, GOP leaders were furious at Greenspan for making the move right before their convention. "There is absolutely no evidence of a serious inflationary surge; that's all press hype," an administration official said. "The Fed move was a mistake," said another.

To the administration's monetarist advisors, any extra growth or price pressures in 1988 was explainable by the rapid money supply growth the Fed had permitted in 1986 and early 1987 when falling *velocity* (the rate at which the money supply turns over) had made the Fed distrust its aggregates. But in the second half of 1987, all measures of money grew below target, and since the beginning of 1988, the aggregates had been well-behaved within their target ranges. To the monetarists, the money supply bubble had been deflated since mid-1987 and was no longer posing an inflation threat, and the prices of oil (down $4 a barrel) and gold (down nearly $50 an ounce) confirmed their strongly held beliefs. They railed against the "Keynesian," "Phillips Curve" mentality that was driving Fed policy. In reality, the FOMC had considerable monetarist representation, and Greenspan was not your typical Keynesian. For Democrats optimistic about recapturing the White House after eight years out of power, the discount rate hike seemed like manna from heaven. Democratic presidential nominee Michael Dukakis blamed the latest rate hike on the administration's deficit spending, making no mention of Congress's role in it. "When we're running deficits of $150 billion a year, it shouldn't surprise you that we're building up inflationary pressures. That's what happens when you live on a credit card for eight years."

Attention turned to Frankfurt and Tokyo to see when the Bundesbank and Bank of Japan would raise rates to keep their currencies from slipping against the dollar. The Bank of Japan, continuing a policy begun in June, nudged up short-term money market rates an eighth of a percent to 4⅛ percent. The Bundesbank waited until its next policymaking Council meeting on August 25 and raised its discount rate for the second time in less than two months to 3½ percent, after raising its key Lombard rate from 4½ to 5 percent on July 28. In reflection, a senior German official says German interest rates were increased "because of internal reasons"—not because rising U.S. rates were causing the mark to fall against the dollar. "We were in a strong boom situation" with inflation pressures rising and the money supply "overshooting. So, the Bundesbank did it not so much because the Americans did it, but because the Bundesbank felt it was for their own interest." But that was not the reason given at the time for consumption in Germany. Soon after the Fed rate hike, Stoltenberg bluntly told reporters in Bonn, "A constantly rising dollar poses problems." At that stage, the dollar had risen as high as 1.92 marks, a roughly 22 percent rise from the start of the year. Other European interest rates and currencies were also under pressure and the cry went up from Paris for greater G-7 "coordination." The Fed was cooperating with the Treasury and foreign monetary authorities to stabilize the dollar through intervention, but so long as U.S. interest rates were on the rise, intervention could have little effect. In announcing the Bundesbank discount rate hike, Poehl declared war on the dollar bulls, vowing to do whatever was needed to halt the mark's plunge against the dollar—implying not just more intervention, but higher rates. As wire reporters scrambled for the phones, Poehl chuckled, "They got the message." Poehl's threat seemed to do the trick. The dollar's climb stopped, giving the Fed greater leeway to raise rates.

At the August 16 FOMC meeting, the Fed paused for a breather, having just raised rates, but tilted its directive toward further tightening. Prell upped the ante on future rate hikes. As recently as March, he had said the funds rate might peak below 8 percent, but now, despite the presumed dampening effect of a strong dollar on exports, he said, "We are looking for a federal funds rate in the 9½ percent range by next Spring and Treasury bond yields in the vicinity of 10½ percent. [B]asically, we have the rates getting up to that level by the second quarter of next year and staying there." Prell said the staff had underestimated economic growth and resource use. With real growth running at 3¼ percent in the second half of 1988, after allowing for the depressing effects of that summer's drought, "it appears that the policy action needed to rein in inflationary pressures may be greater than we earlier thought." Without drastic tightening, there was "the risk of a serious acceleration of inflation." To actually reduce inflation before 1990 would require even bigger rate hikes, said Prell, who acknowledged that even at 9½ percent rates would be high "enough to exacerbate significantly the pressures on the thrift industry. . . ." Prell's presentation startled some Fed officials, but the presidents saw it as confirmation of what they had suspected all along. "We've got a real barn burner on our hands," said Morris. The Fed was "moving too slowly." Better to tighten too much than too little. "If we were to move to a policy that was too restrictive we would have plenty of time to correct it. . . . But if we make the opposite mistake and have a policy that's too accommodating, we may find ourselves way behind the curve and facing a situation in which we only have two choices—accommodating an accelerating inflation or pushing the economy into recession. . . ."

Others weren't so sure. One was just-confirmed Governor John LaWare, a lifelong Democrat and recently retired New England banker, who Reagan had chosen months ago to fill a long empty seat on the Board. Senate majority leader Robert Byrd had dragged his feet on confirming LaWare's nomination. Dukakis was leading Bush in the polls, and Byrd's attitude was, "Why should we deny the new Democrat president the opportunity to appoint a Fed governor?" But Massachusetts senator Edward Kennedy persuaded Dukakis to call Byrd and tell him, "If you don't approve him now I'm going to approve him in January anyway." LaWare was confirmed August 4—just in time to participate in the August 16 FOMC meeting.[4] New on the job but not bashful, LaWare cautioned that the economy and its financial sector were "fragile. It seems to me if we snub the brakes too hard and too fast or oversteer this vehicle, we have a risk of going into the ditch." Heller thought the staff was being overzealous. "Certainly it's not going to be a runaway economy in any sense of the word. We shouldn't tinker all that much." Corrigan was more hawkish but agreed that, so soon after the discount rate hike, "there is something to be said for a short period of gestation here." The discount rate hike had had an unintended and disconcerting "feedback" effect—causing heightened fears of inflation among many bond market participants instead of dampening inflationary expectations, Angell noted. Traders felt that "after all, if the Fed did this drastic thing which wasn't expected—and, of course, it makes the markets a little angry for us to do something they don't expect us to do—then this really must be worse than they anticipated." Greenspan said the Fed would have to tighten again, but did not press the point, and the FOMC voted to leave policy unchanged. Only Hoskins, wanting immediate tightening, voted against the decision.

In fact the Fed kept rates unchanged until mid-December. Some thought it delayed further tightening because of the November election, but the Fed fiercely denies it, and there is nothing in the FOMC transcripts to indicate that was the reason. There was considerable dissension in the ranks over the economic outlook and considerable concern about those financial "fragilities" LaWare talked about. The Fed was a bit unsure of itself. It had by then raised the funds rate 1¼ percent, and officials were growing nervous about how much was enough. The hawks and doves were beginning to square off. Even for those who were most worried about economic overheating and the threat of higher wages and prices it posed, it was difficult to determine how much tightening was needed to restrain demand and cool wage-price pressures, without going overboard and precipitating a recession.

Most Fed officials frankly admit conducting monetary policy is an imprecise exercise—more of an art than a science. Given the lag times and other imponderables, some would say using reserve pressures and rates to bring about a particular growth rate is almost a guessing game. The policy actions taken through August, aimed at dealing with pressures then evident, would not fully take effect for many months, and no one knew what the economy would look like when they finally took full effect a year or more in the future. So deciding in September whether to make additional moves was a shot in the dark. An added complication which made it difficult to read the economy and inflation was that year's severe drought and the growing bank and thrift problems. Even the inflation hawks admitted they had no definite idea how high the funds rate needed to go to bring growth to a more sustainable 2½ percent. Doves were even more leery of boldly raising rates. The net result of these doubts and divisions was that the Fed cautiously groped its way into a hazy economic future. The economy's growth potential was "one of the measurements that we were always looking at," says LaWare, who retired in spring 1995. "But when you ask [the staff], 'How did you derive the 2½ percent potential?' they can't give you a definitive answer, any more than they can give you a definitive answer to the other two unknowns: 'What is the natural rate of unemployment, and what is the lag time for policy to be reflected in the economy?' And when you're dealing with an equation with three unknowns . . . you kind of fly by the seat of your pants under those circumstances." Unlike LaWare, Angell was a trained economist, and he, too, had occasion to dispute the staff's output gap model. Also, while U.S. economic statistics are considered the best in the world, they are known to be sorely inadequate to measure an ever changing economy and are subject to seasonal and other quirks. But the Fed makes do.

When the unemployment rate rose from 5.3 to 5.6 percent in August, amid other signs of slower activity, one Fed hawk said those who derived comfort from the soft-looking numbers were indulging in "wishful thinking." But others were relieved. "I'm not sure the heat is off, but the frenzy is off," said one official. Another said the economy "still has a fair amount of momentum built up" but this "certainly takes the edge off." Johnson told me the "slower pattern of employment" likely represented an economic "softening to a certain extent," so that "things are less pressure-packed than earlier." The net result was to keep the Fed on hold, election or no election. Ironically, the signs of slowing could not have come at a better time for the Bush camp. It enabled them to deflect Dukakis claims that the Reagan-Bush team had generated inflation pressures that the Fed was going to have to use draconian measures to stop.

The Fed was getting pressure from all directions to desist in raising rates. About the time of the August 16 FOMC meeting, the Congressional Budget Office (CBO) forecast 2.7 percent real growth and 4.9 percent inflation for 1989 and warned the Fed it was running "a risk of unintentionally going too far and causing a recession." Administration officials continued their not-for-attribution sniping. "I think they acted too fast" in hiking the discount rate, one said in early September, warning further tightening would damage an economy already slowing of its own accord. Pointing to weak employment numbers, another said the Fed "certainly can't use this as justification for any more tightening. . . . [The data] indicated that the economy is decelerating a little bit, that it is not in the overheated state as the Fed had feared. Inflation fears should be calmed." Robert Ortner, chief economist for the Commerce Department, argued the data "should help alleviate some of the fears that the economy is overheating. . . . they are telling us that the economy is likely to keep growing, but at a more moderate pace [and that] the signs of accelerating inflation are not here yet and that's further in the future, if at all." The business community was also sounding off. Jerry Jasinowski, head of the National Association of Manufacturers (NAM), told Congress on September 8 they "would not endorse any further restrictive measures that might increase the risk of a sharp slowdown." James L. Pate, senior vice president of the Pennzoil Company, conceded "the outlook is definitely for higher wages and prices," but "recent anxiety over inflation has probably been somewhat overdone. . . . While capacity utilization rates are high in several major industries, they are in most cases below the peak rates reached in previous expansions." The Fed's tight money policies were also not playing well in Peoria, where Don Paris, chief economist of Caterpillar Incorporated "urge[d] the Fed to be aware of the risk of precipitating an unwanted recession by clinging to current policy too long. . . . I don't question that the economy is stronger than it was during 1987, but I am questioning whether or not it is worth the risk of a recession and a resurging dollar."

Going into the September 20 FOMC meeting, the Fed's own beige book survey revealed signs of slowing but also "further upward pressure on prices." Prell, who had previously projected a 9½ percent funds rate and said growth would have to be held below its long-term potential of 2½ percent if inflation was to be brought under control, now said drastic tightening, even to the point of bringing on a recession, might be needed if inflation was to be brought down very much. In answer to a question from Angell about what it would take to bring inflation down 1 percent from the prevailing 4 percent, he said, "If I were to aim at the kind of inflation trajectory that you've outlined . . . I would suggest that you would need a substantially greater tightening. . . . I think you'd need substantially greater restraint—probably close to or even into recessionary conditions—in order by 1990 to have an inflation trend down to 3 percent at an annual rate." A number of FOMC members pointed to signs the economy was slowing. Kelley feared what might happen "if the black box kind of thing begins to happen and we slide over into a recession. . . ." In that event, the federal deficit would expand and make the economy's problems even worse, but most thought the moderation was a good thing. Forrestal said, "We should not be lulled by this softening at the fringe" into thinking inflation was not a worry. Riven by doubts and divisions, the FOMC voted to leave its credit stance the same and keep the funds rate at 8⅛ percent but to put a tightening bias in its directive.

On October 7, just when all those who were afraid to swallow more of the Fed's anti-inflation medicine were getting their hopes up that the economy was slowing down, the Labor Department released September jobs figures that pointed to renewed strength: a dip in unemployment from 5.6 to 5.4 percent, along with jumps in nonfarm payroll, hourly earnings, and average weekly hours. Once again administration spin doctors went into action, dismissing Fed fears rekindled by the jobs report and focusing on a loss of factory jobs.

"It doesn't give them any reason to change policy," one official asserted. But Black saw the report as evidence "the August pause was just that. . . . It suggests we're moving on a little faster track." The Commerce Department added more fuel to the fire when it announced the trade deficit had ballooned from $9.5 billion to $12.2 billion on a surge in imports that swamped export gains. To the Fed, the import surge meant consumer demand was too strong, while higher exports meant strains on production capacity. The trade numbers also weakened the dollar—bad news all around. Ortner admitted the import rise showed "the economy hasn't slowed down as much as people thought," but said much of it reflected increased business investment in capital goods which would help relieve strains on capacity. When the Fed announced its capacity utilization index for September had fallen from 83.8 to 83.6 percent, an administration official pounced on it as further evidence the Fed had tightened more than enough.

The Fed maintains it does not base policy on any given month's numbers, but it was hard not to get that impression as the Fed and the administration battled to put their own spin on the data du jour. The administration had a valid point; there were definite signs of slowing activity, and this was confirmed on October 18 by the beige book prepared for review at the November 1 FOMC meeting. Ironically, while the administration wanted maximum growth, the slowing suited its purposes, at least in the short run with the election just a few weeks away. The last thing Bush needed was another Fed rate hike right before the polls opened. Administration officials turned up the rhetoric to ward off further credit tightening. "A slowdown in demand growth [will lead to] a modest further decline in the rate of inflation," Sprinkel said on October 18. Any hint of inflation had been due to a temporary rise in oil prices. "There is no evidence that generalized price pressures are emerging . . . ," the Treasury's Thomas Berger echoed. "The major thrust of the evidence points to some slowing in the rate of rise of total demand in the economy and some abatement in actual inflation and inflation risks in the future."

In reality, as Corrigan now observes, inflation was on a dangerously accelerating trend, reaching 6.1 percent by late 1990. "We came too damned close for comfort in terms of letting the genie out of the bottle," Corrigan says. "You can imagine where it would have gone if we had not done what we did." Nevertheless, the numbers were causing some second guessing that Fall. The dip in capacity utilization and other data looked "pretty cheery," one Fed official confided October 18. "It says that maybe we've landed pretty softly." Johnson was arguing the Fed had probably halted rising inflationary expectations. When the Labor Department reported October 21 that the CPI had risen 0.3 percent in September, doves noted that was a tenth of a percent lower than in the prior two months, while hawks pointed out that the core rate had risen

0.4 percent—twice as much as in August. The best that could be said, the hawks argued, was that inflation was not getting worse, but it certainly was not getting any better. Hawks and doves remained stalemated going into the November 1 FOMC meeting.

Greenspan strongly hinted the Fed was not through tightening in a lengthy correspondence with Proxmire released October 26. "Given the present risks of inflationary pressures in the U.S. economy, we do not consider monetary policy to be excessively tight in present circumstances." He also told Proxmire the dollar was "a very high priority" for the Fed. "The exchange rate is a central price variable in the economy with implications both for U.S. inflation and output and for resource shifts across sectors. We cannot be indifferent toward it nor can we ignore the information it may provide." By late October, the dollar had fallen from its high of 1.92 to around 1.78 marks and from 137 to 126 yen. The Treasury was not inclined to support the dollar, blaming its renewed weakness on technical factors. In truth, according to a Treasury official, there was "a general feeling that adjustment of [trade] accounts is needed, and that is consistent with a dollar that is lower, but the question is the pace." The pace became intolerable at the end of the month after the dollar had sunk to a six-month low against the yen, and the Fed, working with the Treasury, intervened to prop up the dollar, with very limited success.

To the great annoyance of some of its policymakers, the Fed had gotten itself on a seesaw. After participating with the Treasury in a concerted G-7 action to arrest or reverse the dollar's rise, the Fed was forced to turn around and buy dollars to keep it from falling too much. At the November 1 FOMC meeting there was a burst of exasperation from some members over the Fed's foreign exchange dalliances with Treasury. "We have been in on both sides of the markets, which gives an impression that we know what the right exchange rate is," Hoskins exclaimed. "I don't feel comfortable that I know what the right exchange rate is, and I'm not sure anyone around this table does. . . . I think we run the risk of setting up the public and ourselves for a nice fall in the dollar simply based on expectations. . . . [B]y doing this I think we continue to confuse the public as to what our policy is all about and divert attention from our long-term objective of stable prices. And secondly, I think we run the risk of confusing ourselves as to our abilities to influence exchange rates in an appropriate fashion." He also objected to the Fed cooperating with the Treasury to "stabilize the dollar until the election is over with." That had been a factor, Cross acknowledged. "As we moved up toward the election there has been a feeling on the part of a lot of people in the market that the authorities would be particularly careful not to let exchange rates change very wildly, and they succeeded in doing that." But he and Truman defended the recent intervention as designed to produce "exchange rate stability" in a context of G-7 cooperation. "We have to walk this narrow line between trying to encourage a certain degree of stability and to keep the financing for this [current account] deficit occurring until we can move further toward other financing. . . ."

To bolster its case for increasing the funds rate to at least 9½ percent by spring, the Fed staff rolled out a new Trojan horse: a model it called *P-Star* or

P*, not unveiled publicly until much later. Constructed at Greenspan's suggestion, it was a variation on the old quantity theory of money: $MV = PQ$, where M represents the amount of money in the economy, V represents its velocity or rate of turnover and, on the other side of the equation, P stands for prices, and Q stands for the quantity of all goods and services bought and sold in the economy in a given year (GNP). The theory holds that, in the long run at least, the quantity of money multiplied by the number of times per year it is spent is equal to the total of all goods and services multiplied by their prices. Increasing the supply of money, others things like velocity and the supply of goods being equal, leads to higher prices over the long run. P* postulated the equilibrium price level that is achievable given current money supply growth, assuming the economy is growing at potential and velocity is running at its historical average. Actual money supply growth can then theoretically be adjusted to aim actual price behavior toward the equilibrium level. With P*, the Fed staff purported to project where prices were headed given prevailing rates of money supply growth. Kohn told the FOMC the model "paints an eerily similar picture" to the staff forecast of accelerating inflation. The future level of inflation (P*) was headed higher than current inflation. The obvious conclusion was that money growth had to be slowed. In coming up with P*, the Fed staff was turning the tables on Sprinkel and Darby, using their own money supply ammunition against them. Asked years later about the staff's P* concoction in 1988, Kohn just smiled. Some cynics think the model was a sham cooked up to reinforce the rationale for tightening credit and later discarded. "The only real use of P* was to justify a policy move that they would otherwise have taken anyway," says David Jones, chief economist of Aubrey G. Lanston & Company. "It justified their reasoning process." Such skepticism is understandable. The Fed staff has not been known for taking its cue from the monetary aggregates. "By the time P* was created I don't think anybody at the Fed believed the monetary aggregates were a reliable indicator of inflation," says Jones. Though still in use, the Fed has not given P* much weight because of growing doubts about M2's ability to measure money supply and about its linkage to output and prices. In any case, it did its job in 1988.

In seeking to persuade the FOMC to continue raising rates at the November meeting, the staff assured the governors and presidents recession was unlikely. "Our view is that there is more underlying strength in the economy and that a small, further increase in rates would not have the effect of tipping the economy into recession," Prell said. He acknowledged inflationary expectations had declined, as reflected in lower long-term interest rates, but said the funds rate still needed to rise at least 1 percent by "early next year." Some FOMC members were afraid an economic slowdown might turn into something worse. Among the most anxious was LaWare who warned of the "increasing fragility in our financial system which would react very badly to anything that threw us into any kind of recession." Johnson even thought easing credit by the next meeting was "probably a very good possibility." Melzer was worried about recent more sluggish money growth. He warned overdoing it on slowing the economy to cool inflation could backfire. "If we get way out of position . . . in the short run in policy and subsequently we're forced to reverse policy very sharply for short-term reasons, it's going to make the long-term battle a lot more difficult to win." By contrast, Forrestal wanted to counter a "psychological mindset" that 5 percent inflation was "acceptable" and that the Fed was "going to have a very inflexible kind of policy because we can't afford to allow a recession to appear in the economy."

Greenspan was not convinced the economy had really slowed. "What we're going through is a pause . . . the slowing is likely to diminish rather quickly." What's more, "to the extent policy has been the source of this slowing, then it's very crucial that we not be perceived as weakening prematurely." The FOMC nominally left policy unchanged at the November 1 meeting, but since the funds rate was trading an eighth of a percent or so higher than the preexisting 8⅛ percent target, it effectively firmed a bit, leaving the funds rate around 8¼ percent. And it gave Greenspan leeway to raise rates between then and the mid-December meeting. Seger was the only one opposed. Another baby step toward tightening was not long in coming. Three days later, the Fed got an unexpected jolt: a drop in unemployment back to 5.2 percent, coupled with an 0.8 percent rise in hourly earnings. Administration officials, who had unrealistically begun hoping for a rate cut, moved to quell Fed rate hike fever. "It isn't growth that causes inflation, it's excessive growth in total spending and demand, and we're seeing a gradual slowing in the rate of spending as unemployment falls," Sprinkel told me. "The inflation scare evident earlier in the year has abated." Betraying a continued misunderstanding of how committed the Fed was to its anti-inflation course, another official said, "Any easing they might have contemplated will have to wait until after the election. . . . The recent behavior of the dollar very much constrains their action."

The election came and went a few days later with no credit easing by the Fed. Yet Sprinkel continued to argue for lower rates. There was no reason why the economy could not continue to expand without generating inflation, he said on November 8. Darby also got back on the warpath, declaring the economy was perfectly capable of 3 to 3½ percent growth without increased inflation—a proposition wildly at variance with most Fed officials' views. Greenspan said such a growth rate "presupposes an increase in productivity that could happen but is unlikely given the decline in our net capital stock." James Baker was taking a more conciliatory tone. Talking to reporters at the National Press Club right before the election, he pledged the Bush administration would "respect" the independence of the Fed and not seek a deal with the Fed to maintain a given level of money growth. That may have been the first and last olive branch offered to Greenspan from the Bush camp. Bush was headed for the high office amidst considerable hope that, despite his "no new taxes" pledge, concerted efforts would be made to further reduce the budget deficit. But the new administration soon discovered that trying to mollycoddle Congress was a good way to get mugged. Bush's "kinder and gentler" approach to fiscal policy turned out to be a euphemism for runaway deficit spending— just the opposite of what Greenspan and company had been counting on in their effort to increase national savings and plow resources into increased productive capacity to reduce the external deficit.

In case there were doubts about where he stood on fiscal matters, Greenspan told the National Economic Commission on November 16 interest rates would not fall unless "concrete" action was taken to reduce the budget deficit. What's more, he suggested, if the government wanted faster growth it should stop borrowing so much money that it "crowded out" private borrowers and prevented them from making productivity increasing investments. "The markets are waiting for changes in legislation [which show] a longer term solution. To the extent the markets perceive [deficit reduction efforts are] on track and working" two things would occur: "the inflation premiums built into long term interest rates will come down and the instability expectations [built into long rates] also will come down." But until the markets saw "something concrete other than promises, one cannot expect the market to react." In fact, it looked to him like "the downtrend in real long-term rates has become erratic, tending to stall with the level still historically high." Deficit reduction was crucial because overreliance on foreigners to buy U.S. government debt was putting the nation's finances in jeopardy. He warned an eventual loss of confidence in the dollar could occur suddenly; then it would be "difficult to retrench. The danger lies in the fact that what they hold is dollar denominated assets. Should there be a major shift in the desire to absorb dollar denominated assets . . . what you get immediately is a significant drop in the currency which could lead to inflation and other imbalances." The Treasury dismissed Greenspan's concerns in its semiannual Report to Congress on International Economic and Exchange Rate Policy. Fears that foreigners would become unwilling to provide capital without either being paid substantially higher interest rates or being able to buy U.S. assets at cheaper exchange rates were "exaggerated or unwarranted in the current circumstances," it said.

There was a bit of euphoria when it was reported wholesale prices had been unchanged in October, but it didn't last long. In mid-November came news that retail sales and industrial production had risen substantially. The pendulum was swinging back in favor of further tightening. Adding to the pressure was the renewed weakness of the dollar. By mid-November, the dollar had fallen to roughly 1.73 marks and 122 yen, after hitting highs of 1.92 marks and 137 yen in August. The dollar was already on its way down when Bush campaign advisor and Harvard economist Martin Feldstein gave it a big shove from behind, declaring on November 9 that the dollar needed to fall another 20 percent. The dollar's decline in turn precipitated a fall in the stock market. It was not a good omen for the incoming Bush administration. Craig Fuller, codirector of the Bush transition team, rushed to say that dollar depreciation was "not the policy of this administration and it's not going to be the policy of the next administration." When the dollar kept dropping, Bush himself, surrounded by reporters on November 14 as he tried to relax on the beach in Gulf Stream, Florida, after the long campaign, was forced to come to the dollar's defense. He said he planned to pursue the same dollar policy as his predecessor—a "policy built around policy coordination and exchange market stability." Considering the checkered career of Reagan dollar policy, it was hardly a ringing endorsement of a strong dollar.

Fed officials scrambled into damage control mode, abandoning their usual "no comment" policy on the dollar to talk the U.S. currency up. "The fundamentals haven't changed that much," Seger told me November 16. "The thing that bothers me the most about the weakness of the dollar is that it is reacting to psychological factors and statements by people outside the government." "At these levels of exchange rates we certainly seek stability of the dollar," Johnson said the same day. "With the economy at this stage of the expansion I doubt if a drop in the dollar is particularly useful. [Goods from the United States] enjoy strong international competitiveness at these levels." Sounding more like a Treasury political appointee than a central banker, Johnson raised eyebrows when he lashed out at Germany. By increasing its trade surplus with other European countries while decreasing its surplus with the United States, "it places strains on the currencies of the countries in deficit within the European Monetary System. . . . Germany, like Japan, must increase the contribution to growth from internal or domestic sources relative to the contribution from international or external sources."

Just when things were starting to settle down in the foreign exchange market, Brady, who had been designated Treasury secretary in August when Baker left to run the Bush campaign, made his first splash, giving the markets a clue of what the next four years were going to be like under his stewardship of the nation's finances. Just four days after Bush's on-the-beach defense of the dollar, the former Wall Street executive said he was "not concerned" about the dollar's recent weakness and said he was opposed to higher interest rates to support it. Brady's comments were very poorly received by already nervous financial markets, which detected a lack of commitment to support the dollar as well as the makings of a Fed-Treasury rift. Greenspan had just expressed concern about the dangers of a foreign loss of confidence in the dollar. Now here was the guy who would be running dollar policy for the next four years signaling he didn't much care. Once again, Fed officials felt forced to stress that they, at least, did care. "A declining dollar can have adverse consequences for the rate of inflation and therefore can complicate the other major objective of U.S. macroeconomic policy—the preservation and consolidation of the gains made during the 1980s in the area of inflation and internal adjustment," Johnson said later that day.

Hastening to clean up after Brady, a Treasury spokesman said he was really "in favor of stability of the dollar." When Brady said he was "not concerned," he was talking about the volatility in the currency markets and only making the point that "markets go up and down." Fed officials, for the time being, were prepared to be patient and understanding with a man whom Greenspan had recommended for the Treasury post after Brady had impressed him with his stock market crash autopsy. But there was bafflement, as there is to this day, that a man from Wall Street could utter such market insensitive remarks. Their bafflement would only increase. It was not the last time Brady struck a seemingly nonchalant pose on such matters. It soon became a standing joke among reporters covering Brady that, whenever asked about interest or exchange rates, he was likely to respond, "Rates go up, rates go down, I don't really care." After a while, the markets seemed to stop paying a great deal of attention to Brady. Certainly, for better or worse, he was never the market mover Baker had been. Once when I was covering Brady's congressional testimony, he repeated a familiar line about something or other. When diminutive Ed Kean of Knight Ridder Financial wearily rose to go file on the comment, I and a couple of other wire reporters turned to him almost as one and sarcastically said, "Sit down!" Sheepishly, he took his seat, as everyone cracked up. No dunce, Brady nevertheless had a way of putting his foot in it, as, for instance, during a press conference at the end of the 1990 Houston Economic Summit. The White House filing center was crammed with reporters, and in the back a very competent but not particularly feminine scribe kept waving her arm to get recognized to ask a question. As it happened, she was wearing a white sweater with a red valentine emblazoned across the front. "Okay, the woman with the heart on," Brady said to a cascade of guffaws that embarrassed the Secretary and the journalist in question.

On November 22, Greenspan took advantage of market pressures to increase the federal funds rate to 8⅜ percent.[5] He still had theoretical leeway to raise rates further, but in late November it seemed Greenspan would have a tough time mustering a consensus for further tightening, or at least for a further discount rate hike. The hawks and doves were still at it. Heller and Seger were downplaying the threat of inflation in interviews. Heller was "very pleased that the economy continues to perform as well as it is," and that "inflationary pressures are well contained." While the Fed should reduce inflation from the 4.2 percent rate it had registered in October, it should do so "slowly" by "steadily" reducing M2 growth. ". . . What we want to do is have a program that will gradually reduce inflation further. We've got to look at that from a medium-term perspective." Seger did "not think that the economy is growing at such a breakneck speed that somehow or other we're going to break our necks against an absolute capacity to produce." She said she only voted for the August 9 discount rate hike to "send a signal" and calm "the near hysteria" in the markets and "show them that we all had the courage to act." Heller's comments mirrored those of Darby, whose contention was that the Fed was trying to reduce inflation too rapidly. "I thought that they were looking for less than one percent growth, and whether that was zero to one or negative, the models aren't that precise," says Darby. "That's the whole point for going slow. You don't know that much of what's going to go on, so don't add a big disturbance to the system. Be persistent and the system can deal with it, if you're persistent and gradual. If you throw in a big disturbance you may throw in a big problem."

The hawks were still swooping, though. Hoskins told me on November 29 that he "would prefer to see a dampening of domestic expenditures" to contain inflation, which he saw buiding up "both on the wage side and in the price indices." Angell wanted to see the Fed set "a reasonable goal" of reducing inflation a half to a full percent per year while keeping unemployment in the 5 to 6 percent range. Slowing money growth should "forestall imbedding inflation into the wage structure and should enable us to continue the disinflation process to achieve our goal of price level stability." Misleadingly, Angell cautioned against assuming further rate hikes. "Interest rate movements can be a two-way street. If we do our job, the next move may surprise someone. . . . [Developments] might mean that interest rates [go] lower." Hoskins and Angell both felt that if the Fed followed the right domestic policy "exchange rates will take care of themselves." The hawks got some ammunition when the Commerce Department revised up its previous estimate of third-quarter GNP growth from 2.2 to 2.6 percent. Its fixed weight price index showed inflation running above 5 percent.

An obstacle to further tightening was the growing awareness of financial "fragilities." Seidman warned on November 30 about the impact of tight money on the banking system. After saying the government must be prepared to allot $30 billion in 1989 alone to close 100 insolvent thrifts and that up to $100 billion might be needed to deal with all sick thrifts, he said a discount rate hike "wouldn't help, that's for sure." Were banks' cost of funds to go up another 150 basis points, "it would seriously damage the returns of a great number of thrifts." In an effort to improve their profits, banks had just raised their prime lending rate 10 to 10½ percent.

A couple of weeks in advance of the December 13–14 FOMC meeting, the Fed's beige book seemed to strengthen the hand of those reluctant to raise rates further by reporting a "slower pace" of growth and "persistent weakness in many sectors," including retail sales and construction. Loan demand was "flat to moderate." It called wage increases "moderate" and said increased capacity had eased price pressures. But then came a raft of government statistics that gave Greenspan and the hawks ample justification to tighten, beginning with a December 2 report that nonfarm payroll had risen twice as much as expected in November. Kelley was not anxious to raise rates again, but warned, "If we keep pushing for export growth in the hope that this will enable us to grow out of both [deficit] problems simultaneously without any demand restraint on our already very full economy, we may soon risk overheating with an attendant increase of inflationary pressures. . . . This danger could be heightened by a substantial further decline in the exchange rate of the dollar." At the White House, Fitzwater focused instead on a drop in the Commerce Department's index of leading economic indicators and joyously proclaimed signs of an economic slowdown—not your customary fodder for triumphant White House press pronouncements unless your audience is the FOMC.

One of the election results was that scandal-plagued House Banking Committee chairman Representative Fernand St. Germain, the Rhode Island Democrat who had collaborated with House Speaker Jim Wright of Texas to bottle up legislation that would have enabled the Federal Savings and Loan Insurance Corporation to take over insolvent thrift institutions, was put out of office. That left the door open to the committee's senior Democrat, Texas congressman Henry Gonzalez, to take over the chairmanship. The longtime

Fed gadfly, who had once filed a motion to impeach Volcker and who was now to become even more of a thorn in the Fed's side, launched his career as committee chairman with an endless press conference on December 9, in which he minced few words expressing his dislike for the Fed. Lashing out at "the tremendous power" of the Fed, he said he was determined to make it "accountable." It was to be a long six years for Greenspan, responding to the incessant (at times daily) demands of Gonzalez for testimony, reports, correspondence. But it is thanks to Gonzalez that I am able to draw on verbatim transcripts of FOMC meetings.[6]

With discount rate hike speculation raging and the December 13–14 FOMC meeting approaching, both outgoing and incoming administration officials did their best to keep the Fed on hold. Michael Boskin, whom Bush had chosen to succeed Sprinkel as CEA chairman, told reporters on the sixth he saw no signs the economy was "overheating." Although, industry was then running at a historically high 84 percent of capacity, and unemployment was below 5½ percent, "there is still room for the economy to expand," argued Darby, who was about to become assistant secretary of commerce. Capacity was being expanded and there was still "some margin of unemployed labor to fuel increased production."

FOMC members still had misgivings about further tightening, but, after a four-month hiatus, Greenspan was determined to get rates significantly higher, as was the staff. Despite signs of slowing, Prell said inflation pressures were so bad the Fed must "run the risk of some financial distress and economic weakness" to control them. Prell was now talking about a further 2 percent rise in the funds rate by early 1990, which would have meant pushing it to at least 10¼ percent. "Then it flattens out," he told worried FOMC members. ". . . We are not trying to drive the unemployment rate up toward 7 or 8 percent in an effort to slow inflation. . . ." In contrast to other periods, when the Fed would cite relatively low long-term interest rates as a sign the Fed was conquering inflationary expectations or at least slowing the economy, Kohn practically lamented the fact that long-term rates had risen less than a half percent since the previous winter. The modest rise raised "a question about the degree to which monetary policy has applied effective restraint on the economy this year." Some members saw the flat to lower trend of long-term interest rates as evidence the economy was not overheating and inflation was not accelerating, but Greenspan said, "I don't think there's anything involved here other than in part pure luck." The dollar was still under selling pressure, and Truman warned it would fall further if the Fed did not raise the funds rate. Greenspan worried that a stalling out of the trade adjustment process could precipitate a decline in the dollar and said "this strikes me as an area where you can get some destabilization from something cracking in the seams."

Greenspan and his hawk allies got an assist before the second day of meetings started, when a surprising rise in November retail sales was reported. He could also point to a rise in industrial production which pushed capacity utilization to 84.2 percent. But many members still had doubts. Even some of the usually hawkish presidents were nervous. Black saw "very little room for error." Though "concerned about inflation," Melzer said, "Inflation is not going to get away from us. . . . To attempt to wring it out all at once, to try to deal with that too aggressively, is just going to take us off the track of really making long-term progress on the inflation front." Chicago Fed President Silas Keehn thought "the risks are on the price side" but was "not sure just how draconian we need to be." Kelley warned the Fed would face "a terrible dilemma" if it pushed the economy into recession. "I can envision a scenario where if the economy were to go south too far too fast, we might wind up spending many more years trying to get to price stability than we would under some alternative scenarios. . . . It's my hope that as we do go forward here, we'd be very careful as to how aggressive we get. We don't want to wind up with a Pyrrhic victory." Making a seasonal pun, LaWare suggested that, instead of "ringing the gong" by raising the discount rate a half percent, the Fed should content itself with "jingling the bell" by raising the funds rate a quarter point. Contemplating the impact of another 2 percent increase in interest cost on the financial industry, the former bank executive said he was getting "a metallic taste in my mouth. . . . The costs of getting back if we really dump this economy would be terrible." If the Fed was going to "apply the brakes," it should "do it very gently." Johnson revived the threat of a "world-wide ratcheting up of interest rates," predicting Germany and the rest of Europe would follow any Fed rate hike.

Administration officials had continued to fight a losing battle against the Fed's credit tightening right up through the end of the FOMC meeting. "Unemployment has been hovering around 5.4 percent for several months, and there is no indication of greater or lesser pressure" on wages and prices, a senior Treasury official asserted as the FOMC met on the fourteenth. "The consumer price index for the last 12 months has been flat as a pancake." The Fed should not fall prey to "a confusion of growth with overheating." Sprinkel complained the Fed was associating high employment with inflation, when in fact "it's not inevitable that when you reach high employment it's followed by worse inflation. To no avail. Greenspan built a consensus around the argument that the potential costs of not tightening credit were greater than the risks of tightening. "Moving forward and finding that we made a mistake is a possibility, but I think the cost of such a mistake is really much smaller than the cost of doing nothing in the face of what basically is going on" with inflation. He hoped to avoid raising rates 2 percent over the next year because "that's going to create a lot of problems for us," but on December 14 he persuaded the FOMC, on an 11 to 1 vote, to raise the funds rate a quarter point to a range of 8⅝ to 8¾ percent by pushing up the borrowings target another $100 million. There was an understanding that Greenspan would have leeway to raise the funds rate another quarter point to 8⅞ to 9 percent in January.

The first installment of credit tightening became evident the next day, Thursday, December 15, when the Fed failed to supply enough reserves at its late morning intervention hour (*Fed time*, as it's known) to keep the funds rate down at the old level. But hours earlier in Frankfurt, before the Fed had shown its hand, the Bundesbank had done as Johnson had predicted and announced it was raising its Lombard rate from 5 to 5½ percent, effective December 16.

Other European central banks had little choice but to follow suit to keep their currencies from getting out of line with the mark within Europe's semifixed exchange rate grid (the Exchange Rate Mechanism, or ERM). Little more than a month later, following another Fed rate hike, the "ratcheting up" continued as the Bundesbank defensively raised its discount rate from 3½ to 4 and its Lombard rate from 5½ to 6 percent. The virtually simultaneous Fed and Bundesbank moves smacked of interest rate coordination, one of those things central banks like to deny doing. Corrigan, who met with officials of the Bundesbank and other major central banks in Basel shortly before the FOMC meeting, says he can recall no explicit coordination in this instance, but added knowingly, "There's an awful lot of body English" that goes on at the monthly BIS meetings. "It would not surprise me at all, without the words ever having been said, that the Bundesbank . . . had every good reason to think that an increase in rates in the United States wasn't far off. But I doubt that anybody picked up the phone that [Wednesday] afternoon. At least, speaking for myself, it wasn't me. . . . Maybe [Greenspan] did, but I doubt it."

The European rate hikes were not welcomed by the Treasury, which saw them as a harbinger of higher U.S. rates and a depressant on export demand. "It will probably force tightening moves by the Fed, so all in all it seems negative, since the evidence of inflation is rather minuscle—in Germany and here too," an administration official told me. A Fed official disputed that. "Despite what some may say, we don't take orders from Wall Street or from Frankfurt, nor does Frankfurt take orders from us . . . ," he said, but he conceded the European rate hikes would cause the Fed to reevaluate its exchange rate and trade forecasts. Angell said the latest wave of European rate hikes "doesn't put us under any pressure at all. We have our job to do, we look at events and do what we have to do."

The Fed action roiled the already troubled waters of the thrift industry. Dan Wall, chairman of the Federal Home Loan Bank Board (FHLBB), charged with supervising roughly 3,000 savings and loan associations, put a rosy spin on S&L problems in a December 19 interview, claiming 86 percent of the nation's roughly 3,000 thrifts with 90 percent of the assets were profitable and that losses had been diminishing steadily. But he warned the Fed's rate hikes could undermine the S&Ls effort to stay afloat. "We have very much begun to see a turnaround, but to the extent that interest rates go up, losses will be larger." Wall was far too optimistic.

In a sign of conflict to come, Bush policy adviser James Pinkerton told reporters Bush had "a good relationship" with Greenspan, but said the new president would "like to see [interest] rates low and not damaging to economic recovery." It was among the first of many shots the new administration would fire at the Fed over the next four years. Bush himself was trying to take the high, not to say cosmic, road. He seemed to think that, if he could only change the way markets thought, interest rates would come down. In an impromptu news conference at his jam-packed campaign headquarters on Washington's Fifteenth street, the president-elect blamed high interest rates on "adverse psychology" which his administration would work to counteract. "I will just do my level best to send signals to the international markets that we're serious about [deficit reduction], that we're projecting it downward firmly," he said. "And I really believe that once that happens that the adverse psychology that is forcing interest rates up, in my view beyond where they ought to be, will turn around. Once the markets think we're definitely on track, that in itself will be enormously beneficial to world markets." It all sounded good, but it was all to come to naught—at least in the way Bush meant it. Long-term interest rates would eventually come down, despite budget deficits that dwarfed Reagan's, but only because the economy went into the tank.

CHAPTER FOUR

An About-Face

Fed policymakers came into the new year with guns blazing like federal marshalls gunning for cattle rustlers. Christmas shopping season had been strong, and other indicators convinced the Fed the economy had an inflationary impetus that needed to be slowed. Entering 1989, the funds rate had been trading firm—near 9½ percent—due to technical year-end pressures, and many thought the Fed had elevated its funds rate target well above the 8⅝ to 8¾ percent it had set at its December 13–14 FOMC meeting. It had not, but sentiment was building to do so. "It would be a mistake to assume that slower growth in 1989 is going to translate into less price pressures," Parry, a voting FOMC member that year, said in a typical interview. "Nationwide we've been growing in excess of potential for some time. Even with a growth rate of 2½ percent or even slower you're not going to build up much slack." He and others thought it would take more than a year of lower growth to free up enough resources to permit more rapid growth.

On January 5, as prearranged, the Fed raised the funds rate to a target range of 9 to 9⅛ percent. With unfortuitous timing, the move coincided with a House Banking Committee hearing on the impact of rising interest rates on banks and their debtors. Seidman said rising rates were hurting less developed countries and their FDIC-insured creditor banks.

Brady reacted to the rate hike with an odd equanimity. The increases "don't bother me," he said as he released the fiscal 1990 budget four days later. "They will be back down again. I'm not comfortable when interest rates are rising, but I would say that interest rates do go up and down." Brady would take a less sanguine attitude toward rates once the economy turned south. For the time being, the administration in waiting was living in a dreamworld. The economy looked solid, enabling the high-riding Bush team to overlook the severity of the country's financial problems. What's more, they were confident they were going to get Congress to reduce the deficit. In late December, then Director of the Office of Management and Budget (OMB) Joseph R. Wright Jr. had proposed $35 billion in "savings" that would supposedly shrink the deficit to $92.5 billion—well below the ceiling set by the Gramm-Rudman Act. Unemployment had just fallen to 5.3 percent in December. A telltale sign of slowing was a decline in hours worked, but Fed officials brushed it off and focused on what they regarded as tightening labor market conditions and excessive growth.

In an illustration of how monetary policy actions in one country can cause tensions with another country, a row broke out in the first week of January between the U.S. Treasury and the German central bank. By then, Fed rate hikes had caused a substantial dollar rally from its postelection lows. It all started when Bundesbank vice president Helmut Schlesinger declared he could not hope to fight the stronger dollar trend, given U.S. interest rate premiums, particularly when the United States was "in agreement with" a stronger dollar. Schlesinger seemed to be reversing previous Bundesbank policy of keeping the dollar from strengthening above 1.80 marks. Treasury officials made matters worse when they disavowed Schlesinger's characterization of U.S. dollar policy, thereby signalling they wanted a weaker dollar. Schlesinger was "inaccurate and incorrect" in saying the United States wanted the dollar to rise against the mark, I was told. There had been "no change" in dollar policy, and Fed dollar sales done at Treasury's behest proved it. While Treasury was resigned to seeing the dollar float up because of rising U.S. interest rates, it did not want to see it rise to 1.90 marks or more. Despite the squabble with Germany, Brady told a dubious Congress, "We've got an excellent relationship with our G-7 partners."

As if to prove Brady wrong, Stoltenberg reheated the whole stew January 13 while in Washington. When I asked him about the prospect of further Fed rate hikes, he bluntly said "it is desirable that there be no further rise" because "a further rise in interest rates would create problems." Stoltenberg saw "no need" for the Bundesbank to raise rates "from a pure domestic" standpoint, but said Fed rate hikes could force its hand. He said he was worried about the impact of higher rates on world economic growth and debtor countries, but mostly he worried about the depressing effect on the mark. Aside from holding down import costs, a strong mark had immense psychological importance to the German people which no politician could ignore. On January 19, two weeks after the Fed has nudged up the funds rate, the independent Bundesbank raised its discount rate from 3½ to 4 percent and its Lombard rate from 5½ to 6 percent. Fed officials downplayed this verbal crossing of swords and rate thrusts. The U.S. Treasury might have its problems with the German Finance Ministry and the Bundesbank, but there was no rift among central banks. Although Fed rate hikes had led to copycat moves by other central banks, Kelley did not see "much danger" of escalating international interest rate hikes. Nevertheless, this kind of transatlantic tiff, coupled with Treasury protestations that it really didn't want a strong dollar, made Fed officials wince. They had seen what damage these altercations could do in October 1987, and had done their best to stabilize the dollar, not just to kill inflation but to prevent market disruptions. It wouldn't be long before the Fed would wish it had some cushion of dollar strength to fall back on.

The Fed's biggest concern was still the pace of domestic economic activity and the fiscal policy outlook. The Fed was beginning to wonder what it would take to cool things down. Interest rates now ranged from around 8¼ percent on 3-month Treasury bills up to around 9 percent on 30-year bonds, and in theory, such rates were supposed to be slowing the economy, but to all appearances, things were going gangbusters. Firms were hiring as sales of cars and other so-called durable goods surged ahead. Economist Henry Kaufman argued that, so far, "higher rates have not reduced credit availabiity. In our new deregulated financial world, for the central bank to achieve effective restraint it must force a denial of credit at a much higher level of interest rates than when markets were more segmented. Monetary restraint is successful only after considerable scrambling for credit takes place among businesses, households and government. . . . We haven't seen the level of interest rates yet" sufficient to slow the economy.

It was indeed a different environment. Through the seventies, the Fed could rely on *disintermediation* to slow the economy through the credit channel. With the interest banks could pay on deposits capped by Regulation Q, as the Fed raised rates above those ceilings, money began to flow out of bank deposits into more attractive nonbank investments, leaving banks and thrifts less funds to lend. Soon credit availability dried up and so did business activity. With the elimination of Regulation Q, banks and thrifts were at liberty to bid as high as they wanted for deposits to lend out at higher rates. They also had increasing access to "brokered deposits"—large institutional funds seeking the highest rates available on jumbo CDs—and the Eurocurrency market, awash with offshore dollar deposits. From the standpoint of borrowers, the advent of adjustable rate mortgages made it easier to get credit, even when rates soared. What's more, increasingly savvy individuals and firms knew how to get the maximum return on their funds, shifting it among an array of money market funds, CDs, and other instruments to take advantage of market rates. Larger companies were also beginning to hedge their interest rate risks through the use of interest rate swaps and other derivatives.

The Fed hoped the new administration would be able to work effectively with Congress to balance the budget. It was pleased with the administration's proposal to shrink the deficit from $152 billion in fiscal 1989 to less than $100 billion in fiscal 1990. But already there were the makings of big problems, and Bush hadn't even taken office. The budget which the Reagan administration sent to Congress on January 9 and which Bush planned to adopt contained a glaring, built-in conflict with the Fed. The central bank had made clear it would tolerate no more than 2½ percent real growth, and secretly the Fed planned to allow even less. Yet, the budget assumed real GNP would grow 3.2 percent in 1989 and beyond. The assumptions were tailor-made for a clash with Congress, which seized on them as an excuse not to bargain in good faith with the White House on balancing the budget. The CBO had projected 2.7 percent growth in 1989, followed by an average 2.3 percent per year through 1994. I got a hint of the conflict that awaited Bush from House Budget Committee chairman William Gray in December after the administration had released the outlines of its budget proposals. "It makes two economic assumptions I've found no support for," Gray said. "It says that, after six years of economic growth we'll have another five years of economic growth even higher than the six years we've had, and it calls for interest rates to drop two percentage points below their August level and stay there for the next five years." When asked about the contradiction between the administration's economic assumptions and the stated unwillingness of the Fed to allow that much growth, Sprinkel made the further assumption that the Fed would provide for such growth by maintaining growth of the money supply near the midpoint of its target growth range of 3 to 7 percent. "We will not see an aggressive further tightening by the Federal Reserve . . . [at least] I hope not," he said on January 10. "We assume there will not be continued tightening of monetary policy."

In his January 20 inaugural address, Bush pledged deficit reduction with a flourish. "We have more will than wallet, but will is what we need. We will make the hard choices, looking at what we have and perhaps allocating it differently, making our decisions on honest need and prudent safety." There would be "a new engagement" between White House and Congress. "We need compromise; we have had dissension. We need harmony; we have had a chorus of discordant voices." And in a plea for bipartisanship, Bush symbolically extended his hand toward Speaker Wright and Senate Majority Leader George Mitchell and said, "Let us negotiate soon and hard. But in the end let us produce. . . . We must bring the federal budget into balance." Bush's blissful spirit of bipartisanship did not live much beyond that day.

Cooperation with the Fed also died aborning. Even before the inauguration, relations were on the wrong track. Darman, Bush's designated budget director, launched a salvo at the Fed the day before Bush took office. "If the Federal Reserve were excessively tight for an extended period it would slow the economy and increase the [budget] deficit," he told the Senate Governmental Affairs Committee. He urged it not to do so. A few days later, Darman announced OMB would adopt the Reagan administration budget assumption of 3.2 percent growth in each of the next five fiscal years—a direct challenge to the Fed's growth tolerances. The Bush line was not selling at the Fed. "I don't see a lot of widespread evidence of slowing," Richard Syron, who had taken Frank Morris's place as president of the Boston Fed a couple of months earlier, said in a January 17 interview: "I still number myself among those concerned about prices." Voting FOMC member Hoskins accurately warned inflation "could easily exceed 5 percent" in 1989. He felt it was time for the Fed to get serious. "For the past several years we have tolerated an inflation rate that eroded the purchasing power of a dollar by 20 percent to 25 percent. Continuing inflation rates of this magnitude do not seem today to be regarded as a pressing economic problem, yet cumulatively they have eroded the value of our dollars and impaired our economic efficiency." The Fed should seek "zero inflation."

Impatient with ambitious administration growth plans and pronouncements about no further Fed tightening, Greenspan did not wait for his late-February Humphrey-Hawkins testimony to set the Bush team straight. In a January 23 speech he made clear that beating back inflation was the top priority. While the Fed would seek to "support economic growth at a pace that can be sustained as we continue to move toward price stability," he emphasized "inflationary pressures must be contained if we are to avoid the wrenching volatility of the past." The bond market, in keeping long-term interest rates "fairly steady," had given the Fed "an expression of confidence . . . that actions taken now will preclude a more severe tightening later." The next day he threw more cold water on administration assumptions before the House Banking Committee. "It is possible that forces not now visible could impart a significant upward push to productivity," he began charitably. "This could boost potential economic growth beyond 3 percent per year. However, a policy that assumes such outcomes risks significant inflationary imbalances." With nonfarm business productivity growing only 1 to 1¼ percent per year and labor force growth slowing, continued growth at the pace the White House assumed was not possible.

"The longer-run costs of a return to higher inflation and the risks of this occurring under current circumstances are sufficiently great that Federal Reserve policy at this juncture might well be advised to err more on the side of restrictiveness than of stimulus," he said. Factories' capacity use had "risen to levels that at numerous times in the past have been associated with a worsening of inflation," and "if growth were to continue indefinitely at the recent pace, the concomitant tightening of supply conditions for labor and materials would risk a serious intensification of inflationary pressures at some not too distant point in the future." While "labor markets and industrial facilities may well be flexible enough to allow us to operate for some time at higher levels of resource utilization without a visible deterioration in inflation . . . there is little doubt that margins of slack have been reduced." Real GNP had grown by 4.4 percent in 1988, and Greenspan warned, "The risks of greater inflation could be appreciable if real GNP continues to increase at recent rates over the next several years. . . . Containing the pressures on labor and capital resources while continuing to reduce our external imbalance will require a slowing in domestic demand." In a further declaration of political independence, he indicated he would not let worries about what recent dollar strength might do to the trade balance deter the Fed.

Greenspan's message was clear: The Fed had no intention of accommodating the kind of growth Bush was counting on to make his budget work and would soon be raising rates. Bush's reaction was swift. In an interview with the *New York Times* the next day, Bush said, "I haven't talked to Alan lately, but I don't want to see us move so strongly against fear of inflation that we impede growth. We have to keep expanding opportunities for the working men and women of this country." The war over White House budget assumptions was focusing more attention on the Fed's growth targets than it felt comfortable with, and a concerted campaign was launched to disabuse Congress and the public of any notion their central bank had erected a glass ceiling on the economy's ability to grow. The Fed did not like being seen targeting growth, anymore than it liked being seen targeting interest or exchange rates. "One thing that is misunderstood is that the Fed does not have a position on what is an acceptable growth rate," Kelley said. "There is no formal Fed position." "I don't know what the appropriate full employment growth rate is," Johnson echoed. "No one really knows. We're not as a matter of monetary policy committed to any particular growth rate. The Fed will resist inflationary pressures no matter what the growth rate is." But the officials protested too much.

The Fed downplayed the sniping between the Fed and the new administration. "I don't see a rift, and I see no reason to be concerned about a rift," Kelley said in late January. Any differences between Bush and Greenspan were "very minor." Boskin said the Fed and administration were "roughly in the same ballpark." But in his next breath, he delineated the differences by asserting the economy "can grow slightly over three percent." While the Fed had done a good job up until then, he said he would "hope and expect that they will carefully monitor the economy, production and financial markets so we can have maximum sustainable growth." He said the administration's deficit reduction efforts would "provide the Fed with elbow room to provide liquidity." By then, the funds rate was higher than long-term rates, and Boskin said this "inverted yield curve" could only have two meanings: Either "the signal is getting out that we are not going to tolerate inflation" or it could signal a slowdown. "It is only one signal, but it is one that we ought to be concerned about." If the Fed shared Boskin's concern, there was no sign of it. "Some view the inverted yield curve as a possible precursor of a recession," Heller said January 31. "However, monetary restraint has in years past resulted in inverted yield curves without producing a recession."

Greenspan again hit the OMB assumptions before the Joint Economic Committee on January 31. Asked if the economy would grow more than 3 percent in 1990 while interest rates fell 2 percent he called it "feasible," but added, "Is it probable? No, it is not. I certainly wouldn't want to argue that case." Such a growth pace was conceivable if productivity rose enough, but the Fed could not count on that. "I think it is wiser to have 'money in the bank before we spend it' so to speak." Greenspan said the Fed's rate hikes had "suppressed some of the forces that would create instability" and contended the Fed's policies were "more likely to extend out the recovery than to bring it to a halt." Again he served notice the Fed would "err more on the side of restrictiveness than of stimulus" because "containing the pressures on labor and capital resources while continuing to reduce our external imbalance will require a slowing in domestic demand." While slamming its budget assumptions, Greenspan lent support to the administration's effort to reduce the deficit. Action on Bush's budget "shouldn't be protracted indefinitely." If there was quick action, "the effects would be quite dramatic and favorable." He "would prefer sequestration"—automatic spending cuts provided for under Gramm-Rudman—to a budget that did not restrain spending. He found "credible" the assumption that long-term Treasury rates would decline to 7.6 percent in 1990, 6.1 percent in 1991, and 5.2 percent in 1992—provided Congress passed it.

Fed officials had high hopes for deficit reduction, and some held out the prospect of easing. If Congress reduced the deficit it would give the Fed "more room to maneuver" and allow for lower rates by reducing the financing needs of the federal government and reducing demands on scarce capital, Heller said. Cutting the deficit "would release real and financial resources for domestic investment purposes, thereby helping to build additional capacity to keep inflation in check." All of this balanced budget talk was to prove empty. Instead of falling, the deficit rose from $152 billion in 1989, to $221 billion in 1990, to $269 billion in 1991, and to $290 billion in 1992, as government spending far outstripped revenues despite a record tax hike. There would be no relief for the Fed as "the only game in town."

Deficit reduction might some day unburden monetary policy, but in the short-run the Fed had other concerns. On January 18, a big jump in imports which caused the trade deficit to widen pointed to continued strong demand. Although an administration official claimed the imports reflected higher business investment that would expand industry's capacity to export and that lower exports would lessen capacity strains, the Fed saw the wider trade gap as symptomatic of basic imbalances between the United States and its trading partners. Without greater investment and/or less consumption, the U.S. trade balance would not improve much. To redress the imbalance the budget deficit had to be reduced to increase savings and investment. In the meantime, the Fed could not let trade concerns govern its policy. The wider trade deficit prompted speculation the dollar would have to depreciate, and Feldstein's call for a 20 percent dollar drop was still ringing in currency traders' ears. "That's nonsense," a Treasury official told me. "That's definitely not the Treasury's view." Even so, weak dollar talk gave the Fed more reason not to let up in its anti-inflation crusade.

The Fed could take cheer from reports showing both industrial production and consumer prices had risen a mild three-tenths of a percent in December. "Very encouraging," said Black. But producer prices had risen twice as fast, suggesting more inflation in the pipeline. Hoskins was "inclined to doubt that we have made much progress toward an inflation-free environment" and said the Fed should "err on the side of overly restrictive policies until it becomes clear that progress toward that goal [of price stability] is being made." The Fed's beige book for the February 7–8 FOMC meeting dashed hopes the Fed's past rate hikes had slowed things down. It found signs the economy was gaining momentum. Then, in early February, the Labor Department reported a dramatic upsurge in January nonfarm payroll, along with a sizable jump in average hourly earnings.

Four days before the FOMC met, G-7 finance ministers and central bankers met in Washington. Beneath the meeting's tranquil surface lay turbulence caused by Fed rate hikes, which had strengthened the dollar and raised German and Japanese import costs. German officials made little secret of their desire to see the Fed hold the line on rates to take upward pressure off the dollar. A senior Japanese official called the dollar's rise "not acceptable." Greenspan told the FOMC "a vague mild division [was] beginning to emerge" between the finance ministers and the central bankers over monetary tightening, with the other central bankers supporting the Fed, while the finance ministers were opposed. In an apparent reference to Stoltenberg, Greenspan said one finance minister had had "a strong reaction" to Fed tightening. He detected "a relatively laid-back attitude" among G-7 officials about the stronger dollar's likely effect of prolonging trade imbalances. He took this to mean "there is a fairly considerable willingness on the part of these countries both in their private and public sectors to absorb liabilities against the United States. . . . They are sort of delighted with the surpluses and the effect of the claims, especially the buildup of the claims, in an almost mercantilistic power sense." But he questioned whether that attitude would last if the dollar were to resume depreciating, thereby undermining the value of foreign-held U.S. assets. While finance ministers now had "a vague laid-backness about the stalling of the adjustment process" they were beginning to be concerned about the rise of U.S. interest rates and the accompanying rise of the dollar because "there is a latent fear that it could begin to reverse," Greenspan said, "and I think that would accumulate into a fairly significant set of concerns amongst finance ministers and to a much lesser extent central bank governors, who have been largely supportive of general strengthening."

At the FOMC meeting, the Fed staff projected the funds rate at 10¾ percent by the end of 1989. The Fed had already raised it roughly 3 percent to just over 9 percent, and some members were getting jittery about the impact the rate hikes might have. The Cassandra voices of Seger and LaWare continued to haunt the discussions, the latter warning the Fed not to applaud itself too much for fighting inflation. If they ended up "dumping the economy" they would be seen as "black knights" and their anti-inflation credibility "would disappear overnight." Seger warned of the impact of higher rates on unstable banks and thrifts. The hawks were not impressed. "I don't see one structural problem—in the Southwest or with the thrifts or internationally—that would be helped by having an inflation rate of 5.7 percent," Hoskins told her. "It seems to me that we could undo the cost of being overly tight now relatively quickly if we needed to. We can't undo the other. It gets built in."

The compelling counterargument was that if the Fed tightened to the point it drove the economy into recession it would harm its long-term effort to gain price stability because it would be forced to restimulate the economy. LaWare was "very concerned about the fact that there are some significant signs of a turndown in this operation," and felt it would be counterproductive if "we really beat inflation over the head and in the process increase the unemployment rate or dump the economy in some fashion." Melzer, who bowed to no one in his anti-inflationary zeal, took up the cry. "I'm not afraid to take a recession if that's what we have to do" to achieve low inflation, but "I don't think that's where we are. I don't think we're in a situation now where it will be productive in terms of the long-run inflation fight to run too close to the line in terms of a recession." If the economy goes into recession, "the [stimulative] response in the other direction is going to put us so far off a sustained path of monetary restraint that it could take us years to get back to the position I think we're in right now." If the committee heeded staff calls for zero growth in bank reserves and narrow money supply (M1) for 1989, "there's a reasonable likelihood that that will put the economy in a recession in late 1989 or 1990." Kelley also had misgivings. "I think there are some very major problems in the United States and indeed in the world that could be severely exacerbated if we are too aggressive too fast: S&Ls, LDCs, the budget deficit. . . ." Besides, the dollar was "strong," money growth "slow" and inflation "sluggish." Curiously, staffers were themselves pointing to drags on the economy even as they advocated much higher rates. Prell said "the combination of monetary and fiscal restraint produces a substantial slowing in output growth." Kohn noted "very sluggish behavior of the money supply of late."

But such sentiments were overwhelmed by more hawkish committee members. Forrestal told his colleagues, "We continue to think that there is momentum in the economy, that we are operating above our potential and that the vulnerability is on the inflation side." Stern called the economy "very solid" and said, "If you want to get the rate of inflation down it's going to take more than prevailing interest rates to accomplish that." Boehne agreed the economy is "growing too rapidly" and warned "vulnerabilities to inflation seem higher to me now than they did just a meeting or so ago. I think this kind of a situation does require a response from us. . . ." Corrigan wanted to raise rates immediately. "My anxiety level is getting pretty high," he said. After trying to hold onto the belief that inflation would stay in the range of 4 to 4½ percent, "I don't think I can say that anymore without my nose growing." It was possible the economy could slow on its own without further tightening, but the Fed had to "balance the risks" and as far as he was concerned "the algebraic sign on the inflation rate is unambiguous—it's plus. It's not neutral, it's not minus, it's plus." Corrigan admitted the dollar "creates quite a conundrum for us right now." So long as the Fed raised rates it would be strong, and so long as it was strong, it would be hard to reduce the trade deficit. If the dollar was not going to be allowed to depreciate "something else has to give," and that "something else" would be the economy. "I have a real question in my mind as to whether we can make sustainable progress on the external adjustment side given any broadly acceptable pattern of exchange rates without a significant and sustained slowdown in the rate of growth in the economy."

After taking it all in and gently guiding the discussion, Greenspan gave his own lengthy, nuanced presentation, drawing on his own in-depth analysis of order backlogs and lead times in industry and a host of other indicators. He had seldom seen an economy "more balanced than the one that we have" and saw little evidence of the kinds of excess inventory buildup that can precipitate cutbacks in production. "There's a certain momentum in the economy that is very likely to carry us quite a good way." He acknowledged signs of slowing and confessed he was "particularly puzzled" by the weakness the closely watched industrial survey of the National Association of Purchasing Management (NAPM) was indicating. Noting the NAPM index had been "very reliable in the past and has often been the first indication that we have had that the climate of the economy is changing," he observed the January index had pointed to a "relatively sharp decline in [coming] quarters." There were "no signs of general overheating." Nevertheless, "we still have a way to go in tightening. I think the evidence is much too premature to suggest . . . that this cycle of tightening that we've been through is over." He pleaded for a strong consensus to give him leeway to raise rates further. He said the only reason he did not want to tighten right away was because the dollar was too strong to allow trade adjustment. Despite some strong reservations, the FOMC authorized Greenspan to raise rates in the weeks following the meeting. Parry and Hoskins dissented because they wanted to raise rates right away.

It was a peculiar understanding Greenspan reached with the FOMC. The committee authorized him to raise rates under one of two conditions: if the economy did not show further signs of slowing or if the dollar weakened. The chairman asked for and got a directive with a tightening bias "with a recognition that, if the pressure on the dollar that is now there stabilizes or falls and if the current mixed signals such as the NAPM survey and the insured unemployment numbers do not indicate early deterioration . . . it would be wise for the Desk to be instructed to move [discount window borrowings] up $100 million maybe in a couple of weeks or so." Once again, the transcripts show, exchange rates can loom large in the setting of interest rates. Greenspan soon had ample ammunition to exercise his mandate.

On the night of Thursday, February 9, Bush gave a budget address that was not well received by expectant markets, even though Bush proposed a budget with a slightly lower deficit than that proposed by Reagan which met the Gramm-Rudman targets. Spending was to grow no faster than inflation. The capital gains tax was to be cut to 15 percent. But the markets correctly sensed Congress was waiting to ambush Bush. And looming over the usual fiscal mess was the S&L bailout, the cost of which seemed to grow by the minute. The administration had proposed a $50 billion recapitalization of the Federal Savings and Loan Insurance Corporation (FSLIC) which added to market concerns about mounting federal borrowing, as deficit reduction faltered in the face of congressional opposition to the Bush budget plan.[1] Financing all the borrowing that would be required was getting steadily more expensive as the Fed pushed up interest rates. It was reported on the tenth that wholesale prices had risen at an annual rate near 13 percent in January. The markets were unnerved. Thursday and Friday, February 9 and 10, was a bloody two-day period on Wall Street. The Dow industrials dropped 57 points, and bond prices plunged. As investors deserted stocks and bonds, short- and medium-term rates soared. The yield on one-year Treasury bills went to 9.2 percent. The sell-off in the bond market continued the following Monday, pushing the long bond yield to 9⅛ percent. Just two weeks earlier the yield had been 8¾ percent. Suddenly, hopes that the bond markets were signaling diminished inflation fears were dashed. The dollar plunged on Bush's budget address, then recovered on expectations of higher U.S. interest rates. Banks raised the prime from 10½ to 11 percent.

Sensing more credit tightening, Bush moved to head it off. "I would not like to see it," he told the *Wall Street Journal* on February 13. "I don't think the growth is excessive at all." He was "not overly concerned" about inflation. The wholesale price jump had been "an anomaly." While saying he and the Fed were not "far apart at all," he was opposed to "any radical surgery." The president should have saved his breath. The next day, Greenspan played the card the FOMC had dealt him the week before and ordered the New York Fed to start pushing the federal funds rate up another quarter point to a range of 9¼ to 9⅜ percent. The new target was supposed to be consistent with a borrowing target of $700 million per day, but since the open market desk was having increasing difficulty with its borrowing target because of unpredictable swings and shortfalls in banks' adjustment borrowings, the desk was instructed to use "flexibility" in hitting the desired funds rate target. That meant the borrowings target was practically out the window and that the desk was simply fine-tuning the funds rate on a day-to-day basis using open market operations.

A week later, Greenspan was back on Capitol Hill for two days of Humphrey-Hawkins testimony. He announced the Fed had decided to reduce its target for M2 money supply growth by 1 percent to a 3 to 7 percent range. But the Senate Banking Committee wanted to know why he raised rates February 14. Unapologetically and dispassionately, he said the economy was "operating essentially at capacity" and that "monetary policy cannot force demand to expand more rapidly than potential supply without adverse consequences. . . . The current rate of inflation let alone an increase is not acceptable, and our policies are designed to reduce inflation in coming years." So growth had to be restrained. "With the economy running close to its potential, the risks seem to be on the side of a further strengthening of price pressures. Therefore, the Fed remains more inclined to act in the direction of restraint than toward stimulus." If that meant a strong dollar that hurt exports, too bad. The only thing which appealed to the White House was his urgent call for cutting the deficit "by focusing solely on the expenditure side." He said he would "favor going to a sequester" over raising taxes. Interest rates would fall if there was "fairly expeditious passage" of Bush's budget. If not, the buildup of public and private debt together with economic strains and other problems might mean "a significant acceleration of inflation in this country and a set of imbalances that could lead to a major contraction. . . . We have a little time, but we do not have time to procrastinate and hope that it will go away."

A few hours after Greenspan's testimony Boskin did a delicate tightrope walk on the other side of the Capitol, opposing further Fed rate hikes, while maintaining there were no significant differences with the Fed. While conceding inflation had become "a greater risk," he told the House Budget Committee "the current economic data do not yet suggest a permanent acceleration of inflation. . . . I do not yet see a serious increase in the underlying inflation rate." Using a little soft soap, Boskin said he had "great admiration for Greenspan, and I do not believe he is falling into a trap in this regard"—driving interest rates up to an extent that it made businesses' cost of capital too high. "What the Federal Reserve has been trying to do is send a signal to the financial markets that it will not tolerate an acceleration of inflation. . . . I have confidence in the current Federal Reserve, and I'm cautiously optimistic about its ability to maintain economic growth without accelerating inflation." Boskin said "too much has probably been made of the differences of the long-range forecasts by the Reagan administration and what the Federal Reserve considers sustainable growth." In reality, the administration's 3.2 percent real GNP growth forecast was "only slightly above the 2½ to 3 percent range recently cited by Chairman Greenspan." Besides, the Fed's money growth target was "reasonably consistent with real GNP growth in the range of 3 percent or slightly higher." But Greenspan had just said real growth probably could not much exceed 2 percent.

All this making nice with Greenspan was about to come to a halt. Before Greenspan went before the House Banking Committee to give his second installment of Humphrey-Hawkins testimony the morning of February 22, the Labor Department reported consumer prices had risen more than 7 percent at an annual rate. In contrast to the 1994–1995 tightening period when there was little rise in unit labor costs, Greenspan blamed accelerating wage rates as "the reason we're starting to get a stronger inflationary tone" and called the CPI jump "disturbing." That's Fedspeak for "Look out!" Two days later, the Federal Reserve Board voted 6 to 1 (the 1 being Seger) to raise the discount rate from 6½ to 7 percent. Ten of the 12 Federal Reserve banks had requested a rate hike. The Cleveland Fed had asked for a full percent increase. The Board's action had the effect of pushing the funds rate to a range of 9¾ to 9⅞ percent, and for some time the funds rate was to trade at 9.9 percent. Like an army marching at dawn, the Fed struck early on February 24. "I was in Los Angeles at the time," LaWare recalls. "I got this telephone call when I came back from dinner [the previous night]. They said, 'There will be a telephone meeting of the Open Market Committee tomorrow, at 8 A.M. Washington time, five o'clock in the morning Los Angeles time.' So I set the clock and ordered coffee up to the room, and I was sitting up in bed drinking coffee when the call came through, and that was the last notch." About the same time, the Fed ordered its examiners to crack down on bank financing of "highly leveraged transactions" (HLTs). Some saw the move as an effort to discourage lending for mergers and acquisitions and thereby tighten credit through supervision where rate hikes alone had failed. "To the extent banks become more frightened about doing that kind of lending, that's what it would do," said a senior officer of a major money center bank. Corrigan and others deny that was the motivation, but certainly it amplified the effect of higher rates.

The Fed won praise from Wall Street, but elsewhere, the reception was chillier. "They seem to think that the economy growing too fast and too many people at work is inflationary," said U.S. Chamber of Commerce economist Lawrence Hunter. "That's not true. . . . All they're going to do if they persist in this is push us into a recession." There was barely concealed anger at the White House. Darman had previously scheduled a breakfast for reporters—one of a series of soirees known as "doughnuts with Dick." The usually affable and clever OMB chief was steaming after the Fed made its early morning rate announcement. He was seeing his assumption about the cost of financing the national debt (a major component of the budget) go up in smoke, and he was not amused. The Fed's move was "not at all welcome," he said tersely, charging the Fed had acted on nothing more than "a perception" of inflation. At the Treasury, an official I spoke to charged the Fed was going overboard in combatting wage-price pressures. "Obviously this is going to have an effect on the real economy at some point"—maybe not until next year, but "it could bite more suddenly."

President Bush, who always seemed to be in tropical climes when the Fed lowered the boom, was on a trip to Asia this time, and he held a press conference on the tarmac at Tokyo airport on Saturday, February 25, to denounce the rate hike. "I can't say I'm happy about the rise in interest rates," he said. "Higher interest rates are not helpful in deficit reduction." But he tried to defuse the appearance of conflict with the Fed. "We've got a little difference of interpretation at this point as to how you read the indicators on inflation," he told reporters before boarding a plane for Beijing. "That's the only difference we've got. . . . We share the common objectives of needing to get the deficit down, and I still maintain that we are not far apart." In reality, the Fed's rate hikes were taking the White House further and further away from its low interest assumptions, on which it was counting not only to lower the deficit but to save the sinking thrift industry. Boskin, of all Bush's advisors the most sympathetic to the Fed's ends, if not always its means, was more restrained. "In general, I've been supportive of the Federal Reserve so far," but the Fed "has got to be conscious that policy operates with a lag" and that any "extreme" credit tightening could cause a future downturn. The upsurge in wholesale and retail prices to which the Fed had reacted was just a "blip" caused by higher oil prices. He expressed hope that "we're looking at rates that are near their peak." In fact, they *had* peaked.

Black knew intuitively the Fed had finally gotten ahead of the curve. "I'm personally prepared to wait awhile to see whether we are," he told me. "I certainly hope this is enough. I think everybody hopes it is enough." It was to be the last time the Fed raised interest rates in five years. By spring, the pendulum was swinging the other way, and in June, Fed policymakers ignored staff advice and started a long series of rate cuts. The Fed now found itself in nearly the same position it would find itself in February 1995, having just raised the funds rate some 3 percent, except that in 1989, the funds rate was pushed 4 percent above the peak reached five years later. If the Fed proceeded more cautiously in the later period, perhaps it was because memories were fresh of what happened in the earlier one.

Although there were now mounting signs of a slowdown and financial problems, the Fed staff continued to push for yet higher rates. Greenspan himself seemed inclined to go along with them. "With the economy already operating at high levels of labor and plant utilization and given the disturbing signs of strengthening price and cost pressures, the momentum of expansion implies risks that clearly remain on the side of accelerating inflation," he told the Senate Budget Committee on February 28, implying the latest rate hike might not be enough. "We still have work to do if we are to succeed in our task of achieving the goals of balanced expansion and the reduced inflation needed to sustain it." The Fed's goal was not just to stop inflation from worsening but to end it. Far from credit tightening weakening the economy, the surest path to recession would be allowing inflation to get out of hand. If the Fed had not raised short-term rates as much as it had, "long-term interest rates [then around 9¼ percent] would almost surely be higher than they are at the moment." Across town, Johnson gave a speech that diverged dramatically from Greenspan's view that monetary policy should be guided by levels of growth and capacity utilization. "A monetary policy strategy attempting to equate real economic growth with the growth of potential or full capacity is risky at best. It is dangerous to generalize that changes in real economic growth lead to changes in prices. Because changes in real output can be asso- ciated with either supply factors or demand pressures, there is no consisent relationship between economic growth and inflation." If inflation was to be reduced, it had to be reduced "over time and not in any dramatic way that risks disruptive results." He also disputed the view that the economy was incapable of growing more than 2½ percent over the long run without accelerating in- flation. "There is no specific real growth target at the Federal Reserve," he asserted. That night, Angell, appearing on CNN's *Moneyline* program had to deny there was a rift on the Board over how to evaluate the economy and inflation.

Greenspan kept heightening the urgency of his appeal to Congress to reduce the budget deficit in support of the Fed's anti-inflation policy, warning failure to slash the deficit could lead to much higher rates. This was to prove largely a lost cause for the next several years, as the deficit continued to mount, but one Greenspan never tired of fighting. Whenever legislators complained about interest rates, he could simply remind them of the mammoth amounts of money the government was routinely draining from the country's limited savings pool to finance overspending. They, not he, were keeping interest rates high. Greenspan would sometimes reluctantly support raising taxes, as when he told the House Budget Committee on March 2 that he could support an increase in the federal excise tax on gasoline, but only "because it's important to stem our dependence on imports of foreign oil. . . . I'm not convinced that increasing taxes would reduce the deficit." Higher taxes would only lead to yet higher spending, he believed. It was one area where Greenspan and Brady could agree.

The administration was anxious not to give the appearance of being at odds with the Fed but, in its maladroit way, kept highlighting their differences. After wholesale prices had risen 1 percent for the second month in a row in February, Brady said he agreed with the Fed's goal of controlling inflation, but remarked, "People look at different numbers differently." Boskin told the House Ways and Means Committee on March 8 that "a mountain is being made from much less than a mole hill," but proceeded to dismiss Greenspan's inflation concerns. "I do not yet see a serious increase in the underlying infla- tion rate. . . ." By then inflation had risen from less than 2 percent in 1986 to nearly 4½ percent in 1988 and had risen at annual rates exceeding 7 percent in the first two months of 1989. Much as they tried to deny it, a chasm widened between Fed and administration. A band of Republican senators goaded Pres- ident Bush to take a more confrontational approach in a letter released March 14. "We do not deny that inflation has to be controlled. What we do deny is that it is presently out of control," wrote Mississippi's Trent Lott, Utah's Orrin Hatch, Florida's Connie Mack, and others. "If the Fed persists in tightening credit and raising interest rates we fear it will be sowing the seeds of a recession. . . . This Fed-induced recession will cause economic hardship in communities all over America. Furthermore, your plan to balance the budget without raising taxes will be ruined because interest rates will skyrocket and tax revenues will decline."

Many thought it was just a matter of time until the Fed pushed the funds rate above 10 percent. But something about crossing that threshold gave Fed officials pause. Seger said the Fed had already "overdone it." Heller was "encouraged" by a shift away from personal consumption and said the Fed did not need to "stifle" economic growth to control inflation. Despite a big February jobs gain and a drop in unemployment from 5.4 to 5.1 percent, Kelley expected the economy and the rate of inflation would slow "in the near future." This viewpoint got some support from mid-March reports of declines in housing starts and industrial capacity utilization, and even after the producer price jolt, stunned officials were inclined toward caution. While "disappointing," the double-digit price rise was "not totally shocking" because it reflected the delayed effect of past expansion and monetary accommodation, Syron said. The Fed had to look forward and hope the past year's rate hikes would cool inflation. "We've had substantial tightening but there are substantial lags before you start seeing the benefit of that. . . . My belief is that the slowing is going to occur."

Another factor not far from the minds of officials was that the dollar pendulum was now swinging too far in the direction of strength for the good of reducing the trade deficit. Some Fed officials shared Treasury fears that continued rate hikes would push the dollar and the trade deficit higher. Angell said on March 20 that he would not want to see the dollar depreciate but also did not want to see the dollar rise much further. Dollar custodian Mulford, who had been elevated to Treasury undersecretary, continued the administration campaign against higher interest rates on March 21. While "we need to keep the lid on inflation," there is "no clear and compelling evidence that inflationary forces are rising" and "we need to sustain growth." The Labor Department that day said the CPI had risen a more modest 0.4 percent in February. Though still a 5 percent annual rate, Fitzwater said it proved there was no need to worry about inflation. While claiming the White House had "been supportive of the Fed," he said the president "has not always shared the same degree of concern about inflation." Brady echoed the same theme a few days before the FOMC's March 28 meeting, contending, "Inflation is leveling at about a 4 percent increase." If the Fed kept tightening credit it "runs the risk of a recession," an official told me a day before the FOMC met.

The Fed also had to fret about the worsening mess in the thrift industry. What the FHLBB had estimated to be a $15 billion problem the previous fall had burgeoned into something much larger, in good part because of the delay in recapitalizing the FSLIC. The problem was growing worse by the day as sick thrifts were allowed to continue in operation making bad loans and investments, and now the administration was telling Congress an S&L cleanup would cost up to $100 billion. The FDIC was saying $115 billion. (The ultimate cost would be more like $200 billion). In February alone $9.4 billion of deposits had streamed out of the thrift industry, on top of $10.6 billion that had been withdrawn in January. The Fed had announced in late February it was prepared to backtstop the Federal Home Loan Banks and lend to troubled thrifts itself. But many in Congress felt the Fed was worsening the situation by raising rates. On March 22, Greenspan told the House Banking Committee the Fed was taking the S&L situation into account in setting policy but gave no indication he was inclined to ease because of it. On the contrary, the very inflation the Fed was trying to combat was worsening the thrifts' woes. "Obviously we are aware that the inflationary pressures that have moved up interest rates have increased the cost of resolving the S&L problem. Our major concern is that inflationary pressures not drive rates to the point that further costs are incurred in resolving this thrift thing." The Fed had been raising short-term rates to cool inflation and thereby lower long rates. In truth, though, the high cost of funds the Fed was imposing on thrifts and banks was giving policymakers second thoughts about further hikes.

Despite all these concerns, the hell-for-leather Fed staff was spoiling for more rate hikes at the March 28 FOMC meeting. Prell doubted the economy was heading toward a "perfect 'soft landing,' " but he was not referring to signs of economic weakness. He meant the economy was still overheating. "Although we may be on a gradual descent in terms of real growth, it is looking more and more like we've overshot the full employment runway and that we'll need to do some backing up if inflation is to be contained." Prell and his staff projected the funds rate would need to rise almost another full percent by the end of 1989. Kohn said the P* model "gives the impression that monetary policy may have tightened about enough to stop the acceleration of inflation, but may not yet be tight enough to reduce the inflation rate." Prell forecast real GNP growth would slow from 2½ percent in the first quarter to just 1.2 percent in the third and average that anemic rate through 1990 but persisted in calling for higher rates. He acknowledged that recent data showed "economic activity is decelerating somewhat in the first half of this year," but "given our view that growth will have to slow considerably further and remain low for some time in order to reverse the updrift in inflation, we still think it likely that further increases in interest rates will be needed." The Fed staff was playing hardball. In calling for the Fed to push the funds rate up to 10¾ percent by year-end, Prell made no bones about the potential consequences. "We are skirting zero growth here by a small margin. And certainly a small hiccup in the economy in an adverse way could tip this into negative territory. So I would say that with this kind of outlook there is a non-negligible risk of at least a mild downturn in the economy."

Greenspan had been able to pull together a broad consensus over the past year in raising rates to contain inflation, but now here was Prell openly flirting with recession. It did not sit well with some, as this Dr. Strangelove–like colloquy between the blithely draconian Prell and a somewhat aghast Vice Chairman Johnson illustrates:

> **JOHNSON:** We have gotten into these arguments before about what potential is, but I think everybody agrees that [1.2 percent real GNP growth] is well below whatever anybody thinks of as potential. And that's for a significant period of time.
>
> **PRELL:** Let me say first that it takes a period of below potential growth in order for some slack to open up in the labor market in particular. . . .
>
> **JOHNSON:** I know, but there's a year of that kind of slack. And I just wondered. . . .
>
> **PRELL:** But, as you know, in our forecast that only brings the unemployment rate up to about 6 percent. . . . [T]hat's only getting us back to the natural rate. . . . [A]s we move up to the 6 percent neighborhood and edge above it by the end of 1990, we are anticipating that we will begin to see some tendency toward moderation in the underlying inflation trend. . . .
>
> **JOHNSON:** But if you're just saying that we're moving to the natural rate why would you get below potential growth on that?
>
> **PRELL:** Well, to raise the unemployment rate you have to move below potential growth. . . .
>
> **JOHNSON:** . . . The Blue Chip consensus [of private economic forecasters] expect a decline in short-term interest rates by the second quarter whereas we're saying they need to go to a percentage point higher.
>
> **PRELL:** . . . There continues to be some difference of opinion between the staff and that average in terms of how much weakness is likely to occur in aggregate demand as a consequence of the tightening that has occurred already. . . . I think what we have built into the remainder of this year is not very large. In fact, I will venture to say that it might not be large enough. . . .

Melzer was concerned that judging the strength of the economy by looking at the latest months' economic statistics would lead the Fed into "a trap" because of the lags with which past rate hikes would take effect in the future. "By the time we see the weakness it could be too late, and when we do see the weakness we probably will continue to see price pressure. What do we do then?" In a lighter moment after a coffee break, Greenspan informed the committee the dollar, bonds, and stocks were all up and asked, "What do they know that we don't?" "Plenty of confidence in us, that's all," Syron replied. "Well, they're in a lot of trouble," Kohn said. Despite some officials' concerns that the Fed was going too far, others saw plenty of economic strength and saw inflation ahead. Greenspan's opinion was that, while the economic outlook was "generally uncertain, . . . the odds are that what we're going through now is more likely to be a pause rather than the beginning of a downturn." So the FOMC adjourned leaving policy unchanged, which meant keeping the funds rate in the 9¾ to 9⅞ percent range, but it gave Greenspan leeway to raise interest rates if he saw fit.

Greenspan never had to exercise that prerogative. Within the next few weeks, there were further indications in employment, industrial production, auto sales, and other data that the economy was weakening. In their unique way, Fed officials were grateful but wanted to see more. "There are some signs that would indicate there is a slowdown," but "we can't be certain it's baked in the cake," Syron said in an April 7 interview. The economy "has to grow slower than its potential for some time to get back to a rate of price increase that is acceptable." Seger reminded me she "was concerned in February we might be going too far." Around mid-April, allies Angell and Johnson began hinting the Fed had tightened enough; privately they were conspiring to move policy in the other direction. In fact, Angell made a bet with Kohn and Prell that the Fed would be lowering the funds rate before long. There were still some full-throated hawks, like Hoskins, who wanted to reach zero inflation as fast as possible. But most of the hawks were beginning to sound more dovish.

Bush, meanwhile, was being advised that the Fed was about to catapult the economy into recession. At a weekend economic "roundtable" at Camp David in late April, Bush surrounded himself with Brady, Boskin, Darman, and White House chief of staff John Sununu, as well as a number of top economists from outside the administration, including Volcker and Sprinkel. Bush was told the Fed was "running a very big risk of overdoing its restraint, and if it continues at this pace we run the risk of causing a recession later this year or maybe next year," according to a participant. So when, in early May, the Labor Department reported a 0.3 percent leap in unemployment, administration officials were primed and ready. Boskin advised the Fed not to "overdo any monetary tightening and cause a recession" on May 9. He called for a monetary policy which "predictably controls inflation while providing enough liquidity to sustain growth." He hoped the Fed had "paused to see what effects its past tightening moves will have on the economy." Boskin also hinted the president's famous "read my lips, no new taxes" pledge was not as ironclad as it purported to be. "The president wants to be absolutely sure that there is no tax increase in the first year and do everything he can to make sure there is no tax increase in the full four years." It was the first sign that Bush was willing to cut a budget deal with Congress if it meant getting lower interest rates.

At the May 16 FOMC meeting, Angell and Johnson were determined to move the Fed out of its 14-month-old credit tightening posture, but it wasn't going to be easy. Although Kohn had publicly stated there were "a lot of indications that monetary tightening has been having an effect on the economy," putting it "on a slower growth trajectory," the staff still wanted to squeeze growth out of the economy. Though "more confident," the economy was indeed slowing, Prell maintained, "What is in prospect is a period of slow growth, rather than imminent recession." With inflation still threatening, what was needed was "a substantial slowing." Far from easing, Prell told the committee, "We have retained our forecast that the necessary monetary restraint will be associated with somewhat higher interest rates in the second half of this year." Some members were growing impatient with Prell's projections and prescriptions. When he repeated his call for a 10¾ percent federal funds rate by year-end, Heller could not believe his ears: "Mike, what did you say? I didn't hear you. By the end of the year?" Johnson observed that financial markets "have been giving us a slightly different picture for some time now," namely a decline in rates as the economy slowed. He told Prell a further rate hike of the type he advocated "puts you in the recession category." Prell conceded, "We're very close to recession in this forecast in the first part of 1990." Angell pointed to the dramatic deceleration of the money supply. M2 had slowed to a growth rate of only 3 percent in the second half of 1988 and in the first half of 1989 had nearly stopped growing. During the first five months of 1989, M2 grew just 0.2 percent at an annual rate, compared to the Fed's 3 to 7 percent target. Kohn cited a variety of reasons not to be concerned about weak M2, such as the flight of deposits from failing S&Ls and larger federal tax payments, but Angell warned against "the extremism of letting the monetary aggregates fall out of bed" when the economy was already slowing. Just leaving rates unchanged would be tantamount to credit tightening. "Declining monetary aggregates in the face of an economy that shows some signs of slowing actually could give you a tightening of monetary policy while interest rates appear to be stable." Others shared Angell's concerns.

Melzer was "increasingly concerned that, with virtually no M1 [money supply] growth since July of last year, the risks of recession either later this year or early next year are becoming considerably greater. . . . If we wait to see signs of recession, given the lags in the impact of monetary policy, it's basically going to be too late." He called for the Fed to ease, warning fighting inflation would be harder in the long run "if we destabilize the economy through a monetary policy that's too tight." Kelley thought, "We're probably getting to the point where it should be on the table for us to keep a weather eye out to the possibility of a substantially worse result than anyone has heretofore addressed. We now see an economy that is slowing to an extent that I think surprises all of us a little. . . . I'm not sure that we can be very confident that we're not beginning to see the first of some downside momentum here." LaWare warned, "Further tightness may only aggravate some of the problems that we have." He had been warning about the impact of the Fed's tight credit stance on "fragile" financial institutions since the day he arrived, but had never dissented against raising rates. "I was still sort of feeling my way in terms of, 'were my analytical abilities superior to those of my colleagues as well as the staff?' " he explains. "At that point I think I was still learning, and my negative vote wouldn't have meant a whole lot." Now, others were adopting his view, although they still doubted recession was coming.

Greenspan was beginning to give as well. Stoltenberg, among others, had been leaning on Greenspan to lower rates to halt the dollar's rise. The Bundesbank had raised its discount and Lombard rates a half percent to 4½ and 6½ percent respectively on April 20, and he wanted to see the Fed lower rates so their combined actions would narrow interest rate differentials favoring the dollar's rise against the mark. In the same hope, the Bank of Japan would soon raise its discount rate 75 basis points to 3¼ percent. The Germans and Japanese had their sympathizers at the Treasury, where a senior official told me the situation "will be improved if other countries raise their interest rates or if we lower our interest rates." Treasury had a less than consistent position. At the same time, Brady was urging Germany and Japan to avoid "restrictive policies" and stimulate demand.

Greenspan was still not convinced easing was needed. While the economy had clearly slowed, he saw no evidence of a "cumulative" downswing that heralded recession. But, sensing the tide had turned, he told the committee, "We have moved . . . from a tilt toward inflation being more probable and are now closer to some form of symmetry." Then, too, the Treasury bill rate had trended down in anticipation of a lower funds rate, and leaving the funds rate unchanged could mean keeping policy "actually tighter than I think the markets perceive us to be going." The chairman asked for and got a "symmetric" policy directive, abandoning the tightening bias of the March 28 meeting. The funds rate would stay in the 9¾ to 9⅞ percent, but there was no longer a predisposition to raise it further. Angell urged Greenspan to convene an FOMC teleconference before the July 5–6 FOMC meeting if the money supply did not recover. Greenspan agreed there might be a need for an intermeeting conference call because "we are in a very sensitive period." The stage had been set for a 180-degree policy shift. Angell says he and Johnson voted for the February rate hike and the March tilt toward tightening "to put ourselves in a position to be able to lead the charge to bring interest rates down because we knew that monetary policy was sufficiently restrained. . . ." He crows that he "won" his bet with Kohn and Prell at the May meeting, but "whenever the Fed changes policy directions, you have to win in one meeting and let everybody get used to it, and then you get the vote the following meeting. Manley and I carried the day at the May meeting that we had to lower rates, but we didn't get around to doing it until the June meeting."

Two weeks after the May 16 meeting, the FOMC held the first of two conference calls. Greenspan's assessment of economic risks had taken a nasty turn. "I personally am concerned about what in fact is going on out there," he said in the May 31 call. "People to whom I'm talking are indicating to me for the first time a degree of softness, especially on the price side." He proposed to cut the funds rate unless upcoming economic data proved strong. Finally, in a June 5 call, the FOMC took stock of weak money supply, employment, commodity prices, factory orders, and other indicators and decided to lower the borrowings target from $600 million to $500 million with the aim of reducing the funds rate to 9½ percent to 9⅝ percent. It was just the first of a long series of rate cuts that would culminate in a 3 percent funds rate in September 1992. Administration officials were pleased the Fed had finally started lowering rates, but made clear they thought the Fed had a long way to go.

The easing process continued at the July 5–6 FOMC meetings, notwithstanding staff recommendations against further rate cuts. In fact, the staff was calling for a rise in rates, although it had by now abandoned its call for pushing the funds rate to 10¼ percent. The staff forecast allowed for real GNP growth of just 1½ percent, which would mean unemployment would rise from 5.3 percent to more than 6 percent—"enough slack to put downward pressure on wage and price inflation," as Prell said. "Restraint on economic expansion is necessary if there is to be a diminution in the underlying pace of inflation." Although long-term rates had fallen sharply, the economy was not responding, and this worried many officials. Sales of autos and other goods were off, as were orders for big ticket "durable goods." Production had turned flat. The beige book had detected "ebbing rates of expansion." The staff blamed an unanticipated rise in the dollar for depressing export-oriented production. Corrigan scoffed, saying he knew no manufacturers who thought the dollar's rise had crimped their orders.

Many officials who had earlier been worried about too much growth now had a different worry. Boehne was still hoping for a "soft landing," but said, "The chances of a bumpier landing have increased." Greenspan said he sensed an inventory *backup*—an accumulation of unsold goods that can lead to production cutbacks, layoffs, and a downward spiral into recession. The yield curve had become inverted with the overnight funds rate nearly 1½ percent above the yield on 30-year bonds, another danger sign. With the markets expecting lower rates businesspeople and consumers might delay investments and expenditures, amplifying the slowdown. Furthermore, if interest rates were not reduced, the stock market could become "vulnerable to flight," Johnson warned. Indeed, if the Fed didn't "keep up with events," it could find itself in a Depression-type situation where "the Fed drove interest rates gradually down to 0 in the 1930s and it didn't do a blessed thing to stop the economy's decline." LaWare said the Fed dare not disappoint expectations of lower rates. The markets were "extremely skittish" and the financial system "rather narrowly balanced." Corporations had large amounts of debt to service at high rates and pension funds and S&Ls were loaded up with high-yield junk bonds. Depressed real estate values and continued Third World loan problems were pinching bank profits. "So a significant turndown in the economy could cause all that to get out of whack and have a ripple effect throughout the whole financial system that I think could be very severe. . . . I think there are great expecations out there for lower rates, and the disappointment of those expectations could result in an acceleration of the slowdown that could take it out of hour hands."

Others were willing to risk economic weakness if it meant beating inflation. Noting the staff was forecasting 4 to 5 percent inflation through 1991 despite weak growth, Hoskins declared that unless the Fed became "more aggressive . . . we shouldn't kid ourselves that we're after price stability because we're not." Corrigan said the Fed had no hope of stopping inflation from accelerating, much less reducing it, unless it developed "a fair amount of slack in the economy," which is Fedspeak for increasing the rate of unemployment and reducing the pace at which factories were running. He was "quite prepared to accept running some risk of the kind of slow growth that is built into the staff forecast and maybe even growth that is a little slower than that." Aside from wanting to slow the economy to defeat inflation the blunt-spoken New York Fed president said "the external side of our economy still stinks; there's no other way to put it." The U.S. *international net investment position*—the amount of claims Americans hold abroad relative to the claims foreigners hold on the United States—had gone from positive in the early eighties to a negative 12.4 percent in 1989 and was projected to rise to a negative 14 percent in 1990. America had become a net debtor nation because it was spending more than it saved and borrowing the rest abroad. A growing proportion of government securities sold to finance the budget deficit and the interest on old debt was held by, among others, the Japanese, who had billions of surplus trade dollars they needed to invest somewhere. The Japanese just then were buying Rockefeller Center and other high-profile assets. The deteriorating U.S. external position was "trouble looking for a place to happen, and it's going to come home to roost on us sooner or later," said Corrigan. If Congress would not balance the budget, the only way to redress the savings shortfall and stop the slide into deeper external debt was to slow private sector spending.

Faced with the task of molding a compromise between these extremes, Greenspan told the FOMC he had his own concerns about slow money growth and signs of an unplanned inventory accumulation, but did not want to cut rates too aggressively. "The worst thing that can happen to us, as far as policy is concerned, is that we are perceived to be easing too fast and in a manner which would open up the possibilities of inflationary expectations." He persuaded the FOMC to cut the funds rate another quarter percent to a 9¼ to 9⅜ percent target range, with the proviso the Fed would then have no predisposition to either cut or raise rates. The FOMC reaffirmed its 3 to 7 percent growth range for M2, an action Johnson ridiculed. "The way in which we conduct monetary policy, these monetary aggregates are simply passive proxies for what the economy generates through money demand. This is not a money supply process. We are setting interest rates and the economy is reacting to those interest rates and it's demanding money. . . . We are not setting any money supply goal and supplying that amount of reserves to make sure [we achieve it]. . . . And we shouldn't kid ourselves and think that we're supplying levels that are being generated through our policy."

Battle lines were also drawn at the July meeting on an issue that would come to a head a few months later—the degree to which the Fed should be helping hold down the dollar through intervention in the currency markets. The dollar had been shooting up against other major currencies since the start of the year despite G-7 efforts to halt it, and although it was well below its May highs, it was still 10 percent above where it had been in December. From a 1988 low of 121 yen and 1.71 marks, the dollar had risen to as high as 144 yen and 2.02 marks. The administration and some Fed officials were afraid it would make U.S. exports uncompetitive and widen the trade deficit, which had been laboriously worked down to just over $8 billion in April, compared to monthly deficits in the $15 to $16 billion range a couple of years earlier. Were the gap to begin widening again, protectionist fervor in Congress would heat up again. For a while, U.S. authorities had been willing to accept some modest appreciation. On March 24, when the dollar was trading around 1.87 marks and 131 yen, a senior Treasury official told me he did "not think [the dollar's strength was] yet a problem" and that the trade deficit could continue to fall in 1989, though by only half as much as the $30 billion it had been trimmed in 1988. But when the dollar continued to soar, the Treasury hit the panic button. "The longer we have a strong dollar, the greater the likelihood it would have a discouraging effect on our exports," a Brady aide said in mid-June.

The Germans and Japanese, distressed at seeing capital draining out of their economies into dollar assets and at having to pay more for dollar-priced imports as their currencies fell, had pressured Greenspan and Brady to halt the dollar's rise at an April 2 G-7 meeting, both by reducing interest rates and selling dollars. In a communiqué, the finance ministers and central bankers "agreed that a rise of the dollar which undermined adjustment efforts, or an excessive decline, would be counterproductive" and agreed to "cooperate closely on exchange markets." What this new, more assertive language meant was heavier than ever intervention to restrain, if not reverse, the dollar's rise. In addition to selling dollars, the Bundesbank and the Bank of Japan raised rates. The Treasury wanted the Fed to reinforce the German and Japanese rate hikes by lowering its rates to make the dollar less attractive. Even the White House got into the dollar-bashing act on May 22 as the greenback broke through the 2-mark and 140-yen barriers on the upside. Departing from his standard "we don't comment on the dollar" line, Fitzwater said, "The dollar's recent rise against other major currencies is a matter of concern. . . . If the dollar's recent rise against other major currencies is prolonged or extended, it could undermine efforts to reduce global trade imbalances." So the United States would be "cooperating in exchange markets" to weaken the dollar. Even the president expressed "concern" about the dollar's strength.

To stem its rise, the Treasury had cajoled the Fed into selling dollars, not just for the Treasury's account but also for the Fed's account. (Typically, the Treasury and Fed, each with their own pools of foreign exchange, go 50-50 on intervention efforts). Just since the May meeting the two together had sold nearly $10 billion against marks and yen. Since these operations flooded the market with new dollars, the Fed had sterilized them by draining reserves domestically or by not adding as many reserves to the banking system when needed. In acting as the Treasury's agent, the Fed "warehouses" foreign currencies for the Treasury's Exchange Stabilization Fund (ESF). Basically, the Treasury transfers foreign exchange from the ESF to the Fed, which then credits the Treasury with dollars at the appropriate exchange rate. Fed holdings of foreign currencies had grown 50 percent in the space of just a few months to $30 billion, exposing the Fed to potential losses if those currencies' value fell. The intervention had only limited success. By mid-June, the dollar had risen to a two-year high of nearly 149 yen and 2.03 marks, and the administration's effort to talk down the dollar and pressure the Fed into lowering rates became more desperate than ever. Commerce secretary Robert Mosbacher, ordinarily under instructions not to talk about the dollar, said, "The recent strength of the dollar leads us to be concerned about the economy's ability to sustain the excellent [trade] trends seen so far." On June 29, the Bundesbank again raised the discount and Lombard rates a half percent to 5 and 7 percent, respectively.

Increasingly, Fed officials regarded this whole exchange rate rat race as a harmful distraction from the Fed's domestic goals. The Fed had been buying marks and yen covertly, using a commercial bank to make the transactions on its behalf, rather than intervene openly in the name of the central bank. "In operating more discreetly we have been able to kind of encourage the dollar down without appearing to try to take on the market in a direct way," Cross told the FOMC. An outraged Angell pounced on Cross. "I just do not agree that it's appropriate for us to act in ways that are intended to confuse the markets or mislead the markets," he declared. "I just don't hold that these kinds of moves make that much difference. But even if they did, I do not believe it's appropriate for a government agency in a market society to be acting in such a manner." This secretive dollar selling "tended to disrupt the normal market processes," and using a commercial bank as agent created the danger of insider trading. He served notice that if the dollar sales continued he would vote against the usually pro forma approval of the New York Fed's foreign exchange operations.

Johnson even suggested the Fed tell Treasury it would no longer use its own funds to intervene but would only act on Treasury's behalf. Cross and Truman hastened to quash that idea. They were afraid such an ultimatum would cause the Treasury to usurp the Fed's authority in the foreign exchange area. "The worst of all possible worlds would be to give the Treasury the authority to dictate to the Federal Reserve to do it for its own account," Truman warned. "Then the Federal Reserve would have no influence over the amount of sterilized intervention that took place. . . ." For someone supposedly just doing what Treasury had requested, Cross seemed entirely too enthusiastic about intervention. The former Treasury staffer said intervention had been conducted "to attempt to shield the economy and domestic financial markets from the full force of potentially reversible and destabilizing pressures in the exchange market. It is hard to see what possible gain there would be from a further sharp and unsustainable rise in the dollar from the levels it had reached." Seeking to defuse the issue, Greenspan said it looked to him like the dollar's recent strength had been just "a bubble that is going to turn down and make the issue moot at some point." In fact, the issue would be revisited even more vocally at later meetings.

Within a few weeks of the July FOMC meeting, rising levels of unemployment insurance claims, weakening factory orders, and other weak signs convinced Greenspan further rate cuts were needed and couldn't wait for the next meeting on August 22. Predicting the economy would slow in coming months, he warned the House Banking Committee this "softness conceivably could cumulate and deepen, resulting in a substantial downturn in activity." Although the FOMC had adopted a "symmetrical" directive, he informed the FOMC in a July 26 conference call he had used his discretion to lower the funds rate another quarter percent to 9 to 9⅛ percent. At the same time, he advised caution because of a "worrisome acceleration" of the money supply and surging home sales. "Having made this move, we should probably stay put for a while until we see how the money supply works out and how a number of other elements within the economy continue to move." A few days later he told the Senate Banking Committee monetary policy was now "on the right track." The Fed would stay put until mid-October.

The Fed was preoccupied not just with the business cycle, but with the politicized budget cycle. For the Fed to calculate how much credit it needed to provide to sustain expansion, while making progress against inflation, the Fed needed to know how much fiscal stimulus the government would be providing via the budget deficit, but the fiscal 1990 budget was still up in the air. In April, the White House and Congress had reached an agreement that would have met the Gramm-Rudman deficit target of $100 billion, but it had never been implemented. The Fed could only guess at what the deficit would be doing to the economy. A larger deficit would tend to stimulate demand, but the Fed had no way of knowing how much. Adding to the uncertainty, the Resolution Trust Corporation (RTC) had just been created on August 9 as part of the far-reaching Financial Institutions Reform, Recovery and Enforcement Act (FIR-REA) to take over the job of liquidating hundreds of insolvent thrifts—an enormous task that would add to the deficit. Already the RTC had borrowed more than $6 billion to fund the process of seizing sick thrifts, selling their assets (often at deep discounts to their stated worth), and paying off insured depositors. No one knew how much it would all cost or what the economic effect would be of dumping billions of dollars worth of depressed real estate on an already shaky market.

In this uncertain atmosphere, a heated debate took place at the August FOMC meeting over whether the Fed should cut rates further, despite Greenspan's stated preference for a pause in the easing process. The Fed staff was still assuming no change in rates for the forseeable future—an assumption that did not sit well with some. Kelley warned the cost of the thrift crisis "could just go completely out of sight if we get into a recession scenario," and that efforts to reduce the budget deficit would "go into a cocked hat completely." The Fed had to be "careful we don't push our luck too hard." Seger said the construction business had gotten so bad the last job her contractor brother had gotten in Arizona was building a bankruptcy court. Auto dealers had become so desperate to sell cars that "once these new 1990 models come in, if any people can be pulled off the streets into the showrooms to look at the cars, I think they're going to fall flat on the floor when they see the stickers." LaWare was frustrated inflation had not come down more than it had but said, "If the only way to really knock inflation down is to have a recession, that's a very unwelcome alternative option. We talk about a soft landing, but this kind of landing looks more to me like being stuck in the mud." On the other hand,

Corrigan objected to a policy that accepted inflation of 4 to 5 percent "stretch-ing out as far as the eye can see . . . I don't see the light at the end of the tun-nel." The big risk was that the economy might grow too fast to reduce inflation. "Of all the ugly things that we could think about that one gets pretty ugly." Greenspan agreed, "That is the worst scenario that we could face, because I think at that point monetary policy becomes impotent." "Monetary policy that always attempts to preempt recessions is going to end up biasing toward inflation and lower output over time," said Hoskins. The FOMC left rates unchanged but gave its directive a tilt toward easing.

Fed-Treasury tensions over dollar policy continued to fester. Although the dollar was down from its highs, the New York Fed had continued to sell dol-lars when it rallied in collaboration with Treasury, to the annoyance of officials like Angell. Not content with the Fed's cooperation on intervention, adminis-tration officials were also leaning on the Fed to cut interest rates to weaken the dollar as the trade deficit widened. Darman, who had helped Baker manipulate exchange rates, had gone on NBC-TV's *Meet The Press* before the FOMC met and openly criticized the Fed for keeping rates too high and keeping the dol-lar overvalued. Some thought Darman had gone off the reservation in making his unusually direct attack on the Fed until Bush defended Darman's com-ments as "very balanced." Privately, Treasury officials were also leaning on the Fed to soften the dollar. Angell thought the Fed staff was too cozy with Trea-sury on intervention and also objected to the staff's assumption that the dollar needed to fall by 10 percent. Others were also uncomfortable. "You can't ignore your currency, but in terms of letting it guide monetary policy, I don't think we can, particularly at this juncture," Guffey told me. Black had "grave doubts" about what the Fed and Treasury had been doing. "Within the system, there isn't a lot of sympathy for doing any more than we have. Price stability should be our prime goal."[2]

When the G-7 met in Washington on September 22, there was little evi-dence of "cooperation." Less than two weeks before the G-7 met, Mulford, who was basically running dollar policy for a disinterested Brady and was con-tinuing Baker's interventionist policies, blasted away at the Germans, Japa-nese, and anyone else he could hit. The Germans were keeping the mark "undervalued" and building up trade surpluses not just with the United States but with other nations in Europe. France he criticized for refusing to accept any devaluation of the franc and delaying a needed realignment of the ERM currency parities. Japan had not been forthcoming in the "structural impedi-ment initiative" talks designed to make Japan more open to American exports. "We've had no success whatsoever getting Germany and Japan to stop build-ing surpluses with the rest of the world," Mulford said. It was not a message well-received by either country, which felt the United States' own profligate ways were at the root of its deficit problems. Not long ago, the Treasury had been urging those same countries to raise rates to boost their currencies against the dollar—hardly measures likely to stimulate demand for U.S. exports. Despite this rancor, the G-7 cobbled together a communiqué with another new foreign exchange twist: The dollar's rise had been "inconsistent with longer run economic fundamentals." The finance ministers and central bankers "agreed that a rise of the dollar above current levels or an excessive decline could adversely affect prospects for the world economy." The day before the dollar had closed at 1.9510 marks and 145.90 yen, up from 1.8960 marks and 132.65 yen at the time of the April 2 G-7 meeting. Yet this G-7 language was weaker than in April, when the operative phrase was that "a rise of the dollar which undermined adjustment efforts . . . would be counterproductive." The change of wording from "would" to "could" seemed to signify less will among the G-7 to battle the currency markets, whose volume on any given day dwarfed any amount of resources they could bring to bear. Trying to counter a currency trend was like spitting into the wind, and many officials recognized that.

Mulford and his counterparts labored long crafting these communiqués, and it was always a challenge to figure out what the nuances meant. But Brady told reporters after the meeting that "there's no reason" for this ostensibly meaningful wording change. "If we don't change any word at all, we are accused of merely repeating," said Britain's Lawson. "If we do change a single word, people attach great significance to it. This makes drafting a communiqué extremely difficult. Perhaps it would be better to have no communiqué at all." Most forthcoming was French finance minister Pierre Beregevoy, who later committed suicide, albeit not out of frustration with G-7 communiqués. What it meant was that "the dollar is too high, but it shouldn't go too low; we should find something in between." It did not mean monetary policy would be used to realign exchange rates. Lawson, new German finance minister Theo Waigel and new Japanese finance minister Ryutaro Hashimoto were tired of raising rates to hold down the dollar. As Lawson put it, "Each country has to decide what level of interest rates is appropriate for that country in light of economic conditions in that country." They had good reason to suspect the dollar would soon weaken. Meanwhile, the G-7 would keep, well, spitting into the wind.

A rift between Greenspan and Brady became evident at the G-7 meeting. It was obvious that, while Brady felt the funds rate was too high, Greenspan was "still concerned with inflation and thinks it's premature to do anything with interest rates," said a European source. Greenspan was in a difficult spot. The Fed had already cut the funds rate three times, and was prepared to do more, but he did not feel an urgency to cut rates further and did not want to be rushed into doing so to meet the Treasury's exchange rate objectives. Although it was forecasting some dollar depreciation, the Fed feared an excessive dollar decline would worsen inflation; yet it was being dragooned by Treasury into intervening to push the dollar down or at least prevent it from rising. The Treasury was working hand in glove with the Japanese Ministry of Finance to target a lower dollar. "There was a bit of an alliance," says Dallara. "The Japanese were exceptionally anxious not to have the yen falling through the floor at that point. . . . And it seemed to me that although we did not want to go too strongly to the rescue . . . we didn't want to completely ignore their pleas." Greenspan was unenthusiastic about manipulating exchange rates but felt bound by tradition to do as Treasury asked and went along to minimize the damage, rather than provoke an open confrontation. He was not willing to cut interest rates for exchange rate purposes, however, unless it could be justified for other reasons.

Dissension on the FOMC over the degree to which the Fed should cooperate with Treasury on exchange rates boiled over at its October 3 meeting. At the outset, Angell and Johnson led a rebellion against the Fed's collaboration with Treasury to depress the dollar. Cross revealed the New York Fed had been selling dollars along with other central banks with some success. From the time of the G-7 meeting until the FOMC met, the dollar had fallen 3.7 percent against the mark and 4.4 percent against the yen. In that time frame, the Fed had bought, both for its own account and Treasury's, more than $1.4 billion worth of marks and yen. Cross boasted he had performed "a delicate balancing act" between "not driving down the dollar in a falling market" and not selling dollars aggressively enough. "It was recognized by the G-7 that if we operated only to cushion the pace of the dollar's rise and not turn it around, the market's strongly positive attitude toward the dollar would not weaken." He had sold dollars "less defensively than before"—a euphemism for aggressive dollar sales.

This was not what many wanted to hear. "You mentioned that the strategy was generally to resist upward pressure, but there were times repeatedly when there was a concerted effort to drive the dollar lower and then, as it ratcheted down, to hammer it when it even started to show any upward pressure from lower levels," Johnson charged. "So, I think it's a bit of a semantic issue to talk about resisting upward pressure when in fact it was a clear strategy to ratchet down the dollar." Noting the Fed had even sold dollars in the Far East, he accused Cross of "grossly destabilizing" actions. "I thought it was a scary event, and I can't see us condoning that sort of a strategy. I think it's potentially very, very dangerous." Cross denied "hammering" the dollar and said he had merely been acting within G-7 guidelines to "bring about greater stability and to reduce the dollar somewhat." A party to the G-7 pact, Greenspan said it was not meant to fix a lower range for the dollar. "I think the best way of describing the agreement is that there would be moderate intervention and if that intervention knocked the dollar down significantly, which it did, that was fine, but if it did not, there was no agreement to just use unlimited resources to break the market." The central banks had insisted that "any evidence of a cumulative deterioration [in the dollar's value] would have induced a real pull back. It really wasn't country versus country. It was finance ministers against central bank governors."

The day before the meeting, Cross's crew had intervened five times and spent $400 million when the dollar had gone over 139 yen in an unsuccessful effort to keep it from going above 140. Hearing Cross explain his tactics, Johnson cracked, "You can imagine the uncertainty that might be out in the market if we can't even figure out what's going on." Greenspan said, "That's not quite fair." Corrigan told Johnson he was "shooting the messenger." Boehne warned the heavy intervention might make the markets believe the G-7 were planning monetary moves to set exchange rates, since intervention alone would only have a "temporary influence." Greenspan assured everyone he had made no pledges to back up intervention with interest rate changes. He agreed intervention unsupported by fundamental changes was ineffective, but said finance ministers did not realize that. "There is an [adjective deleted] belief now, particularly among the Japanese that, sterilized intervention can put the exchange rate where they want it."

Realizing his colleagues were fed up with taking orders from Treasury to batter the dollar, whose value they were supposed to be defending, Greenspan laid out for them the whole sorry G-7 political picture with which he had to contend. "There is no enthusiasm [for intervention] among any of the central bankers. I don't even think the Bank of France is enthusiastic. The two leading prongs are the U.S. Treasury and the Ministry of Finance of Japan. There has been a pulling and tugging on this of rather large dimensions." Greenspan said he and other central bankers discouraged the finance ministers from greater intervention. Worse, "what we have been fending off, successfully so far, is pressure that was not too subtly brought forth before the G-7 meeting to bring the central banks into this whole game. In other words, essentially the G-7 would start to control monetary policy. And I think that was fended off pretty abruptly. There was a feeble attempt to put that in the communiqué. That was knocked out very quickly before things got moving."

Greenspan continued:

> Our problem, basically, is that at this stage we could probably as central banks— we could at the Fed—create a really big fuss about this. As you know, legally, the presumption is that the president, through the secretary of the Treasury, has full control over the issue of intervention policy. It has never really been tested. We have always had a partial voice; in other words, when Messrs. Brady and Mulford started to talk about [a target of] 125 for the yen and 1.75 for the mark, I protested to a point where I suggested that they would pull the system apart. And I got that eliminated. So they did have targets. The trouble is if we ever tried to get to those targets, we'd have the world's most awful mess on our hands. There is a limit as to what we can do short of confrontation. I don't think it serves either the Fed or the country to try to be actually up front and to bring this operation to an abrupt halt. I think we could do it. In other words, if that were our objective—forgetting all the secondary costs—I have no doubt that we could do it. I just think that it would be far better not to try that and, hopefully, keep this constrained at a level where the damage is minimal.

There were two thorns in his side. Hashimoto, Japan's eventual prime minister, "strikes me as a fixed exchange rate man, an interventionist who is willing to expend large resources to create changes. He came over to me just before the G-7 meeting started and said, if we can't get the Germans to join us we would like to join you, meaning the United States, in extensive exchange rate intervention." Then there was Mulford. "We have had philosophical and other differences with him on this and other issues for quite a while." But he thought he could defang Mulford. "We do have significant influence in that operation. In other words, it's not without possibilities."[3]

Greenspan reassured the FOMC that, "having seen an earlier version of intervention really almost kick over the bond market" (in October 1987), he would not let the Fed get dragged into so much intervention that it would distort monetary policy or let it become directly involved in setting exchange rates. "I don't know what the end result of this thing will be, but if the dollar all of a sudden starts to strengthen I will try as hard as I can to convince Secretary Brady that this is a futile effort, that the markets are trying to tell us something, and that to fight against it is a rather fruitless task," he pledged. "Whether I will succeed, I don't know." Corrigan, whose bank's foreign exchange operations were being challenged, agreed that "trying to beat down the dollar is a very, very dangerous thing," but said something had to be done to reduce trade imbalances and warned against a confrontation with Treasury. Johnson was not mollified. "Why should central banks be participating in this exercise?" Helping finance ministries "ratchet down" the dollar was in direct conflict with the Fed's stated goal of price stability. "We've been making statements about price stability now to the point where I think we have almost been a 'johnny-one-note' on that issue. And people, I think, are starting to believe us. For us to be countering that with this ridiculous approach just doesn't make sense; [it introduces] a potential doubt out there. If central banks continue to participate in this kind of strategy and show even a compromise on it, I think to some extent the markets are going to say this is a joke—in fact, they are balancing the goals of the current account versus price stability."

Greenspan promised to tell Brady how upset the FOMC members were about the intervention, but that wasn't good enough for some. On the table was Cross's request for approval of his operations, and soon he would need additional authority to purchase foreign currencies. The limit on Cross's ability to acquire foreign exchange had already been increased several times to $20 billion, but recent operations had brought him within $1.5 billion of that ceiling. Some did not want to authorize anything. Johnson thought it was pointless to be approving limits on the Fed's foreign exchange holdings when the Treasury seemed to be running the show. "Why do we even care about it? Let's just turn over open market operations on foreign exchange to the Treasury. What are we going through this silly exercise for if we don't have something to say about it?" Greenspan informed him that, although the Treasury had the lead role in dollar policy, the Fed did have 40 percent control. That being the case, Johnson suggested the Fed inform the Treasury it would no longer use its own resources to intervene, but merely act at arm's length as the Treasury's agent. "Acquiring exchange reserves on our account when we are totally opposed to the direction of policy that takes implicates us in the policy," he declared. While cooperation was okay up to a point, "when I perceive that we're getting to a point where we are literally taking risks and we are moving in a direction counter to our whole philosophy, it seems to me that we've got to stand up and be counted here. This whole thing runs the risk of implicating us in something when we are out there saying we are standing for price stability."

Johnson, who had been at Treasury until 1986, had a low opinion of the current occupants. "Continuing to acquire exchange reserves and exposure on our own account is really risky, especially given what I know about people over there running things at the Treasury. I don't think it's Nick Brady myself. I think you have a green eyeshade person in David Mulford over there who doesn't know what he's doing. And I think it's very risky to turn over policy to somebody like that." Although she had been concerned about the strong dollar's adverse trade impact, Seger said she did "not believe the way to get the dollar down is to bomb it through intervention." LaWare likened the dollar to a swimmer. "Sooner or later, even the strongest swimmer is going to go to the bottom if you push his head under water again every time he comes to the surface. And I worry that any kind of a free fall in the dollar in the near future could drive people away from dollar-denominated securities and reverse this interest rate structure very dramatically by forcing the financing of our deficits back into our own markets."

Angell liked the idea of threatening to pull out of joint currency operations with Treasury, and said he planned to dissent against approval of Cross's recent intervention to make the threat real. "The Treasury certainly would be dissatisfied to be without us," Angell said. "The thought that we might pull out of this is indeed some force, and my dissent . . . is to contribute to an environment in which the Treasury recognizes that it may not wish to go it alone. I agree it's best for us not to get out. But sometimes we have to act like we might get out. . . ." The Fed could not have a believable commitment to price stability and help the Treasury beat down the dollar. Others were sympathetic but warned against such brinksmanship. "There could come a time, but I don't think this is the time," said Melzer. "If you really want the worst scenario that we're all so terrified of, I'll tell you how you get it," Corrigan said. "That would be to advocate this and then have our 40 percent taken away so it's nothing. And then you would have your green eyeshade guy running the shop." Truman warned Treasury might go to Congress and get authority to force the Fed to do its bidding on the dollar or simply take away the Fed's authority. Corrigan warned a public fight with Treasury "could precipitate the collapse in the dollar and the rout in the bond markets and the stock markets." Guffey warned that "as soon as the public and the market perceive that there's a split I think we have the real possibility of a currency crunch that we will not want to face."

Ultimately, the committee agreed to avoid confrontation and put its faith in Greenspan, who agreed to tell Brady and Mulford about the FOMC's "real deep-seated concern." It might prove "somewhat useful to have some rumbling of a minor nature at this stage," provided it did not become public and rattle the markets. But it was a temporary abatement of hostilities. The following March, Fed dissatisfaction with Treasury-directed intervention against the dollar would cause a breakdown of joint intervention.

One thing the FOMC did not do to help Treasury soften the dollar at its October 3 meeting was cut interest rates. Prell continued to argue the economy was "overemployed" and therefore subject to wage-price pressures. Policymakers were divided. Melzer said it was "very hard to find businessmen who are worried about the economic situation. Nobody grabs you by the lapels and says, 'This thing is going south and you better do something about it.'" But Kelley said it was "hard to see where meaningful strength can come from and relatively easy to see where weakness can come from. . . . We ought to be rather sensitive to emerging weakness and be quite careful that we don't induce something through policy that would turn out to be counterproductive to society in a larger sense." Others also felt the economy needed stimulus, but ironically, the same administration which was so anxious for the Fed to lower rates had made that difficult for the Fed with its weak dollar policy. Angell and Johnson, who had led the charge for lower rates in the spring, felt further easing was needed but that dollar selling made it wise to wait. "It's unfortunate that the G-7 took away what I think may be a time in which we may need to act," Angell said. "Any attempt to ease now, even if we thought it was the right thing to do, would have great risks because the perception [would be] that our goals were associated more with some dollar level than our view about inflationary risks." Greenspan was dubious whether the economy needed lower rates anyway, but concerns about the dollar clinched his argument against immediate action.

Greenspan knew other G-7 central banks were about to raise interest rates. On October 5, the Bundesbank raised its discount and Lombard rates a full percent to 6 and 8 percent, followed swiftly by the Bank of France and Bank of England. On October 11, the Bank of Japan raised its discount rate a half percent to 3¾. A BOJ official denied it was part of a coordinated rate move and insisted it had been taken "to prevent higher inflationary pressures," but admitted exchange rates had been "one factor." Unlike the Bundesbank and the Fed, the BOJ was then "highly controlled by the Finance Ministry in Japan," which was cooperating with the Treasury to lower the dollar, a former Treasury official says. There was considerable suspicion the Fed would reciprocate with rate cuts to depress the dollar. The Fed would, in fact, lower the funds rate soon, but while Mulford would later insinuate the Fed had been party to a coordinated rate move, there is no evidence Greenspan had made such a commitment to the G-7. He advised delaying rate cuts at the FOMC meeting so as not to give that appearance and because he thought easing was premature. "At this particular stage . . . the argument for moving [the funds rate] in either direction is rather dubious . . . moving down right at this moment [is problematical], in light of what is presumed to be an increase in the Bundesbank rates on Thursday and a coordinated attempt on the part of the G-7 to now put monetary policy on the table and bring the dollar down—and believe me it will succeed; it will go right through the floor. If we were to get anywhere close to moving rates down in conjunction with the Bundesbank move, I'm fearful that we would get too much market response as the new G-7 coordinated monetary policy endeavors to bring the dollar down. And I think that would create some really major problems for us." The FOMC gave a reluctant Greenspan leeway to ease before the November 14

FOMC meeting. His hand would soon be forced by market events and some ill-considered press leaks.

Greenspan did not confine himself to private talks with Brady to express the Fed's misgivings over Treasury pressure to loosen monetary policy and soften the dollar. In an October 10 speech in Moscow, where he had gone to provide advice on monetary reform, Greenspan seemed to be addressing the Fed-Treasury relationship before his Russian audience. Noting the Fed had long enjoyed "considerable independence," he said "independence is most important in cases where large fiscal deficits are likely to occur and the private sector savings are subnormal." Emphasizing the importance of price stability as the most important long-run goal of a central bank, Greenspan said, "Too much attention to short-run output goals may lead to high inflation rates and reduced output growth over the long-run." While there were occasions when "short-run stabilization of domestic financial markets or foreign exchange markets" might be appropriate, such preoccupations "may ultimately be counterproductive if they are allowed to obscure or cause long delays in the achievement of price stability." Whether or not Greenspan intended to send him a message, Brady got it (helped by the fact that the Fed chairman's comments had fueled a fresh upsurge in the dollar). Asked about Greenspan's Moscow comments, Brady fumed, "I can't imagine why a guy would go to Moscow to say something he wouldn't say right here."

By mid-October, the economy had taken a turn for the worse. Factory layoffs had soared. Corporate chieftains meeting at Hot Springs, Virginia, clamored for lower interest rates. "We continue to be at a substantial disadvantage to Japan in terms of cost of capital," American Express Company chairman James D. Robinson III declared. "I hope the Fed soon realizes that they can take those rates down." IBM Corporation chairman John Akers claimed his company was having trouble competing with foreign computer makers because high interest rates had pushed the dollar up. "I worry a great deal about interest rates, largely because of the effect on the dollar," concurred Johnson & Johnson chairman James Burke. Pfizer Incorporated chairman Edmund T. Pratt Jr. said the dollar was "too high from the point of view of the way it draws in imports and makes exports harder, and interest rates are one of the ways you cope with that." But the Fed faced a dilemma. Although the economy was slowing, prices were accelerating. The producer price index (PPI) was reported up at a jarring 11 percent annual rate in September.

Then, with little warning, the Fed had to revisit its October 1987 nightmare. On Friday, October 13, after the PPI release, the Dow plunged 190 points—far more than on the Friday before Black Monday in 1987. Once again, heavy selling of stock index futures coincided with an unloading of shares. There was a sense of déjà vu. This new crash seemed to confirm the worst fears of some Fed officials who had warned uncertainties about interest and exchange rates and bickering among central bankers and politicians would spill over into the stock market. In fact, the Dow's plunge in October 1989 had more to do with market disillusionment with the whole leveraged buyout frenzy, sparked by news that a bid for UAL Corporation, parent company of United Airlines, had fallen through. It was also evident some of the reforms put in place since 1987 had made the stock, futures and options markets less subject to disruption. While not to be taken lightly, there was no cause for panic. But on Sunday, an anonymous "senior Fed official" was quoted in the *New York Times* and *Washington Post* as saying, a la 1987, that the Fed was "prepared to inject massive amounts of cash into the banking system" Monday morning to "prevent a financial crisis." Suspecting who that senior Fed official was, I called Manley Johnson at home that Sunday to get my own confirmation or denial. He confirmed the *Post* and *Times* stories as "generally accurate" but downplayed the provision of emergency liquidity as "all in the normal course of events" and said pumping reserves into the system "doesn't have any implications for interest rates."

Greenspan and Corrigan were furious at Johnson. "Alan got really mad at him," a former official recalls. "Alan had plenty of pressure, and this may have been the last straw. . . . I felt pretty bad that he got chewed out." Corrigan still steams over the incident. "It certainly wasn't taken well by me. Of course, at the time I didn't know who had said what. But I was quite angry about it. It was the absolute, classic, worst case moral hazard and all the rest of it. One of the things you learn with these things is you never, ever, ever, ever, ever tip your hand in advance as to what you'll do or what you won't do and under what circumstances you will or won't do it. And not only does it make for lousy public policy but it also creates the worst possible situation in that if you commit yourself to doing something like that and you do it and it doesn't work your credibility is absolutely destroyed. So you just don't do those things!" Greenspan was "not too happy," a Fed official confirms. "Particularly in the light of fairly recent history of just two years before, I don't think the Chairman was just really delighted to have had that happen the way that it did."

Johnson's comment forced the Fed to ease credit whether it wanted to or not. Greenspan had been contemplating another easing move anyway because of deteriorating corporate profits and factory orders, but he did not like having his hand forced. In the first of a series of daily FOMC conference calls early Monday morning, before the New York Stock Exchange opened at 9:30 A.M., Greenspan said the "unauthorized" pledge of emergency liquidity over the weekend had "severely restricted our options or it could," and he begged the other members to "stay away from the press." Corrigan, who was directly responsible for conducting open market operations, told the committee the press stories had "already done some damage in terms of reducing [our] flexibility and undermining discipline in the marketplace." Whoever had made the comments was "amateurish" and had "undercut the character of the Federal Reserve as I have known it for many, many years." Sternlight said he had planned to drain reserves for technical reasons on Monday, but now "the question will be how far we feel committed [to add reserves] by any expectations growing out of those newspaper articles."

The market rallied Monday, but the Fed injected reserves in the morning because that's what the markets had been led to expect, and the Fed was afraid the market might resume its downtrend. There was particular concern about the illiquid junk bond market, especially "punk junk"—the lowest of the lower-rated corporate bonds. Junk bonds had long been around, but now large quantities had been issued to fund corporate takeovers or sometimes to resist them. A number of investment banks, mutual funds, as well as S&Ls, had invested in these high-yield securities and were now trying to sell them into a market in which there were few buyers. Another concern was the suddenly shaky dollar. Corrigan thought the markets were "better off than we were in '87" and had "no sense of a panicky feeling." Even so, he was worried about possible "spillover effects in high-yield markets; there is always the possibility that with markets as they are now, for firms that are trying to restructure an existing deal in bankruptcy, it wouldn't take much for that kind of situation to get pretty ugly." As the Fed added the obligatory reserves, it became apparent the Fed intended to lower the funds rate from 9 to 8¾ percent. On Tuesday, the FOMC met again by phone, relieved the market had rebounded but still anxious. "The presumption that the worst is over is a nice feeling, but I wouldn't want to bet on it," Greenspan said, ordering the open market desk to "continue to operate flexibly" in supplying liquidity. It soon became clear the Fed's worst fears had been unfounded, and when the FOMC members talked the following day the main topic was not the stock market but the devastating earthquake that had just occurred in San Francisco. At the end of the meeting, Greenspan ordered the desk to make permanent the easier credit conditions the Fed had been forced into, but the whole episode left a bad taste.

The stock slide itself had less economic impact than the earthquake, but there were other worrisome tremors running through the economy. Problems with financial institutions were worsening. In the third quarter of 1989, commercial banks reported an aggregate loss of $744 million—their first in two years—as banks set aside large loan loss reserves against nonperforming Third World loans. Banks were busy creating new problems for themselves with real estate lending. Such loans were accounting for two-thirds of banks' asset growth. New England had supplanted the Southwest as the big trouble spot, and its sick banks were becoming a major Fed headache. Fourth-quarter bank earnings were positive but pitiful, as loan losses hit record levels. Five of the ten largest banks in the country reported full-year losses, and 206 banks failed, down only modestly from 1988's record 221. Bad real estate loans, as well as direct investments in real estate and other shaky ventures, had already taken their toll of thrifts; 205 S&Ls with assets of $100 billion had failed in 1988 alone. The RTC, created by Congress on August 9 to take over from the FHLBB the botched job of resolving the thrift crisis, was only starting to clean up that enormous mess. On the day it came into being, the RTC had become custodian of 262 defunct thrifts in 33 states with total assets of $104 billion and total deposits of $89.3 billion. Congress had authorized it to borrow $50 billion to liquidate them. But it would be months before the RTC got cranking selling the assets it had taken in receivership.

It was a multifaceted nightmare for the Fed. The prospect of huge amounts of property being sold into an already soft market threatened to further undermine the housing market. In turn, financial institutions which had so far weathered the storm would weaken. Credit problems could make banks and S&Ls reluctant to lend, hurting otherwise healthy businesses. What's more, the heavy borrowing the RTC would be doing would swell the deficit and keep pressure on long-term interest rates. These contractionary forces made it difficult for the Fed to focus on reducing inflation, which in spite of the slowdown was rising. The Fed faced a tough choice: Should it throw caution to the wind and cut rates aggressively to jump-start the economy and ease pressure on real estate and lenders? Should it stay on its anti-inflation course? Or could it somehow calibrate a policy that would keep the economy moving while making gradual progress against inflation?

On October 25, Greenspan told the House Banking Committee inflation was unacceptably high but indicated the Fed would balance its lower inflation goals with trying to prevent recession. Hoskins warned easing "would not only support the current inflation rate but would also lay the foundation for accelerating inflation." But Greenspan had decided the better part of valor was to continue lowering rates in small steps as it became apparent the economy was weakening. Other board members spread the word the Fed would strive for "stable prices" *and* "a reasonable rate of growth," as LaWare put it on October 31. On November 6, faced with further signs of weakness in manufacturing and housing, the Fed cut the funds rate to 8½ percent. The Fed had come under outspoken administration pressure in the prior week. Boskin "rejected" the Fed's belief that the only way to get inflation down was to create "slack" in the economy, while Secretary of Housing and Urban Development Jack Kemp said the Fed needed to ease credit to help the housing market. Brady called the Fed's desire for price stability "an admirable goal" but said the administration was "slightly more interested in growth than inflation."

The Fed's disagreement with Treasury on dollar policy had spilled over into the House Banking Committee on October 31. Defending intervention to soften the dollar, Mulford claimed that if the dollar had not fallen prior to the October 13 stock market plunge, it would have fallen even more dramatically afterward and could have "unhinged" the markets. (The dollar closed at 186.70 marks and 141.45 yen October 13, compared to 1.95 marks and 145.90 yen the day before the September 23 G-7 meeting.) Johnson countered that Treasury had been trying to "push the dollar against the fundamentals of the market" and vowed the Fed would not use monetary policy to depress the dollar to lower the trade deficit. The two men reprised their testimony before the Senate Banking Committee on November 16, by which time the Fed had eased. Mulford painted the October-November rate cuts as part of a coordinated G-7 rate move. Boasting that the 8 percent decline of the dollar (to 1.8380 marks and 143.70 yen) that had taken place since the G-7 meeting had been "a reasonably significant accomplishment," he said more than just intervention had been behind the dollar drop. He observed that Germany and Japan had raised their discount rates in the aftermath of the G-7 meeting, and "the U.S. subsequently has reduced its short-term interest rates, although it has not reduced its discount rate since the meeting." Johnson denied the Fed's easing moves were related to G-7 policy on the dollar. "Interest rates have been trending down in the United States and up [in Germany and Japan], but the reasons for those interest rate movements have nothing to do with precise manipulation of exchange rates." The Fed and other central banks "feel very strongly that policy should be focused on domestic conditions in each country."

Dallara has a different recollection. The central banks "wanted the world to understand that, 'well, there really wasn't much coordination,'" but in fact, "there was a real element of coordination under way at that time. And it was not so much that the Fed was trying to base its policies on what Germanay and Japan were doing, but if it seemed mutually beneficial to all parties concerned to take a step in one direction, then why not do it in an at least semi-coordinated fashion. And I would characterize those kinds of actions as semi-coordinated. . . . I think it would be misleading to suggest that there wasn't some real coordination in that, in terms of timing and sequencing and the overall effects of things. . . . I wouldn't say that these things became, in a very structured sense, highly coordinated, but I certainly think there was an element, a strong element of coordination at that time." Either Greenspan or Johnson met with their foreign counterparts monthly in Basel, giving them ample opportunity to "coordinate" or at least learn of each others' intentions. While these meetings were for central bankers, the Treasury was kept informed. "We frequently talked to the Fed before the meetings, during the meetings, after the meetings," Dallara says. "I had numerous conversations with Cross and Truman around the edges of these things." The central bankers "would exchange views about their various intentions and that would be fed back into Treasury behavior."

Although the trade deficit had fallen below $8 billion and the dollar had softened, the war over foreign exchange intervention smoldered on. Jumping ahead to the December 18–19 FOMC meeting, Cross's request to increase the limit on how much foreign currency he could hold from $20 billion to $21 billion prompted Angell and Johnson to make another stand against cooperating with Treasury. By that point, the Fed had sold $22 billion, more than 2½ times the amount it had sold in any previous year. Other central banks had sold an additional $54 billion. The dollar, by then, had fallen to 1.72 marks through a combination of changed interest rate differentials, intervention, and perceptions the U.S. economy was slipping. "I can't see a situation in which we would want to be selling dollars into this market . . . ," Johnson told Cross, who said he had no such plans but needed the authority, if only to allow for accumulation of interest on existing holdings. Angell was unassuaged. "For us to sell and try and affect the yen/dollar relationship is at best naive and at worst stupid. It just doesn't make any sense whatsoever." Both men threatened to vote against raising the limit. Greenspan sympathetically took their point and blunted it. "I think there have been innumerable occasions since the last FOMC meeting when the water they are drinking over there [at Treasury] obviously has had something in it. But they have calmed down, and I can't conceive that they would want to push on this side." He had "tried to convince some of our colleagues [at Treasury], with some success I think [to desist from selling dollars], and we will continue to do so." "Well," Angell asked, "if they say they're going to jump off the cliff, could we promise not to link hands and jump off with them?" "Yes, we could," Greenspan replied. Angell was appeased but said the Fed should retain the threat of nonparticipation in Treasury currency adventures.

Dallara, to whom it was often left to work out the details of intervention with Cross and Truman, says Treasury was "really trying to work closely with the Fed" in 1989 and to "walk a fine line" in controlling the appreciation of the dollar. He claims the Fed and Treasury found "common ground" 98 percent of the time. "The Treasury cannot call up the Federal Reserve and say 'We order you to use Federal Reserve money to intervene,' " says Cross, but "nine times out of ten" the Fed and Treasury did work out their differences." The trouble was many Fed policymakers disapproved of the extent to which the Fed staff was doing Treasury's bidding. Fed-Treasury relations became increasingly strained over the Treasury's efforts to hold down the dollar in late 1989 and early 1990. "I remember Manley [Johnson] being agitated at that time," says Dallara. "Things got a bit testy between Mulford and Manley there over these issues. . . ." Their "falling out" was less of a personality clash than a reflection of "one of the inherent tensions between the Treasury and the Fed. . . . In the end the Fed's view is driven by its anxiety that a depreciating exchange rate imports inflation, and Treasury on the other hand remaining concerned about the current account imbalance and U.S. competitiveness."

On several occasions Greenspan met with Brady, Mulford, and Dallara, accompanied by Johnson or Truman, to resolve the dollar dispute. "Alan would handle these things in his own inimitable style," says Dallara. He simply "put his concerns on the table. . . . I never remember any rabble rousing with Alan." Though not as exercised as some of his fellow policymakers, Greenspan shared their disapproval of the Treasury's intervention practices—in part because he regarded them as ineffective. From experience he knew central banks could not continuously intervene because the amount of reserves they had at their disposal was minuscule compared to the huge volume of currency private traders had. The only way to effectively move the foreign exchange market, in his view, was if the central banks could catch it out of step. Then it was possible to get a large run in the opposite direction, as had been done in January 1988, when the Fed and other central banks caught many traders short dollars and unexpectedly came in with massive dollar purchases that forced the shorts to cover their positions. But if the authorities were so predictable that traders expected them to intervene, the effort would be wasted. This was how Greenspan regarded the intervention Treasury was asking the Fed to conduct in the fall of 1989. He tried to tell Treasury officials their methods would not work, but it took months for them to get the message.

A top adviser to President Bush says Treasury's intervention against the dollar was more than just an effort to "manipulate exchange rates." It was part of "an attempt to pressure the Fed into easing more quickly." However, he doubts whether it affected the timing of Fed rate cuts or, for that matter, independently caused relations between the Fed and Treasury to deteriorate. "I think that the issue of currency intervention was separable from the basic stance of monetary policy, except for the fact that the view of any serious economist is that currency intervention won't do very much unless it's backed up by basic changes in policy. So I think there was a tension. But I wouldn't say that this was as fundamental as the differences between the Treasury Secretary and the Fed on the generic course of monetary policy."

Dallara still defends Treasury's 1989 dollar sales on the grounds that "if you did not avoid an overly sharp appreciation of the dollar, what you were positioning yourself for was a sharp downward correction that would really give you the potential of a psychological or real inflationary impact. . . . One of the strong reasons why I argued in support of some resistance to the upward movement of the dollar then was the concern that if fundamentals didn't support it, and I did not think they did, on the external balance side, that when the market began to focus again on the trade imbalances and current account imbalances, that they would then provoke the potential of another sharp downward movement. And I think that getting that kind of bubble in the exchange market is not healthy." Dallara says, "Brady was never much of an intervention man" and approved intervention only "reluctantly" after he and Mulford urged him to do so. Brady was "resistant of any massive effort to support the yen, because he fundamentally believed that the Japanese stock market was in the process of a fundamental correction. And he didn't think we could stand in the way of it." As it turns out, Brady was right about that. But ultimately, the Fed won its battle for less intervention against the dollar, not because Brady decided intervention was a bad idea, but because the dollar started weakening of its own accord in the spring of 1990.[4]

Before the November 14 FOMC meeting, substantial drops in retail sales, industrial production, and capacity utilization had been reported—just the kind of "slack" the Fed had been talking about, but the Fed decided to keep its powder dry for a while since Greenspan had just ordered a rate cut eight days before the meeting. The administration wasted no time responding to the Fed's no-action. Kemp said the Fed was making "a tragic mistake" in trying to restrain economic growth and had "been too tight and too high [with rates] too long." The committee reaffirmed the November 6 easing move and adopted an asymmetrical directive with a bias toward further rate cuts, but not without some reservations by more hawkish members. Parry worried that "if the economy expands as fast as I think it could, which is around 2 percent, then unemployment will rise only modestly, and I think upward pressures on the underlying inflation rate are likely to persist through the end of next year." Others thought the economy would be feeling the lagged effects of past Fed rate hikes and dollar strength, and the Fed needed to bring interest rates down if recession was to be averted. Kelley saw "disinflationary forces" at work which "could become deflationary and lead us into some really serious problems that might be avoidable." Seger said the same FIRREA legislation that had created the RTC had made it difficult for builders to get loans by imposing limits on how much banks could lend to a single borrower. LaWare thought that "we may be closer to the edge of the abyss than was indicated" in the staff forecast.

Greenspan blamed the Fed's dilemma on fiscal policy. With the government spending more than it was taking in, thereby stimulating demand in the economy and pushing up market interest rates, the onus was entirely on the Fed to control the pace of economic activity and prevent inflation. Ideally, the administration and Congress would help the Fed slow demand by reducing the deficit; then the Fed would have more room to lower its rates, but the Fed could not count on that, despite administration plans to "sequester" spending. So there was a limit to what the Fed could do. "Our fundamental dilemma is . . . that there is no viable clear-cut path that gets us to where we would like to be without some assistance from the fiscal side." Greenspan had told Bush and his advisors that, in the absence of fiscal restraint, "there is a downside limit to how far short-term interest rates can go without retriggering inflationary expectations and a significant recession on the other side of that. . . . The flexibility that we have to achieve the dual goals of declining inflation and still sustainable growth clearly is a window which may in fact not be there." Absent fiscal restraint, achieving price stability "will be very difficult . . . without breaking the back of the economy." While striving over the long run to eliminate inflation, "we also have to be careful not to fumble into a severe recession," he warned with one eye on the stock market. "If the bear market is rather soft and cuddly, that's fine; but if it decides to move rather fast then I think we will get some of the wealth effects in the GNP accounts and the economy will tilt over."

Eight days after the November FOMC meeting, the Fed's secretive operating methods came back to haunt it, when a pre-Thanksgiving reserve adding operation by the New York Fed, intended to be purely technical in nature, set off rumors that the Fed had eased again. On Friday, the day after Thanksgiving, the *Wall Street Journal* flatly asserted the Fed had eased, converting what had been suspicion and speculation to established fact in most people's minds. In fact, it had merely been trying to make sure that, going into a holiday weekend, when heavy cash demands would be draining reserves from the banking system, banks had sufficient reserves.[5] Not until Monday, when the Fed aggressively drained reserves did it dawn on many people that they had been had and that the Fed still wanted the funds rate at 8½ percent, not 8¼ percent. This Thanksgiving turkey of a miscue caused some big trading losses and a lot of fingerpointing.

Publicly, the Fed took a kind of "tough luck" attitude. "We've gotten into a period when the market has devoted more and more attention to reading entrails," said Syron. "They devoted too much attention" to the Fed's open market operations. "I don't think anybody ought to assume on the basis of several days movement in the federal funds rate that we've changed policy," agreed Black. "If I were in the market I would not jump at every uptick or downtick of the market." But behind closed doors, there were recriminations. "Clearly, we misjudged the market's reaction," Sternlight confessed at the December 18–19 FOMC meeting. A Fed staffer told me the open market desk had been "inept. . . . I can't recall an operation recently that's turned out so badly." Outside the Fed, the episode added to the belief the Fed needed to be more open in the way it made policy. It probably contributed to the Fed's decision in 1994 to begin announcing changes in the funds rate.

Part of the Fed's problem in late 1989 was that the relationship between the Fed's target for discount window borrowings and its federal funds rate target was breaking down. Banks' borrowings were becoming erratic and unpredictable. The Fed had been trying to adjust the availability of reserves and in turn the funds rate by forcing banks to borrow a certain amount of reserves each day, but the banks weren't cooperating. A big reason, as Kohn explained, was because banks didn't want to be tarred with the "problem bank" brush. Although the Fed does not announce which bank is borrowing from the discount window, other financial institutions inevitably find out because the Fed always asks banks to bid aggressively for other sources of funds before they come knocking at the Fed's window. Because of such problems the Fed soon dropped the pretense of targeting borrowings altogether.

By the December 18–19 FOMC meeting the Fed had reports auto sales were dropping, factory layoffs increasing, industrial production flat, and housing slipping. Unemployment was starting to rise, while capacity utilization was down further—more of that "slack" the Fed had so earnestly sought. Prell conceded, "The economy has indeed moved down another notch. Consequently, we now feel more assured in predicting that the pace of expansion will be slow enough in the near term to produce a further easing of pressures on resources and thus some tempering of inflationary forces." But he told the FOMC the staff still assumed "you will not engage in any substantial further easing, despite the provocation of a rather soggy economy." More "slack" had to be created. Some policymakers were astonished at the staff's take-it-or-leave-it assumption of no further rate cuts. "Essentially, for the next two years you have subpar growth of under 2 percent and the unemployment rate rising to over 6 percent," Boehne said. "You have a somewhat heroic assumption that there will be no further easing in monetary policy over that period. Yet the inflation trend line is not very good." The staff was projecting a small dip in inflation in 1990 followed by a rebound in 1991. "It seems like a lot lost on the real side and nothing [gained] on the inflation side," Johnson said.

The FOMC discussed at great length a staff study on how the Fed could achieve price stability by 1995 and at what cost. The key to reaching that goal was "credibility." The public and markets had to believe the Fed was determined to defeat the "inflationary psychology" that led individuals and firms to seek higher wages, prices, and rates of return on their money. The study was quite explicit and bears a remarkable resemblence to what actually happened over the succeeding six years. Under one alternative, an "aggressive tightening of monetary policy early on," which had already occurred in the March 1988 to February 1989 period, would be followed by "a small recession in 1990," then a rise in unemployment to 8 percent. Unemployment, in fact, peaked at 7.7 percent in 1992 after the 1990–1991 recession. Another scenario envisioned unemployment rising to 7 percent from the prevailing 5.3. The com-

mittee considered (without formally adopting) the desirability of setting a
fixed timetable for eliminating inflation, complete with "sacrifice ratios," a
euphemism for "how many people we're going to throw out of work," as
Greenspan plainly stated it. Seger went on a rampage. Reminding her colleagues the average American was "more interested in the Redskins football
game yesterday" than in the Fed's doings, she lambasted a suggestion that "disinflation costs were not that great" in the early eighties. "Possibly from Washington, D.C., they didn't look that great, or if you were sitting with the
security of a government job or a government paycheck, perhaps they didn't,
but I can tell you that there are a lot of people who paid dearly for that disinflation. They lost businesses; they lost farms; they lost jobs, and they're still
without them." Kelley advised keeping in mind "the potential human costs" of
beating down inflation, not to mention "the political threat" that might arise if
the Fed brought on a recession. Syron questioned "how long we can squeeze"
the economy without incurring Congress' wrath. "I don't think there is a public or political mandate to go to zero inflation if it means pushing up unemployment and risking a recession," said Boehne, who advised a go-slow
approach. Forrestal said people were already telling him the Fed had "a fetish
about inflation." Corrigan said "betting the ranch" on zero inflation credibility risked a backlash against the Fed.

Some, however, were willing to accept recession as the price of disinflation.
"I don't think that any of us is looking for a recession, but I don't think we
should shy away from it either," said Guffey. Hoskins agreed wholeheartedly.
Angell emphasized the benefits of attaining "zero inflation" over the costs. "It
just seems to me that the case is so strong for wanting the American people to
be able to buy homes at a 5 percent mortgage interest rate." Besides, he went
on passionately, "it's our job to make promises in regard to the purchasing
power of U.S. dollars. To me it's a moral question of integrity. And I cannot
participate—I cannot serve on a Board and an FOMC that doesn't have this
integrity." From the sublime to the ridiculous, Black cracked, "I'm on the side
of the Angells in this!" "I knew someone was going to say that," Kelley
groaned. Greenspan had already testified in favor of the Neal bill to give the
Fed a price stability mandate but had suggested a nonspecific definition of
price stability. Inflation would be deemed to have been eliminated when it
ceased to be a significant factor in personal and business planning. An informal
consensus was reached that it was a good goal to strive for in the years to come.
Greenspan asked members not to tell the press they had even discussed a
timetable for reaching zero inflation.

Although the study seems to have influenced the future course of policy, it
did not prevent the Fed from taking near-term action to avoid recession—an
irony not lost on Hoskins. "It seems to me that in some cases we have forgotten yesterday's meeting," he complained. But the majority was not about to listen to the staff's advice to keep policy on hold. Even ordinarily hawkish
members were getting nervous, not just about the economy, but about the
financial system. In supporting a further small easing move, Corrigan cited the
spread of credit problems. He had "a down-home example: the contractor that

we've used at the Bank for years. We were about to let a contract when his insurance company wouldn't post bond for him for credit reasons. And this is a company we've done business with for 50 years." LaWare pointed to "the real estate fungus that is spreading across the country" and the toll it was taking on banks. "And when you look at how a slowdown would affect the debt burden that we have in the economy in terms of the flow of revenues and the direct effect on cash flow and the coverage of debt service, it seems to me that you see a snowball beginning to roll downhill that I don't like the looks of."

Greenspan adroitly addressed the concerns of each camp. The Fed needed to run a tight monetary policy if it hoped to achieve negligible inflation, but to do that it had to avoid recession. "A necessary condition, politically, for people arguing to do that is that we skim through this particular period without going into the ditch. Because if we could come through this period even with a mild recession, or preferably none whatever, I think the credibility of the institution would be such by the fall of 1990 that we could probably write our own policy ticket in that respect." With new manufacturing orders and unfilled orders declining, with residential construction faltering, and other signs of weakness, the Fed needed to ease again to guard against recession. In theory, cutting rates now would not act soon enough to help avert the weakness that was building in the economy, but Greenspan went against the Fed's own oft-stated premise that monetary policy only operates with "long and variable" lags of 12 to 18 months. "The truth of the matter is that I don't believe that for a minute. I do think that there is a significant longer-term impact from interest rates; but I don't see that monetary policy has no effect in the short run." Needless to say, Greenspan got the last word, and the Fed closed out the year with funds at 8¼ percent. Little did policymakers know they had only begun to ease.

CHAPTER FIVE

The Chickens Come Home to Roost

Although Alan Greenspan will probably be best remembered for the way he responded to the October 1987 stock market crash, his leadership in handling the host of economic and financial problems that beset the U.S. economy in 1990 and beyond was just as critical. The Fed has been blamed for causing the 1990–1991 recession and the "credit crunch," but while not totally unfounded, that criticism is unfair. Problems in the financial industry, including not just banks and thrifts but also securities firms and even insurance companies, had been brewing for years. Intersecting these problems, a radical restructuring was taking place in the corporate sector. Companies were trying to strengthen their balance sheets and unwind the long-term debt burdens many had accumulated, but they still needed access to short- and intermediate-term credit, which was becoming harder to come by, especially for small- to medium-size firms not considered investment grade. Companies were also coming to grips with the reality of global competition, which notwithstanding the dollar's depreciation was becoming acute. Thus was born *corporate downsizing*—a ruthless closing of obsolete or redundant plants, retooling of remaining facilities, and layoffs of both blue- and white-collar workers. As it proceeded, American industry became more competitive than in decades, pushing exports to record levels, but it was a painful process.

Outside some regional recessions, the national economy had had enough momentum to ride out such financial difficulties through the eighties. Now, as the momentum dwindled, these chickens came home to roost. An earlier Fed might have tried to paper over the problems with inflationary money. This Fed set itself a bigger challenge—to provide enough credit to keep the economy growing while it solved its problems and at the same time gradually reduce inflation. The strategy was not carried out flawlessly but, as John Crow marvels, "They were able to in a sense decompress the economy and get a better inflation performance." The country emerged in sounder shape.

From the peak of interest rates in February 1989 through the end of December, the Fed had cut the federal funds rate more than 1⅛ percent—a lot more than some officials would have liked, given that inflation was still on an uptrend. The administration, as well as many on Capitol Hill, did not see it that way. Real GNP had steadily slowed in 1989 from a first-quarter growth rate of 3.6 percent to 0.3 percent in the fourth. Yet from December 20 through July 13, 1990, the Fed left the funds rate unchanged at 8¼ percent. Reports and warnings of the credit crunch were initially downplayed by the Fed staff, as it continued to counsel a tight money policy. By the time it dawned on the Fed the credit crunch was for real, the economy was in trouble. The money supply, so often dismissed by many Fed officials, told the tale. It became obvious as the year wore on that anemic money growth reflected stringency in the credit markets and the Fed's own policies. By keeping the funds rate unchanged at 8¼ percent through mid-July, then keeping it at 8 percent until November, in face of collapsing credit demand, the Fed in effect tightened credit. But the staff was advising the FOMC the economic outlook was relatively bright, the inflation threat real, and the value of the dollar in jeopardy. What's more, a decision was made to use monetary policy as leverage to get the politicians to do their job and reduce the federal budget deficit.

Among the Fed's biggest headaches was the thrift crisis. Greenspan does not regard it as a major direct cause of economic stagnation in the early nineties, but it had countless spillover effects. For years S&Ls had thrived and proliferated in a low-inflation climate taking deposits and making home mortgages—basically borrowing short and lending long. As inflation crept up in the late sixties and seventies, they found themselves locked into low-earning, fixed rate, 30-year mortgages, while having to pay ever higher rates to attract deposits. The market value of their equity collapsed. S&Ls' average cost of funds rose from about 7 percent in 1978 to over 11 percent in 1982, causing 470 S&Ls to fail between 1980 and 1983. Many of those that stayed in business did so by dint of regulatory "forbearance." The minimum capital requirement was reduced from 5 to 4 percent of assets in 1980 to 3 percent in 1982, and under the "Regulatory Accounting Principles" (RAP), which the FHLBB recognized in place of "Generally Accepted Accounting Principles" (GAAP), thrifts could count will-o'-the-wisp intangibles like "goodwill" as capital. Starting in 1981, S&Ls were allowed to defer losses on the sale of bad mortgage loans and mortgage-backed securities. Thrifts were also allowed to issue so-called *net worth certificates*, which the FSLIC then bought with cash or promissory notes.

Some have blamed the lifting of the deposit rate ceiling as a source of the problem, but inflation had made the ceiling obsolete. When market rates rose, depositors simply withdrew their funds from banks and thrifts and invested them at higher returns elsewhere. Repeal was inevitable. What was not inevitable was another congressional decision: increasing the amount of deposits the FDIC and FSLIC would insure from $40,000 to $100,000 as part of the 1980 Monetary Control Act. Compounding the problem, regulators went beyond even that high limit in the case of large failures to cover all deposits. Meanwhile, the 1982 Garn–St. Germain Act lifted some of the restrictions on S&Ls' assets. Now, in addition to mortgage lending, federally chartered thrifts could make a certain number of consumer, business, and nonresidential real estate loans. State-chartered, but federally insured thrifts in California, Texas, and other states were given virtual carte blanche in the types of assets they could hold. None other than Alan Greenspan, while a private economic consultant, praised these direct investments a few years before becoming chairman as a way of diversifying and theoretically strengthening their balance sheets. Soon thrifts were making wild direct investments in everything from speculative real estate developments to windmill farms to junk bonds. The problem was not that their activities had been deregulated but that the government was, in effect, subsidizing them through almost unlimited deposit insurance, as well as access to the Fed's discount window. Reckless and at times unscrupulous thrift operators could make risky loans and investments in the knowledge that, if they failed, the government would bail them out.

Seidman says federal policies on S&Ls created "an attractive nuisance" that drew operators like Charles Keating. When Congress discovered S&Ls could not cope with inflation, "they decided they would try to help them out of that by allowing them to enterprise their way out, grow out of it, by giving them more money to increase their insured deposit level and by allowing them to go into almost anything you could think of. So, as a result of that, two things happened. One was that a lot of S&L guys who didn't know anything about it went into a lot of wild lending, and secondly, it attracted a whole bunch of people who suddenly found out that they could print money if they owned an S&L." The former RTC head also faults Wright and St. Germain for delaying FSLIC recapitalization through 1987 and 1988. "Both of them were very supportive of some of the people in the S&L industry who were our worst offenders. Jim Wright really behaved as though he was just a congressman from Ft. Worth instead of being the Speaker." Because of FSLIC's inability either to pay off depositors of insolvent thrifts or assist their acquisition, the S&L crisis "got worse, because they were losing money and going into deals all the time. Since FSLIC was effectively unable to do anything about it because it didn't have any funding, that simply made it worse."

By late 1988, when collapsing real estate values had rendered hundreds of S&Ls insolvent, the unfunded FSLIC was reduced to issuing its own dubious securities to raise cash. What had been estimated by the Bank Board as recently as the fall of 1988 to be a $15 billion problem was recognized by spring 1989 as a disaster of much greater proportions. By the fall of 1989, Brady was putting the price tag at around $200 billion, including the cost of scores of last minute deals the FSLIC, under the direction of the FHLBB, had made at the end of 1988 as part of its so-called Southwest Plan.[1] By 1990, when the RTC started closing and liquidating S&Ls in earnest, instead of being freewheeling sources of credit, the thrift industry had become a financial black hole. Congress exacerbated the problem in its effort to deal with it. One FIRREA provision required S&Ls to swiftly divest their junk bond portfolios, causing an implosion of the bonds' values and heavy losses on thrifts' balance sheets. FIRREA had also mandated minimum capital standards for thrifts with three components: a 1.5 percent tangible capital requirement, a 3 percent leverage requirement, and a 6.4 percent risk-based requirement. The Fed estimated in early 1990 that 507 then solvent thrifts failed to meet at least one of the requirements and so would not be allowed to expand their assets. In effect, they would be all but forbidden from making new loans.

Bank credit pipelines were also getting clogged. The focus of bank problems had shifted to the Northeast, where in the first quarter banks suffered a $1.1 billion decline in net income relative to the first quarter of 1989, as non-current loans and leases rose $9.4 billion from a year earlier. Their return on assets had dropped 35 basis points to 0.52 percent from the first quarter of 1989, compared to a national average of 0.76 percent. The two previous quarters, they had net losses. New England's supposedly more sober bankers had been competing to offer more generous loan terms, taking ever greater risks in the process to finance a commercial building boom. Before joining the Fed, one of LaWare's last acts as chairman of Boston's Shawmut Bank was to rule on a loan which had been appealed to him. "I was absolutely appalled, because this was a proposition in which we were being asked to lend 100 percent of the expected market value of the building at completion, plus a five percent contingency reserve, plus all of the interest up front. That's how competitive that lending had become. In any case, I said, 'Absolutely not. This is nonsense.' " Federal regulators, particularly the Office of the Comptroller of the Currency, had been overlooking such loans. Like the banks, they "were being lullabied by the same thought that there was no end to the real estate boom," says LaWare. ". . . We were a national bank, and we were not getting any kind of pressure on all of that [loan] build-up. . . ."

Restricted from offering securities underwriting and other services by the Depression-era Glass-Steagall Act and restricted from branching across state lines, banks had sought other profitable lines of business. The vast majority of the hundreds of bank failures in those years were due to real estate lending. Seidman says a contagion spread from the S&Ls to the banks. There was "a very corrosive effect of all the S&Ls getting into their business and not knowing what they were doing. It's very hard to compete when you have a bunch of wild men running around in your business the way the S&Ls were." Banks were not making direct investments in real estate like S&Ls, but had begun to make loans on real estate developments without any "take-out." Normal practice in financing, say, for an office building, was for the bank to lend for the first two years, and after that an insurance company or a pension fund would commit to "take them out" and provide longer-term financing for the building. But, as Seidman recalls, "When they got into this hot period when they were short on things they could do, they started making loans without that, which meant that they were suddenly borrowing short and lending long, and were taking the kind of risk that long-term lenders might take, which short-term lenders aren't supposed to take." With banks and S&Ls competing to finance more and more audacious and fanciful real estate projects, real estate prices became inflated. Office buildings and shopping centers were being built with little prospect of enough occupancy to make them pay, even in good times. Vacancy rates rose steadily throughout the eighties from less than 5 percent to nearly 19 percent by 1991. When the economic slowdown began to bite in 1989 and worsened in 1990, real estate values collapsed, wreaking havoc with loan portfolios. As banks failed or pulled in their horns to keep from failing, lending dried up. Banks were still recovering from their bad Third World loans of the early eighties when the real estate loan crisis hit. Unlike S&Ls, they had not been allowed to invest in so-called junk bonds, but they had made increasingly heavy "mezzanine loans" to finance corporate takeovers.

Another factor complicating banks' ability to lend was the risk-based capital guidelines the Fed had crafted with its fellow central banks in 1986. The idea was that banks would hold capital in proportion to the riskiness of their assets. The Basel Accord set different risk weightings for different assets. Banks were required to hold zero capital to back their holdings of government securities. Mortgage loans loans, however, had to be backed 50 percent. Other types of loans required 100 percent backing. Seidman calls the risk weightings "highly arbitrary. Nobody made a study and said the risk on home loans is twice or is much more than the risk on government bonds." Overlaid on these risk-based capital standards, banks were required to meet an overall minimum capital-to-asset ratio of 8 percent by 1992.[2] To meet that ratio, a bank could increase the numerator by going to market with sales of stock or bonds—an unattractive option in the uncongenial markets of the period. Or it could reduce the denominator by liquidating assets (calling loans, selling securities) or not growing them as fast. Most banks had no problem meeting the 8 percent standard, but some had to shrink their assets to meet it. What's more, the zero capital backing on government securities holdings produced an incentive, under certain market conditions, to hold securities rather than lend. So, despite the Fed's easing moves in the second half of 1989, banks were becoming increasingly reluctant to lend. Just at the time when they were suffering pinched earnings and loan losses, they were being required to meet higher capital ratios. Seidman says risk-based capital standards "had an influence" in restricting lending by banks "pressed" for capital, though not by all banks. Hoskins doubts the Bank for International Settlement (BIS) standards helped cause a credit crunch by encouraging banks to invest in government securities instead of make loans, but says that, to the extent higher risk weightings for loans raised loan rates, "Yes, you would price people out of the market, there's no doubt about that."

The Fed was aware of what was going on. Its November 1989 survey of senior bank loan officers had found "increased credit restraint," primarily because of "deterioration" in the economic outlook but also because of regulatory pressures and capital requirements. Banks were found to have raised their fees for credit lines, charged larger spreads over base rates, reduced the size of lines of credit, tightened loan covenants, and increased collateral requirements. Total bank credit (loans and other assets) had slowed from an annual growth rate of 10.2 percent in 1986 to 7.7 percent in 1987 and 1988 to 6.6 percent in 1989. After growing 8.5 percent in 1986, business loan growth slowed to 7 percent in 1987, 6.6 percent in 1988, 6.1 percent in 1989, and 2.4 percent in the fourth quarter. The greenbook prepared by the staff for the February 6–7 1990 FOMC meeting noted bank credit had contracted at a 2¾ percent annual rate in December 1989, the first decline since President

Carter imposed credit controls in 1980. The Fed was not greatly displeased at this juncture that credit was becoming less available. If banks were less willing to lend, that was seen as not such a bad thing, given past excesses and given the Fed's goal of not just containing inflation but reducing it. Inflation had averaged 4.8 percent in 1989 and was correctly forecast to rise further in 1990. Although it had begun reducing the funds rate to reflect lower market rates and slackening credit demand, the Fed attitude was that it had eased sufficiently.

Pressure was building from the White House and Congress to cut rates. In a late-December report, the Senate Banking Committee had warned, "A policy designed to reduce inflation at all costs, might, given the unprecedented overleveraging in many sectors of our economy, produce a dangerous recession." But the Fed's strategy was to hold growth below its potential to kill inflation. A tightening of credit conditions fit nicely with this strategy, and the Fed turned a deaf ear to complaints about slackening credit demand and reduced willingness to make loans. Some argued for a moratorium on the BIS capital standards. "Without some of the capital constraints at the end of the year, rather than trying to consolidate assets, given the rate structure, [Citibank] would have been more aggressive in augmenting assets," a bank source told me. But Fed sources said loans were still growing, though at a greatly reduced rate, and there would be no backing off on capital requirements. Far from reducing them, Greenspan had talked of even higher capital ratios to discourage risky bank activities.

There were spreading indications of economic weakness. Although unemployment was still just 5.3 percent, job growth had slowed to a crawl. Housing was slumping. The January beige book reported the economy "expanding slowly in most of the nation" with manufacturing "generally sluggish" and retail sales "disappointing." To many, there seemed to be ample reason to continue easing credit, but they did not reckon with the Fed's determination to defeat inflation and extricate itself from the stop-go policies that had exacerbated the peaks and valleys of past business cycles. "I really think we've got, overall, the most dedicated bunch of inflation fighters that we've ever had in the system," Black told me at the time. Fed officials were breathing fire against inflation in early January. Forrestal called inflation a "dark cloud on an otherwise bright horizon." Corrigan said the economy was "in the yellow zone with regard to the potential for some buildup in inflationary forces." He complained politicians did not seem to understand the need to hold inflation in check, "especially when it comes to support for preemptive policies that work to head off rises in the inflation rate before they are actually reflected in statistics and in behavior and expectations." Not part of this chorus was Seger. "Everytime a price moves to me doesn't mean you're off and running on the inflation tread mill." If citrus and oil prices rose, "what are we going to do about it? We sure don't have any control over the weather, and we don't have any control over whether some refinery springs a leak." The bigger risk was that "the tightening of credit standards" was curtailing home and car buying and risking recession. "If we have a continued weak construction picture and if the auto industry really goes into the tank, then I think that could do it." But Seger was a lone wolf on the FOMC, and the markets stopped looking for a rate cut after it was reported wholesale prices had risen at an annual 8½ percent in December. Bond and stock prices tumbled.

The administration saw rising prices as just a lagged effect of past expansion and thought the Fed was fighting the last war. "It is quite unlikely we'll have a recession," Boskin said in mid-January, predicting the economy would "rebound" following "a period of sluggish growth." Prices had "been fairly steady with the exception of jumps in energy prices." CEA member John Taylor told me the Fed should not be unduly concerned about inflation and the steepening of the yield curve. "You have to be looking for it to see increased inflation. Over the course of the expansion we've had stable inflation." When it was reported on January 18 that the CPI had risen 0.4 percent in December, while housing starts dropped 8 percent, the administration said the numbers proved the Fed should be focusing on sustaining growth, not fighting inflation, although the CPI uptick represented a roughly 5 percent annual inflation rate. The Fed should "understand that these numbers are low, and that indicates inflation has remained very steady over the last seven or eight years, and that lower interest rates are justified," said Fitzwater after a skull session with Boskin, Darman, and other Bush advisers. "We aren't trying to tell the Fed what to do," he added lamely. Asked about Fitzwater's comments, Greenspan told the House Banking Committee a few days later he "would not interpret that as pressure from the administration to take action." Bush's spokesman was merely saying, "Lower interest rates would be better than higher interest rates. I know of no one who would dispute that." Kemp said Fitzwater "was not putting pressure on the Federal Reserve" but repeated there was "room for lower interest rates."

As always happens in a slowdown, prices were continuing to rise before turning down. The result was the appearance of "stagflation." The Fed was not surprised. "If you're trying to slow the economy you're going to have so-called stagflation every time," said a Fed staffer. "It's exactly what you want to see. . . . The question is whether you get the desired response of prices eventually, and that takes patience." Patient was just what the Fed planned on being. Meanwhile, bad inflation numbers helped justify its stand pat policy. Fed officials did not anticipate just how weak the economy would become. While planning for subpar growth, the Fed staff did not anticipate an actual contraction. Most policymakers believed the economy would continue to get by with modest growth. I found a sense of optimism and confidence in my conversations with Fed officials that January. The expectation was for slower-paced activity, but not recession. Typically, Parry thought the economy was slowing due to "temporary factors. As things return to more normal patterns economic growth should rebound. . . . The economy still is operating at a level that strains capacity and generates inflationary pressures. In particular, the level of the unemployment rate is likely to remain below the level most economists consider consistent with keeping inflation under control." The Fed needed to "ease inflationary pressures gradually by slowing growth to somewhat below the rate of growth in capacity." Johnson said it was time to "consolidate and watch."

The administration projected more growth than it had a right to expect in the fiscal 1991 budget it released January 29, assuming real GNP would grow 2.6 percent in 1990, then rise to 3.3 percent in 1991. That was not totally unreasonable, except that it also projected rates on three-month Treasury bills, then trading around 7.7 percent, would average 6.7 percent in 1990 and 5.4 percent in 1991. Ten-year Treasury note yields were projected to fall from the prevailing 8.5 percent to 7.7 percent in 1990 and 6.8 percent in 1991. Unemployment was assumed to average 5.4 percent in 1990 and 5.2 percent in 1991, while the CPI was projected to rise just 4.1 percent in 1990 and 4.0 percent in 1991. The Bush budget proposed a deficit of $63.1 billion in fiscal year 1991, down from a projected $123.8 billion for fiscal 1990 and $152 billion for fiscal 1989. The budget was branded "dead on arrival" by Congress. Boskin said he did "not believe these [economic assumptions] err on the side of optimism," but the administration was counting on stronger growth than the Fed was prepared to accommodate. In a February 6 letter to Congress accompanying the annual Economic Report of the President, Bush wrote, "If my budget proposals are adopted, and if the Federal Reserve maintains a credible policy program to support strong noninflationary growth, the economy is projected to expand in 1990 at a slightly faster pace than in 1989. Growth is projected to pick up in the second half of the year and to continue at a strong pace as the level of output rises to the economy's full potential." The report warned the Fed against "setting hopelessly unrealistic goals," a reference to Neal's bill to eliminate inflation within five years which Fed officials were endorsing. "Just as inappropriate monetary policies can damage economic performance by allowing excessive inflation, they also can lead directly to recessions. Excessively tight policies, when demand is already weak and rising inflation is not a threat, may contribute to a recession." Bush was in for a disappointment. As growth slowed, then evaporated, the fiscal 1990 deficit turned out to be $220 billion, up $68 billion from 1989, and the 1991 deficit rose to more than $269 billion. Leaving aside economic assumptions and the fact that the RTC was borrowing heavily to fund the shortfall between the S&L assets it was acquiring and the insured deposits it was paying off, spending was outpacing revenues. In 1989, outlays were 22.2 percent, while revenues were 19.2 percent of GNP.

A day after the budget was released, Greenspan torpedoed its assumptions. He told the Joint Economic Committee inflation was "unacceptably high" and "could divert" Japanese and other foreign investors. He saw only a "temporary hesitation in the continuing expansion of the economy." That's what the administration hoped, but Greenspan meant growth would have to be restrained. He did not foresee a recession barring "some adverse shock not now visible." The message was the Fed had no intention of lowering rates for the foreseeable future. If the deficit was reduced, "then long-term rates would fall fairly quickly and that would pull on short-term rates." The administration was not prepared to be that patient and was not shy about saying so just before the FOMC met. Darman went on television Febraury 2 and said rates could come down if only the Fed would follow a "reasonable policy." Brady complained the Fed was too focused on zero inflation and not on growth. The pressure was unavailing.

At the February 6–7 FOMC meetings, there was sentiment to raise rates, not lower them. Notwithstanding the economic and financial concerns many members had, the staff recommended rates be kept the same or raised somewhat. Under its baseline forecast, real growth was to be restrained to between 1 and 1½ percent in 1990 and to 2¼ percent in 1991 by keeping the funds rate at 8¼ percent through 1990, then raising it in 1991. The greenbook stated that if the FOMC hoped to reduce inflation over time it would "require some easing of pressures on resources, and to keep domestic demand sufficiently in check, the staff projects that real interest rates will have to be maintained at relatively high levels." The accompanying bluebook said the baseline strategy would impose "enough restraint, through moderate upward movement in nominal and real interest rates, to keep real GNP growth below its potential through 1991 and until 1992. This induces a gradual increase in the unemployment rate to 6¼ percent by 1992, somewhat above its assumed natural rate of 5½ to 5¾ percent." This "added slack" was seen reducing inflation starting in 1992, assuming the dollar stabilized. Going beyond its usual exercise, the staff prepared a set of longer-run policy strategies for reducing inflation. Under the baseline strategy, if M2 grew 6 to 6½ percent, inflation would fall to 3¼ percent by 1994. If the Fed wanted to lower inflation to 2 percent, it would need to slow M2 to 5 to 5½ percent and push unemployment to 7 percent. Kohn said the staff "start[ed] from the presumption that the unemployment rate has to rise from current levels to keep inflation from accelerating in an underlying sense." Lower inflation would not come for a while "because you have to get those real interest rates up and keep them up . . . to induce a gap in resource utilization. . . ." The staff assured the committee recession was almost out of the question. "We don't see much sign that the negative elements in the economy are gathering recessionary force," Prell said.

Some FOMC members favored going to the tighter strategy, which envisioned holding GNP growth below 2 percent until 1993. "I would have to conclude that maybe our best efforts should be to cap inflation now with the thought that the only way we're going to get inflation down is with a recession and that quite likely a recession will occur within the next five years—particularly if we hold growth below the trend line for this long period of time," Guffey said. For Hoskins the staff's tighter policy option was not tight enough. If the Fed really wanted to achieve price stability, instead of being "reasonable," he suggested "we be unreasonable once in a while and look at what could happen and take a tighter policy to get to where we say we're going to go, or we shouldn't be saying it's where we're going to go." Boykin, whose once depressed southwestern district was now recovering, wanted to at least tilt toward a tighter policy. Greenspan joked, "That booming district of yours is turning your head."

Seger was appalled. "If we should tip the economy into a recession, Congressman Neal may still be holding hearings on the need for zero inflation, but

434 other people in Congress in the House and 100 people in the Senate are going to be dragging us down there to explain why in an election year they're facing rising amounts of unemployment back in their districts," Others shared her fears. "I'm just worried that we're sliding toward a recession," a self-described "gloomy Gus" LaWare said, describing banking as "troubled," the construction industry as "hurting," and the auto industry as "a hospital case—they're almost on a life support system." Calling herself "a gloomy Gussie," Seger said examiners were "scaring the heck out of bankers" and killing lending. Melzer was getting growing complaints from smaller companies that regulators were "overreacting," causing banks to tighten lending standards. In New England, Syron said, "It's to the point now where if someone calls a financial institution that they haven't had a long-going relationship with to talk about a real estate loan, it's almost like one of these commercials where people on the other end of the line just laugh and say something like: 'You must be kidding! We're not doing any more real estate loans unless we have a well-established relationship with you or unless you have extraordinarily good collateral." Forrestal reported a "very pessimistic attitude" in the Southeast. "There's a very pronounced fear of recession and I would say a distressing lack of interest in reducing inflation." Corrigan said, "There clearly is a pervasive tightening in credit standards in depository institutions of all sizes," and "there is absolutely no question that lenders are alleging that they are being pounded upon by examiners." Banks might be using regulators as a "convenient excuse to say 'no' " to would-be borrowers, but the fact remained credit was tightening. Kelley warned against being "too terribly macho . . . in trying to knock inflation down very rapidly."

Greenspan predicted that sometime between 1990 and 1994, "there is likely to be a recession," and "that may in fact be the easiest way to bring price stability in the 1994–95 period." For now, though, "making any significant moves in monetary policy probably would be ill-advised." Rather than raising rates, "the odds are strongly likely that we will find reasons to move down rather than up," but for now monetary policy was "blocked" by a unique dilemma. On the one hand, the economy seemed to be doing well in its "physical aspects." Looking at income, consumption, inventories, and investment, "we may in fact already have seen the weakest point" in activity. Simultaneously there appeared to be "a general, continued financial balance sheet deterioration." Profit margins were eroding, the financial system was "fragile," and credit was being "rationed." What's more, there were international concerns: the "severe threat to the Japanese stock market" and global interest rate pressures. The best thing the Fed could do was provide "a sense of stability." Greenspan prevailed, and the FOMC voted 8 to 3 to keep the funds rate at 8¼ percent and issue a "symmetrical" directive. Boykin and Hoskins had wanted to tighten, the latter immediately, while Seger wanted an immediate easing.

When Greenspan warned about financial fragilities, he was not just talking about the difficulties banks and thrifts were having. Many financial institutions had been major purchasers of the junk bonds purveyed by investment banks, chiefly Drexel, Burnham Lambert, to both finance and resist corporate leveraged buyouts. In the typical hostile takeover, a would-be acquirer would set up a shell company to issue low-grade, high-yield bonds to raise money that could then be used in a tender offer for a target company's stock. Alternatively, a group of corporate insiders might "take the company private" by issuing corporate debt to buy up the company's stock. Target companies often issued large amounts of debt to buy up their own stock and/or to make themselves less appetizing. Phillips Petroleum saw its debt rise from 30 to 80 percent of capital in the wake of its successful effort to prevent Mesa Petroleum owner T. Boone Pickens from taking control. Commercial banks could not invest in junk bonds, but they loaned heavily to assist "highly leveraged transactions" (HLTs). The urge to merge had been going on throughout the late eighties to the Fed's growing concern. Although some leveraged buyouts (LBOs) were effective in shaking up stodgy management, streamlining firms, and making them more competitive and profitable, others proved the undoing of previously sound companies. The net result of the whole LBO phenomenon was that corporations took on dangerously high levels of debt relative to equity.

If there's one thing the Fed dislikes it is debt. In 1990, corporate debt reached 91 percent of GDP, up from 74 percent in 1980. Household debt rose to 72 percent of GDP, up from 55 percent in 1980. And government debt was 36 percent of GDP, up from 19 percent. Henry Kaufman had warned that "for the Federal Reserve, the dilemma of how to conduct monetary policy during the next recession for an economy laden with heavily indebted corporations will be especially acute." The Fed decided to do what it could to slow, if not reverse, the process. Its February 1989, strictures against HLTs discouraged bank financing of LBOs. Then FIRREA required S&Ls to divest their junk bond holdings. Drexel and other firms were hurt badly by the resulting plunge in junk bond values. Drexel was in trouble. The Fed and other regulators decided to make it an example. Drexel, which had pioneered the use of junk bonds to finance corporate takeovers, had found itself in federal crosshairs since at least 1987, when Drexel client Ivan Boesky pleaded guilty to insider trading after years of profitably relying on hot tips to buy and sell large blocks of stock of companies that were "in play" in the takeover game. Then, in December 1988, Drexel pled guilty to securities fraud and agreed to fire Michael Milken, the wunderkind of junk bonds. The firm was fined $650 million.

The New York Fed had a tough decision to make. Drexel's government securities subsidiary was one of a select group of "primary dealers," banks and securities firms with whom the Fed deals directly in its purchases and sales of Treasury securities. Corrigan satisfied himself the government securities subsidiary "had nothing to do with all these problems" at Drexel and that its capital was well insulated but was still troubled about the parent company's difficulties. After agonizing over whether to take Drexel off the primary dealer list, he decided not to terminate the relationship. Instead he put it on probation, telling Drexel that if it failed to live up to all of the commitments it had made to the SEC and the Justice Department the Fed would publicly stop doing business with its government securities affiliate. It was a "tough call," Corrigan told the FOMC on March 27, 1990, but "had we just overtly, publicly, stopped doing business with them instead of privately putting them on notice and putting them on probation, it's now very clear to me that that action, had we taken it, would have caused the demise of the firm." The firm eventually failed anyway, but Corrigan said he "would rather that it happened the way it did than as a result of some overt action on our part."

Despite the Fed's forbearance, it was all downhill for Drexel after its run-in with the SEC. Aside from its costly legal problems, the bloom was off the LBO rose. In May 1989, Drexel had helped underwrite a record $4 billion of corporate bonds to finance the takeover of RJR Nabisco by Kohlberg, Kravis, Roberts, but that proved to be Drexel's high-water mark. The bottom was falling out of the junk bond market. Investor confidence in them began to collapse as it became evident S&Ls would be dumping them on the market. Debt-laden corporations could not bear the burden of servicing high-yield bonds in a slowing economy. In October 1989, Drexel lost heavily when it was forced to back out of financing an attempted buyout of UAL Corporation by its employees. Its own junk bond portfolio suffered as the market collapsed. Soon it was on the ropes with no one in its corner.

Viewed as an upstart ally of antisocial "corporate raiders," Drexel had made a lot of enemies in the corporate world, on Wall Street and in government, which ironically was one of the biggest holders of its junk bonds, having inherited them from failed S&Ls now in RTC receivership. Many at the Fed, the SEC, and Treasury regarded Drexel the way a narcotics officer regards a pusher. In their eyes, it had inveigled S&Ls and others into buying junk bonds, encouraged corporations to take on excessive debt, and weakened credit standards by spurring competition in highly leveraged finance from banks and thrifts. Its good works, such as providing vital funding for fledgling enterprises like Cable News Network, were forgotten. In mid-1989, nine months before its Götterdämmerung, Greenspan was overheard telling some associates, "I'll rescue the American banking system because I have to, but I'll be damned if I'll rescue Drexel Burnham." Many figured Drexel would be considered "too big to fail," like Continental Illinois. To the contrary, the Fed had decided to showcase Drexel's failure as a display of its Hobbesian willingness to let the market work and let financial kingpins fall. "The problem with Drexel was that Drexel didn't cultivate as many friends in Washington and in the [Federal Reserve] system as it should have in order to survive," says Maria Fiorini-Ramirez, then Drexel's chief economist. "The regulators, who were closing 30 banks per day, were very happy to shut Drexel down. They forced it to close at the margin." All it needed was the ability to roll over a couple hundred million dollars worth of commercial paper, but "there was an unwillingness to let Drexel survive."

On February 5, 1990, Drexel Burnham Lambert reported a 1989 loss of $40 million on revenues of $4.1 billion, on top of an estimated $160 million 1988 loss. Drexel chairman Frederick H. Josephs minimized the loss, but in fact the firm was in worse shape than it seemed. It faced a bad liquidity crisis. Like many securities firms, only more so, Drexel funded itself on a day-to-day basis, borrowing short-term through commercial paper (corporate IOUs). It had an ample securities portfolio, but it was not very liquid, so it depended on banks and other lenders for short-term credit. Drexel Burnham Lambert Group, or DBL Group, parent company for broker-dealer Drexel Burnham Lambert, as well as government securities and commodities subsidiaries, had in excess of $3 billion in debt outstanding. It had issued more than $700 million in commercial paper in 1989, but as its problems mounted in late 1989, its paper was downgraded, the market for it dried up, and Drexel was forced to pay off some $575 million in commercial paper it could not roll over. This left Drexel with insufficient funds to meet other obligations. It began relying on cash from its commodity trading subsidiary, then from the capital account of its broker-dealer. Compounding its problems, Drexel had been paying large bonuses, partly in stock, partly in cash, to keep key employees, aggravating the company's financial squeeze.

By February, with little cash left and with much of its credit cut off, the Fed and the SEC got wind of Drexel's predicament. The Fed had alerted the SEC that Drexel was draining capital from its broker-dealer to meet its obligations. Once again, it was crisis management time for Corrigan. As he had during the October 1987 crash, Greenspan relied on him to oversee the dismantling of Drexel and to make sure it had no untoward effects on the financial system. "It was one of these kind of 'Geez, what happens now?' situations," recalls Crow. "When a securities player fails . . . how do you avoid gridlock, everybody kind of backing off and nothing going through. There were some very challenging issues that fell upon the Fed." The crisis came to a head on February 13, when Drexel was forced to declare bankruptcy. Corrigan had suspected Drexel was in fatal trouble the week before. "When it became apparent that the bonus payments had been made by upstreaming capital from the broker-dealer to the parent and then those bonus payments made through the parent, which was a violation of the spirit if not the letter of the SEC capital rules, then it became very apparent that a slug of commercial paper was going to mature early that next week and the parent company did not have the resources to pay off the commercial paper," he recalls. On Sunday, February 11, Josephs met with a group of major banks and investment banks and asked to borrow $300 million. They were not interested. That evening, while watching a game on television, Corrigan got a call from one of the participants informing him "the thing was coming unravelled and that they thought that what was going to happen next was that the Drexel people were going to try to get me to pressure the banks to make the loan."

"I knew at that point that the thing was history," Corrigan says. "There was no doubt in my mind that the ballgame was over." He also knew the proper response was to resist any Drexel request for assistance. Corrigan called Greenspan and Brady and told them Drexel had reached the end of the line, that he expected Drexel to ask him to pressure the banks into providing credit, and that he intended to turn them down flat. He also informed SEC chairman Richard Breeden. "Sure enough on Monday morning [February 12] I got a call . . . basically saying, 'You have to make the banks make these loans,' " Corrigan relates. "Well, I wasn't about to make the banks make any loans. Even the day the stock market crashed, I never made a bank make a loan. I told them to look at the big picture and all that, but I never said you've got to make a loan. Certainly I would never say you have to make a specific loan. You have to keep the credit wheels turning and all that, but saying you have to make this loan to this guy, I mean, you never can say that. I just couldn't ever, ever do that!" Josephs was desperate. "He called me up too," Seidman says. "I suppose he called everybody he ever knew." But Seidman would not lean on the banks to lend to Drexel, any more than the Fed. Seidman says, "It was more likely the FDIC would say, 'We don't want you to lend money to this account,' or at least we'd say, 'You're going to have to classify this loan,' because of the additional borrowing." When banks refused to roll over its commercial paper or provide other forms of credit, Drexel's fate was sealed. Its only choice was to liquidate its securities portfolio, but as a former Drexel officer observes, "When you're forced to liquidate and there's no bid in the market you can't liquidate."

As Monday, February 12, wore on, it became obvious to Corrigan that Drexel's final demise "was going to happen sooner rather than later." Late that night he called Josephs and told him he had until seven o'clock the next morning to make up his mind what he was going to do, reminding him DBL had subsidiaries regulated by the Fed, the SEC, and the CFTC. At 7:05 A.M. on Tuesday, February 13, Corrigan got a call from Josephs basically saying he would consider putting the parent company and all of the unregulated entities into bankruptcy that morning. Corrigan told him that was "constructive," but advised him, "We're not going to be able to save these regulated entities anyway" because even if the Fed made a statement of support, Drexel would experience a "run" that would make it impossible for the government securities and broker-dealer subsidiaries to survive. "I think it's in our interest, in the interest of the markets and all the rest of it, to really try to cushion that run," Corrigan told Josephs.

Knowing there would be a mad dash by Drexel's creditors to get their money from the failing firm, Corrigan coordinated with Breeden and Drexel to limit the collateral damage. It was agreed late Tuesday morning that the SEC would issue a statement saying the broker-dealer was in compliance with SEC capital rules, which technically it was, and that the New York Fed would issue a statement saying Drexel's government security dealer, a separate legal entity, was in compliance with primary dealer standards. The press releases were synchronized. The Fed statement said Drexel would be liquidating its government securities portfolio in an "orderly" fashion and that the Fed would "carefully monitor" the Drexel situation. Breeden announced the SEC and the New York Stock Exchange were "carefully monitoring the liquidity of Drexel Burnham Lambert Group Incorporated and its registered broker-dealer subsidiary Drexel Burnham Lambert Incorporated. Both the SEC and NYSE currently have examination teams on the premises of DBL. Inventory schedules and other detailed financial information submitted by DBL indicate that at this time the registered broker-dealer has positive net worth and remains in capital compliance. In cooperation with the NYSE, transfers of net capital of the broker-dealer to its parent corporation have been prohibited without prior specific approval. The SEC will continue close oversight of the broker-dealer's ongoing operations in cooperation with personnel of the New York Stock Exchange." Late Tuesday, having defaulted on $100 million in loans, Drexel declared bankruptcy.

Corrigan says his "strategy was predicated on his belief that once Drexel's statement got out there was no way in the world you were going to be able to finance and salvage those two regulated entities, but what you had to do was to buy enough time for a soft landing, to coin a phrase." It was a "very revealing case study" of what can happen to a firm's financing when creditors smell blood. "The minute the statement of Drexel went out and notwithstanding what the SEC and the Fed said about the broker-dealer and the government securities [subsidiary], . . . virtually no one was willing to do the plain vanilla, simple repurchase agreement transaction with the broker-dealer and the GSI [Government Securities Incorporated] notwithstanding the fact that it was book entry, delivery against payment, collateral in hand, margin in hand, I mean, no risk at all! Just no risk! But once that trap door opens it's history. It's a remarkable illustration of the contagion problem and all the rest of it." The final end came swiftly. Ramirez recalls going to the CNBC studios in midtown Manhattan for an interview amid rumors Drexel was having trouble funding itself. "By the time I got back to the office, it was well-known in the firm that the firm was going to shut down." She differs with Corrigan's insistence he could not ask banks to lend to Drexel. "It's not that the Fed can't force banks to do anything; there have been instances where it has either encouraged or discouraged something. [But] Drexel was not viewed as a friendly party to help."

While declining to lean on banks to lend to Drexel, the Fed quietly assured its creditors they could borrow from the Fed if Drexel defaulted on its obligations, and it stood ready to lend securities from the Fed's portfolio as Drexel's government securities subsidiary was liquidated. The Fed's refusal to help Drexel itself laid to rest the perception there was almost no one the government would not bail out and that the Fed gave banks their marching orders. "I've been around it a long time, and if they do it, they sure do it cleverly!" says Seidman. The already soft junk bond market took another hit when Drexel went down, but the markets at large took in stride the firm's bankruptcy and subsequent liquidation over a period of weeks. Sternlight called that "a notable achievement given that this was a major player in a variety of markets with pre-bankruptcy balance sheet positions on the order of $28 billion and similarly large interest rate swap positions off the books." The unwinding of Drexel's operations and positions did not go smoothly by accident. Corrigan recalls "an absolutely extraordinary effort involved in managing the Drexel thing . . . babysitting that thing almost transaction by transaction, to make sure that that [failure] occurred in an orderly way and did not destabilize markets." The Fed's major concern was that Drexel's "difficulties could spread to other firms with potentially disruptive systemic consequences," Sternlight later told the FOMC. "For a couple of weeks rumors did in fact abound in regard to some other U.S. investment banking concerns, with particular focus on those with appreciable junk bond or bridge loan exposure. These firms experienced a more cautious attitude—even a pulling away—by some usual funding sources." More vulnerable firms had to boost their capital or get statements of support from their parent companies. Banks became more cautious in lending to the securities industry. Securities firms became more cautious to avoid getting in similarly exposed positions.

There was speculation Drexel's collapse would spur a Fed easing, but while symptomatic of broader problems, it was digested relatively easily and soon forgotten. The Fed moved on. It still had its eye on inflation. Those who thought the Fed was satisfied with stabilizing the inflation rate at around the prevailing 4½ percent rate were "wrong," Angell said on February 15. Conditions were ripe "to further disinflate" and reach "price stability" within four years. In his February 20 Humphrey-Hawkins testimony, Greenspan played down economic weakness and played up inflation risks. While it was "premature" to say the slowdown had ended, recent economic data was "more encouraging than otherwise," even though just four days before the Fed announced a sharp drop in industrial production and a decline in capacity utilization from 83.1 to 81.9 percent. "The weakest point may have passed," he told the House Banking Committee. Inflation was still "horrendous" and the outlook for restraining labor costs "not favorable." If the dollar weakened, that would be "another impetus to near-term price increases, reversing the restraining influence exerted by a strong dollar through most of last year." Monetary policy could "support further economic expansion without abandoning the goal of price stability," but the Fed would have to "restrain growth in money and aggregate demand in coming years, enough to establish a clear downward tilt to the trend of inflation and inflation expectations, while avoiding a recession."

Fed watchers and the administration did not need to see the greenbook to infer that the Fed had no plans to lower rates further. Greenspan's rhetorical tilt toward concern about inflation was reinforced by the "central tendency" of economic growth expectations among the Fed governors and presidents. The 19 officials were looking for real GNP growth in the 1¾ to 2 percent range—well below the economy's potential, much less than the administration was forecasting. Johnson made it even more plain when he said on February 21 the Fed's pursuit of price stability might at some point necessitate raising the funds rate if it saw a "sustained rise" in bond yields and commodity prices along with a weakening dollar. When the Labor Department announced two days later the CPI had risen 1.1 percent in January, it became even more obvious rates were not going anywhere. In his second day of Humphrey-Hawkins testimony, Greenspan offered another reason why it might be hard to reduce interest rates. The Berlin Wall had come down the previous fall, Germany was reunified, and Communist dictatorships had toppled throughout eastern Europe. Now, Greenspan told the Senate Banking Committee, potential high returns in the former Soviet satellites were attracting Western capital. Eastern Europe's "potential for growth" was extraordinary, "and it is that which has led to pools of savings looking to Eastern Europe as a potential source of great returns." This had forced rates up, as more traditional investments competed for funds. He could only hope the run-up in rates had been "overdone." To some, his citing of European interest rate pressures sounded like an excuse for not easing credit in the United States, but Greenspan's analysis was sound. The yield on 30-year Treasury bonds was then in the neighborhood of 8.6 percent, but would go to 9⅛ percent in late April, before retreating, and there was no question increased competition for world savings had contributed. It was not the only factor. There were still inflation pressures, and the full extent of the impending economic slowdown was not yet evident.

For the moment, the dollar was relatively strong, and Johnson said on March 5 that continued dollar strengthening would give the Fed "breathing room" to lower interest rates. At the time, the dollar was worth more than 150 yen and 1.71 marks. To the Treasury's consternation the dollar would strengthen a good bit further against the yen, but the Fed left the funds rate unchanged. By early March, some of Bush's advisers were so angry at Greenspan they leaked word he was unlikely to be reappointed when his term expired in 1991. Brady and Darman were his biggest foes. Although they tempered their public rhetoric, they were intent on getting lower rates to validate their budget assumptions. Long-term rates had risen nearly three-quarters of a percent since December 1989, and they seemed to think the Fed could somehow bring them down, even though the Fed had limited control of those rates. Inflation was "moderating" and interest rates should reflect that, a "concerned" Brady told Congress. Boskin and Fitzwater downplayed talk of giving Greenspan the boot, saying his reappointment had not even been discussed. Nevertheless, the Fed was feeling the heat. Any hope Brady may have had for Fed rate cuts went aglimmering when the Labor Department reported a big leap in payrolls. Boskin now contented himself with saying Fed policymakers "certainly have flexibility to avoid tightening policy" since inflation was "contained."

The Fed and administration were on a collision course. In a March 12 interview, Assistant Treasury Secretary for Economic Affairs Sidney Jones said there were "not any fundamental differences between the Fed and the Treasury." So long as the Fed "uses judgment" and provides sufficient growth in the money supply, he saw no obstacle to the administration achieving its forecast of 2.6 percent growth in 1990 and 3.3 percent in 1991. "It's no secret the Fed would like to see the economy grow between 1½ percent and 2 percent," but the difference between the two forecasts was similar to "the difference between a running back playing at 204 or 205 pounds." That was wishful thinking. Fed officials I talked to then had made up their minds the only way to make real progress against inflation was to suppress growth. LaWare said the Fed would try to bring inflation as close to zero as possible within five years by holding growth below 2½ percent without causing a recession. Boykin said growth above 2 percent would make him uncomfortable. If the Fed allowed the economy to grow faster it would be difficult "to make any headway on the inflation picture." Parry was worried growth in 1990 would "turn out to be stronger than expected" and might even realize the administration's forecast. "For us to make progress in holding inflation and subsequently reducing it, we've got to see the economy grow less than its potential."

Meanwhile, the economy was moving imperceptibly toward an outcome that would give the Fed more slowness than it had bargained for. The beige book survey conducted for review at the March 27 meeting found growth at a "moderate pace" with signs of strength. But bank credit was giving off ominous signs. Their business and banking contacts were telling the Fed banks about slack credit demand, tightening credit standards, and reductions in all types of lending by financial institutions. "Most districts report that financial institutions are either less willing to extend credit or actually tightening credit terms." Meanwhile, real estate loans were becoming a major concern to bank regulators. Most Fed officials disregarded the danger signals. "I don't find this to be a concern," Parry said. "It's a natural part of the slowdown in the economy. As the economy grows, credit will take care of itself." Whenever the economy slows, businesses borrow less to finance investment in inventories and plant and equipment. Consumers borrow less to finance purchases. But something more was going on. The Fed's HLT rules were reducing business loans. Tight new regulations governing thrifts, such as limits on how much an S&L could lend to one customer or one category of customers, were restricting real estate loans, as was the sheer shrinkage of the thrift industry. Higher mandated capital to asset ratios were forcing them to restrain or even shrink loan portfolios. The only one really warning of a "credit crunch" was Seger, but she was not heeded.

Though not necessarily caused by monetary policy, a monetary policy response would be required. Ultimately, Greenspan acknowledges, the precarious condition of thrifts and many banks that so impaired credit flows motivated an easier monetary stance, but at this stage, the Fed welcomed the constriction of credit as a supplement to its strategy of skating near the edge of recession to combat inflation. The problem was the Fed did not realize just how close to the edge it was skating and did not anticipate the "external shock" of the Persian Gulf War that would tip it over. Even Bush's more softspoken advisers were becoming more vocal in their concern. Sustaining growth had to be the nation's "number one priority," Boskin said March 19. "The monetary authorities must sustain monetary expansion sufficient to maintain growth while controlling inflation." Inflation had been "relatively steady" at 4½ percent. The next day, however, it was disclosed that the CPI had risen at an annual 6 percent rate in February. Heller's departure had given President Bush the chance to appoint one of his own people to the Board of Governors, and on March 23 his nominee David Mullins, then assistant Treasury secretary for domestic financial policy, appeared before the Senate Banking Committee for his confirmation hearing. Mullins, who would soon replace Johnson as vice chairman, had been recruited from Harvard by Brady to work on the S&L crisis and other financial issues. Although he said the Fed was following "the right approach" in maintaining "relatively high real interest rates . . . to break the back of inflation," Mullins would emerge as a force for more aggressive easing. In a hint of that, he said the Fed should fight inflation "in the least costly fashion" and "follow a policy that allows that growth to continue." He swore he had not been asked about his policy prescriptions before being nominated.

Growth was not the only reason the administration was worried about high interest rates. Mulford still wanted lower rates to soften the dollar, particularly against the yen. He was still importuning the Fed to sell dollars. The Fed, while it had no desire to see exports suffer from an overvalued dollar, did not see the dollar as overvalued. Indeed, it saw a firm dollar as an ally against inflation. If it goosed the money supply to lower the dollar/yen rate, it risked inducing a generalized weakness. Selling dollars against yen, aside from being ineffective, sent the wrong signal. When Greenspan took the FOMC's concerns about intervention against the dollar to Brady in late 1989 he hoped that would be the end of it. Greenspan had resisted making threats of noncooperation for fear that if the Fed did not continue its usual 50-50 participation it would lose influence over currency operations. But he made clear many FOMC members were distressed with the Treasury's dollar policies, and Cross and Truman were instructed they should not blindly follow the Treasury's lead on intervention if they determined the intervention was contrary to the Fed's goals and interests. Greenspan's message evidently did not get through to Mulford. When the dollar continued to rise against the yen in early 1990, climbing toward 160 yen, Treasury resumed dollar sales and expected the Fed to cooperate. But by March 2 the Fed had reached its limit, literally and figuratively. After having sold dollars heavily against yen for nearly a week, Cross informed Treasury the Fed would not sell dollars on the Fed's account, only for the Treasury's account. The Treasury continued to sell dollars for yen, with the Fed acting as its agent but not using its own funds. On March 5, Treasury started selling dollars against marks. Once again it asked the Fed to participate. Again it refused. Cross cited the ceiling the FOMC had imposed on how much currency he could buy, but also told Treasury the Fed feared expanded dollar sales against the mark as well as the yen "would be misconstrued as a more generalized effort to reduce the dollar against all currencies." Between the February and March FOMC meetings, the New York Fed sold nearly $1.5 billion against yen and $200 million against marks; all but $325 million were Treasury's.

It was almost unheard of for the Fed to refuse to join the Treasury in intervention, and Mulford and his staff were upset. It was a heady feeling for Fed policymakers as they discussed their little war with the Treasury and what their next move would be at the March 27 FOMC meeting. "My view is that we've had considerable influence standing firm," Johnson said. "The fear at the Treasury of the Fed pulling out of this process in my opinion has been as strong a disciplinary force as anything else." The Treasury had expected the Fed "to engage in the selling of dollars at a time in which no one knew what the down side was in regard to the deutschemark market as we were selling yen, and in this [untenable] position that the Treasury was in I think we had no choice but to separate ourselves from that risk," the combative Angell said, adding, "Mr. Chairman, I'm delighted we have." But Greenspan and others were somewhat taken aback by their own audacity. They worried how the Treasury would react. What if Brady got Congress to order the Fed to do Treasury's bidding in the foreign exchange arena and to eliminate the Fed's international monetary discretion? What if Treasury did an end run around the Fed and entered into an arrangement with the BIS or another central bank to conduct its currency operations? Some had their blood up for a continued feud with Treasury, but Greenspan argued the Fed had made its point and made the Treasury see reason. Now it was time to calm down and be cooperative by increasing the limit on foreign currency holdings from $21 billion to $25 billion and the warehousing limit from $5 billion to $10 billion.

Better to be a participant and have some say in how the dollar was managed and how the supply of reserves was affected than to be out of the loop, Greenspan and Corrigan argued. Yes, Mulford had been "stubborn," Greenspan agreed, but Brady could be made to see reason. "I will tell you that he is not disinclined to scream and yell at us when he doesn't like what we're doing," Greenspan confided, but that had not been the case in his recent talks with Brady on exchange rate matters. Brady had recently flown to Los Angeles to meet with Hashimoto prior to a U.S.-Japan trade summit in Palm Springs, and before he left Greenspan had spent a half hour explaining to him why the yen was temporarily weakening—the fact that money was pouring out of the overvalued Tokyo stock market into international markets. Greenspan had told Brady "the problem was essentially a Japanese problem, that we would in a sense be [spitting into] the wind trying to stop any of this and that we would be perceived as ineffectual in endeavoring to stop any really major move." Greenspan said Brady had taken his advice and resisted Hashimoto's pleading for more U.S. intervention to prop up the yen. Cross said he had detected, since the showdown, that the Treasury had "become much more diffident in terms of the quickness with which they want to jump in and participate in an intervention operation in the yen. . . ." Truman said Treasury had come to "feel that they're better off keeping peace in the family" rather than go to G-7 meetings "at loggerheads with the central bank."

Greenspan said,

To the extent that we at the Board raised concerns to the Treasury, I think we were more heard than not. In effect, I would say that in this most recent endeavor to suppress the decrease in the yen against the dollar about which we raised very strong [objections] and had extended discussions at to why that was desirable or appropriate, it actually paid off. In other words, the Treasury did pull back. As best I can judge, that was largely the result of our reluctance to go along and of the arguments we were making. So, even though in a legal sense we have to interpret ourselves as junior partners, it has been my impression that we do have a significant effect on the overall Treasury decision. Were we to pull away and be strictly [the Treasury's] agent, I think by that very nature we lose completely all of our capability of influencing decisions that could affect our monetary policies. . . . Leaving aside the issue of intervention where it seems appropriate to curb disorderly markets and raising the much broader issues of pegging-type intervention, including G-7 coordinated intervention to drive the dollar down, for example, the question is whether or not we lose our ability to influence those decisions if we pull away. And I must tell you my impression is that we do. Frankly, I would be quite fearful of what they might do if we weren't there to harass them toward some degree of sensibleness.

Truman observed that Treasury officials naively viewed foreign exchange intervention as an effective "instrument of dealing with a trade [deficit] problem."

Some still were not persuaded and resisted raising the foreign exchange holdings limit to $25 billion. The limit had already been raised several times, and some thought it was high enough at $21 billion. Not only was the Fed subject to incurring large losses on these holdings, which could expose it to congressional scrutiny and criticism, but the need to offset large quantities of dollar sales by draining reserves in open market operations could have a disruptive and misleading effect on the money markets. Moreover, Johnson observed, "If I were a market participant and I were sitting out there seeing the Federal Reserve talking about price stability and yet selling massive amounts of dollars, I think eventually I'd decide that was a joke as a policy." The Fed should threaten to "pull out" of foreign exchange operations with the Treasury or deny it warehousing facilities unless it saw things the Fed's way. Melzer did not think it was reasonable to refuse to warehouse currency for Treasury but said, "I think we really have to try to draw some ultimate line in the sand and then work very hard to get a different understanding with the Treasury." Hoskins wanted an even sharper line. He had opposed increasing the forex limit from $10 to $12 billion, from $12 to $15 billion, and from $15 billion to $20 billion. "Now we're going to $25 billion, and much the same arguments were made each time as to why we were going up and the necessity of going up." He was unwilling to vote for any more increases. If the Fed drew that hard a line Treasury would go to Congress and "effectively put us out of the operation," Greenspan told him. "You may find that attractive; frankly I don't."

Finally, Greenspan brought the question of raising the ceiling on foreign exchange holdings and warehousing to a vote after promising the FOMC members he would carry their concerns to the Treasury again and tell Treasury the Fed was reaching the limits of how much foreign currency it felt it could prudently hold. He also pledged the Fed's participation in intervention would be "discretionary, but with the strong presumption that the system will join the Treasury as long as there is reasonable two-way communication about U.S. policy objectives and tactics in this area." If the Treasury tried to commit the Fed to "concerted intervention to drive the dollar down," Greenspan said, "At that particular stage I think we would have a confrontation. . . . When I say we'll have a confrontation I don't mean a big one. We'll have a big dispute and I think the highly likely occurrence is that they would be unhappy but they would back down." The FOMC approved the increases in both limits on 11 to 3 votes, with Angell, Hoskins, and LaWare opposed. For now the Fed-Treasury contention over intervention had subsided, but the issue did not go away. Black's successor as Richmond Fed president, Alfred Broaddus, and his director of research Marvin Goodfriend, writing in the Bank's 1995 annual report argued, "The Fed should be separated completely from the Treasury's foreign exchange operations."

The domestic part of the March 27 FOMC agenda was no less disputatious. To the members' astonishment, the staff had dramatically increased the funds rate assumption in its forecast. It would need to rise a full percent to 9¼ percent by early 1991 "to temper growth in aggregate demand through 1991 and to set the stage for a renewed slowing of the underlying trend of inflation," said Prell, who told an aghast Syron "a one point change in the funds rate really wouldn't look all that dramatic." He had some support among hawks, but others were becoming alarmed about the credit crunch. "We may have witnessed here a transfer of at least part of the control of the growth of the economy as a result of this extraordinarily stringent application of examination standards to the banks," LaWare said. "I'm concerned that that will, in fact, cause a contraction of credit that may deal a greater blow to inflation than our current policy." Greenspan again argued for no tightening. While there was "unquestionably an improving business cycle," he worried about a "deterioration and erosion in balance sheets." He was still agnostic about "whether the credit crunch is real," but said "it has to be partly real unless human nature has been repealed because there has to be a fundamental response to what has occurred." Greenspan had another reason for leaving policy unchanged. While not wanting to weaken the dollar he was wary of driving it higher. The exchange rate effect of higher interest rates "would really be quite a destabilizing force." Angell concurred, adding that "the transmission mechanism of monetary policy is increasingly through the foreign exchange rate." Greenspan got his way. The FOMC left the funds rate at 8¼ percent with no predisposition either to raise or lower it. Boykin and Hoskins again dissented, the former wanting a bias toward tightening, the latter wanting an immediate rate hike.

The Fed-Treasury dust-up over intervention did not end exchange rate concerns. The United States and Japan were then in the midst of one of their perennial rounds of trade talks, and the yen's weakness exacerbated trade tensions. So concerned were G-7 finance ministers and central bankers over the yen's weakness they did not wait for their regular May 6 meeting, but gathered a month early in Paris. Since the September 23, 1989, G-7 meeting, the dollar had risen from just under 146 yen to nearly 160 yen. Neither large-scale intervention nor a 1 percent increase in the Bank of Japan's discount rate had stemmed it. The dollar, meanwhile, had fallen against the mark from DM1.9510 to about DM1.70. So, unlike September, when the G-7 had expressed concern about the general rise of the dollar, concern now centered on the yen's weakness. Going into the meeting, Japanese vice finance minister Makoto Utsumi told me the yen's weakness was "against the fundamentals" and would not likely continue. Japan was beginning to have serious problems. Its stock market had fallen 30 percent in the weeks leading up to the G-7 meeting. In their April 7 communiqué, the G-7 singled out "the decline of the yen" as a source of "undesirable consequences for the global adjustment process" and again pledged to "cooperate in exchange markets." But while the Japanese were still eager to intervene, neither the United States nor Germany wanted to join in efforts to force up the yen that might weaken their own currencies. The Treasury now pinned its hopes on Fed rate cuts to soften the dollar.

The Fed, as turned out, had succeeded all too well in persuading Treasury to be less active in the currency markets. Reporting on the G-7 meeting in an April 11 FOMC conference call, Greenspan said, "What was really quite interesting as we went into it was the increasingly anti-intervention views of our Secretary of the Treasury." Brady had "come into the process with what he called an open mind but had been observing the phenomenon now for quite a while and had concluded in far stronger language than anyone on this Committee has that 'it just doesn't work.' " Brady contrasted the $40 billion that had been expended in a futile effort to support the yen to the daily $650 billion turnover in the foreign exchange market to illustrate the futility of intervention. He had already begun to abandon his support for intervention in his conversation with Greenspan before his March 4 meeting with Hashimoto. Now he and Mulford had seemingly become reborn noninterventionists. The other G-7 officials were also reluctant to engage in substantial intervention at the meeting and instead pressured Japan to raise its interest rates to strengthen the yen—something the Japanese resisted. So, while agreeing the yen was out of line, the G-7 had essentially decided to do nothing about it.

When they held their regularly scheduled meeting on May 6, the dollar was still hovering near 160 yen, and G-7 officials repeated their warning about the weak yen's "undesirable consequences." As it turned out, however, that was the high-water mark for the dollar, not only against the yen, but against other currencies. From then on, the dollar would begin an almost unbroken slide that greatly complicated monetary policy and the Fed's relationship with the Treasury. It would not be long before concern about the dollar's strength would seem rather quaint. The Fed had been relieved to be out from under the Treasury gun on intervention, but it became apparent the Treasury had not had any genuine change of heart on intervention. It merely saw the market moving its way. The administration was determined to work the dollar lower against the yen given the "resistance" it was getting from Japan on lowering trade barriers. Once so eager to intervene to weaken the dollar, the Treasury did not resort to intervention to strengthen the dollar as it began falling dramatically. Treasury's new posture "was partly the fact that, from a trade and current account position, one welcomed an orderly depreciation of the dollar," Dallara confesses. "But it also reflected the fact that Brady increasingly dug his heels in in resisting continued intervention, and I recall clearly that he got exasperated a bit with David and me" for continuing to advocate intervention. Not until the dollar had fallen to 125 yen was Treasury prepared to intervene, says Dallara. "Even we at the Treasury got a bit antsy about it at that point." Then Secretary of State Baker did not like the way Treasury had moved away from his G-7 coordination approach and asked Brady about it. Brady told him he was having "trouble getting the Fed to participate."[3]

The weaker the dollar became over 1990, the more difficult it became for the Fed to ease credit as much as the administration wanted. "We were always trying to urge the Fed to take action sooner," recalls a Brady aide, but Greenspan or another Fed official would respond that, given the dollar's weakness, it could not ease any faster. "We tried to put an awful lot of pressure on them in terms of moving faster, but there's no big hammer that you can pound the Fed with to make them take action. They will take it when they feel it's right." Corrigan says the weak dollar did delay easing in 1990—"not in a decisive way, but nonetheless it was a factor." A big concern at the May G-7 meeting was the upsurge in interest rates worldwide. The yield on the Treasury long bond had gone as high as 9.07 percent the week before. Bank of Japan governor Yasushi Mieno emphasized the need for increased national savings, a polite way of telling the United States to cut its budget deficit.

By then, Bush's commitment to his "no new taxes pledge" was beginning to erode in face of Congress's refusal to accept or even consider his fiscal 1991 budget, which had proposed to reduce the deficit to $63.1 billion by restraining spending growth. On April 26, as the House overwhelmingly rejected Ohio Republican congressman John Kasich's proposal to freeze spending, Boskin was asked whether deficit reduction was possible without raising taxes. "It's conceptually possible, but whether it's politically possible remains to be seen," he replied. "We have made clear we're not fond of tax increases, but we have also said we're reasonable people. . . . We're willing to listen and debate everything on its merits." But it was Darman who was behind the fateful decision to accede to Democrat demands for higher taxes, say several former Bush aides. The OMB director had begun talking to the Democrats in March, and by spring Darman and Sununu had committed to a full-fledged "budget summit." The talks culminated in the biggest ever tax hike just as the economy went into recession, making it more difficult for the Fed to revitalize the economy. Darman "personally cost us the election, and he did it over the objections of, I would say, 95 percent of the senior staff," one former Bush staffer says. "But that's Dick 'I know better than everyone else' Darman." Another aide calls the 1990 budget deal "a mistake" of Darman's making. No one should have been surprised. As a top White House aide in the early eighties, Darman had led a counterrevolution against the Reagan tax cuts, leading to the 1982 Tax Equity and Fiscal Responsibility Act (TEFRA). TEFRA was supposed to have reduced spending three dollars for every dollar of higher taxes, but Congress reneged. The pattern was repeated following tax hikes in 1984 and 1986. Still Darman persuaded Bush to raise taxes on the promise that spending would be controlled.

The Democrats played it smart politically. Senate Budget Committee Chairman James Sasser, House Ways and Means Committee Chairman Dan Rostenkowski, and House Budget Committee Chairman Leon Panetta had been calling for repeal of the Gramm-Rudman Act, with its descending annual deficit targets, because it had slowed spending, but they used Gramm-Rudman as leverage to get what they wanted. To fuel more spending they needed more revenues. So, after rejecting Bush's budget out of hand and producing CBO economic projections that showed the deficit greatly exceeding the $64 billion 1991 target, they and Darman convinced Bush negotiations were necessary to meet the target. It was a slippery slope toward higher taxes. Bush's alternative would have been to use the law's provisions to order a spending sequester to hold the deficit at target, but Darman convinced Bush a sequester would be disruptively big—an estimated $100 billion.

Though not directly involved in the budget talks, Greenspan played a key role. He always expressed a preference for reducing the deficit "on the spending side," but emphasized the important thing was to reduce the deficit by whatever means. The Fed had made clear it would not supply the kind of money the economy would need to realize the kind of growth the Bush budget had assumed. With lower than expected growth, higher than expected interest rates, with the RTC swelling government spending, and with the Democrats unwilling to consider the administration's "flexible freeze" on spending, it became obvious the deficit was going to exceed the Gramm-Rudman target. If the administration was to get the rate cuts it wanted, it was going to have to strike a deal with Congress, and given Democrats' intransigence on restraining spending, that would mean agreeing to a tax hike. The Fed had remained reluctant to lower rates. Consumer prices had risen at a 6 percent annual rate (8½ percent excluding food and energy) in March. Although construction plunged, rising industrial production pushed capacity utilization from 82.9 to 83.3 percent, and despite scant payroll growth, unemployment dipped to 5.2 percent. "It heightens the chances we'll have more inflationary problems than I'd like to see," one policymaker confided. "It's more likely you'll see more upward wage pressure." It was the kind of Phillips Curve thinking that infuriated Bush's advisors. One disputed "the notion there's a trade-off between inflation and unemployment. There's no hard-edged potential GNP rate or unemployment rate that's too high or too low." The administration was not going to win that argument. Getting lower rates would require either a weaker economy or deficit reduction.

The Fed was slow in acknowledging underlying trends toward a weaker economy, particularly the drying up of credit. Through March, business loans had declined four months in a row. Consumer credit had slowed. A survey of 60 senior bank loan officers conducted by the Fed in April found "a decreased willingness to extend overall business credit" among a fifth of them. Three-quarters had tightened credit standards on merger-related loans, and half had tightened standards on nonmerger-related loans. Four-fifths reported a "reduced willingness" to make real estate loans. Three-fifths reported reducing permissible loan-to-value ratios, and so on. The less favorable economic outlook was only one of the reasons banks cited. Under congressional pressure, the bank regulatory pendulum was swinging from laxity to harsh restraint, just as the economy was slowing. Comptroller of the Currency Robert Clarke, an old pal of Jim Baker, had become the self-proclaimed "regulator from hell," and his national bank examiners acquired a reputation for clamping down hard on bank lending. Banks were constantly looking over their shoulders for fear the feds would rap their knuckles for making loans they disapproved of. The OCC had come up with a new category of "performing nonperforming loans"—loans that were still being serviced but were deemed unviable for various reasons, for example, high vacancy rates in an office building being financed. If a building's value had declined and, in the opinion of the examiners, could no longer generate sufficient income to make principal and interest payments, or if the borrower was using loan proceeds to make interest payments on the loan, the examiner classified the loan as *nonperforming* or *nonaccrual*, forcing the bank to set aside loan loss reserves, further reducing its ability and willingness to lend. It was rumored Greenspan had taken Clarke to task for being overly zealous in examining national banks, but he denies any such confrontation.

On April 25, in the first of many hearings on the "credit crunch," House Small Business Committee Chairman John LaFalce, a New York Democrat, complained "well-run businesses, particularly small businesses" were being denied credit because of overly strict regulation. While regulators needed to be tough, "healthy, solvent fiscally well-run companies should not be denied the credit needed to keep in business." Massachusetts Democrat Representative Joseph Kennedy charged regulators were "acting with unprecedented and unannounced toughness." Credit was "in short supply because banks have been required to reserve an excessive amount of cash against loan losses, and regulatory actions have sowed confusion and apprehension in financial markets, thus prompting overly cautious lending practices." A survey of 1,800 small businesses had been conducted by the Massachusetts Industrial Finance Agency, and its executive director Joseph Blair said banks had capped or suspended existing lines of credit; renegotiated the terms of lines of credit; reclassified loans without good reason; reappraised the value of the collateral for loans; and changed or reinterpreted loan covenants. Borrowers were "experiencing unusual delays in the process of applying for a loan" and sometimes were "unable to obtain capital." Banks blamed regulators for imposing "excessively high capitalization rates" in the range of 12 to 14 percent instead of the usual 9 to 10 percent; forcing "drastic discounts on appraisals; requiring banks to take hits to their reserves"; classifying performing loans as nonperforming; making "unreasonably pessimistic assumptions about lease-up or real estate assets"; forcing some real estate loans into nonperforming status even if borrowers were current; and "disallowing the recognition of income on nonperforming loans," thereby driving down bank earnings and equity.

Boskin said he had "heard enough anecdotes [about the credit crunch] that it's no longer anecdotal" and feared it might "get out of hand" and cause "a downturn in the economy." But such prognostications were only beginning to be seriously listened to in April by a Fed still committed to limiting credit expansion to hold down growth and inflation. The big exception was Seger, who had "an awful feeling that [the credit crunch] is going to get worse before it gets better. The reduction in credit availability has become a big problem not just for highly leveraged firms but for normal customers." She felt the Fed needed to offset these credit strains. LaWare warned a "spreading credit crunch" could dampen the economy, but did not think there was much the Fed could do about it. "We can create all kinds of reserves, but we can't make bankers lend. This takes monetary policy partly out of our hands." Even the term *credit crunch* incited debate on the FOMC. There was "a fairly heated discussion over the issue of 'What is a credit crunch and why do you think we have one?' " recalls Hoskins, who "never viewed it as a credit crunch" and "thought that we shouldn't be focusing on that issue, that we ought to be focusing on what policy should be all about, which is controlling money to control inflation." Hoskins, now an Ohio bank executive, objected strongly when Greenspan started using the term *credit crunch*. As far as he was concerned, "All that happened was that the price of credit was going up. It wasn't that banks were cutting it off. It seemed to me they simply either were perceiving more risk or whatever and were charging more. I look at a credit crunch as credit not available at any price. Credit was available; it was the price that people didn't like." Angell considers the term *credit crunch* a relic of the Regulation Q era, where interest rate ceilings caused disintermediation and constricted credit flows. "I never bought into the notion of the credit crunch in the conventional way that it was talked about," says Corrigan. "The conventional way, of course, was that the credit . . . process was grinding to a halt because the banks couldn't or wouldn't make loans. To my way of thinking the problem was much more a demand side problem than a supply side problem. [People were] looking at their balance sheet and saying, 'My God! I have a whole pile of debt here, in an environment of increased uncertainties, of unemployment prospects and income prospects and I have to scale back!' " Semantic arguments aside, something was going on, and the question was what to do about it. "I didn't think we needed to do anything special about it, either in a regulatory way or in a policy way," says Hoskins, who saw the credit crunch as an unwinding of credit quality problems that had arisen when banks adopted sloppy S&L loan practices. "They were doing deals with no equity in them." He remembers a Cleveland Fed branch board meeting where a developer said, " 'Boy, things are really difficult out there. I mean, I actually had to, to get some credit, put five percent equity into this deal!' And the manufacturing guys are starting to laugh around the table, because they've always had to do that!" When the regulators started imposing more rigorous standards, it seemed like a credit crunch.

But Greenspan and others began to realize the regulators had gone too far and were discouraging lending. "We sat there, on occasion after occasion, saying that the Federal Reserve and FDIC and Comptroller of the Currency 'soldiers in the field' were into the carryover restraint mode . . . ," says Angell. LaWare says, "The regulatory authorities contributed to the number of banks that failed because they were too rigid in what they required in terms of the treatment of troubled loan portfolios. I think that all of us erred on the side of 'We're not going to be tarred and feathered with the forbearance label. We're going to be tough. We're going to require these loans be written off, and if that fails the bank, so be it, we're going to fail the bank.' It's totally contrary to the experience of the American banking system to say, 'Hey, you have a borrower in trouble. Shut 'em down.' The whole history of the banking system in this country has been that when you have a borrower who's in trouble you work with him. You restructure the loan. Well, they put up penalties for restructuring the loan, and stigmata were visited on any bank that was doing that. . . . I think the super-punitive attitude of the examiners and the regulatory authorities contributed to the recession. First of all, it dried up credit. And secondly, it brought down a lot of companies that were otherwise viable, if they had been able to rework their obligations."

Another Fed policymaker concedes bank examiners, including the Fed's, overreacted to earlier laxity and helped create a credit crunch, "because they were human beings. Instead of raising the question, 'did they respond more aggressively on the contraction side than one would have expected?' the question is: 'is it even remotely conceivable that they would not have?' " Human nature also made it difficult to undo the Uncle Scrooge face examiners had put on, no matter how hard Greenspan personally tried. "The problem you have, if you're an examiner and things get away from you, even if it's got nothing to do with what you're doing . . . , if things turn adverse, your risk aversion is very clearly toward making certain things do not get worse. When I say it's human nature, it's an almost impossible thing when you're dealing with thousands of people to turn them around, because . . . if the institutions they are examining go into liquidation they are very significantly pilloried—not necessarily by their peers, but by themselves. . . . If you go across the street and almost get hit by a car, the next week when you cross, you're going to be very careful, . . . And we had to try to fight this psychological thing. . . . We tried all different vehicles to counter something we knew that we couldn't counter by just putting an order out, . . . and it turned out it didn't work that well."

"What eventually broke the back of the credit crunch and relieved the pressure on lending officers was lower interest rates," says Greenspan, but not until much later. The question the Fed had to ask in spring 1990 and beyond was how much it should be trying to offset tightening credit conditions by lowering rates. It's still a question that haunts policymakers. "If we had eased more or eased more quickly, would it have been material?" Corrigan asks. "Would it have mattered? My answer is probably and almost certainly not. Because we had to work off all of those credit excesses, on both the part of the borrowers and lenders. And under any circumstances that was going to take some time. We also had to go through that very difficult process of getting these major financial institutions back on their feet. That, in retrospect, went much faster than I thought it would at the time. I thought we had a five-year adjustment process. And in the end, basically, it was about 2½."

There was still serious speculation about the Fed raising rates in late April, despite the looming credit crunch. The Fed had done too good a job convincing the markets the economy's forward momentum was generating wage-price pressures. But Greenspan was beginning to modify his outlook. In an April 30 speech, he deflated 9 percent–plus long bond yields when he described the economy as "like a tire with a slow leak" and said he expected growth to be "somewhere between modest and moderate." It was the first sign his mood was moving toward ease, but the internal debate over credit conditions raged on.

On May 1, Parry maintained real estate finance was actually "less prone to credit crunches" than before thanks to the deregulation of deposit rates, the advent of adjustable rate mortgages and the development of a secondary mortgage market. Although lending was being restricted by bank and thrift problems, he saw this as "only temporary" and thought the Fed should be more concerned that the economy's "very high level" of operation was creating "troubling signs of inflationary pressures." What was needed was "an extended period of slow growth." By contrast, Kelley saw "very little evidence there's going to be a meaningful reacceleration of the economy" and considered the recent inflation bulge "temporary." Seger warned that "by the time [the credit crunch] is obvious to all of us it will be too late to do anything about it." The economic numbers from April were starting to support the doves. Nonfarm payrolls dropped, and the unemployment rate jumped two-tenths of a percent to 5.4 percent. Industrial production, retail sales, and housing starts all fell, as did producer prices, while consumer prices rose just 0.2 percent. Most dramatically, on May 14 the Fed's survey of bank loan officers reported non-merger-related business lending had "virtually ceased." The economy suddenly seemed to be falling apart.

At the May 15 FOMC meeting, incredibly, the staff had upped its forecast of how much the funds rate needed to be raised to 200 basis points by mid-1991, which would have pushed the rate to 10¼ percent, higher even than at its February 1989 peak. Growth had to be restrained, said Prell, or unemployment would not rise enough to lower inflation. "I hate to sound like Ginny Dimwit today," Seger said, but "exactly which sectors are the ones that we have to restrain? I'm having a problem finding such sectors out there." Boehne told Prell there was "certainly no national support for this kind of firming in monetary policy, as best I can tell," and he questioned his forecast that, despite this draconian tightening, inflation would still be in the 4 to 5 percent range. Given the slowing of growth in credit and money, Melzer wondered "whether there's a significant tightening going on already with the funds rate at a constant level." Complaints about credit becoming unavailable were rampant. Corrigan, while skeptical there was a "credit crunch" properly defined, confessed, "I still can't quite shake a sense of uneasiness that there may be something there that we just haven't seen yet." LaWare declared, "The credit crunch is real, and I don't think it's necessarily confined to real estate. I'm convinced that it's going to get worse. . . ." He warned the economy was "very close to the possibility of tipping over into recession," which would cause credit-starved firms to fail. But Prell minimized the credit crunch, saying, "The only significant effects are going to be in the construction area," which was "overbuilt" anyway. He predicted the problem would go away within a year.

The meeting coincided with the formal start of the budget summit, and already a mindset was developing that monetary policy action should be held in abeyance pending budgetary action. Within a couple of months, when the economy had become so weak the Fed was forced to consider easing, it would be argued repeatedly easing must await the outcome of the budget talks. Now, the talks were being cited as a reason to delay tightening. "It seems to me that with the budget summit that is starting today, a tightening of policy before this meeting is concluded might very well reduce the pressures on the negotiating parties to actually restrain the budget, meaning less would be done," Forrestal said. Corrigan said that if there was a budget deal that tightened fiscal policy, "It's going to make things [tightening monetary policy] very difficult for us in an ironic kind of fashion." Adding to the mix, was the weakening dollar. It fell to Greenspan to make sense of it all and mold a consensus out of disparate viewpoints. He resisted the staff's urging to push up interest rates. That might become necessary, but for now his well-honed instincts were telling him it would be the wrong medicine. Although outwardly the economy seemed to be "mildly accelerating," Greenspan had become convinced "we have something more than a merely minor financial disturbance. I think there may well be more to this credit crunch than we're looking at; or to put it more exactly, I don't think we're through it yet." To tighten in face of the credit crunch would be "a mistake." With Hoskins dissenting, the FOMC left the funds rate at 8¼ percent with no bias.

Although the bond market was starting to bet on an economic downturn, lowering the long bond yield from a peak of 9.07 to 8.59 percent by late May, recession was still the farthest thing from most Fed officials' minds. "We're in the midst of a soft landing," Black said in a May 21 interview. "Maybe we've already achieved it." However, June brought evidence of further softness in the labor market and a third straight monthly drop in retail sales. Another concern was the deceleration of the money supply. Earlier in the year, M2 had been growing in the upper part of the Fed's target range of 3 to 7 percent, but now it was growing at the bottom of the range and threatening to go below it. Taylor, ordinarily one of Bush's less critical advisors, told me on June 4 it was time for the Fed to reevaluate in light of this slow money growth. Two days later, at his annual joint press conference with other G-7 central bankers, Greenspan was no longer talking about the threat of inflation due to excessive growth and was hedging his bets on recession. "The signs of the economy at this stage are really quite ambiguous," he told reporters. "It is true that the rate of growth is exceptionally slow, but keep in mind that the unemployment rate has not budged." So far there had not been the kind of inventory accumulation of unsold goods that proceeds a downturn. "We do not yet see the underlying deterioration in that process," he said, but added, "I'm not saying it cannot occur."

After rising at its lowest rate since the 1970 recession in the first quarter, credit had continued to slow. But the Fed and other regulators remained ambivalent. LaWare told the House Small Business Committee on June 6 some slowdown in lending was "appropriate," given credit problems in the real estate market and "slowing business activity," but said the Fed would "monitor" credit availability and would become "concerned if the examination process resulted in an unwarranted decline in lending to creditworthy borrowers or for projects that are economically or financially sound." Clarke heatedly denied his office had invented performing nonperforming loans or had intensified its examination process to crack down on lending in New England. The FDIC's director of supervision Paul Fritts said he had "never seen a banker who will not make a loan for fear of what a regulator might do" and said the FDIC was "very sensitive to . . . the need for banks to extend good, solid credit."

The monetary policy outlook became a bit more uncertain on June 7 with Manley Johnson's announcement that he was resigning "to return to private life." Kelley and LaWare say Johnson left primarily for financial reasons, but there was more to it than that. The 41-year-old Johnson had been increasingly frustrated with his job at the Fed. "Manley got stuck with a lot of things that Alan didn't want to do," says an associate, who says the relationship between the chairman and vice chairman had become strained, particularly after Johnson's unauthorized assertion that the Fed was prepared to infuse liquidity into the banking system after the October 1989 minicrash. What's more, "Manley would have liked to be chairman," and it had become clear that was not going to happen. There was even some question about his being renamed vice chairman. Johnson said he knew of no discussion of his status on the board, but decided to resign after ten years in government service to "head off" the renomination and reconfirmation process. Bush wanted to put his own people on the Board. Reagan appointee Johnson had become fairly hawkish, and the administration was looking for a vice chairman who would "send Greenspan a message" about the need for an easier credit stance, according to an official familiar with White House thinking. Angell says Johnson decided to leave rather than be "dangled" by the administration for reappointment. Some thought was given to making the CEA's Taylor vice chairman, but the respected Stanford University economist was seen as too independent-minded and potentially hawkish and too close to Greenspan, having been a consultant for Townsend-Greenspan & Company. The nod went to Mullins.

Increasingly, the administration was hinging hopes for lower interest rates on a budget pact with the Democrats, and as it drew closer to a tax-raising compromise it knew would slow the economy, it ratcheted up pressure on the Fed. On June 10, Boskin said he expected the Fed to "offset" the impact of the deficit reduction package in the works and said it "would be irresponsible if it didn't." He denied there was any "deal" in which the Fed agree to cut rates in return for deficit reduction. Brady complained the Fed was trying to tackle an inflation rate that largely reflected prices in the service sector which it had no control over. New Mexico Republican senator Pete Domenici, who as ranking Republican on the Senate Budget Committee was a key figure in the budget talks, charged the Fed itself was worsening the deficit by holding down growth and hence revenues. In mid-June, Greenspan said a "credible" deficit reduction package, one without "smoke and mirrors," would lead to "very significant reductions in interest rates." Some thought Greenspan was just talking about the lower market interest rates that would presumably result, particularly on the long end, if the deficit was dramatically reduced, but the clear implication was that the Fed would make rate cuts of its own. "I call your attention to what the chairman said, that if meaningful progress is made on decreasing the budget deficit that he'd support a reduction in interest rates," Black said when I asked him about prospects for a Fed rate cut. "I would read into [Greenspan's statement] that he's saying there is room for ease if we got credible deficit reduction. . . ." Until a budget deal was reached, however, prospects for easing were doubtful. Most of the Fed presidents still saw weaker economic and credit activity as a salutary inflation antidote.

The beige book, released June 20 in preparation for the July 2–3 FOMC meeting, suggested growth would continue at a modest pace but found fresh indications of tighter credit, but Greenspan told the Senate Banking Committee that day greater caution in bank lending was "probably warranted in the current environment." With the economy slowing, it was natural for credit demand to slow. Besides businesses were meeting at least three-quarters of their credit needs outside the banking system. True, smaller businesses depended on the banks, but they were always complaining about getting loans. Outside of the "troublesome situation" in the Northeast, Greenspan did not see "a broad-based squeeze on credit. . . . All things considered, continued modest economic growth remains the most likely outcome, and looking at the economy as a whole, enough credit appears to be available to fuel this growth." But Greenspan was nervous enough about the situation to add a caveat. "Significant problems cannot be ruled out in the period ahead, and we will continue to devote close attention to credit conditions." While there was no credit crunch "yet," one "may emerge." He said the Fed was monitoring credit availability and "focusing very closely" on the "puzzling" economic slowdown.[4]

A good deal of time was spent discussing the contractionary impact of the hoped-for deficit reduction package and the worsening credit crunch at the July 2–3 FOMC meeting. In 40 years of watching the economy, Greenspan said he had never "sat through this type of unravelling of an accelerated financial expansion," where credit growth went from double-digit rates to barely positive. Corrigan had a "nagging feeling that any kind of a shock could knock consumer spending off in the wrong direction." There was "a financial shrinkage" taking place, illustrated by the troubles the rejuvenated Chrysler Corporation was having getting operating lines of credit. A couple of weeks before the meeting, it had been announced Chrysler was being put on a credit watch list for its commercial paper ratings and, within three or four days of the announcement, Chrysler had drawn down its bank lines by almost $3.5 billion to replace commercial paper it could not roll over, even though it had fully paid back-up credit lines with the banks. "The bankers are saying to me point blank that if somebody comes in looking to draw on their lines and they don't have fully paid lines, forget it—the loans simply aren't going to be made," Corrigan said. Ultimately this financial consolidation process would be "healthy," but in the meantime the economy was vulnerable.

Faced with a slowing economy and mounting evidence of credit stringency, a chastened Fed staff had toned down the greenbook's monetary machismo, but while it was no longer assuming a 2 percent increase in the funds rate, it still wanted to keep rates up. It was still minimizing the credit crunch's severity, although Prell admitted it was "retarding aggregate spending." He believed "some increase in resource slack will be needed, and so we have assumed that aggregate demand will be restrained enough to bring about a rise in the unemployment rate." Kohn contended, "Most prices in financial and closely related markets do not suggest that policy is obviously too tight." The mere fact the dollar was near its post-Louvre Accord lows did "not suggest monetary stringency." Asked why the staff had abandoned its assumption of higher interest rates, Prell admitted the economy was "weaker in an underlying sense than we had anticipated," but also the staff was now assuming a budget deal that would reduce growth in coming years. Mullins, among others, thought the economy was "weaker than [the staff had] projected."

After seven months on hold, Greenspan realized the time had come to take a modest easing step. Going against his staff and the more hawkish committee members, he made his case. The economy was undergoing an historic "unwinding from several years of excess credit expansion," and the only reason the process had not flung the economy into recession was that improvements in inventory management had prevented excessive buildups of inventories. Banks concerned about their capital positions were "pulling back" and "rationing" credit, slowing the economy in the process. For the first time, it appeared inflation was "cresting." In this environment, the Fed had been inadvertently tightening credit by leaving the nominal federal funds rate unchanged. "At this stage the odds that we are not seeing some actual money market tightening are very slim indeed. Put another way, the funds market is trying to ease and we are essentially holding it in check." The Fed could not hope to successfully "fine tune" the economy, but it did have to do its job of providing an adequate supply of money and credit. M2, which had been slowing to a crawl, had become key. The time was growing nigh to cut the funds rate modestly. Doing so would not really be an "easing," merely a "holding" of policy in a neutral stance. Otherwise, the Fed would be tightening through inaction.

Greenspan wanted to cut the funds rate a quarter point if the monetary aggregates and other indicators did not improve. His proposal was not well-received by all parties. Angell thought he was giving up too early in the inflation fight. Nevertheless, the committee voted unanimously to give Greenspan leeway to reduce the funds rate from 8¼ to 8 percent. He acted on it ten days later after Brady had publicly urged the Fed to cut rates. It looked like the Fed had caved in to pressure. Greenspan and others deny it. What had happened was that Greenspan had briefed Bush's advisors on the FOMC decision, and the administration capitalized on the heads-up. "We are below the administration's growth goals and we would like to get back on that path again as soon as possible," a forewarned Brady said at a July 5 press conference. "Lower interest rates would aid that." The Fed's inflation worries were overblown and should be "subjugated to a good, strong healthy concern about growth." Brady said he had urged Greenspan and other Board members to cut rates "the sooner the better" and not "wait around" for a budget package. "It's not a wise idea to emphasize an undying, forever attack on inflation if it jeopardizes growth in this country." Brady's actions did not endear him to Greenspan, whose opinion of the Treasury secretary's analyses and policy prescriptions ebbed ever lower. The Fed had eased in spite of, not because of, his pressure. "There were a lot of other reasons for that rate cut at the time," Taylor notes. Greenspan and an FOMC majority had simply realized they and the Fed staff had been overly optimistic in their assumptions.

That did not mean Greenspan was ready to start easing aggressively, as he made clear in his July 18 Humphrey-Hawkins testimony. The purpose of the July 13 rate cut had been to "hold credit conditions the same and, in general, keep markets stable," he told the Senate Banking Committee. The Fed had "increased the risk of recession by a shade" by keeping policy unchanged for seven months while credit conditions tightened, but with the recent rate cut, "I think we've offset most of that." Had the Fed not lowered rates, "we would have increased the chance that the credit system would begin to crush the economy," but "I hope we have alleviated that." The Fed would "remain alert to the possibility that an adjustment to its posture in reserve markets might be needed to maintain stable overall financial conditions" and monitor credit conditions. Greenspan was playing it safe, leaving himself room to ease further if necessary while indicating he was not anxious to do so. While not complacent, he was fairly confident the economy could muddle along at a modest growth pace, somewhat below its 2½ percent potential—just what was needed to get inflation down from the 4 to 5 percent range in which it appeared to be stuck. The CPI for June had risen at a 6 percent annual rate. "If you look at what we've got, the economy is behaving much better than a lot of people feared. . . . Things are not doing all that badly." There was no "cumulative evidence working toward recession." Inventories were in good shape and "if credit tightening does not take place further we should not expect to go off the track we are on."

Greenspan used his Humphrey-Hawkins appearance to again urge the White House and Congress to agree to a deficit reduction package, strongly suggesting that was the key to further rate cuts. He was not loathe to play the numbers game. A $50 to $60 billion package "could be implemented without undercutting growth in the economy." Though spending cuts would be preferable to tax hikes, the size of deficit reduction was more important than the composition. He did not promise further easing but said that "major substantive credible cuts in the budget deficit would present the Federal Reserve with a situation that would call for a careful reconsideration of its policy stance." He could not say how much the Fed might cut rates or when. That would "depend on the constellation of other influences on the economy, the nature and magnitude of the fiscal policy package and the likely timing of its effects. I can only offer the assurance that the Federal Reserve will act . . . to endeavor to keep the economic expansion on track."

In fact, however, the economy was about to jump the tracks with a little help from Saddam Hussein. The National Bureau of Economic Research (NBER), which retrospectively pinpoints when recessions begin and end, says the economy peaked in July 1990 and headed down from there. The start of the recession roughly coincided with Iraq's August 2 invasion of Kuwait, which caused an already climbing oil price to skyrocket. West Texas intermediate crude, having fallen to a low of $15 per barrel in June, had rebounded to $22 per barrel the day before the invasion. Fear Iraq would seize most of the world's oil reserves drove the price to $40 per barrel in early October, before retreating to $28 by year-end. Not until the U.S.-led Desert Storm operation against Iraq did oil return to $20. The oil price spike not only drove up fuel costs, it dealt a heavy blow to consumer confidence. There is no doubt the trouble in the Persian Gulf contributed to the recession. It is still a matter of considerable debate whether the sluggish economy would have gone into recession without it. One thing is clear: economic data had already turned negative. The day before the invasion, the purchasing managers said their index had detected a manufacturing contraction in July. Bush aides urged prompt rate cuts. "It suggests a pretty soft economy," said one. "If you look at the sources of strength in the economy, you don't see any buoyancy in any of them. . . ."

In an interview the day of the invasion, Boskin expressed greater concern about the plunge in the NAPM index than about the oil price surge that had already begun. He estimated a 25 percent rise in the price of oil would trim "a few tenths of a percent" from GNP but said, "Even if the higher price is enforced, our economy today is much better able to absorb price increases than in the past." But the preinvasion NAPM survey showed the economy was struggling along "at a sluggish pace." Anticipating a $50 billion deficit reduction, he said the Fed would have to act "quickly" to offset its additional contractionary effect. August 3 brought news the unemployment rate had jumped three-tenths of a percent in July. An administration official called the jobs report "a strong signal for the Fed to ease monetary policy." Another said the apparent implosion of the labor market before anything had happened in the Persian Gulf showed the Fed had not eased enough in 1990 and needed to cut rates now "regardless of what happens with the budget agreement." The beige book survey, conducted before July 27, though not released until August 8, provided more evidence the economy was headed south before Saddam. Brady, privately fuming, managed to keep his cool in a National Press Club speech, but made clear he wanted Greenspan to loosen the monetary reins. "Inflation is important, but now is the time to focus on growth, and lower interest rates would help that." The money supply was telling the tale of Fed tightness. M2 had grown less than 1 percent at an annual rate in July after growing barely 3 percent since December 1995—the bottom of the Fed's 3 to 7 percent target range.

Some second guessing was going on at the Fed. A Fed staffer confessed the jobs report proved "things are weaker than we thought." Even some ordinarily hawkish officials were concerned. "It may just be that the economy has moved from a higher rate of growth to a lower rate of growth, but the question is: is it too low?" one asked. "One degree below potential is acceptable, but two degrees below potential would not be acceptable; that would threaten recession." But Greenspan decided not to ease right away. The Fed was faced with the dilemma any central bank faces when confronted with an external shock. At a given quantity of money circulating in the economy at a given velocity, a sudden upsurge in the price of one commodity cannot cause all prices to rise. To the extent consumers cannot substitute for the higher priced commodity, demand will tend to fall for other goods, reducing their price. There can only be a rise in the general price level if the central bank increases the money supply. If the Fed accommodated higher oil prices by creating more money it could accelerate inflation. If it did not accommodate it, the higher oil price would tend to reduce consumer purchasing power for nonenergy goods and slow the economy. Prices for nonenergy goods would be held down or reduced, possibly leading to deflation or at least disinflation in some sectors. In the 1970s, the Fed had accommodated oil price shocks to prevent them from depressing other areas of the economy, with the result that the general price level rose sharply. The Fed did not want to repeat that episode. The Fed was not targeting the money supply but pegging the funds rate and basically supplying as much money as demanded at any given rate. If demand rose, the Fed could inadvertently accommodate higher oil prices and prevent relative price adjustments, causing accelerating inflation. So it had to be cautious about lowering the funds rate.

Although wholesale prices had fallen in July, consumer prices had risen at a 5 percent clip, and the Fed knew the August price numbers would be worse. Much as the administration shouted that inflation was a lagging indicator and that monetary policy should focus on the battle ahead against recession, it could not ignore price pressures. The oil price surge, which for all anyone knew would last indefinitely, was causing financial markets to build higher inflation expectations into bond prices, pushing up medium- and long-term interest rates and making it more difficult for the Fed to cut short rates. The markets feared the Fed would bow to administration pressure and ratify higher oil prices by pumping out more money. In a fateful decision, Greenspan decided to keep fighting inflation at the risk of weakening the economy further. As a Fed official explained, "There's nothing the Fed can do to create oil, and if we futilely try to maintain the standard of living against a lower supply curve you get nothing except higher prices." In effect, Greenspan rolled the dice and hoped the economy would skirt recession so he could continue his battle against inflation. He was also determined to see the White House and Congress come through with deficit reduction. Then, too, the dollar had fallen to 147 yen and 1.60 marks, its lowest level in nearly three years.

The choice was not easy to make given the deteriorating financial picture and its dampening effect on the economy. For a while, the Fed had not believed there was "a broad-based squeeze on credit," but "more recently, evidence is building that conditions have become weaker," LaWare told the House Banking Committee on August 8. The RTC was in the midst of liquidating 315 insolvent thrifts. Bank earnings were in the process of falling 29 percent in the third quarter as banks set aside $8.3 billion in provisions for future loan losses on top of the huge amounts already set aside in the previous 12 months. Banks' return on assets had been cut in half. Through the end of the third quarter, net loan charge-offs would be a record-breaking $30.5 billion. Greenspan was asked by the Senate Banking Committee whether the Fed would be able to stimulate the economy out of recession if heavy provisioning for loan losses so reduced banks' capital that they could not lend. While "monetary policy would retain its effectiveness," Greenspan conceded "any Federal Reserve effort to stimulate the economy might be undermined" if banks became so unable or reluctant to make loans that any reduction the Fed made in their cost of funds was used just to improve their profits and capital positions. Eventually, rate cuts would take effect by improving lending margins, raising asset prices, reducing business's nonbank borrowing costs, and lowering the dollar exchange rate, but "there would be some additional uncertainties about the intensity of monetary policy effects. . . ." His words proved prophetic, for the economy would not fully recover until the Fed had cut the funds rate to 3 percent more than two years later. For now, the hawks were determined to stay the course against inflation. The Fed had to be "careful not to overreact to today's weak economic numbers," said Parry, who thought the economy would "continue to chug ahead slowly." If the Fed was to get inflation down from its 6 percent first half pace, the economy would have to be kept sluggish "for some time," particularly given rising oil prices and a falling dollar.

The FOMC had to decide whether to reaffirm Greenspan's steady-as-you-go decision at its August 21 meeting. Faced with a bewildering mix of preinvasion economic problems, an exploding budget deficit that was holding up long-term interest rates, a looming tax hike, a weak dollar, and now surging oil prices and a consumer confidence crisis, the committee incurred the wrath of Brady and sat tight with the funds rate at 8 percent. It kept an easing bias in the directive, but one that would not be used for another two months. The staff was still assuming the Fed would keep rates unchanged through 1993 before lowering them. Prell predicted "both relatively high inflation and very slow growth." There was a great deal of agonizing about how to respond to the combination of weakening economic conditions and price pressures.[5] Some policymakers felt the economy had been dangerously slow before the Iraqi invasion and the Fed had not done enough to offset it. The economy was "weak to begin with," said Mullins. Now the oil shock was "making it weaker." LaWare warned recession "would further undermine the banks at a time when many of them are on skinny ground as it is." Syron knew of a thrift executive who had told loan officers, "If it isn't gold, don't bring it in to me." Several members warned against a "paralysis of policy" in the face of the conflicting economic effects of the Iraqi invasion. But others felt there was little the Fed could or should do to rescue the economy from the oil shock. Although "things are very much on the gloomy side," said Corrigan, "it's not something that is subject to any quick fix by monetary policy." Hoskins took an even more hard-nosed attitude: "There's little that we can do constructively to get more oil. And there's not much we can do constructively to lower real interest rates. There is one thing we can do and that is to keep the long-term inflation expectations from being built into this economy." Angell saw "nothing there that gives me any indication that monetary policy at this moment is too restrained."

In fact, the dollar's depreciation and rising gold prices indicated "we have already eased."

Greenspan said it was "about as difficult a policy discussion as I have ever been confronted with, and I've been around these policy woods so to speak for 40 years." He saw no evidence the economy was in recession. In a statement that would later come back to haunt him, he told the committee, "I think there are several things we can stipulate with some degree of certainty: namely, that those who argue that we are already in a recession I think are reasonably certain to be wrong. . . ." He felt the Fed had to be mindful of other issues: Wage pressures were threatening to push up inflation. War was on the way, bringing the possibility of loss or destruction of the vast Persian Gulf oil resources. Hopes for a budget agreement seemed to have dimmed. All in all, "we are in a sense in economic/political policy turmoil," he told the FOMC. In that environment, the nation needed "some stable anchor in the economic system," but who was going to provide it? "It's clearly not going to be on the budget side. It has to be the central bank. It's got to be we! I think we very clearly have to preserve—which is our fundamental role, mainly—the value of the currency both internally and externally. . . ." This was not a time for the Fed to try to move significantly in either direction. "I would suspect at this point, that the Pentagon has more policymaking clout than we do." Until the military could dispose of Saddam and restore normalcy to the world oil market, the Fed's "tools are limited." He suggested, "The greatest positive force that we could add to this particular state of turmoil is not to be acting but to be perceived as providing a degree of stability." Greenspan was hopeful the credit crunch was "simmering down" or "flattening out," but wanted to pay closer attention than usual to the monetary and credit aggregates. The odds favored the Fed's next move being to lower interest rates, but for now the Fed should leave policy unchanged. He appealed for a unanimous vote to show the Fed's solidarity in time of crisis. He got it.

September brought further contractions in production and sales and higher unemployment. Greenspan convened an FOMC conference call September 7 to consider whether the Fed should take rates lower. Some officials were itching to ease, but with bond prices and the dollar weak, others feared the market reaction to a rate cut would be adverse—"devastating," said Angell. Mullins agreed it was not a good window of opportunity to move, but said it would not get any easier so long as oil prices stayed up, and warned the longer the Fed waited the more radically the Fed would have to ease when it did act. Divided and uncertain, the FOMC agreed with Boykin the Fed was best off "just standing by and not doing anything right now."

The Fed was increasingly fixated on the marathon budget talks going on at Andrews Air Force Base outside Washington. Greenspan was anxious to see a tighter fiscal policy and was determined to help bring it about. He had strongly implied a budget deal to his liking was a quid pro quo for further easing when he told the Senate Banking Committee on July 18 "major substantive credible cuts in the budget deficit would present the Federal Reserve with a situation that would call for a careful reconsideration of its policy stance." The economy's downturn had done little to change his view. Testifying before the House Banking Committee on September 13, Greenspan said banks had gone "over the line" in restricting lending and stressed the need to "make sure we don't induce a regulatory credit crunch," but his only indication of a willingness to ease credit itself came in connection with the budget talks. If a "credible, enforceable" multiyear budget agreement was reached that resulted in lower market interest rates, "the Fed would move toward ease to accommodate those kind of changes in the market place." Greenspan was hinting strongly he would not favor further Fed easing until a budget deal was reached. "I got that impression," the Republican congressman Chalmers Wylie of Ohio said after the hearing. For the Fed to ease, there had to be not only weak economic conditions but a budget "package that brings down long-term interest rates," a Fed official told me. The economy was "fairly flat with small or modest gains, but there aren't any signs of serious deterioration." The Fed had not yet recognized the onset of recession.

On September 17, a vigorous debate ensued among Fed presidents and governors when Greenspan convened another FOMC conference call. Alarmed by the economy's continued deterioration, Kelley joined Mullins, Boehne, LaWare, and Seger in calling for easing without delay, but others wanted to wait. For one thing, the dollar had fallen nearly 7 percent just since the August 21 FOMC meeting. The other big question was whether the Fed should wait until after Congress and the administration had agreed on a budget deal before easing. The dollar's behavior seemed odd. Cross observed that, unlike past crises, the dollar had not benefitted from the "safe haven" effect. It was a true anomaly that, in this mother of all Middle East crises, the dollar was falling instead of strengthening. Past international crises had caused foreign investor funds to flow into the greenback, and rising oil prices would ordinarily be expected to help the dollar, since oil was denominated in dollars. Corrigan had the explanation. He had just visited some London bankers who told him "funds were finding their way into British and other institutions and into non-dollar instruments, not only because of the uncertain macroeconomic situation in the United States but also because of the elevated concerns and perceptions in Europe about the banking situation in the United States." Corrigan was concerned about the impact of a rate cut on the already weak dollar. Greenspan pointedly observed that, unlike earlier in the year, Treasury was not ready to "pull out the intervention club" to help the dollar.

Corrigan wanted to wait for a budget deal before easing. "I'd rather sit it out here a bit longer in the hope that we can do that in the context of something of a positive nature in the budget process." For others, both fiscal and foreign exchange concerns tied the Fed's hands. "The external aspects of what policy should be tend to override the domestic concerns at the moment," said Boykin. "I think it's going to rest pretty heavily on what, if anything, comes out of this budget effort. So I would be a little hesitant to move right away." Forrestal warned of a spreading "recession mentality" and said he would have preferred to ease two weeks earlier, but "in light of what has been happening on the budget side, perhaps it might be better to wait just a bit to see what happens on that score. And, of course, we do have the problem with the dollar to consider." Mullins warned of a "danger in pinning our hopes to a budget accord. Im not very optimistic that we'll get a very impressive deal, and I'd hate to be put in a position of trying to validate a weak deal, at least in the eyes of the market." If the Fed delayed easing it would have to act more aggressively later, he warned. The economy was so weak, "there is not a real substantive danger in being perceived as going up on inflation." Boehne also advised against letting the budget cause monetary "paralysis." It was decided once again to leave the funds rate at 8 percent. By contrast, the Fed would cut rates three times from July 1995 through January 1996, despite a long-lasting budget impasse. In the recent period, lower inflation gave the Fed more leeway, but it had also learned from the earlier budget battle that it was not desirable for monetary policy to be perceived as too closely linked to fiscal policy. There was a perception the Fed had let itself be "paralyzed" by the budgetary inaction in 1990.

If the Fed needed an excuse not to cut rates, it got a good one September 14, when the Labor Department reported producer prices rose 1.3 percent in August. Consumer prices rose 0.8 percent and 0.5 percent even after taking out energy and food. The Fed's concerns were further aggravated when the dollar plunged lower on news the trade deficit had ballooned from $5.34 billion to $9.33 billion. By then it had fallen to 135.8 yen and 1.5380 marks. Seemingly oblivious that a weak dollar was making the Fed reluctant to ease, the Treasury welcomed the dollar's plunge, especially against the yen. When I pointed out to Mulford on September 17 that the dollar had been steadily dropping without he or anyone at Treasury making "so much as a peep," he puckishly responded, "Peep." That afternoon he termed the dollar's 15 percent fall in five months "orderly." The Fed saw it differently. "It raises further concern about inflation and instability," Greenspan said, holding out little hope for lower rates. The Fed might have to make "a significant policy response" if the economy began to experience "modest negative growth," but while the economy was "slowing down and the layoff rate is rising," he saw no "cumulative interactive deterioration." So long as rates were rising in Europe and Japan while the markets anticipated lower U.S. rates, a falling dollar was almost inevitable. After their September 22 meeting, G-7 officials including Greenspan called exchange rates "broadly in line" with the need to adjust trade imbalances, but he was still concerned about the dollar.

For the most part, Brady had suppressed his exasperation with the Fed's policies in public and saved his outbursts against Greenspan for the ears of fellow administration officials. But his antagonism toward Greenspan was evident at the G-7 and subsequent IMF–World Bank meetings. The G-7 communiqué had called for "stability-oriented monetary policies," compromise language between the central bankers and finance ministers that did not satisfy everyone. Beregevoy said he personally would have preferred a statement calling for avoidance of higher interest rates but said that proved impossible because of "the internal debate in the United States. . . . Greenspan is looking at inflation, while Brady is looking at slowing activity. I almost sensed there was a tension between Greenspan and Brady from their glances at each other." Brady had described the communiqué as calling for "balance" in monetary policy. The Fed had to "steer between the two risks" of inflation and recession. Hashimoto urged the Fed to "try to avoid a recession," because it would be "devastating" to the rest of the world. In a September 23 lecture, Volcker urged Greenspan to stick by his guns and continue pursuing price stability. "Even the partial victory over inflation is not secure. Procrastination in dealing with inflationary pressures is twice damned. Beyond a certain point the inflation itself distorts the economy and once inflation is ingrained the dislocations in restoring stability are apt to be larger." But he also warned that "pulling back from excessively aggressive lending practices here and abroad could spill over into a mutually destructive retreat from ordinary prudent credit extensions. That is the kind of potentially contagious behavior that could turn stagnation or a mild recession into much more serious difficulties." He advised the Fed to "consider whether a tendency to contract lending is not exercising an unduly restraining influence on the economy."

Though it was obvious the economy was sliding, the Fed stayed on hold through September and October. There was still a large body of opinion among FOMC members that the Fed had to stay focused primarily on inflation. "The Federal Reserve's anti-inflationary resolve is being tested now," Angell said September 25. "A slowing economy cannot deter the Federal Reserve from pursuing the one goal which will be most effective in stabilizing the real economy." By late September, the administration was forced to trim its economic assumptions. At midyear, the administration was projecting 2.2 percent real GNP growth for 1990 and 2.9 percent for 1991. Now, Taylor said higher oil prices would cut growth in half both years, even as inflation worsened. He warned it would be "a mistake" for the Fed to target nominal GNP at the same rate as before the oil shock, because price increases associated with the oil shock would tend to increase nominal GNP without increasing real GNP. "Increases in inflation could be large but temporary," so "holding the brakes on GNP could be too contractionary."

Perhaps the most important outcome of the G-7 and IMF meetings was that one foreign official after another echoed Greenspan's urgent calls for deficit reduction. It was music to his ears, but it was another painful reminder to Brady and his colleagues that it had to do business with Congressional Democrats. The surreal budget talks had dragged on, and the deeper the economy sank into its torpor, the higher the bidding became for increasing the tax burden. The "kinder and gentler" hand Bush had extended to the Democrats when he came into office was being slowly gnawed off. Over five months of negotiations, Bush had repudiated his campaign promise to not only refrain from raising taxes but to cut the capital gains tax. Over the last weekend of September, the White House concluded a five-year $500 billion deficit reduction agreement with the Democrats, under which federal spending would continue to rise by $1.72 for every dollar of new tax revenues. Putting the best face on it, Taylor conceded the tax-raising package would "tend in the short-run to have a dampening effect, but our hope is that will be offset by reductions in interest rates." The market response was tepid on Monday, leaving the yield near 9 percent, hardly the vote of confidence the Fed had been looking for.

An array of problems—worsening credit availability, soaring fuel costs, the budget stalemate, the weak dollar, the onset of recession, and more—left the FOMC not knowing which way to go at its October 2 FOMC meeting. Although a budget deal was in prospect, it had a face only a mother could love, with massive tax hikes that threatened to worsen the recession. It had become clear the credit crunch was more than an isolated phenomenon. Together, the seven largest money center banks had assets of about $700 billion, and all were afflicted to one degree or another with loan problems. Corrigan, intimately familiar with the banking giants, told the FOMC that, "with only one or maybe two exceptions, for the foreseeable future the growth in assets in these institutions is going to be very, very restrained because of capital considerations." Insurance companies and securities houses were also in trouble. Now came the oil shock to worsen those preexisting problems. Forrestal said the economic outlook in the Southeast had become "quite fragile," and bank credit policies "increasingly stringent." Keehn and Melzer said businesses' and consumers' negative attitudes had caused them to cancel or postpone major expenditures. The staff now agreed the economy was in a "contraction" and revised down its forecast to show "modest negatives" in GNP for the fourth quarter of 1990 and the first quarter of 1991. Prell admitted there was "more [credit] restraint being imposed there than we might have anticipated." But the staff was still assuming an unchanged funds rate. Unimpressed, Boehne predicted a "recession that will be more pronounced than contemplated in the greenbook."

The Fed found itself in a box, partly of its own construction. To cut rates without a budget deal that at least theoretically reduced government borrowing would be risky, particularly now that the Fed had created the impression monetary easing was conditioned on fiscal tightening. The Fed felt obliged to cut rates on a budget deal regardless of its size and composition. Greenspan was explicit about his desire to link easing with a budget pact. He had told the G-7 his intentions and "didn't get too much in the way of concern about that, although I would suspect that if we embarked upon significant ease without a budget agreement, we would," Greenspan said. "To the extent that these people ever express disapproval in anything stronger than moving an eyelash, we would get a double eyelash effect or something like that." The Fed also had to weigh the currency consequences of cutting rates. Cross warned a dollar free fall was now "a real danger."

Patience was wearing thin with keeping the funds rate at 8 percent while the administration and Congress dallied and dickered. Mullins said the Fed had not been maintaining a "constant" policy at all but had, by standing still, tightened money. Credit was getting steadily scarcer. Making matters worse, as part of the effort to rebuild the FDIC's depleted insurance fund, banks' deposit insurance premiums had been increased from 8¢ per $100 of deposits to 19½¢ and were slated to rise to 23¢. The banking industry was headed for "a protracted period of retrenchment." With the economy already "stalled out," he warned "we do have a risk of turning a mild downturn into a fairly ugly situation." The banks had become "really scared" and "demoralized," LaWare chimed in. As for the budget, "If you had walked across the Sahara Desert without a canteen, you would think the water in Boston harbor was potable," but as far as he was concerned the budget deal was "a sham and a delusion." Others still argued for guarding against inflation and dollar weakness.

After listening to the verbal tug-of-war Greenspan said the time had come to provide some credit relief. The evidence had become overwhelming that a "credit implosion" had taken place, and if the Fed was "going to maintain a semblance of monetary stability in an environment in which credit pressures are tightening the market, then I think we have to find some mechanism to ease." What's more, the White House and Congress finally seemed close to a worthy budget package. Even if there were no budget deal, economic and financial conditions justified an easing, although if there were no credit crunch and no budget deal, just an oil-induced downturn, Greenspan indicated he would not favor easing credit at all. The budget deal struck over the previous weekend was not what he would have crafted. "I must tell you there is a disproportionate amount of tax and tax-type stuff in there, much more than I would prefer." But it did promise to reduce the deficit and did contain "enforcement mechanisms" to restrain spending over the next five years. Greenspan asked for and received an odd directive. Policy would be "maintained" for the time being, but there would be a bias toward ease that implied not one, but two rate cuts. On the assumption the budget deal reached over the weekend passed in the coming week, Greenspan would cut the funds rate a quarter of a percent the following Tuesday, October 9 (Monday being a bank holiday). If, in addition, the employment report due out Friday, October 5, proved weak or if other subsequent economic data were weak, Greenspan would in all likelihood lower the funds rate an additional quarter point. Initially, both rate cuts were to be automatic, but in face of opposition, Greenspan agreed the second cut would not be presumptive. For the first time, Greenspan also raised another possibility—cutting reserve requirements, which he said would have a "noninterest rate easing effect" by reducing what amounted to a "tax" on the banks.

Greenspan met fierce opposition, as both hawks and doves objected to basing monetary moves on fiscal policy. Black suggested it might be "wiser to link [the initial easing move] more to those economic considerations so we don't have this precedent of having acted because fiscal policy has acted." Melzer said he'd "hate to see us get into a linkage where we sort of condition people to think that there is always going to be a monetary policy offset." Angell called Greenspan's proposed double-barrel easing "the worst form of fine tuning," not only because it was linked to budget passage but because it was designed to address problems the Fed did not create. Hoskins alleged the Fed was "losing sight of [its] fundamental job." Corrigan said, "The more I think about that [linkage] the more I think it would be embarrassing." But Greenspan was unmoved. "I don't see how we can get around not responding to a real budget agreement," he told his restive colleagues. "This is a real budget agreement. There is no question that there is a significant absorption of purchasing power coming out of the system." The Fed would not be easing purely in reaction to a budget but to the economic conditions in which the budget was passed. The only concession he was willing to make was that he would not make the second cut if the dollar was under severe strain at the time. "If we all of a sudden find that the dollar is loose on the down side, we'd be crazy to move again," Greenspan said. The FOMC voted 7 to 4 to keep policy unchanged for the moment but gave Greenspan authority to cut rates once a satisfactory deficit reduction bill had been enacted. Angell, Boykin, and Hoskins dissented because "such a linkage could establish an undesirable precedent that could limit the flexibility of monetary policy in the future." Seger dissented in the other direction, arguing the Fed should not wait for a budget deal to cut rates.

Some Fed officials have tried to deny there was linkage, but the following verbatim exchange between Keehn and Greenspan demonstrates there was:

KEEHN: Could I ask an operational question to be sure I have this clear? You're suggesting that we ease early next week, say Tuesday. Is the purpose of that easing to respond to the tightening that has taken place in the market?

GREENSPAN: No, that's in response to the budget resolution passing.

The ultimate proof of the linkage was that, when the budget deal negotiated over the last weekend in September fell through, the Fed delayed easing for almost another month, despite the demonstrable needs of the U.S. economy.

The day after the meeting, Greenspan put his qualified imprimatur on the budget plan but gave no indication of when the Fed would lower rates, given doubts about whether it would actually become law. The budget summiteers had "crafted what appears to be a credible, enforceable reduction in the budget deficit stretching over a number of years," he told Congress. "If enacted, the budget package should reduce the drain of the federal deficit on our national savings, lessen pressures in credit markets and enhance investment and the long-run growth potential of the United States." Passage was crucial. While the market response had been positive, it had been "restrained by criticism that seemed to make prospects for enactment less certain." He would have preferred more emphasis on spending reduction, but the long budget talks had "probably unearthed the maximum cut in the deficit feasible at this time with about the only mix possible given the political context. If this agreement is voted down, prospects for coming to grips with the corrosive effects of budget deficits on our economy would be dim indeed. I am fearful that failure to enact the agreement would produce an adverse reaction in financial markets that could undercut our economy—already significantly weakened by the shock of the Middle East crisis and problems in our financial system." Brady said, "It's simple. If Congress passes the budget agreement, interest rates will go down. If they don't pass it, interest rates will go up."

Market skepticism about the budget package's viability proved perceptive. It was doomed. Not only were conservative Republicans up in arms over the tax provisions, which did not include the capital gains tax cut Bush had promised, but Democrats began going back on the deal almost immediately. On October 4, House Speaker Tom Foley and Bush emerged from a luncheon meeting and cooly shook hands for the cameras in front of the West Wing of the White House. Bush wore a grim look. After shaking hands with Foley, he wheeled and reentered the White House without answering questions. Foley stayed behind and talked to us at length. The reason for the tension soon became clear when Foley said the various committees of Congress should feel free to change parts of the budget package that had been hammered out so painfully over four months of negotiations. Appropriations committees had "to have the ability to look at alternative policies that will achieve the same results. We are not preparing to renegotiate the whole agreement, [but] it's always been assumed that when it came to the committees many of the policies [in the package] were for illustrative purposes." It had included $60 billion in Medicare "savings" over five years, but Foley said Congress would feel free to modify that using "the rule of reason. . . . There has to be an understanding that there always has to be flexibility." Foley seemed to be going back on the agreement which had stated any budget reconciliation bill (to bring appropriations in line with the congressional budget resolution) had to be "consistent" with the agreement reached at the budget summit.

In any case, Fitzwater told reporters Bush did not have the votes to pass the package that had been agreed upon, despite having personally appealed to 60 Republican and Democratic representatives for their support. He said Bush was unwilling to consider any changes in the package and would send it back to Congress rather than agree to modifications. If Congress refused to pass it, "the government shuts down" as the government ran out of spending authority under a "continuing resolution" in force through October 19. The implication was that Bush might sequester spending, but few believed Bush, having already broken his "no new taxes" promise, was willing to stand his ground now. The administration was desperate for a deal. When he was asked about the potentially damaging effect of higher taxes on the economy that day, Fitzwater invoked Greenspan. "My answer to that is that chairman Greenspan said it's a grave mistake not to vote for the package and I have great respect for the chairman of the Fed." The night of Thursday, October 4, to few people's surprise, the budget package went down to defeat in the House. The next morning, the Labor Department reported a recessionary drop in September nonfarm payrolls, and a further rise in unemployment to 5.7 percent. Joblessness had now risen a half percent in four months. An alarmed administration official said the Fed could not afford to wait for budget passage. But the Fed had no intention of easing until a deficit-cutting package was enacted. If it had waited this long, it could wait some more.

Whether he intended it or not, Greenspan became Foley's and Mitchell's ally. The administration felt it had to compromise further with the Democrats to get a budget deal, even if it meant abandoning Georgia Republican congressman Newt Gingrich and his troops, who were demanding Bush redeem his promise to cut the capital gains tax rate to 15 percent. The administration's squishiness became evident on October 11, when Fitzwater indicated Bush was willing to sacrifice capital gains tax relief if he could eliminate the so-called income tax "bubble," the 33 percent marginal tax rate then paid by upper middle income taxpayers. Bill Archer of Texas, then ranking Republican on the House Ways and Means Committee, came out of the White House that day after meeting with Bush and said he did not think a budget would get passed with Republican support. "We're not going to be able to sell anything because [the Democrats] want the populist, class warfare issue." Bush signed another continuing resolution extending the government's spending authority through midnight October 24. The administration at this point had almost written off Republicans like Gingrich. When I asked Fitzwater why Bush did not insist on reducing the deficit by restraining spending instead of raising taxes in the teeth of a recession, his response was that the president believed "the best way would be to get a deal with the Democrats that would pass both houses and get the economy moving again."

Like men crawling through the desert toward some distant oasis, administration officials thirsted for the liquidity the Fed would mercifully bestow once they reached a budget agreement with the Democrats. It became a mantra, to the point that the merits of the agreement itself became secondary. Though not an architect of the budget deal—indeed if he had been, it would doubtless have made more sense—Boskin said on October 15 the most important thing the government could do for the economy was to swiftly pass a budget agreement similar to that agreed at the end of September because it would "give the Fed elbow room to lower interest rates without sparking inflation." The economy was suffering not only from higher oil prices but from "the lagged effect of interest rate shock early in 1990." The economy continued to weaken and credit conditions to tighten throughout October. "Banks are running scared of all kinds of lending," LaWare said midmonth. Not only had bank credit slowed, "in some places a contraction has occurred." But the Fed maintained its figurative vigil outside the budget talks. Seger, who would soon leave the Fed, was outspoken against the Fed's inaction. The Fed could "not sit around waiting for Saddam Hussein to be overthrown" before easing nor should it allow itself to be "hamstrung" by the budgetary impasse.

Finally, in the wee hours of Sunday, October 28, after a three-day government shutdown, victorious Democrats pushed through the House and Senate a budget which contained $18 billion more in taxes and $18 billion less in spending restraint than the package that had been defeated three weeks before, and it fell $8 billion short of the magical $500 billion deficit reduction in five years that had been promised. Only 47 House Republicans and 19 Republican senators voted for the package, which Bush reluctantly agreed to sign. The final $492 billion deficit reduction bill (a ten-inch thick monstrosity) raised taxes $164.6 billion over five years, not counting various user fees and other revenues, at that time the largest tax hike in history.[6] It would all prove to be poisonous pie in the sky. Although the spending caps exercised some restraint in future years, the deficit soared from $221.4 billion in fiscal year 1990 to $269.5 billion in fiscal 1991, and to $290.4 billion in fiscal 1992, as government revenues fell well short of expectations, while spending continued to grow out of control. It is hard to say how much the higher tax rates hurt the economy, but it would be hard to find an economist of any persuasion who thinks raising taxes during a recession is a good idea. "Given the state of the economy, this is not the best time to try to reduce the deficit," but if it was going to be done, "I rather see it done entirely through reducing expenditures," said a Fed official. Hoskins says higher taxes took effect faster than Fed rate cuts and contributed to the recession. Like many former Bush aides, Taylor regrets the tax hike. "It was a political decision that it needed to be done to get a budget deal, and I think it was a mistake."

By midmorning on Monday, October 29, the markets had given a lukewarm endorsement of the plan, pushing bond prices up enough to reduce the long bond yield from 8.77 percent at Friday's close to 8.73 percent. It had been as high as 9.17 percent in September. The Fed had little choice but to ease after all the hopes it had built up in the markets. Federal funds were trading at 7¾ percent in anticipation of a rate reduction. Had it not cut short-term rates, there is little doubt bond and stock prices would have plunged. So late that morning, Greenspan used the latitude that had been given him and ordered open market operations to reduce the funds rate target from 8 to 7¾.

The Fed prides itself on making monetary policy independent of the political process, including fiscal policy decisions, except in so far as the budget affects the economy and the structure of market interest rates. Kelley, among others, insists there was no deal of looser monetary policy for tighter fiscal policy in 1990. "I will absolutely guarantee you there was no quid pro quo," he says. "Those don't happen." Taylor, who was involved in talks with Greenspan and his senior staff, says, "There were a considerable number of discussions about the effect of the budget deficit reductions on the economy, on interest rates and the implications for Fed policy," but "I don't recall any formal quid pro quo of that kind at all. [There was] a recognition that, in the event of an agreement, some interest rate change would occur if the economy weakened, but that's all." He adds that, when the Fed cut rates after the budget deal was announced, "a lot of people including me thought there was a good possibility they were related . . . , but it was only a quarter point, very small, and it could be interpreted as part of a continuing decline that should be occurring as we were going into recession. . . ." Angell's recollection is closer to what the FOMC transcripts reveal. "It's an open secret that Alan Greenspan in a sense promised that, if there was a fiscal deal, the Fed would make a monetary [response], . . . and right after the budget deal was done, there wasn't much time that went by before we actually lowered rates." Angell says "it was a terrible mistake" which caused "one of the sharp differences that my friend Alan Greenspan and I had. . . ." It's always wrong to link interest rate changes to budget action, he adds, but "if you're going to make a bad mistake of tying monetary policy to fiscal policy, then you shouldn't use it to encourage the

Congress to do the wrong thing. And for the Fed to say, 'Well, if you'll go out and do this bad tax increase bill, we will reward you with lower interest rates,' I mean, . . . that's when Alan and I had sort of a little bit different track. . . ." Central bankers should not "make the mistake of thinking that they ought to do fiscal policy rather than doing monetary policy." It must be noted Angell himself crossed the line then by advising Senate Minority Leader Bob Dole and Gingrich on tax policy.

The administration saw the October 29 rate cut as a puny downpayment on the easing it thought had been promised. "It was good to see the first step taken immediately," a senior official told me, but "obviously more will be necessary." The economy would need "a multiple of what they've done." On November 2, after the Labor Department announced more job losses, an administration official said "the Fed needs to move a little faster in easing credit." Having cut a deal with Congress, Bush's advisors felt the Fed owed it much more than a quarter percent to help the sick economy. Trying to walk the line between playing down the economy's weakness for the public's benefit and playing it up for the Fed's benefit, Boskin avoided using the "R" word, but said the economy was "at best . . . in a lull" in a November 8 speech. "By taking some of the pressure off of [long-term interest rates] we've given the Fed more elbow room to lower short-term interest rates without putting pressure on the dollar." But administration expectations of a stepped-up pace of rate cuts were not shared by the Fed. Stern, a voting FOMC member, had indicated the day of the rate cut that no "major" easing was in the offing. Boykin, who had voted against so much as an easing bias at the October FOMC meeting, said on November 6 that "rising oil prices, tightening credit markets and increasing uncertainty have now sapped an economy that had already begun to show signs of a slowdown," but suggested there was little the Fed could do about it. "Reducing interest rates will not replace lost oil production, nor will it make it easier to refinance a more than $2 trillion federal debt that has to be financed in global capital markets. . . . The Federal Reserve is doing the best that it can." The inflationary impulse from oil prices would prove "temporary . . . provided that the Federal Reserve System does not try to compensate for slower growth by overly accelerating the expansion of the money stock."

More than ever, Treasury's lower interest rate demands were conflicting with what many considered its "benign neglect" of the dollar, which had continued falling due to the presumption the Fed would have to lower interest rates further and foreign rate hikes. So, eager to push the dollar down, the Treasury was not at all eager to intervene to push it back up. In a sense the Treasury was getting back at the Fed for its noncooperation in March, but was cutting off its nose to spite its face. In his November 13 report to the FOMC, Cross said he had detected some "increased willingness" by Treasury "to consider possible action to halt the decline if it should continue," but so far there had been none. In fact, there had been no intervention since early April. While the weak dollar might give exports a needed boost, it greatly complicated the

Fed's job and G-7 relations. On November 8, when the dollar had fallen to new lows of 128.77 yen and 1.4869 marks, Beregevoy made public his concern about the disruptive effect the weak dollar was having on Europe's ERM, releasing a letter he had written to Brady, urging a special reexamination of exchange rates by the G-7, because "the sharp fall in the dollar does not reflect reality" and could lead to inflation. Germany had also expressed concern when the dollar fell below DM1.50 for the first time on October 18. Treasury was not agreeable to a special G-7 meeting. Its main goal was the maximum possible Fed rate cuts, and if the dollar suffered, so be it. Realizing the weak dollar was an impediment to Fed easing, Mulford said it was "quite incorrect that we are not at all concerned about" the dollar's slide. "Obviously we are concerned about it, but it has not yet reached a point where there are immediate dire consequences." Predictably, his remark fueled more antidollar speculation. In the absence of strong action to support the dollar, it was seen as little more than lip service, but holding up interest rates would support the dollar at the cost of worsening the economy.

Despite the weak dollar, the administration was hoping for another rate cut at the November 13 FOMC meeting, as was Wall Street. The hopes were fulfilled but not without considerable agonizing. The Fed staff, no longer able to disregard the mounting signs of an economic downturn, revised down its forecast of real GNP growth in the fourth quarter from minus one to minus two percent and predicted unemployment would rise to $6\frac{3}{4}$ percent in the first half of 1991. Prell now said the credit crunch had "progressed further than we had previously anticipated" and would continue, making any "snap back" in economic activity unlikely. To significantly improve the outlook "substantial easing" would be needed. Even if the funds rate was immediately cut to 7 percent, unemployment would rise to $6\frac{1}{2}$ percent by spring. Seger, who had been warning of a recession since early in the year, could not resist tweaking Prell, who had scoffed at her concerns. "At the beginning of the year when I was trying to get Mike Prell to tell me why I couldn't see the strength in the economy, he sort of suggested kindly that I needed new glasses. So I just wanted you to know that I went to the ophthalmologist two weeks ago and got an exam and a prescription for new strong lenses. And now that I can read the numbers they look worse!" Prell made no response.

The district-by-district economic condition reports sounded bleaker than ever. Syron called the banking sector in his region "truly dismal. Some asset markets just literally have ceased to exist, and this is not just in the real estate area. I'm talking about loans to small businesses and that sort of thing." But Greenspan found room for some gallows humor. With people and firms unable to pay electrical bills, Syron reported there had been an absolute decline in electrical hookups, correlated with "a significant jump in bankruptcies, particularly among customers of Massachusetts utilities." "It's shocking!" replied Greenspan. "Well, I want to get a charge out of it," Syron came back. "We try to stay plugged in!" As bad as things were, Kohn recommended "a very cautious approach to easing policy at this time," in good part because of the weak dollar. Further ease "risked a sizable decline in the dollar, which would intensify price pressures."

The FOMC was baffled because this was, as Corrigan observed, "a different kind of recession," one not preceded by the usual run-up in inflation and interest rates. What made it different was the constriction of credit that was taking place in reaction to the real estate bubble and other factors. But because of the vulnerability of the dollar, "there are limits at least at this point as to how much can or should be done with lower interest rates." The Fed had to "start looking at other things" to address the country's woes. Corrigan had detected, from his extensive contacts with foreign financiers, a growing lack of confidence or at least nervousness not just about U.S. financial institutions but about AAA-rated corporations. Anything that touched off a sudden plunge in the dollar could spark a liquidity crisis that could jeopardize the enormous flow of funds to the United States, on which the nation depended to make up the shortfall of U.S. savings caused by the swelling federal budget deficit. Cross confirmed that the weak condition of U.S. banks was not only causing foreign investors to steer clear of placing funds in dollar deposits, but also was diminishing liquidity in the foreign exchange market and increasing exchange rate volatility, because other institutions were afraid to be counterparties in foreign exchange transactions with major U.S. banks. One of the most troubled banks was Citicorp, whose medium-term debt and preferred stock had been downgraded by the market. Its ten-year notes had fallen in price so much that the quoted market yield spread over comparable Treasury maturities had widened from 3 to 5 percent.

Officials felt a sense of monetary impotence and questioned whether the Fed could loosen up the credit blockage even if it was willing to disregard international sensitivities. "I don't think there is a lot we can do about the availability of credit," said Melzer. "We can make sure that we provide adequate reserves and that money grows at an appropriate rate, but I think the behavior of credit really is largely out of our control." Angell persisted in his argument that, while the economy was "very soft," it was "not an event induced by a monetary shock event," and he warned that "if we try to jab our way out with a monetary reaction we might very well find ourselves worse off than we were before." The economic cycle had to be allowed to run its course. But that hard-line approach would no longer fly. Yes, it was a weird kind of recession, said Mullins, one with no excess inventory trigger and with unemployment still at "full employment" levels. Nevertheless, the Fed could not deny "we have a recessionary psychology in full bloom." The Fed may not have caused the credit crunch, but that did not mean it should not do something about it. Companies considered less than investment grade were having to pay as much as 1,200 basis points above Treasury yields to borrow, compared to the usual 400 basis points. "There's a great risk that the downturn could become much more severe and longer in duration, given the weakness of the financial system," he warned. "I also think there's a credible case that some lowering of short rates would improve the financial health of these institutions and perhaps at the margin also loosen up some credit and produce a growth rate in the aggregates that would at least creep back into the lower range of our accepted policy."

Greenspan sided with Mullins as he cut through the fog of conflicting and confusing policy considerations in a closing oration. While the economic numbers were not so weak as to suggest the economy was "falling off the cliff as yet," it seemed to be "crumbling very gradually under the financial pressure." Not only was credit demand down, banks, thrifts, insurance companies, finance companies, and other credit providers were "pulling back" and starving the economy of liquidity. The weak dollar, admittedly, was a conundrum, and one that could not be explained merely by looking at yield spreads among the various national currencies. It seemed to be "essentially a vote of no confidence in the United States." The dollar's condition dictated that the Fed be "awfully careful" in addressing the economy's problems, but it could not sit on its hands. "I don't think that we have the choice at this stage of not trying to ease into the markets, being fully aware that at the first sign that we get of negative response we're going to have to stop." By negative response, he meant not just from the foreign exchange market but from the bond market, for if cuts in short-term rates triggered a fall in bond prices, the resulting rise in long rates would hurt the economy, not help it. Greenspan told the FOMC to "remember what a central bank is here for"—"to maintain monetary conditions in a stable manner." Therefore, he concluded, the Fed needed to cut the funds rate another quarter of a percent right away and stand ready to ease again if conditions continued to worsen. However, "if there is any evidence of significant weakness in the dollar, I think we will have to pull back and harbor the thought; it's not inconceivable to me that at some point if we overdo it, we will have to move back up." The vote was unanimous to do as the chairman suggested, and in the next few days the funds rate was brought down to 7½ percent.

Asked if he was pleased with the Fed's action on November 16, Boskin replied, "Yes, so far." Within days the Treasury Department was clamoring for further rate cuts. The administration had also hoped banks would cut their prime lending rate, which had been kept at 10 percent since January, after the Fed action. When a prime rate cut was not forthcoming and when it was further revealed by the Fed's November senior loan officers survey that banks had "increased credit restraint" in nearly all types of lending, Brady resorted to a mixture of encouragement and intimidation in a vain attempt to get banks to lend more generously. "I understand the pressures that come from building capital in a softening economy, but let's not overreact to the economy or the regulators," Brady said November 20 at, of all venues, an Arthritis Foundation dinner in New York City. "Your franchise depends upon your continued willingness to stand by your customers. I urge you not to walk away from those whose trust you have worked so hard to earn." Rather than reduce their loan assets to improve their capital ratios, he suggested they cut costs and dividends, or even "agree to combine with a long-time rival." To regulators, Brady said: "Use some judgment. Apply some balance. Don't use unrealistically negative scenarios in evaluating loans. Don't overreact." Ironically, the biggest regulatory offender was the OCC—a division of Treasury.

The Fed by now recognized it was somewhat behind the curve in combating the recession. Greenspan was prepared to use the leeway the FOMC had given him to cut rates further and also had some other stimulative tricks up his sleeve, but the weak dollar was a continued impediment. On November 20, Brady issued a call for "stability" of the dollar, but a high-level administration source said there was neither the ability nor the inclination to reverse the dollar's depreciation. LaWare did not help matters on November 27 when he told reporters he did not think the dollar had weakened to the point it threatened inflation, nor did he think it had reached the point of maximum benefit for exports. Not pleased, Greenspan took the first chance to say that, while it might "provide some stimulus to our exports and restrain our imports," a weaker dollar was "a cause for concern: it adds upward pressure to import prices, compounds the inflation impulse emanating from the higher oil prices and may put at risk our ready access to net inflows of foreign savings." "With the oil shock and the lower dollar adding fuel to inflation, a significant move towards ease by the Fed might well cause long-term interest rates to rise," Parry concurred.

But something had to give. The Fed could not let exchange rates, worrisome as they were, stand in the way of countering the recession. Although he was still unsure a recession was on, Greenspan saw signs of "further pronounced weakness" in industrial production. The trick was going to be providing enough money and credit to resume growth in the face of an external oil shock and a host of internal shocks without setting in motion a longer-term inflationary impetus. It would be, perhaps, the most difficult tightrope act Greenspan had ever attempted. The October 1987 crash had been an intense, but mercifully brief experience. Now he was in for the long haul. He showed he could be an innovative central banker. *Reserve requirements*—the noninterest bearing funds which banks must hold at the Federal Reserve as a proportion of their deposits—had long been almost an afterthought of monetary policy, something that had gathered rust at the bottom of the Fed's tool chest. Now Greenspan and the Board pulled it out and dusted it off. On December 4, the Fed announced it would eliminate the 3 percent reserve requirement on nonpersonal time deposits and net Eurocurrency liabilities in two steps by December 27. The action added $13.6 billion in reserves to the system.[7]

The beige book for the December 17 FOMC meeting presented an almost irredeemably dreary picture of economic conditions. Activity had declined in many Fed districts and was described as "sluggish" elsewhere. The unemployment rate had risen another 0.2 percent in November to 5.9 percent as payrolls fell 270,000. There was no more denying the economy was in recession. That did not mean the Fed was willing to throw caution to the wind, however. "What concerns many [at the Fed] is that, if monetary policy is not that effective in arresting a cumulative decline, if monetary policy tries to make it all go away by being too lenient, and if unemployment is not headed to 7 percent or 8 percent, then all we buy for our efforts is a much higher rate of inflation," an official told me at the time. "We don't want to have a replay of the seventies. . . . The best course is more of a steady-as-you-go policy with some give, with some sober understanding of what's possible and what's not—a policy that would ameliorate [recession] somewhat, but limit the inflation on the other side." Within hours of the December 7 employment report, Greenspan decided to nudge the funds rate down a quarter point to 7¼ percent. Informing the FOMC in a conference call, he said the money market had virtually forced the action by trading the funds rate at that level for two days, putting the Fed "in the position today of either protesting the rate for the second day in a row or essentially acquiescing to it." Given discount rate cut requests by numerous Federal Reserve banks, he decided to "acquiesce" and lower the funds rate. The funds rate had now been reduced a full percent for the year, but there was no visible impact on the money supply. M2 had grown barely more than 3 percent since the end of 1989, the bottom of the Fed's target range, and since August had contracted. The paltry money growth reflected weak credit demand and supply. Bank credit grew just 2 percent in November. The Fed can provide reserves, but if banks don't lend, deposits aren't created.

Even ordinarily hawkish Fed presidents were now urging a cut in the discount rate, which had been kept at 7 percent since February 1989, but Cross issued a caveat. "Anything that conveyed any sense of panic on the part of the Fed would have the possibility of a very serious impact on the exchange market." Germany and Japan might soon raise rates, and if the Fed simultaneously cut rates the dollar could take a bad hit. Greenspan was off to Basel, Switzerland, the next day for a regular meeting of the G-10 central banker's club where, notwithstanding any squabbles that might be going on among their governments' finance ministries, they could talk in a congenial atmosphere lubricated by good wines and Swiss cuisine. Greenspan intended to get a "clearer picture" of what the Bundesbank and others had planned, which meant if possible getting them to delay any planned rate hikes to give the Fed a window of opportunity to do the easing it needed to do. The trip was successful. The Bundesbank was laboring to control inflationary pressures stemming from German reunification, which had necessitated a highly expansionary fiscal policy, and from the July 1 German monetary union, which had entailed an exchange of greatly overvalued East German marks for West German marks at a one-to-one ratio for most private savings and two-to-one for other money claims and liabilities. The net result had been a sudden 15 percent increase in the German money supply (M3). It had raised its Lombard rate from 8 percent to 8.5 percent on November 1, and it was just a matter of time until it raised rates again. The Bank of Japan, battling inflated asset prices, had increased its lending rate from 5¼ to 6 percent on August 30, and it was widely assumed more would be needed, despite concerns about a Japanese slowdown. Greenspan was told both would delay further rate hikes, enabling the Fed to cut the discount rate in December with less likelihood the dollar would get hammered. The Bundesbank would wait until January 31, 1991, before raising the Lombard rate to 9 percent and the discount rate from 6 percent to 6.5 percent. The BOJ, as it turned out, would not raise rates again.

Coordinating interest rate moves is not something the Fed or its counterparts like to admit doing, but in this case a senior Fed official says it is "quite a reasonable supposition" that the Bundesbank and Fed worked together to avoid the sudden lurch in the dollar-mark rate that would have occurred if the former had raised rates as the latter lowered them. It was "one of the things that went into the decision process, to the extent that you had knowledge of what was going to happen in another major currency." "I suspect that it was another good case of what I would call 'semi-coordination,' " says Dallara. Greenspan told Congress the following February he had been "coordinating" with the Bundesbank so as "not to create galvanic disruptions in exchange rates." Outside of this particular instance, Greenspan has regularly coordinated with other central banks, keeping them informed of the Fed's intentions and being informed of theirs in return, so that neither made moves at cross purposes if they could be avoided. Knowing how the Bundesbank or Bank of Japan was going to move would not change the Fed's basic strategy but might affect its timing. "There is consultation and an exchange of views that goes on all the time," a Fed official explains. Central bankers "develop a pretty good sense of where the other guy is coming from and what he's thinking. . . . Everybody conducts their own monetary policy in their own national interest, but that includes a healthy dose of awareness of what's happening in other nations, because we're all so interdependent with one another these days."

Dissatisfied with what the Fed had done so far, Brady went on television two days before the FOMC's December 18 meeting to say the Fed had "ample room" to cut rates, but the Fed staff did not think that would be necessary. Prell predicted "a relatively mild and brief recession" and a "sluggish" recovery. GNP would be down 3 percent in the fourth quarter, fall modestly in the first quarter, then return to a 2½ percent growth path the rest of 1991 and 1992. "An upturn in activity can occur before very long at current levels of interest rates." Truman warned against weakening the dollar and overstimulating the economy. "The fundamental risk associated with a further substantial decline in the dollar, especially one induced by Federal Reserve ease, is that the resulting recovery of aggregate demand might be so strong that little additional slack would be opened up in the economy and limited progress would be made in lowering inflation."

The staff forecast was greeted with wide-eyed disbelief. Mullins said the economy was in for "a bumpy landing." Seger caustically recalled liking childhood stories with "they lived happily ever after" endings, but reminded the staff their forecast had "sounded too good to be true" all year and still was. "I know that it's nice to assume that [the recession is] a fallout from Saddam Hussein and the higher gasoline prices and the worries over availability of oil, but my sense is that if all those things were taken care of this afternoon and whatever it takes to solve this problem were done, this would not go away completely." Corrigan said "the risks in the second quarter of 1991 and beyond are probably on the south side of that forecast." "While the Greenbook forecast of a relatively mild, short-lived recession is plausible, my guess is that it's wrong and that we will have a longer lasting and a more serious recession," said Boehne, noting that unemployment was up to 9 percent in parts of his district. The Fed hawks were beginning to coo. Black said a manufacturer had called him to tell him "the bottom had fallen completely out of his order book, which is something he had not seen before." Parry, who had earlier maintained the Fed could not let up in its fight against inflation to deal with the economic slowdown, now feared GNP would be down at a 4 to 5 percent annual rate in the fourth quarter, more than could be explained by the oil shock. Inflation "may have peaked." Forrestal said conditions in his district were "universally gloomy."

Voicing a concern that would soon become a familiar refrain, Forrestal feared the Fed's effort to stimulate the economy through rate cuts would be "damped" or offset by the credit crunch and called for "a little more aggressive policy response." By pegging the funds rate at 7¼ percent, Melzer said the Fed was dragging down bank reserves and the money supply. With demand for reserves down, the Fed was draining reserves to keep the funds rate from falling below 7¼ percent, causing reserve growth and in turn banks' ability to lend to further decelerate. The Fed was being inadvertently restrictive despite its recent rate cuts. Corrigan saw no end in sight for a credit crunch which he said was constricting the supply of money to the economy. Banks would eventually start lending again as their margins improved, but there was no sign of it yet, and there were problems elsewhere in the financial industry. He had just been "looking at a broad cross section of data on the insurance industry, top to bottom, and I will tell you, that is pretty grim stuff, to put it mildly." Mullins asked, "Who is going to finance this rebound?" Banks and others were having asset quality and capital problems and were reluctant to lend. Banks were still refusing to lower their prime lending rate—a politically sensitive matter that was becoming an increasing matter of concern to the Fed. Companies not rated AAA could not borrow without paying high premiums. The bank insurance fund was in trouble.

Summoning a sense of history to his aid, Greenspan told the frustrated FOMC the Fed was dealing with a phenomenon "without any parallel in the post–World War II period." It was not a recession, but "a balance sheet suppression." It was "really quite interesting" to watch, he said like a biologist admiring some new virus through his microscope. Because of the restructuring of balance sheets and the unwinding of debt burdens, asset values were collapsing, first in real estate but spreading to other parts of the economy. It was "fairly clear that we're beginning to see a disinflationary process going on. . . ." Once skeptical of the "credit crunch," Greenspan now was convinced "we are seeing a seizing up of some forms of credit availability." In fact, "we have severe recessionary pressures." Money supply had become "extraordinarily restricted" as part of a "very major credit contraction." The Fed could not just stand by and not do its job of keeping the money supply growing at an adequate rate. It had to at least give the economy a chance to grow, and that meant lowering rates more aggressively. But it had to move with caution or "at some point we'll succeed beyond our wildest dreams." The Fed had to "be prepared for the fact that we may, and probably will, overdo it."

Federal Reserve Board chairman, Alan Greenspan.

Greenspan with Treasury Secretary James Baker (*left*), Secretary of State George Shultz (*right*), and then Fed Chairman Paul Volcker, at a reception for Volcker at the State Department, July 1987. Greenspan had been nominated as Volcker's replacement.

The stock market crash of 1987. Traders work frantically on the floor of the New York Stock Exchange as the Dow plummeted over 500 points. It was the biggest one-day loss in history.

A 1988 meeting of the Fed's policymaking Federal Open Market Committee in the boardroom of the Fed's Washington Headquarters.

The chairman with Jack Kemp, then Housing and Development secretary, in early 1991, at a hearing before the Senate Banking Committee during the S&L crisis.

President Bush escorts Greenspan into the White House briefing room to announce his intention to reappoint the chairman to a second term as Fed chief in July 1991.

Greenspan flanked by First Lady Hillary Clinton (*left*) and "Tipper" Gore, wife of Vice President Gore, in February 1993, in the House gallery at President Clinton's first State of the Union address to a joint session of Congress.

Presidents of 11 out of the 12 Federal Reserve Banks at an unprecedented joint appearance before the Senate Banking Committee, March 10, 1993 (*from left to right*) the Cleveland Fed's Jerry Jordan (*not shown to Jordan's left, the Boston Fed's Richard Syron*), Richmond's Alfred Broaddus, Atlanta's Robert Forrestal, Philadelphia's Edward Boehne, Chicago's Silas Keehn, New York's Gerald Corrigan, Minneapolis's Gary Stern, Dallas's Robert McTeer, St. Louis's Thomas Melzer, Kansas City's Thomas Hoenig, and San Francisco's Robert Parry.

Greenspan talks with President Clinton and White House Senior Adviser Mack McLarty outside the Treasury Department in September 1994.

The 1995 Federal Reserve Board (*front row, left to right*) Vice Chairman Alan Blinder, Chairman Alan Greenspan, Janet Yellen; (*rear row*) Susan Phillips, John LaWare, Edward Kelley, and Lawrence Lindsey.

The gold vaults of the New York Federal Reserve Bank.

The Washington headquarters of the Federal Reserve system — the Marriner Eccles Building on Constitution Avenue.

The Federal Reserve Bank of New York, 10 Liberty Street.

E. Gerald Corrigan, president of the New York Federal Reserve Bank until 1993.

William McDonough, Corrigan's successor as president of the New York Fed since July 1993.

One of the trading rooms where the Federal Reserve Bank of New York buys and sells government securities and foreign currencies to affect the level of interest and exchange rates (pre-1997 renovation).

Greenspan said it was his intention to ask the the Board of Governors to lower the discount rate a half percent and asked the FOMC to ease reserve pressures immediately so the funds rate would be brought down a quarter percent. It was an unusual request at the time, for since September 3, 1987, whenever the Fed had cut the discount rate it had cut the funds rate by the same amount. Now Greenspan wanted to "pass through" only half of the discount rate cut to the funds rate. There was still some anxiety about continuing to lower the funds rate at a time of soaring oil prices and depreciating currency, but Greenspan got a unanimous vote. He was already looking ahead to the next shift in policy, knowing the day would come when inflation, not recession or the credit crunch, would again become the proverbial wind against which the Fed must lean. "This is not the tough vote," he said. "The tough vote is on the other side of this." Later that day, the Fed announced it was reducing its discount rate from 7 to 6½ percent to counter "weakness in the economy, constraint on credit and slow growth in the monetary aggregates." The next day, the Fed cut the funds rate from 7¼ to 7 percent. The Fed had now used all three of the weapons in its arsenal: open market operations, reductions in reserve requirements, and cutting the discount rate. The Fed had now reduced the funds rate nearly 3 percent since its peak in February 1989. No one would have bet the easing process had another 4 four percent to go.

Again, it appeared the Fed had bowed to political pressure, but Greenspan and other Fed officials say they would have taken the action regardless of what Brady said. In any event, the administration wasted no time pressing for more. "This sets the stage for additional Fed easing and signals the Fed has shifted away from inflation, which seems to be trending down, to improving economic performance as its main concern," said one official. He was in for a disappointment.[8]

A debate still rages about the recession of 1990. Fed officials doubt there would have been a recession had it not been for the Persian Gulf War. Bush advisers tend to think the Fed's raising of interest rates to near 10 percent in February 1989 and its slowness to lower rates thereafter, combined with heavy-handed banking regulation, made recession highly probable, if not inevitable regardless of the war. Boskin, who says he had only a "slight disagreement" with Greenspan compared to other Bush advisors, says "the Greenspan Fed's overall strategy of engineering a second round of disinflation was exactly right" in the 1988–1989 period but thereafter "they probably should have eased a bit sooner and a bit more rapidly. . . ." He hastens to add that many unexpected events impinged on Fed policy. Aside from the Iraqi invasion, "the Fed didn't know there was about to be a collapse of the Soviet Union and a dramatic acceleration of the defense drawdown. . . . They might have wound up getting pretty close to the same place, with a little less downside to the economy, but at the time that was a debatable, conjectural proposition. . . ." Less charitably, Darby says the Fed was consciously cutting it very close, hoping for a "soft landing" but "aware that there might be a negative quarter. They just didn't want two in a row" so "they wouldn't get called for a recession." Where the Fed went wrong was in ignoring its own monetary aggregates, which he says made the chances of recession at least "50-50" with or without a Middle East crisis. "Alan was unlucky in the sense that it was a flip of the coin thing. For him it was apparently important avoiding the NBER calling it a recession. [His attitude was] as long as you avoid a technical recession you've done fine."

Taylor thinks there was such a fine line between recession and a sluggish "soft landing" that it's almost a moot point whether Saddam caused the recession or not. "It's a small difference, and you could say anything made the difference—the Gulf War, a little bit more on the fed funds rate, not a rapid enough [funds rate] decline. I don't think anybody could say the Gulf War caused the downturn." Whatever the cause, Taylor says the Fed was not as willing as it should have been to lower rates to preempt recession. Although it was admittedly difficult for the Fed to target money growth reliably, he argues the Fed should have been conducting a money supply oriented policy by proxy. Because of money measurement problems, the Fed is "stuck with interest rate targeting for the time being," but when recession appears likely, "you have to be particularly ready to reduce rates as rapidly as they would be reduced if you were targeting reserves or money. In other words, you're not targeting reserves or money, but you know that if you were there would be a very rapid move [downward] in the interest rates, and you sort of want to be ready to do that. It's a matter of just considering all the facts, all the issues, and coming in and perhaps being willing to react with interest rates more rapidly than you normally would when recession starts to come because historically when reserves or money was targeted you got big declines in interest rates when there was weakness in the economy."[9]

Greenspan has no regrets about the Fed's rate hikes in the 1988–1989 period or its subsequent caution in reversing them. As to whether monetary policy caused the recession, he evinces a scholarly doubt. "It's not easy to tell, but what we do know is that the Gulf War very clearly had a shock effect, which in and of itself cannot explain what was a relatively mild recession by historical standards. But that's not the same thing as saying that if the Gulf War had not happened we wouldn't have had a recession. It's clear that a type of shock was enough in and of itself, and you could argue that monetary policy may have been enough in and of itself, so you'd never be able to tell. My own impression, living through that period, was that I thought we'd stopped tightening well in advance of the economy weakening, and in that period we did not see the type of deterioration which usually precedes a recession, so my inclination is to presume that, were it not for the Gulf War, we would not have had a recession, but if you asked me to prove it I would not be able to do so."

"My guess, and that's all it is, is that we would not have had a recession" in the absence of the war, says Kelley. "I believe that we had the proverbial and long-sought 'soft-landing' in hand, and that it was in prospect that we would have had an extended period of slow growth, then, somewhat similar, for other reasons obviously, to what we expect now."[10] Parry acknowledged the Fed had been trying through the middle of 1990 to "orchestrate a slowdown" but that the unforeseen Iraqi invasion exaggerated the slowdown. "If you're trying to pursue a policy of slowing the economy and you throw [higher oil prices] into the equation that's bound to intensify the slowdown." Dallas Fed President Robert McTeer thinks it's no accident the NBER marks the peak of the economic expansion in July 1990 and that the start of recession coincided with the Iraqi invasion in August. "There were a lot of headwinds separately. You had the credit crunch, you had the corporate downsizing, you had the base closings. All of those things added up." But the war probably "tipped the scale."

Angell and McTeer point out that the Fed had begun lowering rates in June 1989—an unprecedented 13 months before the peak of economic activity—but in hindsight concede the Fed could have eased more aggressively. "People said the Fed did too little too late," says McTeer. "I don't think it was too late. Maybe it was too little. . . . Obviously if we had known there was going to be that invasion and all of that happening my guess is the Fed would have been more aggressive prior to August. Once a recession gets started you don't know for awhile that it's started. So it's possible, but I think we got it about right." Had the Fed begun easing earlier in 1989 and taken bigger steps, Angell says "it wasn't necessary to to have any recession in '90–91 at all." But, given the policy that was followed, there would have been at least "a zero growth recession if it had not been for the Gulf War." He thinks the Fed should have worked harder to avoid a recession "because if we hadn't had the recession then we wouldn't have ended up with a three percent fed funds rate."

CHAPTER SIX

"Fifty Mile per Hour Headwinds"

The year 1991 picked up about where 1990 had left off—with rising jobless-ness, worsening bank problems, and heightened anxiety over the credit crunch. On January 4, the Labor Department reported that the unemploy-ment rate had risen another two-tenths to 6.1 percent in December, and three days later, the Fed got more inklings of what the new year was going to be like when the Bank of New England, the third largest bank holding company in the Northeast and number 35 in the nation, failed after experiencing 1930s style bank runs at its Massachusetts, Connecticut, and Maine subsidiaries. The FDIC rescued the bank, guaranteeing all deposits, including those over $100,000, and infusing $750 million worth of capital notes into three *bridge banks*. The bank's troubles had been brewing for some time, causing an out-flow of deposits and a shrinkage of credit availability in the region.

The bank's failure came as no surprise to the Fed, which had been lending to it heavily through its discount window for months—a fact that would be sharply criticized by Congress. What's more, for a year, the Treasury had qui-etly funneled tax receipts, roughly $1 billion of them, into so-called *tax and loan accounts* at the Bank of New England to bolster its liquidity in what a Fed source called "definitely a coordinated action" with the Fed. It was not the first time troubled banks or even thrifts had been used as Treasury depositaries but it still raised eyebrows when it became known. Although the Treasury claimed it "took no special action with regard to the Bank of New England" and that the Treasury placed excess tax receipts from its account at the Fed in banks around the country "at random," that was less than forthcoming. Another source confessed it had been an effort to slip the bank some extra aid, but insisted the Treasury deposits had been fully collateralized by the bank and were not at risk. "It's one more aspect of how we try to cope with bank prob-lems. It's a typical way of responding to a credit crunch."

Like other banks in the region, the Bank of New England had gotten caught up in speculative real estate loans. But the problems were not limited to the Northeast. One hundred fifty-nine banks had failed in 1990, and another 108 would fail in 1991. The effect was a shrinkage of bank assets. In 1990, assets had grown a paltry 1 percent, which meant very little new lending to U.S. businesses and consumers. It would get worse. In the first quarter of

1991, bank assets actually fell $38 billion. On January 5, major banks finally cut their prime rate a half point to 9½ percent after keeping it at 10 percent for nearly a year, but it had little impact on loan demand. Former FDIC chairman William Isaac said the federal government should ease up on capital requirements or at least delay the deadline for compliance. "I don't know how we expect the economy to go through a recovery if banks can't make loans, and banks can't make loans if they can't meet the capital requirements, and banks clearly can't raise capital in the current climate." The need to increase capital-to-asset ratios was forcing banks to make fewer loans or even cut loan portfolios just at a time when the Fed was trying to stimulate lending, Citicorp economist Dallas Batten said. But the Fed downplayed the effect of the Basel capital standards. There could be no backing down from the laboriously negotiated risk-based standards.

The only alternative, in the view of the administration and the business community, was for the Fed to slash interest rates. "When the economy is weakening rapidly . . . drops in interest rates have to be forthcoming if money and credit growth are to be maintained," said an administration official. The Fed's three-fold measures in December, which left the funds rate at 7 percent, were not enough. "High debt service burdens for individuals and firms, along with the weak financial structure is going to make it more difficult to get a robust rebound," the NAM's Jasinowski said on January 8. "It's clear the financial sector is fragile in terms of balance sheets, cash flow and liquidity, which, along with government regulation, have led to more difficulty in credit availability. . . . I hope Greenspan will recognize that the Fed ought to be taking a modestly more aggressive role."

The Fed's anti-inflation fervor was beginning to waver a bit. Forrestal, who had been gung ho for credit tightening in the 1988 to 1989 period, and was now an FOMC voter, said on January 7 it might be necessary for the Fed to "tolerate slower progress against inflation than we had earlier hoped for." He was looking for real growth of only a half percent in 1991. By contrast, Hoskins warned the Fed had to bear in mind that price stability was the Fed's only achievable goal and that efforts to prevent recession in the short run could generate worse economic problems later. On January 8, the Fed surprised many people by going ahead with another quarter-point reduction in the funds rate to 6¾. Once again, Greenspan had used the easing bias in the FOMC's policy directive to act on his own. The Fed had now cut the funds rate a quarter point in each of the last 4 two-week reserve maintenance periods. The Treasury and REFCORP (Resolution Funding Corporation, the entity Congress had created to raise money for the thrift bail-out) were about to come to market with a large amount of long-term bonds which was likely to push up long-term interest rates, and if the Fed had waited until then to cut short-term rates, there was some fear it would further steepen the yield curve. Inflation was ceasing to be a short-term concern. Wholesale prices had fallen in December thanks to a big retreat in oil prices.

The Fed had now lowered the funds rate 1½ percent since July 1990—all but a quarter percent of it just since October—and had eased more than 3 per-

cent since February 1989, yet there was no sign of improvement in the economy. Some Fed officials I spoke with in mid-January were convinced their
effort to stimulate the economy was being thrwarted by banks' reluctance to
lend. Banks' unwillingness or inability to lend "makes it more difficult reaccelerating the economy," Guffey said. "There is liquidity in the system. The
question is are banks and other financial intermediaries creating a credit
crunch because they're afraid to move, and there is some of that." The credit
crunch meant that "for any given degree of monetary stimulus, you get less
impact than you would in other economic circumstances," said Syron. Another
official said the Fed was "pushing on a string." Given "the lousy outlook" it
could not force credit expansion by lowering interest rates and reserve requirements. "How low would the funds rate have to go before a lender would
be willing to lend on the construction of an office tower in Chicago or to get
people in New England to buy new cars?" he asked. "Zero won't do it." Parry,
a voting FOMC member, saw it differently. "Everytime you go into a recession
there's a tendency for people to talk about not being able to push on a string.
That's been wrong in the past, and it stands a good chance of being wrong
again." Less lending was "a normal prudent response to uncertain economic
times. You'd expect lenders to be more leery whether borrowers can service
their debt, and you would also expect borrowers to feel that this may not be the
best time to get into contractual debt."

Overhanging everything was the looming war in the Gulf, of which no one
knew the duration, cost, or ultimate outcome. On January 16, the U.S.-led
allies launched an all-out air assault on Iraq. The market reaction was swift and
favorable. Oil prices plunged from $32 to $23 per barrel on the New York
Mercantile Exchange. Treasury bond prices shot up two and a half points, lowering the bond yield from 8.4 to 8.15 percent. As the war ground on successfully over the next month and a half, the presupposition arose in some quarters
that the economy would come roaring back as confidence was restored in a climate of lower energy costs and interest rates. Greenspan and others fed such
hopes. Such fantasies did not reckon with the severity of the problems facing
financial institutions and the resulting credit crunch. Nor did they reckon with
the Fed's determination to move with great caution. The Fed had been making a "measured response" and that would continue unless and until the economy got worse, according to Parry. In that event, "we may have to reevaluate
our current policy stance."

Testifying before the House Budget Committee January 22, Greenspan
indicated he thought the Fed may have cut interest rates "enough to turn
money growth back to the path" the Fed had targeted (3 to 7 percent). "We
expect that our actions to date will provide support to economic activity in the
quarters ahead." The drop in oil prices would have a "significant effect" on
consumer spending, he predicted, adding that "the downward pressures on
activity may be lessening." The Fed would be watching the money supply
more closely than usual, and if money and credit failed to grow adequately to
sustain economic growth, naturally, the Fed would take further steps, but as of
now, there was no need. "We must take care to avoid a policy that is overly

stimulative." He betrayed some frustration at banks' failure to pass lower funds rates on and make loans to creditworthy borrowers and seemed to echo other Fed officials' concerns that the Fed's easing efforts are being undermined by bank lending restraints.

Greenspan was back on Capitol Hill the next day with other members of the RTC Oversight Board for a routine status report on the thrift cleanup operation before the Senate Banking Committee. Instead, he got a tongue-lashing from Senator Alfonse D'Amato. The Fed's December discount rate cut had been "too little, too late," the strident New York Republican charged. "No one wants to tell you that because you're the big guru." Greenspan had blamed the recession primarily on the Persian Gulf crisis, but D'Amato was "sick and tired of hearing that nonsense." The Fed was to blame for keeping credit so tight "there's no liquidity out there." The Fed had "choked" the banks, and anyway, "what inflation are you worried about? Do you need people to tell you that the real estate market isn't going to come back and needs a jump start? What's wrong with getting the prime down and stimulate? . . . People are going to starve out there and you're worried about inflation." He urged the Fed to cut the discount rate again to 5½ percent right away. Greenspan also got an earful from Democratic Senators John Kerry of Massachusetts and Christopher Dodd of Connecticut, the latter complaining that the New England economy was "hemorrhaging badly" because of tight credit. Greenspan took it all in cool silence.

Meanwhile, the committee was being informed by Brady, the RTC Oversight Board's chairman, that the cost of the thrift crisis would be toward the higher end of the $90 billion to $130 billion range the Treasury had estimated the previous summer. He asked Congress to immediately approve a $30 billion increase in the RTC's funding to cover losses in fiscal 1991, on top of which he said the RTC would be spending $47 billion in borrowed "working capital." It had already spent $53 billion in working capital. The budgetary delay the previous fall had forced the RTC to curtail thrift closings, allowing sick thrifts to continue in operation making bad loans. If the RTC took over a failed S&L with $100 million in insured deposits and assets of only $85 million, the RTC would borrow $100 million to pay off the depositors and take into receivership the assets. Even assuming the RTC was then able to sell the assets at their nominal value of $85 million, which often was not the case, it would end up with a net loss of $15 million, which had to be funded by federal borrowing. Not only was it a fiscal nightmare, it was a drain on the struggling financial system and a major headache for the Fed. Things were not as bad in banking, but were bad enough. At the end of January, Seidman said the FDIC needed $5 to $10 billion to augment its shrinking bank insurance fund.

D'Amato had been reflecting not just the concerns of his big bank constituents but the concerns of the Bush administration, now less than two years away from a presidential election. Bush himself was understandably oblivious to the economy and monetary policy, given his concentration on diplomatic and military initiatives in the Middle East, but his advisers were becoming increasingly impatient with what they considered the Fed's slow, incremental easing policy. If the Fed could get the economy moving again soon, the electorate might forgive and forget Bush's broken tax pledge. If not, the GOP's chances the following year would be doomed. Help was on the way, if it could get there in time. It had become known in early January that White House domestic policy adviser Lawrence Lindsey, an ardent supply sider and foe of Darman's tax hikes, would be appointed to the Fed Board, while former Brady aide Mullins would be moved into the vice chairmanship vacated by Johnson. On January 22, Seger resigned, enabling Bush to appoint another governor. (He chose former CFTC chairwoman Susan Phillips several months later.) The 57-year-old governor's tenure at the Fed had not been very happy, her relationships at the Fed not the best, and she left embittered after being denied an appointment to see Bush to talk about her resignation. Frequently at war with the Fed staff, she could be cantankerous, as when she abruptly informed her assistant that she was fired by posting a note to that effect on her office door. But the six-foot four-inch Seger had an underestimated intellect. Although ridiculed by some, Seger had accurately warned about the credit crunch. Now, in her parting press conference she lashed out at the Fed not only for participating in a regulatory crackdown that had discouraged bank lending while it raised capital standards, but for failing to anticipate that the resulting slow growth of bank assets would bring a parallel slowdown of bank liabilities (deposits) that would starve the economy of adequate money supply. Both Seger's designated replacement, Phillips, and Lindsey were projected to be reliable votes for more aggressive easing, having made no secret of their progrowth leanings, but neither would be confirmed until the end of the year.

The January beige book presented an almost uniformly bleak economic outlook. Contrary to Fed protestations that the credit crunch merely reflected weak loan demand and therefore was not something the Fed was responsible for or could do much to remedy, the beige book revealed that supply was also a problem. Businesses surveyed complained they could not get credit to finance inventories and fixed investments. Banks evinced an unwillingness to lend, sometimes saying interest rates were still too high to qualify borrowers under stricter credit standards. The money supply was getting off to an abysmally weak start for the year, far below the Fed's target growth range. "Good news," relatively speaking, was the Commerce Department's preliminary estimate on January 25 that real GNP had fallen "only" 2.1 percent in the fourth quarter, thanks to strong net exports. A few days later, a fresh plunge in consumer confidence was announced.

The administration had continued to bring pressure to bear on the Fed as the economy deteriorated, but now it really turned up the heat. In his State of the Union speech on January 29, Bush tried to be uplifting, declaring that "the largest peacetime economic expansion in history" had only been "temporarily interrupted. . . . We will get this recession behind us and return to growth—soon." But then he demanded, "Sound banks should be making more sound loans now, and interest rates should be lower now." In what it lamely considered a sop to Greenspan, but in fact was more of an embarrassment, Bush announced he was naming the Fed chairman to head up a task force to study reducing the capital gains tax. Greenspan, who had long favored cutting or eliminating the tax, had been consulted about leading the capital gains mission and reluctantly consented. "When the president asks, what can you do?" an aide said. Like Bush's budgets the capital gains study would turn out to be "dead on arrival." Congressional leaders were determined to keep the capital gains tax rate unchanged, regardless of the revenue effect, and were not about to cooperate with a task force headed by an avowed advocate of lowering it. The American Bankers Association (ABA) wasted no time diverting Bush's call for lower rates in the Fed's direction. Sung Sohn, chairman of the ABA's economic advisory committee, asserted it was up to the Fed, not the banks, to resuscitate the economy. It was not the banks' fault money supply growth was "basically flat."

Bush, in fact, was aiming his message not just at banks but at the central bank, say Taylor and other Bush aides. This did not stop Fed officials from trying to jawbone the banks. "In the current setting banking institutions must see to it that the credit needs of creditworthy borrowers are satisfied," Corrigan told New York bankers on January 31. "Discipline and care in the credit decision-making process are one thing; outright retrenchment is another." Try as it might to lay off blame on the banks, the Fed could not escape political pressure. Administration pressure on the Fed didn't stop with the State of the Union address. In ensuing days, nearly every choirboy in Bush's loft joined in a chorus of calls for Fed easing—timed for the approaching February 5–6 FOMC meetings. One memorable scene was Brady turning to Greenspan and telling him, "There's plenty of room for interest rates to be lower," as the two sat side by side at the House Banking Committee's witness table January 31, 1991. On the spot but unruffled, Greenspan responded that while everyone wanted lower rates, it was up to the Fed and other agencies to pursue policies that "keep the economy in a noninflationary environment." Only under those conditions could rates be as low and growth as high as possible. The Fed had to be careful not to inadvertently introduce inflation into the economy in an attempt to bolster growth. "It's a question of balance," he said.

On February 1, three days after Bush had demanded "lower interest rates" and four days before a two-day FOMC meeting, the Fed cut the discount rate from 6½ to 6 percent, citing "further declines in economic activity, continued sluggish growth trends in money and credit and evidence of abating inflationary pressures, including weakness in commodity prices." The timing looked suspicious, but Fed officials emphatically deny the rate cut had anything to do with Bush's or Brady's urgings. "It was well understood that the Bush administration wanted rates to come down, and they were quite vocal about that, publicly and privately, but in terms of the influence that that had here, on policy, it did not," Kelley says. In fact, Bush had known the Fed was about to lower interest rates, because Greenspan had given the White House strong indications a rate cut was coming. Contrary to the appearance of having lowered rates in response to the presidential plea, it was Bush who, knowing a rate cut was coming, got out in front to take credit. "They were playing games," says an authoritative Fed source. The Labor Department had just given the Fed ample reason to ease with its announcement of a further 0.1 percent rise in unemployment to 6.2 percent. Greenspan would later indicate the credit crunch was the biggest motivating factor behind the rate cut. In the days leading up to the decision, the Fed had become aware of a further deterioration of credit conditions. Its January survey of senior loan officers detected a "further overall tightening" of bank lending.

As it happened, the Fed rate cut came a day after the Bundesbank raised its discount and Lombard rates to 6½ and 9 percent, respectively. The net result was a further weakening of the dollar. The Bundesbank had delayed raising rates for three months despite its mounting concern about inflation and monetary expansion. The German rate action, which Poehl called just a "technical adjustment," angered the French and others who had to follow the German rate hikes to prevent their currencies from falling through their ERM floor. The French and others who had lobbied against any further German rate hikes before and after a January 21 G-7 meeting in New York City, now complained Germany had violated the agreement reached there: "Implementation of sound fiscal policies, combined with stability oriented monetary policies, should create conditions favorable to lower global interest rates and a stronger world economy." Some G-7 officials claimed Germany had promised not to raise rates, but Waigel's top deputy Horst Köhler told me Germany had made no such promise; it would do whatever necessary to contain inflation. The German attitude, as a Bonn official put it, was, "France and the rest of the Europeans are directly benefitting enormously from our strong economy. You can't have both. You can't have low interest rates and a strong economy."

At Greenspan's discretion, the half percent discount rate cut was allowed to "pass through" completely to the funds rate, reducing it from 6¾ to 6¼ percent. Major banks reduced the prime rate from 9½ to 9 percent, but the administration was dissatisfied. Within hours of the Fed action, Deputy Treasury Secretary John Robson said there was "ample latitude for more movement" to lower rates. Robson had been put in charge of a joint regulatory effort to ease the credit crunch. He had been meeting with officials from the Fed, FDIC, and OCC to devise new examination standards to spur lending by spring, with particular emphasis on the nonperforming portions of loans and the use of real estate appraisals. Property appraisals in evaluating loans had become less reliable in a market where there were few buyers and sellers, and Robson complained, "We are seeing appraisals move more and more toward liquidation [value], which doesn't tell you whether you're going to get your loan repaid." The Treasury wanted regulators to take a "bifurcated loan" approach, in which the performing portion of a loan would be divided from the nonperforming portions, so that only part of the loan would have to be classified as nonperforming. The Treasury was not pushing for "funny accounting," Robson insisted. "The idea is to recognize the fact that we have an economy that's troubled and that banks have a role to play as shock absorbers in the system during bad times. . . . This is a time when you ought to look at ways, within the confines of regulatory responsibility, to look at the world as it is today." Robson's efforts eventually produced a set of measures designed to ease the credit crunch, but Greenspan says they had little impact.

The Bush administration took every opportunity to slam the Fed. The president's fiscal 1992 budget, presented to Congress on February 4, implied slow money growth had cooled the economy and widened the federal deficit. Although M2 had grown 3.2 percent for 1990 as a whole, it had slowed to an annual growth rate of just 0.7 percent in the fourth quarter, and this had led to curtailed production, layoffs, and other cutbacks. Brady and Boskin repeated their mantra that there was "still ample room for lower interest rates." The Fed had reduced the funds rate 3½ percent from its peak, but Brady was not impressed. The funds rate had been reduced from a high level, and the money supply was below the bottom of the Fed's target range, which he said was questionable at that point in the business cycle.

The Fed Board's action made the February 5–6 FOMC meeting somewhat anticlimactic, to the mild annoyance of some Fed presidents. They would have preferred being consulted about the amount of the funds rate reduction, but there was "not any knock-down, drag-out fight," despite rumors to the contrary, according to a participant. Greenspan would have preferred to wait until the FOMC met to lower rates, but felt he needed to act without delay. "This was at the height of our moving," he recalls. "We had to be very careful, because when the markets are in turmoil and the economy is moving fast, a few days really matters. In other words, if you are perceived to be dragging your feet when markets are under pressure, you could do some damage which you had not intended. . . . The reason I chose not to wait was that I concluded it was too dangerous to wait since there was virtually no doubt we would move." Greenspan was conscious of his colleagues' desire to move at meetings. "Other things equal, that would have carried weight, but the other things were not equal." The FOMC voted unanimously to maintain the newly loosened policy and wait to assess the effect of past rate cuts before easing further, but it biased the directive toward easing between then and its March 26 meeting. Notwithstanding the unanimous vote, there were divided sentiments, the minutes reveal. Some wanted to put "a high premium on avoiding any tendency for the weakness in the economy to cumulate because they were more concerned about the severe consequences of a potentially deep and prolonged recession than those of a sharp rebound in the economy, especially given current financial strains and fragilities in the economy." But others saw "considerable risks" in "overreacting" to weak economic statistics and warned the Fed had to be ready to tighten promptly at the first sign recovery might reawaken inflation pressures. And there was a lot of concern that further easing would weaken the dollar. The FOMC voted to lower its M2 growth target from 1990's 3 to 7 percent to 2½ to 6½ percent, with Forrestal dissenting in favor of keeping the higher growth range.

It was later reported by the *Wall Street Journal* that the Fed presidents had rebelled against Greenspan at the February 5 FOMC meeting, challenged his authority and attempted to bring greater "democracy" to the Fed. However, there is no evidence anything more than a mild disagreement occurred over Greenspan's use of his discretion. In conversations with a wide variety of presidents and governors, I was told the report was "overblown," and "made a mountain out of a molehill." At most, a president told me, there was "some discussion about how frequently we ought to discuss things." Greenspan pledged to consult with members whenever possible. The notion that Greenspan's discretionary authority was challenged was patently false, because there had never been any question that an FOMC directive with a bias toward ease gives the chairman the power to cut rates as much as half a percent. Even a symmetrical directive has long been understood to give him leeway to cut rates a quarter percent. There certainly is no evidence Greenspan emerged from the alleged squabble with lessened authority. Officials reacted angrily to such suggestions, and it became evident Greenspan was admired, even loved by his colleagues. "It seems to me Greenspan bends over backwards to have conference calls whenever he moves, even though he does have discretion," a president told me. "He is very collegial, very democratic."

The administration kept up the pressure in the Economic Report of the President. The February 12 report sent the Fed a dual message. In the supervisory sphere, it "should not pursue overly stringent regulations that unnecessarily restrict creditworthy borrowers." In the monetary sphere, it said the moderation of inflation gave the Fed "greater latitude to mitigate the recession without causing an increase in inflation expectations." Fed officials had been boasting how much they had "eased" by reducing the funds rate, but the CEA-prepared report advised the Fed that "interest rates tend to fall as the demand for private credit falls in a weakening economy" and that "a decline in interest rates during a downturn may not be a sign of monetary easing, particularly if the growth of money and credit has slowed." To make sure it was providing sufficient liquidity, the Fed should be concentrating on sustaining money supply growth, not on targeting any given funds rate. This is just what Greenspan had said the Fed was trying to do, but Bush's advisors saw no evidence it was doing that. Boskin expressed confidence the economy would rebound by midyear, provided the Fed allowed for adequate credit expansion. If not, the economy would remain sluggish. The economy had gone into recession not just because of the Persian Gulf War, but because of "the lingering effects of a successful effort by the Fed to counter inflation by running a tight monetary policy." Now the Fed must lower rates and spur credit growth to provide for a strong recovery. Though "pleased that the Fed has begun to take some steps to mitigate the downturn" he implied much more needed to be done.[1]

The Fed was only partially getting the message. Easing would continue, but slowly, incrementally and not with the kind of devotion to money supply growth the administration was after. Fixated on the 350-plus basis points worth of rate cuts they had already made, Fed officials were convinced they were on the right track. Even LaWare, one of those who had been most concerned about the credit crunch, was taking a go-slow approach when I interviewed him in mid-February. He hoped the Fed's rate cuts to that point would mean "credit will be attractive to potential borrowers and that wider spreads will make lending more attractive to lenders." The Fed would be "flexible" but would "wait to see what happens with the most recent series of moves we've made. I would hope that at some point banks will return to a more aggressive posture of lending." It became clear as I talked to other officials that this fairly content, wait-and-see approach was the party line. "The lowering that has taken place over the last six to eight months should result in some acceleration of growth in the monetary aggregates," Kelley said. "I would expect a progressive relaxation of the tightness of credit on both the demand and supply sides as conditions begin to improve a little bit later in the spring or whenever that occurs." Black thought that "what we've done to this point has been appropriate and enough. . . . We've got to wait awhile" before deciding whether to cut rates further. Hoskins declared the Fed had "done enough and we should wait until we are able to judge the results of the adjustments we have already made."

Given the Fed's oft-stated belief that the effects of its actions are not fully felt for at least a year or a year and a half, the administration was not pleased to hear that the Fed planned to wait to see the effects of past moves, since all but one of those moves had been made in the past four months, leaving aside the 1989 cuts. The Fed's wait-and-see disposition was reinforced when the Labor Department reported that the core PPI had risen at a 6 percent rate in January, showing that inflation was still breathing despite the recession. Brady was annoyed by the comments Fed officials had been making. He felt a stand-pat Fed policy was unjustified and that further rate cuts were needed without delay. Boskin, who had both better economic training and a cooler head, delivered the administration's message to the Fed in testimony before the House Budget Committee on February 19. Just because the Fed had lowered the funds rate 2 full percent since the previous July did not mean it was providing sufficient money and credit. The Fed still had "latitude to take steps to mitigate the downturn without causing an increase in inflationary expectations. . . . Even though interest rates are coming down, if credit is not forthcoming at these rates the recovery may be stalled." As for the Fed's concerns about the dollar, so long as it did not fluctuate "widely and quickly," Boskin did "not think it's a serious problem."

Greenspan fired back the next day, rejecting outright the monetarist thesis that the Fed had gotten "behind the curve" in lowering the funds rate. "We cannot have been lagging the market," he declared with some force during his Humphrey-Hawkins testimony before the Senate Banking Committee. "At the worst we're consistent with it." If money growth was sluggish it was not because of Fed policy but because of the credit crunch, and the credit crunch was the result of regulatory policies and bank practices unrelated to monetary policy. If the economy was in recession, it was primarily because Iraq had burst the consumer confidence bubble. The Fed would be "flexible" and lower rates again if necessary, but would proceed cautiously for fear of reigniting inflation. The Fed was already "beginning to see results" from past rate cuts and the money supply was "beginning to accelerate." Asked whether the Fed could lower rates again right away. Greenspan responded that the Fed was trying to strike "a proper balance" to put the economy on a path that "would give us the highest probability of maximum sustainable economic growth." The Fed was watching the economy "on and hour-to-hour basis" and would lower rates "if and when appropriate" but "the major danger is inflationary pressures taking off." Greenspan lectured the committee that "major mistakes in monetary policy are made at turning points." That was why the Fed was following a policy that "would enable us to come out of the recession on a non-inflationary track" so that it would not have to induce another monetary crunch and another recession to attack inflation again. There was another reason for going slow: "The exchange value of the dollar has shown unwelcome weakening tendencies at times recently." The dollar had sank to all-time lows of 1.4445 marks and 128.19 yen that month.

The credit crunch was "the most critical thing confronting monetary policy," Greenspan said, denying the Fed's "hands are tied" in addressing it. He was hopeful the credit crunch would soon let up, but for now "it's still there and it's still tight." He was willing to go beyond the usual bounds of monetary policy. It was already known he was cooperating with other regulators and the Treasury to develop what he called "a balanced evaluation process that endeavors to reflect the long term value of an illiquid asset rather than the exaggerated appraisals that have been evident in both the upside and the downside of the real estate cycle in recent years." Now, he went a step further and invited banks to borrow from the Fed's discount window, no doubt causing banks to do a double take. Banks had shown an "increased reluctance" to borrow from the Fed, he lamented. This was not surprising, given its active discouragement of such borrowing. Asked if the Fed ever had a problem in the late eighties with banks trying to "arbitrage the window," that is, borrow at the cheaper discount rate and lend to other banks at the higher funds rate, Corrigan says, "No. We'd slap 'em down so fast they wouldn't know what hit 'em." Banks were afraid to borrow from the Fed unless they were in extremis for fear of inviting the wrath and increased scrutiny of the Fed. Now, Greenspan was practically begging the banks to borrow from the friendly Fed. "The Federal Reserve has no desire to circumscribe the legitimate use of the discount window, and market participants should not intepret such use as indicating underlying problems for the institutions involved."

Greenspan went even further on February 21 and told the House Banking Committee the Fed had seriously considered creating a facility for buying commercial bank loans as a means of easing the credit crunch but had questions as to whether the Fed should "become effectively a commercial banker." Nothing ever came of the idea, but it reflected the growing desperation to overcome the problem. Where innovation failed, scare tactics were tried. Echoing previous comments by Brady, Greenspan warned banks were "threatening their franchise" by refusing to lend. Yes, bank regulators had overreacted and contributed to the credit crunch, and, yes, loan demand had softened, but there was also "a small but significant part of the contraction that reflects unilateral action of bankers and is not related to demand." Bankers were risking forefeiting their "franchise" of taking deposits and making loans under federal deposit insurance protection and other perks. "Commercial banking is a risk-taking activity and it is the jobs of banks to make illiquid loans . . . bankers have pulled back to a point which is not in their interest."

While acknowledging the Fed's and others' regulatory actions had moved in "a cycle from lax to stringent," Greenspan denied the credit crunch had been induced by monetary policy and also denied regulatory stringency was counteracting the Fed's rate cuts.

Greenspan was stung by accusations the Fed had only recently begun to pay attention to weak M2 and that it had not really "eased." "While we are and continue to be concerned about M2 we would not conclude that we are not easing. . . . The effect of the credit crunch on the money supply appears to be easing off." M2 growth had picked up from around 1 percent in January to around 3 percent in February, still anemic, but at least within the Fed's target range. He denied the Fed was merely targeting the funds rate. "That's the tool, not the mechanism," he said. Greenspan also contended the Fed had not been responsible for the meager [0.3 percent] growth of bank reserves in 1990, blaming this on technical factors that had lessened demand deposits against which reserves must be held. Nor had weak reserve growth caused the deceleration in M2 growth to just 1.2 percent in the fourth quarter.

It was one of the few occasions I can recall where Greenspan was roundly criticized, not just by administration officials, but by many Wall Street professionals and even some other Fed officials, for his two days of Humphrey-Hawkins testimony. Many saw it as an exercise in self-justification—an attempt to deflect blame for the recession onto Saddam Hussein and other forces beyond the Fed's control. Greenspan's line of argument about reserves and M2 was branded "totally incomprehensible" by a Treasury official. "I suppose you could postulate some kind of pathological situation where you broke the link between reserves and the money supply, but basically if you keep pumping you get water out the other end of the pipe." Most Fed watchers concurred. Even if the Fed could not completely control reserves or M2, the fact the money supply was growing so slowly in 1990 and the fact that slow money growth was being reflected in the financial system and the economy should have dictated more aggressive easing actions by the Fed.[2]

The end of the "100 Hour War," or Desert Storm, on February 27 heightened optimism at the Fed. Even before the end of the war, Syron told me the victory should "move up" economic recovery by a full quarter. Real estate, joblessness, credit constraints, and other problems would still be there, but the anticipated boost to consumer confidence would get the economic juices flowing again. "I feel very strongly that the return of consumer confidence, which had been clouded by the war, will encourage a return to positive growth of the GNP," LaWare said a day after the war ended. No one was looking for a sharp upturn, but they expected a slow, steady recovery after the economy bottomed out in the first quarter. But this widely held view would prove misleading and disappointing. The belief the economy would more or less recover on its own without a great deal more monetary medicine tended to lull the Fed into a somnambulent sense of overconfidence. Having cut the funds rate a quarter point every two weeks between October 29, 1990, through January 8, then cutting it a half point on February 1, Fed officials were reluctant to do more. Parry said in late February that past rate cuts would boost money growth and add 1 to 1¼ percent to real GNP growth in 1991. As for the credit crunch, it was "not clear that this is a major factor in today's economy."

Although the economy would resume growth, it would be very sluggish, tapering away toward zero by year-end, with worsening joblessness and bankruptcy. The Fed still did not appreciate the severity of the credit crunch or the inadequacy of its response. Looking back, a senior Bush Treasury official says the Fed was "slow in recognizing the credit crunch. If it had seen it sooner it would have moved sooner, and if it had moved sooner the turn would have come sooner." After declining at annual rates of 1.6 percent in the third quarter of 1990, 3.9 percent in the fourth quarter, and 3.0 percent in the first quarter of 1991, real GDP managed growth of just 1.7 percent in the second quarter, 1.2 percent in the third, and 0.6 percent in the fourth. The Fed still had a long way to go—longer than it could have imagined—in easing enough to bring about a lasting recovery.

But in early March, prospects looked bright. Greenspan took an upbeat attitude in March 6 testimony. He felt the Fed had done a lot, cutting the funds rate, discount rate, and reserve requirements. Plus he was leaning on his examiners to go easier on banks and was throwing open the discount window to banks. All these moves "may well prove sufficient to foster the growth of credit needed to finance economic expansion," he told the House Ways and Means Committee, although he added, "We recognize the risk that problems in this [credit] area could persist and could warrant further actions." The end of the war had "removed a troublesome uncertainty and should provide some lift to consumer and business confidence." He saw "a number of elements . . . moving into place that should enhance prospects for recovery." The end of hostilities would mean lower oil prices and higher consumer confidence. There were "anecdotal reports of increased traffic in real estate offices and auto showrooms." Inventories were so "lean" any boost in demand would result "fairly promptly in a higher level of production." Export prospects were bright. M2 was rebounding.[3]

Even if Greenspan had wanted to ease more aggressively, it would have been difficult with hawks like Parry and Angell still fighting the inflation war. "I believe that the central bank serves the best interests of the nation when it holds unswervingly, but not inflexibly to a goal of price level stability," the latter said on March 7. The Fed must avoid "interfering with the economy's own healing process. . . . The central bank, while playing an important role in economic stabilization, must take care not to short-circuit the stabilizers inherent in the economy." The surest way to drive up long-term rates would be "an excessively loose policy, accompanied by rapid money growth and sharply higher inflation expectations." Angell's hard-line approach in midrecession, always presented with a mix of professorial detachment and cock-of-the-walk arrogance, drove some of his colleagues up the wall at times. LaWare says Angell "would accept much more agony for the economy and for people than I would be willing to do in order to get more rapidly toward what he would define as stable prices. . . ." Why? "Wayne comes from a landed family who have a reasonable amount of personal wealth and insulation from the business cycle. . . . So I'm not sure Wayne is totally familiar with or sympathetic with the human effects of some of what would appear like clearcut positive policy considerations, like let's go to one percent on the CPI, let's do it by just cranking up [rates] and making it so dear that we really crank things down and we almost get into a disinflation kind of thing. . . . [But] he surprised me on several occasions after making rather impassioned speeches about which way policy should go, and then seeming to kind of turn over like the friendly dog and let them scratch his belly."

For the time being, flushed with victory in Kuwait, the administration was prepared to share Greenspan's optimism and give the Fed the benefit of the doubt. Sidney Jones, who shared with Taylor responsibility for formulating administration economic forecasts, was convinced in early March that the Fed was doing what was necessary to keep the money supply growing at or above the middle of its target range. Unlike past recoveries, when GDP had risen 6 percent in the first 12 months, this recovery would not be a "dead cat bounce," but the administration was prepared to live with a 3 percent rebound. Both the Fed and the administration were shocked out of their optimistic daydreams March 8 by the Labor Department's report that nonfarm payroll had plunged 184,000 in February, while unemployment had jumped three-tenths to 6½ percent. The administration swiftly resumed pressuring the Fed. The jobs figures proved the downturn shows "no sign of bottoming out," said one administration official. The Fed should "buy some insurance by easing further." The Fed did just that, reducing the funds rate again, but only by a quarter point, that morning to 6 percent. That left the funds rate and the discount rate at the same level, not at all unheard of, but not in keeping with the Fed's operating procedure which was designed to keep the discount rate below the funds rate. Moreover, if Greenspan really wanted banks to borrow from the discount window, there was little incentive to do so if it could borrow at the same cost in the funds market. So speculation immediately began on when the Fed would cut the discount rate.

But once again, the Fed lapsed into a wait-and-see mode, spurred by resistance from both Fed hawks and the bond market. The Fed must not "overreact to the downturn and thereby lose or even reverse hard-won gains on underlying inflation," Parry said. An effort was launched to quash discount rate cut speculation. The discount-funds rate parity was perfectly "manageable," a Fed Board staffer told me. Then on March 13, Greenspan told the Joint Economic Committee the Fed was getting "some resistance" from the long end of the bond market to its previous easing. Bond yields had inched up from around 8 percent to about 8⅜—an ostensible signal the Fed's short-term rate cuts were reviving inflationary expectations, although another explanation was the record amounts of borrowing the Treasury was doing. Greenspan also felt the financial system was "less fragile than six months ago." Clearly, the Fed had no intention of cutting rates again for a while.

Such timidity was not what the administration wanted to hear, particularly after it was reported on March 15 that industrial production and wholesale prices had plunged in February. "There is more room for the Fed to ease," said a Bush adviser. "They should cut the discount rate to 5½ percent definitely. The bottom is still not there." But at the Fed the view was the economy "has bottomed out," in one official's words. In fact, there were "reasons for suggesting there might be a quite rapid recovery." While the producer price index had fallen six-tenths of a percent overall thanks to falling oil prices, the core PPI had risen four-tenths, so the Fed could not relax its guard against inflation. Despite the decline in factory output, Syron thought the economy was starting to turn around and that it was at just such times the Fed had to be wary of inflation. Brady, who saved most of his jawboning for private conversations, said openly on March 18 he was "pushing for lower U.S. interest rates" and pressuring the Fed and other bank regulators to "alleviate the credit crunch." About the same time, auto executives invited to the White House were urged to lean on the Fed. But the Fed turned a deaf ear. Indeed, it was entrenched in the status quo by an unexpectedly large 0.7 percent rise in the core CPI. What's more, M2 had risen nine consecutive weeks and was growing at a 7½ percent rate. Brady would just have to wait—and stew.

Brady's comments were timed to put the maximum pressure on the Fed before its March 26 FOMC meeting, but the committee not only voted unanimously to leave policy unchanged but did not even include an easing bias in its directive. Most members felt the Fed may have already done enough rate cutting to revive the economy. Those past rate cuts had "represented substantial easing on a cumulative basis and most probably had positioned monetary policy to contribute to a satisfactory recovery in business activity." A willingness was expressed to ease further, if economic and financial conditions failed to improve, but preposterous as its seems now, this was overridden by fear that further rate cuts might lead to an overly robust and inflationary expansion. To some members, "the most likely direction of the next policy move was not clear," which is to say some thought the Fed might have to do an about-face and start raising rates. Things did seem to be turning the Fed's way. Although much of the data remained weak, the Conference Board's consumer confidence index was reported up from 59.4 to 81.0 the day the FOMC met, as dramatically improved expectations swamped a decline in current economic assessments. The only problem, as Taylor observed, was "you just don't instantly convert confidence to a car purchase that day." The Fed had to keep the money supply growing and make sure credit was available for consumers to translate confidence into actual consumption. In another hopeful sign, the NAPM index for March was reported up from 38.5 to 40.0, still a very low level, but seemingly on the mend. The Fed's March survey of senior loan officers showed no easing of credit pressures, but the Fed was happy to find "fewer respondents reporting tightening in the six weeks ending in mid-March than in the previous survey."

There were differences of opinion within the FOMC, but not along the neat dividing line of presidents versus governors. "That's always been a figment of the press, it really has," says Kelley. There was no monolithic presidential position. For instance, Black on April 2 said the Fed had to guard against holding the funds rate "too low" and reigniting inflation now that the money supply was growing above target. The next day Forrestal said the Fed might have to allow higher inflation for a while to insure recovery. On the whole, FOMC members were cautiously optimistic the economy was on the road to recovery and worried inflation would become a problem if they overdid cutting rates. They got a reality check on April 5, when the Labor Department reported another large drop in nonfarm payrolls, pushing unemployment from 6.5 to 6.8 percent. "There is no question this suggests additional easing, and they should ease," an administration official told me. Boskin, not content with his usual call for sustained M2 growth, urged the Fed to lower rates "soon." But again the administration would have to wait.

Life was complicated enough for a Fed chairman trying to cope with the vagaries of the business cycle, but another factor began to come into play: Greenspan's term was due to expire in August, and there began the quadrennial game of "dangling" as Angell terms the suspense presidents put Fed chairmen through as they seek maximum leverage over monetary policy. For months, the White House would not make clear whether or not it supported Greenspan's reappointment. Fitzwater was pelted with questions, but laughingly refused to say whether Bush would nominate him for a second term. In hindsight, it is clear the odds of Greenspan not being reappointed were low, but Greenspan, a man who loved his job and wanted to keep doing it, could not be sure of that at the time. He would endure a similarly agonizing process in 1995–1996.

There were other slings and arrows. Congressmen Lee Hamilton and Byron Dorgan, Democrats from Ohio and North Dakota, had introduced a bill that would lift the veil of secrecy from Fed operations, requiring it to immediately disclose changes in policy instead of waiting for six weeks. It also would have allowed a president to appoint his own Fed chairman within a year of taking office; would have required the FOMC to formally consult regularly with the secretary of the Treasury, the chairman of the Council of Economic Advisors, and the director of the Office of Management and Budget, and would have subjected all aspects of Fed operations to audit by the congressional watchdog agency General Accounting Office (GAO). It was one of the first of many threats to the Fed's political independence. In August, Hamilton and Maryland Democratic senator Paul Sarbanes would introduce legislation taking away the voting power of the privately selected Fed presidents. A subsequent variation would make Fed presidents subject to presidential nomination and Senate confirmation—what would have amounted to the complete politicization of the FOMC. Although none of these proposals would go anywhere for several years, the Fed had been put on notice; greater disclosure and greater openness was on the way, although the Fed would manage to hold out against it for several more years.

In a threat of greater immediacy, the administration, as part of a $70 billion plan to beef up the FDIC, proposed that the Fed be required to lend $25 billion to its bank insurance fund (BIF). In the Fed's mind it would prostitute its independent central banker's mission. The proposal "deserves a quick burial," Hoskins asserted April 9. "The Federal Reserve System was set up explicitly to be separate from the Treasury in order to preclude central bank financing of Treasury operations. Large-scale, long-term loans to government agencies like the FDIC are a clear violation of this important principle, and today's violations are likely to invite further violations in the future." Let Congress appropriate sums necessary to recapitalize the BIF and have the Treasury borrow the money through conventional means to finance those appropriations. Hoskins raised the specter of the Fed someday becoming a Third World–style puppet central bank whose main function was to print money for the government. Fed loans to bail out the FDIC "could put us on the slippery slope of monetizing government outlays through central bank financing rather than through congressional appropriations. Breaching the barrier that separates the monetary function of the central bank from the constitutionally based appropriation process could have dire consequences for the future independence of monetary policy and for the control of inflation."[4] A less politically independent Fed might not have resisted so adamantly.

Meanwhile, the short-term policy battle wore on. Mid-April reports that wholesale and retail prices had fallen in March along with retail sales and industrial production brought another chorus of administration calls for Fed rate action. Wall Street lent its encouragement by sending bond yields from 8½ to less than 8.2 percent, but there was still no sense of urgency at the Fed. D'Amato again harangued Greenspan about lowering the discount rate in an April 16 Senate Banking Committee hearing. Greenspan made no reply. Seven days later, D'Amato was even more histrionic, demanding to know why Greenspan didn't just lower the discount rate from 6 percent to 5.5 percent. After all, hadn't the Fed kept the discount rate at 5.5 percent in 1986, when the economy was much healthier? Wearily, he told D'Amato 1986 had been a different time, with different circumstances, notably falling oil prices, and anyway it was the funds rate, not the discount rate that was "the operative rate." Greenspan still sounded (prematurely) optimistic. "While all the evidence we have suggests that the credit crunch is still with us, there is increasing evidence to show that we may be gradually working our way through this." Nonperforming loans were "flattening out" and this would mean banks could become less concerned about their capital positions and start to lend more readily. The economy was "still moving lower but . . . at a diminishing rate." It was "close to the turning point." Nevertheless, Greenspan hinted the Fed might ease by saying the Fed was "doing rather well" on inflation and had its "options open."

Brady, meanwhile, had been cutting a wide swath through Europe. In London for the inauguration of the European Bank for Reconstruction and Development on April 15, Brady said G-7 central banks were worrying too much about inflation and not enough about growth. "We should act on the risks as they are today, not as they were in times past." His comments, which capped a tour of Europe meeting with top finance ministers and central bankers, were aimed not just at the Fed but at the Bundesbank, which had recently raised rates further in an ongoing effort to contain the inflationary pressures stemming from German reunification. Brady's comments were echoed back in Washington by Boskin, who implied certain European central banks were being less than "sensible." But if Brady or Boskin thought Greenspan was intransigent, they were fortunate not to have to deal with Poehl on a regular basis. A few days later, Poehl pointedly said he had no intention of easing monetary policy in a climate of rising wages, prices, and money supply fueled by an expansive fiscal policy that was increasing domestic demand in Germany. Moreover, he was not going to allow the mark, which had been weakening against the dollar, to depreciate further. Brady's frustration with both the Fed and foreign central banks mounted.

A top Brady aide recalls "a very stiff discussion" with Poehl and other officials, as he tried to persuade them monetary and fiscal stimulus was needed to prevent the G-7 economies from sliding into recession. "Not only were we met with dogmatic resistance, but the European officials kind of dismissed Brady's views as being really off the mark. . . ." Only in Paris did he get a sympathetic reception. "It was a difficult time. Brady really struggled through that trip, and he was really almost derided by his European colleagues, and I think misleadingly so." Tietmeyer, then vice president of the Bundesbank, later expressed private regret at the way Brady had been treated. The Brady aide has no apologies for his former boss. "With hindsight he was much more on the mark than many of them, because the U.S. and European economies were slipping into a recession. In fact, it was at least two years before the European economy came out of it, after the Gulf War. And particularly the Germans seemed so fixated on the implications of unification that they failed to see that the whole of Europe was really settling into a bit of a recession. It was a very frustrating trip for Brady, because . . . there was just very little common ground. . . . But I think you have to give the guy some credit. He was probably more farsighted than most people were willing to recognize at the time."

Brady got no support from the Fed. "Alan would never go out and directly, visibly undermine what the Secretary was trying to do; he was too much of a gentleman," says a former Treasury official. "But he certainly didn't support it. . . . It was seen as a bit of a Brady adventure. . . ." Brady's effort to talk down European interest rates was a bit mortifying for Greenspan, who had built good relationships with other central banks. Equally mortifying were reports Brady had been badmouthing Greenspan's policies in talks with European officials. "There was a little wry shaking of heads," a Fed official recalls. "The reaction he got was one that just about anybody could have predicted he would have gotten. So why did he do it?" Greenspan discreetly passed word to Brady that he considered his efforts less than productive.

That the Fed would not support Brady's bashing of other central banks should not be surprising. It was coming in for the same treatment. By this time, Brady was "very, very aggravated with Fed policy and with Greenspan," says one of Brady's assistants. "At that point, he became very insistent that the Fed was missing the opportunity and they needed to ease." Brady and Greenspan were "not able to communicate effectively with one another. It wasn't always pleasant to be around." By this point, the two men "were struggling . . . to sustain any utility" of their weekly breakfasts. "Brady just never really seemed to fully understand that you don't win when you go head-knocking with the Fed. You really have to cajole, to work with, to cooperate, to argue with, you debate and you find tactical ways to pull them down your path, but Brady, too often just wanted to go head-knocking with Alan! And that is just not a winner! Brady's substantive sense was, I think, very sound. His tactical sense was not so strong. . . . The guy just never learned how to function effecitvely in Washington. . . . I hate to say it, but he just never did."

Brady had succeeded only in setting the stage for an acrimonious April 28 G-7 meeting. Though still relatively weak against the yen, the dollar had been surging against the mark since February, rising from DM1.44 to 1.75. Even against the yen, the dollar had risen from 128 to more than 138. Whenever the dollar showed significant strength, one could lay odds the Treasury would start trying to talk it down. This time, the Treasury had to be a little more careful, since it did not want to do anything to foil its main objective—getting lower rates from the Fed. Five days before the meeting, Mulford told me that while he was "not concerned about the level" of the dollar, he was "concerned about the rapidity of the rise." The United States was still "competitive at these exchange rate levels," but markets had to be kept "orderly." Beregevoy, who was not anxious to see the Bundesbank pushing up rates to keep the mark from falling against the dollar, lent Mulford an assist by saying the dollar had reached its "high point. . . . A further rise in the dollar would not be in line with fundamentals."

Brady's main objective was still to get a commitment from Germany and Japan to lower interest rates on the theory this would make it easier for the Fed to lower rates and spur foreign demand for U.S. exports, but he failed. The G-7 communiqué's language on interest rates was bland and meaningless.[5] Brady insisted he was happy with the communiqué, but no one believed him. Brady had even persuaded President Bush personally to join him in pressuring the Germans and Japanese to lower rates, but both men had been firmly rebuffed. It was pathetic. Bush and Brady should have realized that, given the strain of German reunification, it was "absolutely impossible [for Germany] to go down with interst rates in the present situation," said a senior German official, who could not believe Brady had "talked [Bush] into it." He said he "was surprised, given the situation in Europe and given the situation in my country, at the pressure that was [applied] on Germany" and amazed that concern about German interest rate levels reached "so high in this country." The upshot of the latest desultory round of G-7 meetings was that the vaunted G-7 policy coordination process was "more or less over," the official said.

It was neither the first nor the last time Brady's efforts at G-7 diplomacy had come up short. While Brady had "a good grasp on the domestic policy issues," he was "out of his element in many capacities," including international monetary policy, according to a former administration official. "Being a wonderful investment banker does not make you a wonderful Treasury Secretary. Being the consummate gentleman doesn't make you a wonderful Treasury Secretary. . . . He was not an international economist, he didn't have a background in that, and he was very often sort of taken to the cleaners by various parties that Treasury had to deal with." When it came to G-7 meetings and the like, "he was not adequately prepared and it showed." Greenspan, as a result, played an increasingly important role in the G-7 process along with Mulford. He was "absolutely right smack in the center of it," says a Brady aide. Baker had been a major force in the G-7, and Greenspan to some extent let Baker take the lead, but under Brady, he came to the fore. "The Fed's position was always taken extremely seriously. . . . Greenspan personally carried a huge amount of weight. . . ."

Two days after the G-7 meeting, the Fed cut the discount rate from 6 percent to 5½ percent—its first rate reduction in nearly two months. In conjunction, the Fed advertised its intention to lower the funds rate to 5¾ percent. Notwithstanding suspicion to the contrary, the rate cut was taken independently of the G-7 discussions and was not part of any policy coordination campaign. German and Japanese officials made clear they had no intention of following suit and would make their monetary and fiscal policies to suit their own needs rather than the desires of Brady. The Fed said the cut was made to restore the traditional funds rate premium over the discount rate and was "taken in light of continued weakness in economic activity, especially in the industrial and capital goods areas, and evidence of abating inflationary pressures." Publicly, the Bush administration welcomed the action, Boskin saying it "should help ensure that recovery begins sooner and be more secure," but privately officials were less enthused. They thought the Fed had gotten behind the curve and had more easing to do. Although the banks joined in cutting the prime rate from 9 to 8½ percent the day after the Fed acted, the administration was impatient with their slowness to lower lending rates and ease loan conditions. There should not have been any great mystery. Banks were still trying to increase profitability, curb nonperforming loans, and improve capital positions by maintaining wide spreads between their cost of funds and loan rates—exactly what government policies had dictated.

The administration hoped the Fed was now prepared to do whatever it took to end the credit crunch and jump start the economy. Instead, the Fed would wait until the end of August before taking another small easing step. Never having faced quite so intractable a set of problems, the Fed was in unexplored territory. The prevailing attitude was that the credit crunch was on the verge of lifting and the economy on the verge of recovery, but that in any case the credit crunch wasn't the Fed's fault, and there was only so much it could do, having already reduced short-term rates 2½ percent in six months. Greenspan saw the credit crunch as primarily a healthy return to more normal lending standards. "There is more to the credit crunch than weak demand and possible over-zealous regulation," he said on May 2. "When you go from excess credit creation and overly optimistic reserving to more normal practices it can feel like a tightening. . . ." At a congressional hearing the following week, Keehn and McTeer fueled allegations that the Fed was more interested in disavowing responsibility for the credit crunch than overcoming it. "I do not think that monetary policy has been the cause of this [credit] restraint," Keehn said. The Fed had "eased rather aggressively and regularly over the last six months." McTeer said "monetary policy has provided a positive environment" by cutting rates to "very low levels" and increasing the money supply. In reality, M2 growth had begun to tail off by then, but McTeer argued, "The banking system is liquid." It would require considerably more convincing before an FOMC consensus for further rate cuts could be forged.

Brady's frustration mounted, and when he went to talk to Greenspan about it, he came away even more frustrated. One of Bush's advisers recalls a good deal of behind-the-scenes "grumbling" by Brady and others, "but what surprised me was that in spite of it all they did not move aggressively even to send [Lawrence Lindsey's] name up" to the Senate for confirmation as Fed governor. Lindsey had been asked in August of 1990 whether he would be interested in a Fed vacancy, but his name was not sent up until January. It was not until May 7 that the Senate Banking Committee held a confirmation hearing for Lindsey, and the former Harvard professor left no doubt he would be a force for lower interest rates and faster growth. Price stability was just one of the Fed's goals and should be pursued at "minimal cost," he told the committee. Committee chairman Senator Donald Riegle, now best known as a member of the Keating Five, and Sarbanes kept making insulting double entendre references to the rotund Lindsey's girth which had occupants of the press table groaning in embarrassment. For instance, they wanted to know whether Lindsey, who had authored a book on Reaganomics and countless professional papers, was an "academic heavyweight." Both were opposed to confirming the good-natured Lindsey because of his outspoken "supply side" support of the Reagan tax cuts. Susan Phillip's nomination was not sent to Capitol Hill until months later, and there was little effort to push the nominations to a vote, with the result that the two were not confirmed until late December.

Greenspan was getting heat from Capitol Hill, as well as the White House. House Banking Committee chairman Gonzalez never tired of condemning the Fed, its fellow regulators, and the banks themselves for causing the credit crunch. Yet he was the chief sponsor of a bill to recapitalize the depleted FDIC that would, in many ways, make the credit crunch worse. One of its provisions curtailed the Fed's discount window lending to problem banks, of which there were then nearly 1,000. In Gonzalez's mind, Fed loans had kept the National Bank of Washington, the nation's oldest bank before it failed in 1991, operating long after it should have closed its doors, costing taxpayers $500 million. His staff produced a study showing 90 percent of all banks which had received "extended credit" from the Fed subsequently failed; 530 banks failed within three years of borrowing from the Fed, and 320 banks were borrowing at the time of their failure. This was a little like saying 90 percent of people who died had been ill.

Greenspan objected to restricting the Fed's ability to play its "lender of last resort" role. In a May 6 letter, he told Gonzalez his proposal "could seriously handicap the Federal Reserve's ability to ensure the stability of the banking system and prematurely close off liquidity support to viable depository institutions, potentially increasing costs to the federal deposit insurance fund." If the Fed was prevented from lending to a troubled bank for as much as three months, as provided for in the bill (no more than five days in any three-month period) and was forced to insist on repayment of previous loans before it could resume lending to the bank, "the failure to provide funding could result in the closure of the borrowing institution, not always in an orderly fashion, and could have systemic consequences for other institutions and the markets generally." The bill "would also prevent the Federal Reserve from lending to viable institutions that are experiencing only a minor capital deficiency and temporary liquidity pressures." Some Fed officials disagreed with Greenspan. Hoskins was adamantly opposed to the way discount window lending was being used in conjunction with FDIC-directed operations at failing banks. "Use of the discount window for temporary support of insolvent banks has resulted in a situation that, at least in retrospect, appears outside the scope of the Federal Reserve's intended responsibility. The irony is that, lacking a clear set of rules and objectives, the Federal Reserve's discount window activities can interfere with its mandate to protect the efficient and safe functioning of the payment system." Mullins felt that, by the time banks were in so much trouble they had to depend on extended credit from the Fed it was generally too late; there had to be earlier intervention by regulators to prevent problems from festering.

The long hiatus in the easing process following the Fed's April rate cut strained the Greenspan-Brady relationship to the breaking point. Greenspan had recommended Brady be named Treasury secretary after watching him manage the task force on the stock market crash. The two had worked together effectively on the restructuring of the S&L industry and the international debt problem, but when it came to monetary policy, things had been going steadily downhill for some time. It was a tradition for the Treasury secretary and the Fed chairman, as the nation's top two economic and financial policymakers and representatives to the world, to meet weekly for breakfast. But these meetings became increasingly frustrating for Brady, who, despite his Wall Street background, had a weak grasp of macroeconomics. Sources familiar with the Greenspan-Brady sessions say the latter found the meetings exasperating, intellectually intimidating, and ultimately unproductive. A former Treasury official recalls "many occasions where the discussion would get locked onto a monetary policy issue of the day, and the rest of us there would work hard to get it on some more constructive issue because the two gentlemen were just not, clearly, going to find, if they'd spent the entire day at that breakfast table, an accommodation with one another's views." Brady "had to go in and tell the President everyday why the economy wasn't doing well," another Brady aide says. "That get's frustrating." Brady was "generally supportive of Greenspan and the Fed, but I think he became increasingly frustrated over time at the sluggish pace of the Fed response to the economy," says Boskin. "I think it was understandable. He was much more public with his larger disagreements than, certainly, I was, with my much smaller occasional disagreements."

Brady could get nowhere in his efforts to persuade Greenspan to speed up the credit easing process. Greenspan was willing to listen to Brady's arguments but did not think the Treasury Secretary had a particularly good grasp of the economy or any persuasive arguments, merely a one-sided desire for lower interest rates. In contrast to Baker, "Brady was not interested in a lot of reports in the state of the economy," says Darby, who briefly served as Brady's top economist. ". . . The thing that I remember most was that there was a decrease in emphasis on what's going on and, really, the amount of work we had to put in on that." It became painful for Greenspan and Brady when the latter persisted in pressing for more dramatic rate cuts, and the former continually rejected his pleas. "That was not the happiest episode since I've been here as far as the relationships between Treasury and the Fed goes," says a Fed policymaker. "As time went on, the basic relationship got a little bit more and a little bit more and a little bit more difficult." The best a senior Fed staffer could say about the Greenspan-Brady relationship was that it was not as bad as the one between Volcker and Donald Regan, the former Merrill Lynch executive who preceded Baker as Treasury secretary.

Brady was held in disdain by some Fed officials. "Brady should never have been Treasury Secretary," says one. "I don't know how he ever got to be chairman of Dillon Read." Angell is not much kinder on the record. "Here you have Brady coming out of the financial market and Brady just never was with it. . . . Alan just sort of wore out trying to bring him along. . . . On two occasions, Alan Greenspan, Manley Johnson and I had lunch in the chairman's room with Secretary Brady. Well, looking back at it, it really wasn't very fair. I mean, you take Wayne Angell, Manley Johnson and Alan Greenspan, all agreeing, talking to poor Nick Brady. He was just out of his league. The thing just kept breaking down and breaking down until they even stopped having their weekly breakfasts."[6] By all accounts it was at Brady's initiative that the two stopped their breakfast meetings in late 1991 or early 1992. "At some point Brady just said he didn't want to have breakfast anymore," says Boskin. "They found that there was nothing to do," LaWare says. "I mean, what were they going to discuss?"

Brady never blew up at Greenspan in his presence, but back at the Treasury or at the White House he let off considerable steam at the Fed. "Brady was forever upset with them saying that they were too tight and that this was going to cause a recession," says a witness. "Brady was continuously saying both publicly and especially privately that he was going to slow the economy down and it was going to be bad for the country and bad for Mr. Bush getting reelected. . . . He talked a lot about how he disapproved of what Greenspan was doing and how he tried to convince him to change it and so forth." It was an odd break, for the two continued to enjoy a surprisingly good relationship on a personal level, sometimes socializing together even after they had become professionally estranged. The two were seen at parties together and sometimes played golf. Greenspan even got to know the Brady family.

May brought a series of statistical reports on the April economy that were only encouraging in comparison to the uniformly bleak March data. Unemployment fell two-tenths back to 6.6 percent, but that was belied by a continued decline in nonfarm payroll. Industrial production was up, but only a tenth of a percent after falling the prior month. Retail sales had fallen modestly. Inflation appeared to be under much better control, with the core PPI and

CPI rising just two-tenths of a percent. Administration officials jumped on the numbers as proof the Fed still had "ample room" to lower interest rates. One did not need a calendar to know it was FOMC time again. But the Fed turned a deaf ear. At its May 14 meeting, the FOMC left rates unchanged and adopted a symmetrical directive on a unanimous vote. Some had preferred an easing bias but not badly enough to vote against the majority, which felt "the risks to the economy were reasonably well balanced" between inflation and recession. The Fed consensus was that the central bank could not solve all the economy's problems and that its past rate moves had to be given time to work. "What we're seeing is an effort by households and businesses alike to rebuild their balance sheets after the debt binge of the eighties," Corrigan said the day after the FOMC meeting. Monetary policy "under any circumstances is not in a position to deal with that, nor should it. . . . While central banks can create money, they can't create savings." Besides, it looked like the economic downturn was "moderating." Corrigan's remarks coincided with release of survey results showing "a further tightening" of loan standards. With M2 growing within its range, Black said the Fed should probably not lower rates further and, in fact, should guard against holding the funds rate down too long. Not what Brady and company wanted to hear.

Not only did Brady fail to persuade the Fed to step up the pace of credit easing, his pressure on the Fed probably backfired. At the very least, it worried the bond markets and kept long-term interest rates higher than they might otherwise have been, and it may have delayed official rate cuts. "You might get a little stubborn if it puts you in the position of looking like you're reacting to political pressure," says McTeer. "I think we all tried very hard to do what was right and ignore the pressure and the way people would think we were reacting to pressure. I must say the pressure was foolish because the markets are observing and they're listening, and there's a cost built into the interest rate structure." Taylor thinks the public perception of tensions between the Fed and the administration, which he contends were overblown, may well have been counterproductive by making it appear monetary policy and administration economic policies were working at cross purposes. "If you lose that cohesiveness . . . policy is not as effective. You get more uncertainty in markets; bond prices can be more volatile, and the effect of monetary policy can be more uncertain. That's why it's important to articulate a coherent whole for policy, and when you have public friction it deteriorates from that."

Greenspan and company did not know it at the time, but they still had not cut rates nearly enough to overcome the depressing effects of the credit crunch and other drags on the economy. It is easy, in hindsight, to look at the economy's continued doldrums and fault the Fed for not having cut rates more aggressively, but at the time they were groping their way along, frankly not knowing when the upturn would come or how strong it would be. "In retrospect, if everyone knew the state of the economy that we do now the Fed would have acted differently," Brady's undersecretary for domestic finance Robert Glauber says. "It was very difficult to know what was going on. Everyone was saying there was a credit crunch, but when you asked the National

Federation of Independent Business what its members were saying, it said there was no credit crunch. The credit crunch was seen as a demand problem. We now know it was more than demand." It was a different kind of recession, and the Fed was in the dark. This confusion was illustrated by a Fed policymaker I spoke with a week after the FOMC meeting. "I don't see any evidence that an upturn has begun at this point, but it's possible we could be near the bottom. We might be in the trough—at best. We might be headed lower."

Greenspan acknowledged on May 20 that neither the recession nor the credit crunch was over. What's more, inventory liquidation by business was now holding down activity. However, he thought recovery was probably at hand. Once inventories had been worked down, any pickup in demand would necessitate increased production, and off the economy would go, fueled by the liquidity the Fed was already providing. New orders for durable goods seemed to be bearing out Fed hopes for recovery, shooting up 2.9 percent in April after falling 4.5 percent in March. If recovery was, indeed, just around the corner, monetary policy had best not give it an impatient shove and plant the seeds for a new round of inflation. This was the fear that nagged at many policymakers, with fresh memories of the inflation pressures that had built up in the late eighties. "Let's not do what we've done every time before and pull out all the stops," Melzer said. The Fed could get inflation below 4 percent if only it stayed on course instead of rashly stimulating the economy. "Underestimating the strength of the recovery" and failing to raise the funds rate when recovery begins to take hold "has been the most common error in the past," another official agreed, but "I don't know if we're anywhere near that point now."

One of the Fed's biggest policy constraints was long-term interest rates, more important than short-term rates in driving economic activity. Mortgage rates determined housing affordability; the higher the rate the less willing were people to buy homes or build new ones. This in turn dampened sales of appliances, building materials, and other goods, reverberating through the economy to hold down growth. If cutting short rates merely increased inflation expectations and drove up long rates, it gained the Fed nothing. To some extent the Fed had put itself in a box by conveying its attitude that increased economic activity inexorably strained the economy's resources and led to wage-price pressures. This perception had become ingrained in the bond markets, so that even in the midst of the recession, a strong number could depress bond prices and push up yields. In the spring of 1991, although the economy was very weak, long-term rates remained stubbornly high—nearly 8½ percent—and always threatened to go higher. Forces largely outside the Fed's control were contributing to this upward pressure, including rising global demand for capital, heavy federal borrowing and lack of confidence in the dollar. The Fed could not escape the suspicion that the high level of long-term rates cast doubt on its own credibility as an inflation fighter.

It was something Brady never seemed to grasp. The Treasury attitude, as expressed by Glauber, was that federal borrowing had largely caused high long rates, and that the Fed should not let that influence its policy on short rates. Likewise, a Senate Banking Committee report on May 24 blasted the Fed's dilatory rate cuts and advised the Fed to ignore the bond market and "err on the side of credit easing" to end the credit crunch and the recession. Bank loan portfolios were down more than 50 percent from 1990, and net lending to business had declined almost 66 percent. Not just bad risks were being denied loans but "worthy borrowers" as well. It was up to the Fed to alleviate the situation. The committee deplored "a tendency by the Fed to follow the market, to wait until the market is properly prepared for a change. If it means only occasional, short delays, little damage is done, but regular and long delays when a policy change is appropriate should be resisted. Even if bond yields do not decline immediately following a reduction in short-term rates, the decrease in short-term rates has some effect by itself." This same committee had contributed to the credit crunch by legislatively overreacting to earlier thrift and banking problems. Chairman Riegle had accepted large campaign contributions from Charles Keating, one of the smarmiest of the thrift operators and, along with four other senators, had intervened on Keating's behalf to prevent the FHLBB from snooping into his affairs.

The Fed continued to delay further rate reductions, as modestly improved economic indicators kept upward pressure on long rates. In early June, an uptick in the NAPM May index of industrial activity seemed to confirm Fed hopes that economic recovery had begun. Kelley said the economy had bottomed out and that while "prospects are for a somewhat slower recovery than in the past," he saw "no reason why it should not be sustainable." Parry saw "a lot of signs that the recession has spent itself" and said it was "hard to see what would cause the economy to grow briefly then lapse back." Two other officials, who did not want to be identified, were equally confident the worst had passed and that the economy was on its way up. There was "no reason why it should be a false start." M2 money supply was growing at about 4½ percent and that should insure recovery, they felt. It was time to start worrying more about inflation. "What we have to be careful of is that we don't get overly complacent and somehow lay the foundation for a resurgence of inflation," Kelley said. They said there was no cause for long rates to rise out of concern about inflation.

Greenspan struck an even more optimistic note on June 5. While the economy was "not yet clearly in an upswing," he said "the probability of a stronger-than-expected recovery is rising slightly." The employment report released by the Labor Department the next day seemed to support his contention. Although the unemployment rate rose again to 6.9 percent, nonfarm payroll was up (59,000) for the first time since June 1990, and there was even a 12,000 manufacturing job gain. "Hot dog, it feels good to be right every once in awhile," exclaimed an administration official who had been heralding the beginning of the recovery for months. Retail sales and other indicators also turned up in April, adding to the upbeat mood. All of this optimism would prove premature. Even as officials celebrated, the money supply had begun to decelerate markedly, reflecting the fact that credit was still not flowing to a struggling economy. But for the time being, the Fed remained firmly on hold, convinced it had done enough. LaWare saw "signs of a general economic turnaround" and said further rate cuts would not contribute to speeding the recovery. By mid-June M2 had slowed from an 8 percent growth rate in March to barely 4 percent—below the midpoint of the Fed's target range on which the Fed and administration had put so much emphasis. With core inflation running at 4 percent or more, 4 percent M2 growth would provide for little, if any, real growth. But the Fed did not take this slower M2 growth too seriously. With recovery in progress, Fed officials reasoned, the velocity of M2 was sure to increase as people started spending, so less money could fuel growth by turning over faster. Anyway, the Fed did not want to see rip-roaring growth; 2 or 2½ percent would do nicely.

Mullins, now undergoing confirmation as vice chairman, gave strong indications the Fed would not be lowering rates again soon when he told the Senate Banking Committee on June 18 that money growth "should be more than sufficient to accomodate the growth foreseen in the rebound," because "typically velocity growth speeds up at this stage of the cycle." Brady had hoped Mullins would lead him to the promised land of lower rates, but now Mullins was saying past rate cuts appeared "adequate," that the economy was "squarely in the positive" and that it was "not apparent there is room in the current environment" to cut rates further. In fact, Mullins was just biding his time. When Lindsey and Phillips arrived on the scene he would lead a charge for the most dramatic rate cuts yet, but he would have to wait for awhile.

As long as the Fed could point to strong money growth, it could plausibly tell the administration it was doing what was necessary to fuel recovery, but as M2 continued to decelerate that became difficult. Bush's top economists could not quarrel with the Fed's arguments about velocity. Boskin and Sidney Jones acknowledged 4 percent money growth would be sufficient if the rate at which that money turned over increased, but they doubted this velocity increase would actually occur. Boskin said on June 19 the Fed "seems to be counting on an increase in velocity that often occurs" during economic recoveries, but this could not be counted on. If the increased velocity did not materialize, money supply "would not be adequate," Jones told me. The Fed had to be prepared to goose up money growth through lower rates if its risky assumption about velocity didn't pan out. The administration faced a dilemma. It wanted to be upbeat about the economy as the last year of Bush's term approached, partially as an exercise in amateur mass psychology. If enough people could be convinced the economy was recovering, they might actually start behaving like robust economic players and create a self-fulfilling prophecy. On the other hand, it wouldn't do to be so upbeat the Fed would feel complacent and not do what the administration wanted. So, administration officials would alternately talk about the continuing credit crunch and other risks to the recovery in an effort to buffalo the Fed into easing credit.

There continued to be hopeful signs, and on June 18, Greenspan all but declared the recession over. "It's very difficult to get around the data of the last several weeks which are strongly suggestive that the bottom is somewhere in the second quarter," he told the House Ways and Means Committee. The Fed found signs housing, consumer spending, and manufacturing were "improving modestly" in its beige book survey, compiled for use at the July 2–3 FOMC meeting, but it also found that "bank lending continues to be weak. . . ." The FOMC voted unanimously to stay on hold and in neutral, but there was a lot more anxiety over the slow pace of M2 growth and a lot more doubt about whether higher velocity would take up the slack than Fed officials had been letting on. "On balance, growth of [M2] thus far in 1991 had fallen short of what might have been expected on the basis of historical relationships with nominal income and interest rates," the minutes state. Members recognized slow money growth reflected "quite sluggish" growth of debt and "the contin-uing redirection of credit flows away from depository institutions. . . . Consid-erable uncertainty continued to surround the demand for money and the behavior of velocity."[7] The money supply continued to dry up, so that by the end of July, M2 had grown less than 3 percent relative to the end of 1990, and since April had not grown at all. With that kind of M2 growth, M2 velocity was almost academic.

The Fed's foes in Congress chose this time to fire a shot over the Fed's bow. Hamilton and Sarbanes, joined by a host of cosponsors, introduced legislation to strip the Fed presidents of their vote on monetary policy. Hamilton, who had bought the superficial line that the presidents were a bunch of hawks who were tying the hands of the more dovish governors, said his bill was aimed at "a handful of individuals representing private interests impeding efforts by responsible government officials to conduct monetary policy in the best inter-est of the nation's economy." But there was a schizophrenia to the Democrats' approach. If they really wanted an easier Fed policy, why not rush to confirm Lindsey? Instead, they were finding excuses not to. The Senate Banking Com-mittee had voted to confirm Lindsey on July 10, despite the opposition of Riegle and other critics of the Fed's anti-inflationary policies, but did not report his nomination to the full Senate until August 29. North Carolina Democrat Senator Terry Sanford vowed to fight Lindsey's nomination because, although he had been appointed from the Fifth Federal Reserve Dis-trict, covering the region stretching south from Maryland through the Caroli-nas, he was in fact a northerner whose only acquaintance with the South was Washington's Virginia suburbs. Lindsey was eager to get on the Board to cut rates but was being stymied.

Weak money growth was one thing, but when the Labor Department reported on August 2 that unemployment had jumped from 6.8 to 7 percent the Fed knew it had waited long enough. Clearly the modest recovery Greenspan had virtually promised was not coming to pass. On August 6, with the next FOMC meeting two weeks off, the Fed faced facts and took another baby step, lowering the funds rate from 5¾ to 5½ percent, its first rate cut since April 30. Though not released until the day after the rate cut, the Fed knew the contents of its latest beige book survey. What little improvement in economic conditions there had been was occurring at "a slow, uneven pace" with no inflation pressures. The credit crunch, which the Fed had for so long tried to wish or define away, was found to be a very real problem dragging down the economy. This was no mere anecdotal phenomenon. The Fed's own statistics showed clearly what was going on and had for months. Business loans had fallen 3.3 percent over the previous 12 months, and consumer credit had fallen 0.5 percent. For months the Fed had been delaying cutting rates in fear that doing so might trigger a bond market sell-off. In the event, just the opposite happened. The day after the rate cut, a bond rally already in progress gained momentum. The long bond yield, which a couple of weeks earlier had been above 8.5 percent, fell to 8.17 percent.

Three days after the discount rate cut, President Bush, vacationing in Kennebunkport, Maine, finally got around to reappointing Greenspan as Fed chairman after allowing him to twist in the wind for months.[8] Bush had "dangled" Greenspan to the last possible moment in an effort to extract as much stimulus from the Fed as possible. To Greenspan's embarrassment, the nomination announcement had the appearance of being a reward for the discount rate cut. Long-time associates say Greenspan was willing to go to great lengths to insure his reappointment in 1991 and again in 1996, but Greenspan had more than enough reason to cut rates on this occasion. It has been asserted that Brady opposed Greenspan's reappointment, but I have found no evidence of this in conversations with senior White House and Treasury officials. For all his grumbling about Greenspan, Brady stopped short of recommending he be replaced. Bush called together his advisers to discuss whether Greenspan should be given a second term. Sununu and Darman argued he could not be trusted to provide enough monetary stimulus to allow the economy to rebound at a healthy pace. They warned he would keep policy tight to hold down growth and control inflation. Boskin countered that, given the current condition of the economy, Greenspan was not about to suppress growth. Brady was lukewarm about renomination, but did not oppose it. He told the president he believed he could get assurances from Greenspan that, given prevailing economic and financial conditions, he would be willing to foster a modest recovery of about 3 percent without having to worry about inflation pressures. Baker urged a second term, clinching his renomination.

The August 6 rate cut left the funds rate on top of the discount rate, setting the stage for a discount rate cut to restore a funds rate premium. The Fed was ready to cut both the discount rate and the funds rate again, but wanted to see further evidence of weakness. As far as the administration was concerned, there was more than enough evidence. Fitzwater told reporters shadowing Bush's vacation in Kennebunkport, the Fed rate cut had been "an encouraging sign," and declined to say whether the Fed should cut rates further because "we won't try to tell the Fed what to do." But privately, the administration was doing just that in increasingly strident tones. Bush's advisers were quite unhappy about the Fed's management of the economy and were "putting an arm on the Fed" to cut rates further and faster, as one source put it. They were rubbing the Fed's nose in the fact the money supply had shrunk "back to March levels." The latest quarter point rate cut was simply "not enough," an administration official contended. "The whole problem of capitalization of banks and the need of banks to raise capital all suggests that it will take more Fed action to get each unit of economic advance. It suggests the Fed needs to be more active." The Fed had been offering a variety of explanations for the dearth of money growth, such as portfolio shifts out of bank deposits into bond funds. The administration was having none of it. "Even money that goes into bond funds ultimately goes back into the banking system," said an official. "You'd see it somewhere. When you start looking for excuses when you have evidence this strong, you're on thin ice."

It was an exasperating time for Greenspan and the FOMC. They felt they had done more than enough to ease the credit crunch and get the economy moving. They had now cut rates a cumulative 2¼ percent over the past year and even cut reserve requirements. They had leaned on their examiners to go a little easier. Yet banks were not responding. Greenspan and others took every chance they could to urge, if not beg, banks to lend. But the credit crunch dragged on, and as it did, money growth continued to stall. "If you're sitting at the Fed, you have to be wondering what happened to all that stimulus," Nikko's Bob Brusca marveled. "It's like it went into a black hole."

When the FOMC met on August 20, it had in hand a bewildering mix of information to consider, including an attempted coup against Russian president Boris Yeltsin that threatened to hurt consumer confidence. There had been positive reports on retail sales, housing starts, industrial production, and exports, but credit conditions and the money supply were as weak as ever, and that proved to be the overriding consideration. M2 had just fallen below the bottom of the Fed's target range for the year. Although portfolio shifts were cited as the cause, the FOMC finally faced up to the reality that such technical factors could not explain away the underlying credit problems afflicting the nascent recovery. "Of potentially greater concern and significance for policy was the evidence that some of the weakness of the monetary aggregates stemmed from unusual constraints on the amount of credit provided by depository institutions and implied restraint on the overall supply of credit." Many members indicated continued weakness in M2 would be "a matter of increasing concern, especially given questions about the strength of the economic recovery." The Fed was also getting a bye from the inflation indices, CPI having risen just two-tenths of a percent in July. Many thought the FOMC would decide to ease again. The FOMC was not prepared to do that, but it was sufficiently concerned about money and credit conditions to shift away from the symmetrical directive it had had in place for months, giving Greenspan a green light to cut rates when he saw fit. Black was frank to tell me, "If we don't get a satisfactory rate of M2, I'm going to be in favor of cutting the [funds] rate" again.

Things did not get better. The senior loan officer survey released August 29 found continued tightening of credit standards by banks, widening of interest rate spreads, and "weaker than usual" retail deposit growth. Money supply growth continued to decelerate, giving the administration an easy target. Fed policymakers, particularly those of a monetarist bent, "have got to be embarrassed by money growth below two percent," an administration official told me. "When you've got to look hard for explanations your gut should be telling you something. . . . Interest rates are still too high to spur demand." The bond market seemed to be giving the Fed a golden opportunity, with 30-year yields below 8 percent, but the Fed waited, hoping the monetary drought would end and the forces of recovery would assert themselves. In early September, officials as various as LaWare and Parry were asserting the money supply problems were temporary and technical, that the economy was in the early stages of recovery, and that it was at just such times the Fed had to be vigilant against the longer-term inflation threat. On September 6, the Fed breathed a sigh of relief when the August employment report showed a modest job gain. Treading that thin line between hailing good news and keeping the heat on the Fed, Boskin said the data pointed toward recovery but the Fed had to get M2 back up.

When the Fed's calculations showed another $9.7 billion weekly drop in M2 on September 12, the Fed could wait no longer. It also had in hand a favorable CPI report, showing retail prices had risen just 0.2 percent overall. What's more, bond yields were now holding below 8 percent. Not even the hawks could resist cutting rates again. Indeed monetarists like Black and Hoskins were in the vanguard of those saying the Fed had to act to expand the money supply to prevent an economic contraction. "Troubled" by the anemic growth of M2, Hoskins blamed the Fed's operating procedure. "If you peg the funds rate, money growth is a residual. . . . You've got to supply whatever reserves the economy is demanding at that rate." If demand for reserves was weak, "you may cause money to decline" inadvertently in the process of draining reserves to prevent the funds rate from falling below target.

On September 13, the Board cut the discount rate from 5½ to 5 percent— lowest level since February 26, 1973. The funds rate was reduced from 5½ to 5¼ percent. Banks responded by reducing the prime from 8½ to 8 percent. The administration's enthusiasm was restrained. "As we've been saying for some time, they had to move to get the money supply up well into the middle of their target range," Boskin told me after the rate cut. "Sluggish growth of the money supply has been one of the major problems in the economy, so obviously it was a correct move." Privately, Bush's people made clear they wanted more. One official was so fed up with the Fed's gradual, incremental easing approach he was sputtering with exasperation. Why had the Fed done yet another quarter-point cut? This level of rates should have been reached months before. Yet, in the aftermath of the rate cut, Fed officials were uttering their usual admonitions against "overdoing it" and saying the Fed would have to "wait and see" if further rate cuts were warranted. Unable to get a stimulative capital gains tax cut from Congress, monetary policy was, as usual, "the only game in town." Something had to be done to light a fire under Alan Greenspan.

On September 27, Greenspan was summoned to the White House for a meeting in the Cabinet Room with Bush and his Economic Policy Council. Present, besides Bush and Greenspan, were Brady, Boskin, Darman, and other advisers. Bush, who had been amazingly aloof from domestic economic developments but who was now starting to hear loud complaints from some of his biggest fundraisers, told Greenspan he was concerned about the economy's sluggish pace and would like to see more stimulus. This credit crunch he had been hearing about could have a "chilling effect" on the recovery, mightn't it? Brady and others seconded the notion. Greenspan informed the president the economy was "moving into a 50-mile per hour headwind." Although the economy was "fundamentally sound," the financial system was "under strain." He made no promises. The "50-mile per hour headwind" comment reverberated around the room. It was a phrase the Fed chairman would later repeat publicly many times. Actually, Bush was informed, there were different gusts of wind that were hindering the economy's progress, chief among them the adverse climate in the banking industry. Bank balance sheets were under "severe stress," and "bankers were becoming much more cautious about what they were really lending" for, on top of which bank regulation had become more strict. The economy was also suffering the after effects of tax law changes which had slowed the pace of depreciation allowances and radically restricted passive losses on real estate investments.

Participants describe a strange mood. Greenspan had, in effect, handed the president a death warrant on his reelection chances. But, while his advisers were taken aback by Greenspan's matter-of-fact but alarming presentation, Bush reacted sedately. Sitting with his back to the window facing Greenspan, with his economic and political experts arrayed around him, Bush was just "taking it all in," said one Bush aide, who was chagrined at Greenspan's remarks. "Given the background of the meeting, all that struck me was how calm and subdued it all was." Another says Bush did not seem "jolted" by the Fed chief's comments. "I don't remember it as being a contentious meeting. I mean, there was not an obvious 'magic wand' that was proposed. I think the President was probably looking for that." Although Brady made his usual assertion that rates were too high, Bush and his team largely treated Greenspan with deference. "The other fact that should have been discussed more vociferously, but was not, was the fact that [the Fed] should steepen the yield curve," says a Bush adviser. "That's ultimately what happened, so that banks could make money, to help them build capital," but not until later would the spread between short and long rates become wide enough to prompt banks to lend.

One reason for Bush's seeming nonchalance, a former aide says ruefully, was that some of Bush's more restive advisers held their tongues. One of those "headwinds" was the record tax hike Bush had reluctantly agreed to the previous fall at Darman's urging. Another, the credit crunch, was partially the outgrowth of the FIRREA legislation, another Bush baby. Now the president was on the verge of signing into law another massive bill, the Federal Deposit Insurance Corporation Improvement Act (FDICIA), which, in the process of recapitalizing the FDIC, changed bank rules in ways which some Bush advisers were convinced would do further damage. "The administration had just shot itself in the foot a couple of times, . . . but no one was willing to say it quite as bluntly as that. The first thing they did was pass this retraction [of Bush's 'no new taxes' pledge], which was exacerbating the recession, and no one was willing to touch that one. . . . And the other thing was they had just signed FIRREA and were . . . negotiating FDICIA, and both of those basically codified the headwinds. . . . They certainly had a chilling effect on banks' lending, making directors personally liable and carting some off to jail and what have you. It was a stupid thing to do . . . I mean, [with] FIRREA we really shot the bullet, and now we were about to pull the trigger for the third time. . . . In retrospect, it was all very obvious. You've blown fiscal policy, you've blown regulatory policy. The only thing left was to allow banks to print money, and that was what happened when the balance over at the Fed changed."

The whole episode lent credence to the charge Bush was out of touch with the concerns of ordinary Americans. What had happened, according to White House insiders, was two things. One, Bush had spent enormous amounts of time and energy fighting and winning the war in the Persian Gulf and then managing the aftermath of victory. On a couple of occasions Brady had gotten him engaged on economic issues, but only temporarily. "It was natural he'd be preoccupied," says a former White House staffer. After the decisive defeat of Saddam Hussein, Bush was riding an almost unprecedented crest of popularity in the polls that seemed impervious to economic or other difficulties. "The thought that he wouldn't be reelected hadn't occurred to him." Second, Bush had been virtually shut off from communication with most members of his economic team. This was a residue of the "budget summit" which Darman and Sununu had persuaded Bush to enter into with the Congress the previous summer. "Prior to that time, it had been a model of how a White House should operate, with communication up to the president and back down to the staff," a former Bush aide recalls. "It was going beautifully; it was textbook." However, this all changed with the start of the budget talks. Once those negotiations began in earnest, the once open White House "went on a war footing" to prevent the administration's budget bargaining positions from leaking to the press. Sununu and Darman became bottlenecks to the free flow of information from the staff to the president, walling the president off from contrary points of view on the wisdom of tax hikes. "The president, temporarily, had to accept the price of being deaf, blind and dumb." Some officials, who continued to tell outside groups Bush was against raising taxes were caught flatfooted when the president abruptly announced he would do just that.

Once the budget deal was signed, Bush continued to be walled off from vital economic information, according to a Bush aide. "Once you monopolize power in the hands of Dick Darman and you've broken the channels of communication, it takes a real creative effort to open them, and they didn't open up. As a result, by the time the September '91 meeting came about the president had been going on for almost 15 months without having had the kind of regular information flow that a President needs to know what's really going on." White House staffers began to connive to get what they considered to be urgent advice on economic policy before Bush. "It was a scheme: 'how do we get it in to the President and around Darman?' [Vice President Dan] Quayle was one such mechanism." Quayle had lunch with Bush once a week. "That was one way through the bottleneck, but it was at that level of desperation to get information to the President." By late September, the economic and financial problems had become so acute Bush was beginning to hear about them from the *Eagles*, Republican backers who gave upward of $100,000 to the president's campaign. "They were starting to complain to him, and he wanted to know what was going on," says a Bush aide. "He had heard it enough! When you give $100,000 you have the right to ask the president a negative question or two and he was hearing it a lot! So this meeting was set up so the President" could hear from not only Greenspan but his own economists. "Given a 15 or 18 month hiatus of information to the President, this was a very subdued move." The Fed's response was also subdued. Not for another month would the Fed cut rates again, and a Fed official says there was little or no linkage to the Bush appeal. "We would have [eased] anyway." That is not to say Greenspan ignored Bush the way he largely ignored Brady. "When the president hauls you in and says we need some teamwork here if you know what I mean that's a different matter."

The Fed did not need any additional distractions, but it was saddled with an embarrassing scandal that cost incalculable amounts of staff and policymaker time, political capital, and institutional credibility. It had been announced on August 9 that Salomon Brothers, one of the most esteemed names in investment banking on Wall Street and long one of the Fed's top primary dealers, had been caught trying to manipulate Treasury note auctions. The Fed's critics on Capitol Hill had a field day accusing the New York Fed, and Corrigan in particular, of neglect. The scandal could not have come at a worse time for the Fed. It had engaged for months in an old-fashioned Washington turf war with Treasury, which contended additional regulation of the government securities market was needed. The Fed maintained the market was doing fine under the watchful eye of the New York Fed and the SEC, respective supervisors of bank and securities firms operating in the huge government debt market. Treasury's rulemaking authority in the area should be renewed, LaWare had testified in mid-June, but it did not need additional power to promulgate "sales practice rules" and other regulations. Now came word Salomon Brothers had admitted to violating Treasury rules governing the submission of bids at its auctions. The firm disclosed that in a December 1990 auction of four-year notes and a February 1991 five-year-note auction, bids were submitted by Salomon in the names of persons who had not authorized such bids, and that Salomon then purchased the notes allocated to those bids. In this way, the company had gotten around Treasury limitations on one bidder purchasing more than 35 percent of any given issue. The firm had been lobbying Treasury since July of 1990 to get rid of the rule, and when it did not succeed apparently decided to circumvent it. For months, there had been reports off and on of "squeezes," in which dealers who had committed to deliver securities had to bid up prices to obtain them from a handful of holders. Now here was proof a major firm had tried to corner the market right under the New York Fed's nose.

Salomon discharged two managing directors and promised to sin no more. Initially, the Treasury said Salomon Brothers' confession had "cleared the air." But as the uproar grew, the Treasury announced that, henceforth, Salomon would only be allowed to bid for its own account at auctions. An angry Corrigan forced Salomon Brothers chairman John Gutfreund and president

Thomas Strauss, among others, to resign and be replaced by billionaire investor Warren Buffet. He also launched a review that ended in a two-month suspension of the firm's primary dealer status the following summer, a costly blow since most large bids by institutional investors were routed through the 39 primary dealers. The SEC launched a full-scale investigation into possible widespread manipulation of the government securities market, including alleged collusion and price-fixing. When Congress came back from its August recess, there was the usual round of hyped-up hearings, in which indignant legislators who often knew next to nothing about the government securities market railed against Corrigan and the Fed for letting this scandal happen. The prescheduled reauthorization of the 1986 Government Securities Act provided a ready-made vehicle for trashing not just Salomon but its overseers.

Mullins defended the Fed's oversight in a September 4 hearing before a House Energy and Commerce subcommittee. Far from proving inadequate, "existing enforcement mechanisms appear to have been instrumental" in uncovering Salomon's false bids. Corrigan said the New York Fed had notified the Treasury in February that Salomon, in conjunction with S. G. Warburg & Company, had exceeded its bidding limits. Assistant Treasury Secretary for Domestic Finance Jerome Powell confirmed Treasury had learned that Salomon had submitted a tender at the February five-year-note auction for a customer identified as Warburg Asset Management and that the Warburg parent company had simultaneously submitted a tender of its own. Together the bids exceeded 35 percent.

The SEC's Breeden criticized Treasury for not following up. Subcommittee chairman Representative Edward Markey, a Massachusetts Democrat, branded as "unacceptable" the behavior of the regulators and the Fed in particular. "Salomon Brothers felt no heat until April. Nothing was done to prevent the May squeeze." The Fed and Treasury had both been "derelict" in supervising the market, Congressman J. J. Pickle declared at a later House Ways and Means Committee hearing.

Corrigan felt the New York Fed had done all it could do to detect, report, and respond to Salomon's misbehavior, but Mullins said it could have been more meticulous in monitoring government securities dealers' positions. The New York Fed got reports on dealer positions in securities that were about to be auctioned by Treasury, but "these reports were not actively monitored," said Mullins. Henceforth, they would be. So, "while this has been a troubling episode, it is not apparent that sweeping changes in regulation are warranted." Corrigan argued it was "premature to come forward with any broad-based plans for regulatory changes or legislative proposals with respect to the government securities market." Despite the incident, the market had functioned smoothly with no disruptions or loss of confidence. But the Fed was fighting a losing battle this time. Ultimately, a number of reforms were made. The Fed and Treasury increased scrutiny of dealers' securities positions. The Fed began spot-checking large bids. Treasury began allowing all government securities dealers registered with the SEC to submit bids for customers at Treasury auctions, instead of only primary dealers and banks. Treasury improved automated bidding and payments procedures to make it easier for investors small and large to buy securities without going through a primary dealer and increased the amount of securities it would award to "noncompetitive bidders" at the average accepted tender. Treasury instituted a new policy of "reopening issues," or issuing more securities in the event a particular issue became subject to a squeeze. It brought into the sunshine Treasury's suspect routine of getting advice behind closed doors from a select group of primary dealers known as the Treasury Advisory Group of the Public Securities Association on the types and amounts of securities Treasury should auction. The healthiest result of the scandal was the opening up and modernization of the whole auction process.[9]

Corrigan, now a Goldman Sachs executive, is still bitter over allegations that he and his staff were asleep at the switch. "That's bullshit!" he exclaims from a leather-bound chair in his office just blocks from the Fed. "I mean, here you have a situation in which you had false statements being given to the Fed at the time, in terms of the auction forms themselves. The fact of the matter is that it was a fairly low level clerk at the Fed who noticed the first irregularity in the thing, in March, and the Treasury made some followup inquiries and couldn't find any evidence of any irregularity at the time. But the suggestion that there's even a smidgen of reason to suspect something irregular or fraudulent in that timeframe in which the fraudulent auction reports were submitted, which actually went back to '90, and the time when the whole thing came to light is just preposterous. . . ." Corrigan concedes, "In retrospect, we probably should have had another level of checks and balances and reverifications of some of the information that was submitted with the auctions, but we didn't. You always learn, thank God, in retrospect, things could have been done a little bit better."

While the Fed was handling the fallout of the Salomon fiasco, the economy careened along on its unsteady way. If it was headed into a "50-mile per hour headwind," as Greenspan had told Bush in his visit to the White House woodshed, then surely the Fed would be moving aggressively to counter those winds, the administration thought. But Greenspan had given Bush no assurances of further monetary ease and had stressed the need to "focus on the regulatory side" to ease credit constraints. There had been great unanimity on the September 13 rate cuts. Even Angell had voted to cut the discount rate, citing lower commodity prices. Super-hawk Hoskins had taken the view that, given weak money growth, the risks were now "on the side of being overly restrictive," according to a Hoskins aide. But most Fed officials were still reluctant to escalate the size or timing of credit easing, and they were reluctant to believe all of their past rate cuts would not soon begin to have the desired effect. At an October 1 FOMC meeting, members found it "particularly difficult to assess the overall state of the economy," but they concluded that "on balance the evidence was consistent with a continuing though still sluggish recovery in economic activity and that the prospects remained favorable for a sustained expansion at a moderate pace over the next several quarters." They "generally felt that monetary policy was on the right course under currently prevailing and immediately foreseeable economic and financial circumstances." They decided to maintain (with an easing bias) prevailing policy, which they felt "provided an appropriate balance between the risks of a faltering economic expansion and the risks of little or no progress toward price stability."

This sounded a lot like what had been said at earlier FOMC meetings. It proved there was still an ingrained caution in the current cast of FOMC characters, and the Senate was still keeping Lindsey and Phillips offstage, to the annoyance of not just the nominees but Bush's increasingly worried advisers. Phillips would not even face a confirmation hearing until October 25. "There was a good deal of frustration that rates were not coming down as rapidly as we had hoped, and part of that was Congress's intransigence in acting on our appointees, including Larry," says Roger Porter, Bush's domestic policy adviser. One top Bush counselor is convinced the Democrats delayed confirming Lindsey and Phillips precisely because they knew those two would push for more aggressive monetary stimulus which might help the economy and enhance Bush's reelection prospects. Some of the biggest critics of the Fed's cautious easing approach, like Sarbanes and Sasser, were also among the biggest opponents of Lindsey. "They knew the administration was trying to push a more pro-growth policy and they were moving very slowly on it. It certainly looked deliberate."

Now more engaged on the economy, Bush renewed his call for cutting the capital gains tax September 30, but if Senate Democrats were not going to confirm progrowth Fed nominees, they certainly were not going to pass a progrowth tax cut, even though both houses of Congress had in the past approved some variant of capital gains tax relief. Increasingly desperate, the administration seriously explored using an executive order to index capital gains for inflation and thereby lower the effective tax rate, an idea ultimately nixed by the Justice Department. On another front, the Treasury was leaning on other G-7 nations to spur growth. If they could not get the Fed to spur domestic demand, maybe they could convince other nations to spur their demand for U.S. products. Brady and Mulford did not get far with Germany, which by October had opened up a 4 percent short-term rate spread with the United States. Germany had repeatedly served notice it would not be shamed into loosening monetary policy. Talking to German officials at that time, it became clear their top concern was controlling inflation and stabilizing their economy as they absorbed the states of former East Germany. For emphasis, the Bundesbank had raised its discount rate from 6½ to 7½ and its Lombard rate from 9 to 9¼ percent in mid-August. Each time it raised rates, other European nations had little choice but to raise theirs or see their currencies weaken more than the 2½ percent that was then permitted under the rules of the ERM. The French and others grumbled, but went along rather than formally devalue their currencies and adjust their exchange rates. So growth was dampened throughout Europe, softening demand for U.S. exports. If Germany was willing to ignore the pleas of its neighbors, it was fatuous for Brady to expect Germany to heed his.

Germany was also focused on economic and monetary policy coordination within Europe. Such coordination ended at the European coastline, Lutz Stavenhagen, a top aide to Chancellor Helmut Kohl, suggested in a briefing for a group of American reporters. The G-7 forum was nothing more than "an exchange of views. It should not be seen as an enormous instrument for economic harmonization." In those halcyon days before the European Monetary System virtually fell apart, when prospects for European Monetary Union and a single European currency seemed bright, Stavenhagen boasted the day was coming when Europe would be "less of a junior partner and more of an equal partner" with the United States. "The dollar will have to define itself in relation to the European currency," Waigel assistant Gunter Grosche told me. "It's our objective to create a single currency at least as stable as the Deutschemark, and if we keep it stable, then I'm sure it will be the leading currency in the world."

With Germany (and Europe) basically a lost cause in the G-7 arm-twisting competition, Brady and Mulford zeroed in on Japan, which had shown a bit more flexibility, cutting its discount rate from 6 to 5½ percent in July. They wanted much more. Their main objective was to drive up the yen. In February, the yen had appreciated to as high as 128 yen per dollar, a level which some had feared reflected undue dollar weakness, but had since fallen as low as 139 yen per dollar. They determined to push the yen back up. Although a stronger yen would tend to hurt growth in Japan, it was hoped it would work to lower America's gaping trade deficit with Japan. Accompanied by Greenspan, Brady and Mulford flew to Bangkok for the annual meetings of the IMF and World Bank, stopping on the way in Tokyo to meet with Hashimoto. Although the Greenspan-Brady policy rift had become quite wide by that point, the two were seen joking and talking amiably on the long flight across the Pacific. By the time the G-7 finance ministers and central bankers met on October 12, the yen had in fact risen back to 129 per dollar, a level which Japanese Finance Ministry officials deemed acceptable. Following the meeting, best remembered for marathon discussions with Russian economic policymakers, the G-7 communiqué stated that "recent exchange market developments were broadly in line with continued adjustment of external imbalances." The subtext was that the dollar was expected to depreciate further against the yen. Greenspan could only hope the United States did not get too much of what Treasury had sought. When it came to macroeconomic policy, there was little pretense at coordination. "The ministers and governors emphasized the importance of fiscal and monetary policies which, while reflecting the differing situation in each country, provide the basis for lower real interest rates and sustained growth with price stability in a medium term perspective." As Frederick the Great once said, "In Prussia everyone must get to heaven in his own way."

Back home, a dreary economy awaited Greenspan, as reflected in the beige book released October 22 in preparation for the November 5 FOMC meeting. Business and banking contacts in the 12 Fed districts had told the Fed the economy was "weak or growing slowly" with little or no improvement in retail sales, modest if any expansion in factory output, and still "weak" lending activity. A NAM survey of manufacturing executives suggested the Fed had gilded the lily. The Commerce and Labor Departments provided confirmation with late-October reports of plunging factory orders and home sales and surging unemployment claims. The administration abandoned its line that recovery was on track and renewed its demands for Fed rate cuts. Greenspan had seen enough. Although he had privately voiced doubts about the strength and sustainability of the recovery, he and other Fed officials had publicly maintained a fairly hopeful attitude, talking in terms of 3 percent real economic growth in the second half and beyond. In an October 28 speech, he confessed the recovery was "demonstrably sluggish." For the first time in public, he used the imagery he had employed at the White House a month earlier: The economy was trying to advance into "a fifty-mile-per-hour headwind" and was therefore "having significant difficulty bouncing back." The following day, the Conference Board reported a plunge in consumer confidence. The Commerce Department estimated the economy had grown 2.4 percent in the third quarter, but even this paltry growth rate coming out of a recession, would later be revised down to 1.2 percent, following second-quarter growth of 1.7 percent and three straight negative quarters before that. The fourth quarter then in progress would regress to just 0.6 percent—far too weak to prevent unemployment from rising. The administration was hoping the inevitable rate cut would be more than the usual quarter percent. Robson complained the Fed had moved "too slowly." It was disappointed when the Fed cut the funds rate from 5¼ to 5 percent on October 30.

Fed officials still believed the economy was suffering not from a lack of monetary thrust but from a mélange of factors that were preventing banks from performing their financial intermediation function. Syron said the Fed and other regulators needed to "lean against the wind" in applying regulatory standards to ease the credit crunch. The Fed was considering taking another whack at reserve requirements to encourage banks to lend. Some thought the Fed should start paying banks interest on the reserves they kept in Fed accounts up to 12 percent of their demand deposits, but number crunchers at the OMB and in Congress frowned on this because it would have reduced the profit the Fed annually funneled into Treasury's coffers.

The onslaught of bad economic news continued in November. Nonfarm payroll was down along with hours worked and hourly earnings. The phrase *double-dip recession* began to come into vogue to describe an economy that recovers only to go back into recession. That never quite happened, but to many it seemed that way. Tinkering with reserve requirements and browbeating examiners into going easier on loan portfolios might help at the margin, but ultimately there was only one thing that would get banks back in the lending business and that was to continue cutting rates, and Greenspan knew it. Around the FOMC table on November 5, nevertheless, officials disagreed on the need to continue lowering rates. Through the end of October, the Fed had now cut the funds rate 3¼ percent over the past 15 months and had cut the rate virtually in half from its February 1989 peak. That seemed like a lot to many, and some resisted continuing the process. At some point, they would be inviting trouble. But confronted with sluggish money growth and sluggish economic numbers, the divided and dismayed policymakers voted to cut rates again. With Angell dissenting, it was decided by the board members that the discount rate would be reduced the next day from 5 percent to 4½ percent, and the full committee voted to simultaneously make another quarter-point reduction in the funds rate to 4¾ percent. The FOMC also approved an easing bias. Angell and Kelley dissented, fearing an adverse bond market reaction.[10]

If the Fed expected gratitude it had another thing coming. The administration welcomed the rate cuts, but implied more was needed. Boskin called it "a responsible move in the right direction." While glad to see any easing, however small, Treasury officials criticized the timing as "clumsy" and "panicky." The moves had come in wake of a disastrous Treasury three-year note auction, in which a relative shortage of bids had led to a high yield—good for investors, bad for Treasury. Many suspected the Fed had cut rates when it did to salvage what was left of the quarterly refunding auction, which continued the day of the rate cuts with $12 billion of 10-year notes and a similar amount of 30-year bonds the following day. Echoing many market players whose trading positions had been undermined by the surprise rate cut, a Treasury official said that "it would have been preferable if they had done it before the auctions or after the auctions," not during them. When the ten-year note auction also went poorly, Treasury officials again alleged the Fed had torpedoed the issue. "We warned that you need to be careful when you make changes," one said angrily. The Fed did not take umbrage, feeling it was not its responsibility to maximize the prices Treasury got for its securities—a long-since-abandoned policy known as *even-keeling*. It had not cut rates to bail out the quarterly refunding auctions, and it certainly had not cut rates to hurt them. Slack economic activity and money growth had given the Fed ample reason to cut rates when it did. Uncertainty about Fed policy undoubtedly affected the auction results, but so did other factors. Complaints about Fed moves during refundings did prompt the Fed subsequently to try to avoid rate changes in midauctions, however.

Brady waited only a day before going on television to declare that rates should "continue to come down." At the same time, he accused Democrats of trying to "jawbone down the economy." Senator Mitchell had compared Bush to Herbert Hoover. Brady said he wanted to see not just further Fed rate cuts but a reduction in capital gains taxes. In fact, though, Brady aides revealed the Treasury secretary had persuaded Bush not to push for capital gains tax relief just yet. Treasury officials were quietly lobbying against capital gains reform bills in Congress in the belief they would reduce government revenues, even though past capital gains tax cuts, such as those signed into law by Presidents Kennedy and Carter had had just the opposite result. Now was not the time, Brady told Bush. The votes weren't there, and the bond market might not like it. The upshot was another broken Bush promise and another lost opportunity to get the economy moving sooner. The president's budget had called for reducing the capital gains tax rate from 28 to 19.6 percent, but now the proposal was shelved.

But Brady was willing to consider other measures, some of which can only be described as bizarre. A former Fed official recalls participating in a meeting at which Brady was brainstorming ways out of the credit crunch. "Brady said, 'How can we get these banks to start lending again, instead of buying government securities?' And he paused, and he thought about if for a minute and he said, 'I know, let's reopen the tax code and tax them higher on the earnings on Treasuries than on a loan.' The Secretary of the Treasury, in an open meeting, with representatives of several different agencies including his own in the room, I mean, my hair stood straight up on end, I'm sure, and I just couldn't believe what I was hearing." The Treasury had tried to devise innovative, not to say suspicious-looking, regulatory responses to the credit crunch. A March proposal to "split" loans into performing and nonperforming segments so that the performing part would not have to be written off had been abandoned as unworkable in late July. But Brady and company forged ahead, looking at such schemes as a liberalized definition of bank capital and a board of appeals where bankers could contest examiners' "unfair" loan classification rulings. One thing not seriously considered was backing away from the 1988 BIS capital standards, with their zero capital backing requirement for government securities.

Throughout November, the Brady-chaired Economic Policy Council explored other measures, including a tax credit for purchases of American-built cars. Brady also weighed abandoning the sale of Treasury 30-year bonds on the theory that would reduce long-term interest rates. The wheels were starting to come off. At one session of the EPC, the normally cool and collected Boskin erupted at Sununu for making the administration look "like a laughing stock" by persuading Bush to call for lower rates on credit cards. Senator D'Amato had dutifully introduced a bill to cap credit card rates, which sailed through the Senate and was blamed for causing a 120-point plunge in the Dow on November 15. One Bush aide blamed Sununu for producing a "discombobulated" response to the economic slump.

What passed for good news was a Fed finding in its November 13 senior loan officers survey that credit conditions had slowed their rate of deterioration. Although some banks were still tightening credit, most had left their lending standards unchanged. It was cold comfort. Business loans were on their way to a 4.8 percent decline for the year—the first annual decline since a 3.8 percent fall in 1975. Inflation had practically disappeared. The CPI had risen just a tenth of a percent in October. What on earth was the Fed waiting for, Brady wanted to know? His deputy Robson minced few words in a November 20 address. "If you look at the charts showing what the Fed has done meeting its monetary targets they're not on the chart. They're off of it." He advised the Fed: "The downside risks of easing are very modest . . . the impact on inflation is not something you have to concern yourself with."

The Fed's December beige book confirmed anecdotally what statistics had been saying, that consumer spending and manufacturing activity, two prime ingredients in any recovery remained in the doldrums. The recovery was suffering from what the Fed delicately called "flagging momentum." After rising earlier, orders for autos and other goods had dried up. Layoffs were on the rise. Lending was weak. Housing activity, the one semibright spot, was growing "slowly." On December 6, the Labor Department announced nonfarm payrolls had plunged 241,000 in November. Later that morning, the Fed cut the funds rate another quarter point to 4½ percent, a rate not seen since mid-1972. Greenspan admitted that day he had misread the economy. "The economic recovery, which seemed to be gathering momentum and spark during the summer, more recently has shown signs of faltering. The normal forces of economic expansion are running up against countervailing forces that I have likened elsewhere to a 50-mile per hour headwind." What had first seemed like a healthy tightening of credit standards had gotten out of hand, and now "many creditworthy borrowers face significantly stiffer terms and standards, and some find credit simply unavailable." He was not prepared to admit the Fed had goofed, however. The Fed had "eased monetary policy considerably over the past 18 months or so," but the Fed was being frustrated in its effort to grow the money supply. He offered a number of explanations for slow money growth, without quite dismissing it.[11] Greenspan's explanations were reasonable, but did not satisfactorily explain to Fed critics why it had lowered rates in dribs and drabs in a process one administration official labeled "Chinese water torture."

It was no accident the Fed took a gradual, incremental approach to cutting rates. LaWare says the Fed committed itself to a slow pace of easing because "to have eased more rapidly would have signalled a real crisis in the economy which I don't think was there. We had no way, at that stage of the game, of appraising what the effects of the Gulf War would be, whether they'd be stimulative or be depressive or what have you. So I think it was a deliberate series of moves toward ease that were well designed. They could have been accelerated at any time anybody felt they should have been. I don't remember any of us—making a strong argument that that was the case." Another Fed governor says the decision to lower the funds rate a quarter percent at a time was "not made on some predetermined path," but "was done piece by piece." However, each small easing "was done in the context of people realizing that we were probably still basically in an easing mode and hadn't gotten through with it yet" and that further easing should be "incremental or piece by piece." In trying to look beyond discouraging monthly data then coming in and project trends one to two years in the future, "there was a lot of faith that the economy would get going, and we didn't want to overdo it." There was no explicit, preordained strategy to take small bites out of the funds rate month by month, says a Fed staffer. "It not like [professional football coach Joe] Walsh where you call the first 25 plays of the game." However, there was an understanding at each successive FOMC meeting that more rate cuts were going to have to be made, but that it should be done slowly so as to avoid disrupting the markets. "There was a kind of understanding that we'll take this step today, but more will be needed in the future, because this just isn't enough, and when we meet again we'll do more."

The go-slow approach was consciously motivated by a desire to "make hay while the sun shines"—that is to say beat down inflation while the economy was in recession, says the staffer. "There was a lot of talk about 'speed limits' and 'can we risk too rapid a recovery? Should we take advantage of the war? Should we take advantage of the circumstances and use this slowdown to get inflation down?' " What's more, there was a genuine "fear that inflation was rising and that we'd overshoot full employment for too long. . . . There was clearly a lot of pressure on the Fed to ratchet that inflation down. . . . So nobody was in a hurry to stoke up growth." Only late in the game did the Fed realize it had underestimated the downside risks and had to shift gears to a faster easing pace. "Initially [the easing] was quite slow but then when it became clearer, in late '90, that the economy was really struggling, then we went down, certainly again in small increments, but rather rapidly," says a Fed governor. "But you can't plan that in advance." After fearing a drawn-out Middle East crisis would keep oil prices high and damage the economy, the Fed became overly optimistic after the speedy allied victory in Kuwait. "As it turned out, none of the extremes that we expected were there and the Gulf War was not a prolonged proposition," says LaWare. "It was over so promptly, and the psychology of the country was so upbeat coming out of it that a faster process of easing just didn't seem appropriate.

Greenspan says that "the state of the bond markets was crucial in those days" in slowing the pace of easing. "We wanted to get long-term interest rates down and it was by no means clear whether that was most effectuated by holding short-term rates [steady] or lowering them, because the evidence is mixed in that regard. What we did know was that long-term rates were a crucial issue." Although the Fed has been faulted for not doing more to prevent or alleviate tight credit conditions, Bank of England governor Eddie George says that, of all the "enormously impressive things" Greenspan has done, "One of the most impressive of those things was the way in which he handled what came to be called the credit crunch, the kind of pressures that resulted from the collapse in property values and the way in which he combined . . . low short-term interest rates with higher bond yields, which had the effect of easing pressures on the American banking system. I think that was one of the remarkable episodes of sound central bank management. . . . It was a domestic issue, but the American banks operate all around the world. So we had an interest from that perspective. . . . Also, low interest rates would have been a factor influencing the dollar. . . ."

Despite what the monthly indicators were saying, the Fed's models were telling it its rate cuts would provide enough fuel for a moderate, noninflationary recovery. This general approach continued into December. Although the economy was clearly not responding well to the Fed's many rate cuts, totaling 3½ percent since July 1990, Fed officials were optimistic. True, the economy had "certainly hit a slow path in here," but there was "still a substantial amount of stimulus ahead of us from actions taken over the past year or more," Kelley said in a December 9 interview. Both cyclical problems, like excess inventories, and structural problems, like the "debt overhang" on consumer and corporate balance sheets, were being worked out. Households were paying off their debts, and corporations were gradually reducing their debt-to-equity rations. "There's every prospect we'll see slow improvement as we get through next year." While "pessimism was pretty prevalent" just then, Black said his business contacts were upbeat about prospects "six months down the road." Mullins joined in this general refrain. When he said December 10 that past rate hikes "should be sufficient to put us back on the path of moderate growth" now that business balance sheets were improving, many came to the conclusion the Fed had finished cutting rates. Ten days later he would lead the charge for the biggest rate cut the Fed had made in years.

The administration was anything but optimistic or patient. The way Boskin saw it, the economy was going to be "sluggish at best for the next several months," and faced a number of "downside risks": the continued lack of credit; the "strained" financial position of households; state and local government fiscal problems; continued low money supply growth; and a possible drop-off in net exports due to slower growth abroad. With inflation "down and declining," he told the Senate Finance Committee on December 12 that the Fed still had "ample room" to lower rates. Above all, the Fed had to keep its mind on expanding the money supply, which was still creeping along at an annual rate of about 2½ percent. The Fed had to "recognize that a decline in interest rates during a period of soft economic activity may not be a sign of monetary easing, especially if the growth of money and credit has slowed." Dole echoed Boskin in his characteristic staccato monotone: "We have to take a look at monetary policy. . . . Has it lagged behind, can it do more—I think so." He complained the Fed had been "timid" about easing and had had "to be pushed and nudged" to lower rates.[12]

Brady, appearing with Boskin, was angry at the Fed not just for its monetary policy but for what he perceived as its failure to follow through on relaxing banking regulation. He complained examiners from the Fed, as well as other agencies, had resisted implementing the new examination guidelines that had been finally released after months of delay. Brady said the key to raising real estate values, which he considered the leading problem with the U.S. economy, was getting regulators to appraise real estate collateral for loans based on its long-term potential, not just its current liquidation value, but regulatory personnel were sabotaging the guidelines their higher-ups had ageed upon. "I'm frank to tell you, they don't like the changes we've made." He was determined to root out this "insensitive handling" of real estate assets. Charles Bowsher, comptroller general for the General Accounting Office, had warned the Treasury guidelines were excessively lax and threatened to revive the problems of the eighties. "I don't know where Mr. Bowsher has been during the real estate crisis," Brady said. "To say regulators must be stricter, he must be living in a different world than I am." Brady's anger at the Fed was misplaced. Greenspan had been fully cooperative in trying to counter the credit crunch through more flexible examination procedures.

As the FOMC convened on Tuesday, December 17, the White House made a strategic decision: It would no longer pretend the economy was recovering.

"From any practical standpoint, the recession does continue," Fitzwater said. "The people of this country know that the economy is in trouble and it doesn't make any sense to play games." Or as Bush himself mellifluously put it, "I am less interested in what the technical definition [of recession] is. People are hurting. When there's this kind of sluggishness and concern—definitions— heck with it. Let's get on with the business at hand." The next day, as General Motors announced it would close 21 plants over four years to cope with $15 million per day losses, Greenspan told the House Ways and Means Committee the economy had "faltered" and was "struggling." The economy had come "half way back" from recession but had "stalled." He acknowledged he had known the economy was in trouble for months. By late summer, "it became clear that the cumulative upward momentum that characterized previous recoveries was absent." The propensity of households and businesses to reduce their debt burden "was a signal that the balance sheet restraints, feared by many for a long time, had indeed taken hold, working against the normal forces of economic growth." Why then had the Fed not eased more aggressively? Nobel Prize–winning economist James Tobin had described Fed rate cuts as "nibbling around the edges." Greenspan bristled when asked about Tobin's allegation. On the contrary, the Fed's rate cuts had been "really quite extraordinary. . . . It is true that we have chosen to go down in small increments, but we do it often." He blamed fiscal policy. "The heavy demand the government is already placing on the credit markets is a significant factor in the persistence of historically high real bond yields and mortgage rates, which is making the private balance sheet adjustment process all the more difficult."[13]

The markets had been looking for a cut in the discount rate and funds rate following the FOMC meeting, but none had been forthcoming, and the committee members wanted to know why. Cryptically, Greenspan told them the Fed was looking "very closely" at lowering rates further. In fact, he was actively arranging the biggest rate cut in a decade. There had been a very different chemistry at the Tuesday meeting. After months of delay, Lindsey and Phillips, both of whom had made clear they would vote for lower rates, had been confirmed and sworn in, Lindsey on November 25, Phillips on December 2. The FOMC was concerned about "retrenchment" associated with balance sheet restructuring, "sluggish" consumer spending, falling consumer confidence, and weak money growth. There was a predisposition to ease, but disagreement on how much. Some argued for "a more substantial move" than the Fed had been making, but others "expressed reservations about the urgency to ease in the near term and especially the need for a sizable move." Still others wanted no easing. The FOMC voted not to change policy right away, but approved a directive with "an especially strong presumption that some easing in reserve conditions would be implemented unless improvement in the economy became evident fairly promptly or there was significant evidence of a pickup in M2 growth." LaWare dissented because he "preferred not to prejudge that need [to ease] but to wait and assess the effects of the considerable easing actions undertaken earlier." The seeds had been planted for dramatic early action.

Corrigan recalls telling the FOMC it was "time to ring the bell," that is, slash the discount rate. "What I meant was that economic fundamentals, at least as I saw them, were quite respectable, but we just were in this funk, and talking about 'ringing the bell,' to me, it was kind of like a wakeup call or a school bell." Mullins had come to the same conclusion. During a coffee break, Corrigan somewhat rhetorically told Greenspan, "You know, what we ought to do is reduce the discount rate by a full point!" Corrigan says Greenspan "looked at me a little bit surprised, and we talked about it a bit, and then Mullins came into the room. We talked about it a bit more. And by then I actually had convinced myself it was a pretty godamned good idea! And, of course, the rest of it is history." Mullins talked further to Greenspan about Corrigan's idea, then sounded out each of the governors. Phillips had only been in office for a couple of weeks when Mullins dropped by. "I remember David Mullins came down here and we sat in this very office, and we talked about it and I said, 'You know, we need to move.' So he said, 'What would you think about a one percent move?' And I said, 'If we can do it that would be great, but I don't think it can be done. I don't think the votes are there.' And he said, 'Well, we'll see.' " Lindsey also gladly gave Mullins his support. LaWare and Kelley were iffy, and Angell was a lost cause.

There was only one problem. While the Board had received numerous requests for a half-point reduction in the discount rate, it did not have in hand any requests to cut the Fed's lending rate by a full point. Corrigan told Greenspan he could convince his board of directors to request a 1 percent rate cut, but Greenspan wanted two requests. Coincidentally, Greenspan had been scheduled for months to sit in on an upcoming two-day meeting of the Chicago Fed's Board of Directors. "Terrific," said Corrigan. Following his Wednesday congressional testimony, Greenspan flew to Chicago, returning Thursday afternoon, December 19, with the 1 percent rate cut request in hand. Meanwhile, Corrigan was extracting a similar proposal from the New York Fed board. Some of the governors had vacation flights scheduled the next morning, so Greenspan summoned them to the board room Thursday evening to consider the two requests. With Lindsey and Phillips backing Greenspan and Mullins enthusiastically, Kelley voted with them to cut the discount rate from 4½ to 3½ percent. Somewhat sheepishly, having just a few days earlier voted against an easing bias, LaWare went along. Angell refused. Announcing the rate cut Friday morning, December 20, the Fed said it had been "made on the basis of cumulating evidence, notably monetary and credit conditions, as well as current economic conditions, that point to a receding of inflationary pressures." Together with previous rate cuts, the action was expected to "provide the basis for a resumption of sustained economic expansion." That same morning, Greenspan convened an FOMC telephone conference, in which it was agreed the funds rate should be reduced half as much as the discount rate, taking the funds rate from 4½ to 4 percent. It was a bold move and not taken lightly. The Fed had to consider how it would be received by the markets. A panicky-looking move could backfire, sending bond and stock prices plunging and undermining the dollar. Fortunately, that did not occur.

Lindsey recalls waiting for a flight at Baltimore-Washington International Airport after the rate cut announcement. "The Dow was up 100 points or so, and I felt like I had done what I was supposed to do. That was quite an exhilarating feeling." Phillips concurs. "It was great! It was great! And it was quite a break [from past Fed strategy] because the Fed had been moving in smaller increments. . . . The economy had shown positive growth, but it was very paltry." One of the Reagan appointees now insists the Board would have cut the discount rate as much as it did even without the addition of Lindsey and Phillips, because "the Chairman and Mullins were very strongly in favor of doing it." But Lindsey and Phillips are convinced they, along with fellow Bush appointee Mullins, made all the difference. "It was obvious that Mullins had worked very hard to try and get rates down, but it was dragging," says Lindsey. "There was a lot of inertia . . . [in] what had been a very cautious Board, with LaWare, Kelley, Greenspan and Angell. Phillips and I were anxious to cut rates, as was Mullins."[14]

The Fed had made its monumental move despite the fact that the Bundesbank had raised its discount and Lombard rates to 8 and 9¾ percent respectively on Thursday, but the Fed did not let that affect its timing on this occasion. "We knew darn well the Bundesbank was considering it," according to a Fed official. "When they went ahead and did it, we decided nevertheless to do what we had to do." Not surprisingly, the dollar fell, which was fine with the administration. "It will be a big boost to export growth," said a Treasury official, who was happy to see the Fed put the needs of the domestic economy uppermost. "It shows the name of the game is to get the economy back closer to full potential in 1992 and beyond." The administration was also glad to see banks cutting their prime rate a full percent to 6½ percent. Other officials were more grudging with their praise. "It's about time," said one, who called the rate cuts "necessary but not sufficient" and said the administration would still have to push for fiscal stimulus measures. "It finally sank in that the incremental approach was not having sufficient effect both in real economic terms and in psychological terms," an embittered official said. "They've obviously come to terms with the fact that there's a real economic and psychological difference between an equal value of incremental changes summed up and an equivalent one-time change."

The eleventh hour discount rate cut left a bad taste in some Fed mouths. "That whole thing stinks," one senior Fed staffer confided, alleging Greenspan bowed to political pressure from the White House to engineer the rate cut after he and Mullins had given strong indications no rate cuts were imminent. An administration official did tell me two days before the discount rate cut "the pressure on the Fed is just irresistible at this point," and other officials later crowed about having persuaded the Fed to move away from its "baby step" approach to easing. But I have no reason to believe Greenspan capitulated to White House pressure. On the contrary, if Corrigan is to be believed, it was his idea to do the full point cut, and Corrigan is a Democrat.

CHAPTER SEVEN

The End of a Recession—
and a Presidency

By the beginning of 1992, the Fed had cut the federal funds rate 5¾ percent from its February 1989 peak, sliced the discount rate from 7 to 4 percent, and eliminated some reserve requirements, but the U.S. economy remained in its torpor, still overcome by credit and other problems. Civilian unemployment had risen to 7.1 percent, as growth ground to a virtual halt. The payoff was that the Fed had finally started to make real progress against inflation. After rising by 6.1 percent from December 1989 to December 1990, consumer prices rose 3.1 percent from December 1990 to December 1991. That progress proved to be lasting. Just as the Fed staff had been saying for several years, creating "slack" in the economy would cause a deceleration of inflation. To make these gains, the Fed had not responded aggressively to recession and stagnation until late 1991. If the Fed had lowered rates earlier and faster, there might have been no recession, or, if there had been, the recovery would have been stronger and more lasting but inflation probably would not have come down as much as it had.

The Fed paid a high political price for its reluctance to accelerate its easing pace. The Fed had overplayed its hand. The economy had proved much softer than Greenspan and most of his fellow policymakers had expected and now seemed stubbornly unresponsive to their ministrations. Having failed to pre-empt recession, the Fed would feel compelled to lower rates to levels it had never imagined. In the process the U.S. dollar would get into serious difficulties. If the Fed knew then what it knows now—that the economy would steadily accelerate its recovery in 1992—it might have stopped lowering interest rates in December 1991. But having finally convinced itself the economy was mired in financial quicksand, it continued the easing process, though not right away. As the year began, it looked like the economy would continue to stagnate. On the second day of the year, the NAPM index of industrial activity was reported down sharply to 46.5 in December, as new orders, production, and employment all weakened.

Things also still looked bleak for the banking industry. The GAO's Bowsher told Congress on January 3 that the industry would be unable to raise enough money through higher deposit insurance premiums to repay the $70 billion Congress had authorized the FDIC borrow from the Treasury unless the economy improved. Bowsher had been a bit of a Chicken Little on banking problems, but this was one area where the Fed did not want to take chances. Once more, Congress had made matters worse for banks by passing FDICIA in late 1991. Fed officials could barely restrain their contempt for the legislation. Congress had held endless hearings on the credit crunch and had directed much of the blame in the Fed's direction, yet with this legislation it had sent the credit crunch into extra innings. Its primary purpose was to recapitalize the depleted federal deposit insurance fund, but it did not stop there. Greenspan complained it attempted to "micromanage" banks in the guise of increasing "safety and soundness." In the process it counteracted the Fed's efforts to ease the credit crunch.

Signed into law December 19, 1991, FDICIA provided for "prompt corrective action" against undercapitalized financial institutions. Banks were categorized into different capital zones, and if a bank found itself in one of three "undercapitalized" categories, it had to submit a detailed plan for rebuilding its capital position without increasing its risks. If the bank did not follow the plan to the letter or if it became "significantly undercapitalized," the bank's regulator must require it to issue new stock or subordinated debt or be acquired by another institution. The law also prescribed restrictions on transactions with affiliated institutions; on interbank credit transactions; on how much interest a bank could pay to attract deposits; on dividends; on asset growth; and on executive bonuses or raises. What's more, the regulators could restrict any activity deemed to pose excessive risk to the insurance fund; replace directors or senior executive officers; and require divestiture of any part of the bank that posed a risk. Ultimately, the government could seize the bank and put it in receivership. FDICIA also imposed personal liability on bank directors and officers and an array of other intrusive guidelines covering nearly every aspect of bank operations. Loan documentation after FDICIA became "grotesque," according to LaWare. Other provisions narrowed regulators' flexibility to react to problem bank situations, strictly limiting the Fed's ability to lend to troubled banks and ending the so-called "too big to fail" doctrine, under which the FDIC had previously protected uninsured depositors. Annual on-site examinations of all FDIC-insured institutions were required. Bank regulators were to determine how much "interest rate risk" banks were running and augment capital requirements accordingly.

Having just signed the legislation, President Bush could not very well ask Congress to repeal it. Instead Brady stepped up efforts to have the regulators do everything they could to minimize the burden FDICIA had mandated. Greenspan was willing to cooperate, short of disobeying the law, and put Phillips in charge of the Fed's effort to work with the administration to soften the blow of FDICIA. New to the game, she was "horrified at some of the provisions that were in FDICIA. I thought they were really quite Draconian." Fed officials, working with other regulators, came up with the idea of giving banks a quota or "basket" of "character loans" they could make. Banks had virtually stopped making such loans, which did not carry with them the usual standards and documentation, for fear examiners would mark them down. Greenspan himself wrote a letter to examiners practically pleading with them to be less strict and to take a longer view with regard to the value of loan collateral. But such efforts were largely unavailing. FDICIA inclined examiners to be even more hard-nosed. Examiners were looking over their shoulders, knowing their supervisors were likely to be reviewing their work and reporting to Congress, particularly if a bank failed. About the time FDICIA was passed, the Senate Banking Committee blocked Comptroller of the Currency Clarke from serving another term regulating nationally chartered banks. Phillips thinks that "had a fairly profound effect on the examination community," leading them to believe even tougher examinations were expected of them. The result was a "reign of terror" that discouraged bank lending.

More than 230 banks with some degree of capital inadequacy, as defined by Congress, became subject to FDICIA's harsher provisions, and another 520 banks with 30 percent of total bank assets were subjected to some capital constraint, according to Phillips, who said the new law removed regulators' discretion and forced them to impose harsher measures than they might otherwise have chosen. Greenspan, who would often drop into LaWare's office, prop his feet up on the coffee table and talk about banking with the former bank CEO, complained FDICIA raised bank costs and "discouraged healthy as well as unhealthy risk-taking in lending decisions." There is no question the law complicated and undermined the Fed's mission by prolonging the credit crunch and delaying true recovery. Some of the more onerous provisions of FDICIA were later repealed, but not until 1993. Total bank credit in 1992 grew 4.1 percent, a slight improvement over the 1991 pace of 3.9 percent, but still quite weak by historical standards. It was actually much weaker, for bank investments in government securities swelled the total credit figure. There was essentially no growth in bank loans and leases in 1992, after an anemic 1.9 percent rise in 1991. By contrast, total loans and leases grew 16.4 percent in 1984.

The dearth of loans was a big factor restraining money growth. Banks finance loans by issuing *time deposits* or *certificates of deposit* (CDs), and when few loans are made few CDs are sold. The ongoing closure of scores of banks and thrifts compounded the problem. Another 108 banks had failed in 1991, and almost as many would fail in 1992. The RTC would liquidate 69 thrifts in 1992 on top of the 232 liquidated in 1991. Typically, a failed institution's deposits and assets were assumed by a healthier institution, but often only a small portion of the failed bank or thrift's loan assets were worth holding and lending on. Only about a fourth of the assets of RTC-resolved thrifts were accepted by acquiring institutions, while the acquirer took over all of the failed thrift's deposits. Often these were high-cost *brokered deposits*. As a result surviving banks and thrifts often ended up with more deposits than they needed or wanted to fund their loans and investments, particularly in a climate of slack loan demand, so they worked to reduce their deposit liabilities by cutting interest rates on deposits and in some cases abrogating large time deposit contracts. As customers removed their deposits and invested them outside the banking system, the M2 money stock tended to shrink.[1] M2 growth had steadily dwindled from 5½ percent in 1988 to 5 percent in 1989, to 3.2 percent in 1990 to 2.9 percent in 1991. In much of the second half of 1991, M2 barely grew at all. It picked up somewhat in early 1992, but then decelerated again, so that by midyear it was growing at an annual rate of less than 1 percent. That was a major problem for the Fed, politically, because the M2 target was its most conspicuous monetary policy commitment and one the administration was determined to hold it accountable for; and economically, because, despite its measurement problems, M2 had shown an undeniable connection to the recession.

At the beginning of 1992, the Fed could not be sure how serious the credit crunch would continue to be or how much momentum the economy would have. Having reduced rates substantially, it had every reason to believe it had improved banks' margins sufficiently to encourage lending. In their private counsels, officials talked about the possible need to cut rates again, but they were disinclined to move so soon after December's discount rate action. They hoped the economy would at last pick up steam. "I don't think we're in a recession," Forrestal said on January 6. "But if we were to fall back into a recession, I think we would respond appropriately." In an unusual joint session of the Senate Banking and Budget Committees on January 10, Greenspan kept all his options open, too. Past rate cuts had been "very considerable" and it was his "best judgment" they would be "far more than enough to turn the economy around." The "stretched balance sheets" that had been restraining the economy would return to normal. But Greenspan confessed, "My best judgment is not as good as I would like." "Disinflationary forces" were still "retarding the economy," so the Fed would "continue to monitor the situation carefully and stand ready to take steps necessary to foster sustainable economic expansion." The economy had "come back half way [from recession] and gone flat." If it turned down, the Fed would have to resume easing.

Despite the weak signals the money and credit aggregates were sending, Greenspan and associates were hopeful the economy was starting to perk up. Consumer and business balance sheets really were starting to improve, helped by lower debt servicing costs, and households had more liquid wealth to spend, helped by gains in the stock market. Loan demand was showing signs of increasing. I talked to Lindsey, Boehne, new Kansas City Fed president Thomas Hoenig, and others in mid-January and they all predicted the economy was headed for real growth in the 2 to 3 percent range that year. Some saw even stronger growth. This time, the Fed optimists would prove accurate. The economy would grow 2.6 percent for the year, accelerating to a growth rate of 5.7 percent in the fourth quarter. However, they had proved wrong before. So Greenspan remained on the alert to lower rates again—and not just because he wanted to avoid another lapse into recession. As perhaps the most fiscally conscious Fed chairman in the central bank's history, he was also anxious to avoid giving the administration and Congress any excuse to resort to fiscal stimulus. Notwithstanding the 1990 budget deal, the federal deficit had climbed to a nightmarish $269.5 billion in fiscal 1991 and was headed toward $290.2 billion in fiscal 1992. But the administration and some in Congress were proposing a variety of tax cuts designed to rejuvenate the economy in time for the November elections. Greenspan had not been happy with the degree to which the 1990 budget deal had relied on higher taxes, and he had always been a believer in reducing or preferably eliminating the tax on capital gains, but regarded the tax rebates and other measures the Republicans had in mind as pure poison. "What we do not need at this particular stage are fiscal policies that restimulate the debt process," he said.

Brady continued to pressure the Fed, publicly and privately, but did not confine himself to giving unsolicited advice to the U.S. central bank. Despite having been slam-dunked by Poehl the previous spring, he reprised his assault on high German interest rates at a January 25 G-7 meeting in Garden City, New York, out on Long Island, as Greenspan looked on. Going into the meeting, the Treasury had twin objectives: further yen appreciation and lower European interest rates. In the past year, the dollar had fallen from as high as 141.59 yen per dollar to 123.80. Inevitably, the dollar drop was not confined to the yen; it also fell from as high as DM1.75 to DM1.5940 at the time of the meeting. But administration officials wanted further dollar depreciation to spur exports. They also wanted "expansionary policies" by all U.S. trading partners, on the theory that would increase overseas demand for U.S. goods and services. The Bank of Japan had lowered its discount rate a half percent to 4½ percent in late 1991, but the Bundesbank had given no signs of any inclination to loosen its tight policies. It was still trying to cope with the rapid money supply growth and expansionary fiscal policy stemming from German reunification. Brady and Mulford seemed oblivious to those concerns. Once again they vainly hoped to shame the Bundesbank into lowering rates. Its "interest rate policies are putting great pressure on other European economies," a senior administration official told me near the outset of the G-7 confab. "We understand they are very concerned about wage pressures, but if those can be dealt with that ought to open the door to a lowering of interest rates and an easing of monetary policy. We would like to see an easing of monetary policy as would other European countries. Current German policies are putting great strains on the European system." It was embarrassing for Greenspan to listen to Brady's ham-handed demands, as indeed it was for other G-7 officials.

Brady and Mulford were soon set straight. Although the communiqué contained a phrase stating that with inflation diminishing there is a "basis for an easing of monetary conditions and interest rates," which Brady pointed to triumphantly, it soon became clear the phrase did not apply to Germany. "It would be a mistake if you were to focus only on German easing," Köhler, Mulford's German counterpart, told me. "We have to stick to our near-term [fiscal] consolidation line. That is the basis for possible easing in the future." In other words, the Bundesbank had no intention of easing until the German budget deficit was reduced. Mulford conceded he and Brady had made no headway with Poehl and Waigel. "There was a broad discussion of interest rates but everybody knows what the German position is on interest rates now." Far from easing, the Bundesbank would raise rates further. German rate cuts were more than a year away. In the meantime, rising German rates and falling U.S. rates would put heavy downward pressure on the dollar and strain the European Monetary System to the breaking point.

The dollar was in for a long descent, particularly against European currencies—a source of concern to the Fed, particularly given the Treasury's relative lack of concern. A weak currency meant not just potential inflationary pressures but a potentially destabilizing loss of confidence in U.S. financial assets. The Fed had to make another difficult choice. Basically, it was decided the dollar would have to take care of itself while the Fed dealt with the credit crunch and the domestic economy. If the Fed could engineer a noninflationary recovery, improved fundamentals would eventually undergird the dollar. The Fed had failed to bring the economy in for a soft landing after its inflationary flight of the late eighties, but it did not want to make matters worse either by gunning the engines into another inflationary takeoff or by keeping the economy grounded in an effort to protect the dollar. It was a tricky matter of providing enough fuel to get the economy off on a trajectory neither too steep to control inflation nor too shallow to reduce unemployment.

It was not just to reduce joblessness that the Fed wanted to revive the economy. The recession and stagnant recovery were combining with profligate spending and the costs of the thrift cleanup to drive the federal deficit into the stratosphere. The fiscal 1991 deficit had been a record $269.5 billion, including an estimated $66 billion in deposit insurance related outlays. The fiscal 1992 deficit was then projected to go to $365.2 billion. Now, on January 29, the White House was presenting a fiscal 1993 budget that projected a deficit of $332.7 billion. The problem was not revenues. In fiscal 1991, government receipts were 18.7 percent of GDP, only modestly less than they had been for many years, but outlays were 23.5 percent of GDP. The Fed could do nothing about Congress' penchant for spending money it did not have, but it could lessen demand for some social programs and increase tax payments by allowing more job creation. The fiscal 1992 deficit would in fact come in at $290.4 billion, a record but far less than feared, thanks to the recovery that finally began in earnest in the spring, and the fiscal 1993 deficit would decline to $255.1 billion, nearly $80 billion below projections. The administration, in its fiscal 1993 budget, saw the need for the Fed to continue cutting interest rates to achieve its economic vision: real GDP growth of 2.2 percent in 1992 and 3 percent in 1993; unemployment falling from 7.1 to 6.9 percent in 1992 and to 6.5 percent in 1993; inflation averaging no more than 3.3 percent from 1992 forward, and ten-year Treasury notes topping out at 7 percent in 1992 then falling to 6.6 percent. As it had said at every step along the way, the administration still asserted there was "ample room" for the Fed to lower rates. Those assumptions underlay a budget containing a capital gains tax cut, increased tax exemptions for families with children, tax credits for first time home buyers, and other tax incentives.

The day the budget was presented, Greenspan was before the Senate Banking Committee for his long overdue second-term confirmation hearing. He was in an uncomfortable position. His term as a member of the Board of Governors ran through the end of January. Bush had belatedly renominated him as chairman during a congressional recess the previous August, effective the day before his chairmanship would have expired. This so-called *recess appointment* allowed Greenspan to continue serving until he was reconfirmed by the Senate or for that matter until the end of the 102nd Congress, even if he had not been confirmed. So the Senate Banking Committee had been in no particular hurry. Now, on January 29, two days before the exipiration of his term as governor, Greenspan was being grilled by Riegle, Sarbanes, and other Fed gadflies. Not content with his lengthy testimony and responses to questions, they gave Greenspan a long list of questions to answer in writing. With insufficient time to respond and be confirmed, Greenspan would go into the February 4–5 FOMC meeting a quasi-lame duck.

Greenspan was cautiously upbeat at the hearing, expressing hope the credit crunch would soon ease and that money growth would quicken, but said the economy, while not declining, was "flat" and had "no bounce." He took exception to complaints the Fed had not eased credit sufficiently. The Fed had done a lot, perhaps "enough" to do the job, but was ready to ease further if necessary. Greenspan was anxious to head off any fiscal stimulus measures that might further widen the deficit and terrify Wall Street. So he did not want to leave the impression monetary policy had retired from the fray. However, many market participants interpreted Greenspan's comment that past easing moves "should be sufficient" as ruling out further easing, prompting the Treasury to redouble its Fed bashing. "Finally, after a year of taking quarter-point baby step decreases, the Fed dropped the discount rate a full point last December," but rates were still too high to spur recovery, particularly in the real estate sector, Robson told a group of mortgage bankers on February 3. "That's why we have been continuously pressing the Fed to bring the rates down. . . . With inflation so clearly under control, there may well be more room for even further easing by the Fed to stoke the fire of our slow-burning economy."

Alarmed by the reaction to his Senate testimony Greenspan told the House Budget Committee on February 4 he was "frankly surprised at the market interpretation of what I said last time." He feared a tax cut "bidding war" to stimulate the economy and wanted to reassure Congress the Fed was not on the sidelines. He had said "nothing new" at the earlier hearing, he stressed. Past easing moves would likely lead to a "quickening pace" of economic activity as balance sheet adjustments "dissipated," but if the economy did not respond as hoped, "then further action would be desirable." The Fed was "continuing to evaluate" whether more rate cuts were needed. Greenspan was willing to go well beyond ordinary monetary measures to insure recovery and preempt the fiscal stimulus furor. With heavy federal borrowing driving up long-term interest rates he said the Fed might buy and hold more long-term Treasury securities in an effort to push up their price and lower their yield. In fact, the Fed had done just that in 1991. Greenspan also supported the Treasury's decision to sell fewer long-term notes and bonds, but urged it not to lean too heavily on short-term financing. That was not all. The Fed also had under active consideration a further reduction in reserve requirements. Greenspan's reassurances that the Fed had not forsworn further easing did not get the administration off his back. The Economic Report of the President, whose release coincided with the FOMC's second day of meetings February 5, blamed the Fed for prolonging the recession. Monetary policy "should have been geared to lowering interest rates faster and earlier." With short-term interest rates still above the inflation rate, the Fed was still too tight; the Fed needed to bring rates down to the level of inflation (a little over 3 percent) or less.

It was a concerned and uncertain group of Fed governors and presidents who gathered for the first FOMC meeting of 1992 to set policy guidelines not just for the next six weeks but, provisionally, for the year. "The members generally agreed that enough monetary stimulus probably had been implemented to foster the desired upturn in economic activity without further policy moves. Nonetheless, the high degree of uncertainty surrounding the outlook suggested that the Committee needed to remain alert to the possibility of developments that might require additional easing." They voted unanimously to keep policy unchanged but gave Greenspan leeway to lower rates again if he saw fit before the March 31 FOMC meeting. Greenspan had a green light from a substantial fraction of the committee. "The persistence of a weak economy might well have especially severe consequences, and, in the view of some members, signs of such an outcome would call for prompt action." Others felt there should "not be an unusually strong presumption" of further easing. The committee did not dare reduce its M2 growth range from the previous year's 2½ to 6½ percent.

Greenspan did not avail himself of the latitude the FOMC had given him, despite continued signs of economic gloom, such as a 91,000 decline in January nonfarm payrolls and a survey of senior bank loan officers that indicated no relaxation of credit conditions. The best that could be said was that fewer banks were tightening loan terms and standards. There had been a temporary resurgence in money growth, and Greenspan was determined to give past rate cuts a chance to work. It was a sentiment shared by most other Fed officials. There was a feeling that, as Boehne put it in mid-February, the Fed should "not move too sharply" in trying to push the economy out of its doldrums. Phillips and Lindsey had brought a new attitude to the Fed. "There was a time when inflation was an invidious problem, . . . but when inflation is not a problem, which it's not right now, growth has to be the major concern," the former said February 13. Greenspan kept reminding Congress the Fed was ready to "take other actions," as he wrote to Riegle on February 11, to take out "additional insurance." One stimulative measure Greenspan could not countenance was devaluing the dollar to give exporters an edge in world markets. It was fairly rare for him to express himself publicly on exchange rate policy, but he did not hide his displeasure with the proclivities of some in the administration and in Congress to seek a weaker dollar. "While the dollar has depreciated substantially in recent months, partly in response to the easing of the U.S. monetary conditions, a policy that seeks to depreciate the dollar against the yen or any other currency is not an appropriate way to stimulate the U.S. economy," he wrote. Doing so "may distort the effects of other policies and have adverse effects on our own economy and could lead to a counterproductive pattern of competitive depreciation."

The first few months of 1992 were a period of great ambivalence among Fed officials, so the Fed settled into one of its periodic wait-and-see modes. Greenspan's familiar line that the Fed may well have eased enough but was prepared to do more sounded obfuscatory, but it was an accurate reflection of the chairman's and the whole FOMC's thinking, according to Black. "Everybody on the committee would say the same thing. We hope we've done enough, but if we find out we haven't we're prepared do do more." The Fed had done "one whale of a lot" of stimulus, but "it takes time to affect the economy." Part of the ambivalence had to do with the bond market. After falling from a 1991 high near 8.6 percent to 7.3 percent by year-end, the long bond yield had climbed back to 7.9 percent with parallel increases in mortgage rates. It would have been difficult for the Fed to cut short-term rates in that climate without risking a further rise in long rates that would kill in its crib any housing recovery. Then, too, economic statistics were sending mixed signals. A day after the Commerce Department reported an encouraging rise in retail sales for January, the Fed reported a big drop in industrial production. M2 had so far shown more strength than it had in a long time.

There was a feeling the Fed had to do something, even if it was not ready to lower rates again. So on February 18, the Fed Board decided to cut reserve requirements on transaction accounts from 12 to 10 percent to "reduce funding costs for depositories and strengthen their balance sheets" in the hope that eventually "these costs savings will be passed on to depositors and borrowers." It was made effective April 2. This first major change in reserve requirements on demand deposits put in place by the 1980 Monetary Control Act might or might not spur more lending, but at least nobody could accuse them of sitting on their hands. Greenspan was set to present his Humphrey-Hawkins report the next day, and while Fed officials deny the action was timed to soothe a restive House Banking Committee, it certainly did not hurt Greenspan to have another antirecessionary action he could point to. The administration praised the Fed's apparent easing move. In truth, the reduction in reserve requirements was intended less as a direct easing of credit than as a boost to bank profits and capital positions, which might indirectly loosen up credit. Lindsey said the Fed had acted to reduce a "distorting tax" on the banking industry, which would now have to keep fewer noninterest bearing reserves in idle Fed balances. It appeared the Fed had lowered reserve requirements to stave off actual monetary easing. Not so, says Greenspan. "The motivation was technical in the sense that reserve requirements were higher than were appropriate at the time. . . . It was not a substitute for a rate cut. It has the effect of creating profitability for the banks, but it does not change the short-term rate structure."

Armed with lower reserve requirements, on top of a 60 percent reduction in the funds rate, Greenspan was ready to do battle with the House Banking Committee. It was obvious from his testimony the Fed had done all the easing it intended to do for a while. The economy was still "troubled," and the outlook was still "uncertain," in part because the credit crunch had still "not been eliminated" and balance sheet "restructuring" was ongoing. It was possible the recovery could again "peter out," as it had the previous spring. But there were "reasons to believe that business activity will pick up." There had been "stirrings" in the real estate and retail sectors. Spending was "starting to firm." Balance sheets had strengthened. The Fed had used all the tools at its command: open market operations, the discount rate, and reserve requirements. Now, he implied, it was time for the Fed to rest and wait for its good works to prove fruitful. The Fed would "monitor" and be "sensitive" to incoming economic and financial data, and stand ready to pursue "alternate policies" if they proved disappointing, but (and this was the key sentence) "the monetary stimulus already in train is expected to provide effective support for economic growth this year." Adroitly turning the tables on his congressional critics, Greenspan reminded the committee, "The large stocks of federal debt that have been built up likely have adversely affected our economic prospects by putting upward pressure on real interest rates and thus stunting the growth of the capital stock on which our future incomes depend." No one laid a glove on him.

When Greenspan talked about corporate *restructuring*, he was talking about a multifaceted process that was going on throughout the business world. It involved not just the unwinding of excessive debt burdens and the rebuilding of equity. It also involved closing down obsolete or superfluous plants and retooling those that remained. And, of course, it involved the painful human process of laying off many thousands of people, not just blue-collar workers, but senior management. Companies were streamlining, getting rid of extra layers of management. The ultimate result was a far "leaner and meaner" corporate sector ready and able to compete globally, but while it was at its height, it was a wrenching experience for individuals, communities, and the economy as a whole. For the most part, the Fed and the government generally let this market process work. Breakneck pump-priming measures were rejected, as were protectionism and *industrial policy* proposals that would have put American industry and labor into European-style straitjackets. None of which is to say the Fed's job was made easier by this laissez-faire approach. One of the Fed's big problems, which came through again and again in my conversations with Fed officials was the difficulty in differentiating between job losses related to the business cycle and job losses related to corporate restructuring. As Phillips observed, it was "going to take a longer time to see considerable improvement" in employment because cyclical job losses were being amplified by longer-term payroll trimming. These trends cast doubt on what "full employment" meant in a changing economy.

Greenspan got a more rigorous going over when he gave his second installment of Humphrey-Hawkins testimony before the Senate Banking Committee February 25. Still cautiously optimistic, despite a "quite disturbing" plunge in consumer confidence, he was hounded by Sarbanes and others on when the Fed would cut rates again. He had repeated his assertion that past rate cuts should be sufficient to fuel recovery, but was forced to admit, "We may be mistaken: more might be required. . . . It's much too soon to make the judgment that the economy is solidly on a growth path." The Fed would lower the funds rate again if need be. Indeed, the Fed was making a "day-by-day evaluation" and asking itself "Are we having enough effect and is more required?" Greenspan wanted to see "definite signs" that the economy was reviving "sometime in the second quarter." However, the Fed had to be sure not only that more rate cuts were needed but that they would be "positively" received. The financial markets were already anxious over the high level of federal borrowing and the possibility Congress would pass a fiscal stimulus plan. He urged Congress to act soon one way or another to end the uncertainty.

Greenspan was adept at reminding Congress of a fact they would just as soon forget. Because of its own deficit spending over many years, Congress had given the markets an effective veto over both fiscal and monetary policy, and there had been no effective effort by the White House to rein it in. With a nearly $300 billion deficit to finance in 1992, not to mention the accumulated $3.7 trillion national debt that had to be serviced at that point, no president, no Congress, no Fed chairman could afford to ignore the opinion of domestic and foreign bond traders and investors. Once upon a time, when the U.S. budget deficit was small and the United States was a creditor nation, the bond market had been a sleepy backwater. Now there was a raging torrent of government paper changing hands with breathtaking speed in this constantly growing, constantly mutating worldwide marketplace. Even the hint of a policy move that threatened to increase the amount of debt or undermine its value instantly registered in the form of falling bond prices, skyrocketing interest rates, often spilling over into the currency and stock markets. This ferocious monster, which Washington had created, sent its calling card in October 1987, and woe to the politician or policymaker who did not heed it.

The market monster had snorted flame again when the Fed cut reserve requirements. Mullins was astonished at the resulting drop in bond prices. For heaven's sake, "it was almost a technical adjustment, not any attempt at policy," Mullins said on February 26. Nevertheless, it did "say something about the fragility of the bond market." It was a common refrain among other officials I talked to. Here the economy was struggling to climb out of recession, yet every member of the FOMC was conscious of the run-up in bond yields that had occurred and of the danger that one wrong move could send them yet higher. Since the beginning of the year, long-term interest rates had climbed nearly three-quarters of a percent. "The obvious question that leads to is 'do you have any room to do any more [easing]?' " Syron said. That is why the Fed needed to see weaker economic data—not just for proof more easing was needed, but because only economic weakness would prepare the bond market to accept an easing. Hoenig, who had succeeded Guffey at the Kansas City Fed five months earlier, saw it a little differently. "Anyone in the business of central banking has to be alert to the fact that its actions also affect the bond market, and you have to be sensitive to the effect of your actions, but I don't think you say 'we'll take this action now because it will have this effect.' "

In spite of the continuing credit crunch, Greenspan saw "hopeful signs" in early March that a recovery which had been "little more than glacial" was gaining momentum. Like crocuses popping up in the spring, one statistic after another seemed to confirm his optimism that monetary policy was "working." The NAPM index went back above the crucial 50 level to 52.4 in February. The housing market was starting to improve. Although the unemployment rate rose from 7.1 to 7.3 percent in February, more attention was paid to the fact that nonfarm payroll had risen 164,000, its largest increase in nearly two years, and that the average workweek was up. Retail sales and industrial production had also risen strongly. Inflation, though relatively quiescent, could not be forgotten. Core consumer prices rose at an annual 5 percent rate. "The jury [was] still out" on the sustainability of the recovery, as Mullins said on March 9, but these types of numbers left the Fed firmly on hold, watching and waiting with rising expectations for an economic rebound mixed with dread that its old nemesis inflation could reawaken at almost any time. It began to look like the Fed had done all the easing it was going to do.

There was another factor keeping the Fed from lowering the funds rate further. Fed officials were being pulled in opposite directions by the money supply's bewildering behavior. After being raked over the coals for two years for letting its favorite aggregate, M2, grow at or below the bottom of the target range, the Fed had succeeded in returning it to a growth rate roughly in the middle of the 2½ to 6½ percent target range during the first two months of 1992. Although Greenspan downplayed M2's short-range importance in the Fed's calculations in a March 6 letter to Congressman Neal, the fact was the Fed was greatly relieved at its resurgence and wanted it to continue. Five percent M2 growth was seen as appropriate, together with an anticipated increase in M2 velocity, to provide a modest economic rebound without reaccelerating inflation. It was "a healthy sign," said Mullins. The trouble was other measures of the money supply, which the Fed had officially deemphasized but could not ignore, were exploding. M1 grew more than 20 percent from December through early March. The monetary base (bank reserves plus currency in circulation) had grown more than 13 percent. After a long monetary drought, which had exposed the Fed to terrific criticism, the Fed was now getting too much of a good thing. Apart from any actual inflation it might cause, it appeared to be a contributory factor to high long-term interest rates. The Shadow Open Market Committee, a group of monetarist economists which until recently had included new Cleveland Fed president Jerry Jordan, declared it was time for the Fed to start tightening credit to staunch money growth and avert an outbreak of inflation. Some Fed officials shared these concerns. "I'd be more comfortable if it wasn't growing so fast," Black said in a March 11 interview. Although M2 had proven to be "a better indicator of the impact of monetary policy, M1 has really taken off with a vengeance. . . . We have put out a whole lot of reserves no doubt about it. It could be we've put out more money than we meant to."

There were various explanations for what was going on with the various monetary aggregates, none of them totally satisfactory, and the Fed did not know quite what to make of it. That made it tough, for the Fed had resolved to pay greater attention to the money supply and to hit its M2 targets after allowing it to slow to a crawl in the 1990–1991 period. "We're a little adrift to find reliable monetary policy instruments," confessed John Davis, then director of research at the Cleveland Fed. "Thirteen years ago I would have stood here and defended to the death the use of M1. Today, I'm hard pressed to defend the use of M2." There was a relatively simple explanation for what was going on. Rapid M1 growth primarily reflected a shift of funds out of time deposits, now that interest rates had fallen so much, into more liquid transaction accounts, and this necessitated increased bank holdings of reserves, which in turn increased the monetary base. The Fed had merely been accommodating banks' increased demand for reserves as the public had increased its demand for reservable deposits. To some, the bulge in M1 and reserves was nothing more than a natural consequence of economic recovery. Others worried there might come a point where the Fed was increasing reserves too much for its own good. A major pitfall of the Fed's funds rate pegging procedure was that it basically provided as many reserves as were demanded at a given funds rate. The Fed had to be careful not to "get stuck into not changing the funds rate for a long period of time," San Francisco Fed economist Bryan Motley said, because "if you persist in having very rapid reserve growth it would tend in the long run to push up M2 growth." The Fed would continue to have difficulty reading the divergent monetary aggregates.

The administration knew the high level of long-term interest rates was discouraging further easing measures, yet it continued to do and say things that worsened the long rate spike. On March 11, President Bush said he was more concerned about stimulating the economy than about long-term rates and said higher long rates were "manageable." Predictably, bond prices plunged on the comments, sending the yield on the Treasury long bond above 8 percent briefly. Even at this late date, Bush just "didn't get it." Nor did Brady. When I interviewed the Treasury secretary the following day he claimed the bond market's reaction had been "a function of retail sales, not the president's comments," a reference to the relatively strong sales increase reported the morning after Bush's comments. Those retail sales figures proved there were "robins on the lawn"—a metaphor for recovery Brady was fond of repeating. (About the same time he was citing rising sales of lightbulbs as proof Americans were opening their wallets again, and we used to joke about Brady's "lightbulbs on the lawn.") The bond market would just have to learn that good economic news did not necessarily mean inflation. "I think that long-term rates will come down when people realize that you can have recovery and at the same time not have inflation." He still had not learned that Wall Street does not respond to exhortations from the secretary of the Treasury, even when he is an alumnus. The long bond would fall back below 8 percent by April, but in May jumped back up to 8⅛ percent before beginning a long descent.

A noninflationary recovery is exactly what the Fed was hoping to achieve. It was just that achieving it might be easier if the administration would stop scaring the markets with nonstop chatter about monetary and fiscal stimulus. Fed policymakers I talked to in the third week of March expressed growing confidence a noninflationary recovery was in prospect. If they had failed to achieve a "soft landing" perhaps they could at least achieve a smooth takeoff. Thanks to slack in product and labor markets, Lindsey predicted, "We will continue to see lower inflation rates even as growth picks up." Syron, a voting president that year, still had his doubts about the strength of the recovery, given the slowdown in Europe and Japan, but was "more encouraged" than he had been just a month before that the recovery was for real. With unemployment relatively high and capacity utilization relatively low, he was "not that worried about" inflation. Black thought "things are going to work out reasonably well" in terms of improved economic growth without an acceleration of inflation. Mullins, LaWare, Kelley, Phillips, Parry, Stern, and Forrestal had a similar view, although they placed different emphases on the impact of weaker foreign growth on exports and other factors that might dampen growth. This conditional optimism was validated when the beige book reported "some improvement in economic conditions" around the country with "few indications of significant upward pressures on retail and wholesale prices of goods." Even the administration, treading its usual thin line between bashing the Fed and not trashing the economy, had to be more restrained in its demands. The economy was "clearly improving," but the Fed should "stand ready to make sure we have sustainable money growth" and "take the necessary steps" if money growth diminished. Insufficient money growth was the least of the Fed's worries.

So it was not surprising when the FOMC, at its March 31 meeting, left the funds rate unchanged at 4 percent, while retaining an asymmetrical directive with a bias toward ease. The majority felt "a steady policy course, at least for now, was . . . desirable in the context of encouraging evidence of a strengthening economy and the outlook for continuing expansion at a pace that was deemed likely to be consistent with further progress toward price stability." Although the economy was only starting to show signs of recovery, there was concern overeasing would backfire by causing inflation fears. "The members acknowledged that the uncertainties in the economic outlook were considerable, but given the ongoing stimulus stemming from earlier easing actions, they agreed that for now an unchanged policy represented an appropriate balancing of the various risks to a satisfactory economic performance." It was felt that "substantial further easing at this time might well fail to provide much added stimulus; indeed, it could prove to be counterproductive because of adverse repercussions in financial markets. Moreover, too much easing at this juncture could establish the basis for unduly rapid growth of money and credit when the economic expansion gathered momentum." Some wanted to drop the bias toward ease which the FOMC had kept in its directive, but it was decided this would be "premature. . . . While the members generally anticipated that economic and financial developments during the intermeeting period would not call for an adjustment to policy, many remained concerned about the vulnerability of the expansion to a variety of risks."

In fact, though, the seeds for a rate "adjustment" before the next meeting had been planted. The much maligned monetary aggregates were sending maddeningly conflicting signals. M1 and the monetary base were still expanding wildly (nearly 20 percent for the former), making some FOMC members think policy was now too loose. However, more closely watched M2 was starting to wither. Through early March, it had grown almost 6 percent at an annual rate, but by the time of the FOMC meeting, its growth pace had slowed to 3 percent. The alarmist view of the ballooning narrow money supply was outweighed by concerns that broader money was running out of gas. The FOMC had taken notice of M2's deceleration, and "it was suggested that a persisting shortfall in the growth of M2 and M3 could signal that monetary policy was not positioned to support a satisfactory expansion." Two days after the meeting, the Fed announced M2 had fallen by $10.2 billion in the latest reporting week, on top of a $4.6 billion drop the week before that. Even M1 fell by $4.8 billion. All of a sudden things seemed to be going awry. The Fed was forced to reexamine its assumption that its past rate cuts had been sufficient to propel adequate money growth. The following Thursday, April 9, would bring news that the money supply had fallen again, but the Fed did not wait until the late afternoon announcement to act. Knowing what the money supply had done and having also seen a disappointing March jobs report, Greenspan consulted the other members of the FOMC by telephone, then ordered the open market desk to push the funds rate down a quarter percent to 3¾. Before the Fed showed its hand in the market late that morning, my Fed sources had confided their concern about the money supply and the pace of recovery. "Just because rates are as low as they have been in 20 years, it may not be enough; we may need more," said one. "This recovery may require more priming." Market News Service subscribers liked the quote.

It was an odd state of affairs. Although there were, as always, mixed signals, it was becoming increasingly evident the recovery was picking up steam, and yet those pesky aggregates seemed to be pointing in the opposite direction. The once-burned, twice-shy Fed, looking as it must toward economic conditions a year to two in the future, saw the slowdown in money growth as a possible harbinger of another faltering in the recovery, another false start. People were talking about a "triple dip." It wasn't just weak money growth that kept the Fed on the edge of its chair. It knew the credit crunch had never really gone away, nor had the other "headwinds" of which Greenspan had spoken the previous September. Companies were still streamlining and downsizing themselves physically, organizationally, and financially. Household balance sheets were still being rebuilt. The post–Cold War build-down of the military was in progress, hurting the economies of California and other states dependent on large defense installations and contracts. Defense spending had fallen from 6½ percent of GDP in 1986 to 5 percent before the Persian Gulf War, and after a brief upsurge, had resumed its decline. It was scheduled to fall to 3.7 percent by 1997 under Bush's fiscal 1993 budget. The real estate sector, particularly commercial real estate, was still trying to recover from the bursting of its bubble. In Boston it was said overbuilding had created enough excess office space to last for 20 years. Higher rates in Europe and more deep-seated problems in the Japanese economy were hampering growth abroad and threatening exports.

It was not your usual business cycle upswing. So while Fed officials tried to sound optimistic, it was optimism tinged with doubt and hedged with a readiness to act again. The Fed could not afford to suffer a further loss of credibility by allowing the economy to sink back into recession. Typical of the attitude was that expressed by Lindsey in one of a series of interviews conducted four days after the rate cut. "The odds are we will have continuing sustained expansion, but there are risks. We'll have to keep our eyes on it." Phillips was less confident. "We're starting to see the recovery take hold, but the question is whether it will be sustained. There is a lot of downside uncertainty. It will require continuous monitoring." LaWare, on the other hand, was "one of the cockeyed optimists who believe we're in a recovery." With his keen banker's eye, LaWare could sense the animal juices beginning to flow. He would prove accurate as the economy got stronger quarter by quarter, but in the early spring, those robins on the lawn Brady kept talking about looked pretty sickly. From January 1 to April 1, for instance, commercial and industrial loans had fallen from $291.6 billion to $288 billion, a 4 percent rate of decline. It was hard to get much M2 growth when banks were not creating deposits to make loans. In a wilderness of uncertainty, the Fed could only hope it had done enough. Once again, it sat back to watch and wait.

The same could not be said for an administration now just seven months away from election day. Less than artfully, Bush's advisers talked out of both sides of their mouth. The economy was in recovery and had "turned the corner" on the credit crunch, Robson averred April 21, but the Fed had to keep pumping out money "to ensure that it continues." A notable exception to this kind of talk who deserves to be mentioned was Treasury's Jones, who consistently declined to parrot the Brady line that there was always more room for the Fed to ease. On the contrary, the independent-minded Jones said on April 29, the Fed could not be expected to cut rates much more because of "the inflation risks of monetary accommodation." He did say there would be no need for the Fed to tighten policy "for the foreseeable future" as the economy gained strength because wages would remain "under control."

While the administration was anxious to maximize growth, the internal Fed debate as the second quarter brought continued signs of improvement was how fast a recovery it should allow. In May, a debate began to rage among policymakers and their staff advisers over what "speed limits" the Fed should set on the pace of expansion. Some "hawks" were content with projected real growth rates of 2½ to 3 percent and felt not much more than that should be permitted if inflation was to be contained. Other more "dovish" members favored a "more typical" recovery of 4 to 4½ percent to get unemployment down faster. It was a rather odd debate to be having, since there was still tremendous uncertainty about whether the recovery would even be sustained. The Fed was groping its way along in a statistical fog, unable to see what was ahead, only what was behind, and even that was hazy. In early May, for instance the Commerce Department had estimated real GDP had grown 2 percent in the first quarter, and initial indications were that the second quarter would be no better, maybe worse. The purchasing managers reported that production and new orders for manufactured goods had slackened in April. The beige book reported "uneven" economic conditions. M2 seemed to be pointing to sluggish growth at best. With the benefit of final revised figures, we now know real GDP (using 1987 dollars) rose 3.5 percent in the first quarter of 1992, slipped back to 2.8 percent in the second quarter, then accelerated to 3.4 percent in the third and 5.4 percent in the fourth. At the time the Fed had no way of knowing this, anymore than it knows at this moment how fast the economy will grow over the next quarter or two. This is why monetary policy is an art, not a science.

Greenspan capsulized the Fed view in a May 7 speech. "Things are improving," but because of the "extraordinary strains" caused by balance sheet restructuring in both financial and nonfinancial companies "we still have a ways to go." When the May 19 FOMC meeting rolled around, "things" were looking better. The unemployment rate for April had been reported down a tenth to 7.2 percent, as nonfarm payroll rose more than expected. Retail sales and industrial production had also risen handsomely, although housing starts plunged. M2 was making a small comeback, but was still near the bottom of the target range. Consumer prices, after rising a scary five-tenths of a percent in March had risen just two-tenths in March. To further spice things up, Olympia & York Developments, a giant Canadian real estate developer active in the United States, declared bankruptcy, exposing major banks to losses and causing the New York Fed to throw open the discount window to banks needing emergency liquidity. It was all grist for a lively debate between hawks and doves. The former, notably Angell and Jordan, argued the economy was gaining such momentum it would be foolish to cut rates again. The doves argued the recovery was still shaky and there was no inflation to worry about, so why not "buy some more insurance" by cutting the funds rate another notch. They wheeled out the dusty P* model to help make their case.[2] Lindsey, for one, argued the model was "consistent with substantially lower inflation" in the future—roughly 2 percent instead of 3 to 4 percent. "P* suggests that inflation will come down a lot further, and that's what I believe," Black said. But a Board staffer poured cold water on the model, noting it was based on M2 and "everybody is suspicious of M2."

No longer united by an obvious need to combat recession, the FOMC was splintered. A great deal of time was spent debating the monetary aggregates. Some expressed alarm at the weakness of the broad money supply and cited it, along with projected declines in defense spending and exports, as a reason for continuing to tilt toward ease. Others dismissed M2's sluggishness and said the economy could do fine with less money growth and a higher rate of velocity. They pointed to stronger orders for nondefense capital goods, a pickup in business fixed investment, improved business confidence, signs of "a more accommodating climate" in loan markets, gains in consumer spending, and other signs of strength. Some thought it was time to go to a directive biased toward tightening. After a great deal of wrangling, the deep divisions were resolved by agreeing on a symmetrical directive, under which Greenspan could tack in either direction. It was the first time the FOMC directive had not had an easing bias since July 1991.

Whoever likened the legislative process to watching sausage being made never contemplated the conduct of monetary policy. Few areas of policy are so dependent upon forecasting the future and therefore so subject to second-guessing. It is virtually always a thankless job, and never more so than in the period we're talking about. It goes without saying that politicians of both parties were almost impossible to satisfy, and there was no shortage of criticism from professional Fed watchers, but it didn't stop there. There were those within the system who also questioned the way Greenspan had steered policy. The main charge: unpredictability. "Being unpredictable means people build a cushion into the prices [of bonds] and it costs Treasury money," said a top trader for a primary dealer. "If you're uncertain about what goes on, you'll tend to try to buy things cheaper." A senior Fed staffer at a key Federal Reserve Bank, who needless to say did not wish to be identified, complained that in "trying to keep the market off balance," Greenspan and other policy-makers had "thrown business off." Not knowing whether the Fed intended to cut rates further or leave policy on hold, there was a tendency by businesses, investors, and ultimately consumers to put their economic activities on hold. What's more the Fed bore some responsibility for keeping long-term interest rates up by keeping the market off balance. "Why say that the economy is still having problems, but then say the Fed has done enough?" asked the staffer, referring to the occasions in early 1992 when Greenspan and Mullins had talked about continuing weakness in the economy but implied the Fed had provided sufficient liquidity, only to go ahead and ease credit anway. "It makes no sense for the Fed to be so unpredictable." Another staffer said the Fed was "adrift" in early 1992 for lack of a reliable monetary measure and therefore lacked "credibility."

The Fed was accused of playing a cat-and-mouse game with the markets after December's 1 percent cut in the discount rate cut, first failing to pass through more than 50 basis points to the federal funds rate, then leaving the funds rate unchanged at 4 percent for four months while unleashing a barrage of conflicting and confusing statements—talking optimistically about recovery and the ample monetary stimulus "in the pipeline"—only to cut rates again when the supposedly unreliable and discredited money supply ebbed away. Throughout this period, a Fed staffer alleged, Greenspan and Mullins had spread uncertainty in the markets, helping hold up long-term rates and under-mining business confidence. Paul Kasriel of Northern Trust Company said he "would rather pick the lottery numbers" than try to predict Fed policy. Former Fed governor Lyle Gramley agreed statements by different Fed officials had been "confusing" to the market, but doubted it had affected market rates or the economy very much. The biggest problem, according to Gramley, was the "abominable" forecasts the Board staff had been providing to the FOMC. "They sat all during the summer [of 1991] and didn't see the weakness that was coming. . . . The Fed has consistently underestimated the seriousness of the credit crunch. The economy faces a major problem—not enough private credit flows—and when I talk to people at the Fed I don't get a sympathetic ear." These criticisms all have a ring of truth, but they fail to come to grips with the fact the Fed was facing an incredible array of problems and changes that made it very difficult to read and forecast the economy.

After the May meeting, the debate between hawks and doves and those in between continued at a low boil. Nearly everyone was talking hopefully about economic prospects, but Phillips and Lindsey questioned the strength and sustainability of the recovery, laying the groundwork for another rate cut. Others would take some convincing. They saw the economy recovering, led by business spending on heavy equipment, and saw no shortage of liquidity to finance it. This group got some support in late May when an encouraging senior loan officer survey gave the first sign in many months that the credit logjam was beginning to break up. For the first time in a long time, more banks reported easing credit standards than reported tightening, and loan demand was up. Small- and medium-sized businesses, which had been hardest hit by the credit crunch, were starting to face somewhat easier credit conditions. It was not the only straw in the wind. The purchasing managers index continued to improve in May. However, signs of weakness were not hard to find, and bit by bit the doves built their case for another easing.

The administration was still bending the Fed's ear, and M2's continued weakness gave it all the excuse it needed. It had slowed to an annual growth rate of less than 2 percent since the end of 1991, and since March, it had actually fallen. "If the Fed pulls down the level of the money supply in 1992 as was the case in 1991 when the first appearance of growth came, then we're taking a chance with the recovery," Brady told reporters covering the big bankers' annual International Monetary Conference in Toronto on June 1. Greenspan was also in Toronto to participate with other G-7 central bankers in their annual joint press conference. He had a different theme. The economy was in a "gradual but persistent expansion," and the major risk was "the inflation threat embodied in long-term interest rates." In reality, there was "almost no evidence of inflation emerging over the next two to three years." The reason long-term rates were so high for this stage of recovery was the huge budget deficit, which was contributing to "a persistent view that over the longer run there will be latent but persistent pressure" on prices.

As if to prove the Fed chairman wrong, the Labor Department announced on June 5 that the unemployment rate had leaped from 7.2 to 7.5 percent in May. The administration dismissed the rise in joblessness as a statistical quirk caused by the growth in the size of the labor force and the number of job applicants. There were indeed positive elements of the jobs report. Nonfarm payroll had risen again, as had hours worked. Even so, it was one of those bad PR numbers that was difficult for the Fed to shrug off. What's more it came a day after M2 plummeted another $10.7 billion in a single week. This too could be explained away as a New York Fed staff study attempted to do. Authors John Wenningner and John Partian wrote that M2's "unusually weak" growth had been due primarily to flows out of small time deposits into other types of accounts and into nonbank instruments in response to falling yields on CDs, which in turn was related to banks' lack of need for deposits to fund loans. In other words weak loan demand was fueling weak money supply growth. That thesis begged the question of which came first: the loan demand chicken, or the money supply egg? Either way, weak M2 was a reflection of soft economic conditions or at least of weak bank lending activity. The Fed could only hope businesses and consumers were able to meet their credit needs outside the banking system. There was reason to believe they were, but with an important difference. Unlike banks, other lenders do not have banks' ability, through the magic of fractional reserving, to create money through the so-called *multiplier effect*. To illustrate, given a 10 percent reserve requirement, for each $1,000 deposited in a bank, that bank can lend $900, keeping $100 as reserves. If, hypothetically, all of that $900 loaned by the first bank were deposited in a second bank, that bank could loan out $810, keeping $90 in reserve. A third bank that received the $810 in deposits, could lend out all but $81 and so on. To the degree credit extensions bypassed the banking system, that multiplying process was short-circuited. The Fed had to count on an increase in the velocity of money to make up for the lack of money creation.

Although unemployment rose while consumer spending slumped in May, industrial production had skyrocketed by 8.1 percent—the fourth consecutive monthly rise. As economic data continued to zigzag from encouraging to discouraging and back, Fed governors and presidents were divided on whether the economy needed another jolt of monetary stimulus. In fact, the FOMC was divided into three camps: those who believed the economy could not grow any faster without reigniting inflation; those who thought the economy was growing well below potential and could grow faster with no danger of spurring inflation, and "a third camp who believe the economy is capable of doing no more because of financial impediments," said a Fed official. For the third camp, "the speed limits [for growth] are not enforced by fear of inflation, but by what we can reasonably expect from our economy" given the level of debt and the need to restructure financially. Those divisions made it hard to forge a policy consensus. Official comments revealed the divisions that existed. LaWare, on June 10, questioned whether additional Fed rate cuts would do any good in terms of stimulating the economy and might serve only to worsen the inflationary expectations that were holding up financial markets. The Fed had to "convince the market" it would keep inflation down. Phillips, on the other hand, saw no cause for concern about inflation and emphasized her doubts about the sustainability of the recovery. Hoenig thought the recovery had "its feet firmly planted," and while the recovery would be moderate, the "silver lining" was that inflation would stay low.[3]

Always looming over the Fed was the bond market, which was keeping long-term interest rates stubbornly high out of concern about the deficit and disbelief that inflation would be kept under control. News that retail sales had risen a meager 0.2 percent in May, while consumer prices rose just 0.1 percent gave bond prices a boost, but the long bond yield remained above 7.8 percent—a high level for an economy climbing out of recession. The United States had made "considerable progress toward price stability," but there was still "a significant inflation premium" built into bond yields, a frustrated Greenspan said June 16. Heading into the June 30–July 1 FOMC meeting, the beige book survey found anecdotal evidence the economy was continuing to improve, particularly in manufacturing and residential construction. Despite the pick-up in activity, it found that "price stability in the retailing and manufacturing sectors seems to be the rule across districts."

Reading all these entrails, many Fed watchers concluded the FOMC would leave monetary policy unchanged. They were in for a surprise. In the week leading up to the meeting, M2 had fallen $14 billion, leaving its growth rate since the beginning of the year less than 1 percent. The Fed staff argued sluggish money growth "did not appear to have the usual implications for the economy," because velocity was rising as balance sheet adjustments and other factors curbed demand for money assets relative to spending and income. However, many members were not prepared to simply ignore money's dramatic deceleration. The FOMC was sharply divided. One group favored immediate easing, but agreed to support a bias toward ease. A second group favored an unchanged policy stance, but nevertheless said they could accept a bias toward ease, and a third group was opposed even to a bias toward ease. The third group feared another rate cut would hurt the dollar and drive up long-term rates. By a 10 to 2 vote, with LaWare and Melzer opposed, the committee voted to keep policy unchanged but to go back to a bias toward ease, little more than a month after it had gone symmetrical. The next morning, the Labor Department announced that the unemployment rate in June had risen from 7½ to 7.8 percent—the second straight month the jobless rate had jumped three-tenths of a percent. There was also a huge drop in nonfarm payrolls. Suddenly the divisions among policymakers were erased. Semishell-shocked, the Board voted to cut the discount rate from 3½ to 3 percent. Without a conference call, Greenspan decided to push the funds rate down a half percent to 3¼ percent. It was the lowest discount rate since July 1963, a level no one could have foreseen. Nor could they have foreseen there was more easing yet to come in this most unpredictable of all business cycles.

One thing the Fed's July 2 rate cuts proved is that, in the final analysis, domestic considerations take precedence over exchange rates. By then, the dollar had become quite weak. At the April 26 G-7 meeting, the dollar had been relatively firm around 1.65 marks and 134 yen, compared to 1.595 marks and 123.5 yen at the January G-7 meeting. In response to U.S. pressure, the Bank of Japan had cut its discount rate by three-quarters of a percent to 3.75 percent on April 1 at the same time the government announced a $113 billion package of accelerated public works spending to stimulate the Japanese economy, which had the tendency of making the dollar more attractive. The perpetually dissatisfied Treasury immediately made clear it wanted further measures to stimulate Japanese demand for U.S. exports. There was a built-in contradiction to the Treasury's attitude. It wanted lower Japanese interest rates, but when lower rates caused the yen to weaken, it complained the yen was not strong enough. At U.S. insistence, the G-7 communiqué stated the yen's decline was "not contributing to the adjustment process." Meanwhile, Brady and Mulford had tried again to pressure Germany into goosing up its economy at the April 26 meeting, making light of its preoccupation with inflation, but had again been rebuffed. Mulford did not help the Treasury's cause when, three days before the G-7 meeting, he charged Germany was forcing the rest of Europe and the world to pay the cost of its reunification. The combination of its large fiscal deficit and tight monetary policy was "having spillover effects. It is causing high interest rates, high unemployment and slow growth. . . . The true cost of unification has yet to be borne by the German people [but was being imposed on] the rest of Europe and elsewhere in terms of slower growth." Köhler called Mulford's comments "one-sided," "wrong," and "unacceptable." As for Mulford's complaint that Germany's budget deficit was too big, Köhler hinted that people who live in glass houses should not throw stones. Just another red letter day for the Bush administration's international monetary policies.

From April on, the dollar went into a long slide, so that by the time of the July FOMC meeting it was trading below 1.55 marks and 126 yen, causing some members to hesitate about lowering rates to help sustain the recovery. After the July 2 rate cuts, the dollar devaluation gained momentum and became a hot side issue at the G-7 nations' annual economic summit in Munich, where Brady's futile demands for lower German rates served to weaken the dollar further. As frequently happens when G-7 officials are about to congregate, the big three had all done some fancy policy footwork: the United States, with its rate cuts; Japan, with a further 7 trillion yen fiscal stimulus program; and Germany, with a pledge to hold federal spending increases to 2½ percent. Mulford told me all three nations' policy initiatives were "very real and very substantial" efforts to "foster growth," but Brady could not resist calling on Germany again and again to lower rates. Neither the Bundesbank nor any other central bank was represented at the summit, but a German official pointed out his country's 4.6 percent inflation rate and 9 percent money supply growth rate did "not leave the Bundesbank any maneuvering room to drop interest rates." Brady also got a stiff-arm from Waigel: "We are aware of the problems in the U.S. economy and of the slow recovery, but one can surely not attribute the problems of the U.S. economy to German interest rates." The perception that the rate spread between the U.S. and Germany would, if anything, widen further in favor of Germany, further undermined the dollar. On Monday, July 6, the first day of the summit, when the dollar closed at 124.23 yen and 1.5133 marks, Mulford dismissed the dollar's drop since the rate cuts as a "normal" market reaction. The next day, however, when an aide told Mulford the dollar had plunged below the 1.50-mark level, and had gone below 124 yen, Mulford exclaimed to aides, "Gee, it's headed to an all-time low! The market is collapsing!" Publicly, he was saying the dollar was "still in the range of the past year."

The dollar was indeed headed for an all-time low. Ignoring the advice of Brady and others, the Bundesbank on July 16 raised its discount rate from 8 to 8¾ percent, effective the next day. This gave new impetus to the mark's rise against the dollar and created problems for the rest of Europe. As the mark climbed against the dollar, other European currencies tended to weaken relative to the mark and test the limits of their allowable fluctuation bands in the

ERM. To stay within those bands and avoid devaluation, Italy and other European countries with vulnerable currencies had to raise their interest rates or keep them high. This in turn threatened to sap the strength of Europe's economy and hurt vital U.S. export markets at the worst possible time. So it was not easy for the Fed to ignore the dollar's weakness. On July 20, a day before Greenspan was to present his midyear Humphrey-Hawkins report to Congress, the dollar sank to within a hair's breadth of the record DM1.443, set in February 1991. Only massive coordinated selling of marks for dollars by the Fed, Bundesbank, and others temporarily held the dollar above that level. Testifying before the Senate Banking Committee, Greenspan indicated how he regarded the Brady-Mulford dollar policy. "I see no net benefit from depreciating the dollar further." Calm as usual, Greenspan knew, or at least suspected, the Bundesbank was finished raising rates. It had not raised the key Lombard rate, which had much more bearing on German market rates, when it raised its discount rate, and he had gotten indications it would not be doing so. Within a few months, the Bundesbank would reverse course and begin a long easing process.

It was an impatient, sometimes angry Senate Banking Committee that heard Greenspan explain why the economy had not responded as hoped to the 23 separate easing steps the Fed had taken over three years. The economy was beginning to look like the little engine that couldn't, and all Greenspan could do was repeat what was holding it back and what it had going for it. The recovery was still being hampered by the "restructuring" of corporate and household balance sheets, as well as by defense cutbacks, state and local government fiscal problems, the slowdown abroad, and still "stagnant" bank lending. "Clearly the structural imbalances in the economy have proven more severe and more enduring than many had previously thought. The economy still is recuperating from past excesses involving a generalized over-reliance on debt to finance asset accumulation." Balance sheet restructuring had rendered monetary policy less "potent" than in the past. Had the Fed attempted to ease more aggressively than it had, it only would have increased inflation fears and driven long-term interest rates higher. As it was, investors were "inordinately worried about future inflation risks." Although his past promises of recovery had proven premature, he again expressed optimism. With household finances being adjusted "quite rapidly," the economy was "reasonably close" to a pickup in consumer spending. Production was on the rise. The only reason unemployment looked so high was because the labor force had increased, and puny growth of the money supply was a largely technical phenomenon that would not prevent recovery. "Economic expansion will soon gain momentum," he told skeptical Senators. Although Democratic presidential candidate Bill Clinton was already going around the country talking about "the worst economy in fifty years," Greenspan was right. The economy *was* coming back. As subtle and imperceptible as it may have seemed, the economy had embarked on a strong second-half growth spurt.

Anything but subtle were Brady's efforts to goad the Fed into more election-year easing. In an early August interview with the *Wall Street Journal*, Brady crossed the political aisle to virtually endorse Congressman Hamilton's Fed "reform" proposals. He said Hamilton's plan to let the president appoint his own Fed chairman, strip Fed presidents of their voting power, and inject the Treasury secretary more formally into FOMC discussions deserved "useful exploration" in the interest of "bringing Fed deliberations closer to the actual circumstances in the economy." Democrats who had cosponsored the Hamilton bill, while delighted Brady had given it impetus, were astonished at this latest act of desperation, as were some of Brady's aides. "He has never mentioned it to me, and I've never been in a meeting where it's been discussed," a senior Treasury official told me. It was probably "just a throwaway line. . . . I don't see that it's a realistic strategy in any overarching plan . . . the relationship between the Secretary and the [Fed] Chairman has deteriorated." Exasperated with the slow growth of the money supply and the sluggishness of the recovery, Brady thought the Fed presidents were primarily responsible for delaying Fed easing. For Congress or the administration to try to limit the Fed's independence would be "counterproductive and almost embarrassing given the deplorable fiscal management," said another Treasury official. But Brady was serious. He told the Senate Banking Committee the policy role of the Fed presidents should be "thoroughly discussed."

Although August brought significant job gains and other signs of the increased momentum Greenspan had promised, economic and monetary data were still sluggish enough and inflation low enough that further Fed easing was a topic of speculation. However, with the election approaching, it was felt the Fed would feel compelled to stay on the sidelines. Moreover, the dollar was so weak many figured the Fed would not dare cut rates again. The Treasury, once happy to see the dollar depreciate, had undergone what a source called "a change in attitude" and was trying to stabilize the dollar and give the Fed leeway to ease. On August 10, Brady at long last said he did not want to see any further fall in the dollar. On eight occasions through August 11 he had authorized repeated rounds of intervention in support of the dollar. Sources say the objective was not purely to keep the dollar from going to new lows against the mark and yen, but to undergird U.S. securities markets and discourage an outflow of foreign capital that would drive long-term rates, which had retreated to about 7¼ percent, back up. A cheap dollar could make U.S. securities attractive to foreign investors "as long as you don't think it's going to get a lot weaker," but "you wouldn't want it to get away from you on the downside," said a source. "If it begins to get away from you you're really in a dilemma. . . . It would limit the Fed's ability to ease any further." In short, if Brady and company were to have any hope of getting lower rates out of the Fed they had better be more protective of the dollar. Then, too, a weak currency doesn't look good at election time.

As August brought cheerier economic indicators from the prior month, there seemed every reason for the Fed to content itself with having lowered the funds rate more than 6½ percent in three years. Aside from improving employment, retail sales had done better than expected. Industrial production had risen 4½ percent for the fifth month out of six. Bob Brusca joked that an upsurge in coal mining either suggested that "we're trying to dig our way out of recession" or that "we're preparing lumps of coal for Republican Christmas stockings." Housing starts were down, but with mortgage rates falling that was expected to change. For the most part the picture was brightening. Why cut interest rates again with things seemingly on the mend and the dollar vulnerable? That was just the question some Fed policymakers asked pointedly at an August 18 FOMC meeting. LaWare and Melzer felt the Fed had done enough easing and voted against a policy directive that left policy unchanged for the time being but contained a bias toward ease between then and the October meeting. They argued for "a more patient monetary policy—one that was less predisposed to react to near-term weakness in economic data and that allowed more time for the effects of earlier easing actions to be reflected in the economy." They warned another easing could exacerbate inflation concerns and "have adverse repercussions on domestic bond markets and further damaging effects on the dollar in foreign exchange markets." Others opposed an easing bias but not strongly enough to vote against it.

The FOMC gave Greenspan the green light to make one last rate cut because it did not know then what we know now—that the economy had in fact turned the corner as Greenspan had so often said. There was still so much uncertainty about the outlook, given the inexplicably weak growth of the money supply, that the FOMC weighed the risks and decided the Fed could afford, if necessary, to take another easing step without sparking inflation. Since the spring, the CPI had registered consistently modest increases and risen at a mild 1.7 percent annual rate in July. The staff projected only a "subdued expansion" in the near-term followed by a "gradual pickup" in 1993. Members dwelled on impediments to stronger growth like cutbacks in defense spending, expected state and local tax hikes, continued "restructuring" by financial institutions, corporations and households, weak consumer and business confidence, and the slowdown in Europe and Japan. At the time it appeared "the rate of economic expansion had slowed to a relatively subdued pace since the early months of the year" and that "the economic expansion was likely to be on a slightly lower track over the next several quarters. . . ." In fact, it was about to accelerate dramatically. Perhaps the biggest factor swaying the Fed toward ease was the positive bond market response the Fed had gotten to the July 2 rate cuts. Since then a sustained bond rally had brought down long-term rates roughly half a percent, alleviating many members' concern that short-term rate cuts would ipso facto cause long rates to rise. This helped take the sting out of the dollar's woes. Finally, the Fed had some well-informed inklings that, before long, the Bundesbank would be lowering rates, making it more comfortable for the Fed to do so without undue disruption to the bond or currency markets.

Within a week of the FOMC meeting, even though the Fed had not lowered rates, the dollar avalanche resumed, fueled by a 6½ percent German interest rate premium. After breaking through the old DM1.443 level, and making Mulford's nightmare come true, it continued downward, falling through the DM1.40 level on August 25. The administration felt helpless.

"Our options are limited," an official confided. "As long as the Bundesbank insists on maintaining high interest rates relative to their inflation rate there's not much we can do," said another. By September 2, the dollar had gone as low as DM1.3870, a post–World War II record. Currencies like the British pound and Italian lira were on the floor of their EMS exchange rate bands, putting enormous pressure on the Bank of England and Bank of Italy to expend foreign exchange reserves and raise interest rates to prevent an ignominious devaluation of their currencies. Surely now the Fed would have to leave rates unchanged. Even the administration had given up on further rate cuts. "There is very little chance now of the Fed easing," an administration official said, because both the Fed and the Treasury "worry about the dollar going into some kind of tailspin." Some even speculated the Fed might have to raise rates to prevent inflation and market instability.

But this time the Fed was determined to do what it always claimed it had and not let exchange rates skew monetary policy. I talked to several Fed officials the day the dollar hit its low point. Weighing the depreciation of the dollar against the needs of the economy, one said the dollar was "an important, but not a primary consideration." It helped that the bond market seemed to have made its peace with the weak dollar. The yield on the long bond had fallen below 7.4 percent. On September 4, after the Labor Department had reported a 183,000 drop in nonfarm payroll in wake of a renewed bout of M2 declines, Greenspan used his discretion and reduced the funds rate a final quarter percent to 3 percent, the same level as the discount rate. It was the lowest funds rate level in nearly 30 years. Greenspan has no regrets about the last rate cut. Asked whether he would do it again, he says, "Yes. We didn't get evidence of real weakening of the credit crunch until the summer of '93. So the pressure was still there." McDonough concurs. "It made a good deal of sense in that it was the last—what turned out to be the last—of a series of moves that, in my view, created a monetary policy environment which was highly instrumental in permitting the restructuring of the U.S. economy and the U.S. banking system." McTeer says that "in retrospect the banking system needed that." LaWare, on the other hand, thinks the final rate cut "was totally unnecessary. I argued both privately as well as in the committee that it was kind of overkill and that I didn't think we had allowed the necessary time for all the easing that we had done to grab hold. . . . What we were doing was putting short-term interest rates in real terms at zero, and I thought we were overdoing it." He adds that the Fed may have "needed to . . . send that kind of a signal to really get things cranked up." Angell says that if the Fed had begun easing more aggressively in 1989 there never would have been a recession, and a 3 percent funds rate would not have been needed.

With the threat of lower U.S. interest rates no longer overhanging the market, the dollar started to recover. What's more, the Bundesbank had shot its wad on monetary tightening. It could not continue to keep interest rates at such high levels. It would have to reduce rates, not out of any altruistic desire to help its neighbors, although it was anxious to preserve the European Monetary System's Exchange Rate Mechanism as a stepping stone toward European Monetary Union, but because those high rates were attracting so much capital into Germany they threatened to aggravate the very problem the Bundesbank was trying to correct, the inflationary expansion of the German money supply. If France and others had been willing to devalue their currencies against the mark and agree to a long-overdue adjustment of the exchange rate bands, the speculative frenzy that was tearing the EMS asunder could have been defeated, at least for a while, but devaluation was out of the question as far as the French government was concerned. It had staked too much political capital on its "franc fort" policy. Ten days later, the Bundesbank lowered its discount rate a half percent to 8¼ and its Lombard rate a quarter to 9½ percent, effective September 15. It was the first of a long series of German rate cuts. Other European central banks followed suit. The dollar jumped above DM1.50.

The Bundesbank action, taken at an extraordinary Monday morning session of its policymaking council, came only after the European currency crisis had come to a head. The system of semifixed exchange rates was coming apart in the face of speculation against the weaker European currencies. In effect, currency traders were betting the monetary authorities of Italy, Great Britain, and other countries would not have the resources or the will to support their currencies at what many regarded as unrealistic official levels. After central banks had raised rates and expended huge amounts of foreign exchange reserves, not to mention credibility, high-rolling speculators such as George Soros won. At an emergency meeting on Sunday, September 13, European authorities agreed on a realignment of the EMS currencies on the condition Germany lower interest rates. As part of the deal, the Italian lira was devalued 7 percent. It was not nearly enough. The lira, as well as the pound and the Spanish peseta, remained under heavy downward pressure. The Bank of England twice raised rates to 12 percent on Wednesday, September 16, to keep the pound from falling through its ERM floor, only to see speculation against the pound continue. British prime minister and former finance minister John Major had sworn he would not devalue, but later Wednesday, he withdrew sterling from the ERM, letting it float free to whatever exchange rate the market saw fit. While the Bank of England thereby regained its freedom of action and began lowering rates, other European central banks continued to battle currency traders. Bundesbank president Helmut Schlesinger encouraged new rounds of deutsche mark buying when he said there was "no room for more" German rate cuts, despite enormous pressure from other European officials, the U.S. Treasury, and the IMF. By relieving pressure on the Bundesbank to intervene in support of the pound, Britain's exit from the system made the Bundesbank less inclined to lower rates, and when a big bulge in German money supply was reported, further German rate cuts became even less likely.

In the wee hours of Thursday, September 17, the European Community (EC) Monetary Committee announced further steps to stop the bleeding. The peseta was devalued 5 percent, and the lira was allowed to "temporarily" float. With the pound and the lira effectively out of the ERM, ten currencies were to remain bound by the requirement that they not rise or fall more than 2¼ percent. Mulford hailed the latest moves and proclaimed "stability is returning" to the currency markets. IMF managing director Michel Camdessus declared that "in spite of the formidable turmoil of the last few days, the system has once again demonstrated its remarkable resilience." They were a bit premature. Having driven the pound and the lira out of the ERM, speculators began training their guns on the French franc and other units on September 17. To protect the krona's link to continental currencies, non-EMS member Sweden's Riksbank pushed a key short-term interest rate to 500 percent before relenting and eventually abandoning the ERM peg. The Bank of France, on September 23, raised interest rates 2½ percent to 13 percent and intervened heavily to beat back speculation against the franc. Some countries, like Spain, resorted to capital controls to protect their currencies. The Bundesbank alone spent roughly $30 billion of its reserves, just to support the pound and the lira. In coming months there would be more devaluations—of the peseta, the Portuguese escudo, the Irish pound—and the Norwegian krone would be cut loose from its ERM peg. But the European currency problems continued to fester until, the following summer, the silly effort to keep the currencies of countries with widely divergent economic fundamentals from finding their appropriate market levels was effectively abandoned. On August 1, 1993, the allowable band of exchange rate fluctuation for EMS member currencies was widened to plus or minus 15 percent.

Meanwhile, with speculators focused on driving the mark up against other European currencies, the dollar remained relatively firm against the mark at roughly DM1.50, but now it was plunging to record lows against the yen. It fell below 120 yen per dollar for the first time on September 23, as Japanese investors repatriated their funds. Mulford didn't help matters when he said he was "not that concerned" about the dollar-yen rate. The focus of dollar weakness had merely shifted, but it is doubtful the dollar weakness would have prevented further Fed rate cuts if they had been deemed necessary.

A big motivating factor behind the September 4 Fed rate cut was that bank lending was still stingy. Chastened by strict bank capital requirements, harsh examination procedures and the threat of personal liability suits, bankers had pulled in their horns and were actually contracting their loan portfolios. For the 12 months ending September 9, 1992, business loans had fallen nearly 8 percent. The administration was frantically trying to gin up more loans by goading examiners to get off bankers' backs and blaming Congress for the harsher provisions of FDICIA. (Like the 1990 tax hikes, it seemed, Congress had made Bush sign the bill.) Lowering banks' cost of funds was welcome, but would not get banks to lend if, as Treasury Undersecretary Powell told Congress September 10, laws and regulations were having "a chilling effect." Greenspan had urged Fed examiners to lighten up, but with very limited results. The only solution seemed to be to pump reserves into the banking system and keep banks' margins wide enough, long enough so that when loan demand appeared, banks would find it more profitable to make loans than invest in government securities. To that end, the Fed was prepared to lower rates even further, although many FOMC members were disinclined to until after the election. A sharply divided FOMC approved a bias toward ease at its October 6 meeting. Jordan and Lindsey wanted an immediate easing, while LaWare and Melzer did not even want to tilt toward ease. Not wanting monetary policy to appear influenced by the election cycle, Greenspan went so far as to hold a rare press conference October 10 to "set things straight." News articles "implying we were shutting down monetary policy until after the election" were off base, Greenspan told reporters covering the annual Business Council conference in Hot Springs, Virginia. "It would be an irresponsible action on our part were we to do that. We at the Federal Reserve will continue to observe and evaluate the economy the way we always do and we will not, if we believe it to be necessary, abstain from actions solely because there is an election under way."

It sounded like Greenspan might be setting the stage for more rate cuts. The White House was demanding them. "I would just like for once to see them get out in front instead of behind," an administration official sputtered. "They have fallen into the trap of incrementalism—just following the market, which doesn't have any effect. . . . They can't worry too much about what the official inflation rate is. The long rate goes down every time the Fed lowers the short rate so the market is telling us there's plenty of room to cut further without inflation pressures." Notwithstanding what Greenspan had said, however, it would have taken considerably worse economic indicators than expected for the Fed to cut rates again before the election. That is not what happened, and further rate cuts proved unnecessary. Although the credit crunch dragged on, spending, jobs, housing starts, output, and other aspects of economic activity became increasingly positive. Even M2 began to grow. Alas for the defeated George Bush, the economy's strength became even more evident after the election. And on November 18, Greenspan said (a bit prematurely) the credit crunch "may finally be retreating." A still-divided FOMC retained an easing bias at its November 17 FOMC meeting, and Jordan dissented again in favor of another immediate rate cut, but sentiment was moving rapidly away from that posture. At its December 22 meeting, the FOMC abandoned its easing bias and shifted firmly into neutral. By then the guessing game had started as to when the Fed would start tightening credit.

CHAPTER EIGHT

Working with a Democratic President

Perhaps the most remarkable period of the Greenspan years, in purely political terms, coincided with the administration of President Bill Clinton.
Having weathered a stormy relationship with the Bush administration, the
Republican-dominated Fed did not know what to expect from the first Democratic administration in 12 years. As it turned out, relations between Clinton
and the Fed were relatively smooth, at least on the surface, even after the Fed
resumed raising rates in February 1994. Indeed Greenspan's relationship with
Clinton and his cabinet seemed so close at times that some have suggested
Greenspan practically became a member of his economic team. In fact, it was
more complicated than that.

Greenspan says he enjoyed "cordial" and "friendly" relations with both
Clinton and Treasury Secretary Lloyd Bentsen, but disputes the notion he collaborated with them or gave them policy advice. The former Arkansas governor showed more savvy in dealing with the Fed than his predecessor had
developed in three decades around Washington. Clinton adviser and later Fed
Board vice chairman Alan Blinder says he, Bentsen, his deputy Roger Altman,
National Economic Council chief Robert Rubin, Council of Economic Advisors chairwoman Laura Tyson, and nearly everyone on the Clinton team "had
the view that it was not good policy to bash the Fed. I think that was right, and
I think the administration held that line extraordinarily well. Now, it's also
been the case, of course, that the economy has done well. This policy might
have been strained if the economy did poorly, but it has done well." Bentsen
says that, in contrast to his predecessor, he "had an excellent relationship with
[Greenspan] both officially and personally." The two resumed the weekly
breakfasts Brady had abandoned. "I had breakfast with him in my office one
week, and then we'd have breakfast next week at his office." Greenspan frequently played tennis with the former Texas Senator and Senate Finance
Committee chairman on the White House courts, and inevitably monetary
policy was batted around along with the little white ball.

But appearances are a bit deceiving. The Fed got along better with the
Clinton administration than with the Bush administration, but to say the Fed
was free from political pressure during the Clinton years does not reflect real-

ity. A kind of triangulation was at work, with Clinton at the top and Congress and the Fed at the base. Greenspan's aim was to protect the Fed's ability to pursue its long-term goal of price stability. The aim of Clinton and his allies on Capitol Hill was to keep rates as low as possible as long as possible. The difference from the Bush years, aside from economic recovery, was that Clinton was less clumsy in pressuring the Fed. He orchestrated the most clever campaign to manipulate monetary policy in memory. Equal parts cooption, intimidation, and propaganda, some think the strategy kept real short-term rates at zero or negative levels throughout 1993 and beyond. Clinton's loyal troops were determined to keep the funds rate at 3 percent, if not lower. What emerged, whether by design or not, was a kind of good-cop-bad-cop approach. While administration officials professed their respect for the Fed's independence and their desire to work with it, Congress put more heat on the Fed than ever. Well before Clinton was inaugurated, Democrat leaders set up a clamor against the Fed daring to take one step away from 3 percent (unless it was down), while threatening "reforms" the Fed considered inimical.

Clinton, whose image as a hard-money Democrat had helped get him elected, knew it was important to win Greenspan over. Rubin and other advisers stressed the importance of keeping interest rates across the maturity spectrum as low as possible, and had warned that picking fights with the Fed would not serve that end. If the markets perceived the administration was pushing inflationary policies, long-term rates would soar and undermine the Clinton economic program. In late January, the yield on the Treasury long bond was about 7.3 percent, 4.3 percent over the funds rate. Greenspan blamed inflation concerns in his January 27 congressional testimony. More than any other administration, the Clinton team was focused on the care and feeding of the bond market and was willing to do whatever was necessary to assuage its concerns to get bond yields down, whether that meant shifting more Treasury borrowing to short-term securities or kissing up to the Fed.

Even before the election, Clinton showed an adroit awareness of the need to tread lightly with the Fed. In his first debate with Bush on October 11, 1992, Clinton was asked whether the Fed needed to be made more accountable. "Frankly, I don't think that's the problem today," candidate Clinton responded. "We have low interest rates today. At least we have low interest rates that the Fed can control. Our long-term interest rates are still pretty high because of our deficit and because of our economic performance. But I think the important thing is to use the powers the president does have on the assumption that, given the condition of this economy, we're going to keep interest rates down if we have the discipline to increase investment and reduce the debt at the same time. . . . I don't have to worry, I don't think, in the near-term about the Federal Reserve. Their policies so far, it seems to me, are pretty sound." It was typical Clinton. In a single statement, he had managed to imply respect for the inflation-fighting central bank's independence and a commitment to deficit reduction, while reserving the right to increase "investment" (a Clinton euphemism for social spending) and to gripe if rates rose. It was easy for Clinton to say Fed policy was not a problem "so far" when short-term rates were at 3 percent and the economy was in recovery. His view would change somewhat when it came time for the Fed to start raising rates.

After his election, Clinton really turned on the charm. The president-elect, who was planning on pushing a fiscal stimulus package even as he talked about deficit reduction, did his best to kill Greenspan with kindness in the hope he could get the Fed on his side or at least keep it on the sidelines. In mid-December, after Greenspan visited him in Little Rock, Clinton said the two had a wonderful discussion. "It's an important relationship, and I will do what I can to work on it." He said he respected the Fed's independence and wanted Greenspan to serve out his term. Fed officials were optimistic about a good relationship with the incoming president. "I see no reason why it shouldn't be just fine," Kelley told me. "Our constituency is the American economy. What we're trying to do here continues to be good public policy for the American economy in either administration." "There is no reason for things to be any different," agreed another. Clinton had taken a "hands-off the Fed" approach during the campaign and talked of "the need for monetary discipline." They appeared to understand "the impossibility of getting real rates much different in one country than another." Greenspan "took the job to do monetary policy, and there is nothing a Clinton administration can do to frustrate him," said a third, although "if he can appoint enough new governors to make things dicey for him, things might change."

Meanwhile, congressional Democrats went into action. On November 19, 1992, Gonzalez announced plans to submit legislation requiring Fed presidents, who had always been selected by the boards of directors of the Banks and approved by the Board of Governors, be appointed by the President of the United States and confirmed by the Senate, like board members. The Banking Committee chairman also threatened to curtail the Fed's budgetary independence, raising the possibility Congress might curb Fed operations if it didn't like its policies. His legislation also would have forced the Fed to immediately release FOMC minutes—something that was anathema to the secretive central bank. Meanwhile, Gonzalez was carrying on a running battle with Greenspan over slow growth in the money supply—a remarkable complaint given that the Fed was pursuing the easiest policy it had run in decades. In a December 1 letter, he accused Greenspan of "undermining the Federal Reserve's credibility" by letting M2 fall below the Fed's target ranges, then downplaying M2's reliability. In fact, Greenspan had told Gonzalez in a November 27 letter that one of the reasons the Fed had eased credit was precisely because M2 had been below the 2½ to 6½ percent target range, even though the Fed had its doubts whether the shortfall of money growth was meaningful in light of the rising level of spending. What really set off Gonzalez was Greenspan's hint that he might lower the M2 target growth range because of the apparent increase in M2 velocity. It was largely a technical matter as far as the Fed was concerned, but Gonzalez saw it as a Fed threat to tighten policy. Not only had Greenspan "engineered slower money growth," he had admitted he was "considering moving the money growth target down even farther. . . . The American public has the right to ask just what is going on at the Federal Reserve, our nation's central bank." Gonzalez vowed to force "an end to the aura of secrecy and confusion" by requiring the Fed to videotape its closed meetings and make it public.

It would have been one thing if only long-time Fed gadfly Gonzalez was going after the Fed, but he had plenty of company. In the House, Joint Economic Committee (JEC) Chairman Hamilton was still pushing legislation to strip the Fed presidents of their voting rights, make the Fed chairman's term run concurrent with that of the President and subject the Fed to congressional budget control. Wisconsin Democrat David Obey, who would succeed Hamilton as JEC chairman, was among its backers. Senate Banking Committee Chairman Riegle and Senate Budget Committee Chairman Sasser, along with senior Maryland Democrat Senator Paul Sarbanes and others were preparing similar bills. A top aide to one Democratic Senator made clear before Clinton's inauguration the strategy was less to pass the legislation than to keep the heat on the Fed to play ball with the new administration. "I would guess that if the Fed conducts monetary policy to give us some growth it probably doesn't have a whole lot of chance of passage, but if the Fed starts screwing up and thwarting what the President is trying to do, there would be more support for legislation to create a Fed that's more sympathetic." Another congressional Democratic source made explicit the quid pro quo the Democrats had in mind. The hope was that the bills would "have the effect of sending a signal to the Fed" to cooperate with Clinton. The president was "hoping to enjoy good relations with the Fed" so he would "wait to see how things turn out" before supporting them. He might support the bills "if the administration is trying to stimulate the economy and the Fed tries to tighten."

After Clinton was sworn in, congressional Democrats formally introduced their bills, making vituperative speeches and beginning a round of hearings on the Fed's "accountability" which would carry on sporadically throughout the year. The message that came through loud and clear, not just from backbenchers but from key committee chairmen, was that the Fed had better "cooperate" with the administration or else. It became a steady drumbeat in Greenspan's ears, as when he appeared before the JEC January 27. "We are starting a new year with a new president committed to stronger growth," Obey said. "I hope the Fed will cooperate with him." Greenspan had been meeting with Bentsen, and Obey hoped the meetings would "lead to closer cooperation between the administration and the Fed and to a reversal of the anemic economic performance that we have had to endure during the past three years."

The next morning, after Greenspan met with Clinton, White House spokesman George Stephanopoulos said the two shared the same goal: "getting growth in this economy." From the White House, Greenspan went before the Senate Budget Committee, where he was harangued by Sasser. The White House, Congress, and Fed needed to be "singing from the same Psalm book." If Congress and the White House were going to reduce the "daff-uh-sit," as Sasser always called it, "Congress needs the Fed to offset the contraction by using its tools to keep the economy going." After the 1990 budget deal, "the opposite proved true. The Fed neither acted quickly, nor supported expansion sufficiently. It timidly followed the lead of the credit markets. The Fed's help came far too late and was far too little. Though the recession is over, the wreckage it left is still strewn across the nation. I have no desire to embark on a new round of deficit fighting only to discover that the Fed has left our right flank exposed again." Sasser alleged the Fed's plan to lower its money growth target constituted a monetary tightening, not just a technical adjustment to reflect faster velocity as Greenspan had maintained. "No action, more baby steps, or worse, monetary contraction, will without a doubt in my mind, lay a killing frost over the economic spring that President Clinton is trying to force. The success of our economic recovery and deficit reduction will depend greatly on getting the Fed, Congress and the White House pulling together as a team." Sarbanes blasted the Fed along the same lines.

Greenspan got the none-too-subtle message. He told Sasser the Fed "would respond" in the event deficit reduction created a "fiscal drag" on the economy. He saw "no need for immediate" easing in response to the kind of deficit cuts being proposed, but said easing "might be required at some later date." The Fed conceivably might not even wait for fiscal drag to appear if a deficit reduction package was well received by the markets. "To the extent, in the short-term, there is a decline in long-term interest rates, then obviously monetary policy would adjust to that as well." It would be wrong to conclude Greenspan was caving in to pressure from Clinton and Congress. He was giving textbook central banker responses to budgetary eventualities. When Sasser pressed Greenspan to have the Fed take the lead in cutting rates rather than "taking its cue from the market," Greenspan told him, "It's important to understand what monetary policy can and cannot do." The Fed "cannot force the market in a manner which would almost surely fail." What the market needed for rates to come down was "specific, hard-wired" deficit cuts.

Republicans were dumbfounded at the Democrats' nerve, considering it had been their bad luck to see the economy surge a real 5.7 percent in the fourth quarter, after it was too late to save Bush's presidency, and considering that the funds rate was being held at a trifling level. The beige book on January 21 had reported "continued improvement in economic conditions" yet Democrats were demanding the Fed ease. "Efforts to demand action now to lower short-term rates, while ignoring the legitimate fears of rekindled inflation that could easily drive long-term rates higher, not lower, is yet another example of the wisdom of keeping the Federal Reserve an independent agency," Senator Kit Bond said on January 28. "After completely messing up fiscal policy, now some want to share their wisdom on monetary policy too. Instead we should be concentrating on the huge deficit and debt which is our responsibility and quit trying to shift blame for our economic woes." Fed officials were also taken aback by the ferocity of Democratic attacks on their policies. Publicly, they held their tongues. Privately, one official said, "Sarbanes will never be satisfied with anything. His purpose in life is to bitch and moan."

Hill Democrats were not propitiated by Greenspan's pledges to ease credit if deficit reduction caused the economy to slow or caused market rates to fall.

In a February 8 letter, Gonzalez warned Clinton not to trust Greenspan's pledge of cooperation. "Although Federal Reserve Chairman Greenspan gives the impression that he wants to cooperate with your administration, the actions of the Federal Reserve point in a very different direction. While he praises your budgetary proposals, his approach to monetary policy heavily risks economic stagnation and recession." To back his allegation, he noted M2 was "now taking a dive downward," falling by a 1.7 percent annual rate in the three months prior to January 18, 1993, and growing only 1.6 percent the prior 12 months. Greenspan had explained on several occasions the Fed could safely reduce its money targets without reducing economic growth because, for a variety of reasons, a given amount of money supply had been fueling an increased amount of spending. But Gonzalez persisted in casting Greenspan's intentions in dark and suspicious terms. "To confirm his startlingly new position, Chairman Greenspan has indicated to me that the Federal Reserve may even lower its targets to fit its slow money growth performance. This threatens to place the economy on a Procrustean bed with growth cut off to fit a rigid framework that equates growth with inflation." Gonzalez urged Clinton to "use your office to persuade the Federal Reserve to go to the middle of its present target range, 4.5 percent money growth, to foster healthy economic growth without increasing inflation." He advised the president to "watch carefully the actions of the Federal Reserve and do all you can to dissuade them from adopting a course that would choke off the chances of a recovery strong enough to substantially reduce the nation's high level of unemployment."

Clinton, meanwhile, was playing it cagey, neither supporting nor totally disavowing the Fed reform bills. A top aide to one of the bills' sponsors says his boss was informed by the White House that Clinton liked the proposals to make the Fed "more accountable," but "didn't want to pick a fight with the Fed in his first year." Not until much later in the year did Clinton make his position on restructuring the Fed clear—or, at least, as clear as Clinton ever gets. In the meantime, the Fed was left to wonder whether the administration would back it up or not. While Hill Democrats were slapping the Fed around, the White House concentrated on doing everything it could to cozy up to the Fed and inveigle Greenspan into its fiscal policy schemes. Bentsen appeared on NBC's *Meet the Press* on January 23, and when no one brought up the subject, the Treasury secretary went out of his way to "make another point that you fellows have not touched on, and that is cooperation with the Federal Reserve." He had already had a couple of breakfast meetings with Greenspan, and he said the Fed chairman "is a friend of mine, and I'm looking forward to a cooperative effort between the Treasury Department, the administration and the Federal Reserve and seeing that we keep inflation down and we get this economy moving again." Next came the tête-à-tête between Greenspan and Clinton at the White House the morning of January 28, strategically timed before the former gave his important Senate Budget Committee testimony.

Since well before the inauguration, Clinton had been conferring with Greenspan, and there was widespread speculation a "deal" was brewing between the Fed and the White House—that in return for the deficit reduction Greenspan had long sought, the Fed would hold the line on interest rates or even reduce them further. Though not nearly as shrill as the Hill Democrats, administration officials were letting it be known they would expect a looser monetary policy if they "tightened" fiscal policy. Such talk embarrassed Fed officials, who uniformly denied it—and do to this day. I asked Forrestal and Boehne shortly after the inauguration whether there was any truth to the rumors about a fiscal/monetary policy deal. Forrestal was "not aware of any conversation along those lines with the administration. . . . We will of course be looking at what the administration may or may not do in fiscal policy . . . then come to a judgement about what's the appropriate policy." Boehne said it should not be assumed a tighter fiscal policy would automatically prompt a looser monetary policy. "I don't think one can say if fiscal policy does this monetary policy has to do that or vice versa. I think we need to keep our eyes on the fundamental objective," namely sustainable, noninflationary growth.

But to the annoyance of some Fed officials, Greenspan kept doing things that created the impression he was, in fact, wheeling and dealing with the White House. In the ultimate bid to coopt Greenspan—or at least make it appear that way—Hillary Clinton invited him to be her guest in the gallery overlooking the House of Representatives as Clinton gave his first State of the Union address the evening of February 17. To the surprise of everyone who watched the proceedings that evening, there front and center on national TV sat the Fed chairman between the first lady and vice president Al Gore's wife, Tipper. Heads are still shaking over that (in many people's eyes) unseemly episode. "What I worry about is even the unintentional perception of a lack of independence on the part of the Board, . . . the possibility that anybody is going to conclude that the Board is an instrument of the Treasury or an instrument of the administration or, perhaps worse still, an instrument of Congress," says former Fed governor John LaWare. "That has to be jealously defended, and I can't imagine, to this day, how Alan Greenspan got himself euchred into sitting in that box with Hillary or Billary or whatever her name is, for the President's first State of the Union message. I think that was a serious mistake." A Fed staffer said, "I'm sure he wishes he hadn't been asked." Greenspan felt he had no choice but to accept the first lady's invitation. He did not expect to be seated next to Mrs. Clinton, but elsewhere in the box, as he had before. Others take a more cynical view. "If you assume that Alan Greenspan is a naive person, then you accept his explanation of it, which is that he got a call from the First Lady, 'Will you come and join us in the box?' and that was an invitation that somebody couldn't turn down, and that he only knew when he got there that he was sitting in the front row between the two ladies," says a former Fed official. "I believe that Alan Greenspan is so dedicated to trying to get himself reappointed that he is willing to compromise some of his independence in order to do so. He desperately wants to be reappointed."[1]

In his address, Clinton proposed to raise taxes a record $250 billion over five years while reducing the rate of spending growth by $220 billion. (These "spending cuts" included $29.1 billion in higher Social Security taxes.) Gone was the middle class tax cut he had promised during the campaign. In fiscal 1997, the deficit was to be $206.5 billion. Since a January 11 public television interview, Clinton had been pledging to reduce the deficit by $145 billion within five years, a pledge later modified to $140 billion. By projecting a wildly inflated fiscal 1997 deficit of $346 billion (compared to the $319 billion projected by the CBO and $290.2 billion deficit actually posted in 1992), Clinton could claim to be keeping his promise.[2] Senator Domenici labeled it a fraud, among other things noting that $123 billion of the spending savings had already been contained in the 1990 budget deal. "As part of a bipartisan approach to deficit reduction, I voted for some tax increases to get those spending cuts—I shouldn't be asked to vote for some more taxes to get the same cut again."

Two days later, Greenspan cemented the perception he had been coopted when he closed his Humphrey-Hawkins testimony before the Senate Banking Committee by reading a special, three-page statement broadly praising Clinton's budget proposals. "Leaving aside the specific details, it is a serious proposal, its baseline economic assumptions are plausible, and it is a detailed program-by-program set of recommendations as distinct from general goals. . . . How the deficit is reduced is very important, that it be done is crucial." Spending had to be slowed if the deficit was to be brought under control. Despite his disavowal of the specifics of doing this, Greenspan expressed hope "the president's endeavor to rein in medical costs will contribute importantly to this goal." Not only did he praise Clinton's deficit cutting plan, he refrained from criticizing his $30 billion "stimulus" plan, which would have worked in the opposite direction by increasing spending in the first two years. Given the economy's size, such a stimulus package was "not of particular concern to us," he said. The administration just wanted "an insurance policy on economic growth." The Fed would "monitor closely" the impact of fiscal policy on the economy to decide what the Fed response would be. He hedged on whether the Fed would ease because the economy was showing "noticeable momentum," but said he shared the administration's economic goals and promised the Fed would "provide sufficient liquidity." Four days later, before the House Banking Committee, he said the Fed "would respond."

In his book *The Agenda*, Bob Woodward calls Greenspan "the ghostwriter of the Clinton plan" and says he recommended the $140 billion deficit reduction goal as the minimum that would be acceptable to the bond market. This account makes Greenspan cringe. He feels he did little more than reinforce Clinton's own view that the deficit needed to be lowered. He had told Bentsen he would expect long-term interest rates to come down if the deficit was reduced, and Bentsen had passed this on to the president. Greenspan did not originate the $140 billion figure. He had been asked whether that amount of deficit reduction would be considered "significant" by the market and had replied that it would. The Fed staff did compute a handy rule of thumb to advance the cause of cutting the deficit, which Greenspan conveyed to the administration. "Other things being equal," the administration was told, for every $1 billion of deficit reduction, long-term interest rates would come down by one basis point, that is, $100 billion of deficit reduction would reduce long rates by 100 basis points or 1 percent.

Bentsen says Greenspan "was not big in" the evolution of Clinton fiscal policy. "He was obviously very sympathetic to what we were doing and supportive of what we were doing, but he was not involved in the specifics." He says the details of the package were worked out by himself, Rubin, Budget Director Leon Panetta, and his then assistant Alice Rivlin. "From my vantage point, the role of Chairman Greenspan was quite minimal, from what I could see, which is consistent with what Greenspan has said and not with what Woodward has said," says Blinder, who was intimately involved in the evolution of Clinton's budget plan and in consultations with Greenspan as a member of the Council of Economic Advisors. Another top Clinton adviser also denies the $140 billion figure came from Greenspan and says Woodward "overstated the closeness of the relationship" between the White House and the Fed. His description of Greenspan's role in the preparation of the 1993 budget package was "much more explicit and formal than I experienced."

Nonetheless, an impression arose that Greenspan and Clinton had an understanding, if not a quid pro quo, that deficit reduction would be rewarded with lower interest rates. This is vehemently denied by Fed officials. "There was no [deal]," says Phillips. "That's just not true. That's just not true." Lindsey says he has "no knowledge that there was any deal." The funds rate was left at 3 percent throughout 1993 because "we had just learned the lessons of '92 and '91. We knew that the headwinds were still there, and we also, in early '93, had terrible economic numbers. So I'm not sure what would have set us up to change." The Fed always considers the impact of fiscal policy, but "in terms of a quid pro quo, those don't happen," Kelley asserts. McTeer, an FOMC voter that year, is equally emphatic. "We weren't coaching the chairman on a deal or being briefed on one either. I am positive that I wasn't conscious of any horse trading, and I'm almost positive there wasn't horse trading going on. I read the Woodward book, and what I get out of it is that here you've got a new president looking for a fiscal policy, and Alan Greenspan is head of the central bank, and he's a natural person for you to consult with, and what I gather he advised the president is: try to reduce the budget deficit. That's certainly not a radical proposal coming from a central banker. I gather it was along the lines of: how you do it is important, but that you do it is the most important thing, and I think everybody knows that if you do something that will effectively reduce the budget deficit that puts downward pressure on interest rates, and it doesn't mean that you made a deal. It just means that it affects the market that way."

Corrigan says he would have known if there had been any kind of monetary-fiscal policy trade-off between the Fed and the administration and says that, not only was he "never a party to any such discussion or negotiation," but also "nothing ever came to my attention that suggested a deal . . . in the literal sense in which I think you are raising the question. I would have opposed any such literal deal. . . . I was only there for half of '93, but it sure as hell didn't have any effect on my thinking, I can tell you that!" Corrigan says it would be foolish for the Fed to base policy on presumptions about the effect the budget might have on the economy—in 1993 or any other year.

> Obviously you have to be sensitive. For example, if you are looking at a situation in which, other things being equal, there is a big move in fiscal policy that really is going to be a drag on the economy, obviously you have to be prepared to take that into account in your policy actions. But it is never clear—never clear—that is necessarily going to be the result of some kind of a fiscal package, because, among other things, if the fiscal package is really credible, one of the things that almost surely happens, all by itself, is that long-term interest rates come down, which by itself can essentially neutralize the restrictive actions coming out of the first round effects of a fiscal package. By the same token, a truly credible fiscal package can have a very salutary effect on business and consumer confidence, that produces a higher rate of spending. . . . So while you've got to be sensitive to the potential implications of a major change in fiscal policy, to commit literally to a particular course of action, without providing at least a framework within which you can evaluate how these other things sort themselves out, I think is a mistake.

McDonough, who succeeded Corrigan July 19, 1993, says he does "not have any reason to believe that there was, in fact, an arrangement with the administration. . . . I do think that fiscal policy has an effect on the formulation of an appropriate monetary policy, but I don't think that there has to be any sort of dealmaking between the Federal Reserve and either the administration or the Congress. The better, sounder, more sensible fiscal policy is, the more monetary policy has the ability to avoid an outbreak of inflation with lower interest rates. If you have a very expansive fiscal policy, monetary policy usually has to be a lot tighter than it would otherwise have to be. If you had a very restrictive fiscal policy, monetary policy would probably be appropriately more accomodating. . . . I think what you really want is a very sensible, well managed, fiscal policy and a very sensible monetary policy and then the country really benefits."

Bentsen and other administration officials echo the Fed denials. "I was never cognizant of any such deal, if there was such a deal," says Blinder. A senior official still in the administration says,

> To my knowledge there was not an explicit or a tacit deal. I would say, rather, there was an understanding that if fiscal policy took a more contractionary course that would create room for monetary policy to ease, for interest rates to fall. But to say that it would create room is not to say that it would occur, because there are other variables than the easing or the tightening of fiscal policy which would affect monetary policy decisions. . . . Certainly the administration, in its deficit reduction approach, made the argument and believed the argument that this would allow for a climate of lower interest rates and anticipated that a climate of lower interest rates on the long end would also be conducive to a climate of low interest rates across the interest rate spectrum. . . . The understanding was

that this was going to be a time when monetary and fiscal policy would be working toward the same goal, and this same goal would mean that if we took certain actions on the fiscal side that would create a climate which would allow for a different interest rate situation. But I always felt that it was characterized as much more explicit and formal a relationship in "The Agenda" than I experienced.

Nevertheless, an impression grew that Greenspan was tight with Clinton. In one respect at least, Greenspan did display the Fed's independent streak. Notwithstanding congressional complaints, he told both banking committees the Fed had followed through on its intentions and reduced the M2 growth target a half percent to 2 to 6 percent. Although largely technical, the Fed had been gradually reducing its money growth targets year by year to signal the markets it was aiming for price stability, but the move had little or no short-term policy significance. That did not prevent Sarbanes and others from making fresh howls of protest. Gonzalez said it "leaves no doubt in my mind that the central bank is working against the administration's economic plan, no matter how much lip service it pays our new president."

Greenspan had declined to elaborate on the details of the president's budget plans at the February 19 hearing because it was not "appropriate for any of us at the Federal Reserve to be involved in the debate" on fiscal policy. And yet that is exactly what Greenspan had done in many eyes. Wall Street read Greenspan's statement on the budget more as a validation of the Clinton plan's credibility than as a reflection on Greenspan's lack of independence, and the decline in long-term rates that had been going on since the previous fall continued. The long bond yield, which had been as high as 7¾ percent in November, fell below 7 percent. But there had been raised eyebrows about Greenspan's conspicuous collegiality with the White House ever since his "double date" with Hillary and Tipper. Soon Greenspan would backtrack and deny he had endorsed the Clinton budget. Bentsen helped redeem Greenspan on March 3 by saying there was no pact of easier money in exchange for a tighter fiscal policy. "No, no, no. You don't lock up that with the Federal Reserve, and I understand that. They preserve their independence, and they should." But he said the Fed and the administration were "in broad agreement" and had a "good relationship."

Meanwhile, Congress was keeping pressure on the Fed. Gonzalez, who was already pushing his bill to politicize the FOMC and bring its budget under congressional scrutiny, had come up with another way to tweak the Fed that was equally well calculated to worry Greenspan and company. On March 4, he introduced legislation that would have stripped the Fed of its cherished authority to regulate bank holding companies and some state chartered banks. Later in the year, the administration signed on to the idea despite the Fed's insistence that it needed to have a hand in supervising banks if it was to properly manage the nation's financial system and conduct monetary policy. Another bill, sponsored by Democratic congressman Joseph Kennedy II of Massachussetts and cosponsored by Gonzalez, would have forced the Fed to make direct loans from its discount window to ailing insurance companies.

In the ultimate grandstand play, Riegle summmoned all 12 Fed presidents before his committee to testify March 10. I spoke to a number of them before the hearing, and if Riegle's purpose had been to put the fear of God into them, he had certainly succeeded. There was an undercurrent of suspicion about what Riegle was up to. Some were convinced he and other committee members were working hand-in-glove with the administration to keep rates down and were using as leverage their threats to strip them of voting power or turn them into political appointees. They were determined to hang tough and present a united front at this "circus," as one called it. It was quite a spectacle, with the 12 white male Fed presidents lined up across the witness table in the harsh glare of TV lights like a latter day "Last Supper." It was really more of a Kangaroo Court with Riegle the hanging judge. Since the Fed presidents were not appointed by the president and confirmed by the Senate like the governors, they were not "accountable" but were "nevertheless significant players in policy" at an important time in the interaction of fiscal and monetary policy, and monetary policy had to be made to "fit" with Clinton's fiscal policy, with its simultaneous deficit reduction and stimulative spending proposals, Riegle declared, glowering down on the presidents from his raised dais. "While we're adjusting fiscal policy there is a need to make sure all other policies fit into it. . . . We can't be at odds with one another. . . . Monetary policy has to fit with that, or we're not going to make much progress."

"That gets into the question of accountability . . . ," the notoriously long-winded Riegle went on with the subtlety of a sledge hammer. "Even the minutes of your meetings aren't public. . . . We need some teamwork here. . . . If we end up going off in different directions, we're not going to have a very happy economic future, and the public is not going to stand for it." There had been no carrot proffered, but now came the stick. "Maybe there ought to be Senate confirmation and maybe your minutes ought to be made public." At the very least, he told the 12 he would summon them back up to testify in another six months to "talk about how things are going." Sarbanes at one point demanded, "Who are you to be making these decisions?" If deficit reduction had a contractionary effect on the economy and the Fed did not counteract it with monetary stimulus, there would be no growth impetus. Florida Republican senator Connie Mack, who had been friendly to some Fed reform efforts, objected to the browbeating. "It would be dangerous to get into a situation where we politely jawbone monetary policy in the direction that we want to work with fiscal policy." That road led to "stagflation." Mack accused the Democrats of trying to intimidate the Fed into doing the administration's bidding. It was an ordeal for the 12, and a number looked visibly chastened as they made their way to the elevators after the hearing. Others were steaming. Belying its public love fest with Greenspan, an administration source indicated the White House was not displeased to watch the Fed having to squirm a bit.[3]

Two days later Greenspan gave a speech which caused Fed watchers, who were still talking about Greenspan's balcony scene with Hillary, to wonder whether the Fed chairman's head had been turned. He said a strong February jobs report "overstates the improvement in the labor market," that "the news on inflation has been favorable," and that "the possibility of further setbacks [to economic expansion] . . . cannot be dismissed out of hand." Greenspan's comments startled economists. The Labor Department had reported a whopping 365,000 gain in nonfarm payrolls and a 5 percent rate of increase in producer prices, allaying recession fears and dampening rate cut talk. Other Fed officials had made much more upbeat comments on the numbers. It was "one more piece of evidence that the recovery isn't mired at 2 percent [growth] for the time being," one said. Not only had the Fed chief been consorting with administration officials, he had begun to sound like one. His emphasis on continued uncertainty about the recovery, lack of job growth, and low inflation was similar to what administration officials were saying to justify their fiscal stimulus plan and coax rates lower. "Greenspan is on the brink of losing his credibility," said David Jones. "He's near the border of propriety in terms of maintaining his independence." Greenspan had "tailored his comments to mesh with the administration, and the objective is to talk down rates." Greenspan's desire for good relations with the White House was understandable, but he was "in danger of going too far." Jones speculated Greenspan wanted to be able to "call Clinton and say, 'I did you a favor by holding policy stable; now do me a favor and get Congress off my back.' "

Greenspan's comments worried bond traders that the Fed was not sufficiently concerned about the sizable rises in wholesale and commodity prices that had been announced. "His timing was awful," said Robert DiClemente, money market economist for Salomon Brothers. "Inevitably there's got to be a certain amount of diplomacy when you're trying to preserve the independence of the Fed, but it's hard to believe that in order to preserve independence he'd give up the ship." By mirroring Clinton rhetoric on the uncertain nature of the recovery and the inadequacy of job growth, Greenspan was cooperating with Clinton's effort to "downplay any signs of strength in the economy for political reasons" so Clinton could justify his stimulus program and take credit for an improved economy later on, another top economist said. Greenspan was "playing some political games" for fear that if he did not "the administration won't be in his corner" when Congress considered Fed reform legislation. Greenspan was mistakenly gambling his tactics would "not cost much" credibility. "We all know that the Fed is under a lot of pressure to play ball with the administration," said Richard Berner, chief economist for Pittsburg's Mellon Bank, but Greenspan would lose credibility if he neglected price stability.

As if to confirm Wall Street suspicions, the *Washington Post* carried an article about Greenspan's "Unlikely Alliance" with Clinton, which portrayed Greenspan enjoying the closest relationship a Fed chairman had had with a president since his mentor Arthur Burns had advised Ford and his Economic Policy Board. It was all getting a bit too cozy, and some within the Fed began to grumble privately about the perception they thought Greenspan had carelessly created. Others never lost faith in him. "He has not sold his soul to the administration," said one official. "I think he's got too much integrity for that. I'd give him my proxy to vote in a second." Perhaps sensing Greenspan's credibility was getting tarnished, Rubin came to his aid March 23 when I asked him about the the Greenspan-Clinton relationship. "A lot of people [in the administration] know Alan Greenspan pretty well, and there is a lot of talk back and forth. We have a very good relationship, but the Fed has assiduously maintained its independence, as it should." Rubin went out of his way not to oppose the various Fed reform bills. Asked whether his earlier comments implied Clinton would oppose Riegle, Gonzalez, and company, he slipped off the question and simply reiterated that Clinton "believes in the independence of the Fed."

On March 24, before the Senate Finance Committee, Greenspan went to great lengths to allay the "alliance" talk, insisting his initial statement calling Clinton's budget "serious" and "credible" had been widely misinterpreted as an endorsement of its particulars. "I commended him for putting it on the table, because it's crucial to get the deficit down. His program is serious . . . it's a detailed program, and the markets have responded in quite a serious way because they see it as a major commitment to reducing the deficit. . . . I commended him for putting the issue on the table because it is a serious proposal, but that's not the same thing as saying I endorse it. . . . We [at the Fed] have a very distinct interest in bringing the deficit down because it's a corrosive force, but how that is done is a political issue." Going further to distance himself from the Clinton plan, Greenspan expounded on the futility of trying to reduce the deficit through higher taxes and warned that unless spending was reduced the deficit would go on ballooning out of control. In March 25 testimony before the House Small Business Committee, Greenspan sounded more upbeat on the economy as well, saying "an improved economy" and lower long-term interest rates would soon bring greater lending activity.

It wasn't long before Greenspan's reassertion of his independence from "good cop" Clinton prompted "bad cop" Congress to lean on the Fed to hold rates down, undeterred by mounting evidence the economy was gaining momentum and feeling price pressures. A report issued by the JEC issued on April 1 asserted: "The economy is already growing too slowly to produce any significant reduction in unemployment. To avoid further slowdown, the administration's deficit reduction program needs to be accompanied by both cooperative action by the Federal Reserve and an investment and stimulus package which moderates fiscal contraction by a small amount. . . . The Federal Reserve [must] make the maintenance of adequate growth its central concern in the next few years." Gonzalez launched another salvo against the Fed's allegedly contractionary management of the money supply. Despite such complaints, the economy was in a steady upswing. After surging 5.7 percent in the fourth quarter of 1992, real GDP growth slowed to 1.2 percent in the first quarter of 1993, but rebounded to 2.4 percent in the second and 2.7 percent in the third, then exploded 6.3 percent in the fourth.

Greater confidence in the economic outlook inevitably spurred greater concern about inflation, but Greenspan called the consecutive 0.5 percent jumps in core consumer prices in January and February "aberrations." But in late-March interviews with Lindsey, Kelley, Phillips, Hoenig, and others, I detected a shift from near dismissal of inflation as a concern to a grudging acknowledgment that it had come back to haunt them. As one put it, there was now "a whiff of inflation where it had been completely dormant. It just sticks my antlers up." Greenspan continued to minimize inflation, even telling Riegle in an April 5 correspondence that "we may not be very far from" price stability. But by the time he spoke on April 19, Greenspan had modified his message. Though "quite close" to price stability the Fed would need to remain "especially vigilant" against a reemergence of inflation, even though core producer and consumer prices had risen just 0.1 percent in March.

Suddenly in May there was good reason to be vigilant, when it was reported producer prices had risen 0.6 percent overall and 0.4 percent on a core basis in April, while the CPI had risen 0.4 percent by both measures. All talk of easing disappeared. Some Fed officials argued it was time to start raising rates. Angell and Lindsey had dissented against keeping rates unchanged at the March 23 FOMC meeting because they wanted an immediate tightening. Sensing this mood, Clinton dropped his hands-off-the-Fed pretense. There was "no cause" for inflation to rise and "no reason" to believe it would, he said at a May 14 Rose Garden press conference. The Fed would "have to have more evidence before they raise interest rates in an economy with capacity [utilization] at 80 percent." Other administration officials, who seemed to think they had a deal with the Fed, were privately saying much the same thing in less diplomatic terms, and continued to do so through May and June. As far as some Clinton aides were concerned, the Fed should be lowering rates, not raising them. Respect for the Fed's independence was a fair-weather policy which the administration felt free to discard when things did not go its way.

All this concern at the White House and on Capitol Hill was a bit overwrought. In reality, the Fed was a long ways from raising rates. The Fed was badly divided at its May 18 FOMC meeting. Although the Fed gave itself leeway to raise rates, officials were split over whether the inflation outlook had deteriorated to the point an actual tightening was needed. Greenspan, presciently, did not really believe inflation was making a comeback. He thought the unfavorable price indices were reflecting seasonal distortions, but believed the Fed had to make a statement of concern by adopting a tightening bias. Lindsey was appeased by the bias and voted with the majority, but Angell dissented in favor of an immediate rate hike. Boehne dissented because he felt the Fed should not be leaning toward higher rates. Most members hoped inflation would remain under control, and some felt it would take a lot to justify pushing the funds rate above 3 percent. Gone were the hopeful predictions of several months earlier that inflation would approach the vanishing point in 1993, but even the most hawkish were not forecasting dramatic price increases. Hoenig "took note of" the rapid price rises of the January-April period, but doubted that pattern would be sustained because "we still have an unemployment rate of 7 percent, so there is still slack in the labor market, and there is still excess capacity in most sectors."

In late May, Greenspan was in Dallas to make a speech. (This time he actually got to make it.) Prophetically, he said the economy was in "an early stage of a major expansion in employment." Soon thereafter, the Labor Department announced a healthy rise in nonfarm payroll for May and a 0.1 percent drop in unemployment. Rate hike speculation increased, as did pressure from the administration and Congress. "We're trying to have a more restrictive fiscal policy and our hope is we'll have room for a more expansive monetary policy," he said on May 26. Assistant Treasury Secretary for Economic Policy Alicia Munnell, former research director of the Boston Fed who often participated in Bentsen's regular meetings with Greenspan, was not shy about advising her former employer when I interviewed her June 15. The May core CPI had risen a modest 0.2 percent, and she said this proved the Fed had no excuse to raise rates. "We never saw any reason to raise interest rates. I didn't see any increase in inflationary pressures reflected in the labor market, in capacity utilization or any other part of the economy." Administration officials were doing their best to poor-mouth the economy to strengthen their case for a fiscal stimulus package and lower rates. Tyson was saying first-quarter GDP might well be revised downward from the initial 0.9 percent growth estimate. (In fact, it would be revised up appreciably.) When I spoke to Munnell a couple days later, she insisted the administration had "a cordial and very good relationship" with the Fed, and said, "We don't want inflation any more than the Fed, but our substantive judgment is that at this time there are no dangers."

In a June 9 meeting at the White House, Clinton and his advisers asked Greenspan about his policy intentions. A participant says he gave no assurances he would hold the line on rates but made "a conditional statement" along the lines of, "You all are creating a climate for me to keep inflation low. I may have to do something because of something else, like inflationary expectations. I may have to, but because of what you are doing, I won't have to do that much." This top Clinton adviser adds, "I never thought that there was a quid pro quo."

To the consternation of Clinton and some of his advisers, the bond market had become fixated on the figure of $500 billion in cumulative deficit reduction over five years, after the House and Senate, in March, had passed a version of the Clinton plan that reduced the deficit more than that amount.[4] Clinton was told he dare not disappoint the market. One administration official says the magic $500 billion "took on a life of its own, among even the congressional Democrats, not because anybody could tell a convincing story that the difference between $480 billion and $500 billion was a difference that mattered to the economy, but because the difference between $480 billion and $500 billion was a difference that mattered when you went out and told your constituents what you did." Tyson recalls telling Clinton, " 'Look, there's no reason to [insist on $500 billion]. We don't know for sure how the bond market is going to respond to this.' And certainly, when you're down to the last $20 billion or $30 billion, to argue that you know that the difference between 470 and 500 is somehow going to make a profound difference to the economy, I think is to say that you know something you cannot know. No one knows. And I thought we were paying too much attention to these very, actually small—over the course of five years—differences. So in that sense I think we were being too sensitive to the market, but it wasn't to say I thought that the bond market was driving our policy. I didn't. I thought people were using the alleged reaction of the bond market to effect an outcome that they wanted, and I thought the alleged effect on the bond market was uncertain at best."

It was to meet the $500 billion expectation, after the CBO had "scored" Clinton's budget much lower, that the administration decided to make its tax increases retroactive to January 1, prompting Clinton in October 1995 to say "I raised your taxes too much." At the time, Tyson and others opposed doing so, particularly after Congress rejected the stimulus package. "Because we had lost the stimulus package, we had already become, on net, more contractionary, because we hadn't changed the deficit reduction package," an administration official recalls. "So we had essentially added, by dint of losing the stimulus package, $30 billion to the contractionary effect." At that time the Commerce Department had estimated real GDP grew just 1.6 percent in the second quarter, after growing 0.9 percent in the first quarter, and Tyson and others argued it made no sense to raise taxes retroactively to hit the $500 billion mark. "We wouldn't have had to have retroactivity on the tax increase if we simply let a little of that number go," says the official, who recalls telling Clinton, "You don't have to do this! It doesn't matter. It simply doesn't matter."

However, many Democrats were saying they would not vote for the package if it was less than $500 billion, and people like Bentsen and Rubin were telling Clinton the markets would react badly to a lower amount of deficit reduction, so Clinton "felt he had to," an aide said. Greenspan added to the pressure by publicly urging no backing away from the $500 billion deficit reduction promise. The administration had sold itself on the long-rate reductions the Fed had said might be possible (a tenth of a percent for every $10 billion of deficit cuts). Greenspan had also said each 1 percent reduction in long rates would generate between $50 and $100 billion in increased output. The Fed's numbers were treated by Clinton and some of his advisers as "almost a certainty, that if you get this much in deficit reduction you'll get this much in long-term interest rate reduction. And some of us thought that was overselling what economists know."

Not content with Greenspan's assurances and determined to do whatever he could to hold rates down, Clinton aimed a message at the Fed June 23, declaring, "There's no inflation in this economy that we can see." Two days later, Panetta joined in. The Senate had just narrowly passed its version of the Clinton budget, which proposed to cut the deficit $499 billion.[5] Panetta acknowledged the bill's $249 billion in tax hikes (not counting higher Social Security taxes) were apt to be contractionary, but said they would be offset by lower interest rates. "I think right now, since we are on the threshold of putting the package in place, it behooves everybody to be steady-as-you-go, including the Fed," Panetta said. If House and Senate budget conferees agreed on a $500 billion plan, "the ability to kind of hold interest rates at a low level is going to be more assured."

Included in the budget were $16.5 billion in lower debt servicing costs predicated on greater reliance on short-term Treasury borrowing. On May 5, against the advice of primary dealers, the Treasury had announced a new debt management strategy. It moved from quarterly to semiannual auctions of 30-year bonds, abandoned sales of 7-year notes, and relied more on short-term notes and bills, not just to save interest cost but to reduce the supply of long-term government debt flooding the market in the hope bond prices would rise and their yields fall. The new strategy reduced the national debt's average maturity and enabled the administration to take advantage of the lower short-term rates then prevailing, but that meant the Treasury would have to roll over its debt more often and eventually pay higher rates to service the debt. Over lunch with senior Treasury officials, Greenspan and other Fed officials had cautioned Treasury against shortening maturities too zealously. They did not want to be put under additional pressure to hold down short-term rates to prevent a widening of the deficit. The new debt strategy "turned out to be a pretty stupid thing to do," says a Board member, interviewed when bill rates had risen to about 5.4 percent, while bond yields had fallen to near 6 percent.[6]

The Fed was beginning to chafe at the White House's low interest rate harness. At its July 6–7 meeting, the FOMC left rates unchanged but with a tightening bias, which Greenspan felt was needed to reflect concern about rapid first-half price increases, although he strongly suspected they would prove temporary. Angell dissented in favor of an immediate rate hike. On July 20, as House and Senate conferees continued to negotiate the differences between their respective budgets, Greenspan gave his midyear Humphrey-Hawkins testimony before the House Banking Committee. Greenspan warned the markets would react negatively if Congress did not pass the $500 billion in promised deficit reduction. But he gave little solace to administration officials hoping for perpetually low short-term rates. Although May and June price figures had "helped assuage concerns that new inflationary pressures had taken hold, the news on inflation this year must be characterized as disappointing." Inflation had "at best stabilized," and growth was now picking up. The most hopeful aspect of his testimony from the White House point of view, ironically, was that the economy was still completing its "balance sheet restructuring" and battling those "headwinds." But the Fed chief was not buying the administration theory that deficit reduction was going to be ipso facto contractionary and therefore deserving of monetary accommodation. "The timing and magnitude of any net restraint from deficit reduction is uncertain." Moreover, monetary policy had already been "quite accommodative" considering that real short-term rates had "been in the neighborhood of zero over the last three quarters." The implication was that this could not go on. In a defiance of his congressional critics, Greenspan announced the Fed had decided to further lower its M2 target range a full percent from 2 to 6 percent to 1 to 5 percent. There was also an indirect slap at the administration's disregard for the dollar's value, a troublesome issue throughout this period.[7] "I believe we are on our way toward reestablishing the trust in the purchasing power of the dollar that is crucial to maximizing and fulfilling the productive capacity of this nation. The public, however, clearly remains to be convinced." It was not what the administration wanted to hear.

A "very disappointed" Gonzalez went ballistic over the lowering of M2 targets. The Fed had "failed to meet its own targets for a year and a half, and now is moving the targets down to actual recession levels of money growth," the House Banking Committee chairman wrote in a July 22 letter to Clinton. Worse, the Fed had lowered its projected real GDP growth range from 2½ to 4 percent in February to 2 to 3½ percent. "Instead of this continued policy of virtual no-growth, this is the time to urge the Federal Reserve to follow a monetary policy that is consistent with your policies to put our citizens back to work." It was time to bring the Fed to heel. "I urge you to consider changing the composition of the Federal Open Market Committee which decides our nation's monetary policies. The current Federal Reserve decision makers are seven Reagan-Bush appointees at the Board of Governors. The twelve Federal Reserve presidents are selected by their bank board of directors, who mostly represent commercial banks. In general, the Federal Reserve decision-makers are bankers or friends of bankers." In short, it was time to put people more congenial to the Democratic Party on the FOMC. He urged the president to "consider changing the law so that the 12 Federal Reserve Bank presidents would be appointed by the president and approved by the Senate." He reminded Clinton he would have a chance to replace Angell when his term expired January 31, 1994.

The House-Senate conferees reached a budget compromise on July 29, settling on a 4.3 cent per gallon gas tax. The bill, designed to reduce the deficit $496 billion over five years by raising taxes $241 billion, restraining spending, and reducing interest costs, was passed 218-216 in the House on August 5, and on August 6, Vice President Gore broke a 50-50 tie for final passage.[8] Now that taxes had actually been raised, some Fed officials began worrying fiscal policy might weaken the economy. With or without political pressure, they were coming to the conclusion it behooved the Fed to hold the line on rates rather than gamble on tipping the economy back into recession. Uncertainty about the budget had "clearly put a damper on spending and planning" by business, and uncertainty about the president's expensive health care reform proposals was "going to be around for some months to come and is apt to prove more troublesome to medium and small-sized businesses," Boehne said August 11. Keehn said the just-passed tax hikes and the prospect of more to finance health care reform would be "an inhibitor" of growth, making employers reluctant to hire for fear of higher government-imposed payroll costs. Better-behaved inflation reinforced the monetary status quo. Producer prices fell for the second straight month in July, while consumer prices rose just a tenth of a percent.

At the August 17 FOMC meeting, most officials were content to leave the funds rate unchanged. Views differed, but as a group Fed officials felt the prevailing mix of slow growth and relatively low inflation was about the best that could be expected. While some would have liked to see faster growth, they saw the Fed having limited power to spur business activity in the face of fiscal and other constraints. And, to one degree or another, FOMC members were anxious to do nothing to stir the slumbering inflation dragon. Ten days after the meeting, Lindsey told me inflation and the weak dollar would bear "close watching." Mullins described the Fed's stance as "very accommodative" and was not comfortable with the level of inflation. These former doves were leaning increasingly toward tightening. But for the moment, there was no consensus to move in either direction. After having had a tightening bias in its May and July directives, the FOMC reverted to symmetrical language. The Fed had not knuckled under to political pressure. Greenspan and others simply felt a bias was no longer needed now that spring's false inflation signals had evaporated. Those earlier directives, along with congressional testimony, had been designed to help cool inflation psychology in the bond market. They reflected "a determination on the part of this committee not to leave the punch bowl on the table too long and that if the numbers continued as they had we were prepared to move to forestall an inflationary bulge," LaWare said.

Greenspan and his senior staff were already thinking ahead to when it would become necessary to raise rates. When the time came, the Fed might well have to make larger rate moves to have the desired impact, Greenspan said at the Kansas City Fed's annual Jackson Hole, Wyoming, conference August 20. Because depository institutions now accounted for a much lower share of the total provision of credit, "the fairly direct effect that open market operations once had on the credit flows provided for businesses and home construction is largely dissipated. Nonetheless, the Federal Reserve can still affect short-term interest rates and thus have an impact on the cost of borrowing from banks, from other intermediaries and directly in the capital markets. While this effect may be more indirect, take longer and require larger movements in rates for a given effect on output, the Federal Reserve and other central banks still have the tools required to implement monetary policy." I later talked to Kohn, who said financial market innovations meant "rates may have to move over a larger range." *Securitization* (the bundling of loans into securities for sale in a secondary market) had made borrowers "not so dependent on intermediaries [like banks]. If rising interest rates made an intermediary less profitable [and less eager to lend] there are other ways of getting money through the securitization process." As a result, the Fed was apt to find it harder to constrain credit flows by pushing up the funds rate.

There were forces at work keeping the Fed from tightening for now. On September 1, the NAPM announced its index fell for the third straight month in August to 49.3, indicating an industrial contraction. Output had risen, but employment had fallen, reflecting reluctance to hire for fear of increased taxes and regulation. Many businesses had resorted to contract workers and paying overtime to existing workers instead of adding to their permanent payroll. "In spite of the fact that business may have picked up, companies are not anxious to make new hires because of anticipated health care costs," said a Fed official. "There has been a lot more reluctance to hire than has been typically the case," said another. "We've been hearing a lot of things from employers about the costs of adding payroll, coming at the same time when they've been spending on investments to augment productivity." Foreign demand was also soft, and officials felt there was enough "slack" in terms of unemployed labor and underused capacity to hold inflation at bay. But it was just a matter of time until the Fed had to switch direction, as Greenspan signaled in a September 2 letter to Riegle: "The current real short-term interest rates of about zero are below the levels toward which they ultimately will need to move to be consistent with achievement of the nation's economic objectives over time." He was hazy about when the Fed would have to raise rates. "When and by how much real short-term interest rates will eventually need to rise will depend on economic developments and inflation pressures. . . ."

With the approach of the September 21 FOMC meeting, the beige book found only "slow to moderate growth" around the country, and the Labor Department reported a 0.6 percent drop in producer prices (0.1 percent excluding food and energy). M2 was falling from week to week, leaving its growth rate for the year at an anemic 1 percent. Congressional Democrats clamored anew for an easier Fed stance and were not quieted when consumer prices were reported up 0.3 percent. They demanded rate cuts to offset deficit reduction. Administration officials were more subtle. Rubin's tack was to minimize inflation risks and talk market rates down. "I think we've changed market psychology," he told a small group of reporters. "The markets believe we've gotten our arms around the deficit and gotten inflation under control." Panetta was more direct on September 14, telling the House Budget Committee the administration was counting on "low interest rates into the future," saying the administration expected the Fed to pursue "a steady policy path." Parry spoke for many when he said the Fed was already doing its part to "offset" the "contractionary" effects of fiscal policy and slow growth abroad. The Fed "has cut short-term interest rates substantially—if cautiously—in the past few years." Many Fed officials were growing uncomfortable with the Fed's "steady" path and with the perception it was in Clinton's pocket. Having labored mightily to get inflation down to 3 percent, they were not going to tolerate a reacceleration. Broaddus, who had become Richmond Fed president January 1, thought inflation risks outweighed those of a downturn. Some officials were becoming concerned about fueling a speculative bubble in stocks and bonds by being too easy with credit. The White House didn't like this kind of talk and dismissed the Fed's concerns.

The Fed was catching it from all directions. The Shadow Open Market Committee accused the Fed of being too "expansive" because M1 and the monetary base had been growing at double-digit rates. One of its members, the former Cleveland Fed president Lee Hoskins, noted that, despite the Fed's stated goal of price stability, the Fed governors and presidents had increased their "central tendency" of forecasts for 1994 inflation a quarter percent and were not taking steps to counter it. "You have a Fed that says it wants price stability, yet their own forecast is for higher inflation. . . . It's not like inflation is something that falls out of the sky at night." It was something the Fed had direct control over, and his message to his former colleagues was: "You have the lever, push the lever." At the real FOMC's September meeting, monetary policy was seen as "quite accommodative," but there were sufficient "uncertainties" about economic prospects and sufficient confidence inflation was still "subdued" that it voted unanimously to leave policy unchanged with no tilt toward tightening or easing.

Still hanging over the Fed was the threat of congressional "reform." No one took it completely seriously, but, like a toxic waste dump in one's neighborhood, it couldn't be entirely ignored either. The administration had been content to let the Fed stew over this menace. Aside from the ritual lip service to the Fed's independence, neither Clinton nor any of his top advisers had ever once and for all disavowed the threats from Riegle, Sasser, Gonzalez, and others. Finally, in a September 20 letter to Gonzalez, Clinton said he would not support making Fed presidents political appointees just then, but left the door open. "Your suggestion has merit; there is no doubt about it. But there are also arguments on the other side, and we are not writing on a clean slate. On balance, I am disinclined to seek a change in the Federal Reserve Act at this juncture. There are several reasons. Perhaps the main one is a general feeling that the System is functioning well and does not need an overhaul just now. Changing the way bank presidents are elected at this time runs the risk of undermining market confidence in the Fed. Finally, there is virtue in having the Federal Open Market Committee input [and votes] that truly come from outside Washington. Still, you raise a valid point about legitimacy and representation, and I shall keep it in mind." Clinton had staked out both sides of the issue, withholding support for politicizing the Fed right away but giving the "reformers" hope he might back them in the future. Implicit in Clinton's letter, a Democratic source says, was that, if things did not go as he hoped, he might support the bill.

Gonzalez was "not upset" but on the contrary drew comfort from the Clinton letter because he detected "wiggle room" in the president's position, an aide said. The letter had been "pretty nondefinitive." Another Democratic source said the president's letter "clearly leaves him room to change his mind if he gets upset at the Fed. It's another little warning shot: don't step out of line or I'll change my mind." Far from being dissuaded, Gonzalez felt encouraged to continue his assault on the Fed with a series of hearings. Gonzalez was trying to draw strength from the administration's "reinventing government" theme to "reinvent" the Fed. He was determined to "educate the White House" on the need to rein in the Fed, an aide said. Over two weeks in mid-October, Greenspan, other Fed governors, and many Fed presidents were required to testify on why they opposed changing the way the Fed is constituted and operates. Gonzalez's bill had 20 cosponsors, and Hamilton and JEC chairman Obey had cosponsored their own bill. In the Senate, Sarbanes, Riegle, Sasser (all committee chairmen), and Dorgan were pushing legislation to strip the presidents of their voting rights. A House Democrat predicted, "It's inevitable something is going to be done" at some point. "It's probably headed somewhere, but not on a fast track. If they keep at it, and they're getting more and more attention and support, all it takes is for the Fed to make some enemies and they'll get big-time support." In the meantime, the Fed reform bills were serving their purpose. "One of the intentions is to paralyze the Fed. . . . The intention is transparent, to put the Fed on notice that never again must we see the federal funds rate above 3 percent." Gonzalez could not be taken lightly just because he had been "singing the same tune for so long," said Brusca. He had backers, and "just because Clinton has said he doesn't want to see the Fed tampered with doesn't mean it won't be. He has proven himself to be malleable."

Greenspan was surprised Clinton was willing to go as far as he did and was satisfied he had given Gonzalez only lukewarm support. Other Fed officials remained concerned. Forrestal called Gonzalez's bill "a clear politicization of the central bank. History around the world indicates independent central banks are highly desirable. . . . It has worked extremely well in this country, and I for one would be very sorry to see any diminution of it." LaWare said, "The part that puzzles me is that, if there were a general perception that monetary policy had failed there would be more of a concern about the structure of the FOMC, but in my opinion, on balance, over a long period, monetary policy has been pretty successful by comparison with almost any other industrial country. To mount an attack on the central bank solely on the basis of a narrow constitutional argument does not seem to have a lot of merit." Officials were astonished to come under such fire when, as LaWare put it, the Fed was being "very accommodative." "We've been extraordinarily easy in terms of monetary policy," said another Fed official. "We've supplied a tremendous amount of reserves."

On October 13, Greenspan warned the House Banking Committee passing Chairman Gonzalez's bill would be "a major mistake." The 80-year-old Fed system might not be perfect but it struck "a balance . . . between the need for sound farsighted monetary policy and the imperative of effective accountability by policymakers." Taking away the Fed presidents' vote or making them subject to presidential nomination and Senate confirmation would disrupt that balance and "politicize" the Fed. Likewise, making Fed operations, including FOMC policy deliberations, subject to audit by the GAO, an arm of Congress, "could peal away a layer of the central bank's insulation from day-to-day political pressure" and "impede the process of formulating policy. Whatever its intent, legislation of this type would have precisely that deleterious effect." A more politically influenced Fed would be more inclined to give in to short-run temptations to "gun the economy," and "giving in to such temptations is likely to impart an inflationary bias to the economy and could lead to instability, recession and economic stagnation." As a result, "interest rates would be higher." As for claims it was unconstitutional for Fed presidents to vote on policy because they had not been appointed by the president or confirmed by the Senate, Greenspan pointed out Congress itself had given the presidents a policy vote in 1935. "In often difficult economic circumstances, the Federal Reserve has implemented policies aimed at improving the nation's economic health. We have not always been entirely successful, but we have learned from experience what monetary policy can do and what it cannot do. In my view, current Federal Reserve policy is promoting conditions vital to maximizing the productive potential of the U.S. economy."

If Greenspan was hoping for wholehearted support from his friends at the White House, he was disappointed. They continued to toy with the Fed. At an October 15 briefing which coincided with Gonzalez's two-week assault on the Fed, Tyson again suggested the Fed had no business thinking about raising rates. Economic statistics were "consistent with a path of low inflation, low interest rates and steady economic growth. . . . Right now the economy seems to be performing more or less as forecast, the inflation rate has come down, and there is no danger of inflation rising. . . . I would assume the Fed will read the evidence the same way." When asked whether the administration would support the Fed's independence and help it fend off congressional reformers, she replied, "We have not had an administration discussion . . . we've not even asked ourselves that question. . . ." Blinder observed that Clinton had only addressed the question of making presidents subject to appointment and confirmation and noted there were a number of other Fed reform proposals, and "the president has not opined on any of the others." Such comments were hardly contrived to put Fed minds at ease. The Fed had no immediate provocation for raising rates. The September CPI was unchanged overall and up just 0.1 percent on a core basis. The PPI was also unchanged. Industrial production and retail sales rose modestly. This was good news for the Fed, but in that political climate made it all the more difficult to justify the inevitable preemptive tightening.

Greenspan was back before the House Banking Committee October 19, this time in the company of 14 other Fed governors and presidents. Not to be outdone by Riegle's March show trial, Gonzalez had called the FOMC's entire voting membership plus some. The main issue was "disclosure." Gonzalez and others wanted the Fed to release policy directives within a week of its meetings instead of with a six-week delay and wanted videotapes or verbatim transcripts within 60 days. At the same time, Gonzalez was concerned about alleged policy "leaks" to the press and the markets. Although the only real decision that year had been to go from symmetrical to asymmetric and back, Greenspan suggested some of the "leaks" of policy decisions taken by the Fed may have come from the administration. He said his "contacts with [the Clinton administration] have been exceptionally extensive and have worked very well." He defended the Fed's secrecy compared to foreign central banks, which he said had "far less elements of openness than we have." The Bundesbank did not release minutes of its meetings for 30 years. He was ambivalent about the proposal to make the Fed chairman's term begin at the start of a president's term.

He was anything but ambivalent about the proposal to immediately release FOMC's directives and/or transcripts. The FOMC phrased its policy directive in terms of *"contingency plans."* If its decisions were made public soon after the meetings, instead of at a six-week lag, "markets would tend to incorporate the [contingent policy] changes immediately, preventing the policies from being effectively carried out as planned." Immediate disclosure "would tend to produce increased volatility in financial markets, as market participants reacted not only to actual Federal Reserve actions but also to possible Federal Reserve actions." Immediate disclosure "would impair the usefulness of the directives, as committee members concerned about the announcement effect of a directive biased either toward ease or tightening, would tend to shy away from anything but a vote of immediate change or of no change at the meeting. An important element of flexibility in the current procedures would be lost." Releasing video tape or transcripts "would so seriously constrain the process of formulating policy as to render those meetings nearly unproductive." Angell told the committee officials would be "much less willing to conjecture about future economic and financial developments, to explore alternative policies or to challenge others' view." Jordan said he would have no desire to be a Fed president if it meant being a political appointee, nor would he be interested in serving if the presidents were made an advisory body with no policy vote. Kelley said the Fed is "a creature of Congress" and should fulfill its will, but "needs a clearer mandate" to fight inflation, not the mixed signals it had been getting.

The Fed officials were grilled on what records they kept at FOMC meetings. As they had previously agreed, they either denied taking any notes or said they destroyed them or locked them away for safekeeping. McTeer, who in prepared testimony said he scribbled "doodles" during the meetings, afterwards joked he had been prepared to distribute these "doodles." Phillips cracked, "Only his psychiatrist knows for sure." Greenspan said he took "very brief, rough notes on the views expressed by participants" to help him "keep track of committee sentiment as the meeting progresses and thus in judging where a consensus may be reached with respect to monetary policy." These notes were kept "in a locked file cabinet." In passing, he disclosed that "the meetings are recorded electronically" and "these audio tapes are used to assist in the preparation of the minutes that are released to the public following the subsequent meeting; thereafter the tapes are recorded over. . . . In the process of putting together the minutes, an unedited transcript is prepared from the tapes, as are detailed notes on selected topics discussed in the course of the meeting. These materials generally are seen only by the staff involved in preparing the minutes, and the documents are kept under lock and key by the FOMC secretariat."

It had all been a bit of a charade, an exercise in damage control. Realizing the Fed was going to have to go part of the way in Gonzalez's direction, Greenspan had organized an FOMC conference call four days before the hearing. For the first time, Greenspan had revealed to stunned FOMC members that the Fed had been secretly keeping verbatim transcripts of FOMC meetings since 1976. Some officials were angry this had been kept from them and that they had made unguarded remarks not knowing they were being recorded. FOMC members were anxious for the transcripts not to be made public, and some suggested destroying them, but the Fed's general counsel Virgil Mattingly informed them they stood on shaky legal ground in withholding the transcripts once they became known. Under a new Justice Department policy, "the chances are not good of withholding material more than three years old." With Gonzalez and his staff sniffing around for notes and tapes, it was agreed that, at the October 19 hearing, Greenspan would "matter of factly" disclose that FOMC meetings were taped and transcripts prepared purely for the purpose of preparing the minutes, but that the tape was then erased and the transcripts locked away unseen by all but the staffers who prepared the minutes. It was hoped his innocuous description of the process, buried in lengthy testimony, would somehow suffice, but a memorandum prepared by one of the participants shows Greenspan worried about how Gonzalez's "extravaganza" would go; he feared the Fed would be "at risk" in having to hand over the transcripts and that the Justice Department would be on Gonzalez's side.

Predictably, Gonzalez jumped on Greenspan's disclosure that the Fed had been secretly taping and transcribing FOMC proceedings. A few weeks later, he trumpeted his "discovery" of the transcripts and claimed he had caught Greenspan and his colleagues in a lie. Gonzalez had a point. He had been probing the Fed for nearly a year on what records it was keeping. He had asked Greenspan in late December 1992 whether members of the FOMC objected to having their comments and votes recorded in detailed minutes and then made public. Greenspan spoke against the idea on behalf of the other members, telling Gonzalez the FOMC consensus was that there would be "serious drawbacks to releasing at any time a literal record of FOMC deliberations" because it would "constrain" and "circumscribe" discussions. When Gonzalez accused him of being "evasive," Greenspan asked each member to provide his own response. Naturally, each member echoed Greenspan. In late September 1993, Gonzalez asked each FOMC member to provide a "detailed description" of any notes or records they had made or were aware of others having made. They all said they had no notes, other than minor scribblings, and knew of no notes or records kept by anyone else. Now that he had stumbled over the Fed's secret, he accused Greenspan of "lying" and "stonewalling." He demanded all transcripts be immediately turned over. There ensued a long bargaining process, which culminated the following year in the release of transcripts with a five-year time lag—a goldmine in writing this book.

Meanwhile, the administration kept up its subtler pressure tactics. Blinder, already the frontrunner to replace Angell, said in an October 20 interview he could foresee no rise in inflation, and "that being the thing that would be the most likely to arouse the Fed to tighten, it seems not to be on the horizon." He suggested the Fed had come around to the administration's view that inflation was not a great concern. "The two of us are on the same track in that what we want to happen to the economy in the near and medium term is very consonant with what they want to happen to the economy. For example, you hear less these days of cries to drive the inflation rate to zero. We would all like it to be zero if we could wave a magic wand, but there isn't any evidence that the Fed seeks that as an urgent priority and wants to contract the economy to make that happen. If they were doing that you'd probably see more friction between the Fed and the administration, but they're not." He contended the administration's deficit reduction had "taken a lot of the pressure off the Fed" and said he could envision further drops in long rates. In fact, the long bond yield had bottomed at around 5¾ percent and was destined to go above 8 percent in 1994.

The next day, like a tag team wrestler, Sarbanes jumped into the ring. "My own view is that they could ease further from where they are. There is no basis to tighten. There is no inflation, and the economy is obviously not moving." With the budget becoming "more contractionary," the Fed had to be "accommodative." Sarbanes, who was due to replace Riegle as Senate Banking Committee chairman when the latter retired in 1994, claimed there was a public perception of the Fed's "illegitimacy" that needed to be remedied by taking away the Fed presidents' vote. "We need more accountability. . . . I don't think we'll act legislatively this year," but looking ahead to 1994, "it's always possible."

It was becoming obvious the Fed was going to have to move away from its expansionary credit stance to something more appropriate to long-run economic trends, but Greenspan seemed in no hurry. "The 50 mile per hour headwinds have now come down to about twenty to twenty-five miles per hour," he said on October 22. Less cash flow was being diverted to loan repayment, but a "major" corporate restructuring was continuing. Eventually, the process would add "a couple of tenths or so of a percent to our long-term growth rates," but in the meantime "the announcements of companies downsizing their workforce are likely to continue." The pressure seemed to be having its effect on Greenspan. Some were growing impatient with his seeming sycophancy to the administration. In an October 25 *Wall Street Journal* column, Harvard economist Robert Barro asked how much longer Greenspan could, in good conscience, "remain as part of an administration team that is basically promoting socialism." He likened the Fed chairman to the Alex Guiness character, Colonel Nicholson, in the movie "The Bridge on the River Kwai," who, having built a railroad bridge for the Japanese army in Burma, realizes at the last moment that he has been aiding the enemy and asks, "What have I done?" just before falling on the detonator and blowing it up. "It would be better if Mr. Greenspan left the government a little further in advance of the explosion." About this time, Wall Street economist Maria Fiorini-Ramirez recalls asking Greenspan at a party about the prospects for tightening. He told her that "the only country in the world where inflation seems to be a problem is China."

The economy was looking increasingly strong, fueled by the Fed's highly stimulative policies. On November 5, the Labor Department reported a bigger-than-expected rise in October's nonfarm payroll, coupled with upward revisions to the two previous months. But the Fed was being cautious. Fed officials deny political pressure from both ends of Pennsylvania Avenue had any effect, but at the time one said, "It would be nutty to raise rates before Christmas, then find out the economy is weaker than we thought and have to cut rates. That looks bad, especially with Gonzalez on your tail." He said the Fed had to wait for unambiguous evidence of accelerating growth, even though this meant allowing inflationary pressures to build.

The administration was beginning to see the handwriting on the wall. Greenspan had informed Bentsen and others some rates hikes were inevitable and could not be delayed indefinitely. After a long period of no change, a small increase in the funds rate would be salutary, he argued. Clinton was advised to make the best of a small rate hike in the hope it would have a tonic effect in restraining long-term rates. But the administration was determined to keep any rate hikes to a minimum. The line that evolved was that there was no reason for any significant rise in rates. Altman, who would soon resign after misleading Congress on what he had told Clinton about the RTC investigation of Madison Guaranty Trust Company's loans to the Whitewater development, said after the jobs report he did "not see any basis for sustained upward movement of interest rates." Three days later, after meeting with Greenspan, Bentsen said, "I won't try too speak for the chairman of the Federal Reserve, but with this relatively low inflation rate, I don't see any reason for any major increase in interest rates. I don't agree that the Fed has very aggressively lowered interest rates. I think that the underlying economic fundamentals have brought about that reduction in the interest rates and that's the way it ought to be." Bentsen had just refinanced his house with an adjustable rate mortgage and said, "If I thought we were facing a situation of higher interest rates, I wouldn't have done that. What we're seeing is no serious threat of inflation."

By mid-November, it was obvious the economy was headed for a much faster fourth-quarter growth pace. Capacity utilization was beginning to alarm the Fed. It jumped 0.5 percent in October to 82.4 percent; traditionally 82 percent had been regarded as a level beyond which price hikes could be expected to accelerate. Such indicators as the gold price and the yield curve were flashing inflation warnings. But at the November 16 FOMC meeting, a chastened and somewhat paranoid Fed again left funds at 3 percent—a real rate of roughly zero. There was growing sentiment for a token rate hike, or at least a tilt toward tightening to indicate the Fed's vigilance against inflation, but that would not have made dealing with Congress any easier. The directive was left symmetrical. It was agreed "inflation had not changed sufficiently to warrant an adjustment in monetary policy" at that point, but several members were already looking forward to the need to consider a "move from the currently stimulative stance of monetary policy toward a more neutral policy posture, should concerns about rising inflationary pressures begin to be realized." A *neutral* policy stance implied a funds rate above 3 percent. The members generally "recognized the desirability of taking early action to arrest incipient inflationary pressures before they gathered strength, especially given the committee commitment not just to resist greater inflation but to foster sustained progress toward price stability. . . ." But that would have to wait.

Now conscious they were being recorded and that their remarks might be made public, FOMC members were more reticent about going beyond prepared statements in expressing opinions and disagreements. Much of the meeting was devoted to how to appease Gonzalez with his insistent demands for transcripts. Gonzalez had demanded Greenspan hand over past tapes and transcripts immediately, and the day of the meeting he publicly released embarrassing notes he had obtained from Jordan of the October 15 conference call showing Greenspan and other FOMC members talking about how best to handle the as-yet-unrevealed transcripts of past meetings and what to do in the future. On November 17, Greenspan informed Gonzalez the FOMC had decided to release edited transcripts with a five-year lag, saying any earlier release would impede the frank and open discussion that was "essential to sound monetary policy." Early release would "succeed only in stifling originality, new ideas and the give and take debate that so often open up new insights for the FOMC as a whole." Gonzalez branded this response to his demands "wholly inadequate." The five-year delay was "arbitrary and without any rational basis." The Fed still did "not understand the meaning of accountability." He threatened to force the Fed to release the transcripts. "The members of the FOMC are greatly mistaken if they have decided to disregard the committee's demand for those materials." Hardly a day went by that Gonzalez did not unleash a blast at the Fed.

Speculation intensified that the Fed would need to move away from its lax monetary stance. As of the close of trading on Friday, November 19, the yield on the Treasury long bond had risen roughly 60 basis points from its low point just a couple months earlier, and the administration's regularly repeated boast that interest rates were at their lowest levels in 20 years was beginning to ring a bit hollow. Aside from the positive tone of economic data, traders reasoned: The best is behind us, so let's lock in capital gains from 1993's historic rally now. Market psychology was also changing because of a perception the administration had renounced its own budget-cutting promises. In August, the White House had promised more spending cuts to sway wavering Democrats like Senator Bob Kerrey of Nebraska and Congressman Tim Penny of Minnesota to vote for its budget plan. That ballyhooed deficit reduction package was even slimmer on spending cuts than reported at the time. In September, the CBO estimated it would lower the deficit by $433 billion, not $496 billion. But the administration came up with only meager amounts of extra spending cuts. After initially proposing $10 to $12 billion in cuts over five years it was now talking about $37 billion. When Kerrey and a bipartisan group of 14 other senators came up with $109 billion in proposed cuts, one administration official after another warned such cuts would harm the economy and devastate Hillary's health care reform, although her plan was supposed to save money. Penny and Kasich got the same treatment when they put together a similar package of cuts in the House. Meanwhile, Clinton winked at budget-busting efforts by the Democratic leadership. New York Republican congressman Gerald Solomon estimated the president agreed to "pork barrel" projects costing roughly $50 billion in his effort to win votes for the North American Free Trade Agreement (NAFTA). Throughout the bond rally, the administration had maintained yields were falling not because the economy was still soft but because of its fiscal policy. Now that yields were rising, the administration blamed not its fiscal shortcomings but the stronger economy.[9]

The run-up in long rates signaled the Fed it was time to raise short rates. Another sign the zero real funds rate was obsolete came November 22, when the Fed's senior loan officers survey showed the credit crunch was evaporating.

Banks had eased loan terms and standards and become more willing to lend. Demand for credit was up.

The administration chose this moment to add to the Fed's worries with a surprise proposal to strip it of its authority to supervise the nation's largest banks. Both Gonzalez and Riegle had introduced legislation to do that, and now the administration decided it was time to restructure the labyrinthine bank regulatory system by consolidating supervision and regulation into one super regulator: a *Federal Banking Commission*. The Fed, which had long regulated and examined bank holding companies and many state banks, would be left with no bank regulatory authority. Aside from Democratic threats to its monetary independence, nothing could have been more calculated to aggravate the Fed and cow it into compliance with the administration's low rate wishes. Kicking off his proposal with an op-ed article in the *Washington Post*, Bentsen claimed a consolidated banking agency would not affect the Fed's conduct of monetary policy or its operation of the payments system. But Fed officials felt that, unless the Fed had its finger on the pulse of banking through regular examinations and unless it could affect credit availability through regulatory channels, bank regulation might work counter to monetary policy goals at the worst times. They also argued the Fed needed to have firsthand knowledge of the major banks so it could perform its lender-of-last resort function in times of crisis. The Fed also favored preserving the so-called *dual banking system* of state and nationally chartered banks regulated by different agencies.

Reducing duplication of effort in the hydra-headed bank regulatory system made sense. Besides the bank and thrift supervisors in each state there were four federal regulators, who divvied up responsibility for regulating, supervising, and examining the nation's thousands of banks and thrifts. The OCC had charge of nationally chartered banks. The FDIC, aside from insuring nearly all banks, regulated most state-chartered banks. The Fed shepherded the remaining state banks and had supervision of bank holding companies. Finally, there was the Office of Thrift Supervision (OTS), successor agency to the defunct FHLBB, which watched over surviving savings and loans. Often, the Fed found itself treading where a state regulator and/or a federal regulator had already been. So in July, when Greenspan, LaWare, and Undersecretary of Treasury for Domestic Finance Frank Newman were having dinner at Comptroller of the Currency Eugene Ludwig's house, and Ludwig suggested streamlining the system, Greenspan and LaWare were amenable, provided the Fed's role was protected. "We all agreed that some effort to simplify it and make it more logical would be in everybody's best interest," LaWare says, "and so, at the agreement of all concerned shortly after that, Ludwig and I began a series of meetings interspersed with get-togethers between Greenspan and Newman, during which we tried to examine what the basic issues of the organization of the federal regulatory apparatus were and to try to come up with some solutions." Ludwig, like Newman, a Clinton appointee, started with the proposition there should be a single agency. Greenspan and LaWare told him that was unacceptable. There followed a series of meetings involving huge amounts of Fed and Treasury staff time, culminating in a compromise. The FDIC would be largely stripped of its regulatory powers and left as strictly a deposit insurance provider. The OTS would be absorbed by the OCC, which would regulate all nationally chartered institutions. The Fed would retain hegemony over its state-chartered banks, while the OCC would inherit other state banks from the FDIC. Bank holding companies would be regulated by whoever regulated their lead bank.

The Fed thought it had a deal. "Obviously, it sounds like a Chinese puzzle," says LaWare, "but it looked like it preserved the dual banking system and it looked like it would give banks a choice of federal regulators, which we felt was important, not because of competition in laxity but rather complexity in innovation." Having put the finishing touches on the laboriously constructed compromise, Ludwig left LaWare's office the afternoon of Thursday, November 18, after getting LaWare's home phone number in case he needed to consult with him over the weekend as he presented the plan for final approval to Treasury and White House decision makers. LaWare never got a call and assumed it was a go. But on Tuesday, November 23, the Fed was informed by Ludwig and Newman the administration had decided to ditch the two-agency plan. Bentsen was going to announce a proposal for one Federal Banking Commission (FBC) with a five-member board, all named by the president. Greenspan and LaWare felt betrayed. "We were quite surprised and somewhat dismayed by the fact that this sounded like something very different than what we'd been working on—certainly more like the proposal that had been put on the table which we could not accept," says LaWare. "Alan just dug in his heels and said we're just going to use up some of our influence to try to scotch this thing."

An energized Greenspan was determined not to give in to this joint administration-Hill effort to subjugate the Fed. On November 23, he ordered the issuance of a rare Fed statement opposing the Bentsen proposal: "It is the long-held conviction of the Board that a hands-on role in banking supervision is essential to carrying out the Federal Reserve's responsibilities for the stability of the financial system and is vital for the effective conduct of monetary policy. While the Board recognizes the overlaps in bank supervision that have emerged in recent years, it is essential that any proposal for change preserves the important benefits of the current system." There ensued a battle of op-ed pieces, speeches, and testimony. In a December 15 *Wall Street Journal* article, Greenspan wrote, "Certainly a major factor in our decision to ease interest rates from 1989 on was our increasing awareness, importantly gained through the examination process, that banks were rapidly tightening their lending terms and standards." Without "our hands-on bank supervisory activities, we might not have been aware of the seriousness of this problem until later." There was another unstated reason for the Fed to be concerned. What Bentsen was proposing was a bank regulator, run by presidential appointees, which would be under the thumb of the executive and subject to political pressure—whether to encourage easy credit policies or to quash investigations of embarrassing insider loans. A single regulator under the influence of the executive could conceivably promulgate lenient capital requirements and pursue lax examination procedures to spur lending when the Fed was trying to restrict credit or vice versa.

Gonzalez rushed to support the Bentsen proposal, and an aide scoffed at the Fed's contention it needed hands-on involvement in bank supervision, maintaining monetary policy "would be improved if it weren't doing regulation." The Fed could rely on examination reports prepared by the new FBC. On the contrary, a Fed official told me, "secondhand knowledge is not sufficient. When you have a crisis and you have to get information and know what's going on, if you don't have people who understand a bank and its balance sheet you can't get up to speed by reading somebody else's report."

The administration's regulatory gambit looked like a transparent effort to gain further leverage over monetary policy. It was almost as if Clinton and his advisers had sat around and asked, "What can we do to terrorize the Fed into being more cooperative?" Charitably, Greenspan does not see it that way, but merely as an administration effort to control the bank regulatory apparatus. LaWare feels likewise: "I don't think it was so much of a vendetta against the Fed, but when they got going on that path they simply didn't want to share the thing, and I think they had always squirmed under the fact that a bank holding company, regardless of what the lead bank was or what any of the banks was, was under the supervision of the Fed." But Fed officials had to wonder, if Clinton was capable of backing the Gonzalez-Riegle bill to take away the Fed's supervisory powers, might he not back their bills to disenfranchise Fed presidents, end its budgetary independence, and so forth? A top Clinton adviser says the proposal was motivated purely by a desire to streamline regulation and says the decision to revert to a single regulator after agreeing to a dual-regulator compromise was not aimed at influencing interest rates. Administration and Fed officials say the fight over Fed regulatory authority soured their relationship somewhat thereafter. If the administration was serious about regulatory consolidation on its merits, it had a funny way of showing it. After a six-month cat-and-mouse game, it quietly dropped the whole idea. Gonzalez moved on to other forms of Fed harassment.[10]

Meanwhile, the administration kept pumping out antitightening rhetoric. The economy was in "a very good phase"—recovering but not generating inflation, Rubin said on December 1. When the Labor Department reported a seldom-seen 0.4 percent plunge in unemployment to 6.4 percent two days later (lowest since January 1991, accompanied by a substantial rise in manufacturing and other jobs and a rise in the average work week), Kelley told me the Fed was now on a "vigilant" watch for price pressures. But Tyson downplayed the good unemployment news as "just one month's number." There were still downside risks. It was up to the Fed to "look at what signs the economy is giving about the underlying rate of inflation," but "we don't see anything to suggest" higher inflation. Inflation would increase a bit in 1994, which would cause the market to push up short-term rates, but no more than a half percent. In fact, the Fed would raise rates 2½ percent by the end of 1994 and 3 percent by February 1995.

On December 7, Pearl Harbor Day, Mullins, who had led the charge for the steep rate cuts of two years earlier, dropped his annual bomb—the clearest signal yet that the days of 3 percent funds were numbered. Monetary policy was "at a crossroads." It was time for the Fed to reconsider its "accommodative stance." While it was true inflation was still under control and while there were still "contractionary influences" at work, the Fed could not afford to be complacent. "Early warning signals are starting to twitch," among them rising bond yields, commodity prices and money supply. The Fed had to be particularly wary of rising bond yields because "the only stimulative component in the current economic environment remains the capital market environment. If inflation starts moving and interest rates move up it hurts not only long-term growth prospects but likely hurts near-term growth prospects." The Fed could not afford to wait until inflation actually appeared, because "once inflationary pressures are clearly visible, . . . once you can see clearly the visible signs, it's awfully late." Therefore, "it's time to carefully assess developing trends and balance risks, and that's what we're doing."

But other officials were sending conflicting signals. The same day, Kelley said that, while the Fed did not want to "get behind the curve" on inflation, he did "not see any definitive indications" of inflation, and there was "still a good deal of slack in the economy." He did "not believe the Fed will make a preemptive move" against inflation but would "have to see more conclusive evidence" of rising inflation before tightening credit. The Fed would have to weigh the need to head off inflation against the need to sustain growth and "make a judgement call." Forrestal was opposed to a "preemptive strike" against inflation. He wanted to see "evidence inflation is in fact becoming a problem. . . . We are in a period, and will be in a period for some time to come, of moderate growth with low inflation." Market participants were confused and skeptical. Some recalled that in December 1991, Mullins had implied the Fed was finished easing—just ten days before it cut the discount rate a full percent at his urging. As if to prove the skeptics right, Mullins said on December 9 there was no compelling evidence of inflation pressure, and the Fed was "not on the precipice" of tightening. Some FOMC members worried all the talk about "preemptive strikes" against inflation could create an inflationary psychology and a self-fulfilling prophecy. Too much talk about improved growth leading automatically to inflation could create a climate in which businesses tried to make higher prices stick, leading to an upward spiral of prices and wages that would force the Fed to act. Although the CPI rose just 0.2 percent overall and 0.3 percent in November, producer price numbers bore out concerns inflation was in the pipeline. Core finished goods prices rose 0.4 percent, and crude goods prices rose 1.7 percent. Bond yields rose further on the news.

I found myself across the table from President Clinton as part of a group of reporters called to the White House for a round of briefings December 14, a week before a crucial FOMC meeting. When I asked him how he felt about indications the Fed was about to raise rates to preempt inflation, Clinton said, "It would be a mistake because there is no inflation threat in this economy. Core inflation is down at quite a low level. Energy prices have fallen so much that overall inflation is quite low, wages are not going up very much, and unemployment is still well over 6 percent. So there is no indication of a return of inflation, and we need more jobs and higher income. Until a combination of employment, economic activity and rising wages presents some real threat of an inflation rate that is too high, it would be inappropriate for us to choke off a recovery that has already had a false start or two and didn't move forward in earnest until this past year." He claimed his deficit reduction plan had laid the foundation for economic expansion "without inflation." Besides, "no one can say with a straight face that 6.4 percent unemployment is a good rate for America." Asked whether it would be appropriate for the Fed to act preemptively to tighten credit before inflation actually showed up, Clinton said, "I just think that right now we don't need it. I would hate to see us take another step back in the first two quarters of next year. We need sustained, disciplined growth. If we really get to the point where growth gets so robust . . . there will be ample time to make corrections without having to go to a restrictive policy." A top White House staffer tried to downplay Clinton's remarks, observing there were different points of view within the administration about Fed policy and often what Clinton said on economics was derived from "the last person who saw the president," but it was not an isolated remark.[11]

Clinton told us he fully supported the Fed's independence but backed Bentsen's call for eliminating the Fed's bank regulatory role, despite the Fed's vehement opposition. He had earlier said he was "deeply sympathetic" with congressional efforts to make the Fed more "accountable." Clinton's comments were part of a coordinated effort to keep the Fed on hold. Bentsen, Rubin, and Tyson gave us the same message when asked whether the Fed needed to preempt inflation. Bentsen said he was "quite comfortable with the numbers as they are now. In so far as capacity utilization is concerned, there is sufficient play there, and I don't see any pressure there. Even at 6.4 percent unemployment we have a surplus of people willing to work, and that keeps any serious threat of inflation from being anything to be concerned about. I look for sustained low interest rates both in the short-term and the long-term." Tyson said, "Inflation remains moderate and subdued." Rubin said that with "overcapacity" in the United States and abroad "there doesn't seeem to me to be any basis for thinking inflation is going to reignite and in fact I think it will be very moderate. The economy can absorb any rate of growth that seems likely without reigniting inflation." Bentsen said he was "very much interested in the Federal Reserve continuing as an independent agency and having access to information," but said the Fed could get by without its own bank examination reports.

It was obvious Angell was not going to be renominated by Clinton when his term expired at the end of January, and although he had not formally announced his intention to retire, Clinton told us he intended to replace Angell with someone "who understands that we don't want to get ourselves back into the position of the late 1970s and early 1980s" when inflation was at double digits, "but neither do we want to cure inflation at the expense of chronic recession." His appointee would "have to be sensitive to the obligation not to let the economy get out of hand," but also willing to "let the economy get into gear." Rubin wanted someone "with a sense of reasonableness," not "an extremist who wants zero inflation and anytime inflation is above zero gets upset."

As the FOMC meeting drew closer, Bentsen continued to jawbone against near-term Fed rate hikes. Dismissing Fed inflation concerns December 16, he said, "Some of their predictions have not exactly been on target. I also get concerned about any tightening up and raising interest rates if you don't see inflation as a threat. I'm comfortable with where we are right now." The economy was merely experiencing "gradual, sustainable increases in growth with low inflation. Over the long term—remember I said over the long term—you're going to see a gradual increase in short-term rates, and the situation is right now I'm comfortable with short-term rates." Bentsen also continued to press his case for ending the "Balkanization" of banking regulation and didn't particularly care if the Fed liked it or not. He "would like to have" the Fed's support for regulatory consolidation, but "I don't consider it essential. Both banking committees are very interested in reform." Ignoring the Fed's substantive reasons for wanting to continue regulating banks, he said the Fed was merely "defending its turf."

What it all boiled down to was that the administration's much proclaimed respect for the Fed's independence was pure hypocrisy. It would respect the Fed's independence only so long as it kept rates where it wanted them. The administration and the Democratic Hill leadership were like Tweedle Dee and Tweedle Dum, although the latter were more shrill. In a joint letter to Greenspan in advance of the FOMC meeting, Sarbanes and Sasser asserted it was "incomprehensible" that the Fed would consider raising interest rates "despite the absence of inflationary pressures. . . . It would be a tragedy. . . ."

An annoyed Greenspan penned a hard-hitting letter to Gonzalez on December 16 angrily denying allegations he and other Fed officials had lied to the committee and complaining Gonzalez had refused to meet with him to discuss the transcript issue. Far from conceal the taping and transcribing of FOMC meetings, he claimed he had volunteered it at the October 19 hearing. "I am unable to understand how you could suggest that we concealed this information. . . . You have made statements on this subject that I believe are inaccurate and that might have been avoided had we spoken personally. Had you agreed to meet, I would have assured you once more that I and the other members of the FOMC have not made any false statements to you or to the Banking Committee." He repeated his opposition to early release of the transcripts. It "would do serious damage to the deliberative process of the FOMC and its ability to conduct the monetary policy of this nation." Why did Gonzalez want to "single out" the Fed when other agenies also discussed sensitive matters in private. If anything, the FOMC "releases more information about sensitive deliberations—in the form of minutes—more than any comparable body in our government."[12]

The Fed went into its December 21 FOMC meeting under more than the usual amount of fog about its intentions, amplified by the politically charged atmosphere which had been created. Out of nowhere, the day of the meeting, Bentsen said he did not think Greenspan should resign because of his differences with the administration. With the president publicly warning the Fed not to raise rates, his Treasury secretary trying to take away a key Fed prerogative, and Congress threatening to limit its policy latitude, Fed officials were especially attuned to the need to justify any tightening. If this was a friendly administration, who needed enemies? While vowing not to bend to pressure, Fed officials acknowledged they would need to be able to point either to increasing prices or accelerating activity. The upshot was that, despite urgent appeals for credit tightening, the Fed again left policy unchanged. In fact, the FOMC did not even adopt a tightening bias. While officials had sincere reservations about raising rates, it is hard to believe group thinking was not influenced by the mix of intimidation, cooption, and propaganda Clinton and congressional Democrats had employed.

It is hard to otherwise explain how the policymakers managed to justify continuing to hold the funds rate at recession levels. There was strong sentiment for a more restrictive credit stance. Lindsey and Angell dissented in favor of an immediate rate hike. Others wanted at least a tightening bias. "Many of the members commented that the committee probably would have to firm reserve conditions at some point to adjust monetary policy from its currently quite accommodative stance to a more neutral position, and that such a policy move might have to be made sooner rather than later to contain inflation and continue to provide a sound basis for sustained economic expansion," the minutes state. It was observed that "downside risks to the expansion had diminished considerably" and that "borrowers and lenders had strengthened their financial positions substantially. . . . Moreover, the low level of real short-term interest rates and in the view of some members the continued rapid growth of reserves or increases in a variety of commodity prices provided evidence of a quite accommodative monetary policy. Overstaying such a policy would incur an increasing risk of fostering greater inflationary pressures that in turn would undermine the sustainability of the expansion." But it was decided the Fed would wait to see whether fourth-quarter strength carried over into the first quarter, in part because "any tightening move would represent a turn in policy that might well have a greater-than-usual effect on financial markets." Many Fed watchers saw political capitulation.

Most disappointing was Mullins's retreat in the face of fire. After saying the Fed had reached "a crossroads" at which it was time to "reassess" the Fed's "accommodative" policy before it was "too late" to prevent inflation, he had completely changed his tune by the time of the meeting. Had the administration gotten to the former Democrat from Arkansas, some wondered. The week before the FOMC meeting, Mullins had expressed concern about Gonzalez's bill, in particular its requirement that the Fed immediately release transcripts of its meetings. He told the *Washington Post* the Fed needed to deal with the issue and "get it fixed once and for all." When the Fed had to take "unpleasant, politically unpopular actions," it couldn't afford to have them challenged on the grounds of Fed secrecy rather than their merits.

Some FOMC members regret not having raised rates in late 1993. "If you want to talk about second guessing yourself, what I would have done was change directions and start going back up sooner than February of '94," says one. "In the light of hindsight and what we've seen happen subsequently I would have turned monetary policy around maybe in November of '93 instead of February of '94." But he defends the delay. "I think a decision is a good decision if, in hindsight, it still makes sense in the light of what you knew at the time the decision was made." At the time, "we did not know yet the durability of that surge we were getting into there, and it didn't become clear until late January of '94 that the economy was still moving forward very strongly and that we were in an incipient financial bubble that was in danger of getting away from us. And I think it would have been better, knowing what we know, if we had done that earlier. . . . Some members of our own group criticized us for not having started earlier. But I think that we started as early as we responsibly could myself. . . . In the light of what was known at the time, to have gone much earlier would have been a gamble." As for whether political pressure delayed easing, he declares, "I would absolutely not agree with that." Nor would Greenspan. He was bothered by public administration statements on Fed policy but tried not to let them influence monetary policy. He worked to discourage the running commentary on what the Fed should or should not do, and as the administration matured, he was glad to see it become less frequent.

That key elements of the executive and legislative branches of the Democratically controlled government were trying to manipulate monetary policy is beyond doubt. The extent to which there was a well-mapped-out and coordinated strategy is less clear. Bentsen says that, as far as he was concerned, "I wanted to retain the independence of the Fed." While there were some in the administration who were content to see the Fed twist in the wind awhile in the face of congressional threats, "that was not my position." A senior White House staffer acknowledges there was discussion between the administration and sponsors of the various Fed reform bills and that, while the White House provided little active encouragement, it did little to discourage them. Clinton did not explicitly oppose the Gonzalez and other Fed-bashing bills because he wanted to "leave open the option" of supporting them in the future.

It's impossible to measure how much impact congressional threats and the possibility of eventual administration support had. Fed officials vociferously deny that either Hill threats or White House blandishments affected their actions and insist there were perfectly good reasons to keep rates as low as they did as long as they did. They make light of the pressure they were then under. "No, I really don't believe that had an effect on monetary policy," says LaWare. "I really believe that we pursued monetary policy as we thought it ought to be pursued at the time, irrespective of the political pressures from one side or another, as we were going forward." Although Greenspan left the impression he had struck a deal with Clinton, there was none. As for threats from the Hill, "I don't think in any showdown vote that they would have the capability of really emasculating the Fed as to its independence." Riegle, Sarbanes, and Sasser were taken seriously, but Gonzalez "has been an embarrassment even to his own colleagues in the House. He's talked about the usual populist arguments about a great, big, secret organization affecting everybody's life and so forth and so on. And I don't think anybody pays any attention. There were a lot of arrows flying but none of them were anywhere near the target."

Phillips recalls "a lot of hearings, Fed bashing" and rate cut demands, but doubts it had much effect. "If you actually looked at how many people showed up at those hearings, you have to question how much broad interest there was in that proposed legislation. My impression was this was not something that had broad support in the committee, subcommittee or the Congress generally. So we recognized that." The Fed had no choice but to "respond to these loads of legislative inquiries that were coming in, but we also recognized that it appeared to be very strongly held views by some people, but not very widely held views. So I think that we all tried to put that into perspective and respond as best we could. I think that this was a case where there were a lot of folks on the Hill who weren't voicing their opinions but simply didn't agree with those kinds of positions. . . . It is in any administration's interest to have an independent Fed. If things are going well that's good for them. It's going to reflect on the administration. If things are going badly they can blame the Fed." Angell does not "believe that the chief factor has ever been the political influence." As long as the Fed had a consensus "we were really able to do what we needed to do." He doubts there was much collaboration between Clinton and Democrats in Congress. "I mean Senator Sarbanes, how in the world can a Democrat President control those rascals? I mean those guys—so you really can't put it down as a total kind of conspiracy to do the Fed in. What you have is a lot of independent players, and you have the Democrats in Congress harassing the Fed, an on-again, off-again deal, and I suppose it's always there, that if the Fed makes a mistake and has a recession, you're going to get that, and everybody at the Fed knows that's there."

McDonough says he did "not have any impression that there was a good cop/bad cop combination going on," a view shared by Greenspan, who always managed to remain on friendly terms with Clinton, his senior advisers, and people like Riegle and Sarbanes. "If that was their strategy, I don't think that was what was driving policy," says Lindsey. "I can't tell whether it had a subliminal effect." McTeer "doubt[s] that the rhetoric from Mr. Gonzalez, while it caused anxiety and consternation and so forth, had an impact" on keeping the funds rate at 3 percent. "The timing was just coincidental. . . . The economy, and in retrospect the banking system, needed that, and I don't think there was any connection between that and Mr. Gonzalez's issues." On the other hand, "the criticism coming from the Senate side—the Sarbanes, Riegle, Sasser group—I don't mean to imply that their threats had an effect on policy, but their criticism had more to do with policy than Mr. Gonzalez's. Mr. Gonzalez just doesn't like banking in general and the central bank in particular, and to me it didn't seem to have much to do with what policy was, but with the others, their goal seemed to be to get us to ease." Whatever their motivation, "policy was what it was independent of all that."

But a congressional source observes, "It did seem like after that [threat to the Fed's independence] we got a lot of cooperation." One fact is undeniable: Throughout 1993 and into 1994, the Fed kept both the discount rate and the federal funds rate at 3 percent, long past what many thought was prudent given an increasingly expansive economy. To conclude absolutely that the combination of White House pampering and congressional persecution succeeded in keeping the funds rate down would be to fall prey to *post hoc, ergo propter hoc* logic, but one would be hard-pressed to find another period where the Fed resisted the temptation to tinker with the funds rate for 17 months. There was at least the appearance the Fed had been alternately wooed and walloped into holding rates down. The Fed was successful in defeating the administration regulatory consolidation plan with the help of lobbying by bankers, and the Fed got even by organizing bankers to defeat administration efforts to make more onerous the Community Reinvestment Act's rules on what banks must do in the inner cities. It convinced enough pols it was not in their interest to take on responsibility for the bad, as well as the good, effects of monetary policy. However, it had to make major concessions on disclosure. And it all took its toll—this death of a thousand cuts inflicted by the White House and Congress. At the very least, fighting off regulatory restructuring and other proposals was a big distraction from the Fed's main mission.

If the Clinton team had learned from Bush that it was counterproductive to be too brazen about bashing the Fed they had not learned the lesson that it is counterproductive to bash the dollar. Despite its denials, the administration from the start used dollar depreciation as a tool of trade. Democrat LaWare credits the Clinton administration for being "very responsible about monetary policy," but adds, "on the other hand, on the dollar it's a different story. Here was Bentsen. Whether he really understood what he was saying or not, about 'We have to get the dollar down,' I think he was focused on the trade implications of that. And at the other end of the spectrum was Rubin's statement [in October 1995] that a strong dollar is in everybody's interest, blah-blah-blah, without committing himself as to what is a strong dollar." Since the dollar's purchasing power was ultimately in the Fed's safekeeping, the Clinton weak dollar policy was an indirect slap at the Fed, and it was not pleased to hear Bentsen and others talking down the dollar. As 1933 wore on, the Fed became aggravated by this policy. Its public utterances were relatively mild and few, but the Fed privately made clear it did not like the weak dollar rhetoric.

Supposedly, Clinton and his "new Democrats" were going to pursue hard money policies. When I spoke to one of Clinton's key campaign advisers, who would later become chief architect of his international monetary policy, a month before the 1992 election and asked him whether a Clinton administration would favor a weak dollar to advance U.S. trade interests, he said, "It would be hard to bash the dollar harder than Brady has been bashing it over the past year." No, a Clinton administration would be "pretty careful" in its management of exchange rates. But it proved to be an empty promise, to the

Fed's dismay. Even before Clinton took office, it was obvious his administration would go Brady one better in pounding the dollar down. In a December 7, 1992, interview, a member of the Clinton transition team told me the administration would have to be on guard against a stronger dollar. Recovery "could spark a dollar rally. The danger is that the dollar goes too far on the upside; it's not hard to foresee the dollar rising to counterproductive levels by early summer." Were that to happen "it would behoove the Clinton administration to keep the dollar from getting excessively strong and to use G-7 coordination to that end."

It is rare for a president-elect to talk about exchange rates, but not for "policy wonk" Clinton. During his marathon economic conference in Little Rock on December 17, 1992, Clinton made clear there were limits to how much dollar strength he was willing to tolerate. "I'm for a strong dollar if it is supported by the competitive realities of our underlying economy." What Clinton was saying, according to a source close to his economic team, was that "until a strong dollar is justified by competitiveness, a strong dollar is something that should be regarded as a problem." As a senator, Bentsen had sometimes been an outspoken proponent of a weak dollar. In 1989, he had called for a 10 percent dollar drop. A key campaign adviser was C. Fred Bergsten, who as Carter's assistant Treasury secretary for international affairs, had presided over a deliberate dollar depreciation and had consistently advocated a weaker dollar in the years since as head of the Washington-based Institute for International Economics. He would continue to exercise influence in the Clinton administration as an informal adviser with close ties to former Vice President Walter Mondale, whom Clinton named ambassador to Japan. Bergsten never ceased calling for a sharply lower dollar-yen rate. Another adviser was MIT Professor Rudiger Dornbusch, who told the Little Rock Conference, "We certainly cannot afford a stronger dollar." The Fed "should be committed to not raising interest rates just because they see growth, and to let that fact be known. Only if they let it be known can we avoid an unproductive dollar rally." At that point the dollar was hovering around 123 yen and 1.60 marks per dollar, up from a September all-time low of 1.38 marks. Dornbusch told me he was convinced Clinton "would not let the dollar get out of line." That proved to be true only on the upside. The dollar would get badly out of line on the downside and complicate the Fed's job.

At his January 12, 1993, confirmation hearing, Bentsen seemed to favor a strong dollar. "Some people say we should devalue the dollar," Bentsen told the Senate Finance Committee, but the dollar's value "should be based on market forces—on the productivity of the country, on its fiscal responsibility, on its interest rates." Moving too fast to reduce the budget deficit could cause "a run on the dollar" that would force up interest rates to defend it. But it soon became clear that, at least against the yen, Bentsen did not want a strong dollar. The administration was preparing for a trade war with Japan, and it was decided the dollar had to depreciate sharply against the yen to reduce the large trade deficit with that country ($46.9 billion in 1992). On February 12, Bentsen discussed trade and exchange rate issues with Japanese finance minister Yoshiro Hayashi, and a Japanese official said the two had merely agreed the dollar-yen exchange rate "should reflect fundamentals." A week later Bentsen told the National Press Club, "I'd like to see a stronger yen." The yen had already risen some 5 yen against the dollar and was trading between 119 and 120 yen per dollar before Bentsen's speech. Bentsen's Friday afternoon declaration caused the yen to surge to 115.94 on Monday, and that was just the beginning. Japan was alarmed. "I don't think that far and rapid an appreciation is justified given the relative strength of our economies and interest rate differentials," a Japanese monetary source confided. "We would like a gradual appreciation of the yen . . . [but] if it is rapidly appreciating it's going to be destabilizing."

Bentsen had been advised by other members of the Clinton economic team that if the U.S. current account deficit with Japan was to be reduced, the dollar would need to fall, but did not want to call for a weaker dollar, so instead made a "flippant remark" about wanting a "stronger yen," without foreseeing the full consequences, says a close associate. Bentsen has few apologies for his exhortation. "What I said at that time, I also meant," he says, "but I must tell you at that moment I had not fully accepted the differences between my comments as a Senator and my comments as Treasury secretary." There was a feeling within the administration the dollar needed to decline significantly, at least against the yen, and Bentsen admits, "I was sympathetic to that at that point, but it went beyond what it should."

Clinton policy toward Japan was a mass of contradictions. The administration was simultaneously calling upon Japan to stimulate its economy and strengthen the yen. With Japan's once vibrant economy sinking deeper into recession, it wanted Japan to stimulate its economy through additional fiscal and monetary measures, thereby theoretically inducing greater demand for foreign goods and reducing the trade surplus. But cutting interest rates was not likely to contribute to a stronger yen. And if the yen were to go on strengthening, the result would be to further weaken the Japanese economy and demand for exports. This is just what happened. At a February 27 G-7 meeting in London, Bentsen said he would prefer stimulus measures to yen appreciation as a way to cut Japan's trade surplus, and said he would prefer fiscal over monetary stimulus, because it would work faster. But Hayashi said Japan had "no intention [of adopting] further stimulus measures" on top of the $88 billion stimulus plan it had adopted in 1992 and the $120 billion stimulus plan then under consideration.

Although Bentsen abstained from further talking up the yen in London, the administration had not abandoned exchange rate manipulation as a tool for achieving its trade goals. Lawrence Summers, who had been designated Bentsen's undersecretary of Treasury for international affairs, said on March 23 that "exchange rate movements do and should reflect movements in fundamental values" and added "exchange rates must not be thought of as policy instruments." In fact, the administration was cheering on the dollar's depreciation against the yen, which took it to 112.75 by mid-April. A source told me, "Treasury has been very quiet and satisfied with the yen's appreciation." In advance of a visit by Japanese prime minister Kiichi Miyazawa, Japanese Ambassador Takakazu Kuriyama said the yen's "sudden" rise "does not help the Japanese economy" and therefore could actually increase its trade surplus. At a press conference following his April 16 meeting with Miyazawa, Clinton removed any doubt about his dollar policy when he listed yen appreciation as "number one" among factors he expected to reduce the deficit with Japan. The dollar promptly fell further to a record low of 110.75 yen per dollar. A few days later it had fallen below the psychologically important 110 level. Some put Clinton's damaging comment down to inexperience. But it was part of a pattern of comments that continued for months. The administration waited 11 days before doing anything to clear up the impression Clinton had left.

At the Fed, the dollar's escalating slide was raising hackles. Kelley, in an April 23 interview, said he was "not pleased to see the dollar going down as rapidly as it has been against the yen." At that point it had dropped to a new all-time low of 109.58 yen. Rather than weaken the dollar to reduce the trade deficit, "I would hope that we can address that imbalance more through a stronger two-way exchange of real goods and services than have our currency depreciate so much that it winds up being adjusted on the currency side." Kelley was not alone. Another Fed source said the administration had been engaging in trade "brinkmanship" with Japan by encouraging the dollar's fall. Treasury officials were hoping to isolate the dollar's weakness against the yen and keep it from spreading to other currencies, but that was a risky proposition in the Fed's view. The danger was that dollar weakness could become more general. "It's hard to get one cross-rate moving independently of the world structure of exchange rates," said a senior Fed official. Pushing the dollar down as a trade weapon was "a road easier to get going down than to stay down. If you start at the presidential level leading down that road, then you have trouble referring it to subordinates at a later date. It's hard to understand the advice that would lead to that [Clinton] statement." For some Fed officials the dollar's weakness was another reason to resist calls for lower interest rates, but that seemed lost on the administration.

The Fed's concerns were only temporarily and partially heeded and then only because the administration began to worry that its desire for a weaker dollar was starting to conflict with a more important goal—keeping long-term interest rates low. After falling from 7.4 percent at the time of the election to as low as 6.4 percent, the yield on long-term Treasuries was back up to 6.6 percent in late April amid speculation continued dollar weakness would erode foreign investor demand for Treasury securities. In an April 27 appearance before a Senate Foreign Operations Subcommittee, Bentsen claimed it was a "misperception" the administration was pursuing a weak dollar policy. Exchange rates should "reflect economic fundamentals" and should not be "artificially inflated or manipulated." That morning, under heavy pressure from its G-7 partners, the Treasury had the Fed intervene to support the dollar. It recovered from an all-time low of 109.25 back up to 111.60. Summers said Clinton's comments about yen appreciation being a key to reducing the trade deficit had been misperceived. In fact, it was "not the policy of this administration to artificially manipulate exchange rates." The United States was "ready to cooperate in exchange markets with our G-7 partners as conditions may warrant" to prevent "excessive volatility." He repeated administration demands that Japan reduce its trade surplus. Under the circumstances, Bentsen's and Summer's comments were the bare minimum needed to stop the dollar's slide, and to some they seemed not only belated, but half-hearted and insincere. A source close to the administration told me Bentsen's comments were mostly "a conciliatory gesture in advance of the G-7 meeting . . . a tactical and short-term oriented measure." As the administration kept hitting Japan with increasingly hostile rhetoric, punctuated by hints about the desirability of a weaker yen-dollar rate, a perception was created that the administration wanted the dollar to fall much further. When they weren't making public comments, officials were making no secret of their desires privately. The same day Bentsen and Summers issued their denials of deliberate dollar depreciation, I was told the administration would not mind seeing the dollar go as low as 105 yen per dollar and would only be concerned "if it moved rapidly to that territory." Treasury had been generally happy with the yen's rise so far and merely wanted to be sure further moves were gradual.

When the G-7 finance ministers and central bankers concluded their April 29 meeting with a reiteration of their "commitment to close cooperation in exchange markets" and opposition to "excessive volatility" in currencies, the markets took it as an indication the leading G-7 nation, the United States, was not serious about staunching the dollar's bleeding. There was an air of smugness about U.S. officials' comments on the dollar. The day before the G-7 meeting, Bentsen was asked about his call for "a stronger yen" in February and jocularly told reporters, "Well, it looks like those remarks turned out very timely." In supporting G-7 injunctions against "excessive volatility" and "cooperation on exchange markets," Bentsen and Summers were not contradicting earlier statements that had precipitated the dollar drop. They refused to say whether the G-7 communiqué implied a floor for the dollar against the yen, below which the United States would take steps to support the dollar. There were no assertions from the Treasury or the White House that the dollar had fallen enough or had fallen to "appropriate" or "competitive" levels or other statements of the type used in the past to oppose adverse dollar trends. To say "excessive volatility" was undesirable was not to say the dollar should not fall further. It was no accident the administration chose the language it did. The semantic significance was not lost on the markets. Nor did the intervention the Fed undertook April 27 "represent an administration effort to draw a line in the sand or to define the upper limits of the yen," said a source, who said further dollar depreciation against the yen would be welcomed if it was orderly.

As far as Bentsen was concerned he had "cleared the air" on the yen-dollar question. With some tutelage from the Fed, the Treasury refrained from dollar bashing for a while. It was made clear to Bentsen that, given its reserve currency status, a weak dollar could cause havoc in the financial markets and drive up long-term interest rates. But, to Greenspan's chagrin, other officials felt free to pursue an open mouth policy on exchange rates. Commerce Secretary Ron Brown, notably, appeared to have been given free rein to talk about the dollar's value as it related to the trade deficit, and the currency markets took notice. On May 13, after his department announced a jump in April retail sales, Brown said a 3.1 percent rise in auto sales and rise in the market share of domestic automakers was "evidence that the administration's willingness to let the dollar find a competitive, market-driven exchange rate on world markets will have an important payoff for domestic manufacturers." Four days later, Brown railed against Japan's trade surplus. Without mentioning the dollar specifically, he said the administration would use "every vehicle at our disposal" to persuade Japan to reduce its surplus. Brown's comments might ordinarily have been innocuous, but given the administration's record of seeking a stronger yen, they were viewed in a different light. To currency traders it sounded like another veiled threat to use a weak dollar to gain trade concessions from Japan. "It seems this policy of accepting, endorsing and condoning a stronger yen is very much in place," said one. Instead of disavowing Brown's remarks, a Treasury spokesman simply said, "We have nothing to add." The dollar fell from around 112.5 yen to 111 yen after Brown's comments.

On May 19, Brown was at it again. After his department announced the deficit with Japan had jumped from $4.1 billion to $5.3 billion in March, he said that "we must correct this imbalance" through "market-driven exchange rate corrections," as well as through "prompt fiscal stimulus in Japan" and "negotiations that remove the structural barriers to improved trade between our nations." This time, the dollar fell below 110 yen before rebounding near 111. Summers refrained from echoing Brown's comments, but neither did he disavow them. He said the wider trade deficit showed the "urgent need" for Japan to stimulate its economy. Brown's implications that the dollar needed to fall further against the yen were not disavowed because they accurately reflected the administration's desire to see the dollar continue to sink. Brown's comments were "consistent with the general administration approach" on exchange rates and were "useful" in promoting the goal of a stronger yen, a source confided. So long as the dollar did not fall so rapidly it disrupted financial markets, the administration was happy to see it depreciate. Brown's comments "would be inconsistent only in a situation where the dollar-yen rate was at a record level and the administration was trying to slow the appreciation. Then you would have a clash, but we're not in that situation." A Brown aide said he had not been asked to stop talking about the dollar and saw no inconsistencies between Brown's comments and administration policy. Brown would feel free to continue to call for "exchange rate corrections." On May 24, Brown said exchange rates were "a Treasury matter" but exchange rate adjustments were part of the solution to the deficit with Japan. "The Japanese economy has proven resilient" to the more expensive yen and that was "why much greater changes in exchange rates haven't had the same effect as in the past," implying a need for yet larger dollar declines.

Brown said the administration needed to "work with the Federal Reserve" because its policies "could be undercut by the Federal Reserve." But key Fed officials felt the administraton's undisciplined exchange rate rhetoric was undercutting its policy of stabilizing the purchasing power of the dollar by eroding confidence in it around the world. They wished Brown and others would unite around a sound dollar policy. It had to have been clear to the administration by now that its loose talk was unnerving the markets. But the administration kept pushing its luck. On May 25, the Treasury issued an exchange rate report which, while it repeated G-7 boilerplate exhortations against "excessive volatility" and currency "manipulation," said the Japanese surplus would fall if the yen's rise was "sustained." Predictably, the dollar sold off. Summers's plea that the Treasury had not intended to signal a desire for a stronger yen and his assertion that "you cannot devalue yourself into prosperity" were disbelieved. The next day, Summers and Rubin scrambled to contain the damage. Rubin, who behind the scenes had been counseling a hawkish trade stance that included driving up the yen, said, "Talking down the dollar is not part of this administration's economic policy." Summers maintained the report had been misinterpreted and that there had been "absolutely no intention to signal any alteration of U.S. policy toward exchange rates." In fact, "the U.S. is not seeking a further appreciation of the Japanese yen." For an administration supposedly laden with Wall Street acumen, some were astonished how little its officials seemed to understand the impact of their comments. In reality, they understood all too well.

By May 27, the dollar had fallen to a new all-time low of 107.65 yen, and Summers was forced finally to say the dollar had fallen "too far, too fast." It was the kind of statement that should have been made long before, but then that might have stemmed the yen's rise too soon. What forced the change in rhetoric was a change in the administration's bond market fortunes. Long-term Treasury yields were back near 6¼ percent by the time Summers made his statement. Gold had surged to $383.40 an ounce, highest since January 1991. His comments had only limited effect. In early June, the dollar sank to 106 yen, riling Japanese authorities trying to stimulate their trade-oriented economy, as the U.S. had demanded. The yen had risen "too far, too much," Akira Nagashima, executive director of the Bank of Japan, said. "Certainly the current mood in the markets is not based on fundamentals, but on expectations of future talks with the U.S. on the trade balance."

A senior administration official who cooperated in the writing of this book was quite explicit in acknowledging that the administration was only concerned about dollar weakness to the extent it hurt the bond market. "When the dollar was showing its greatest weakness what we were all looking for were signs that this might represent a threat to other financial markets, . . . and so long as it was just sort of the dollar being weak and wasn't a suggestion that somehow or other we were on the brink of a big asset sell-off we didn't worry." The Fed remained uncomfortable about administration dollar policy. "It's bad when exchange rates change too rapidly," Kelley said on June 8. On June 22, Syron said, "It's one of those things, I'm not saying it's a matter of great concern, but we always have to watch. The earlier dollar drop led to some increase in prices for Japanese products and provided an umbrella for U.S. producers" to raise prices.

Then came the Tokyo Economic Summit, where President Clinton and his advisers largely abstained from trashing the dollar, contenting themselves with Japan-bashing. Though Japan had launched two stimulus packages, Bentsen said the Japanese had "made a start but need to do more." Japan had to lower its trade surplus or face "protectionism." At the end of the summit, Clinton announced a major "breakthrough" in its market-opening talks with Japan—a so-called "framework agreement" for reducing Japanese trade barriers, but it soon became clear not much had been accomplished on trade in autos and auto parts, government procurement, and other areas. The buildup in expectations was followed by more than a year of rancorous negotiations, deadlines delayed and exceeded, threats of retaliation, and so forth—the net result of which was that the dollar would eventually plunge to once unimaginable lows, not just against the yen but against other major currencies.

With trade tensions mounting along with confusion over dollar policy, the dollar fell to an all-time low of 100.90 yen on August 16. It was a matter of time until the dollar fell below the psychologiclaly important 100 yen level, but Treasury officials conspicuously avoided any expression of displeasure with the dollar's level or pace of decline. Summers said he had no desire to "characterize recent exchange rate movements" and had nothing to add to previous G-7 exhortations against "excess volatility" and "manipulation" of exchange rates. It was no accident Treasury was letting the dollar's fall to historic lows go unremarked. "Given our objectives, it's a sensible thing to abstain from comment as long as things are going as you like and the markets are not disorderly," said a source. Another said that, while a further strengthening of the yen would not make much direct difference in trimming the nearly $5 billion per month Japanese trade surplus with the United States, it would be useful in terms of exerting "continued pressure on Japan to open up [markets] and to stimulate." A source said that "it wouldn't necessarily upset anybody in Treasury" if the yen continued to appeciate, at least until Japan adopted further fiscal stimulus measures, cut the discount rate, or both. If and when the Japanese government took such measures, Treasury would become more supportive of the dollar. He said Treasury was not unduly uncomfortable with the dollar's decline because, unlike times in the past, the decline had not undermined demand for U.S. government securities or driven up long-term rates. A G-7 official told me the administration wanted "concrete measures" from Japan to reduce its trade surplus and that until those measures were forthcoming it would not move to take upward pressure off the yen. In the meantime, "whether it is the intention of the Clinton administration or not [to drive down the dollar], the Clinton administration is not quite unhappy about how things are happening." Despite its disclaimers, Treasury was "manipulating" exchange rates, the G-7 official said, aided by low U.S. interest rates.

Japanese and other G-7 officials warned the U.S. policy of tolerating, if not encouraging, the yen's rise, was having the self-defeating effect of undermining Japan's economy. The view was shared at the Fed. The United States had been more vociferous than any government in insisting Japan stimulate demand in its economy. But the yen's rise was having an increasingly depressing effect on Japanese demand. In the second quarter, Japan's GDP contracted 2 percent. In July, Japanese retail sales fell 5 percent from a year earlier. Industrial production was down, and unemployment was starting to rise in a country that had hardly known joblessness. The administration strategy seemed to be that "if the rising yen inflicts enough pain on exporters, they will get their government to pump up demand," said a Fed staffer. "The presumption is that if the pain gets bad enough they will do something to offset the pain." The government had already increased spending and cut the discount rate, but administration officials were not satisfied. They wanted the Japanese government to give its people what they were unwilling to give Americans: a tax cut.

Finally, on August 19, Summers said, "The rapid rise in the value of the Japanese yen could retard growth in the Japanese and world economies." He renewed the pledge to "cooperate with our G-7 partners in foreign exchange markets." The same morning, the Fed began buying dollars. But Summers's statement and the accompanying intervention came only after it was announced new Prime Minister Morihiro Hosokawa and his economic ministers had agreed to produce a package of measures by mid-September to stimulate the economy and reduce the trade surplus and after the Bank of Japan had cut short-term rates with the promise of more stimulus to come. Heavy hints were dropped by Japanese officials that a discount rate cut and other steps would not be far behind. The transparent timing of Summers's statement and intervention confirmed what had been suspected all along—that the U.S. Treasury was using a weak dollar to extract concessions from Japan. Sensing this, the markets kept the dollar from recovering greatly. As the dollar remained weak in late summer, Fed officials again expressed public concern. Lindsey, in an August 27 interview, said the dollar's depreciation was "a matter that bears a lot of careful watching. Of course, a lot of the weakness has taken place rather recently. It will certainly be a topic at the next meeting." Mullins told the Japanese newspaper *Nihon Kesai Shinbun* the Fed did "not share the notion that one can devalue one's self for prosperity, that an ever-dropping dollar is a road to great riches."

Throughout this period, administration and congressional pressure on the Fed to hold down interest rates had the effect of keeping the dollar down, which ironically made some Fed officials all the more anxious to raise them. Fed anxiety about the dollar's weakness continued to fester. On September 8, Margaret Greene, senior vice president of the New York Fed, suggested administration comments on the dollar had been ill-considered. "When new people get into new positions, they may [make such harmful comments] without realizing that the rest of the world is looking at their comments as indicative of policy." She was briefing reporters on the Fed's quarterly report on foreign exchange operations which reported the Fed had bought dollars May 27–28 and June 15 "to show that [U.S. authorities] were willing to cooperate with other monetary authorities as appropriate and were not favoring a weak dollar as a matter of policy." Altman responded that "the Federal Reserve comment wasn't well conceived."

On September 16, Japan announced an emergency economic stimulus package totaling 6.15 trillion yen in extra spending, as well as various tax incentives and deregulations. This was on top of a 10.7 trillion yen package announced in August 1992 and a 13.2 trillion yen plan unveiled in April 1993.[13] Administration officials wasted no time calling it insufficient. The best that could be said, according to one official, was that it was a "step in the right direction." Five days later, in a further effort to pacify the United States, take upward pressure off the yen, and revive its economy, the Bank of Japan announced a 75 basis point cut in its discount rate to the unheard of level of 1.75 percent. Bentsen welcomed the rate cut and said, "This, along with last week's stimulus package and other measures now under review, should contribute to higher Japanese growth and lower current account surpluses."[14]

The dollar had already risen to 104.5 yen in anticipation of Japan's discount rate cut, and when it rose to 107.32 yen a couple of days after the discount rate reduction, the administration began to fear the lower Japanese rates they had sought might become a double-edged sword and undo the yen appreciation they had sought. The administration would have preferred more fiscal stimulus. That way demand might have been stimulated without weakening the yen. But the Japanese Ministry of Finance, unlike the U.S. government, was fervently opposed to deficit spending. The administration still saw a stronger yen as a key to reduce Japan's surpluses, at least until it could batter down Japanese trade barriers. The administration was anxious not to see the yen weaken markedly from the levels that had prevailed before the rate cut. "The administration probably would not say anything so long as the dollar did not strengthen much beyond the 106–107 level, but if it went to 109 or 110 or threatened to go higher it would certainly say something at that time," one source told me prophetically. Another told me 110 was not an absolute ceiling, but movement much beyond that level would cause concern, the degree of which would depend on the degree of progress in trade talks. A third flatly stated a dollar-yen rate in the 110 to 115 region would be "wrong."

For a short time, Bentsen was "comfortable" with exchange rates, as he said on September 23 in advance of the annual IMF–World Bank meetings. For the time being he turned his attention to Europe, where he said lower rates were needed. The next day, though, Brown complained that "unrealistic exchange rates" were among the "non-tariff barriers" causing the United States to run a big trade deficit with the Asian members of the Asian Pacific Economic Cooperation Organization (APEC). He did not say who he meant, but the most important Asian APEC nation was Japan. Only later, after he had once again roiled the currency markets and irritated Japan, did a Brown spokesman say he had not intended to imply the yen-dollar rate was unrealistic. The amazing thing was that, in the face of all these comments, the administration tried to maintain the pious pretense that it was above "manipulating exchange rates" and acted hurt when anyone suggested anything to the contrary.

Bentsen may have been "comfortable" with the dollar at 105 to 106 yen, but the Japanese clearly were not. After the September 25 G-7 meeting, Japanese Finance Minister Hirohisa Fujii said that "the rapid rise of the yen has been having a negative effect on the Japanese economy" and said his government had used "all possible measures of intervention in the economy and stimulus measures and monetary policy at this time." Just a block away, Bentsen was claiming Japan had not complained about the effect of the strong yen on the Japanese economy. He also made clear the administration was still not satisfied with Japan's stimulus measures. Japan needed to undertake "tax reform" and "far-reaching deregulation" of its economy. It was rather ironic coming from an administration raising U.S. taxes and regulation. Fed officials were anxious to keep the dollar's limited gains. "The stabilization of the purchasing power" of the dollar was the Fed's main concern, Angell said on October 5. "A continuing, firm monetary policy assuring stable gold prices and, consequently, a stable exchange value of the dollar, will assure a path toward a stable general price level."

It soon became clear the administration did not want to leave it to market judgments of "economic fundamentals" to set exchange rates. On October 6, the Competitiveness Policy Council, a commission chaired by Clinton campaign adviser Bergsten which included Tyson, recommended locking in the lower exchange rate of the dollar against the yen. It said the yen's rise against the dollar had "helped to correct the yen's earlier undervaluation" and that "currency reference ranges around current levels might assist in maintaining a competitive level for the dollar and ensure against renewed yen depreciation." The administration denied this report reflected official policy. A Tyson spokesman said she "didn't take any part in creating that document," but "I'm not saying she's distancing herself" from it. Bergsten said he had in mind maintaining a "reference range" of 100 to 110 yen per dollar, centering on 105. Summers declined to clarify the administration's position on the commission recommendation, leaving the impression he did not disapprove of it. On October 8 the often surly Treasury undersecretary lapsed into one of his cute moods and joked that the U.S. trade deficit could fall "because the dollar falls through the floor and we become competitive the Somalia way," but other methods were preferable.

U.S. pressure on Japan was relentless. On October 14, Summers said Japan's stimulative "actions have not yet been sufficient to turn the corner. . . . [Japan] still has plenty of room for more expansionary fiscal policy." What's more, Japan had to open its markets. Bentsen continued the theme November 23. "The Japanese government must act promptly and decisively to carry through on its commitment at the Tokyo Summit to implement fiscal and monetary measures that ensure strong domestic demand and reduce its trade surplus." He also urged Europe to slash interest rates. Bentsen was commenting on a Treasury foreign exchange report, which predicted the U.S. trade deficit would continue to widen despite "historic highs" for the yen, due to slow growth in Japan.

On December 8, the Fed disclosed it had spent a paltry $165 million to support the dollar in August. Foreign exchange traders credited the Fed for doing as good a job as it had in temporarily changing the mood of the market, but the report was a measure of how little the Treasury was prepared to defend the dollar. Angell said it was his understanding some in the administration wanted the dollar to fall as low as 80 yen per dollar to reduce the trade deficit—a policy he called "foolish" because it would cause "deflation" in Japan. An administration official denied Angell's allegations, saying "there is nothing in that." But in April 1995, the dollar would fall below 80 yen. Angell, who advised the Bank of Japan to target a 120 yen exchange rate, was not alone. Lindsey said Japan's deepening recession "shows the error of our efforts to talk down the dollar earlier in the year. . . . The problems they're having suggest that was not the best thing to have done." Recalling Bentsen's call for "a stronger yen," he cited the aphorism, "Don't wish for something too much or you might get it." Other Fed officials privately warned it would backfire against the administration by further weakening the Japanese economy, squelching demand for U.S. exports, and widening the trade deficit—just the opposite of what the administration wanted to accomplish. The dollar had rebounded to around 109 yen, but the Fed was still worried.

On December 16, with the dollar near 110 yen, Bentsen again said he was "comfortable" with prevailing dollar-yen levels. On December 21, when the dollar had actually hit that level, he said he had no plans to push it back down. But the next day, as predicted, Bentsen expressed concern the dollar was getting too strong against the yen (even though it was still 11 percent down for the year). After the dollar had risen to 111.65 yen, he issued the following statement: "In light of recent cyclical and exchange rate developments, we at Treasury are concerned that Japan is not meeting its commitment to achieve domestic demand led growth and a significant reduction in its external surplus."[15] Bentsen's surprise statement brought Clinton dollar policy full circle. After setting off a sharp dollar decline in February, the administration appeared to have backed off its weak dollar policy. Since August there had seemed to be an awareness that a strong yen might be counterproductive to the U.S.-Japan trade imbalance and that a weak dollar was not a good thing for the U.S. economy. When the yen began to retreat from its highs, that had seemed acceptable to the administration. But once the dollar exceeded 110, it became agitated that the dollar had gotten out of the 100 to 110 range. Treasury sources left no doubt Bentsen's statement was meant as a signal Treasury did not want a rise of the dollar, given its lack of progress on trade talks with Japan and the failure of stimulus measures to jump-start the Japanese economy. It confirmed the administration wanted exchange rates to "reflect fundamentals" only so long as the yen stayed below 110 per dollar. It was not the last time the Treasury would play such games.

Foreign central bankers strain to be diplomatic about the Clinton administration's handling of the dollar. "When politicans are talking about exchange rates, whatever they're saying, there is a sense among the central bankers that it's better to keep quiet about those developments than talking in one direction or another," says Eddie George. "The less said the better. . . . To that extent, I'm sure that people would have felt, 'Well, I wish they'd shut up.' But I don't think there was a feeling that the American government was deliberately going out to talk down the dollar against currencies in general to get some kind of competitive advantage. There was a sense that the Japanese surplus was disproportionate, that the Japanese economic policy was unnecessarily tight and that you needed to see deregulation in the Japanese market in order to achieve a longer-term equilibrium between Japan and the rest of the world, and there would have been quite a lot of sympathy among other finance ministers and other central banks for that position at that time." Leigh-Pemberton says Bentsen was respected as "the grand old man or the linchpin of that new administration," but "didn't approve" of his talking down the dollar, "because I don't really approve of anybody deliberately devaluating or allowing devaluation. It improved the competitive position temporarily of that particular country against the rest of the world. And to that extent I thought perhaps it was rather a populist move, but maybe an understandable one given the state of the U.S. economy." There was dissatisfaction within the G-7 at Bentsen's comments, "but I think we also knew that there was not much we were going to do about it. I could hear him saying, in so many words, 'I can't go to the Congress and say I'm going in for a stronger dollar kind of monetary policy.' "

Trichet declines to criticize the U.S. Treasury, but says there was a harmful perception that "the administration as a whole was more or less playing a weak dollar strategy, in relationship with the Japanese trade negotiation. . . . The Fed was not at all in agreement, of course, with that, because a central banker knows that the currency questions are really a matter, crucially, of confidence, that when you speak of money and currency you speak of confidence and credibility and that it is absolutely futile to tolerate a minute that you are talking down your own credibility and your own solidity and the confidence in your own production." Another top European central banker says he "had the impression that Bentsen did not have very much experience in the market area, and probably some of his comments were made not taking fully into account what was the possible reaction by the market." In any case, to get its way in the trade talks, "there was pressure from the Clinton administration on the Japanese, and they used, to some extent, even the exchange rate policy by making some comments, and in my view this is very dangerous, to be frank. One should never use exchange rate policy in policy controversies and politics. Never, never. One should not do that. The exchange rate is too sensitive a question, and I have always asked for verbal discipline."

The dollar's long slide after Bentsen's call for "a stronger yen" "illustrated how what amounted to not much more than one remark can get into people's heads and will come back to haunt you for months and months and months and months, if not indeed for years," Blinder said, in a November 1995 interview. "It took the administration a long time—I think it's finally succeeded—to shake out of the markets the notion that the United States was trying to push the dollar down." Phillips says, "People don't realize how fragile reputation is, and once one's reputation goes in one direction, no matter what you say, it's very difficult to get it back going another direction." Once markets believed the administration wanted a weak dollar, "that was difficult to work out of." McDonough thinks that "during most of the period . . . the market perception was not an accurate reflection of Treasury policy." Others say that's being too charitable. Perception or reality, the dollar's chronic weakness against the yen, which eventually spread to other currencies, made life more difficult for the Fed. "To the degree that what I think was mainly a misperception of policy on the part of the market resulted in a weaker dollar, I would say it somewhere between slightly and somewhat complicated the use of monetary policy," says McDonough. Since February 1994, the dollar has not had "a very significant effect at all." That's a matter of dispute. The dollar continued to plummet in 1994 and into 1995, and in the minds of some it was a factor in raising the funds rate from 3 to 6 percent over a 12-month period. Greenspan voiced both private and public concern about the dollar's weakness, so it seems doubtful it was a nonfactor.

CHAPTER NINE

A Preemptive Strike

Although they had been given ample signals that the days of 3 percent money were about to come to an end, many market participants were poorly positioned to absorb the shock of a Fed shift toward higher interest rates, and that meant tightening was going to be a delicate and treacherous operation. The administration knew the change in direction was coming, but certainly did not like it.

With interest rates ranging from 3.06 percent on 3-month Treasury bills to 6.35 percent on 30-year bonds in the first week of 1994, many investments had been predicated on the continuation of low rates. The long bond had retreated from its peak, when the yield had gone as low as 5.77 percent, but vast sums had continued to flow into the bond market, fueling a worldwide rally. The stock market was also humming, as it usually does in a low-rate environment. Investors kept pouring money into equities and fixed income securities like there was no end in sight.

The Fed was ambiguous about its intentions. Many of the comments Fed officials made in early January gave little indication of the tightening to come. The economy had just finished a strong fourth quarter (it was eventually calculated real GDP had grown 6.3 percent in 1987 dollars), but officials downplayed the strength and called it premature to say the economy was generating price pressures worrisome enough to necessitate tighter credit. "One of the things that happens in your profession and the economist profession when you get this kind of recent fourth quarter information is that you immediately react by saying we're going to have inflation pressures, and we're going to have to do something," Hoenig said on January 5. "I think we have to look at a longer-term perspective." So far, he saw "little, if any sign, of worsening wage-price pressures." Parry forecast an increase in real growth for 1994, but said that "we're in a good position to make further gradual progress on inflation." He did give one clue the Fed was getting impatient keeping the funds rate barely above the inflation rate. This "zero real interest rate" situation "would bear watching." Mullins said the Fed could not "wait until inflation is clearly imbedded and moving up," but added that "there is no convincing evidence at this time that inflation is becoming imbedded." Lindsey said the Fed's preferred policy would be to "stop inflation before it starts" but also said the

Fed's "leading indicator" on inflation would be "when we start to see price increases start to stick."

The administration was also still in denial. In the first days of the new year, Clinton's advisers continued to jawbone against rate hikes. On January 3, for instance, Altman declared, "There is no basis either in meaningfully higher inflation or in much greater credit demand to expect that interest rates would rise in a sustained way this year. We expect that interest rates will stay in a relatively subdued fashion in 1994." He could not have been more wrong. On January 5, the administration faced reality. Bentsen predicted "a modest increase in short-term rates" was on the way. He knew whereof he spoke. Greenspan had given Bentsen a heads-up on what the Fed was likely to do at its February 3–4 FOMC meeting so the Treasury would not be blindsided. The administration had known for some time higher rates were coming.[1] Now, Bentsen was no longer disavowing those expectations.

If the Treasury secretary wanted to minimize increases in interest rates he might have given some thought to keeping the dollar strong. Instead, he took another stab at talking it down. After falling from 125 yen to as low as 100 yen between January and August of 1993, the dollar had rebounded to more than 113 yen in the first days of 1994. As I reported January 4, the administration was again concerned about the yen's "weakness." The next day, after the dollar had risen to 113.55, Bentsen declared: "Allowing the yen to slide is not an acceptable way out of recession for Japan." In case anyone might have missed that part of his speech to the Brookings Institution, a Bentsen spokesman carefully pointed it out to reporters in the Treasury press room. "We want to see Japan's surplus reduced significantly, and this will require strong domestic demand in Japan, more open markets and exchange rates that reflect the underlying cost competitiveness of Japan and its trading partners." Japan could "not look to the United States and other countries to make up for slack demand at home." Bentsen's comments had the immediate desired effect, dropping the dollar as low as 112.30. As the year wore on, it would go much lower. What never ceased to amaze me was the way Bentsen and other administration officials would make these kinds of comments, then flatly deny there had been any effort to manipulate exchange rates, as a senior Treasury official did two days later. In reality, all the talk about not manipulating exchange rates and letting fundamentals determine currency values only applied so long as the dollar was trading cheaply enough to suit the administration.

The Fed had a tough enough choice to make without worrying about the dollar. The CPI had risen a mere 2.6 percent in 1993 (2.8 percent excluding food and energy), and there had been few signs of acceleration. It would be difficult to justify tightening to fight invisible inflation. There was even reluctance among some Fed officials. However, Greenspan knew that if the Fed continued to accommodate strong demand in the economy, shortages of skilled labor and materials would begin to develop; strains on the nation's production capacity would grow; plants would begin to have trouble filling orders; and wages and prices would start to accelerate. This was the lesson of the eighties, when by the time Greenspan took office, the reinflation process was so far advanced the Fed could not tighten fast enough to prevent inflation from rising to 6 percent. If inflation was to be held down, the Fed would have to be preemptive. It had already waited too long for some, who had advocated higher rates for months.

Greenspan had been willing to hold the funds rate at 3 percent to help the banking industry recover. Now, thanks to the wide spread the Fed had maintained between banks' cost of funds and their lending rates, banks were coming back strong and were starting to lend aggressively into an expanding economy. Under these new conditions, he told both the administration and his Fed colleagues, a 3 percent funds rate was dangerously low. His message was that the funds rate had to be raised—how far he could not say—both to preempt inflation and to prevent an expansion that carried the seeds of its own demise. He was concerned that the expansion would lead to an excessive inventory buildup that would then precipitate a recession and determined to moderate those forces. The widespread adoption of "just-in-time" inventory procedures had brought inventory-sales ratios down throughout the early 1990s, and Greenspan was concerned that once those ratios hit bottom, as sales increased, there would be a dramatic upsurge in inventory investment that would fuel a major economic expansion. If that expansion were not capped, he feared, inventories would climb to unsustainably high levels and need to be liquidated, leading to painful production cutbacks, layoffs, and so forth. Already he saw signs that this syndrome was developing as lead times on deliveries began to stretch out, a phenomenon that continued as the year wore on.

By late January, notwithstanding their public ambiguity, nearly all Fed policymakers recognized the Fed was pushing its luck keeping funds at 3 percent. A broad FOMC consensus emerged that the Fed could not wait for inflation to actually appear. However, divisions persisted about the immediacy of the threat and how soon to act. There was uncertainty about how fast the economy would grow relative to its potential and how fast rates of employment and capacity utilization would rise to danger levels. Unemployment, still 6.4 percent at the end of 1993, down from 7.4 percent in 1992, could hardly be called inflationary, and it would not be easy to explain why it was necessary to push rates up when joblessness remained relatively high. Capacity utilization was a different story. It had risen from 81.7 percent in August to 83.5 percent—highest since June 1989. In the past, as the rate at which plants operated approached 85 percent, inflation rose. Technological change and the growing importance of trade had cast doubt on the validity of that traditionl yardstick, but the Fed still took it seriously. Most FOMC members were not willing to assume that excess capacity in the slower economies of America's trading partners would restrain price pressures stemming from strained domestic capacity.

There was also concern about how a policy shift would be taken by the financial markets. The administration was particularly anxious that Fed tightening not cause long rates to soar. Bentsen's comments had been intended to set the stage and soften the blow. "He was not opening the door to a Fed move" and was not trying to "give the Fed a green light," said an administration source, but "we have to get the word out at some stage" that a rise in rates is unavoidable and to convey to the markets that "short-term interest rates could go up without having much, if any, impact on long-term interest rates." Bentsen wanted to get across "the administration view that short-term interest rates could go up without hurting the economy." However, Bentsen's comments in no way indicated an eagerness to accept the kind of rate hikes the Fed had in store. The administration had forecast a half percent rise in short-term rates, and the administration's feeling was that rates "should not rise beyond what we predicted, not beyond what is natural given increased demand for money," an administration official confided.

The Fed needed to point to evidence the strong fourth-quarter growth pace was continuing in 1994. Its January 19 beige book had a notably more expansionary tone than usual. "Economic activity continued to expand with signs of acceleration in some sectors." While the survey found "little upward pressure on wages and prices," all the traditional inflation warning signals were flashing: plants operating at or near capacity, shortages of skilled workers, some pickup in wages and prices. It also found rising credit demand. Increased loan demand eventually leads to increased credit flows and more rapid money supply growth, which in turn can feed price pressures. Broaddus said, "The economy seems to have finally achieved sustainable growth." Or as LaWare put it, Greenspan's 50 mile per hour headwinds had slowed to "a mild breeze." Broaddus foresaw real growth in the 3¼ to 3½ percent range for the year, far above what the Fed considered sustainable for long without accelerating inflation. The Fed wanted to get inflation "as close to zero as possible. . . . If we at the Federal Reserve signal we are satisfied with three percent inflation, the credibility of the Federal Reserve would be undermined." The economy could grow above potential without inflation rising, but only so long as "slack" remained in the economy, in the Fed view. The question was, when would unused plant capacity and labor be diminished to the point that faster-than-potential growth led to price-wage pressures? Opinions differed, but most felt the Fed could not afford to gamble that it would be later rather than sooner.

As the FOMC meeting approached, the administration continued to minimize inflation pressures. "We don't see any change in the economic fundamentals that would cause inflation to rise," Tyson told reporters January 28. The Fed might have to raise rates "sooner or later," but "it's not going to be sooner." Greenspan had met with Clinton's economic team and strongly indicated the Fed was going to have to raise rates. His message was not uniformly well received. "He never said, 'I'm going to do this on this date' or anything like that, but he described his interpretation of the economy, and led one to think that some move would occur," a Clinton staffer recalls. "He made a preemptive argument and some people thought it was a little early to be preemptive." Many of Clinton's top advisers thought it would be premature for the Fed to raise rates. The perennial dichotomy between Fed and White House was over which kind of error was worse—acting too soon, or acting too late. Tyson and others in the administration were loathe to act too soon. Greenspan was loathe to act too late.

Having put the White House on notice, Greenspan felt it his duty to inform Congress and the public. On January 31, three days before the FOMC was to meet, he dropped some heavy hints rate hikes were coming soon. Although there were only "very marginal" signs of wage or price pressures, he told the Joint Economic Committee, "Monetary policy must not overstay accommodation." The FOMC would have to decide "when is the appropriate time to move to a somewhat less accommodative level of short-term interest rates. . . . Short-term interest rates are abnormally low in real terms. . . . Absent an unexpected and prolonged weakening of economic activity, we will need to move them to a more neutral stance." Bentsen said he "wouldn't be surprised" if the Fed raised rates, but "if the Fed takes any action, I would think it would be modest, and I think it would be more of a preemptive strike trying to anticipate that some time in the future inflation may climb a bit."

When the FOMC convened, it was absent two members. Angell had resigned January 18 to become chief economist at Bear-Stearns, and Mullins had resigned February 1 to start an investment management firm. Angell had led the charge for higher rates, and Mullins was leaning in the same direction. Rubin wanted to replace them with people who would strive for low inflation with "reasonableness." Many thought the departure of Angell and Mullins would mean a less hawkish FOMC, but their absence made no perceptible difference. Although there was some discussion of the "retarding effects" the 1993 tax hikes and slow growth abroad might have, the overwhelming focus was on the dangers of inflation as the economy continued to grow above potential. On February 4, Greenspan stated the FOMC had "decided to increase slightly the degree of pressure on reserve positions. The action is expected to be associated with a small increase in short-term money markets. The decision was taken to move toward a less accommodative stance in monetary policy in order to sustain and enhance the economic expansion."

It was quickly recognized the Fed intended to increase the funds rate a quarter percent to 3¼ percent. The New York Fed had already set the stage in the way it conducted open market operations. In the past, this had been the only way the markets could divine the Fed's intentions. Now, for the first time, the Fed had promptly announced a policy change. Gonzalez took credit. February 4 also began a new practice of changing the funds rate primarily at FOMC meetings, instead of between meetings at the chairman's discretion. Intermeeting moves were not ruled out, but since then there has been only one intermeeting change. "There was this general, broad perception that the presidents were more comfortable doing it at the meetings when that was possible, and those of us here respected that, and the chairman, I think, respected that and has basically tried to do it that way," says a Fed governor. "It's his call. And I think that largely it was in response to that expression by the presidents." The presidents had often told Greenspan they would prefer that he wait until meetings, and he felt he could do as they asked now that the turbulent late eighties and early nineties, when he frequently felt he had to react swiftly to events, were behind him. Besides, from now on he intended to stay ahead of the curve and not let policy be dictated by the course of events.

The first rate hike in five years had taken courage. That morning, the Labor Department had announced a 0.3 percent jump in unemployment to 6.7 percent, and although the rise was skewed by a change in household survey procedures, other aspects of the report had also looked weak. Although the FOMC voted to hike rates unanimously, it was divided over how much. While the majority wanted to go up just a quarter percent, others "indicated a preference for a somewhat greater firming action that would move monetary policy closer to a desirable neutral stance." They felt "a more decisive policy move at this juncture would in fact reduce uncertainty, because fewer discrete actions would be required and they would have a more pronounced and desirable effect in curbing inflationary sentiment and thus in minimizing upward pressures on longer-term interest rates over time." A big reason why the argument for a larger rate increase was rejected was fear of what might happen to overpriced stocks and bonds. Mirroring concerns that had surfaced at the December FOMC meeting, advocates of a slight tightening "felt that a somewhat greater policy adjustment would incur an unacceptable risk of dislocative repercussions in financial markets." The directive contained no bias toward more rate hikes.

A decade or so earlier, Greenspan's statement that the rate hike was made to "sustain and enhance the economic expansion" would have seemed odd, but the Fed had learned that allowing inflation inevitably leads to recession as market forces drive up interest rates and kill off interest-sensitive spending. Greenspan had done a good job spreading that doctrine. He recalls that when he first came to Washington arguments in favor of price stability as the main goal of monetary policy were "at the cutting edge. . . . Now, they are boilerplate." In a less noticed preventive measure, which may someday prove to have been its smartest ever, the Fed Board voted February 9 to extend the hours of operation of its electronic payments system Fedwire from ten to eighteen hours. It would not be long before central banks got fresh reminders of the need to solidify the payments system.[2]

Although the White House had been given ample warning, Clinton was not pleased by the Fed's action. There was no presidential fit of temper, but a top aide says Clinton was bothered by the decision, and his advisers had to explain to him why the Fed had done what it did. Clinton was "concerned" that higher interest rates would slow the economy down, and his advisers told him that "to a certain extent that was bound to happen anyway, because once you got through the bringing of resources back out of unemployment or excess capacity into the system, that there were going to be some limitations on what the economy's growth rate would be anyway. . . ." Bentsen, the most conservative member of Clinton's cabinet and a man with a financial background before coming to Washington, says he was less bothered by the Fed's gearshifting. "I supported it. I wanted to be sure we had inflation well under control." At the time, he said the rate hike "was not unexpected. We don't anticipate that a modest increase like that will inhibit growth." Tyson, swallowing her misgivings, said the Fed's move was "consistent with expansion of three percent." In fact, the administration had allowed for a half percent rate rise in its economic forecast. What she had no way of knowing was that the Fed would be raising rates another 2¾ percent before it was through. Clinton's relationship with Greenspan would never be the same.

On Capitol Hill, Sasser and Sarbanes blasted the Fed rate bump, accusing it of having "a highly skewed policy" that would undercut the recovery. "The Fed has a hair-trigger response when it comes to fighting inflation," Sarbanes fumed. "They are tightening before there is evidence of inflation, even before there is a real threat of future inflation. . . . It defies understanding." There were dark murmurings about "the Republican Fed." Gonzalez said the Fed's action was "not a wise or compassionate move when millions of Americans are in dire straits and nearly seven percent of the labor force is unemployed," but he "congratulated" the Fed for promptly announcing its decision. Apparently deciding he'd been too soft, he later accused the Fed of "extreme malfeasance" in raising rates. Nor was big business appreciative. On Wall Street, the reaction was swift and negative. Despite all the warning signals, many investors and traders, including supposedly sophisticated portfolio managers, were caught flat-footed. Government securities sold off, pushing medium- and long-term yields up a quarter percent or more over the next week. On February 4 alone, the long bond yield went from 6.31 to 6.45 percent at one point. The Dow dropped 96 points in the hours after the late morning announcement. Large trading losses were incurred by major banks and investment houses domestically and internationally, as the prospect of higher rates began bursting the speculative bubbles that had developed in Third World "emerging markets" and elsewhere.

George marvels at the Fed's handling of the February 1994 policy shift. "The signalling of the tightening which came in '93 and then the beginning of the tightening in 1994 was handled extremely gently, in order to try to minimize the impact of the change in sentiment in the bond markets. I mean, it still had quite an impact but I don't think it could have been handled any better frankly." Phillips says it was her most difficult time as a Board member because "everybody was lined up on the other side of the market. . . . People got lulled into that three percent money for such a long time, and we had had those fading spells at the beginning of 1992 and 1993. . . . So people thought the same thing would happen in '94 and were betting on a continuation of the three percent money. So, the turning point—'when are you going to change directions?'—I think is difficult." She said it was also tough to decide whether to raise rates a quarter percent or more. No matter how much the Fed moved, "we knew we were going to surprise the market, but it had to come sometime." Kelley's only regret is not tightening sooner. McDonough looks back on the credit tightening that began then with a sense of institutional pride that the Fed had the courage to begin tightening well in advance of any palpable price pressures. He is equally proud that, subsequent to the 1994–1995 tightening period, the Fed began easing credit before it saw signs of an actual downturn. "I think one of the things that is different . . . is that the Fed is really making monetary policy adjustments which are considerably more anticipatory than in previous history." This was less the case in 1987–1988 and even less the case in the late

seventies. "Now, the market is becoming accustomed to our being more anticipatory. I would doubt very much that the market today would be as surprised
as it was in February of '94 by our move then. I think now they realize that
we're very much looking a year to two years into the future."

In presenting its fiscal 1995 budget February 7, the White House assumed
three-month Treasury bill yields would average 3.4 percent in 1994, compared
to 3 percent in 1993, then rise to 3.8 percent in 1995, while ten-year Treasury
note yields would average 5.8 percent in 1994 and 1995, compared to 5.9 percent in 1993. This was not even close to what actually occurred or should have
been expected. By the end of 1994, three-month bill yields had reached 5.62
percent, and the ten-year note 7.8 percent. In spite of its faulty rate assumptions, the budget deficit for fiscal 1995 would actually come in $12.2 billion
below the administration's projected $176.1 billion, partially because of higher
taxes but largely because, despite them, the economy grew faster than the
2.7 percent the administration forecast. What's more, the RTC was winding
down its work and, instead of being a drain on the Treasury, was actually contributing as it sold off assets in receivership. The problem was that, in the "out
years," the administration was proposing higher deficits. After dipping further
to $173.1 billion in 1996, the deficit was projected to rise to $187.4 billion in
1988 and to $201.2 billion in 1999.[3]

Now that the Fed had started raising rates, the only question was how far it
would go. Greenspan and his staff did not start with a presumption the funds
rate would have to be doubled to 6 percent. They did not know at this stage
how high the funds rate would need to go or how long it would have to stay
there, only that it would have to be raised substantially further. As the year
progressed, the staff came up with different levels the funds rate might have to
reach to cap the expansion and prevent the kind of inventory-related instabil-
ities Greenspan feared. Analysts were already speculating the Fed would push
the funds rate to 5 percent, and as the year wore on, some thought it would
have to go well above 6 percent, but the Fed hoped to be able to avoid that.
One thing was for sure. There was no way the Fed was going to restrain rates
as much as the administration hoped, not when most policymakers were
expecting real growth in excess of 3 percent. Clinton's advisers knew this,
but argued against anything more than "modest" rate hikes. The Economic
Report of the President on February 14 declared that, at most, short-term
rates would "drift slowly upward." Deficit reduction would hold down long-
term rates and allow "a less restrictive monetary policy." The Fed should be
able to "reduce future real short-term interest rates." Notwithstanding the
administration's projections that the deficit would begin rising again in a few
years and notwithstanding Greenspan's desire to see the budget in balance or
even in surplus, the Report said further deficit reduction would be unacceptably contractionary. For the same reason, it opposed a constitutional balanced
budget amendment. Greenspan warned uncontrolled "entitlement" spending
would make the deficits of the eighties look puny and argued there was no better time than an expansion to begin getting a grip on these longer range problems, but the White House figured it had done its bit for lower deficits.

It soon became clear the administration's hopes for nothing more than a half percent rise in rates were naive. The Fed's new credit stance was "not tight by any means" with the funds rate at 3¼ percent, Kelley said February 16. Phillips said the rate hike had only made policy "less accommodative." None of those I talked to saw the rate hike making the slightest dent in the expansion or moving the Fed far from a stance they considered unduly stimulative. The funds rate would have to go a good bit higher just to achieve *"neutrality,"* that is, the real rate consistent with noninflationary growth. Fed officials did not want to cause a rise in unemployment to restrain inflation. They realized the economy's momentum would carry unemployment to much lower levels. Their goal was to keep the economy from reaching and surpassing full employment too rapidly. In his Humphrey-Hawkins report to the House Banking Committee February 22, Greenspan said that, while there was "no immediate evidence" of rising inflation, he did not want to provide "the financial tinder" for it. Even 3 percent was not a "long-term stable rate of inflation"; it would accelerate from there "if it goes on indefinitely." There was "increasing evidence that the economic recovery is well-entrenched," hence the rise in long-term rates. In that climate "the question really gets to the issue of what basis do we have for continuing an accommodative" policy. The economy appeared headed for growth in the 3 to 3¼ percent range, and new orders for manufactured goods were on the rise. "In past periods that has tended largely to create pressure on capacity, shortages and price inflation. . . . To promote sustainable growth, history suggests that real short-term rates are more likely to have to rise than fall from here."

Although it was not the guiding force, the dollar's vulnerable condition weighed on Fed policymakers' minds and contributed to their willingness to raise rates—something the administration still did not seem to understand. Fed officials had cringed when Bentsen went out of his way to talk the dollar down in December and again in January, and even after he desisted from direct comments on exchange rates he and others continued to take jabs at Japan for running a roughly $60 billion trade surplus with the United States, for not stimulating domestic demand, and so on—all of which kept the currency pot boiling. Seldom did their circumspection allow them to comment publicly, but on February 17, Jordan said that "maintaining the purchasing power of the dollar is critical" to maintaining its role as a "monetary anchor" in the world. "The challenge is to regain the credibility that the value of the dollar will stay the same." The administration was embroiled in the so-called "framework" talks with Japan. As they dragged on through 1994, they became an increasing source of dollar instability. Trade negotiators from the United States were demanding Japan open its markets to various categories of exports and insisting on quantitative goals for Japanese importation which Japan rejected as "numerical targets." Traders were convinced that, if the United States did not get its way, it would drive the dollar to new lows against the yen. Administration officials did little to counter that impression. Their claims that they were not trying to manipulate exchange rates were belied by statements deploring yen "weakness" whenever the dollar rose much above 110 yen. The dollar had fallen from above 113 to below 109 yen by the February 4 rate hike, and because the market believed the administration was keen to depress the dollar, the Fed action gave it little support.

The administration could not resist playing exchange rate games. The president himself got into the act. On February 11, he met with Hosokawa in an effort to iron out the two nations' differences in the five negotiating areas that were due for a progress report under the "framework agreement" they had entered into the previous July. The meeting was a flop, and at a stiff joint press conference late Friday afternoon, Clinton listed exchange rates three times as one of the things the United States would have to look at in monitoring progress on trade with Japan. Later, he remarked cryptically that the administration was considering "a number of options . . . including some that have not been widely discussed." When the markets opened Monday, February 14, the dollar began plunging, falling all the way to 101.10 and appeared primed to go below 100 for the first time. The Treasury made no effort to support the dollar through intervention and waited until 9:30 Monday night before making a bland statement that dollar policy was "unchanged from that already stated by Secretary Bentsen. We don't believe in managing exchange rates." Currency traders scoffed. Saying policy was unchanged from the way Bentsen had stated it was not saying much. As for not managing exchange rates, who were they kidding?

Fed officials were becoming increasingly anxious and frustrated with the administration's devil-may-care attitude toward the dollar. This was serious business. Not only was the dollar weakening against the yen, it was beginning to slip against other major currencies, and there was a danger Japanese and other foreign investors would pull their funds out of U.S. securities, destabilizing markets and driving up U.S. interest rates. Hadn't the administration noticed the shakiness of the bond market? The administration was "playing a game of chicken" with the Japanese on exchange rates, said one Fed official. Lindsey said the dollar's "politically driven" drop could be inflationary under certain economic conditions. Foreign central bankers were displeased too, and not just the Japanese. "It is a pity some officials talk up a currency [because] it creates in the markets some disturbances," Jean Zwahlen, a member of the governing board of the Swiss National Bank, said. "Whatever the level of the yen is, is subject to the market and [officials] should not speak of it for political reasons." When the Fed privately conveyed its concerns to the Treasury, it was assured the administration was not seeking a weaker dollar, but the market did not trust the administration, and for good reason. In truth, it was delighted with the dollar's fall against the yen and was prepared to see it go a lot lower so long as it did not undermine the bond market.

In the final week of February, a chaotic sell-off rocked bond markets worldwide. Part of the explanation was the growing realization the Fed would be pushing rates higher to keep the economy from overheating. Fed officials had anticipated some increase in bond yields. Indeed, while they did not advertise the fact, they were convinced bonds and stocks had become wildly overpriced and needed to be deflated. But they had not expected as much correction as was occurring and were alarmed at the market reaction. "It seems to me that the level of long-term interest rates have to anticipate a stronger economy and greater inflationary pressures than I see," McDonough told me February 25, as the long bond yield pushed toward 6¾ percent. "My own reading of the situation does not show the robustness of the economy or the price pressures that seem to be embodied in long-term interest rates." Obviously there were other explanations. It was no accident, in the Fed's view, that much of the run-up in long rates occurred after the administration had released its disappointing budget, then followed it up by underscoring its fierce opposition to a balanced budget amendment and to bipartisan congressional efforts to enact additional spending restraints. Nor did the CBO's negative fiscal assessment of the Clinton health care plan go unnoticed.

Jitters over the weak dollar and the belief that U.S.-Japan trade talks would spawn continued weakness were another factor. At the height of the sell-off, U.S. Trade Representative Mickey Kantor added fuel to the fire by endorsing a Gephardt bill to impose import targets on Japan and require retaliatory trade penalties if they were not met. And Bentsen again slammed Japan for not opening its markets and stimulating its economy. When a report came out of Tokyo that the United States and Japan had agreed to stabilize the dollar at 110 yen, he called it "a total fabrication." Such reckless comments stirred fear of a trade war, kept alive talk the United States would seek a lower dollar, and fueled market anxiety. When I raised these issues with Tyson late that February she claimed "perceptions of our [dollar] policy are not consistent with reality," but by that point perception had become reality and was undermining both the dollar and dollar assets. It wasn't so much that a weaker dollar implied more inflation, as that investors in dollar-denominated securities, not knowing what the dollar's value would be when they cashed in their investments, demanded higher yields. As U.S. rates went, so went rates in other nations, whose economies were not as robust. Alexandre Lamfalussy, president of the European Monetary Institute (forerunner of the planned European central bank), told me Europe had suffered "a spillover effect" from the U.S. bond sell-off. A major cause had been "the development of the dollar-yen exchange rate. That has certainly played a role. There is no doubt about it, along with the trade war perception. That too has frightened the markets." Whatever the cause, "the upward movement [in European long-term rates] was triggered by what's happened in the United States. We have absolutely no revival of inflation. On the contrary." What was obvious to everyone else was denied by the U.S. Treasury. A day after lambasting Japan again for "draining demand" from the world economy, Summers claimed the global avalanche in the bond market was just a "speculative correction" reflecting rising credit demands.

Even sophisticated institutional investors lost big during this period. Soros Fund Management, which had racked up billions by testing the limits of the ERM in 1992 and 1993, bet that rising U.S. interest rates would strengthen the dollar against the yen and lost an estimated $600 million on February 14 when the unexpected breakdown of the U.S.-Japan trade talks kept the dollar heading south. Former top Soros trader Robert Johnson, who faults the U.S.

Treasury for using the dollar "as a crowbar" to pry open Japanese markets, recalls, "Everyone followed us, and when Soros was wrong, nobody else had anything to hang their hat on. They all walked off the diving board with us." Some blamed speculators for triggering the selling. But Lamfalussy said that "we have to live with" the increased volatility in the bond markets. "We have now reached the stage of a highly activist portfolio management strategy all over the world" where portfolio managers use "high-speed decision-making techniques. Whenever they come to the conclusion that bond prices are not going to rise any longer or that interest rates are not going to fall any longer, they sell, and they all do it at the same time." Bond markets had become subject to the "instantaneous price adjustment" the stock market had long manifested.

Summers's "speculative correction" set the stage for a disaster late in 1994, which would again test Greenspan's mettle. Mexico and other "emerging markets" had been the recipients of large capital inflows attracted by yields that were high compared to those available in the United States and other industrial nations. Mexico had seemingly gotten control of its finances at last, restructuring its debt, beating inflation down to relatively low levels, and solidifying its currency. Investment in privatized Mexican companies, government securities, and the like were attractive. Mexico, Argentina, and Brazil were no longer seen as high-risk places to invest. As a result, spreads between paper issued by developing countries and the U.S. government narrowed dramatically. In 1989, the yield on five-year Mexican government bonds had been 8 percent above the yield on comparable U.S. Treasury securities. By the end of 1993, the spread had fallen to less than 1½ percent—still enough of a premium to attract capital from hungry banks and investment houses in New York. Economic activity and hence demand for capital was sluggish throughout most of the industrialized world. Nations like Mexico seemed logical places to invest, especially since their governments were effectively insuring against exchange rate risk by fixing their currencies against the dollar and since the IMF and the U.S. Treasury had shown a willingness to bail them out if anything went wrong. According to the IMF, countries which had experienced a net outflow of $116 billion during the 1983 to 1989 period, received a cumulative net inflow of $200 billion from 1990 through 1994. Mexico alone received $31 billion worth of capital inflows or 8 percent of its GDP in 1993. When tighter Fed policy, improved U.S. growth prospects, heightened inflationary expectations, and dollar depreciation sent U.S. interest rates up, money rushed out of Mexico. Suddenly the hard currency reserves it had depended on to finance its current account deficit and keep the peso steady started evaporating. It was a ticking time bomb that would go off in the faces of Treasury and Fed officials that December.

Global market turmoil made a dreary backdrop for the March 22 FOMC meeting. Once more the Fed found itself in a dilemma. The long bond yield by then was approaching 7 percent, compared to 5¾ percent less than five months earlier and as low as 6⅛ shortly before the February 4 rate hike. If it raised short-term rates again, it risked driving long rates up further and aggravating the rush out of stocks and bonds that was proving so problematic. But if it did not raise them, it risked creating the impression the Fed lacked the will to head off inflation, causing markets to build a higher inflation premium into long rates. Fed officials kept the markets guessing. Lindsey said the first rate hike might be "enough" on February 28, but a few days later, he was contradicted by Parry: "Since short-term real rates still are quite low, it's unlikely one step is going to be enough."

Four days before the meeting, Greenspan was scheduled to fly to Houston to make introductory remarks at a Dallas Fed conference, but at the last minute he canceled the trip so he could meet with Clinton and members of his National Economic Council. The sudden change of plans gave the appearance that Greenspan had been summoned to the White House for a pre-FOMC lecture. In fact, Greenspan, the president, and his advisers had been trying for some time to find a mutually suitable date for a meeting. Greenspan was not particularly anxious to fly to Houston that day, so he said, "Let's do it." Had he known so much was going to be made of his being supposedly "called on the carpet" he would have gone to Houston instead. It was still the administration's contention that there were no signs of inflation and no cause for rates to rise. Greenspan's message was that capping the funds rate was no prescription for restraining long rates and that if the Fed did not succeed in preempting inflation, long rates could go much higher and ultimately snuff out the recovery. For now there was no danger of a slowdown. Unemployment had fallen two-tenths back to 6.5 percent in February. Industrial prdouction had climbed 5.4 percent, pushing capacity utilization up to 83.4 percent. Housing starts had jumped. Producer prices had risen nearly 6 percent annually.

The FOMC decided to "increase slightly the degree of pressure on reserve positions" to effect "a small increase in short-term money market interest rates." This meant another quarter percent rise in the funds rate to 3½. Many market participants were perturbed the Fed had announced the rate hike shortly after the Treasury had auctioned two-year notes, causing some to lose money as the prices of the securities they had just bought dipped, but the Fed had little sympathy. As in February, the committee was divided. All members agreed on the need to move to "a less accommodative policy stance." Being accommodative had been "appropriate earlier in the economic recovery, when constraints such as the widespread rebuilding of balance sheets and business restructuring activities were strongly inhibiting the expansionary forces in the economy," but now "those constraints had greatly diminished and the expansion clearly had gained considerable momentum." The economy had escaped the clutches of the credit crunch and banks were starting to lend more aggressively. In such a climate, "maintaining an accommodative monetary policy could be expected before too long to foster growing pressures on labor and capital resources with a resulting pickup in inflation. While actual inflation remained subdued and credit growth was still damped, it was only a matter of time before the current monetary policy induced a surge in credit extensions that could fuel an outbreak of inflation." The committee concluded "monetary policy needed to move fairly quickly toward what might be characterized as a more neutral position." Just what constituted a "neutral" funds rate "could not be defined with precision," but "the members generally concluded that such a policy stance was still some distance away, and the key issue facing the committee was not whether but how promptly the necessary policy adjustment should be completed."

That's where consensus ended. Although there was unanimity on the need to raise rates, opinions clashed on how much, how soon. Some wanted a "relatively sizable" rate hike, either a half percent increase in the funds rate or a half percent discount rate hike accompanied by a smaller rise in the funds rate. They argued for stronger action "to underscore the committee's commitment to its price stability objective" and counteract increasing inflationary expectations. They contended market expectations of further Fed rate hikes "were themselves contributing to market instability" so it was better to make a larger rate move and end the uncertainty. Although that course might prove wrong, "they viewed the greatest risk at this juncture to be a policy that allowed inflationary pressures to gather momentum." They felt it would be easier to correct a policy that proved too tight than one not tight enough. But the majority insisted on a quarter percent, mainly out of concern about "a possible overreaction in financial markets that had become quite sensitive and volatile since early February." Jordan and Broaddus dissented. Although the directive was symmetrical, there was a presumption the Fed might need to raise rates again before the May 17 meeting. Greenspan agreed to consult the FOMC if he so decided.

There was disagreement over whether to continue the policy of announcing FOMC decisions. Some did not like this break with the Fed's secretive tradition, but a majority decided "a useful purpose would be served in reducing or eliminating potential misinterpretation of the committee's policy decision and the related risk of overreactions in the financial markets. . . . The news of the committee's action would be conveyed unambiguously to the entire public at once and not filtered through the financial markets' interpretation of open market operations." The precedent was established and has been followed ever since. The meeting had taken place under the shadow of the new policy Greenspan had adopted under congressional pressure of providing transcripts of the deliberations, and although they were to be released with a five-year lag, the knowledge they were being recorded for posterity combined with the fear that Congress might require quicker dissemination had a "chilling effect" on debate, a participant said. FOMC members were much more reticent about expressing themselves.[4]

The bond market reaction this time was mild. In fact, bond prices actually rose. Administration reaction was basically uncritical, couched in paeans to the Fed's independence. A glib Clinton went so far the next day as to tell reporters covering his morning jog he realized the Fed was raising rates to dampen inflation fears and hold down long-term rates. He had obviously watched the market's behavior. "Mr. Greenspan says the long-term interest rates should actually be lower and that maybe this action by him will make it clear that inflation is not on the rise and that long-term interest rates are dropping.

That's what I think he thought would happen the first time. It didn't. It did happen a little bit yesterday. We'll just have to hope that there's a closer connection between the two actions this time than there was last time. He believes that there's no inflation in the economy, that growth is strong and that this may actually result in a decline in long-term interest rates. It happened yesterday, so we have to hope that that condition will stand because there's good growth and no inflation."

But just when the Fed seemed to have pulled off a market-friendly credit tightening, fate intervened. Mexican presidential candidate Luis Donaldo Colosio was assassinated, sparking a crisis in confidence that caused Mexico's financial situation to deteriorate further. After falling 9 percent in February, the Mexican Bolsa fell another 14 percent in March, and capital outflows were forcing the Bank of Mexico to dig into its foreign exchange reserves to prevent a devaluation of the peso, which the Institutional Revolutionary Party (PRI) government considered unbearable—at least before the elections. The market repercussions were not confined to Mexico. The value of Mexico's *Brady bonds*, the U.S. Treasury collateralized securities banks had gotten from the Mexican government in exchange for their outstanding loan claims, plunged, and the U.S. bond market was buffeted by rumors of heavy sales of Treasuries by the Mexican government and by Brady bond holders. Bond yields soon shot above 7 percent. Bentsen could also see the economic promise of the North American Free Trade Agreement (NAFTA) he had spearheaded through Congress going up in smoke. He decided to enter into a $3 billion "swap" agreement with Mexico, essentially enabling it to borrow dollars from Treasury's Exchange Stabilization Fund to support the peso, and he convinced Greenspan to pony up a matching amount. Although Mexico had some $28 billion in reserves before the assassination, it was going through them fast. So on March 24, Greenspan called an FOMC telephone conference. The Fed already had a $700 million swap agreement with the Bank of Mexico, but now Greenspan wanted to increase it to $3 billion. Some members were less than thrilled, but only Broaddus voted "no." Later that day, Greenspan and Bentsen jointly announced establishment of a "temporary" $6 billion swap facility to aid Mexico. A month later, with great fanfare, Greenspan and Bentsen, together with their Mexican and Canadian counterparts, announced these enlarged swaps had been folded into a trilateral currency swap agreement among the three North American nations. But there was no doubt which country would be primarily responsible for bailing out Mexico when the time came. The swaps would be just a small downpayment on what was eventually needed.

By the end of March, the Dow had fallen nearly 400 points (roughly 10 percent) from a January 31 high of 3979.36, and long-term rates had risen a full percent. Would the combined loss of wealth and increased debt financing costs cool the economy sufficiently to make further Fed rates hikes unnecessary? Fed officials thought not. Many took a detached, and as it turned out sensible, view of these scary market developments. "It is relevant that while the markets have gone down a lot in the past few weeks we're basically just retracing the gains of the last few months," McTeer told me. "People may be losing nominal or paper wealth, but it's paper wealth that has risen substantially the last few months. I doubt the wealth effect will be very much." Besides, the market was overreacting. "The fundamentals appear good." In fact, the Fed had raised rates not just to preempt inflation but to take some air out of the market's sails. As one official put it, the market had gotten "pricey" by the time the Fed started tightening, and "our move caused them to sharpen their pencils and take another look." Another said the stock market's record run-up had been "a paper thing," whose reversal would not hurt the economy. "It doesn't worry me that much." They were not saying so publicly, but Fed officials increasingly believed a 4 to 5 percent funds rate would be needed to keep policy from being overly stimulative and were prepared to go much higher.

Evidence was not long in coming that the economy's momentum was unbroken. On April 1, the Labor Department announced a startling 456,000 leap in nonfarm payroll. Rather than hail the job gains, Labor Secretary Robert Reich said it was important not to "exaggerate" its significance. The report prompted renewed selling of bonds and stocks and alarmed Fed officials. Hoenig shook the markets by saying employment and capacity utilization were "at the threshold" of generating inflation. The administration got so rattled a few days after the jobs report, when the market opened down 63 points, that a Treasury spokesman said the department was "watching it." The Fed's continued maunderings about inflation annoyed some administration officials, who felt the Fed itself was building an inflationary psychology and unhinging the markets. Some insinuated the Fed alone had caused the spike in bond yields. This angered Fed officials, who felt only a small part of the rise in long rates was due to their action. Much more of the blame went to the administration for its mishandling of trade and exchange rates and for its fiscal policies. Administration officials regularly implied the Fed was on the wrong track by asserting there was no need to fear inflation. Joining in was soon-to-be Fed vice chairman Blinder. The belief Blinder would blunt the Fed attack on inflation worried Wall Street, needlessly as it turned out.

From the Fed's standpoint, if inflation was not a threat, it was thanks to its preemptive actions. In fact, though, most Fed officials believed inflation was a real threat and were not dissuaded by reports that the producer and consumer price indices had risen modestly in March. They were more concerned with continued signs of above-potential growth and lessening "slack." Capacity utilization had risen again to 83.6 percent. Delivery lead times, which Greenspan watched religiously, were lengthening. By mid-April, inflation fears had pushed the long bond yield above 7¼ percent. The dollar remained under pressure, hovering not far above 100 yen per dollar amid continued suspicion about the administration's commitment to protecting it.

By April 18, Greenspan had seen enough and convened an FOMC telephone conference. He asked for and received acquiescence in another quarter point rate increase in the funds rate to 3¾ percent. The FOMC now saw "considerable momentum in economic activity and further reductions in already limited margins of unutilized labor and other production resources." What's more, stocks and bonds had declined to the point "speculative excesses had been reduced, and ongoing portfolio realignments probably were shifting long-term financial assets to firmer hands. As a result, financial markets now appeared to be less likely to overreact to adverse developments or to policy actions." As major banks increased their prime rate from 6¼ to 6¾ percent, congressional Democrats blasted the Fed for killing growth.

Bentsen, who of all Clinton's advisers was most understanding of what the Fed was trying to do, declared there was "no economic justification" for the rise in market rates. The action proved Greenspan had lost none of his authority or ability to forge consensus. The *New York Times* had run a story April 8 claiming Greenspan was losing control of the FOMC and that his inter-meeting discretion had been curtailed. The story was branded "nonsense" by FOMC vice chairman McDonough. Lindsey said that "there has been no change in any Fed policy with regard to the Chairman's prerogatives," but rumors persisted until Greenspan put them to rest by demonstrating his ability to act between meetings. Greenspan did not make the April 18 rate hike to "flex his muscles," however, sources say.

No sooner had the Fed acted than speculation began about the next rate hike. Voting FOMC members Parry and Broaddus fueled it by saying policy was still stimulative in an economy growing faster than potential and running out of surplus resources. The IMF, never shy about giving gratuitous advice, urged further rate hikes. Chief Economist Michael Mussa said the Fed needed to raise the funds rate to 4 to 5 percent, just to make it "neutral." If not, "continued strong growth would tend to create inflationary presures later this year or in 1995." He was preaching to the choir.

On April 22, President Clinton ended the suspense by naming Blinder to take Mullins' place as Fed Board vice chairman. He also nominated University of California at Berkeley economist Janet Yellen to fill the governorship Angell had vacated. Bentsen billed the two as "pragmatists" who would "put our nation on the path to sustainable economic growth." A wave of concern rippled through the markets, particularly since Blinder was seen as a potential successor to Greenspan when his term expired in March 1996. Clinton aide Gene Sperling said Blinder would be "a contender" for the chairmanship. The former Princeton professor's writings as a *Business Week* columnist and his remarks since joining the administration convinced many he did not have the requisite concern about inflation and would water down the FOMC's price stability commitment. He seemed to confirm their fears when, still speaking for the administration that day, he said, "We just don't see signs of an imminent acceleration of inflation . . . except of the most trivial magnitude. . . . They are just not there." Yellen was less well known, but she too was stereotyped a dove. These concerns proved largely unfounded. Indeed, both would bend over backward to disprove suspicions they were soft on inflation. What's more, their Keynesian bent meshed with the Fed's effort to restrain demand to control wage-price pressures. "Once you've grown enough for a certain period of time, you start pressing on capacity and labor markets and you get price pressures," Blinder said March 4. The main thing distinguishing him from other Fed officials was his belief the economy could sustain lower unemployment without generating inflation.

"The whole idea that it's the administration's goal to appoint a bunch of doves to the Fed who have no desire but to do anything other than pump money into the economy and create jobs couldn't have been further from the truth," says Yellen, who has become a respected and influential governor. When she was interviewed by Rubin for the job she got the impression "the administration was very anxious to appoint people to the Board . . . who in reality were concerned about the traditional goals of the Federal Reserve with respect to preserving price stability. . . . I think if I had ever answered the question by saying, 'the heck with inflation; I don't care about that,' that would have been absolutely the end of it." Yellen says she and Blinder, being academic economists, "understand, appreciate and abide by economic reasoning. . . . I consider it in no way respectable to make arguments that are inconsistent with the data, whatever I might like to be true." Greenspan greeted Blinder and Yellen as "eminently qualified." For the most part they would prove that, regardless of economic doctrines or political leanings, once one joins the Fed one becomes a central banker. The two would make their mark, but not in the way expected.

The April rate hike emboldened the Fed's enemies on Capitol Hill. When, on April 28, the Commerce Department's "advance" GDP report showed a 2.6 percent rise in the first quarter, down from what had then been estimated as a 7 percent rise in the fourth quarter, Sasser and Sarbanes seized on it as evidence the Fed had zapped growth. Sasser said the Fed's rate hikes were generating "accelerating enthusiasm" for Fed "reform." Rather than preempting inflation, the Fed had launched "a preemptive strike on growth and jobs." They vowed to push legislation to either remove district presidents from the FOMC or require they be confirmed by the Senate. However, Fed officials were not persuaded the economy was slowing dramatically. Phillips pointed out that, had it not been for a drop in government purchases, real GDP would have grown 4.6 percent, and an adjustment for bad weather would have raised it more.

Another bout of dollar weakness now took a hand in hastening the next Fed rate hike. Greenspan met with his fellow G-7 central bankers and finance ministers Sunday, April 24, under auspicious circumstances. Despite the administration's incessant saber rattling against Japan, the dollar seemed to have stabilized between 103 and 104 yen. Although there was interest and mild concern about Fed rate hikes, especially from France, rumors Greenspan had been "grilled" about where he was taking rates were unfounded. British chancellor of the exchequer Kenneth Clarke expressed astonishment at the hubbub over the Fed's three tightening moves. "It does not seem to me that Greenspan's moves are out of line with previous expectations of policy. It was my belief that everybody expected American interest rates were going to start going up this year" from what had been "remarkably low levels." The bigger concern was that the dollar was still soft despite the Fed rate hikes and expectations of more to come. A senior Treasury official's dubious explanation was that the dollar had failed to strengthen because of "changes in perception of European and Japanese monetary policy." In other words, because markets did not expect European and Japanese rates to fall as much as before, the dollar and foreign currencies had maintained their relative positions despite U.S. rate increases. Even this illusion of stability would soon be shattered.

Speaking for the G-7, Bentsen said, "Exchange rates have remained relatively unaffected during the period of rising long-term interest rates. We continue to believe exchange rates should reflect economic fundamentals and that excessive volatility is undesirable. We'll continue to cooperate closely in exchange markets." This boilerplate concealed considerable concern and dissension. Japanese officials were alarmed at the upward pressure on their currency against the dollar at a time when they were struggling to revive their stagnant economy. They felt the Clinton administration was trying to devalue its way into Japanese markets and manipulate the yen higher to make Japanese goods less competitive. Japan's Finance Minister Hirohisa Fujii told Bentsen further appreciation of the yen would make it impossible for Japan to boost growth as he kept demanding. Some European authorities feared renewed dollar depreciation would become more generalized and cause further growth-stunting increases in interest rates. They were right to be concerned. Five days after the G-7 met, foreign exchange traders tested their will to support the dollar. They drove the dollar down to within a hair's breadth of 100 yen and pushed it to a low of 1.6430 marks, compared to 1.6940 marks the Friday before the G-7 met. Bentsen authorized the Fed to purchase dollars against the mark, but only later did he authorize buying dollars for yen. A Japanese official said Treasury's failure to support the dollar against the yen until it threatened to go to new all-time lows confirmed the administration's "benign neglect" of the dollar where Japan was concerned.

Bentsen said the intervention had been undertaken to "counter disorderly conditions" in currency markets, but the dollar had fallen in a "disorderly" fashion against the yen before. What was different this time was that, as feared, the dollar was now weakening against other currencies, undermining investor confidence in U.S. assets. The main motivation for the intervention, I am told, was to prevent the dollar's weakness from weakening securities prices and driving up interest rates. So long as it did not weaken bond prices, the administration was content to see the dollar drop—an attitude many Fed officials regarded as foolhardy and dangerous. Medium- and long-term rates jumped more than an eighth of a percent as the dollar fell, a cost the Treasury could not afford as it regularly came to market with huge amounts of debt. As Scott Pardee, former head of the New York Fed's foreign exchange desk who was now vice chairman of Yamaichi America (International), observed, "It is hard for me to sell Treasuries when other parts of the administration are likely to start talking the dollar down again." When trading resumed the following week, U.S. and G-7 resolve to support the dollar was tested again. The dollar took a beating on Tuesday, May 3, particularly against European currencies. It fell near DM1.63, prompting a rare Tietmeyer statement that the mark's rise against the dollar threated the German economy. The dollar hovered precariously around 101 yen. In the midst of it all, Bentsen took the occasion to again slam Japan's economic and trade policies. To market observers, it seemed the Treasury secretary wanted to keep selling pressure on the dollar. Finally, Fed officials and others prevailed upon Treasury to change its rhetoric and tactics. Helping to sway Bentsen was word that Japanese investors had liquidated nearly $4 billion worth of Treasury securities in January and February alone. After feverish overnight consultations, the Fed and Treasury joined 15 other central banks in repeated rounds of intervention to push up the dollar Wednesday morning. Bentsen did what he should have done long before and issued a statement saying the administration saw "no advantage in an under-valued currency." The dollar had fallen "beyond what is justified by economic fundamentals." It was the first time he had unequivocally stated the dollar had fallen far enough.

For a while thereafter, the administration was more careful what it said. The dollar steadied, but the market mood was that there was only one way to stabilize the dollar and bond prices, and that was for the Fed to raise rates more aggressively. "As long as we know the Fed is not through tightening, I'm not going to buy bonds yet," said a fund manager. Anything less than a half percent increase in the funds rate would be viewed as half-hearted and inade-quate. The Bundesbank did its part to take pressue off the dollar on May 11 by cutting its discount and Lombard rates a half percent to 4½ and 6 percent, respectively. The Bank of Japan had already lowered money market rates to 2.2 percent. That set the stage for the Fed to raise rates, making the U.S.-German rate spread more favorable to the dollar. Fed officials did not want to raise rates simply to help the dollar. They considered the dollar's weakness a function of administration Japan bashing, careless exchange rate statements, fiscal policy, and capital losses by foreign investors and felt the best way to help the dollar in the long term was, as one put it, "to run the most prudent domes-tic monetary policy possible." However, the dollar's near-term weakness was both a symptom and a cause of financial market stability that could not be ignored. Plus, it was a potential source of inflation. So when the FOMC con-vened on May 17, the dollar's condition was the center of attention.

Many of the April economic figures the FOMC had going into the meeting were not obviously conducive to another rate hike, let alone a large one. Wholesale prices had fallen, while retail prices had risen at an annual rate of just 1.6 percent. Retail sales had fallen, as had housing starts, and the combi-nation of higher borrowing costs and losses in household wealth cast doubt on future consumption and home buying. Industrial production had risen only modestly with no change in capacity utilization. Nonfarm payrolls had grown handsomely, pushing the unemployment rate down a tenth to 6.4 percent. The FOMC was less divided than before. Members were convinced the economy was on track for solid growth, which if not held in check would reduce slack in the economy and raise inflation risks. Moreover, if the Fed did not deliver a substantial increase in rates, they knew the market response could be very neg-ative. They cited the weak dollar as one of the principal factors undercutting bond prices. That afternoon the Fed announced the Board had decided to increase the discount rate from 3 to 3½ percent (the first change since July 1992) and that the FOMC had decided this half-point increase should "show through completely into interest rates in reserve markets." That meant increasing the funds rate from 3¾ to 4¼ percent. The Fed was relieved when bonds rallied. The long bond yield fell from 7⅝ to 7⅜ percent. It had been a gutsy call. Its earlier rate hikes had gotten a mixed response, and the Fed could not be sure how a larger move would be taken. But the members figured decisive action would have "a settling effect."

The currency market reaction was less satisfying. To the Fed's frustration, the dollar, which had rebounded to more than 1.67 marks and 104 yen, fell despite further rate cuts by Germany and Japan and dollar buying by the Bank of Japan. To some extent "buy the rumor, sell the fact" was at work. Now that the Fed had made its move the threat no longer overhung the market, but the reaction also showed confidence had not been restored in U.S. dollar policy. Also, while the Fed had raised the funds rate 1¼ percent, it had not really "tightened credit." It was providing all the reserves demanded at the new funds rate level, and as lending picked up, the money supply expanded. Reserves had grown more than 11 percent since December. Business loans had grown 9½ percent. Credit, ironically, had been tighter when the funds rate was 3 percent, but banks were reluctant to lend. The funds rate was still below the level consistent with an acceptable growth rate. Both the Fed and the administration were projecting 3 percent real growth and 3 percent inflation, or a combined rate of 6 percent nominal GDP. (In the previous two quarters, nominal GDP had grown an average 6.8 percent.) Yet the funds rate was just 4¼ percent. Lindsey, among others, thought the Fed should be shooting for 5 percent nominal GDP growth. The markets sensed monetary policy, while no longer easy, was by no means tight. The dollar's continued vulnerability frustrated the Fed. "The underlying strength of the economy would lead you to think the dollar would be higher, and our interest rates are going up, and that would lead you to think the dollar would be higher," said a high-level source, who blamed the dollar's weakness on the confrontation with Japan. "There's no doubt that's a strong factor." Lindsey warned on May 25 that "the United States cannot assume that the international role of the dollar is unassailable" and that the dollar could be undermined by "an interventionist trade policy." Two days later, Greenspan said, "The behavior of the dollar has been a source of concern."

In announcing the rate hikes May 17, the Fed said the actions, together with its earlier rate hikes, were intended to "substantially remove the degree of monetary accommodation which prevailed throughout 1993." Bentsen, who had been given strong indications of the FOMC's likely decision and its rationale, nevertheless said he hoped the Fed was "ready for a respite." Another Clinton official said the Fed should be "finished for awhile." The administration's "respect for the Fed's independence" was wearing thinner. On June 13, Bentsen said the Fed had raised the funds rate sufficiently to put it in "a neutral position" and that further rate hikes would be "contractionary." Greenspan got an even less sympathetic reception when Riegle summoned him to defend his policies before a hostile Senate Banking Committee on May 27. He stood his ground, patiently explaining why the Fed had done what it did, but refusing to say whether or when it would raise rates again. Greenspan was able to deflect most criticism because "the economy is doing well. . . . We're looking at an economy that is growing at a respectable pace, is balanced and can go on for quite a long period of time." The best way to sustain growth was to prevent the growth of "imbalances" in the economy, such as excessive inventory investment, that would then have to be unwound. There would have been "no reasonable purpose" in keeping policy stimulative. Had the Fed not raised rates, market rates would have risen anyway, perhaps more.

Greenspan acknowledged the Fed had been out to deflate what he called "speculative" rises in bond and stock prices since February. "Lured by consistently high returns in capital markets, people exhibited increasingly a willingness to take on market risk by extending the maturity of their investments." Investors had shifted funds out of bank deposits and money market funds into stocks and bond, "and some of those buying the funds perhaps did not fully appreciate the exposure of their new investments to the usual fluctuations in bond and stock prices." Of course there were many badly burned investors, including supposedly sophisticated ones, who would have preferred Greenspan had not had their interests quite so much at heart. Lest anyone think the Fed was trying to play nanny, Greenspan said the Fed had acted because, "to the degree maturity extension was built on a false sense of security and certainty, it posed a risk to financial markets once that sense began to dissipate." The Fed's rate hikes had been "instrumental in radically altering perceptions of where interest rates were going and of the risk of holding longer-term assets."

Contrary to White House hopes, the Fed had not finished raising rates by a long shot. But for several months, the Fed paused to gauge the impact of what it had done. Having started raising rates relatively early in the game, Fed policymakers felt they had averted the need to raise rates as high as if they had waited, and they felt they could now watch and wait for a while. The data, while not soft, were not so strong the Fed felt it had to move again right away. Most signs pointed to continued growth above what it considered to be "sustainable." Any slowing, said Forrestal, was "marginal." In fact, real growth was eventually calculated at 4 percent or more in each of last three quarters of the year. But at midyear, the Fed could not be certain of that. Not only had there been signs of moderation, growth in the money supply had slowed dramatically. On the other hand, each succeeding survey of senior bank loan officers showed an increased willingness to lend on easier terms, and while consumer prices remained well-behaved, commodity prices were growing at double-digit rates. Inflation had been "clearly restrained," but "that's history; monetary policy is forward-looking," Greenspan told reporters covering the International Monetary Conference in London on June 6.

Adding to the conundrum, the dollar started to come under assault again in mid-June as the U.S.-Japan trade talks dragged on. The residue of stability imparted by the massive May intervention was wearing off, and Lindsey said the dollar's weakness was "a constraint" on monetary policy which the Fed would be "watching closely." Kohn confessed that, even though the Fed did not target exchange rates like other central banks, it "still needs to pay considerable attention to the foreign exchange market." It wasn't just that the lower dollar would tend to raise import costs and erode foreign investor confidence in U.S. assets, it would also tend to spur foreign demand for U.S. goods and further strain factory capacity. The administration remained torn between a desire to avoid bond market destabilizing dollar depreciation and a desire to keep pressure on Japan to reduce its trade surplus. Bentsen claimed June 13 that the intervention he had entered into so reluctantly (and which probably would have been ineffectual in the absence of Fed rate hikes) had "stabilized" the dollar. It was the kiss of death. From then on, the dollar's "stability" steadily eroded, until, on June 21, it fell below the 100 yen level for the first time. The Fed, while concerned about the dollar's weakness, was disinclined to raise rates again so soon. Adding to the selling pressure, the Commerce Department had reported a sharp widening of the U.S. trade deficit. Sensing that, not only had the Fed suspended raising rates, but that there was a limit to Treasury's ability or willingness to support the dollar, traders drove the greenback from 102.21 to 99.90 yen per dollar and pushed it to a nine-month low 1.5887 marks. There was no word from Treasury and no intervention. Dollar weakness fed a flight from long to short-term Treasury securities.

After conferring with Bentsen, it was agreed Greenspan should give the dollar some verbal support. After all, the markets had not been impressed with Bentsen's comments. It was the kind of thing Greenspan tried to avoid doing, but he could not stand by and watch the dollar go into free fall. On June 22, while testifying before the House Budget Committee, he said he and Bentsen had "been following developments very closely because we cannot be indifferent to major movements in our currency." Separately, Bentsen put out a statement declaring the good fundamentals of the U.S. economy were "what is important," but saying he was "concerned by recent movements in the exchange markets." Bentsen said he would be "carefully monitoring developments," stay "in close communication with our G-7 partners," and "be prepared to act as appropriate." Greenspan's statement gave the dollar a temporary boost because of its implicit threat that more than mere sterilized intervention might be on the way. But while they anguished over what Broaddus called "the nagging weakness" of the dollar, Greenspan and his colleagues had no intention of raising rates in a panicky way to prop it up. For one thing, as the ERM crisis had shown, there was no guarantee higher rates would do the job. Broaddus told me the Fed was giving exchange rates "more weight" than usual, but it realized interest rate differentials were only one influence on the dollar. Greenspan had infused his fellows with a calm confidence that, if the Fed continued to pursue sound policies, the dollar would eventually rise above the more ephemeral factors holding it down. For now, it was decided to stay on hold and take a hard look at how the economy performed in June and July before raising rates further.

With the Fed on the sidelines, the dollar continued to suffer. On June 29, it fell below 99 yen, shaken by the arrival of yet another new Japanese govern-

ment. The long bond yield had now reached 7½ percent. Administration officials had heedlessly reverted to their combative rhetoric. The G-7 Economic
Summit was coming up in Naples, and Bentsen said he and Clinton would
press Japan's new Socialist Prime Minister Tomiichi Murayama and Finance
Minister Masayoshi Takemura to "stimulate their economy." There was no
way the United States could reduce its trade deficit "unless we solve our problem with Japan." He said that "the dollar is not a tool of our trade policy" and
that "a stronger dollar is better for our economy," but his words were not taken
at face value. The weak dollar's inflationary implications were the focus of a
great deal of concern at the FOMC's July 5–6 meetings, where Broaddus urged
a further immediate rate hike. However, the majority agreed it was too soon.
It was decided "policy should not be focused narrowly on the dollar alone."
There had continued to be mixed signals on the economy, making the majority cautious about continuing to tighten credit until they could be sure the
economy was not slowing excessively. What's more, M2 growth had slowed to
an annual rate barely above 1 percent, the bottom of the Fed's target range,
and had actually fallen the past couple of months. The most that could be
agreed upon was a tightening bias. When the meeting ended with no rate hike,
traders sold dollars.

Exchange rates were supposed to have been a nonissue at the Naples Summit, held July 8–9 at a palace built by the Spanish Bourbons in the late seven-
teenth century. Instead they became a central focus. Bentsen and a top Clinton
aide set the stage for another run on the dollar by telling reporters the administration did not want to see further Fed rate hikes, despite the dollar's weakness, because growth was more important. It was bad enough for the Treasury
secretary to make such comments, but then the president himself got into the
act. At a Friday, July 8, press conference, he answered questions about the dollar at length, and the more he talked the more traders sold dollars—pushing
the dollar below 98 yen and 1.56 marks. Clinton said the dollar's fall was
mostly a function of the yen's strength and that its fall against the mark was
"well within historic variations." He gave the impression the United States
was disinclined to support the dollar by minimizing the effectiveness of intervention. "Sometimes they work a little bit." He said there were "macroeconomic reasons" for the dollar's weakness beyond U.S. control, chiefly "the
persistent existence of the trade surplus that Japan has with the United States."

Clinton made matters worse by undermining the Fed. The Labor Department had just announced a much bigger than expected June jump in nonfarm
payrolls, but Clinton urged the Fed not to raise rates to avoid inflation. "I
don't think we should do anything to undermine the recovery when we have
still Americans who need jobs, we have still Americans who are working part-
time who wish to work full-time, we have parts of America that have not felt
the recovery, and we have no evidence of inflation. . . . I don't think we should
reverse course. . . . We don't want to adopt a strategy in the short-run that. . . .
could choke off growth. . . ." With an open line to Market News Service's
Frankfurt bureau, I was flashing headlines as the president spoke, and as they
went out over the wire, the desk was informing me almost instantaneously that

the dollar was ratcheting down on each Clinton utterance. When he finally finished, Bentsen and Summers scrambled to undo the damage, telling reporters the administration really was concerned about the dollar, that it still shared the Fed's objectives, and that intervention had not been ruled out. But when trading resumed Monday July 11, the dollar sank to new lows of 96.60 yen and 1.516 marks.

Back in the States flabbergasted Fed officials could only shake their heads in dismay. Greenspan made clear how he felt in his July 20 Humphrey-Hawkins testimony. The dollar's drop "clearly signals more inflation pressures," he told the Senate Banking Committee. "To the extent that it is a symptom of potential inflationary forces beginning to emerge in our domestic economy, that has to be something we are focusing on. . . . When you have an economy like the U.S. that is so intricately involved on a global basis with the world financial markets . . . any evidence of weakness in that currency is neither good for the international financial system nor good for the American economy because of what they say about what is going on in the American system. . . . If we allow the dollar to weaken as a reserve currency, we will have consequences not only in our domestic system, but I think we will have significant problems with our responsibilites as a world leader." In an indication of the importance of exchange rates to monetary policy, he added, "I would be quite concerned about a dollar that did not show significant strength." Greenspan was signaling the credit tightening hiatus was coming to an end. The dollar meshed with other factors pushing the Fed to raise rates. There was still little actual inflation, but its precursors were evident and were showing up both in exchange rates and bond yields. With unemployment having fallen to 6 percent and capacity utilization near 84 percent, slack had "become relatively small." The economy was in "a rapid expansion" and was growing "appreciably above its longer-run trend."

At the August 16 FOMC meeting, it was a foregone conclusion the Fed would be raising rates. The only question was how much. In the days before the meeting, administration officials had resorted to more of the high-pressure tactics they had putatively disavowed to head off a rate hike. A spokeswoman for Bentsen said, "He doesn't think it's necessary at this time."[5] Munnell had recently said interest rates had reached "equilibrium." Rubin and other administration officials were asserting the Fed had no reason to worry about inflation. The Fed's beige book said otherwise. Greenspan had continued to express concern about the dollar, telling Congress the Fed did "not very specifically" target the dollar's value, but its "primary" goal was to "insure the stability of the currency. . . . It is very important that the dollar be a strong and viable currency." To that end, it was vital U.S. "rates of return be sufficiently attractive to induce foreigners to hold dollar-based assets." The FOMC shared his concern. The dollar's depreciation, which the minutes diplomatically attributed to "evolving perceptions of the degree to which U.S. authorities were concerned about further weakness in the currency," was seen pushing up prices directly via import costs and indirectly by stimulating production for export when factories were already operating close to capacity. Industrial production and housing were surging. M2 had rebounded. A big July payroll rise tightened labor markets. Consumer spending was still in doubt, but business fixed investment in plant and equipment more than made up the difference. The possibility that all this investment, together with excess capacity abroad, would alleviate capacity constraints was acknowledged by Fed officials, but they were not prepared to bet the ranch on it. They felt "a more decisive policy move might reduce the need for further tightening later." After a unanimous vote, the Fed announced another half percent rise in the discount rate to 4 percent and a rise in the funds rate from 4¼ to 4¾ percent. In a phrase it would come to regret, the Fed said its actions were "expected to be sufficient, at least for a time, to meet the objective of sustained, noninflationary growth."

Bond prices stabilized but only temporarily, and the action gave the dollar only a temporary boost. Administration sources blamed the Bundesbank's failure to ease for the dollar's continued weakness against the mark and other European currencies, but at 4.85 percent, the Bundesbank's *repo rate*, the German equivalent of the federal funds rate, was only 10 basis points above the funds rate, and yields on 10-year German government bonds had been trading within a hair's breadth of comparable U.S. Treasuries. Real rates were not much different. So the dollar's weakness could not be explained in terms of rate spreads. Ongoing U.S.-Japan trade tensions were part of the explanation, but could not fully explain the mutually reinforcing weakness of the dollar and Treasury prices. The Fed had done everything it reasonably could do to defuse inflation. That left fiscal policy. The administration boasted it had cut the deficit in half, and indeed the deficit was falling. However, for market participants, including foreign investors taking a currency risk when they bought U.S. paper, it was the "out-years" that mattered most, and even under optimistic OMB assumptions, the deficit was due to start ballooning in 1996. They felt the administration was not doing enough to curb future deficits.

While the markets had great faith in the Greenspan Fed, there was an unavoidable suspicion that some future Fed would accommodate federal financing needs at the expense of the dollar's purchasing power. It was frustrating for the Fed, knowing no matter how responsibly it conducted current policy, the markets had built an ingrained distrust of future policy into interest and exchange rates. This fact of life forced the Fed to worry more about the dollar than it cared to. Like it or not, admit it or not, the Fed was forced to base policy partially on exchange rate concerns. "It was a consideration," though not the dominating influence, Blinder says. "Some say it was never a factor, it was never discussed, it was never on anybody's mind, and monetary policy just blithely went along as if there was no such thing as the exchange rate. I don't think that's correct."

August 16 was the first meeting in which both Blinder and Yellen participated, and their concurrence with the rate hikes quieted most talk about their dovishness, but not all of it. Two weeks later, Blinder addressed the Fed's Jackson Hole conference, held in the shadow of the magestic Grand Tetons—aptly enough, since the *New York Times* made a mountain out of a molehill over differences between Blinder and Greenspan on the question of what the Fed could or should do to maximize employment. Greenspan said a central bank could not be expected to push unemployment down where it has become a "structural" problem. To the extent joblessness was not cyclical but due to factors beyond the reach of monetary policy (like overly generous unemployment benefits, payroll taxes, and government regulations) there was a strict limit on what a central bank could do to generate jobs without inducing inflation. "Any tendency to seek a bit of macro policy relief by pushing on the outer limits of monetary policy risks longer term financial instability." Blinder saw a greater role for monetary policy in bringing down unemployment by spurring demand, but only when unemployment was well above the country's *natural* rate (NAIRU). "The job of the central bank is to push or pull or guide the unemployment rate to its natural rate and not higher." There was little practical difference between what the two top Fed officials were saying. Neither believed it possible to push unemployment below a certain point without causing inflation. The only question was where the natural rate was—an imponderable economists had disputed for years. Blinder thought it was close to 5.8 percent, but with unemployment then at 6.1 percent, he said the economy was getting "extremely close" to full employment, a view also held by Greenspan. But the *Times* portrayed their academic discussion as a "clash" that had made other officials angry at Blinder.

The story perpetuated Blinder's dove reputation. It also advanced the notion Blinder was at odds with Greenspan and the rest of the Board and was out to usurp Greenspan's power. Before he decided to return to Princeton, Blinder told me he had been the victim of "backstabbing" by both other Board members and senior staffers which contributed to what he called "the media frenzy" over his remarks in Jackson Hole. He would not name names. For the most part, though, he enjoyed "very cordial and polite" relations at the Fed and denies any serious rift or rivalry with Greenspan. "The rivalry is greatly exaggerated." Although the two had differences on other issues, when it came to monetary policy, "there's no disagreement." As for his alleged ambitions to succeed Greenspan, he says that "there was no understanding" when he accepted the vice chairmanship he would be in line to become chairman, "nor any such expectation. I was well aware that no vice chairman has ever become chairman in this organization. It is not a stepping stone toward the chairmanship."

While their policy differences with Republican appointees were exaggerated, Blinder and Yellen did take a different approach. They experienced culture shock when they arrived. Blinder, who had been away from academia a year and a half, found the Fed to be "even more formal, even more hierarchical . . . than I realized from the outside." He could not get used to always being addressed as Vice Chairman Blinder and having to address others as Governor this or President that after having sat around the White House calling President Clinton "Bill" and the Treasury secretary "Lloyd." Formality permeated the institution. After about the eleventh time the Fed's switchboard operator said, "Mr. Vice Chairman, I have a call for you," Blinder asked her to please call him Mr. Blinder or Dr. Blinder. "The next phone call she said either Mr. or Dr.

Blinder or something, but by the second one she had reverted back to Vice Chairman. It was too informal, she just couldn't do it." Already under pressure to conform to prove he was not "soft on inflation," Blinder soon found there was "a tradition around here . . . that dissent is a huge deal, that you only dissent on a really fundamental disagreement. . . . You sort of feel that around here. It's in the water." Even the Supreme Court, he notes, has dissenters.

Yellen found the same "cultural bias" against dissenting and says she "would only dissent if I thought I had a significant disagreement. I see an awful lot of people voting yes when they're not really getting their first choice. They clearly have qualms from time to time about what they're being asked to do, and they go along with it." For her the pressure to go along was even greater. "My own perspective on it is I walk into a situation where I'm perceived as a dove, and [others are asking] 'what are the Clinton people going to do? Are they going to go along? Is there going to be a big policy split?' I figured if I dissent it's taken by the outside world as a definite, significant, policy difference. I don't want to dissent unless I regard that as the appropriate interpretation, so I would reserve . . . it for a time when I want the outside world to understand I didn't agree."

They were also astonished at the power and inaccessability of the Fed staff. "I found the Fed bureaucracy harder, much harder, to penetrate than I thought it would be," says Blinder. "I think the staff has enormous influence around here and tries constantly to have even more." Blinder and Yellen were not the first to be surprised and dismayed at the status of senior staffers, who in 1995 were paid $170,700, compared to Greenspan's $133,600, and other governors' $123,100. LaWare says it sometimes seemed "the governors worked for the staff instead of the other way around." The staff exercise great influence in shaping the governors' views with their weekly, Monday morning analyses of the latest economic numbers and set the terms of debate at FOMC meetings. LaWare says he "never had the feeling the staff was really dominating monetary policy," but had a "suspicion that the presentation of the [short-run policy] alternatives and the effects may have been designed to support whatever the Chairman was going to come up with." Greenspan always defends his staff and his relationship with it. "The strength of the Fed down deep lies in its staff," he said April 22, 1996. "While it may appear I take unilateral action with the staff, that is never done without [FOMC] consultation," he told the Senate Banking Committee on March 26, 1996.

Blinder and Yellen discovered that, as board members appointed by the president and confirmed by the Senate to help run the nation's monetary policy, they were to be virtually walled off from Fed staffers as they closeted themselves to prepare their forecasts for each FOMC meeting. Yellen says the Fed staff is "a marvel of government" with its "huge repository of expertise," but she found it frustrating not being able to freely communicate with them. "The ethos behind what the staff does is that the governors, the Chairman, nobody, is supposed to mess with them. And they go off in their own room, and they talk things through, where things are headed, then they set it out in front of us, and you can take it or you can leave it. Early on, I asked if I could go to the

meetings where the forecast was prepared, and I was told that I could not."
Yellen wanted to better understand the process the staff used to come up with
its detailed economic forecast and the monetary policy assumptions on which
it was based, but was told the staff was an independent group of economists
who worked for the FOMC as a whole to produce the best possible objective
analysis and that any single FOMC member who got involved in the process
"would influence the process in an unhealthy way." Greenspan became concerned when he saw Yellen talking to the staff, fearing she might "impurify"
the staff forecast.

"The staff is not anxious to lay forth their reasoning process, uncertainties
and doubts and internal controversies in front of the governors," says a Fed
official. "They protect the information they have." The staff's attitude was
"decide what your position is, and when you have a position come to the governors and tell them what it is and then they can say yes or no. But staff don't
argue in front of the governors. You're not supposed to air your 'dirty laundry'
in front of the governors." Having come from milieus in which vigorous, open
debate was encouraged, Blinder and Yellen had trouble coming to grips with
the staff's cloistered preparation of its forecast. They expected the staff would
present several alternatives to consider and then engage in discussion with
them and other officials over the merits of each before a decision was made.
That was not how things were done when they arrived. Staffers debated
among themselves over the economic and policy assumptions that went into
their forecast, but did not inform the policymakers what they had considered
and rejected. The FOMC debate then centered on a sanitized forecast, contained in "the greenbook," along with short-term policy alternatives contained
in "the bluebook."

They were astounded to learn the staff's forecast of how the economy
would behave over the next one to two years, which they would not glimpse
until just days before they had to vote, was conditioned on a single assumption
about the course of short-term interest rates and ordinarily made no effort to
present alternative economic scenarios under different policy assumptions—
only very short-term policy options. Blinder and Yellen wondered how they
could decide whether or not they liked the forecast without seeing some alternative outcomes based on alternative assumptions about where rates were
headed. "I was shocked when I got here to see it wasn't being done already,"
says Blinder. "This is hardly a revolutionary idea. It's hardly an idea." Although
supposedly the staff did not give policy advice, the new arrivals learned the
staff was choosing an assumption about the funds rate path that would generate the kind of outcome, in terms of growth, employment and inflation, that it
thought the FOMC ought to be moving in or that it thought the majority
wanted. "That appeared to me to be a strong piece of policy advice being given
without really defending it," says Yellen. "It's a judgmental forecast, and it's
really pretty difficult, if you've not participated in it and [known] the guts of
where it came from. I didn't feel that much attempt was made to show what
would happen under alternative monetary policy assumptions. I considered
that to be very strong but unstated policy advice. . . ."

Not everyone was dissatisfied with the old system. "The FOMC takes the assumption that the staff has used in order to make its economic projections as a baseline from which it starts its own analysis, and there is no compunction at all, on the part of the committee, about going a different route than the staff may have gone in the assumptions that it has made," one policymaker says. "Sometimes the committee will wind up in exactly the same place; sometimes it will be different." The staff's forecast is "taken very seriously," but "they do not make a recommendation and the committee does not approach their analysis as being a recommendation."

However, it galled Yellen and Blinder that the typical greenbook did not, for instance, show how the Fed could move more rapidly or more slowly towards price stability than the staff assumed. Although the bluebook at each meeting presented options for what the Fed could do between then and the next meeting (basically tighter, looser, or no change), the Fed's longer-term strategy was based on a forecast conditioned on one rate path. Ironically, the less politically accountable Fed presidents, while they too were shielded from the Board staff prior to FOMC meetings, had their own economists and got the benefit of more open discussion of policy pros and cons than the governors. Unlike the presidents, the governors could not hold mock FOMC meetings with their staff prior to the real event. Rarely could governors ask for advice from a Kohn or Prell or give it. What was true of those division directors was even more true of their subordinates. "The division directors want to know what the governors are hearing, and they want to make sure that the governors are hearing ideas that have been fully vetted internally," says an official. "Let's say staff member X has some wild idea. Staff member X is not supposed to go talk to a governor and trot this wild idea out on the governor. It's supposed to have gone through all the levels of the establishment before it hits the governor. . . . There are rules in place that the staff members are not supposed to even talk to governors unless they have division officers with them."

All this struck Blinder and Yellen as a bit crazy. Other governors had been dissatisfied with established procedures, but for the most part had chosen to grin and bear it. The two Clinton appointees set about to change the system but met staunch resistance. "I and a few others were very insistent . . . that alternative forecasts under different monetary policies be considered," says Blinder. "I don't see how you could possibly make a monetary policy decision without doing that frankly." Blinder cannot recall any objections from Greenspan but says the staff resisted tooth and nail. Finally, they agreed to append to each forecast an examination of how the economy would behave under alternative policy assumptions, albeit only in summary form. "It came about because myself and some others stomped their feet and started breaking windows, figuratively speaking," says Blinder. "To me it's so axiomatic that to go back in the other direction is unthinkable. If anything we need to be going further in the direction we've moved—more detailed exploration of alternatives. I can't speak for everybody, but I think there's a strong feeling that it's better to have these alternatives." In the face of considerable resistance, Blinder and Yellen also were able to break down some of the traditional firewalls separating governors from staffers, inviting them to their offices to discuss policy issues without clearing it through the boss. The information flow remains constricted, however. The staff, in preparing the greenbook, still keeps its deliberations secret. The many memos they write and discussions they have concerning forecast uncertainties and exigencies are kept secret. Low probability events, like stock market crashes and Mexican financial collapses, are still given relatively short shrift in the preparation of forecasts.

The seeds of dissent sown by Blinder and Yellen took root. In early 1996, after Blinder had left, Lindsey, Kelley, and Phillips joined Yellen in complaining to Greenspan that they were being left out of the loop by the chairman, Truman, and other staffers, especially on international financial issues. Greenspan later called the confrontation "no big deal," but acknowledged he had taken steps to route staff documents to all the governors to assuage their concerns.

Having raised the funds rate 1¼ percent by mid-August, the Fed again paused to assess the economy's momentum before moving further. Many officials hoped to avoid making rates restrictive, rather than "neutral," and were hoping past rate hikes would slow growth enough that the economy would not overshoot capacity and full employment. Barring a big surprise in the economic numbers, they decided no further moves should be made until the November 15 FOMC meeting. That this was after the election was pure coincidence, officials insist. For a while, the numbers cooperated. Unemployment stayed just above 6 percent in August. In a series of interviews after the August 16 FOMC meeting, officials as various as Blinder, Hoenig, Kelley, Lindsey, and Phillips expressed relief the expansion was "moderating." Blinder thought there was "at least a fighting chance" the Fed had raised rates enough to achieve "a soft landing." Many observers began to think the Fed had done all it was going to do. Wholesale prices were rising rapidly, but most officials were prepared to overlook this as a delayed reaction to the easy policies the Fed had now corrected, provided growth was moderate. The CPI was rising at a more comforting 0.3 percent. The dollar was still soft, but there was little the Fed could do so long as the U.S.-Japan trade dispute was overhanging the market. Officials tried to take comfort in the fact that, against the currencies of trading partners like Canada, Mexico, and the United Kingdom, the dollar was firm.

The Fed got a jolt September 19 when a strong August gain in industrial production pushed its measure of capacity utilization to 84.7 percent—a tenth of a percent shy of its previous cyclical peak and near the traditional inflation flashpoint. Administration officials, knowing the FOMC would meet in a week, minimized the inflationary implications. To be inflationary, capacity utilization had to "get into the 85 to 86 to 87 percent range and stay there for some time," Tyson said. At most, there might be a small "cyclical uptick" in inflation. Nevertheless, the long bond yield shot up to 7.8 percent. Many Fed officials became convinced they would have to raise the funds rate at least another half percent, a view reinforced by the dollar's weakness. Summers kept the exchange rate pot boiling by threatening retaliatory trade sanctions against

Japan September 21, holding the dollar around 98 yen. Nor had Ambassador to Japan Mondale been terribly diplomatic, declaring on September 6 that his host country's "massive current account surplus denies other countries export and growth opportunities" and complaining it had not done enough to stimulate demand. New Boston Fed president Cathy Minehan said the potential inflationary impulse was "definitely something we need to watch and take into account." But most policymakers were not ready to take another step up the rate ladder. There was too much uncertainty. The economy was still exhibiting "fairly solid underlying growth," Greenspan told the Senate Banking Committee September 22, but it was "clear the rate of growth is slowing" and it was "unclear the extent to which the diminishment is proceeding." At the September 27 meeting, the FOMC was concerned the economy would not slow soon enough to head off accelerating inflation, but not concerned enough to raise rates right away. The staff was projecting a slowdown, and the money supply was weak. So, except for Broaddus, they contented themselves with a tightening bias.

A few days later, Greenspan flew to Madrid for the fall meetings of the IMF and World Bank, including the usual G-7 meeting. The IMF's Mussa said the Fed would need to raise rates further if the dollar continued to weaken. Aside from threatening inflation, the dollar's weakness against the yen was hindering Japan's recovery, a viewpoint Takemura was only too happy to echo. As the G-7 met on Saturday, October 1, the United States and Japan reached a partial trade agreement covering insurance and government procurement, which gave the dollar a small boost. Bentsen said he would not mind seeing a "slightly stronger dollar," as it rose from 98 to 100 yen on Monday. People wondered "Why did he say 'slightly'?" When I talked to him a day later, Bentsen confirmed he meant to say he wanted "a slightly stronger dollar." He reminded me he had called for "a stronger yen" in February 1993, but "we have a different ratio now . . . I am comfortable where it is." Bentsen thereby kept alive the old question of where U.S. dollar policy really stood as the most critical segment of the "framework talks" with Japan, covering autos and auto parts, dragged on. A Bentsen aide told me Bentsen's words "speak for themselves. . . . The Secretary chooses his words carefully." That was just what the Fed was afraid of.[6]

The dollar's "strength" was short-lived. By mid-October, it was plunging. It fell to a two-year low against the mark below 1.49 marks and hit a record 96.10 yen by November 2. Bentsen finally ordered intervention to little effect. The depreciation would have been fine with the administration, except that again it was undermining financial assets. By the end of the month the long bond yield was near $8\frac{1}{8}$ percent—$2\frac{1}{8}$ percent higher than a year earlier. True to form, administration officials sallied forth to give the dollar vocal support. In his strongest language yet, Summers said allowing the dollar to depreciate "would be a dangerous policy." A strong dollar was needed to control inflation and to "promote stability." Moreover, "the dollar's role as a reserve currency makes the pursuit of stability especially important." Such protestations did not ring true. Bentsen had just recently said he was "comfortable" when the dollar would buy just 100 yen—a 25 percent loss of value since he came to office.

Having planted and watered the seed of doubt about its commitment to a strong dollar, the administration now could not understand why the economy's sound fundamentals were not lending it more support. The answer was simple. Fundamentals, not rhetoric or intervention, do ultimately determine a currency's value, but if investors believe a government wants it lower, they naturally presume the government will act to make it lower and will demand higher yields in compensation. Crow observes:

> I think a concern that's always been there, and it's probably the case that the Fed is more sensitive to it than the Treasury, is the question of confidence among holders of claims in U.S. dollars. If people know that you want your currency to decline in the future, they're going to want to hold it at a higher rate of interest than they do now, given that knowledge, because they're going to be losing value in terms of their own currency. If people get the impression, "Well, the only way the U.S. dollar, or the Canadian dollar for that matter, can go is down," that will show up in your bond market in higher bond yields. Now, that's one way one could persuade the Treasury to tread carefully in regard to what is said, because you don't want to pay more for your government debt than you have to. . . . The Fed wouldn't engage, as a matter of principle, in talking down its currency. . . . It would be concerned to not leave holders of claims in U.S. dollars, including Americans, feeling that they're holding a depreciating asset, because that will show up in some ways you won't like, if they really come to believe that fully, in terms of higher interest rates. Everybody is more aware of this relationship of domestic financial markets to exchange rates now than they used to be, as markets have become more global.

Fed officials were alarmed at the dollar's fresh deterioration and accompanying plunge in bond prices. They had already gotten evidence of stronger growth than they had bargained on, although inflation remained moderate. Unemployment dropped from 6.1 to 5.9 percent in September. "It's quite clear the economy is chugging along very well and that whatever slowdown we thought had occurred in the third quarter probably didn't," an FOMC voter confided. Broaddus said the markets were telling the Fed it had "not completed the job" and still had "a ways to go." Support built for further tightening measures. By late October, some were prepared to raise the funds rate three-quarters or even a full percent. They felt the Fed had waited too long already. The dollar's depreciation had taken some of the sting out of the Fed's rate hikes, since it had a stimulative effect on exports. Many were ready to back Greenspan if he wanted to tighten before the November 15 FOMC meeting. "What are we waiting for?" some wondered. But there was reluctance to move so close to the elections. Meanwhile, administration officials continued to dismiss Fed inflation fears. When the Commerce Department announced a 3.7 percent rise in third-quarter real GDP (later revised to 4 percent), while one of its inflation measures took a quirky drop below 2 percent, Panetta declared one "couldn't ask for a better set of numbers." In fact, inflation was threatening. Commodity prices were soaring, and the beige book found "increasing reports" of rising wages and of manufacturers passing along higher raw and intermediate material costs in higher finished goods prices. The price component of the purchasing managers index rose to 79.9—its highest level since July 1988—in October, as the total index of industrial activity jumped sharply. Average hourly earnings rose at an 8½ percent annual rate, as unemployment fell to 5.8 percent, its lowest level in four years.

Then came the November 8 election, ushering in the so-called "Republican revolution." The election results would make the Fed's job easier in some respects. There would be less badgering and no threats to its independence from incoming committee chairmen, and the election would turn out to be the high-water mark for long-term interest rates (near 8¼ percent), as the focus began to turn toward GOP efforts to eliminate the federal deficit, as promised in their "Contract With America." At long last, it appeared Greenspan would get his balanced budget. However, the Fed was in for a long and stormy year as an interested observer in the fiscal battles to come between President Clinton and the first Republican Congress in 40 years.

With the election behind it, the Fed had a near-term choice to make, and it did so with little hesitancy at the November 15 meeting. It raised the discount and funds rates three-quarters of a percent to 4¾ and 5½ percent, respectively. The actions were called "necessary to keep inflation contained and thereby foster sustainable economic growth." The dollar's weakness was not mentioned in the announcement, but had been an ingredient in the decision. Absent was any mention of the rate hikes being "sufficient," although the FOMC reverted to a "symmetrical" directive, presuming no further rate hikes until at least the December 19 meeting. The only question was how much to raise rates. Some thought anything more than a half percent would be overkill, since the economy had yet to feel the impact of the five previous rate hikes. They warned a large move could damage consumer and business confidence and dislocate markets. But the majority argued "an unusually sizable firming of monetary policy was desirable" to "improve the prospects for curbing intensifying inflationary pressures before they gathered further momentum" and "contribute to market stability." There were no dissents. Gonzalez and other Democrats issued their usual jeremiads, but House Speaker-to-be Newt Gingrich endorsed the Fed action. The Georgia congressman was "prepared to argue that part of the long-term change we're going through ought to be to have a very severe effort to move towards a very stable money environment." Gingrich also put the Fed on notice that, far from being a reckless tax cutting legislature that would balloon the deficit, the new Congress was going to go all out for balanced budgets. He suggested Greenspan "talk to [incoming Senate Majority Leader Bob] Dole and me and see what our general plans are, and they might come to the conclusion that we're going to be fiscally fairly restrained." He also said the Humphrey-Hawkins Act should be amended to give the Fed a price stability mandate.

Reborn hawk Blinder told me he had voted for the rate hike to avoid an "overshooting of capacity" and was prepared to do so again, a view shared by Kelley, LaWare, and others. Unemployment had dropped to 5.6 percent in November, near the bottom of what even its most optimistic aficionados believed NAIRU to be. Industrial production, retail sales, home sales, and producer prices rose sharply. Greenspan told the Joint Economic Committee on December 7 the economy was "stronger than we had anticipated." Inventories were still modest relative to sales, implying no downward pressure on production. "Extraordinary" corporate profits were encouraging heavy investment in plant and equipment. Higher interest rates had yet to "pass through" to borrowers because of easier bank loan terms and conditions, and the Fed was "monitoring carefully" the resulting credit explosion. It was a signal the Fed would start leaning on banks not to adopt lax lending standards. Soon Lindsey and others were hinting the Fed might tighten less if banks stopped lending so aggressively. Sarbanes, who would have become chairman of the Senate Banking Committee but for the election results, told Greenspan he was exaggerating the inflation risk and said, "Leave the economy be." Greenspan told him the Fed "cannot ignore experience." Some Fed officials feared rates would have to go much higher to cool the economy. Some wanted to raise rates again at the December 20 FOMC meeting, by which time the unemployment rate had dropped to 5.6 percent. But the Fed had raised rates 2½ percent, and no one could be sure if that was enough. Besides, the Fed had a worried eye on developments in Mexico. The time had come again to pause.

CHAPTER TEN

Coping with a Peso Crisis
and a Fiscal Fiasco

With all its concerns about the U.S. economy, the Fed did not need to worry about anyone else's, but Mexico gave it little choice. After hemorrhaging foreign exchange reserves trying to keep the peso within a narrow 4.4 percent band of fluctuation against the dollar, America's third largest trading partner had belatedly faced reality and devalued on December 20. Two days later the government let the peso "float," a nice way of saying it sank like a stone. From 3.3 pesos per dollar before the devaluation, the Mexican currency fell to 5.7 per dollar by the year-end—a 42 percent plunge in purchasing power in a matter of days. That was just the beginning. In the new year, it continued to depreciate, reaching a low of almost 7.5 pesos per dollar. The result was a collapse of confidence in Mexican financial markets. The inflows of capital on which Mexico had come to depend dried up. In a desperate effort to stabilize the peso, prevent a bad outbreak of inflation, and restore investor confidence, the Bank of Mexico sharply increased interest rates. The Mexican economy slid into a deep recession.

Trade with Mexico was a not inconsequential factor for the U.S. economy, particularly for states bordering Mexico. The United States had shipped some $50 billion in merchandise exports to Mexico in 1994 and run a net surplus of $1.5 billion. Financial institutions from the United States and other investors had invested $34 billion in Mexican government securities, many more billions in Mexican stocks, as well as $53 billion worth of direct investments, and while the Fed had no desire to protect individual investors, it could not ignore the destabilizing effect on the U.S. and world financial system posed by the crisis. The Fed also feared there would be a "contagion effect" from the Mexican crisis spreading throughout Latin America, which collectively absorbed nearly a fifth of all U.S. exports, and other "emerging markets." The loss of investor confidence in Mexico had spread quickly to Argentina, Brazil, and other nations, collapsing their stock markets, torpedoing the value of their Brady bonds, undermining their currencies, and threatening their hard-won prosperity.

Although many foreign investors, who had poured money into high-yielding Mexican securities, were foolishly surprised, the crisis had been brewing for a long time and certainly should have come as no surprise to the Fed or the Treasury. They had gone to Mexico's aid the previous March by expanding their currency swap lines with the Bank of Mexico. Mexican Brady bonds had fallen more than 12 percent even before Colosio's assassination, though they were collateralized by U.S. Treasury zero coupon bonds. Other Mexican debt and equity securities had fallen much more than that. Matters got worse after the assassination. The Fed's Truman called for "a greater degree of policy coordination" among the United States, Mexico, and Canada to guard against "increased risks associated with systemic disruptions." Mexico pledged to strengthen its monetary, fiscal, and regulatory policies and increase its domestic savings to make itself less dependent on foreign capital. It also reaffirmed its commitment to pegging the peso. Things settled down, and the markets got constant reassurances from the Treasury and the IMF that Mexico's finances were "fundamentally sound."

The Clinton administration, which had expended considerable political capital getting NAFTA ratified, wanted to believe Mexico would succeed in its economic reforms and become a growing market for U.S. companies. In fact, things were rapidly deteriorating, as both the Treasury and the Fed well knew. Summers admitted the Treasury and the Fed had been "actively engaged in watching developments in Mexico" throughout 1993 and 1994 and had made "repeated warnings" to Mexican officials that their policies were unsustainable in March 10, 1995, Senate Banking Committee testimony. He told an angry Chairman D'Amato he had kept secret his concerns about Mexico, which had "become more serious" by early summer 1994, because he did not think it appropriate to "undermine the currencies of other countries by making statements about the policies of other countries"—this despite Treasury calls for greater "transparency" by countries in keeping markets informed about their economic and financial conditions. It was no great secret that, with its elections approaching in August, the Mexican government, ruled by the PRI party for a half century, had been playing fast and loose with the country's finances and papering over its deficit financing with heavy issues of a new kind of debt known as *Tesobonos*—short-term notes denominated in pesos but indexed to the dollar.[1] Fund managers loved them because they bore a substantial premium over comparable U.S. Treasury securities but seemed free of foreign exchange risk. This kept money flowing into Mexico's coffers, enabling it to finance a widening current account deficit, as Mexicans used their increasingly overvalued pesos to buy more goods abroad than they could export. But foreign investors' nervousness about uprisings in the Chiapas province and other signs of political instability kept capital from flowing in at the rates of previous years. The Bank of Mexico, unwilling to weaken the economy by tightening money enough to strengthen its currency, steadily depleted its dollar reserves to buy up pesos and stave off a preelection devaluation. The government gambled that, after the election, money would pour back into Mexico.

Things only got worse in January, despite President Ernesto Zedillo's announcement of an austerity plan coupled with an $18 billion basket of credit lines. On January 3, the Fed and Treasury jointly announced they were expanding their swap line with Mexico from $6 billion to $9 billion, while the

Bank of Canada added $1 billion. The G-10 central banks contributed $5 billion from their General Arrangements to Borrow (GAB) fund, via the BIS, and a group of ten commercial banks contributed another $3 billion. The IMF hinted it would expedite a $7.8 billion loan to Mexico. Greenspan said he would "doubt very much" if the Fed and Treasury would need to provide further credits. Summers was making even rosier pronouncements. Such hopes proved premature, as Mexico's crisis continued to deepen. It soon became evident $18 billion was far from adequate. Rubin, who had been designated Treasury secretary after Bentsen retired December 22, enlisted Greenspan's support for something much more ambitious.

This presented Greenspan with a dilemma. As he'd shown in the Drexel affair, it went against his grain to bail out anyone, much less a sovereign nation. He believed rescuing people from the consequences of their misbehavior encouraged more such behavior. This view was shared by other Fed officials. There was still an FOMC aversion to expanding currency swap lines. Greenspan and his colleagues also feared being accused of bailing out the big banks and other fat cats with investment exposures by giving Mexico the wherewithal to pay its debts and stabilizing Mexican securities prices. On the other hand, Mexico was not only a major U.S. trading partner, it was America's neighbor. It was a source not only of cheap goods but of plenty of potential problems which could only get worse if its economy fell apart. A Dallas Fed economist estimated growth in the Southwest would be reduced by a half percent because of Mexico's difficulties. Tyson estimated national GDP growth would lose 1 percent if the U.S. government did not come to the rescue. Other nations which had pursued sounder policies than Mexico were undeservedly suffering spillover effects that threatened to destabilize the world's interdependent financial system. Greenspan also had to consider the potential blow to global growth as developing country markets for industrialized nations' exports evaporated. The IMF, which had a great deal of egg on its face for not having foreseen or warned of the Mexican crisis, had projected in 1994 that the economies of developing countries would expand a real 5.5 percent in 1995, providing a major impetus to growth in the rest of the world. Now such hopes were vanishing. Mexico had $81 billion worth of debt coming due that year, and the Mexican government owed U.S. government agencies $8.1 billion. There was the real threat of a Mexican default.

Much as Greenspan would have preferred letting Mexico and its investors take their lumps in a freely operating market, he felt that option had already been foreclosed. "Once you have a system with a safety net underneath it, creating a lot of moral hazard, you don't have a choice at that time to say, 'Well let's support laissez-faire,' " he says. "Once you construct a financial market with all sorts of fail-safe mechanisms supporting it, preventing the system from working by itself, you're forced to regulate, because you effectively have shut down part of the self-correcting mechanisms of the market. That was very clearly the case in the Mexican situation." He decided the United States had no real choice but to assist Mexico and made up his mind to help the administration persuade Congress to authorize a $40 billion aid package. He stood side by side with Rubin in the White House press room January 12, as the new Treasury secretary announced the administration's intention to seek congressional approval of the unprecedented bundle of loans and loan guarantees, which Summers termed the use of "massive financial force" to overcome the problem.

Greenspan, Rubin, and Summers had made the rounds on Capitol Hill the day before, cajoling Gingrich, Dole, and key committee chairmen, as well as Democratic leaders to support the plan. Indiana senator Richard Lugar, chairman of the Senate Agriculture Committee, said Greenspan had stressed the Mexican crisis's "importance to banks here and financial markets across the world." The announcement strengthened Mexico's currency, stocks, and bonds. Greenspan became a fixture on the Hill as he and Rubin made the rounds of the House and Senate office buildings testifying and lobbying in support of the package. There was "very close cooperation" between Fed and Treasury, says a top Fed official. By all accounts, Greenspan played a key role in persuading Republican leaders to back the plan. House Banking Committee chairman Jim Leach says Greenspan was "absolutely on target on Mexico." A senior Clinton adviser says Greenspan thought of the Mexican financial crisis in the same way he regarded the 1987 stock market crash. "He believed and believes to this day that this was a threat, a significant threat to the global financial system, and he thought it imperative to do something. And it wasn't a matter of coaxing him. That was his analysis of the situation, and it conformed with ours." A Fed governor confirms, "Greenspan felt very strongly that this was the way to go and that it was necessary to do it, and he was in very strong support of it."

The Fed chairman was putting his credibility and, some said, his independence on the line. The FOMC was divided on what role the Fed should play. Some thought it unseemly for the chairman to be lobbying Congress. "There was quite a lot of debate in the FOMC about how appropriate it was for us to become involved," recalls one Board member, who supported Fed involvement but was "uncomfortable" with Congress's reluctance to aid Mexico. "There were a lot of skeptics in the Federal Reserve system on that Mexican deal," LaWare says. "I was disappointed when Greenspan allowed himself to be persuaded to go up to the Hill with Rubin and talk to the Democratic caucus and the Republican caucus in favor of both the first program and the final one. That is something that I would wager Paul Volcker would never have done. It politicized the Fed to the extent that we were asked to endorse a political settlement or agreement. And I think that was a mistake. . . . It was a compromise of Federal Reserve independence and something that we have obviously jealously guarded for a long, long time, and I think it was compromised by being a party to that." Greenspan backed Rubin "to be reappointed, to be a friend of the guy who has the power to keep him in power." Blinder does "not think it 'compromised' the Fed's independence in any way. After all, at least putatively, both the congressional leadership, which was Republican, and the administration were on the same side of the issue. So it wasn't a partisan issue." Blinder notes Greenspan was giving "his own opinion in his own words," not speaking for the Board.

Greenspan made his best case for the loan guarantees before the Senate Foreign Relations Committee on January 26. Mexico had been a star pupil, putting itself through "a major economic metamorphosis toward significant improvement in its economic and financial structure." It had "shed what was an inflation prone, highly unstable economic structure with excessive government involvement" and become "a vibrant economy oriented toward open markets." But its exchange rate policy had had "little tolerance for policy error or capacity to absorb shocks." Yes, Mexico had followed unwise policies, but now it needed help. "Unless Mexico's efforts to restore economic stability and financial market confidence succeed, years of economic reforms in Mexico would be threatened by pressures to reimpose controls in many areas of its economy and to reestablish governmental interference in Mexico's increasingly vibrant private sector." Beyond that, Mexico's problems were causing withdrawals of capital from other countries. "If economically advanced Mexico is having difficulties, it is being argued, perhaps the outlook for other nations dependent on foreign capital inflows is suspect more generally." The Fed had hoped the $18 billion short-term credit lifeline which the Fed and Treasury had put together January 3, together with Mexico's own efforts, would calm the markets and restore confidence, but the problems had "continued to fester." Now the more ambitious package was needed "to halt the erosion in Mexico's financing capabilities before it has dramatic impacts far beyond those already evident around the world." It was "the least worst" solution to "a very unsettling international financial problem."

Greenspan met with considerable skepticism from both parties. Some accused the Fed of causing Mexico's problems by raising rates. Others blamed the Fed and Treasury for encouraging Mexico to devalue. He told them the Fed's rate hikes had had no more than "a marginal effect" and that Mexico's attempt to hold the peso at 3.5 per dollar had been "unsustainable." The legislators were worried about the potential cost if Mexico defaulted on the proposed loans and the impact the additional debt might have on U.S. interest rates. They feared rescuing Mexico would set a dangerous precedent. They doubted Mexico would observe the tough policy conditions Rubin had vowed to impose on Mexico. They argued the government should not be, in effect, bailing out private investors by bolstering the value of Mexican securities. And many just did not want to take responsibility for a politically unpalatable decision. Mutual distrust between Republicans and Democrats ultimately prevented a bipartisan agreement.

When, despite the support of Dole and Gingrich, it became clear at the end of January that the $40 billion program was foundering in Congress, the peso took a fresh plunge, accompanied by sell-offs in securities markets throughout Latin America and elsewhere. The Treasury had been cooking up a much larger alternative bailout plan. Late the morning of January 31, as Greenspan was about to testify before the Senate Banking Committee in a last ditch effort to win passage of the old plan, President Clinton without warning invoked his executive authority to put this roughly $50 billion plan into action after meeting with the congressional leadership and being told chances of passage were bleak. The centerpiece of the aid package was $20 billion of U.S. foreign exchange reserves held jointly by the Fed and the Treasury's ESF, which would be used to make short- and medium-term loans and loan guarantees to Mexico. The IMF would add a $17.8 billion loan unprecedented in both size and speed of approval. Just days earlier, the Fund's Executive Board had given the go-ahead for a loan of just $7.8 billion. There was also to be $10 billion from other major central banks acting through the BIS, as well as $1 billion from the Bank of Canada and another $1 billion from a group of Latin American countries. Mexico would be required to pay loan origination fees and funnel receipts of its oil sales into an account at the Fed to be held as collateral against default. Clinton's new plan did not come as a surprise to Greenspan, but he told Senator D'Amato he could not provide details. He had distanced himself from the construction of the second package with its raid by fiat on U.S. reserves. Although he had provided advice on its overall economic impact, and his staff had provided technical assistance, as befit the Fed's role as Treasury's fiscal agent, he was reluctant to make recommendations on a strategy with which he felt uncomfortable. Nor would he be vocally supportive.

Far more surprised had been Germany and five other European nations who on February 2 abstained on a vote to approve the expanded IMF loan out of pique at not having been consulted on its size or on the funds they were expected to contribute through the BIS. Administration officials claimed there had been no time to consult them. Rubin and Greenspan had to mend fences at a G-7 meeting held in Toronto February 3–4. On the plane back from Toronto, Greenspan and Truman huddled with Summers and his aides. They were relieved differences had been smoothed over and hoped the package would stabilize the markets but still feared Mexico was in for severe economic pain. Less than a week later I asked German chancellor Helmut Kohl at a press conference with President Clinton if he was satisfied with the way the package had been put together. His response was that, while he agreed with the decision, "It could have been taken more elegantly." George said Greenspan helped make up for the lack of communication by Rubin. "He took tremendous care to actually explain to the central banks the situation of Mexico and the attitude towards it, partly because, actually, the government-to-government communication wasn't working as well as it might have done, and I certainly appreciated that."

Now that the initial package had been discarded, Greenspan took a lower profile. Greenspan was no longer to be seen prowling the halls of Congress. LaWare says, "We went underground because we agreed to do this backup thing for the Treasury and let the Treasury be out in front." If anything, Clinton's controversial decision to bypass Congress made the political issues for Greenspan even more sensitive. Greenspan was seen as complicit in what many considered not just an unwise use of reserves but an unconstitutional abuse of executive power. Hoskins, who had bitterly contested earlier Fed-

Treasury efforts to help Mexico while on the FOMC, did "not believe that is something that the Fed ought to be doing. It infringes on the independence of the Fed, and it creates a moral hazard problem." Fed officials were divided. Some resented being dragged into a foreign exchange operation that posed both short- and long-term risks and which they saw as an improper use of reserves. They were concerned about the amount of money the Fed would be putting on the line and whether, if it was not enough, how much more might be needed. Even those who were broadly supportive worried how the Fed might be perceived participating in an operation Congress had refused to support. "It was upsetting to me that they [Congress] were walking away from a problem I thought they should be dealing with," one policymaker recalls. It raised a dicey political issue: "Should the administration and the Fed step in and attempt to put into place a policy the Congress doesn't support? It was certainly something that I think was unquestionably within the appropriate powers of the Treasury and the Fed to do, but one always feels more comfortable, like sending the troops to Bosnia, if Congress agrees with it."

In the end, most Fed officials supported aiding Mexico with various degrees of enthusiasm. "I thought there were dangers in the Fed's becoming involved and the administration becoming involved when the level of congressional support was dubious, but I feel it was the right policy," says one. "I thought there were grave risks to the international financial system, and I was very pleased to see a package put together in which we would participate." Phillips says she had no qualms about the Fed's participation. "We are not independent of government; we're independent within government, but it is one government. Independence is particularly important with respect to domestic policy, but when you're talking about international kinds of things, I think that all the relevant parts of government should be at the table." Another Fed governor says Greenspan "had the Fed solidly behind him, but that's not to say that there wasn't discussion around here about 'what are we getting ourselves into?' But he certainly had the support of everyone at the end of the day because it was considered that something had to be done. . . . This is a critically important country on our southern border that has a very special relationship with the United States, and the judgment was that the best thing that could be done to help Mexico get through a really, really difficult situation was the policy that was, in fact, put in place, and it was worked over and worried over in great detail and required a lot of selling, and Greenspan and the Fed were deeply involved in that process."

At a stormy FOMC meeting the day after Clinton had already announced the Fed's participation in the Mexican bailout, Greenspan had the unpleasant task of asking for approval of this unusual use of reserves. He asked the committee to increase its swap facility with Mexico from $4.5 to $6 billion and to raise from $5 billion to $20 billion the amount of foreign currencies the Fed would *warehouse* for the Treasury, that is, how many dollars the Fed would give Treasury to lend to Mexico in exchange for marks and yen Treasury had in the ESF. Only grudgingly did some members go along with these measures, and Lindsey and Melzer voted no. "They did not believe that the committee had been provided sufficient information to assess whether developments in Mexico threatened U.S. financial stability" and "considered it inappropriate for the Federal Reserve to participate, directly or indirectly, in intermediate to long-term financing to facilitate debt restructuring," say the minutes. "They were concerned that such participation in a fiscal policy might compromise, or appear to compromise, the independence of the monetary policy response."

Only time will tell, but some Fed officials fear the Fed's participation in the Mexican bailout could have dangerous long-term repercussions. These credit extensions involve both market and credit risk, and the credit risk "can be substantial when a loan is made to assist, say, a country managing its external debt or one with a serious balance of payments problem," Broaddus and Goodfriend wrote in the Richmond Fed's 1995 annual report. To the extent credit extensions are inadequately collateralized or other entities like the IMF (International Monetary Fund) do not take over the credit line from the Fed, "taxpayers are at risk." This exposes the Fed to political risk. "The Fed's financing of foreign exchange operations without explicit direction from Congress exposes it to potentially harsh criticism if an initiative goes badly. Unfavorable outcomes would obviously undermine public support for the Fed's financial independence." And there is "a more subtle risk, even if foreign initiatives funded by the Fed go well. Some will ask whether, if Fed financing of credit extensions to foreigners is beneficial, it might also be desirable for the Fed to support worthy domestic objectives." Down that road lies danger. "The publicity for the Mexican rescue put the Fed's off-budget funding powers on the radar screen, along with the potential risks described above. . . . If, over time, developments in Mexico turn unfavorable, the result could be an erosion of public and congressional support for the Fed's financial independence." They urged legislation to disengage the Fed from all joint foreign exchange operations with the Treasury. Greenspan feels it is better for the Fed to stay involved in foreign exchange operations so it can influence the process.

The Mexican aid package would not be finalized in an elaborate Treasury ceremony until February 21, but by then Mexico had already begun drawing on swap lines to redeem billions of Tesobonos held by foreign investors. When Treasury, Fed, and Mexican officials finally finished negotiating the exacting terms and conditions under which Mexico could receive assistance, Rubin made a big show of it. It was a humiliating scene for Mexican finance minister Guillermo Ortiz and his entourage as they were herded into the historic and ornate Treasury Cash Room, jammed with reporters and TV cameras. As we waited for the festivities to begin, a reporter drew on what one of the bandits told Humphrey Bogart in "The Treasure of the Sierra Madre" in imagining what one of the Mexicans might say if asked to show his security badge. "Badges? We don't need any stinking badges!"

Greenspan now warned there was not going to be enough cash around for the next Mexico-style crisis and that other solutions needed to be sought. Over the next year, he and Rubin spearheaded efforts among the G-7 and other industrialized nations to put in place facilities and procedures to deal with future sovereign liquidity crises. On April 22, 1996, the finance ministers and central bankers of the so-called Group of Ten nations pledged to double the GAB to roughly $49 billion to serve as an emergency financing mechanism supplementing IMF lending resources in the event of a crisis. The IMF was to strengthen its "surveillance" of member nations, pressure them into making public more and better economic and financial data, and generally act as an early warning system so that problems such as Mexico's would not go un-heeded. More controversially, the G-10 urged the IMF to do more of what it had done occasionally in the past: lend to countries in arrears on old loans from both commercial banks and official creditors. What's more, it gave its stamp of approval to nations suspending debt payments "in exceptional cases" and on a "temporary" basis. It also left the door open a crack for the creation of some kind of bankruptcy facility for wayward nations, saying the idea deserved further study.

Most press accounts emphasized another aspect of the G-10 report, its statement that neither debtors nor creditors should expect to be "insulated" by official aid in the event of a liquidity crisis. "*Moral hazard*," the proclivity of nations and their foreign investors to take excessive risks in expectation of a bailout, was not to be countenanced. The idea was to forestall a worse crisis. If we only allow countries to suspend debt payments when they get into trouble and give them more IMF loans anyway, the reasoning went, maybe we can keep the steam from building up and blowing the lid off. The counterargu-ment was that the G-10 had just turned the heat up under the kettle. Banking industry critics warned that encouraging the IMF to lend into arrears and giv-ing countries a green light to suspend debt payments was an invitation to more defaults, more bailouts, more moral hazard. They were astonished Greenspan and other central bankers would go along with the G-10 report. One senior Fed staffer conceded, "It pushes the envelope."

Greenspan admits the moral hazard dilemma is "a legitimate issue, which is crucial to this whole debate," but says it is not easily soluble. "Everyone is in favor of lowering moral hazards. Everyone is in favor of lowering extensive credit packages to sovereign nations, either through the IMF or other vehicles. Everyone is in favor of increased surveillance to try to remove the probabilities of international systemic crises. None are capable of being done simply; they're all trade-offs. . . . If you have created a whole set of moral hazards, there are two ways to combat them. You can either lower the degree of moral hazard, or you can increase the regulation." The same is true in the domestic banking field, the reluctant regulator adds.

Meanwhile, the Fed had to maintain its focus on the domestic economy. It was widely speculated Mexico's difficulties would keep the Fed on hold at its January 31 to February 1 FOMC meeting since a further rise in rates would aggravate that country's problems and indirectly slow the U.S. economy. But Greenspan was determined not to be diverted from his inflation fight. Just before the FOMC meeting he told the Senate Banking Committee the best thing the Fed could do to help Mexico was to "create an American economy with sustained long-term economic growth." That meant containing inflation. The only question was whether the economy still had enough momentum to make inflation a continuing concern. The signals were mixed. The Commerce Department had estimated a 4.5 percent real GDP growth rate for the fourth quarter. Industrial production in December had shown its biggest upsurge in more than two years, pushing capacity utilization to 85.4 percent, the highest since October 1979. Unemployment had fallen from 5.6 to 5.4 percent. But retail sales had fallen, and there were signs inventories of unsold goods were piling up. Housing demand was starting to slip. There were still few signs inflation was straying from the 3 percent area, but the beige book had found "more widespread" price increases and "somewhat higher wage increases." Greenspan said the CPI overstated inflation a half to one percent, that the economy was "close to price stability," and that the economy was slowing from its previous "torrid" pace, but there were still "reasons for some concern" on inflation.

The FOMC was less unified than a year earlier. "It was a tough judgment call," one policymaker recalls. "It looked as though the economy was never going to slow down, and we were very conflicted about it. We were beginning to get some signals of a slowing, but it was unclear whether or not a slowdown was at hand or not. We had a debate about whether or not to wait for additional information before proceeeding with that last move." Blinder and Yellen argued there was no obvious need to raise rates and urged the Fed to hold off until it was sure the economy was continuing to grow rapidly. Yellen thought the economy was in an inflationary "danger zone," but also saw downside risks, considering that nowhere near the full effect of past rate hikes had been felt. She had begun to argue that, just as the Fed needed to tighten before the first signs of price pressure to preempt inflation, it would need to ease preemptively against recession. But most felt that if the Fed waited until the March 28 FOMC meeting to move to what the minutes call "a more clearly restrictive stance," they "would incur an unacceptable risk of allowing further inflationary momentum to develop" and they were disinclined to move between meetings. "There was a reasonably long lag [until the next meeting], and we were there, the market seemed to expect it, we were poised to do it, the information we had in hand seemed to point to it, although there were unusually large question marks, and people just on balance felt that we should go ahead, that the risks were more that inflation would rise than that we would be surprised on the downside, and that it seemed to be called for," a participant recalls. "We had previously expected slowdowns to occur. We had consistently been disappointed, in the sense of the numbers coming in stronger than we thought, and I think the predominant feeling was we had waited long enough, the time has come to move, we have to move. You can always wait forever. So eventually you have to call the shots even though you're uncertain."

There was another big reason for this sense of immediacy. The dollar's seemingly intractable weakness continued to bedevil the Fed. It had been speculated increased imports by Japan to repair damage from the mid-January Kobe earthquake might lend strength to the dollar, but the dollar had remained below 100 yen and was around 1.52 marks. The perception persisted that the administration was using a weak dollar as leverage in its ongoing trade dispute with Japan, and now the peso crisis was rubbing off on the dollar. "Part of the risk [of delay] involved a potential further decline in the dollar at a time when there already was considerale concern about rising pressures on prices," the minutes state. The markets expected the Fed to raise rates again, and if it did not it would "raise questions about the credibility of the System's anti-inflation resolve and generate some unsettlement in financial markets, notably in the foreign exchange market where the dollar already appeared to be vulnerable to further weakness."

After the meeting, the Fed announced a half percent increase in the discount rate to 5¼ percent and in the funds rate to 6 percent. Both votes were unanimous. The Fed had now completed a doubling of the funds rate in 12 months, and the FOMC voted not to lean toward further tightening. It had been an agonizing vote for some, especially the two Clinton appointees. They considered dissenting because they were beginning to suspect the Fed's previous rate hikes were starting to take effect. They did not do so because they lacked enough evidence to dispute the staff's forecast, which assumed rates would have to go higher to prevent inflation in an economy operating above potential. They agreed the economy needed to be slowed and that rates would probably have to go higher, but were unsure about the size and timing of further rate hikes. They wanted to wait for more information to remove any doubts. However, the economy had outperformed expectations for months. So they suppressed their misgivings and went along.

Soon they and others would be second guessing their decision. Two days later, the Labor Department reported a 0.3 percent rise in unemployment to 5.7 percent—the first of a series of weak first-half numbers. To this day, policymakers are divided on what proved to be the last rate hike. "As things turned out, I think that was the point at which it was clear things were slowing," one says ruefully. "In retrospect knowing what I now know, I wouldn't have voted for it. . . . My feeling is we somewhat overdid it. . . . I feel we put a little bit too much restraint in place at that point. . . . I think that was a mistake. . . . I simply have the sense of regret that it was a wrong call." Blinder leaves little doubt he feels likewise. "It's an open secret I've been one of the more enthusiastic FOMC members for cutting rates in '95." Others, including Greenspan, have no regrets. "I don't think we had a lot of choice," says Lindsey, who would soon become one of the more vigorous proponents of easing. "If it was wrong it probably was wrong by not much," says Phillips. McDonough, who would also become a force for easing, says he "was quite convinced at the time that we should make the final move to six percent. I think one could easily predict that at some stage during 1995 we would have a weak quarter because of the inventory adjustment. It happened to be the second quarter."

Greenspan defends the Fed's preemptive tightening of monetary policy in the February 1994 to February 1995 period. Had the Fed not doubled interest rates as early and as aggressively as it did, the economy "would have gone into very severe inventory excess," which in turn would have led to "a marked cyclical decline," he told the House Banking Committee February 20, 1996. By tightening credit, the Fed had actually "prolonged the recovery quite a considerable period of time." Otherwise, long-term interest rates would not have fallen by roughly 2 percent from later 1994 to late 1995. "The timing was pretty reasonable the way it worked out. At times we were a little bit ahead of the curve, at times a little behind it," but "on average [we did] pretty well. . . . The evidence is pretty persuasive." New York Democrat Representative Maurice Hinchey asked what inflation pressures the Fed was trying to preempt. Greenspan told him "lead times on delivery of products started to rise very rapidly" and factory overtime hours "rose very dramatically." He likened Fed actions to building sandbag dikes against a flooding river. Having prevented the river from overflowing one could not say the effort had been unnecessary. Hinchey claimed there had not been a flood, but barely "a trickle." Greenspan responded, "I put my scuba diver stuff on, so I got a pretty good look at it."

Many thought there would be more Fed rate hikes. An American Bankers Association panel of economists predicted a 6½ percent funds rate by midyear. Forrestal told me two weeks after the February 1 move the Fed's "challenge" would be to know "when to stop" raising rates to avoid slowing the economy too much. Some officials were skeptical whether activity was moderating enough, despite the Fed's own report of a "widespread" slowing of manufacturing. Greenspan saw only "mixed" signs the economy was showing the desired deceleration. The Fed was haunted by the ghost of the previous August when, encouraged by signs of slowing, it had said a rate hike would be "sufficient" for a while. Even Tyson said another rate hike "remains an open possibility." Producer prices for crude and intermediate goods were rising at double-digit rates in an economy near full employment, and many expected the Congress to cut taxes without offsetting spending cuts, stimulating the economy, and forcing the Fed to raise rates further. That was not what Republican leaders intended, but at the time, only glimmerings of the titanic clash over GOP efforts to balance the budget could be seen.

Greenspan realized the "Republican revolution" did not mean exploding deficits. He had been well received by a joint session of the House and Senate Budget Committees on January 10, where Senator Domenici and Congressman Kasich, heads of the two panels, assured him they planned to eliminate the deficit, not increase it. "This majority is one hundred percent committed to decreasing the size and scope of the federal government," Kasich said. "We are going to review every program in an unprecedented way, and we are going to start this deficit on a downward trend, and you should know that." Greenspan responded enthusiastically, stressing the need for early action to harness entitlement spending before the baby boomers came of age and bankrupted the system. But Greenspan had a sense of foreboding about GOP tactics. Using the statutory limit on how much the Treasury can borrow to finance the national debt to curb spending, as Gingrich had threatened, would be "a very heavy club" which could have "significant potential adverse effects" in the markets if there was a chance a debt limit might not pass, forcing Treasury to default on its obligations. It was the White House that was pursuing a loose fiscal policy. It had proposed $200 billion deficits for fiscal 1996 and beyond. It flatly rejected a balanced budget constitutional amendment, which passed the House of Representatives overwhelmingly January 26. The stage was set for a long, costly battle in which the Fed played oft-ignored referee.

The February 1 rate hike gave no lasting support to the dollar, which by the end of the month was sliding anew. With U.S. reserves on loan to Mexico, speculators were emboldened to test U.S. willingness to defend the dollar, despite Fed and Treasury assertions they had adequate resources to support it. As the dollar fell back below 97 yen, Greenspan spoke out. "Our concern is that the American dollar be a viable, solid, strong basic currency," he said in February 22 Humphrey-Hawkins testimony. If not, the dollar would lose its status as the world's most important reserve currency and "create very significant problems for us domestically. It is incumbent upon us as the central bank to make certain that it is a stable, non-inflation-ridden, solid currency." Greenspan told the Senate Banking Committee he still favored the gold standard. "I've been recommending that for years." A gold-backed dollar would be "very beneficial. . . . I would personally prefer it." As the dollar kept sliding, an astounded Blinder told me it should be appreciating, not depreciating. At his January 10 confirmation hearing, Rubin had said, "A strong dollar is very much in this nation's economic interest." However, the administration was continuing to reap the fruit of its past weak dollar policy. Despite the weak dollar, bond yields continued the decline they had begun the previous November as it became increasingly obvious the economy was slowing. Also, it became increasingly clear Congress was serious about balancing the budget. From a peak of 8.17 percent the previous November, the long bond yield had fallen below 8 percent by February. There would be occasional spikes when the dollar had a bad day, but by midyear, it would be at 6½, and by year-end at 5.97, despite an economic rebound.

With the dollar on the ropes and core consumer prices rising at a near 5 percent rate in January, Greenspan held out the possibility of further rate hikes. Yes, there were signs of slowing, but "the jury is still out" on whether the deceleration would be enough to contain inflation. But he said the Fed might have to revise its thinking. There might come a point where the Fed would have to start easing credit even in the face of continued "adverse" inflation numbers. Just as the Fed had started raising rates before there were visible signs of worse inflation, it would have to start lowering rates before there was an outright economic downturn. Many market players were taken aback by this pronouncement, but Yellen had told Market News the same thing weeks before. Blinder was also ruminating about a preemptive easing. They were expressing a precept developed by longtime Greenspan associate John Taylor, who had returned to Stanford University after leaving the Bush administration. Within a long-term strategy of achieving price stability, the *Taylor rule* would justify the Fed lowering the real funds rate to combat subpar economic growth or rising unemployment even if inflation was above target. Yellen says the Fed has been operating "within the broad contours" of the Taylor rule for years.[2]

Clinton had mostly held his tongue when the Fed raised rates, but as the economy slowed, he could not restrain himself. In his February 27 radio address, he blamed "the unelected Federal Reserve" for having raised rates seven times and "added more than $100 billion to our deficit" through higher interest payments on the national debt. He did not mention it had been his Treasury's decision, against the advice of primary dealers, to shift a greater portion of borrowing to short-term debt and away from long-term debt in a shortsighted effort to take advantage of the low short rates prevailing when Clinton took office. Now short rates were twice as high, while long rates were falling.

Clinton blasted the Fed and Congress in the same convoluted breath. "This balanced budget amendment, therefore, could give the unelected Federal Reserve the power not only to raise your interest rates but also to cut spending on things like Headstart, childhood immunization and educational opportunities for all of our children."

As yet, the Fed was not ready to implement a Taylor-style policy response. Although there was "gathering evidence" of slowing, as Phillips and Lindsey said in late February interviews, most Fed officials would have to be convinced the Fed needed to reverse course. Indeed, Lindsey said past rate hikes were "not necessarily sufficient." The dollar had continued to fall, and not just against the yen. By March 3, it had hit a new low of 93.65 yen and had dropped to 1.4225 marks, its lowest level against the mark in years. One reason was what BIS general manager Andrew Crockett called the market's "changing mood. Whereas six months ago the markets were expecting additional increases in U.S. interest rates in order to restrain the very strong U.S. economy and futher reductions in European interest rates to stimulate the still rather weak European economy, that has turned around to a considerable extent. With the growing evidence that U.S. interest rate increases are having their effect in slowing the economy, the prospect for further increases has receded. In Europe, with the economy picking up, prospects for further rate reductions in order to stimulate economic growth is in its turn receding, so that the balance of probabilites about a shift in interest rate differentials has changed." With Japan still in the doldrums, it could scarcely be argued higher rates there were in prospect, but "actual and prospective inflation is very low in Japan, or negative, and that over the course of time requires an exchange rate adjustment just to maintain real interest rates." Crockett emphasized "the importance of retaining confidence in the U.S. dollar, maintaining the strength of the U.S. dollar. That is important not just to preserve the U.S. dollar's international role, but it is important for the internal stability of the currency and therefore for the longer term health of the U.S. economy."

The U.S. joined in some halfhearted intervention with other G-7 nations to support the dollar March 3, while Rubin expressed a belated wish for "a strong dollar," to little effect. There was still a school of thought in the administration that a depreciating dollar was not such a bad thing. Rather than echo Treasury's "strong dollar" line, one Clinton adviser I talked to in the midst of this latest dollar debauch was licking his chops at the thought of Japan importing more U.S. goods, while exporting less under the influence of an overvalued yen. But this assumed a level of Japanese demand that did not exist, partially because it had been dampened by the yen's rise. When I spoke to the BOJ's Nagashima that day, he was quite concerned at the impact the "excessive" rise his currency had taken would have on Japan. Fed officials were no less dismayed. A "perplexed" Forrestal said economic fundamentals dictated "a stronger dollar" and warned "a depreciating currency does create inflation, and that's always a Fed concern." In short, there was no way the Fed was going to fulfill lower rate hopes as the dollar sank rapidly. On March 7, Summers told Congress the Treasury's ability to support the dollar had not been diminished by the diversion of foreign exchange reserves to help Mexico, but was greeted with extreme skepticism as the dollar sank below 90 yen and 1.37 marks.

The dollar's weakness was "both unwelcome and troublesome," Greenspan told the House Budget Committee March 8, after the dollar had set all-time lows of 88.75 yen and 1.3450 marks. He urged Congress and the White House to work together to slash the budget deficit. "Dollar weakness, while very likely overdone, is unwelcome because it adds to potential inflation pressures in our economy. . . . Dollar weakness is also troublesome because it is doubtless symptomatic of some of the underlying problems confronting the longer term health of the economy: inadequate national savings, continuing large budget deficits and a persistent current account imbalance." Repeating past admonitions, he said the United States could not continue to rely on foreign capital to finance its deficit. "Indeed, given the recent weakness in the foreign exchange value of the dollar, world capital markets may be sending us just that message. This suggests that a key element in dealing with the dollar's weakness, is to address our underlying fiscal imbalance convincingly."

The administration was increasingly anxious for the Fed to ease, yet the dollar depreciation it had spawned made that difficult to justify. The administration had helped trigger the run on the dollar by its strident opposition to a balanced budget amendment, which it succeeded in defeating by one vote in the Senate March 2. The next day the big dollar sell-off began. Rubin denied the obvious connection, while repeating his commitment to "a strong dollar," but Greenspan was convinced the amendment's defeat had been a "crucial action" sparking dollar selling. "The fervor to get the deficit down was perceived to be significantly undercut," he said March 10. Still not taking the hint, Rubin accused Congress of being "monodimensional" in its desire to cut the deficit on March 21. The dollar had just hit another low against the yen, and Rubin was asked about it at the White House press room. "Yeah, against the yen it was somewhat lower," he responded breezily. "It depends on what you look at. It wasn't higher against the peso, because there is some sort of holiday and the peso isn't trading." Boasting of the dollar's prowess against the peso and the Canadian dollar, as Rubin frequently did, left the impression Treasury remained casual about the dollar's steep drop against major currencies. With each lower plateau the dollar reached, the Fed became less inclined to ease. Indeed, speculation was rife the Fed would raise rates. In the minds of many officials, fighting inflation and protecting the dollar were two sides of the same coin. "There is no dilemma for the Fed," one said. "It all comes back to one goal—a sustainable rate of growth with low inflation. If you have too high growth and you have inflation you flunk both domestically and internationally."

The Fed and its fellow central banks had gotten another scare February 27, when Barings PLC, the 232-year-old British investment bank, went bankrupt after billions of dollars worth of stock futures trades made by a 28-year-old trader in its Singapore branch went sour. Stocks dropped 4 percent on the Tokyo Stock Exchange and lesser amounts on other exchanges. At first glance, there seemed to be the potential for a chain reaction of losses and failures as Baring's counterparties' missed payments. The damage was contained, largely through the efforts of the Bank of England, in consultation with the Fed and others. Officials breathed a sigh of relief and said it proved the financial system could weather such a storm. Phillips and CFTC commissioner Sheila Bair said a Barings-style failure could not happen in the United States. Even so, Barings's failure revived the specter of "systemic risk." It was not the first time large derivatives-related losses had rattled the markets. Orange Country, California had gone bankrupt the year before when its Treasurer indulged in interest rate speculation with county funds. These and other incidents gave rise to the usual cries for stricter regulation, but the Fed decided that was not the way to go. The array of futures, options, and swaps which had accompanied the growth and internationalization of financial markets had introduced new dangers or enhanced old ones and had arguably complicated the way the Fed made monetary policy by making it easier to offset the impact of rate changes. But they had also made markets more efficient and enabled financial institutions and their customers to hedge risks.[3]

To try to freeze these rapidly evolving markets in place and bind them with uniform rules, the Fed believed, would be counterproductive, not to mention nearly impossible in a world of offshore financial centers eager to take business from Wall Street. With a notional principle estimated at $7.5 trillion at the end of 1992, it was a little late to be putting the genie back in the bottle. Instead the Fed worked with central banks, securities and commodities regulators of other nations, the so-called Group of Thirty, to enhance supervision within broad guidelines. The emphasis has been on insisting that traders and users of derivatives have adequate capital and install risk management systems, and on making sure payments systems are strong enough so that if losses occur, they do not reverberate around the world and shake the system apart. So far, so good.

Under the direction of Greenspan, who educated himself in this complicated field, the Fed has spent enormous resources of time and money just to keep up with market mutations. While it has given the market its head in the sense of not confining its evolution, it has adopted a no-tolerance policy for reckless practices. This came out at an Atlanta Fed conference on derivatives on March 4. McDonough said he did not want to "put derivatives in a straitjacket." But when a young economics professor with a "go for it" attitude announced he had advised banks not to worry too much about entering into risky swap trades with companies, so long as they had high credit ratings, it got the New York Fed president's Irish up. The derivatives market "isn't helped by people taking a frivolous attitude toward systemic risk," he exploded. Such an attitude "will bring the regulators down on you." Many Fed officials felt derivatives could not be blamed for the stupidity of their users. If an instrument promised an above-market return, investors should "ask if something is wrong," said Atlanta Fed research director Sheila Tschinkel. "There shouldn't be a guaranteed rate of return for anything." Corrigan said his response to anyone who complained about losing money on high-yielding derivatives would be, "Give me a break." He and McDonough argued for improved risk management, greater disclosure, same-day settlement of transactions, and, where possible, the use of clearinghouses to settle trades. Given the young age of many derivatives traders, Corrigan said there was another thing that would help prevent problems—"grey hair."

Throughout March, April, and May the economy continued to weaken, as soft consumer spending, particularly on cars and other durable goods, caused factory orders to slacken, leading to inventory buildups and production cutbacks.[4] Relief that the slowdown had finally arrived and self-congratulatory talk about a soft landing began to give way to concern that the slowdown might turn into recession. Even though the beige book had confirmed a "moderation" of economic activity and retail sales had plunged, the FOMC went into its March 28 meeting amid serious talk about Fed rate hikes, given the dollar's condition, sharply rising prices at lower stages of production, and continuing high levels of employment and capacity use. A widening trade deficit added to selling pressure on the dollar.[5] Absent was LaWare, who had resigned the day before. The Fed staff told the committee the economy would be growing below potential "for some period ahead," and the policymakers agreed, but differed on the extent of the slowdown. Clouding the picture, no one knew how restrictive fiscal policy was going to be, how bad Mexico's recession would become, or how serious an inventory correction was likely. Some were more confident than others that the economy retained plenty of momentum and would benefit from the retreat of long-term rates, the rise of the stock market, and the weak dollar's stimulus to exports. Officials felt the dollar could only aggravate the inflation they saw already in the pipeline. The result was a standoff. With the economy clearly slowing, although it was estimated less than two-thirds of the Fed's rate hikes had worked their way through the economy, members did not want to tighten, but were not ready to risk easing. They left policy on hold but gave Greenspan leeway to raise rates before the May meeting. Bonds and the dollar sank.

Two days later, the Bundesbank lowered its discount rate from 4½ to 4 percent, and a day later the Bank of Japan cut money market rates a half percent, while leaving its discount rate at 1¾. Besides their domestic motives, they hoped to boost the dollar by enhancing U.S. rate premiums. The dollar did surge after the March 30 Bundesbank action to as high as 1.4213 marks and 90.23 yen from recent lows of 1.3450 marks and 88 yen. But when Treasury policymakers ignored advice to buy dollars on the rally and drive it up further, it slipped back and fell to a new low of 86.23 yen on March 31, despite the Japanese rate cut. Not until April 3 did the Treasury ask the Fed to buy dollars, with very limited success. There was much head wagging over this lost opportunity at the Fed. "This would have been the proper time when coordinated action among the three major financial centers would have been in order," IMF chief Camdesuss said. Treasury officials claimed D'Amato, angry over the lack of cooperation his Senate Banking Committee was getting on requests for information about the Mexican aid program, had caused the dollar rout by threatening to curtail use of the ESF to help Mexico and in the process casting doubt about Treasury's ability to support the dollar. In a tirade on the Senate floor March 30, the New York Republican had charged Treasury was "using funds set aside to stabilize the American dollar to reward a corrupt, dictatorial Mexican regime and bail out speculators. . . . Who will bail us out if the dollar continues to fall, the Japanese?" But D'Amato was not saying anything not already on currency traders' minds. The real problem was that traders believed Treasury was, at best, immobilized by indecision and poor judgment and, at worst, pursuing a policy of benign neglect. Though Rubin kept saying he wanted "a strong dollar," he had not intervened. Kantor had continued to foment trade tensions with Japan, and said "it's up to the Japanese," if they wanted a stronger dollar, to stimulate their economy and import more U.S. goods. Worst of all, the White House was fighting Republican efforts to balance the budget, which the Fed saw as the only way to redress America's savings-investment imbalance. So the dollar continued to fall, going below 84 yen on April 7.

The Fed's policy dilemma deepened as the economy softened. Unemployment had risen in March, as factories laid off workers and cut back on hours in response to slack demand and the need to work down inventories. But with the dollar aggravating inflation risks and stimulating production for export, the Fed had to hold open the option of raising rates. Yellen, in an April 10 interview, said the Fed could not be sure the economy had slowed enough to prevent accelerating inflation. When the dollar had fallen further to 81.28 yen and 1.36 marks on April 18, Camdessus kicked off the IMF's spring meetings by advising the Fed to raise rates. He felt the Fed should have raised rates when the Bundesbank and Bank of Japan lowered theirs. He drew "no comfort" from the dollar's strength against the peso or Canadian dollar and said its plunge against the major currencies not only "threatened" the U.S. economy but caused "instability" in world markets. On April 19, the dollar hit rock bottom, falling to 79.85 yen and 1.3440 marks. It had now lost more than 36 percent of its value in yen terms since January 1993. Clinton's response was to say there was not much that could be done to strengthen the dollar in the short run. He put his faith in the fundamentals to support the dollar "over the long run." That was not what the market or the Fed wanted to hear. The latter feared the dollar could become a frightful short-run problem.

There was a disturbing amount of disarray. The U.S.-Japan auto talks had broken down April 18, and Japan had threatened to suspend the talks if the United States did not back off its threat of sanctions. There was talk of Japan boycotting U.S. Treasury auctions. But Kantor and other U.S. officials were in no mood to be conciliatory. There would be "no backing off" from demands for more importation of U.S. autos and auto parts and more stimulus to lower the U.S. deficit with Japan. The BOJ had cut its discount rate to a record low 1 percent April 14, while the Japanese government announced a package of spending and deregulatory measures, but the administration was not satisfied. In return for U.S. demands that it run pump-priming budget deficits, Japan told the United States to cut its deficit and raise rates to bolster the dollar. Europeans were also clamoring for sounder U.S. fiscal policies. French prime minister Edouard Balladur, in a letter to European Union president Jacques Santer, implied Europe's best response to the weak dollar's impact on its export-oriented industries was to resort to protectionism. There were signs of a flight from dollars. Some Asian central banks had been selling them. The German shipping concern Hapag-Lloyd AG was reported talking to shippers about quoting its freight rates in marks and other units instead of dollars. OPEC was said to have considered shifting away from pricing oil in dollars.

When Greenspan participated in the April 25 G-7 meeting, he had more sympathy from his fellow central bankers, at least on the budget, than from Rubin. He felt a credible, multiyear commitment to eliminating the deficit was critical to strengthening the dollar. Though Rubin paid lip service to reducing the deficit, he kept pointing backward at the deficit reduction since 1993 and the deficit's reduced share of GDP. But the administration was proposing endless $200 billion deficits. Other G-7 officials pointed out the contradiction. Most vocal were Takemura and Bank of Japan governor Yasuo Matsushita, echoed by the Germans, French, and others. Nor did Rubin have a sense of urgency about exchange rates. "While the temptation is to focus on exchange rates . . . what is critical for the future of the world is that we get beyond the question of the moment" and "look at strategic issues," he said before the meeting. That was not good enough for others. Takemura said there was "a sense of crisis" around the table over the "uncertainty" and "instability" the dollar was causing in Japan, Europe, and elsewhere. The upshot was what Rubin called a "sophisticated" but Clarke called a "bland" G-7 communiqué expressing "concern about recent developments in exchange markets" that had carried exchange rates "beyond the levels justified by underlying economic conditions in the major countries." They called for an "orderly reversal of those movements" and agreed to "continue to cooperate closely in exchange markets." There was only a vague suggestion some countries needed to lower their budget deficits. Rubin said he had managed to convince the G-7 the United States had made "progress" in reducing its deficit; this had been "not entirely understood before." Canadian finance minister Paul Martin aptly summed it up. "Each country has to do what it has to do." The dollar, which had recovered to 81.75 yen the day of the meeting, gained a little ground afterward, but stayed in the low 80s all spring.

When it met May 23, the FOMC was faced with an economy showing palpable weakness. Nonfarm payrolls had decined in April, and the unemployment rate had jumped from 5½ to 5.8 percent. There had also been declines in retail sales, production, and sales of homes and motor vehicles. Some thought the "headwinds" were back and the Fed would have to reverse course and cut rates after raising them in February. But the Fed saw warmer winds blowing. The predominant view was that a "soft landing" was at last within the Fed's grasp and that the economy would settle down to a 2½ percent growth path. Most officials had little concern that a 6 percent funds rate would cause recession. They felt the economy would maintain sufficient strength to generate satisfactory job growth; 125,000 to 175,000 per month would do nicely. The economy's slower pace was seen lessening price pressures, but officials were not ready to relax their credit grip given continued high rates of resource use and the chance falling long rates and the soft dollar would spur demand for housing and manufactured goods. Before the meeting, Broaddus predicted the economy would be "stronger than projected." Parry said that, despite slower growth, the Fed could not "just sit back and relax." Many believed the economy was just "taking a breather."

Others feared the inventory correction would last long enough to precipitate a classic cycle of self-reinforcing production cutbacks, layoffs, loss of consumer demand, and so forth, but most agreed with Greenspan that this was a temporary phenomenon and that any softness would be leavened by the stimulative effect of lower long-term rates, the cheaper dollar, and stock market wealth gains. Nor could the Fed ignore the fact that the CPI had risen at a 5 percent annual rate in April. Greenspan had continued to closely link the behavior of the dollar, the budget deficit, and the trade deficit. In a May 16 speech directly contradicting administration statements, he had made clear he did not consider the deficit reduction that had taken place over the past two years adequate and said it was "essential that the momentum toward reducing and eventually eliminating the deficits be accelerated." The United States could not rely on foreign savings to make up for government dissavings; the dollar's collapse was "sending us just that message." The FOMC voted to keep the funds rate at 6 percent, but to abandon its bias toward tightening in favor of a symmetrical directive.

Fiscal policy had been a big topic. Two weeks earlier, the House and Senate Budget Committees had passed plans to balance the budget by 2002, the first such action in three decades, and battle lines had been drawn with the White House, which was sticking by its $200 billion deficit plan. The FOMC wanted deficit reduction, but preferred some predictability to how and when it would be achieved, a vain hope. "Fiscal policy was seen as a major uncertainty in the economic outlook. . . . The extent and timing of fiscal restraint could not be determined while federal deficit reduction continued to be debated in the Congress." Some members expected more deficit reduction than others. Lindsey told me later the planned deficit cuts would be a "net plus" which could expand the economy's growth potential, but in the short run would be a drag on growth. It was agreed, in an understatement, that "the course of fiscal legislation undoubtedly would continue to affect financial markets and, in the opinion of some members, would need to be taken into account in the formulation of monetary policy."

Within days of the meeting, the Fed began hearing what one official called "alarm bells." On a grim statistical morning June 1, first-time claims for unemployment benefits shot to their highest level in two and a half years, and the purchasing managers index fell from 52 to 46.1, deep in contractionary territory. Orders, production, and other aspects of industrial activity had plunged. There were large job losses. Heightened speculation the Fed would have to lower rates took the starch out of a dollar rally which the G-7 had tried to jump start May 31 through coordinated intervention. Suddenly, Fed officials were not quite so confident of their "soft landing." Now their comments were couched more in terms of hoping the economy was only experiencing a "mid-course correction," as Broaddus put it. The international bankers gathered in Seattle the first week of June to hobnob with the G-7 central bankers, and there was a mixture of hope for lower rates and anxiety about the weak dollar. "There's a lot of deceleration," Citicorp chairman John Reed said. "If they're looking, they should be looking to ease." Tietmeyer and Nagashima complained about the harm the weak dollar was causing their export-oriented economies, but they felt it was up to U.S. fiscal policy, not monetary policy, to strengthen it. Greenspan told the bankers there was less risk of recession than in past cycles because inventories had not built to such high levels that a major, disruptive inventory adjustment would be necessary to bring inventories and sales back into a more normal ratio. The Fed had started tightening to slow the economy early enough that the kind of inventory overbuilding that had often preceded past recessions had not been allowed to develop. The slowdown had become "quite pronounced," Greenspan said June 7, but "there isn't now the tinder to create the type of recession we've had in the past." Because the economy had slowed and the adjustment of inventories had begun before they reached high levels, "the probability of an inventory recession in the immediate future has declined very significantly."

Nevertheless, Greenspan had used the "R" word. It was a clear signal the Fed would soon shift gears. The administration was not shy about hurrying him along. When asked June 12 if the Fed should ease, Panetta said, "It would be nice to get whatever kind of cooperation we can get to get this economy going." On June 20, when Sarbanes demanded what he was going to do to spur the economy, Greenspan told him "a few bumps in the road" were to be expected as "part of the process" of reducing growth from a "frenetic" pace. But later he said the risk of a "modest near-term recession" had increased and that the Fed was "intensifying our normal surveillance and analysis of ongoing developments to gauge whether policy still is appropriately positioned to foster sustained economic expansion." Greenspan reemphasized the need for the Fed to guard the dollar's "key reserve currency" role, but it was evident purely domestic concerns now took precedence. The dollar had been making a mild comeback. The G-7 had shown more willingness to cooperate in the dollar's defense and reiterated their determination to buck up the "out of synch" dollar at their Economic Summit in Halifax, Nova Scotia, June 17. More than anything, growing aspirations for a balanced budget helped stabilize the dollar around 84 yen and strengthen it against European currencies. When an eleventh-hour breakthrough was finally reached in the U.S.-Japan auto talks on June 28, just as the administration was about to slap 100 percent tariffs on Japanese imports, selling pressure was relieved, and the dollar began digging out of its deep hole. By early August, the dollar would climb above 90 yen, boosted by a "yen stabilization package" which increased demand for dollars by liberalizing Japanese foreign investment. By mid-September, after the Bank of Japan desperately slashed its discount rate to 0.5 percent, it would go back above 100 yen as the Bank of Japan performed what amounted to unsterilized intervention by pumping out yen to revive its economy. The dollar's recovery freed the Fed to focus more singlemindedly on the sluggish economy. GDP had seemingly slowed to a crawl in the second quarter, if it had grown at all.

Few were surprised when the FOMC decided July 6 to lower the funds rate a quarter to 5¾ percent, but the vote had not been unanimous. Hoenig, who favored an unchanged policy, was the sole dissenter, but others felt the same. Meanwhile Blinder and Lindsey had argued for more aggressive easing. "A move from what they saw as a restrictive monetary policy toward a more neutral policy stance was somewhat overdue in their view," say the minutes. The FOMC compromised on a modest rate cut, along with a bias toward further cuts, primarily because members saw diminished inflation pressures, thanks in part to "the recent stability of the dollar." McDonough says the Fed lowered the funds rate "not so much because of the weakness in the second quarter, but rather because the price performance was looking even better than one might have anticipated. That was what led us with good reason to think that we could reduce the nominal Fed funds rate and have, as you got into 1996, somewhat of an insurance policy on getting a little bit better real growth, without concern about inflation picking up."

Another policymaker had a different justification, which would become increasingly important. While the near-term inventory adjustment that was slowing the economy was "baked in the cake," the Fed had to insure against continuation of the slowdown over the longer term. "It wasn't so much the 'Gee, we've got some weak numbers, let's see if we can do something to turn those weak numbers around quickly.' " Monetary policy does not work that fast. Rather, it was a matter of reinforcing the favorable climate of lower long rates that had developed in part out of hope the Fed would ease to offset a likely fiscal contraction. Not doing as the markets expected would have risked a damaging rate rebound. "On balance, it seemed to me . . . we should do essentially what the markets were widely anticipating at that point because they had gotten the reasoning correct and the lower levels of long-term rates were precisely what we were going to need to support the economy now and next year." Explaining the action in his July 19 Humphrey Hawkins testimony, Greenspan pointed to the abatement of labor cost pressures, capacity utilization, commodity price surges, and dollar depreciation. "The success of our previous policy tightenings in damping prospective inflation pressures set the stage for our recent modest policy easing. Because the risks of inflation apparently have receded, the previous degree of restriction in policy no longer seemed needed." He put the markets on notice not to expect further easing anytime soon by saying the economy appeared to have "passed the point of maximum risk" of recession and had "upside risks" of a strong rebound.

No one knew it at the time, but the Fed was finished easing until December. Although Blinder and Lindsey would soon be chafing to lower rates again, most Fed officials tended to agree with Kelley that the economy now had a "good chance" of reaching and sustaining "an acceptable, sustainable cruising speed" of about 2½ percent. The budget now grabbed center stage while the Fed looked on with hope and fear. The Fed did not want to hinge monetary policy on fiscal policy, but had to factor it in. Indeed, it had figured in the FOMC's recent decision. Clinton had shown his resistance to reducing the deficit, first by vetoing legislation that would have trimmed $16.4 billion in previously approved fiscal 1995 spending, then putting forth a laughable scheme to balance the budget over ten years—a political eternity. The House and Senate had approved the outlines of a plan that would bring the budget into balance in seven years, using more realistic CBO assumptions. The growing likelihood of deficit reduction was seen restraining demand in the short run, while lowering market interest rates and stimulating growth in the long run. The problem was that during the transition, there would be great uncertainty. What the Fed did not know was just how much the uncertainty would be aggravated by the political battle royal about to ensue.

Gingrich had foolishly thrown down the gauntlet earlier in the year, threatening to hold an increase in the debt limit hostage to passage of a balanced budget. That was a game of chicken the administration was quite willing to play and play to win. Notwithstanding their scorched earth tactics, what the Republicans were really talking about was a gradual approach to bringing the budget into balance over seven years by restraining the growth of spending—not "cutting" it, just reducing its projected growth. For example, under the Republican plan, Medicare spending would have risen 6 to 7 percent per year instead of the 10 to 11 percent per year Clinton had proposed. In the final analysis, it was Clinton and the Democrats who were willing to play hardball more than Gingrich and company. If the Republicans were willing to threaten suspending the government's spending authority and shut the government down, the Clinton team was willing to endure it and exploit it, with the full support of government employee unions. If Republicans were willing to threaten letting the government's borrowing authority run out and bring it to the brink of default, the White House was willing to go to that brink, if not over it. This was a battle for survival for the Democrats' constituencies, and Clinton successfully mustered all of the forces of bloated government to combat what he labeled the "extremists" of the GOP. Any effort to curb a program's growth was labeled a "mean-spirited" effort to "starve the children" or "hurt the poor" or "destroy the environment" so as to fund nonexistent "tax cuts for the rich." Commenting on GOP efforts to curb runaway Medicare spending, Clinton spokesman Mike McCurry averred that Republicans would really like to see the elderly get sick and die.

By late summer, this high stakes game had begun in earnest. The 1995 fiscal year was racing to an end on September 30, and Democrats and Republicans were barely talking to each other about the fiscal 1996 budget, other than to hurl insults. By "sometime in October," Rubin was saying, the Treasury would run out of borrowing authority if Congress did not legislate an increase in the $4.9 trillion debt ceiling. By September the "drop-dead date" had been extended to November 15. In any case, it was getting to be put up or shut up time. Rubin had received letters from 180 House Republicans and two Democrats saying they would not vote to increase the debt limit unless Clinton accepted their budget plan. In an August 10 speech, the Treasury secretary decried the Republican plan as "arbitrary" and unacceptable. He demanded Congress pass a continuing resolution to allow the government to continue spending at fiscal 1995 levels and raise the debt ceiling. If it did not meet those demands, there would be a financial "train wreck," and Republicans would be blamed despite the administration's unwillingness to present a balanced budget or anything close to it. This was the administration's bargaining position, to which the GOP response was to plow ahead with passage of a balanced budget. While issuing ever more dire default warnings, Rubin was preparing such measures as tapping government pension funds to avoid it. A June 27 memo obtained by the *Washington Times* showed Assistant Treasury Secretary Darcy Bradbury had advised Rubin how he could draw on trust funds to avert default.

There had been real excitement at the August 22 FOMC meeting, as members contemplated the prospect that Congress might succeed in "reducing the federal deficit substantially over the years ahead." One thought that "the political dynamics might very well result in larger reductions than many now anticipated." Greenspan may not have liked Republican tactics—indeed, he warned both publicly and privately against flirting with default—but there was little doubt where his heart lay. That year's Fed Jackson Hole conference Labor Day weekend was devoted entirely to the budget. Instead of focusing on the short-run dangers posed by Rubin, Greenspan delivered an impassioned appeal to eliminate the deficit. Failure to do so would push the national debt to such high levels it could cause a "financial breakdown" and undermine the Fed's credibility. "Such risks exist because there are limits to the amount of debt that foreign and domestic investors willingly accept." Once debt rose beyond this limit there could be a "collapse in the demand for financial assets that has dire financial and real economic consequences." Already, the 50 percent ratio of debt to GDP had cut output as much as 6 percent.[6] Worse, deficit spending would eventually subvert the Fed. "With sufficiently high debt ratios the pressure or temptation to use money growth as a source of finance for public spending can undermine the credibility of anti-inflationary monetary policies." Time was running out. "The costs of maintaining social spending commitments are certain to worsen as adverse demographics make an increasing fraction of the population dependent on the government for income support and the costs of providing health care continue to rise." There needed to be immediate and ongoing action. "Today's actions and commitments are only the first step to fiscal reform that must be consolidated by future legislators.

Indeed, the will and means to follow through are at least as important as the initial commitment to deficit reduction."

Greenspan suggested the Fed would cut rates as and when the deficit was actually reduced. This was misinterpreted to mean the Fed would wait until a balanced budget was actually enacted before cutting rates again. In 1990, the Fed had waited until enactment of a budget that promised deficit reduction before cutting rates, and it was a mistake no one wanted to make again. Equally, Fed officials did not want to be perceived as hinging monetary on fiscal policy, irrespective of economic exigencies. Yellen, among others, vigorously disputed the notion the Fed was withholding further rate cuts until the budget debate was resolved. "The Fed is very much in a watch the economy, continue to look at how growth and inflation are proceeding [mode] in deciding what is the appropriate course of monetary policy," she told me September 5. "There is more going on in the economy that matters to monetary policy than just deficit reduction." Not everyone felt that way. Broaddus counseled waiting to see how Congress and the White House settled their budget dispute and how the markets reacted. Lindsey, eyeing weak job growth and other signs of continued sluggishness, argued the Fed should cut rates right away in anticipation of a fiscal contraction and lower market rates. "The markets are a lot more sensitive than we are smart," said McTeer. "As the likelihood of fiscal tightening occurs, the markets will automatically adjust. If there is significant progress on the budget the markets will reduce interest rates" and "as that occurs the Fed would validate that." However, if market rates did not decline enough to offset any fiscal drag on the economy "the Fed would help it along." Most officials were ready to ease again, regardless of the fiscal state of play, if the inflation picture improved and/or if growth was modest. Conditions would not be judged ripe for months.

An optimistic Greenspan plumped for balancing the budget in September 22 Humphrey-Hawkins testimony. Two days earlier, Gingrich had said he did not "care what the price is" to get a balanced budget, even if it meant default. "I don't care if we have no executive offices and no bonds for 60 days—not this time." Greenspan took Gingrich's and Rubin's saber-rattling in stride, chalking it up to the usual political hyperbole. "If I didn't hear it, I would be discouraged," he told the Senate Banking Committee. "If it were not as contentious as it is, I'm not sure we'd be making any progress at all." After all, the Democratic Congress had played brinkmanship on the debt limit with Republican presidents in the eighties, and in the end there had been no default. So, while a default was "not something anyone should take in a tranquil manner," he preferred to stress the need to balance the budget without fear it would hurt the economy. Indeed, the economy would benefit. By then, the long bond yield had fallen to 6½ percent, due to "the growing probability that a program of credible multi-year deficit reduction plan will be adopted. The declines in rates are already helping to stimulate private, interest-sensitive spending—providing, in effect, a shock absorber for the economy." Sales of homes, cars, and other big ticket items had rebounded, pushing up production and hiring. Inflation remained quiescent. The Fed would "take into account" the economic impact of deficit reduction, but he had "no doubt that the net result of moving the budget into balance will be a more efficient, more productive U.S. economy in the long run." But if Congress and the White House failed to come to terms, "a very marked part" of the reductions in long rates that had occurred in anticipation of a balanced budget deal would be lost with "disturbing" effects on the economy.

Greenspan was confident a balanced budget was, at last, within reach. Never, in his 20 years in Washington, had he been so optimistic about "pulling this off, and without default." But Greenspan did not reckon with the intransigence of the two parties. With the end of the fiscal year approaching September 30, no agreement had been reached on a 1996 budget or on extension of the debt ceiling. Congress passed and the president signed a stopgap measure extending spending authority through midnight November 13, but that was the last gesture of cooperation. Fed officials bent over backward not to take sides in the budget war, but privately some felt it was Clinton, not the Republicans, who were endangering the nation's financial health. "We need a grown-up" was how one succinctly put it.

Greenspan had much to rejoice over. The economy had resumed noninflationary growth, and falling long-term interest rates were reflecting not only balanced budget hopes but also a vote of confidence in the Fed. In short, it was time for an embarrassing bank scandal. On September 26, it was revealed the New York branch of Daiwa Bank had lost $1.1 billion on unauthorized bond trades over a period of years. The New York Fed, its supervisor, moved against the bank the following week, eventually shutting down its U.S. operations under authority granted the Fed after the 1991 Bank of Credit & Commerce International (BCCI) scandal. It soon came out that the Japanese Ministry of Finance had known about the Daiwa losses since August 8 but had not informed the New York Fed until September 18. Furthermore, it was reported the Fed had been warned about the suspicious activities of rogue Daiwa trader Toshihie Iguchi two years earlier but had not taken adequate steps to prevent the losses. Greenspan later told Congress, "We did not succeed in unearthing Daiwa's transgressions where we might have. There were some clues that were missed." The Fed is sensitive to suggestions it failed to detect and correct the Daiwa trading violations and that it responded slowly. "Daiwa really surfaced in a year when we first hired two hundred agents to examine foreign banks," says Ernest Patrikis, first vice president of the New York Fed. The Fed's foreign bank examination capacity is "a lot more mature now than it was then. Under the circumstances we did fairly well. . . . I thought we did a better job than everyone else in terms of seeing the smoke. We just didn't get the extra inch." As for why the Fed waited a couple of weeks to send examiners into Daiwa after being notified by Japanese authorities, Patrikis says the Fed waited for McDonough to return from a trip before going to the U.S. Attorney with its suspicions and only later sent in examiners. "We didn't want to pollute our case" by rushing examiners into Daiwa at the outset. Since the Daiwa scandal, the Fed has worked to strengthen audits of foreign banks in collaboration with other bank regulators. But a question remains for bank supervisors as they try to root out wrong-doing without going overboard: "How cynical should you be in examinations?" I am told the Fed will be far more alert and less tolerant of such abuses in the future.

The Daiwa scandal made a bad situation worse for the rest of the Japanese banking industry, which had been experiencing problems that made those experienced by U.S. banks a few years earlier pale. They had gone whole hog into real estate speculation both directly and through loans to Japanese savings banks and now had a mountain of bad assets. Daiwa's difficulties increased the so-called *Japan premium* Japanese banks were already having to pay when they borrowed in international money markets, further squeezing their profits and threatening their solvency. As angry as the Fed was at Japanese authorities for keeping them in the dark on Daiwa, this was a crisis in the making with potential global ramifications it could not ignore. Japanese banks had huge U.S. operations, competing successfully for loan customers with U.S. banks and investing heavily in Treasury securities. A failure of one or more of these banks could have serious repercussions. The Fed quietly worked out an arrangement with the Bank of Japan to assist Japanese banks if they got into trouble. "What we're trying to do is sleep at night," a Fed official confided. "We have to ask, 'do we want to insure that problems in Japanese banks don't lead to problems in branches of other Japanese banks and, in turn, in U.S. banks?' The answer is 'yes.' " When word of the secret arrangement leaked, rumors about the Fed bailing out Japanese banks flew, embarrassing the Fed and the BOJ. But what the Fed was prepared to do was nothing that unusual.

If a Japanese bank ran into liquidity problems during the day, the Bank of Japan had more than adequate resources to aid it. It held billions of dollars worth of U.S. Treasury securities, which it could sell or borrow against to obtain funds to lend to any Japanese bank in trouble. But what would happen if a New York branch of a Japanese bank found itself short of funds to settle its interbank obligations at the end of the day after the government securities market had closed, making it impossible for the BOJ to effectively tap its stockpile of dollar assets? Japanese banks, like all banks operating in the United States, had legal access to the Fed's discount window, but neither the Fed nor the BOJ thought it appropriate for the U.S. central bank to be making emergency loans to Japanese banks if it could be avoided. "We had discussions with the BOJ," a Fed official says, and "both we and they recognized it was in our common interest to have the Japanese government deal with this problem rather than the U.S. government." After a series of confidential meetings, a technical agreement was reached whereby the Fed would stand ready to purchase the BOJ's government securities overnight. So if, at 5 P.M., a Japanese branch was unable to clear its payments, the BOJ would be able to liquefy its holdings of T-bills or whatnot and lend to the troubled bank to tide it over until the following day. In effect, the Fed was prepared to act as a banker to the BOJ so it could be lender of last resort to its banks. Had the situation arose, which it never did, the Fed would most likely have entered into a customer repurchase agreement, much like the ones it does routinely as part of its open market operations, under which it would have bought the BOJ's T-bills and resold them to the BOJ over the next few days at a lower price—in effect, lending it dollars at a small profit. If the repo fit in with the Fed's reserve-adding needs, so much the better. If not, it would be offset. "The whole spirit of this was that we should not be put in the place of bailing out Japanese banks—not by design and not by accident," says a Fed source. "They [at the BOJ] have had a public commitment to backing any bank that engages in international business. They want to be seen as honoring it. So if it ended up a bank of theirs got in trouble, it would be politically disastrous for them and for us."

Notwithstanding its concerns about the budget and the Japanese banking situation, the Fed had seldom had so much reason to feel content with the effectiveness of its policies. Not only had it seemingly achieved its long-awaited "soft landing," it had brought about favorable market conditions: a firmer dollar and declining medium- and long-term interest rates. But all this good news had not made policymakers completely comfortable. They could not quite believe things were as good as they seemed. Whether it was the Fed's need to think and act preemptively or just a yearning to tinker, officials were looking ahead to what policy moves might be needed to keep the economy on an agreeable course a year or more in the future. They were not necessarily thinking along the same lines. In late October interviews, Lindsey and Blinder said they favored resuming the credit easing process. Blinder was looking to cut rates a "sizable" amount, depending on the final composition of the budget package. Yellen was a kindred spirit, and others were moving in their direction. A 5¾ percent funds rate—a real rate approaching 3 percent—might be okay to sustain growth for now, but a year or more in the future this camp felt such a rate would restrict growth and jobs. And since monetary policy operated with "long and variable lags" the Fed had to start acting soon to put in place prospectively less restrictive monetary conditions. Besides, falling market rates were telling the Fed its rates were too high. Not only were long rates rapidly approaching 6 percent, the entire market rate structure had come down dramatically. While they did not believe the Fed should always feel obligated to take its cue from the market, Blinder, Yellen, and Lindsey felt it was sending the correct signal this time about where the funds rate should go. If the Fed did not "validate" these lower rates, they feared, market rates would go back up. Others were less inclined to ease again, even with enactment of a balanced budget, unless they became convinced the economy was not going to overshoot its long-run potential. They needed to see signs of weaker growth, along with continued good inflation behavior.

Meanwhile, budgetary uncertainties were getting worse. On November 6, Rubin had said the Treasury would run out of borrowing authority and would be forced to default. Congress was prepared to raise the debt ceiling, but only if the White House agreed to work with it to enact a package that ended the deficit by 2002 using CBO economic assumptions. Congress was in the process of putting the finishing touches on a comprehensive seven-year plan to do just that by slowing the rate of spending growth while providing $245 billion in tax relief. At the same time, it was working on appropriations bills to fund various sectors of the government for fiscal 1996. As of the end of

October, it had completed action on four of thirteen appropriation bills, of which Clinton had signed two. On October 31, with the Treasury scheduled the next day to announce its quarterly refunding auctions, Rubin wrote to Gingrich threatening to suspend issuance of savings bonds and dip into the Federal Employee Retirement System's Government Securities Investment Fund unless Congress raised the debt limit. He banned *"when-issued"* trading—the position-taking government securities dealers do in advance of Treasury auctions.

On November 1, Treasury made $31.5 billion in three- and ten-year note sales contingent on passage or assurance of passage of a debt limit extension. Republican leaders said they would raise it if Clinton agreed to bargain on the budget. McCurry retorted that the consequences of GOP spending restraints would be "worse than default." Gingrich was not taking default seriously either. If it occurred, "the market would understand this is not a financial default. This is a political struggle. There's a huge difference." Treasury's advisory committee of securities dealers had warned a default would have "horrific and longlasting" effects, permanently raising government borrowing costs. But the two sides were focused on their respective budget priorities, not the country's creditworthiness. When Gingrich, Dole, and others met with Clinton that afternoon, the president accused them of wanting to "destroy the federal government." Republicans said they merely wanted to stop it from engorging the country. "This is a joke," Domenici exclaimed. "The president of the United States this year has gone from sending us a budget that did nothing on the deficit, ignored it, to one that he sent up that the claimed got to balance and did not get to balance and got zero Democratic votes in the United States Senate." Treasury suspended its auctions when Congress had not raised the debt limit by November 6, even though House Majority Leader Dick Armey promised action soon. On the tenth, Congress sent Clinton a bill raising the ceiling by $67 billion, but he vowed to veto it because it limited Rubin's ability to tap government pension funds and other assets. Rubin found a way to continue financing the government anyway and ruled out default before December 12. He said he could use cash balances destined for the trust funds to avoid default "for some period of time."

Greenspan was getting much less sanguine about default. These politicians were not kidding around. "There are many avenues to an agreement and the full faith and credit of the United States need not be part of the process," he wrote to D'Amato on November 9. Failure to make timely payment of interest and principal "would put a cloud over our securities that would not dissipate for many years. Investors would be wondering when we would next allow our creditworthiness to become embroiled in controversy. Breaking our word would have serious long-term consequences." D'Amato brandished the letter as proof "the President should stop playing politics and talking about vetoing the debt ceiling extension. He should start working constructively with Congress to balance the budget." On November 12, Congress passed its seven-year balanced budget blueprint, which would have slowed growth in entitlement spending while providing tax relief. The next day, with the government's interim spending authority about to expire, Congress sent the president another continuing resolution to avert a government shutdown. Clinton vetoed both the debt limit bill and the spending bill, complaining the latter would have raised Medicare premiums. With all but two departments unfunded, some 800,000 federal employees were furloughed November 14 as the government inched ever closer to default.

It was against this unnerving fiscal backdrop that the FOMC gathered November 15 to reconsider monetary policy. At the August and September FOMC meetings, there had been no consensus for lowering the funds rate, and the committee adopted symmetrical directives at both, abandoning the easing bias it had approved in July. Now pressure was building to take it down another notch. Although third-quarter real GDP growth had been estimated at 4.2 percent, the fourth looked more discouraging. The purchasing managers index had fallen again in October, job growth was anemic, retail sales and industrial production had fallen, and the beige book pointed to a slowdown. Consumer prices had risen 0.3 percent in October, but producer prices had fallen. But, try as it might to transcend the nasty fiscal debate, monetary policymakers found it impossible. Lindsey, more vociferous than ever about the need to ease, estimated the proposed GOP spending restraints would subtract 0.6 percent from GDP growth, if enacted. Congress and the White House had made no progress in resolving their differences. On November 2 Greenspan had "remain[ed] optimistic" but no longer displayed the ebullience he once had about prospects for a balanced budget. "If, for some unforeseen reason, the political process fails, and agreement is not reached, it would signal that the United States is not capable of putting its fiscal house in order, with serious adverse consequences for financial markets and economic growth."

The FOMC was torn. Whatever was eventually agreed on the budget, the government shutdown was sure to dampen an already slowing economy, Lindsey and others argued. However, in wake of the third-quarter rebound, the majority felt any fiscal drag effects "would not be sufficient in themselves to arrest the expansion" unless they continued indefinitely. It was agreed monetary policy remained restrictive, but some thought that was desirable to achieve price stability instead of continuing to coast along with 3 percent inflation. It was decided to leave rates unchanged with no bias toward lowering them. It seemed the Fed had delayed easing because of the unresolved budget—either to put pressure on the politicians or because the fiscal outlook was too uncertain to formulate policy. This misimpression bothered Fed officials. In fact they had "agreed that the Committee could not freeze its policy options while it awaited the outome of a prolonged federal budget debate. . . ." Belief that the Fed had been frozen into inaction would help create a groundswell of support for a rate cut, budget deal or no budget deal. The Fed had to "do whatever is appropriate for the economy" and reject "the concept of the Fed on hold until something happens down the street," Yellen told me in late November. The drop in long rates anticipated not just a lower budget deficit but also an easier monetary policy. "That means we have to ask ourselves whether or not, in the absence of such a policy, long-term rates could increase above current levels, which would endanger the growth projection." The larger Fed concern was that disappointing the market's lofty budget expectations would trigger a bond sell-off that would send long rates soaring. So far, Wall Street had disregarded the Washington squabbling. Choosing to believe Congress meant business and that the White House would sooner or later capitulate, it pushed bonds ever higher.

Four days after the November 15 FOMC meeting, Clinton promised Republican leaders he would work with them on a plan to balance the budget in seven years under CBO assumptions, so long as it protected health, education, and the environment. On that presidential promise Congress passed another short-term spending bill, which Clinton signed, to reopen the government until December 15—long enough, Republicans hoped, to reach a deal. The two sides began negotiations in late November, reinvigorating market hopes. By the end of November, the long bond yield had fallen to 6⅛ percent, and momentum would carry it below 6 percent by year-end, but the Fed knew the rally could not last if budget hopes were dashed. It soon became apparent Clinton's promise had been empty. He was holding out for $475 billion more spending over seven years and using ambitious White House assumptions about corporate profits and interest rates to make his budget balance. The talks broke down. On December 6, Clinton vetoed the GOP seven-year budget plan and the next day presented his own seven-year budget, which Republicans charged fell $400 billion short of balance. Even the *Washington Post* called it "a disappointment." The White House became self-righteously indignant when Gingrich warned of a stock market crash if a balanced budget accord was not reached. But administration officials had used worse rhetoric, prompting one Fed official to say they seemed to be "trying to cause a financial crisis." Gingrich was doing little more than echoing Greenspan's November 30 warning of a "shattering of expectation" that would cause a "quite negative" market reaction.

Greenspan was reflecting a growing Fed exasperation with both sides. By relentlessly working to reduce inflation expectations it had reduced the implicit default premium in long-term rates only to find itself facing an actual "default risk." There was great sympathy among some Fed officials for what Congress was trying to do and a realization that, if it had not been for the Republicans' 1994 election victory, there would be no balanced budget discussion. The White House was seen not bargaining in good faith with Congress or doing its part to avoid the "train wreck" Clinton, Rubin, and Panetta kept warning against. But much as individual Fed officials may have sympathized with the GOP goal and disliked the lack of cooperation from the executive branch, there was an institutional tug of loyalty that could not countenance risking default. The Fed was the Treasury's fiscal agent, handling billions of dollars in government securities transactions and making a market for them. Working together, Fed and Treasury had a responsibility to insure the smooth, predictable functioning of government financing, and that was what mattered most to the Fed at that time.

Republicans and Democrats on the Board and on the FOMC disagreed on the particulars of how to balance the budget, but put such differences aside. "We tend not to discuss at the Board issues such as how much of a tax cut would you want to see or what do you want to do about welfare spending," says one official. There was general agreement that a balanced budget agreement would be good for the economy. But the process of getting there complicated the Fed's job in numerous ways. "Certainly the budget situation affects GDP, affects how much money people are going to spend, . . . but until it's done we don't have a very clear picture," Phillips said late that November. "It's not fully clear how much [spending restraint] is backloaded [into later years]. At first blush it appears that the bad news is pushed back further. So it may well be that some of the effects of the adjustment, when they're enacted, may be delayed. And the other piece is that . . . if they go for some kind of capital gains reduction or indexation or something along those lines it could end up being stimulative. If the markets were to perceive the budget situation as credible and healthy, long-term rates could come down even further, which would be another form of stimulus. . . . You have to take into account what happens on fiscal policy, but you have to take a pretty close look at what they're actually doing and what other reactions are occurring in the economy."

Many questions plagued another Fed policymaker:

To what extent have long rates fallen in expectation there would be an accord? To what extent would we be encountering a fiscal drag on spending coming out of an accord and when would it materialize? Would it materialize quickly, necessitating a relatively near-term response from the Federal Reserve or over a longer period of time, meaning the appropriate path of adjustment for us would be very little and spread over a long period of time? So if there were a budget agreement what would the path look like and what would be required of us in order to support the economy in light of the growing fiscal drag? And could it be we'd end up with a tax cut soon, so that instead of fiscal drag, in the near term you'd have a fiscal stimulus? Would the markets do enough on their own? Could they be counted on to do most of the work? What would be left for us? Then we had a problem of "gee, they're not going to reach an agreement, we're going to have a government shutdown." Well, that's going to have an effect on the economy. And we have continuing resolutions, and CRs may be tighter from a fiscal point of view and from a spending point of view than if we had a budget agreement.

There was also the necessity of including in the Fed forecast a government spending projection. "This is a line with a huge amount of uncertainty that's changing from week to week and that we can't pin down with any precision, and it's becoming a tremendous uncertainty for us in the forecast," an official confided. A by-product of the budget stalemate was that statistical agencies stopped pumping the Fed's lifeblood of economic data, fogging the Fed's ability to read the economy. "Completely outside of the numbers . . . of the impact of fiscal policy . . . it is not a healthy thing that we do not seem to be able to govern ourselves in a mature and rational and calm manner . . . and that can have economic impacts as well as social impacts over time as it goes on," another official says. "It is not healthy for the body politic to see this sort of wrangling going on interminably in Washington and on a basis that is perceived as being narrowly and unattractively partisan between the two parties, and the concern is that that could have sort of a debilitating effect on the confidence of the people that make up the economy going forward."

The sand was running swiftly through the hourglass as far as government spending authority was concerned, and Rubin was facing increasing difficulties, including threats of impeachment, in his effort to fund government operations without new borrowing authority. The House Ways and Means Committee passed another $67 billion increase in the debt ceiling on December 8, but the White House again vowed to veto it because it "tied the Treasury's hands." On December 13, Rubin angered Republicans by announcing his intention to hijack a $14.5 billion interest payment due to the Civil Service Retirement Trust Fund. The same day, Congress sent Clinton another appropriations bill—this one a $12.2 billion natural resources spending package—but the president vowed to veto it on the grounds it threatened the environment. Compromise seemed out of the question. Gingrich offered to reduce by $116 billion proposed reductions in Medicaid spending and make other concessions to get a budget deal, but that was deemed insufficient. Republicans were determined to hold the president's feet to the fire and refused to pass another CR without making substantial progress in the budget talks. So at midnight on Friday, December 15, unfunded agencies had to furlough nonessential employees, and for the second time the government shut down, this time for 21 days. When the markets opened Monday, December 18, the market responded as the Fed had feared. The Dow plunged 101.52 points, and bonds lost 1½ points, raising the yield to 6.20 percent, partly on the presumption the breakdown in the talks would preclude a Fed rate cut. The dollar fell.

It was a loud warning signal of what might be in store to the FOMC, which met the following day. Fed officials deny any direct connection, but the FOMC voted unanimously to cut the funds rate a quarter point to 5½ percent, although some had preferred an unchanged policy. A relieved market rebounded, and on Decebmer 26, the long bond yield fell below 6 percent. Announcing the move, Greenspan said it had been taken because "inflation has been somewhat more favorable than anticipated," but there was more to it than that. Faced with sluggish consumer spending, production, and employment and having realized it could not depend on low long rates to sustain growth in face of a budgetary stalemate, the FOMC decided it could not wait for fiscal action. Many officials feared "an unchanged policy was likely to lead to a backup in intermediate and long-term rates." There was also a desire to get out in front of the politicians on the budget rather than appear to be reacting when a budget pact was finally reached.

A Fed official said:

Another worrisome problem from our point of view has been getting ourselves tied up in the politics of the thing. The Federal Reserve is supposed to be independent, and we can't be put in the position of withholding monetary policy changes in order to throw out thank-you's and bones to the dog for doing the right thing. You can't say, "gee boys, we want you to cut the deficit, and if you do we're going to give you a reward." That line began to become very, very prominent in the Fall, and we began to read stories that the Fed was unlikely to cut this month because they're going to want to wait for a budget deal. This became very troubling, wrapping the Fed up in the politics of the budget deal, making it look like we're trying to be political. This is a very subtle issue because on the one hand, the Fed doesn't want to be political. It's up to Congress and the President what they do with fiscal policy. We may have our view as to what's best for the economy, but Fed policy shouldn't be geared toward trying to extract behavior from those parties with respect to fiscal policy moves. But on the other hand, fiscal policy moves do have an impact on the economy, so . . . monetary policy does depend on fiscal policy simply from the point of view of keeping the economy on track. And, other things being equal, if fiscal policy is going to turn tight, monetary policy ought to be looser. Just trying to figure out what is the appropriate stance of policy depends on the forecast, and fiscal policy goes into the forecast. . . . So you're sitting there thinking, "boy, it sure would be easier to figure out what we ought to be doing if we knew what was going to be happening to fiscal policy," and that leads you to "why don't we wait a little while, and maybe they'll get it resolved, then it will be clear what lies ahead and we'll know what we ought to do." But the longer you wait for it to be resolved the more the press is saying "they're waiting because they don't want to reward Congress or the president with an interest rate cut until they've done their job." So the whole thing became a nasty wrangle.

The December rate cut left many Fed officials feeling the funds rate was still somewhat restrictive. Although the dearth of data combined with severe winter weather to create a statistical haze, available indicators suggested a weak economy. Money and credit growth had slowed, causing monetarists like Jordan to form a marriage of convenience with Keynesians like Yellen in favor of lowering the funds rate again at the January 31, 1996, FOMC meeting. Just as rising credit demand and related rising demand for bank reserves led monetarists to favor raising the funds rate in the February 1994 to February 1995 period to keep policy "neutral," falling credit demand and demand for reserves now necessitated lowering the funds rate. Erring toward restrictiveness would risk a downturn that would force the Fed into expansionary policies. There was little sign of worsening inflation, either from the yield curve, price indices, or the dollar (now solidly above 100 yen). The budget battle was still raging with just enough signs of progress to fuel later disappointment. The government reopened January 6 after Republicans, chastened by bad opinion polls, approved yet another stopgap spending bill, and when that one expired on January 26, they gave the White House another extension until March 15. Greenspan met with Armey January 23 and urged him not to withhold an increase in the debt limit. Eight days later Congress gave Treasury $30 billion new borrowing authority. It all went for nought as far as yielding any meaningful work on balancing the budget, although the administration and Congress finally reached agreement on a 1996 budget on April 24, seven months into the fiscal year.[7]

The Fed was determined not to be diverted from its main focus. Greenspan was relatively confident the economy would rebound and grow at least 2 percent in 1996, but could not be sure. Rather than risk recession, the Fed decided to take out what Greenspan called "insurance" by cutting rates again January 31. The discount rate was reduced from 5¼ to 5 percent, while the funds rate was cut from 5½ to 5¼ percent. Kelley and others now felt the Fed had achieved monetary "neutrality," although Lindsey and Yellen still considered policy "slightly restrictive." The Fed had cut rates despite the absence of the dovish Blinder, who had resigned to return to Princeton University. Clinton now had two vacancies to fill, including the one left the previous March when LaWare retired. Moreover, Greenspan's term as chairman was fast expiring, and there had been no word from the White House about its intentions.

Within five weeks would come convincing proof that the economy had shaken off its winter doldrums and the effects of an inventory correction, just as Greenspan had predicted.[8] By May, many Fed watchers were predicting the Fed would have to raise rates to keep the economic rebound and an upsurge in oil prices from causing inflation. But the administration was impatient for more rate cuts after the Fed's January 31 move. It was an election year, and although Clinton boasted in his State of the Union address about "the best economy in thirty years," the administration was actually quite worried about conditions. The Economic Report of the President, released February 13, dropped heavy hints the White House expected the Fed to continue easing both to accommodate expected deficit reduction and to cut unemployment. CEA chairman Joseph Stiglitz and staff contended the unemployment rate which could be sustained without rising inflation (NAIRU) had gone as low as 5½ percent so that the Fed could provide for lower unemployment with little risk inflation would rise. "If policymakers reduced unemployment in the belief that the sustainable rate had fallen but were wrong and inflation increased, inflation is unlikely to 'take off,' and the cost of returning inflation to its earlier level would roughly equal the benefit of having temporarily lowered the unemployment rate. The gain, of course, if policymakers were right and the sustainable rate had fallen would be lower unemployment with unchanged inflation." Stiglitz said GDP could grow faster than the Fed assumed.

The report posed other justifications for an easier Fed stance. On the premise the budget would be balanced, it suggested the maximum benefit in terms of greater private investment could only be achieved if the Fed provided "an accommodative monetary policy" to "validate" expected declines in real long-term rates. "When market participants are forward-looking and anticipate [correctly] that the monetary authority will accommodate future credible deficit reduction, real long-term interest rates fall by more than when market participants either do not view future deficit reduction as credible or believe that monetary accommodation will not be forthcoming." Some Fed officials were thinking along similar lines, but few were prepared to blithely assume NAIRU had permanently fallen or that the economy's growth potential had increased and to make policy gambles. Nor were they prepared to be overly "forward-looking" in easing on the basis of what a haywire budget process might produce.

Conspicuously absent from the report was any real recognition of the key role the Fed had played in controlling inflation and creating a climate for lower long-term interest rates. The credit for lower rates was mendaciously, not to say absurdly, given to Clinton fiscal policy. In a speech two days later, Clinton himself took an indirect slap at the Fed by calling for a "national debate" on whether the economy can grow faster than 2½ percent without accelerating inflation. Fed officials deny these election-year attempts to pressure them had any impact, but thereafter Greenspan and others went to great lengths to deny they wanted to restrain growth.[9] With Greenspan's future in doubt, it was hard not to get the impression the administration was "dangling" Greenspan, just as Bush had done, to obtain a looser election year monetary policy. The White House had accused Senate Republicans of playing politics with the Fed by blocking the nomination of investment banker Felix Rohatyn to replace Blinder, but the charge boomeranged on the White House the longer it delayed naming Greenspan to a third term. His term as chairman was to expire March 2, but repeated questions from reporters about his fate were greeted with week after week of ambiguity and ambivalence from Clinton and his aides. Nor had they uttered a word of praise for the job Greenspan had done. He was left to twist slowly in the wintry wind.

Some members of the administration, Democrats on Capitol Hill and Democratic Party activists wanted Greenspan gone. As a Democratic insider explained, "He's not one of us." Although Clinton had boasted about low inflation and job creation during his administration, some Democrats blamed Greenspan for keeping a tight lid on growth and being too slow to lower rates. Clinton's reelection chances could ride on the state of the economy. There had been little or no real wage growth for some time. Real disposable income had been stagnating, and only mounting household debt had sustained consumer spending. The Economic Report of the President had proudly pointed to minuscule increases in unit labor costs as some kind of accomplishment, but while that was good for inflation, it was political poison. So Clinton was trying to wriggle out of his bullish pronouncements by suggesting the Fed was not providing enough growth to generate comfy wage hikes for everyone. It was just possible some of this stagnation had to do with Clinton's own tax and regulatory policies, as well as its running budget battle with Republicans, but it was easier to blame the Fed.

In the final analysis, however, Clinton knew he had to reappoint Greenspan. A major fracas would develop if he did not. His delay was adding to jitters on Wall Street. The chairman was also held in high regard by Senate Republicans, some of whom indicated they would settle for no one else. Florida senator Connie Mack, a sometime Fed critic who had introduced a bill to repeal the Humphrey-Hawkins Act and replace it with a price stability mandate, said, "Greenspan has great, great support among Senate Republicans, and frankly I don't think Clinton or the Democrats have any choice but to reappoint him." But not until after Greenspan had hinted, in his February 20 Humphrey-Hawkins testimony at the possibility of further "insurance" rate cuts did Clinton announce his renomination. Perhaps it was only coincidental, but two days later, he named Greenspan to a third term while also appointing his budget director Alice Rivlin to replace Blinder and respected economic forecaster Laurence Meyer to fill the LaWare vacancy. Before he was renominated a former Fed official told me, "Alan Greenspan is so dedicated to trying to get himself reappointed that he is willing to compromise some of his independence in order to do so. He desperately wants to be reappointed." But it would be hard to make the case that Greenspan engineered either the December or January rate cuts to that end. Greenspan's fellow Board members, Clinton and Bush appointees alike, rejoiced at his reappointment. Yellen said she was looking forward to continuing to work with "a very wise leader."

But the Democrats were not finished jerking Greenspan around. Those Clinton advisers who had fought Greenspan's nomination had their allies in the Senate who were determined to delay his confirmation as long as they could. If they could delay his confirmation long enough, perhaps beyond the election, maybe Greenspan would resign in disgust. Or maybe a reelected Clinton would change his mind, withdraw the nomination and appoint a loyal Democrat, say Bob Rubin. The Senate Banking Committee approved Greenspan's nomination, along with those of Rivlin and Meyer, on March 27, three weeks after Greenspan's 70th birthday, and their nominations were expected to sail through the full Senate. But Iowa senator Tom Harkin and three other Democratic senators put a hold on Greenspan's confirmation. By threatening to filibuster any effort to bring the nomination to a vote, they succeeded in delaying his confirmation for another three months. Not since Marriner Eccles in the 1950s had the Fed chairman been in such a spot.

Greenspan arrived in Harkin's office late on the afternoon of April 18 to keep an appointment with the four, hoping to assuage their concerns. He was subjected to a petty display of senatorial discourtesy. Greenspan was left cooling his heels in Harkin's outer office, as reporters, photographers, and television camera crews observed his discomfort through a glass wall. After pacing the office for a few minutes, Greenspan sat down between a television set and a half-filled popcorn machine and waited to be invited into the senator's private office. As he waited, he glanced at a television set tuned to C-SPAN coverage of a Senate health care debate. Several Harkin aides spoke briefly to Greenspan, and a trickle of interns passed through the office to gawk at the famed Fed chairman. Eventually, he was escorted into Harkin's office by an aide. Harkin did not bother to come out to greet him. After some further delay, Senators Paul Wellstone of Minnesota, Byron Dorgan of North Dakota, and Harry Reid of Nevada showed up. The hour and a half meeting was cordial, but afterward, the lawmakers, anxious to score political points with their prairie populist constituents, said they still had "questions" which only lengthy floor debate could resolve. They felt the Fed had been too tightfisted. Harkin was also trying to get back at the Republicans for subjecting Dr. Henry Foster, Clinton's nominee to be surgeon general, to three days of debate before rejecting him in 1995. Surely, Harkin argued, a post as important as Fed chairman deserved at least as much debate. "I've got a lot of stuff on Greenspan, stuff going back years and years, back to the time he worked for Ford," he told Market News Service. "I want to lay it out in a nice, orderly fashion."

The unflappable, Washington-wise Greenspan took the indignity in stride. He considered it the senators' constitutional right to delay his confirmation. Besides, it was no skin off his back. The Board had voted him chairman pro tempore, and he could serve in that capacity almost indefinitely.[10] The clock on Greenspan's third four-year term as chairman would not begin ticking until he was actually confirmed, and the later his term started, the longer he could serve as chairman. John Ryding, senior economist at Bear-Stearns, joked that the country should thank Harkin for prolonging Greenspan's reign. Greenspan and his colleagues were unfazed. "At least in the limited dealings I've had with the chairman, he certainly doesn't give any hint that this is causing him any anxiety," Broaddus told me in late May. "He's still doing his job and doing it well, and I think morale is still quite high in the system." If anything, outside the coterie of Greenspan enemies in the White House inner circle, the administration seemed more anxious to get the Greenspan nomination moving than the Fed or Senate Republicans. Tied to his nomination were those of Rivlin and Meyer, and Rivlin was clamoring to have her status clarified. Rubin and Panetta urged Harkin to expedite the nominations, and, finally, on May 21, Clinton himself called Harkin and told him he wanted Greenspan and the others confirmed "as soon as possible." But another month was to go by before Harkin and company would agree to bring the nominations to a vote.

While Greenspan's nomination was dangling, the Clinton administration demonstrated once again that it respects the Fed's independence and refrains from applying political pressure to monetary policy—except when it chooses to behave otherwise. The president himself was about as brazen as he could be in pressuring the Fed to stay on hold and leave the federal funds rate at 5.25 percent. At a June 7 Rose Garden news conference, after the Labor Department had announced strong May payroll figures, Clinton noted that the Fed would be considering what to do with short-term interest rates at its July 2–3 FOMC meeting and asserted, ". . . If they see that we are producing this kind of job growth without inflation, I would think the interest rates should stay down, not only the Fed rates but the rates that the market sets." As so often happened in the Clinton administration, the president's remarks were later disavowed, as if he had never made them. "I don't think that's what he said," Treasury Secretary Robert Rubin told reporters two weeks later when asked about Clinton's remarks. "I don't think he jawboned the Fed." In the next breath, Rubin put his own more subtle form of pressure on the Fed by saying it should look at "low inflation" and other factors in judging whether to change rates. The day before, at the National Press Club, Rubin anticipated that the addition of Rivlin and Meyer would lead to a "vibrant debate" at the Fed on the economy's ability to grow. Rubin was following through on Clinton's February call for "a national debate" on growth, which some of the White House's Senatorial friends had taken as a mandate to battle Greenspan's renomination. Meanwhile, Summers gave a speech in which he declared, ". . . We cannot and will not accept any 'speed limit' on American economic growth. It is the task of economic policy to grow the economy as rapidly, sustainably and inclusively as possible."

After Bob Dole retired from the Senate to pursue his presidential campaign, and Senator Trent Lott of Mississippi took over as Senate majority leader on June 12, a deal was struck to proceed to a vote on the Greenspan, Rivlin, and Meyer nominations after three days of debate. On June 13, 14, and 20, Harkin, Dorgan, Reid, Wellstone, and others took turns bashing Greenspan. After insisting their opposition was "not personal" and that they "admired" Greenspan, they proceeded to harshly upbraid him. Harkin charged that Greenspan's "blind pursuit of inflation control" at the expense of growth was "cold to the needs of families," and that his policies were "leading to great social unrest." Greenspan "has an economic philosophy that simply does not focus on the problems of average people." What was needed was a Fed chairman with "more balance" and less "religious fervor" about fighting inflation. He charged that "throughout his entire adult lifetime," Greenspan had been "wrong on the economy" and, after failing to anticipate recessions, had "failed to act decisively" to counter them. Greenspan, Harkin went on, has a "hair trigger" in reacting to potential inflation. He accused him of being too oriented to the needs of investors and averred, "What is good for bondholders is not necessarily always good for America. . . ." While accusing Greenspan of "stifling" growth to combat inflation, Harkin claimed he really had not made much progress against inflation and that what little there had been was due to global competition and mass marketing, not monetary policy.

Dorgan alleged that Greenspan, by holding the funds rate higher than he deemed necessary, was "causing every American to be taxed . . . with an interest charge that they did not have any part in being able to debate or talk about. . . ." Only bankers, he contended, had any input in the setting of rates. If the Fed were to restrain real growth to 2.2 percent per year instead of 3.2 percent, it would cost the economy $3 trillion over 20 years, he said. "What we have is a policy that works great for bondholders, great for Wall Street, but does not work well for families in our country," said Wellstone. Senator Kent Conrad of North Dakota argued Greenspan had "made a profound series of mistakes: raising rates time after time, killing the energy in this economy, and doing it on an old, tired notion of an economic theory that no longer relates to reality." The Fed chairman was "killing a chance for American workers to receive the increases they so justly deserve."

Reid said Greenspan should not be reappointed because he was "under a cloud" of suspicion over what he called the Fed's "mismanagement." The General Accounting Office, at Reid and Dorgan's behest, had just released an audit of the Fed, showing that its operating expenses had risen about 50 percent from 1988 to 1994, and that the Fed had built up a $3.7 billion "slush fund." Greenspan had already explained that the Fed's rising expenses reflected the need to beef up its technology and pay higher salaries to run an increasingly complex payments system. As for the alleged "slush fund," the Fed had prudently built up this surplus—over and above the $16 to $24 billion it returned annually to the Treasury Department during the Greenspan years—as a safeguard in the event of loss. But this did not stop Reid from alleging the Fed was "running amok." Greenspan and his colleagues, he continued, "are bloated. They are gluttonous." Playing into the hands of Greenspan's opponents was an accounting disparity at the Los Angeles branch of the San Francisco Fed revealed in early June involving a $178 million series of miscounts of the amount of cash in circulation reported to the Federal Reserve Board in late 1995. The Los Angeles Fed branch, like others, puts new currency into circulation and destroys old, then makes monthly reports to the Board in Washington so it can track the money supply. John Moore, chief operating officer of the San Francisco Fed, acknowledged that there had been discrepancies, but called it a "statistical problem, not a financial one." As this was written the Fed was investigating whether staffers had falsified reports to force balances to add up.

Republicans countered Democratic arguments that the Fed was holding down growth by blaming excessive government spending, taxation, and regulation. "If the people who raise questions about the impact of the Federal Reserve . . . would put their muscle and shoulder behind having a sound fiscal policy passed by the Congress of the United States then they would not have to be so concerned about the Federal Reserve," said Iowa Republican senator Charles Grassley. D'Amato, a past critic of Greenspan's policies, said Congress should "not hold responsible the Chairman of the Federal Reserve for our failures. . . . Instead of blaming the Federal Reserve, we ought to look clearly at ourselves. We ought to look at what we spend our money for, how much we tax our people. Are we spending enough of the tax dollar in productive activities, or are we spending it just exchanging money between our citizens? Do we have an education system that is feeding into our production machine students of all ages ready to take the jobs that we have today, with retraining and high skills being required? Do we have regulations that are too severe, that are not worth the costs that we are imposing?" Mack observed that "Congress had made a mess of fiscal policy. If Congress gets more involved in monetary policy it would be a disaster for the country."

A few Democrats spoke in Greenspan's favor, some more grudgingly than others. Senate Minority Leader Tom Daschle of South Dakota pledged his support only after complaining that the Fed was holding interest rates too high and "should consider lowering interest rates now, this year, this month"—this at a time when nearly everyone was looking for the Fed to raise interest rates to ward off an upsurge in wage-price pressures. Senator Daniel Patrick Moynihan of New York was more enthusiastic in his support, calling Greenspan "a national treasure." He pointed out that, at the same time inflation was running around 3 percent for the fifth year in a row, unemployment was under 5 percent in more than half of the states and under 4 percent in ten states. Given the low level of unemployment in the sixth year of expansion, "the issue is not whether 2.5 percent growth is acceptable, but rather is any higher rate possible," he said. Senator Frank Lautenberg of New Jersey, who had once run a company (ADP) that sold the Townsend-Greenspan database, said, "These criticisms of the Federal Reserve are nothing more than an excuse not to adopt sound fiscal policies like a balanced budget and a pure flat tax. . . . It is clear to me Mr. Greenspan is being made a scapegoat for individuals who will not adopt sound fiscal policies."

Finally, on June 20, 1996, after three days of off-and-on debate, Greenspan was confirmed to a third term, running through the same date in the year 2000. The vote was an overwhelming 91 to 7 in Greenspan's favor. Meyer was confirmed 98 to 0. Rivlin, by virtue of her high-profile role defending the administration's budget policies, did not fare as well. Clinton's budget director became vice chairman on a 57 to 41 vote, but only after Senator Christopher Bond of Missouri and other Republican insurgents questioned her integrity. Bond charged that Rivlin was "willing to subvert her professional judgment in submitting a budget to the political directives of the White House to avoid any cuts. I am sorry to say that I do not believe we can afford to have someone willing to subvert their professional judgment to political directives serving on the Federal Reserve Board." Bond's complaint was essentially that Rivlin had defended the president's budget, which purported to balance the budget by the year 2002, but which postponed the great bulk of spending restraints until after 2000. The heads of the Veterans Administration, NASA, and the Environmental Protection Agency had appeared before Bond's Appropriations Subcommittee and testified they had been assured by the White House they would not have to come up with the projected spending cuts in the "out years." When Bond questioned Rivlin about this in late May, Rivlin responded that the administration would "continue to revisit decisions about specific programs one year at a time." Bond called her response "most disappointing. . . ." Senator Robert Bennett of Utah, who had committed to support Rivlin, announced with "great personal sadness" that he had changed his mind. He accused her of participating in a White House budget "shell game."

During the vote on Rivlin's nomination, Bond and D'Amato hovered near the well of the Senate and actively lobbied Republicans to oppose Rivlin. After receiving Bond's and D'Amato's entreaties, Budget Commitee Chairman Domenici walked off by himself for several moments, apparently anguished as to whether he should oppose Rivlin, with whom he had worked closely for more than 20 years on budget issues. Eventually Domenici voted with the majority to confirm Rivlin. Thus ended a drama that further shifted the balance of power on the Federal Reserve Board in favor of a president who had deemphasized the need to worry about inflation. Only time would tell whether the two new Clinton appointees would significantly alter the direction of monetary policy, but at a watershed July 3 meeting, the reconstituted FOMC decided not to raise interest rates despite speculation that the Fed would need to tighten to insure against inflation. It remained on hold at the August 20 and September 24 meetings, but by then the economy had begun to show signs of a slowdown—just as Greenspan had prophesied.

Epilogue

By the time Greenspan was confirmed to a third term, he had compiled an enviable record, notwithstanding complaints about the slow pace of economic growth. In 1995, the consumer price index had risen 2½ percent overall and 3 percent excluding food and energy—the fifth year running that inflation had averaged around 3 percent or less. In the first half of 1996, although an oil price spike temporarily pushed the overall CPI up to an annual rate exceeding 4 percent, the core CPI rose less than 3 percent, notwithstanding the fact that unemployment had fallen as low as 5.3 percent and real GDP had rebounded to an estimated 4.2 percent growth rate in the second quarter.

But sad to say, Greenspan's third term did not get off to an auspicious start, through no fault of his own. By the time he was reappointed in the midst of an ongoing budget squabble in the Washington sandbox, long-term interest rates were soaring, well before early March brought signs of a resurgent economy. From less than 6 percent at the beginning of 1996, the long bond yield had climbed to 6½ percent by late February, 6¾ percent in March, and above 7 percent in early May. The stock market demonstrated its discontent with occasional sharp drops in stock prices (171 points on March 8). The markets were doing just as Greenspan had repeatedly warned they would if the White House and Congress continued to dawdle over balancing the budget. Jack Guynn, president of the Atlanta Fed, bespoke the bitter discouragement of many at the Fed. "Earlier this year, I had great hopes that Congress would hash out the difficulties in balancing the budget and reducing the deficit," he said March 11. "But both Congress and we as a nation seem to have lost momentum. I'd like to say as strongly as I can that we must not lose our nerve."

No matter how astute and courageous monetary policymakers are, the economy is still ultimately at the mercy of the taxing, spending, and regulating powers of our elected representatives and the hundreds of thousands of unelected bureaucrats they have empowered to oversee nearly every aspect of our lives. In the final analysis, the Fed cannot and must not be "the only game in town."

As this was written, the outcome of the budget debate was undecided, and while it did not look encouraging, there was hope the two sides would agree to balance the budget over a period of years. Oddly enough, the person most optimistic about the eventual outcome is the person one might think has the least reason to be. Greenspan is encouraged by what he sees as a major change in the political climate, which has dictated that both Democrats and Republicans shift toward more fiscal responsibility. When, in the spring of 1996, the two parties were debating whether to repeal the 4.3-cent increase in the federal gasoline tax included in the 1993 budget package, he was gratified that neither side was willing to do so without offsetting savings on the spending side.

If there is an agreement to eliminate the deficit consisting of something more than accounting gimmicks and further levies on an already overburdened populace, it will be cause for rejoicing, but as the Gramm-Rudman experience showed, any pact is only as good as our collective will to live by it.

If and when the president and Congress come to terms on a balanced budget it would likely revolutionize the way monetary policy is made in this country for years to come. If the deficit is actually eliminated, the Fed will find itself living in a virtual central banker's paradise, and so will the rest of us (not that all of our problems will disappear). As the financial markets have already anticipated, a world of balanced budgets—who knows, perhaps even eventual surpluses, as Greenspan has urged—would be a world of low and stable interest rates. Unless some future Fed decided to run a foolishly expansionary monetary policy that generated inflation pressures, there would be every reason for the United States to return to the kind of interest rate environment of the 1950s, where 4 to 5 percent fixed-rate mortgages were the norm and when corporations could issue long-term debt at 3 percent or less. Not just incidentally, the cost of financing the accumulated national debt would decline dramatically as well.

Despite the Fed's hard-fought and largely successful effort of the past 17 years to achieve price stability, interest rates have remained relatively high in both nominal and real terms because of what monetary economists call "default risk." The concept refers not so much to the risk of outright default by the government as to the fear engrained in the collective subconscious of market participants that, no matter how responsible today's Fed policymakers may be, the year-by-year accumulation of deficits will eventually create an overwhelming impetus to monetize the debt via inflation. Even at today's relatively low rates, these inflationary expectations have built in a 3 to 4 percent premium above inflation. What's more, most people now recognize federal borrowing "crowds out" private borrowers. Given America's relatively low savings and our reliance on imported savings, federal borrowing unquestionably bids up the price of capital, pricing out of the market some private investment. By reducing interest premiums, a balanced budget could be expected to unleash an avalanche of investment that would increase productivity and in turn the economy's noninflationary growth potential. (No more 2½ percent ceiling on how much the economy can grow without the FOMC getting the shakes.) The Fed would have to take this into consideration. It would have to redefine "full employment" or NAIRU to allow for lower unemployment and higher growth.

With such a huge quantity of debt to service and another seven years until the budget is putatively balanced, the money markets will remain lively for years to come, but one can even envision the day when the bond market will return to being the sleepy backwater it once was. With reduced demands on foreign capital, America's balance of payments would cease to be a worry. Some think the lower interest rates that would come with a balanced budget would cause the U.S. dollar to depreciate. But it seems more likely, as Greenspan has postulated, that the dollar would strengthen. In any event, exchange rate volatility would probably diminish, and any doubts about the greenback's primacy as a world currency would vanish.

It's been nice having Fed chairmen of heroic proportions like Greenspan and Volcker, but we could go back to the days when nobody knew the name of the Fed chairman—or cared.

I am not prophesying the end of monetary history. The Fed's biggest challenge in this brave new world of fiscal responsibility would probably be avoiding the temptation to tinker with the economy and screw up the business cycle. And it will always be a challenge to maintain a consensus in favor of "price stability." Amid election year pressures to maximize economic growth, the Fed made "Achieving Price Stability" the theme of its 1996 Jackson Hole conference. But while there was broad agreement on the desirability of that objective, there was enough difference of opinion over what constitutes price stability and how to achieve it that one former Fed official suspected a "reevaluation" of the Fed's goals was under way. Given that the CPI overstates inflation by ½ to 2 percent, some said the Fed should settle for an inflation range of 1 to 3 percent and not insist on zero inflation. Some endorsed an "opportunistic disinflation" strategy in which the Fed would not actively seek to lower inflation while the economy was enjoying full employment and modest growth, but would wait for recessions to bring down inflation. Such talk prompted Mullins to express concern that the Fed was getting "cold feet" about actually achieving price stability.

But surely a balanced budget would make the lives of future Fed officials easier. Until that day of fiscal sanity arrives, the United States and other nations which depend so much on it will remain subject to the kind of shocks and potential disasters which we have seen during the Greenspan years. We can only hope Americans like Greenspan will be there to hold us back from the brink.

Endnotes

ONE: *The Makings of a Central Banker*

1. Greenspan served on President Nixon's Foreign Intelligence Advisory Board, the Commision on Financial Structure and Regulation, the Commission on an All-Volunteer Armed Force, the Task Force on Economic Growth, the Security and Exchange Commission's Central Market System Committee, and the Office of Management and Budget's Gross National Product Review Committee.

TWO: *Hitting the Ground Running*

1. Democrats Bill Bradley of New Jersey and Kent Conrad of North Dakota were the only two opposed. The former said Greenspan was "a man of ability and great integrity," but objected to his advocacy of rapid banking deregulation.

2. The Fed's operating procedure prior to the October 1987 crash and again after things returned to "normal" entailed targeting how much banks as a group were expected to borrow, on average, from the Fed's discount window each day. Banks are required to hold a certain percentage of reserves behind their deposits (at that time 12 percent on transaction account balances above $40.4 million), in addition to which banks generally desire holding a certain amount of "excess reserves" over and above their reserve requirements to meet their own liquidity needs. By calculating the total amount of reserves banks needed and then adjusting upward or downward the amount of reserves banks borrowed at the discount window, the Fed could affect the level of overall reserves in the system and, in turn, overall credit conditions. If the system was flush with reserves, banks would be more inclined to make loans on good terms and low rates, whereas if reserve conditions were tighter, banks would be less inclined to lend. In practical terms this meant restricting the amount of nonborrowed reserves in the banking system to essentially force banks to the window. There, banks could post government securities as collateral and borrow short-term for reserve "adjustment" purposes or to meet "seasonal credit" needs at a discount rate set and announced by the Federal Reserve Board of Governors. Where the rubber met the road, so to speak, was that banks don't like to be seen lining up for loans at the window because it invites scrutiny from federal bank examiners and because the Fed has been known to figuratively slam the window shut on their fingers. The stock market crash temporarily forced the Fed away from using the window as a means of restricting reserve conditions and raising short-term interest rates.

3. Under a new method of measuring gross domestic product, adopted in late 1995, known as the *chain weighted* method, GDP growth rates have tended to be less. Consequently, calculations of the economy's growth potential have also been adjusted lower to a range of 2 to 2¼ percent. Also note that in 1991, the Commerce Department shifted from calculating gross national product (GNP) to reporting gross domestic product (GDP). Unlike GNP, GDP excludes foreign source income and counts only output generated domestically.

4. In a curious sidelight, the one-time advocate of the gold standard, endorsed a Baker proposal, made at the IMF meeting, to use a gold-based commodity price indicator in the G-7 policy coordination process. In fact, Baker had cleared the gold idea with Greenspan before unveiling it. Greenspan called gold "a useful indicator of the flight from currencies." Unfortunately, gold was just then acting as an all-too-accurate barometer of the crisis of confidence in the dollar. The noninterest earning precious metal was en route from around $460 per ounce to around $490, having started the year just above $400.

5. Its rate on securities repurchase agreements (the *repo rate*) had risen from 3.5 to 3.85 percent since midyear, and the rate on one-month funds had risen from 3.6 to 4 percent. Long-term rates had risen somewhat more.

6. Stock index futures contracts are an ingenious variation on the basic futures concept, which has been successfully employed for more than 100 years. Traditionally, for a commission, you can put up a small amount of earnest money, or *margin*, and buy (or sell) a large quantity of, say, wheat, for delivery at a certain date in the future, paying a premium or *basis* over the cash or *spot* price. If prices move up between when you buy the contract and the future delivery date, you profit by selling a wheat futures contract at the higher price. Making the market in any commodity are *hedgers*—commercial interests wishing to fix the price that they will have to pay. In the case of wheat, a flour mill, not wanting to gamble on what it will have to pay for grain in six months, can end most of the guesswork by buying the requisite number of wheat futures contracts for delivery in six months. If grain prices rise during that time frame, the additional cost the mill has to pay farmers for their wheat will be cancelled out, net of commissions, by the profits it will have made by selling higher-priced wheat futures to offset its *long* position. A wheat farmer, on the other hand, not knowing how much the wheat will sell for in six months time, may want to sell (*go short*) wheat futures, so that if the price of wheat falls, the farmer is protected. The lower cash price obtained from selling the wheat is roughly cancelled out by the profit made from buying lower-priced wheat futures to offset the short position. Stock index futures work in basically the same way, except that in place of a single commodity, the contract represents the fluctuating value of a diverse group of stocks, such as the S&P 500. Delivery is made in cash. The contract's value is based not only on the value of the actual stocks in the index, but the time remaining until the contract expires and the *carrying cost*, or interest and dividends foregone on the funds invested.

7. Although much of the selling on Black Monday was futures related, most of it was not. "Program" sales unrelated to futures trading accounted for 51.7 million shares, compared to 37.5 million for index arbitrage, according to the CFTC. The SEC says the selling was "broad-based," with institutions accounting for 50.7 percent, including portfolio insurance selling, mutual fund liquidations, margin liquidations, and selling by foreign accounts. The retail public accounted for 33.3 percent of the selling, while proprietary trading by securities firms for their own account accounted for 16 percent.

8. Each exchange operates its own clearinghouse, which functions as an intermediary, essentially acting as the buyer toward every seller and as the seller toward every

buyer, enabling traders to trade with abandon in the knowledge the clearinghouse will sort everything out at the end of the day. The following day net payment or *settlement* is made to the previous day's winners and losers.

9. Jointly owned by the New York and American stock exchanges, the Chicago Board Options Exchange, and the over-the-counter National Association of Securities Dealers (NASDAQ), the OCC issues, clears, and settles all stock options, which give an investor the right to buy or sell a stock at a certain strike price within a limited period of time in exchange for a small premium.

THREE: *"Deep Root Canal Surgery"*

1. Adding to the Fed's headaches, Republic National Bank, one of Texas's proudest financial institutions, was just then hitting up the Fed for huge amounts of *"extended credit"*—the Fed's euphemism for longer-term loans it extends to troubled banks, often before they go down for the last time. To add insult to injury (and to prove that Congress could be just as obnoxious as the White House), Montana's Democratic senator John Melcher announced on March 15 he intended to add an amendment to the Fed's cherished bank reform legislation to strip Federal Reserve Bank presidents of their power to vote on monetary policy. (Unlike members of the Board of Governors, the Bank presidents are selected by their own boards of directors, not by the president of the United States, and are not subject to Senate confirmation.) Melcher never got anywhere with either his legislation or with a constitutional challenge that was eventually struck down by the U.S. Supreme Court.

2. The directive was "symmetrical" in stating that "somewhat greater reserve restraint or somewhat lesser reserve restraint would be acceptable depending on the strength of the business expansion, indications of inflationary pressures, developments in foreign exchange markets, as well as the behavior of the monetary aggregates." It is now known the Fed increased its target for discount window borrowings by $100 million to $300 million with the intent of nudging the funds rate from the 6¼ to 6⅜ percent range to a range of 6½ to 6¾ percent. In reality, funds had been trading around 6½ percent going into the meeting, so the tightening was slight indeed.

3. The current account deficit was headed toward $128.2 billion that year—down from 1987's $167 billion, but still massive—and Greenspan said the deficit showed "how much more deeply in debt to the rest of the world we are sliding each year. The consequence of this external imbalance will be a steady expansion in our external debt burden in the years ahead. No household or business can expect to have an inexhaustible credit line with borrowing terms that stay the same as its debt mounts relative to its wealth and income. Nor can we as a nation expect our foreign indebtedness to grow indefinitely relative to our servicing capacity without additional inducements to foreigners to acquire dollar assets—either higher real interest returns or a cheaper real foreign exchange value for dollar assets or both."

4. Early in the year, LaWare had just come out of his doctor's office for a physical and gotten into his limousine, when his chauffer told him, "Call the White House." LaWare responded, "Yeah? What saloon have you been in while I was in getting my check up." He called the White House personnel office, and the next thing he knew, he was Reagan's choice to fill a seat vacated by Henry Wallich, but that was just the beginning. There was a long, onerous struggle for both the White House and for LaWare, who, for three months before his nomination had been announced in May 24, had been put through an excruciating background check. "The FBI actually asked me to recreate every time I had been out of the country—the dates and the purpose. I was interviewed

by three different FBI agents. One of them even followed me down to Sea Island [Georgia] where we have a house on the shore." Then came two months of delay before the Senate Banking Committee acted on his nomination, "and here we are sitting on tenterhooks, wondering if the whole thing was going to get dumped, and we were trying to get financial things in order and arrange for blind trusts and do all that kind of stuff." Massachussetts' two Democratic Senators Edward Kennedy and John Kerrey had generously introduced the former chairman of Shawmut National Corporation, a regional bank holding company, at his confirmation hearing, and the Committee finally approved his nomination on July 13. But Senate Majority Leader Robert Byrd dragged his feet on a full Senate vote until Kennedy persuaded Dukakis, also of Massachussetts, to intervene on LaWare's behalf.

5. By November 22, the Fed was having great difficulty operationally keeping the funds rate from rising above its target range because the relationship between the funds rate and its borrowings target had broken down. Nominally, at that time the Fed had a $600 million borrowing target, which was presumed to be consistent with keeping the funds rate in the $8\frac{1}{8}$ to $8\frac{1}{4}$ percent range, but actual borrowings had been running considerably lower. Yet the funds rate had been drifting higher, to about $8\frac{3}{8}$ percent. Seizing the opportunity, Greenspan organized a telephone conference November 22, in which he persuaded the FOMC that the firmer funds rate was justified by renewed strength in the labor market. He had the open market desk lower its borrowings target by $200 million per day (ordinarily a sign of easing), but hold the funds rate at around $8\frac{3}{8}$ percent. Rejected was a suggestion by Angell that the borrowing target be set at $500 million which would have carried with it a presumed funds rate level of $8\frac{1}{2}$ to $8\frac{3}{4}$ percent.

6. "Gonzo," as we in the press affectionately called him, was a colorful congressman from San Antonio who hated central banks and banks in general with as much fervor as Andrew Jackson or any other figure in American political history. Even before becoming Committee chairman, he took to the floor of the House, as he frequently did, to deliver a long harrangue against the Fed, calling it "the most awesome power in the history of mankind in any country, in any clime, in any time in the history of mankind, unaccountable to anybody except to itself. It does not account to the Congress because it says, if we do, we lose our independence, and you don't want the politicians handling your money, do you?" The Fed was not a federal agency at all, but "a system of the private commercial bankers," he alleged. "Everybody acts as if it were heaven sent." To describe the Fed chairman, he quoted John Adams's invidious reference to George Washington: "He thinks that he should be elected like the ancient Hebrews used to elect their kings, by their height, the tallest, but also he thinks he's heaven sent, booted, spurred and ready to ride on the hapless backs of mankind."

FOUR: An About-Face

1. Under the plan, the Resolution Trust Corporation (RTC) was to sell $17 billion of bonds per year to be defeased through purchase of zero coupon bonds. The plan was predicated on healthy S&Ls being able to pay increased deposit insurance premiums, but deposits were flowing out of the industry in a panic. That week the government took control of six more insolvent thrifts under President Bush's rescue plan, and the Federal Home Loan Bank Board (FHLBB) announced there had been $8.1 billion in net withdrawals from thrifts in December, a record to that point, with $3.4 billion coming from one large thrift that had been presumed healthy.

2. The Shadow Open Market Committee, a group of monetarists including later Cleveland Fed president Jerry Jordan, estimated the Fed had realized and unrealized losses of $5 billion on its foreign currency operations in the year ended in July.

3. Greenspan did not feel on completely solid ground in arguing against intervention. "Part of the problem is that analytically we have been projecting a declining exchange rate for quite awhile on the grounds that we've always perceived it as being out of sync and too high. And the failure [of the dollar] to do that has led us to temporize on this issue on the grounds that it would cure itself eventually. . . ."

4. Angell has not lost any of his fire as he thinks back on these events either. "Any central banker worth his salt knows that you have a monetary policy problem if you have a weak currency," he asserts. "Whatever was right policy domestically would also be right policy internationally. . . . The problem with exchange rate intervention is that you get a group at the Fed, either the Federal Reserve Bank of New York, at the desk, or the international division here [at the Board], and somebody comes into Treasury, like a Mulford or a Dallara, and you get people that want to play!" The Fed's involvement in exchange rate policy is "so important because the Fed is not willing to give up its independence by doing monetary policy for exchange rate purposes, because if the Fed does monetary policy for exchange rate purposes it has to ask the [Treasury] Secretary's permission. . . ."

5. By adding reserves (using five-day system repurchase agreements) when the funds rate was trading at 8⅛ percent (an eighth of a percent below the Fed's target), many people jumped to the conclusion the Fed was taking the funds rate down to 8¼. Even when the Fed stepped in to drain reserves on Friday, many persisted in the belief that the funds rate target was now 8¼. Indeed, many took Friday's draining of reserves (through matched sales) when funds were trading at 8¾₆ as confirmation of the lower target rate. Not until Monday was the Fed able to convince the markets that it still wanted the funds rate at 8½.

FIVE: *The Chickens Come Home to Roost*

1. In what looked like sweetheart deals, but were probably just born of desperation on the part of ill-starred Bank Board chairman Dan Wall, heavy hitters like Texas billionaire Robert M. Bass acquired billions of dollars in assets for a fraction of their value. With its insurance fund depleted, the Bank Board resorted to merging insolvent thrifts and selling them to the highest bidder using a scandalous variety of inducements. It attracted bidders for sick thrifts by giving them federal tax deductions and guaranteed returns on the assets they bought at fire sale prices. In a highly questionable procedure, it issued FSLIC notes, the proceeds of which it used primarily to subsidize purchase of S&Ls it had in receivership. Thus, in the sale of $30 billion American Savings and Loan Association of Stockton, California, to the Bass Group in September 1988, the Bank Board agreed to provide roughly $2 billion in assistance over ten years, including giving the Group a $500 million note which it could use as collateral to raise cash. Bass invested $550 million, for which he got a tax deduction and a guaranteed return.

2. Half of the capital, known as *tier one* capital, had to consist of common stock, retained earnings, and perpetual preferred stock. The other half (*tier two* capital) could consist of limited life preferred stock, subordinated debt, and loan loss reserves up to a set amount.

3. When he was Treasury secretary, "we actively met and worked hard to try and take coordinated action and mutually reinforcing action," Baker recalls. "Then, Alan

supported all that. I never recall any instances where he challenged that or questioned that. It was . . . during the Brady tenure at Treasury, that the Fed became . . . a little bit more reluctant to adopt an activist approach toward exchange rates because they felt it would restrict their freedom of movement in monetary policy. . . . I don't know why we got away from it in the Bush administration but we did. I guess it was because maybe the Fed decided they didn't want to do it anymore. . . . But I think that much of the instability that has resulted in the exchange rate since then is a consequence of not really working as hard as we should at international economic policy coordination." In reality, G-7 coordination faltered because "it was different people and a different era," says Dallara. Brady was "pretty much of a skeptic . . . on the whole process of policy coordination, which he viewed as largely a Baker invention." Moreover, "the favorable conditons for coordination which existed after the Plaza Accord were not quite as present in the late eighties and early nineties." For one thing, "the entire German decision-making apparatus became preoccupied with German unification, and then all of Europe became preoccupied with efforts to move toward European monetary union, and that made it much more difficult. . . ."

4. As he testified, the International Council of Shopping Centers held a press conference to complain that nearly half its members' recent loan applications had been turned down, that existing loans had been called or "modified unilaterally," that banks were taking longer to make loans and were charging higher fees. William Taylor, director of the Fed's Division of Banking Supervision and Regulation, said the Fed was "working to avoid regulatory actions that would prevent creditworthy borrowers from receiving loans" but said banks had "overreacted" to regulatory pressures.

5. Kohn suggested the Fed target a constant growth rate of nominal GNP and essentially let its two components—real growth and inflation—sort themselves out. "Focusing on nominal GNP imparts a self-correcting aspect to policy—that is, it limits the possibility of cumulating shortfalls in output or sustained acceleration in inflation." If the economy weakened and depressed prices, causing nominal GNP to fall, the Fed could ease policy, but if prices started to turn up, tending to push nominal GNP above the desired path, the Fed would automatically tighten. But, as Kohn freely acknowledged within the safe confines of the Fed boardroom, the Fed had never been willing to target nominal GNP in good part because of "the desire not to be accountable for an objective that is difficult to achieve." The idea went nowhere.

6. Nominally, the top tax rate was set at 31 percent—up from 28 percent for upper-income Americans, down from 33 percent for upper-middle-class taxpayers. In fact, due to curbs on itemized deductions and personal exemptions, the marginal rate for the "wealthy" (those earning over $100,000) could go a good bit higher than 31 percent under the new law. All Americans were hit with a variety of higher excise taxes. The capital gains tax rate was reduced from 33 to 28 percent. The supposed "spending cuts" amounted to little more than phantom reductions in previously authorized entitlement spending increases. Medicare spending was to grow $42.5 billion less than had been projected over five years. "Discretionary" spending on defense and other programs were to be subjected to binding "caps" over the next five years. Under the plan, the fiscal 1991 deficit was to be reduced by $41.4 billion, but that would still leave a projected record deficit of $254 billion—quite a contrast to the $64 billion deficit targeted by Gramm-Rudman and by Bush's initial fiscal 1991 budget.

7. The cut in reserve requirements was partially symbolic, since the Fed had decided to offset, through open market operations, much of the reserves thereby added. The reserve requirement on demand deposits (checking accounts and the like) was left at 12 percent, but only for the time being.

8. The Fed's decision may have been helped by the fact that the dollar had firmed modestly. From a low of around 127 yen per dollar, it had recovered to around 133 yen as the FOMC convened, compared to 160 yen in the spring. Just before the FOMC meeting, a senior Treasury official told me the dollar had reached "competitive" levels. He denied Treasury had been pursuing a policy of "benign neglect" but said recent administration statements of concern about the dollar did not signify an increased willingness to support it in return for further Fed easing.

9. Under a policy of reserve or money supply management, interest rates are allowed to find their own level, and when the central bank is increasing the money supply, there is a tendency in the short run for interest rates to fall, at least until inflation expectations build and push them up.

10. Kelley was talking to me on January 16, 1996, when the consensus forecast was for an extended period of slow growth.

SIX: "Fifty Mile per Hour Headwinds"

1. The administration was now forecasting real GNP growth of just 0.9 percent on a fourth quarter to fourth quarter basis with unemployment averaging 6.7 percent and CPI inflation of 4.3 percent.

2. Greenspan "devoted a great deal of effort to trying to defend the Fed's record, which is indefensible," remarked Robert Chandross, then chief economist of Lloyds Bank. "The question is why it took them so long to recognize what was going on and why they waited from July to the end of October to do something and why they did nothing before July." David Resler, chief economist for Nomura Securities International, asked, "Why did the Fed tolerate slow growth in the monetary aggregates for as long as it did? If the Fed wanted to get faster growth of the monetary aggregates it should have lowered the funds rate sooner. To say that slow money growth is not a consequence of monetary policy is just not true. It's a result of stated policy. Why deny it?" David Jones, chief economist for Aubrey G. Lanston & Company, said the Fed "didn't respond soon enough to the signals of slow money growth, economic slowdown and credit stringency. They didn't react aggressively until December. I would fault them for not seeing the signals clearly enough, not for causing it."

3. Through February 25, M2 had risen for six straight weeks and had grown at an annual rate of nearly 8 percent for the month. It seemed headed back toward the middle of the Fed's target range. But much of the increase was in currency in circulation and in nonbank money market funds, as opposed to transaction accounts at banks, not a sign of confidence in the banking system or of increased economic activity.

4. Short of compromising the Fed's independence, Fed loans to the FDIC would have complicated Fed operations, because to keep them from distorting the money supply, the Fed would have to drain reserves from the banking system through sales of government securities.

5. Noting "the persistence of high real interest rates and the slowing of economic activity in those countries which until recently had been experiencing strong expansion," the G-7 finance ministers and central bankers agreed on "the importance of monetary and fiscal policies which provide the basis for lower real interest rates and a sustained global economic recovery with price stability." The nations were to pursue these mom-and-apple-pie goals via a "medium-term strategy" with emphasis on "increasing global savings." In other words, nothing was going to be done anytime soon.

6. By contrast, Angell says, "Even Jim Baker didn't have as much of a financial background as Brady had, and yet Jim Baker was a very quick study and a quick learner. I mean, I could always sit down with Jim Baker and go over it with him and he could understand the pragmatic, the practical effects of what we were doing. . . ." Reflecting further, Angell admits, "I suppose we weren't very smart with Brady, and I was probably the worst of all." A former Brady aide says, "Baker, I think, under the same sort of cirumstances, would explode and demand and get probably at least part of what he was demanding. Because of his personality, Brady didn't do that. He wasn't that kind of man. His frustration wouldn't be expressed to his immediate staff." Darby, who served both Baker and Brady, puts it a different way. Baker would take the approach with Greenspan of 'let's reason together, and here's what I think is your job. Here's what I think and here's why.' And maybe Brady was less given to that approach." Dallara calls Baker "a dealmaker from the get-go . . . if he could cut a deal with somebody that he felt was in the interest that he was trying to pursue, he was not one to let personalities or ideology get in the way." Brady, on the other hand, "would sometimes get something in his craw, and he just wouldn't let go."

7. As always at the midyear FOMC meeting, the committee had to set tentative money supply target ranges for the following year. Here the committee was divided between those who wanted to keep the 1991 range of 2½ to 6½ percent M2 growth and those who wanted to lower the range. The majority voted to keep the 1991 ranges, but Angell and Black dissented. They wanted to lower the range to 2 to 6 percent to "provide a timely signal of the committee's continuing commitment to price stability, thereby reinforcing and extending the progress in curbing inflation anticipated over the next several quarters."

8. Bush made what is known as a *recess appointment* while Congress was not in session. Greenspan's term as chairman expired August 11, 1991, and his term as governor on January 31, 1992. Announced August 9, the recess appointment took effect August 10. Not until March 2, 1992 was Greenspan formally designated to a second four-year term, expiring March 2, 1996. He was also given another full 14-year term as a member of the Board of Governors, expiring January 31, 2006.

9. The Treasury made it easier and more attractive for banks and nonbanks to bypass the primary dealers and make direct competitive or noncompetitive bids. Non-primary dealers had been able to submit direct bids under the old rules, but nonbanks had to post a letter of credit equal to 5 pecent of the bid in order to do so. Moreover, large and presumably sophisticated institutional investors had preferred to go through primary dealers—partly because of the not unfounded belief that the primary dealers had inside information and partly because the antiquated system formerly in use discouraged them from making direct bids. Dealers phoned their bids to runners at the New York Fed, who then wrote down the bids and placed them in bid boxes at the last possible second. The more technologically advanced system since introduced has made nonprimary dealers more willing to submit competitve bids directly, bypassing the elite primary dealers club.

10. Angell argued the Fed was inviting a rise in inflationary expectations and long-term interest rates, which would undermine growth. To maintain its credibility in the financial markets, the Fed had to demonstrate its commitment to price stability. Then long rates would come down and spur recovery more than if the Fed cut short rates. Kelley, who had voted for the discount rate cut, was against cutting the funds rate and positioning the Fed for more rate cuts because he believed "a steady policy" was in order. He thought "the outlook for continuing expansion in economic activity remained favorable, and he saw considerable risks in further easing at this time." Cut-

ting short rates would not effectively counter Greenspan's "headwinds," could counterproductively raise long rates, and could put the dollar under downward pressure, thus worsening inflation.

11. For one thing, Greenspan said, banks and thrifts with impaired capital positions had sought to limit asset growth and in the process had reduced their demand for deposits and other liabilities. The consolidation of the banking and thrift industries had also been "depressing" M2. "Perhaps it is not too surprising that when bank or thrift institutions merge or when one institution's deposits are assumed by another, the resulting entity will have lower asset totals, and therefore will require lower liabilities than the sum of the two original institutions." What's more, some bank customers had been using deposit balances to pay down consumer credit obligations or were moving out of bank deposits altogether into such vehicles as mutual funds, a trend accelerated by the decline in deposit interest rates. Yet another explanation was that businesses had been borrowing in the securities markets or elsewhere instead of from banks, with the result that new deposits were not being created to fund the loans.

12. Boskin was appearing jointly with Brady and Darman to testify belatedly on a "growth package" proposed by House Republicans before Thanksgiving. The package contained a capital gains tax cut and other measures to stimulate the economy. Boskin, a leading expert on tax policy before joining the Bush administration, endorsed cutting the capital gains tax. He said it would increase the value of assets and thereby induce more spending and investment, producing no revenue losses and possibly gains. "Responsible stimulative policies can be enacted in a context of fiscal discipline." But Brady and Darman gave the package only very lukewarm support, warning against measures that would widen the deficit and push up long-term interest rates. The best Brady could say about the package Gingrich and other House Republicans had crafted was that it "showed the way to the answer." Nothing was done. The package was shelved until 1992, when it would get even shorter shrift from Democrats, who were happy to see the Bush presidency sink into an economic morass.

13. The administration was seriously considering a $300 tax rebate for each taxpayer. Greenspan implied that was a bad idea, but lent support to cutting the capital gains tax. Any tax cuts should be "revenue neutral," he said.

14. Greenspan's defense of his gradualist monetary tactics before the Ways and Means Committee led some at the time to believe Greenspan had been reluctant to back the 1 percent discount rate cut, but sources say this was not the case. As one put it, "Greenspan was not dragged kicking and screaming." As for whose idea the 1 percent discount rate cut was, one FOMC member describes it as one of those ideas that "just kind of percolate up, and it's very hard to say that on a given day that a given individual came up with this idea and it went on from there. I don't think that's usually possible. I don't think that's how it happens. It just kind of generates over time. . . . You find out that a lot of people were getting the same notions at about the same time and you kind of become aware of each other's thinking, then find out that they were kind of running along parallel before they were expressed openly. That happens all the time. Somebody will say something and you'll say, 'Yeah! yeah, I've been thinking that too!' "

SEVEN: The End of a Recession and a Presidency

1. A Fed study, prepared in December 1991 to deflect accusations that the Fed had been supplying insufficient reserves, found that "weakness in broad monetary aggregates that is attributable to depository closings . . . appears to result mainly from the tendency of depositories to downsize their balance sheets following a closing, implying

not only runoffs of managed liabilities, but also an exodus from the monetary aggregates of retail deposits of closed institutions that earn much reduced rates of interest following transfer to an acquirer." Paul Kasriel, chief economist of Chicago's Northern Trust Company, and Chicago Fed economist Robert Laurent argued that was only part of the story. They maintained that as bank and thrift deposits fell, causing a drop in M2, an excess of bank reserves resulted, since banks no longer had as many transaction accounts to reserve against. To keep these excess reserves from depressing the funds rate below the Fed's target, the Fed had drained reserves to keep the funds rate from falling, resulting in an inadvertent tightening of reserve pressures that cramped economic activity.

2. Reiterating, the P* model purported to show the long-run equilibrium price level (P*) implied by recent levels of M2 growth at a constant rate of velocity and real GDP growth at potential.

3. Lindsey on this occasion sounded like anything but the automatic rate cutter he had been stereotyped as. Though "slow," the economy was doing "remarkably well," under the circumstances, he said. "The economy has had a lot of problems to resolve. If I had said to you in 1989 that we were going to have the kind of banking problems we've had, that we were going to fight a war in the Persian Gulf, that we were going to see [stock values on] the Tokyo market cut in half, that we were going to have a fiscal contraction and that the money supply was going to slow down like it has, we'd be talking about whether unemployment was going to be 15 percent or 20 percent."

EIGHT: *Working with a Democratic President*

1. The former official was interviewed in early October 1995, four months before President Clinton announced his intention to reappoint Greenspan.

2. Clinton's plan included an energy or BTU tax; a rise in marginal tax rate from 31 to 36 percent for family incomes over $140,000 and to 39.6 percent for incomes above $250,000; higher business taxes; and taxing 85 percent of the Social Security benefits paid to upper-income elderly instead of 50 percent. This last was counted as a "spending cut." Also counted as a "spending cut" were $16.5 billion in lower debt servicing costs predicated on greater reliance on short-term Treasury borrowing. It contained $160 billion in increased social spending, labeled "investments."

3. Covering that Senate Banking Committee hearing had also been quite a challenge for wire service reporters, who first had to rapidly sift through and file stories on a fat stack of lengthy formal remarks by the 12 presidents, then run and file on their responses to questions, while trying to keep straight who had said what when all we had, aside from the backs of their heads, was our hastily scrawled seating charts and our familiarity with their voices. It was not something one wanted to do every day of the week.

4. Subsequently, on April 1, Congress approved a budget resolution that would reduce the deficit by $496 billion over five years. In early March, the Congressional Budget Office had estimated Clinton's budget plan would reduce the deficit $61.4 billion less than he had projected, prompting the House and Senate Budget Committees to add roughly $60 billion in additional taxes and spending restraints, most of which were then dropped from the final budget resolution. Once this budget "blueprint" was passed, the House and Senate began work on a budget "reconciliation" bill to transform the goals of the budget resolution into actual tax and spending policies.

5. The House had passed a budget May 27 designed to cut the deficit by $496 billion. It included a BTU tax designed to raise $71.5 billion. By contrast, the Senate bill

contained a 4.3¢ increase in the federal gas tax. The two versions now had to go to a House-Senate conference committee to resolve differences with the House-passed bill.

6. Treasury was forced to change its debt management strategy May 1, 1996, lengthening the average maturity of the debt by moving to sales of 10-year notes six times a year instead of four and to sales of 30-year bonds three times a year instead of two. On May 16, 1996, Treasury did what the Fed had long advocated and launched inflation indexed bonds, but not to give the Fed a barometer of inflationary expectations. Its goal was to save borrowing costs and to entice more individual investors to participate in Treasury auctions.

7. Treasury Secretary Lloyd Bentsen had in February set off a precipitous drop in the value of the dollar that was to continue throughout the first two and a half years of the Clinton administration and complicate the Fed's task of maintaining the dollar's purchasing power. This is explored in depth later in chapter 8.

8. The final budget raised the top tax bracket from 31 to 36 percent, and imposed a surtax on upper-income Americans that took the effective marginal rate to 39.6 percent, retroactive to January 1. The gasoline tax was raised 4.3¢ per gallon. It also increased corporate taxes, Medicare payroll taxes, and taxes on Social Security benefits and reduced or eliminated a number of deductions. The $255 billion in projected "spending cuts" included a $65 billion lower interest cost assumption. Medicare spending was to rise $56 billion less. Most of the other "spending cuts" came in defense. The deficit was projected to be $213 billion at the end of the fifth year.

9. It must be stipulated here that the deficit has come down more than expected. In fiscal 1995, the deficit came in at $163.9 billion and, at this writing, was projected to be $117 billion in 1996, but this deficit reduction has had less to do with the 1993 budget deal than with other factors: economic recovery, lower interest costs owing primarily to the Fed's success in holding down inflation, the transition from net RTC spending to net RTC inflows, and, following the 1994 election, the continuation of spending at 1995 levels due to the budget stalemate between the Republican Congress and the White House.

10. On December 1, Gonzalez released a report showing that women and minorities were greatly underrepresented at the upper echelons of the Federal Reserve system, and he demanded that the Fed take "immediate action" to increase hiring and career advancement of women and minorities. "Women and minorities at the Federal Reserve are almost completely excluded from high salaries and promotions," Gonzalez declared. ". . . the Federal Reserve Banks are merely paying lip service to the concepts of equal employment opportunity and affirmative action." The Banking Committee report found that the top ten highest paid employees at the Federal Reserve Board were all white males, and of the highest 10 percent paid employees, minorities accounted for 6.2 percent and women 17.6 percent. Of the lowest paid 10 percent of employees, 6.67 percent were women and 91.2 percent were minorities. Greenspan had already told Gonzalez at the October 13 hearing that he had seen advancement of women and minorities as "one area in which I see a major need for change" and said he was already "working diligently to improve opportunities for women and minorities throughout the system." Gonzalez was also taking aim at the Fed's allegedly extravagant spending on entertainment and at alleged acceptance of expensive gifts and meals from private bankers.

11. Three days earlier, Clinton held a luncheon for a group of reporters at Blair House and told the late Hobart Rowen of the *Washington Post* a Fed rate hike "would be a big mistake." And he again hedged when presented with the opportunity to clearly place himself in opposition to the various Fed reform bills making their way through

Congress. Although "our administration has made it clear that we were not working for the legislation," Clinton said he was "deeply sympathetic with the objectives of Senator Sarbanes and Congressman Gonzalez. . . ."

12. In an unrelated development on December 14, the Fed complied with an earlier congressional action curtailing its policy flexibility, by adopting new rules to limit discount window advances to troubled banks to comply with FDICIA. The Act made the Fed liable for losses to the Bank Insurance Fund when a bank forestalls failure by borrowing from the Fed, then fails anyway. As of December 19, when the Fed lent to a nonviable, undercapitalized bank that had borrowed at least 60 out of 120 days or if it lent to a critically undercapitalized bank five days after getting such a rating, the Fed would become liable for losses to the BIF caused by the advances.

13. There was a certain amount of overlap and double-counting in these Japanese fiscal packages, but the sum total drove Japan from budget surplus into deficit. It could be argued the United States pulled Japan down to its level of fiscal recklessness.

14. The Bundesbank, on September 9, had cut its discount and Lombard rates 50 basis points to 5.75 and 6.75 percent respectively. The Bundesbank lowered rates six times in 1993, a total of 2.75 percent for the Lombard rate, as the German economy sank into recession. As a result, the dollar remained fairly strong against the mark until 1994.

15. All of this Japan bashing ignored the fact that the actual volume of Japanese imports had risen and its exports fallen, but because Japan's trade was expressed in terms of dollars rather than yen and because the yen had strengthened so much against the dollar, the Japanese surplus when converted into dollars looked larger.

NINE: *A Preemptive Strike*

1. Indeed, in its midsession review of the fiscal 1994 budget, released the previous September, the administration had forecast the three-month Treasury bill rate would rise from 3.1 percent in 1993, to 3.6 percent in 1994, followed by further rises to 3.9 percent in 1995, 4.2 percent in 1996, and 4.5 percent in 1997.

2. Effective in early 1997, it voted to keep the system open to settle transactions among banks from 12:30 A.M. to 6:30 P.M. EDT, instead of 8:30 A.M. to 6:30 P.M. Although the world's financial system seemed relatively stable at the time, the Fed was conscious of the explosion of ever-more-complex international transactions. Markets had become truly global, with so-called *hedge funds* and other institutional investors moving money rapidly in and out of different currency instruments. The breakdown of the EMS was a reminder of how deceptive market tranquility could be. The Fed lived not necessarily in fear but in healthy respect for Herstatt Risk. When a German bank of that name failed in 1974, its foreign exchange counterparties had made deutsche mark payments to the bank to settle foreign exchange contracts, but did not receive payments in dollars before the bank closed at the end of the German banking day, causing a damaging ripple effect throughout the financial system. Since 1974, settlement of foreign exchange transactions across borders had not basically changed, but their volume had grown exponentially, and the Fed staff advised the Board that the risk that a settlement failure could trigger a financial crisis had risen commensurately. "In the case of yen-dollar foreign exchange contracts, the yen amounts due on a particular banking day would be paid and settled in Tokyo before the start of that banking day in New York. U.S. dollar contra-payments would be initiated early in the U.S. banking day and settled with finality at the end of the U.S. banking day, some 18 hours after the close of business in Tokyo. Similarly, payments in most European currencies would be made

and settled hours before U.S. dollar payments are either initiated or settled with final-ity." Fed staffer Bruce Summers said extending Fedwire hours was "a necessary, though not sufficient condition" for reducing the risk that one or more banks could fail if the full principal amount of a foreign exchange contract was lost because of inability to get timely payment.

3. The budget assumed passage of Hillary's doomed health care "reform" would save $58 billion over five years. The CBO said the plan would raise the deficit at least $74 billion.

4. Not until the February 1, 1995, FOMC meeting, would the Fed formalize its procedure of announcing policy changes the day they were made and of releasing tran-scripts of meetings with a five-year lag.

5. She later issued a retraction.

6. The finance ministers and central bankers agreed the latter would be given a larger role in the G-7 process, but it was never clear just what this meant. Blinder said, "It just means we'll talk to each other more."

TEN: *Coping with a Peso Crisis and a Fiscal Fiasco*

1. Greenspan, in January 26, 1995, testimony, said it had become "increasingly clear to many observers during the autumn [1994] that the prevailing level of Mexico's exchange rate could not be sustained short of a significant further tightening of mone-tary policy. . . ." Writing in the March 1996 Federal Reserve Bulletin, Truman says that after mid-1994, "It became clear that the outstanding stock of tesobonos was larger than Mexico's foreign exchange holdings." In the same article, Truman acknowledges that private investors, who "did in fact understand what was happening in Mexico in 1994," nevertheless "benefitted from the actions [to bail out Mexico] taken to stave off a larger crisis."

2. Under the "Taylor rule," the Fed should be willing to hold the real federal funds rate (the nominal rate minus inflation) unchanged or even lower it if economic growth falls short of potential or unemployment rises more than desired. Taylor postulated that at 2 percent the real funds rate would be "neutral" (neither restrictive nor stimula-tive) and that the Fed should adjust the real funds rate above this neutral level by an amount which depends on the deviation between actual and potential output and the deviation between actual and target inflation. If there is no gap between actual and potential growth and no gap between actual and target inflation, which Taylor assumed to be 2 percent, the Fed would hold the real funds rate at 2 for the last four quarters, or a nominal funds rate of 4 percent. However, if real output were to rise above potential or inflation were to rise above target, the Fed would move the real funds rate up by half of whatever the resulting gaps were, so that if actual growth increased to 1 percent above potential, the Fed would raise the real funds rate a half percent. It would do the same if inflation rose 1 percent above target. But if actual output fell below potential output, the Fed would adjust the real funds rate down by a similar amount, even if infla-tion were above target. Yellen, in a March 13, 1996, speech, said adhering to the Tay-lor rule should give the Fed "credibility in the public's mind for its anti-inflationary resolve" while at the same time maintaining the Fed's latitude to counteract dips in employment and real output. The rule "could help the Federal Reserve communicate to the public the rationale behind policy moves and how those moves are consistent with its objectives. For example, if inflation were at its long-run target and output were below its potential, the Fed might well choose to adopt an easier-than-average stance of policy. Making reference to the Taylor rule or some similar framework might help

the Fed communicate that such a stance was consistent with its long-run inflation objective." Yellen said the Taylor rule is "a positive description of how policy actually has been conducted over the past decade or so." The major exceptions have been in the 1992–1993 period, when the Fed held the nominal funds rate at 3 percent and the real rate near zero to counteract "50 mile per hour headwinds" and the 1987 stock market crash, when the Fed provided emergency liquidity that pushed the funds rate lower, even though inflation was accelerating. "With the Greenspan Fed's policies often approximating the predictions of the Taylor rule, the American economy has enjoyed a period of remarkably good economic performance. Progress has been made toward price stability, although the business cycle has not been fully conquered." The rule is a "useful benchmark" for assessing the setting of policy and "can warn against any tendency for the Federal Reserve to go too far in tightening or easing policy or to overstay a tight or easy stance longer than desirable."

3. There are thousands of permutations, especially when one gets into cross-currency swaps, but to take a simple "plain vanilla" example, a party which is borrowing at variable interest rates and is therefore vulnerable to rising rates may enter into a mutually beneficial swap with a counterparty which has borrowed at fixed rates. They simply exchange variable for fixed payment flows.

4. It was the beginning of a process which Yellen described better than I can in an April 17, 1996, interview: "Most of 1995 has been about the economy being weighted down to a pace of growth which has been below what I think growth potential is because of the decline in inventory investment. The level of inventory investment depends on how fast the economy is growing, how fast sales are growing. When sales begin to grow more slowly, the level of inventory investment needs to drop off. While it's dropping off from a high level to a lower level it is a drag on the growth rate of the economy, and you end up with a period in which GDP is growing less quickly than final sales. That's exactly what 1995 was about. 1994 was a year in which the growth of the economy was greater than the growth of final sales because inventory investment was rising. 1995 was a year in which GDP growth was below the growth rate of final sales because inventory investment was coming down."

5. The merchandise trade deficit (goods only on a balance of payments basis) was initially reported as $17.19 billion for January 1995. This was later revised down to $16.01 billion. The new record was set in May 1996 of $16.79 billion.

6. Greenspan was drawing on research by economists Laurence Ball and Gregory Mankiw.

7. After going through 13 short-term spending measures, Congress and the White House compromised on a $163 billion bill that completed action on the fiscal 1996 budget in late April 1996. The budget reduced discretionary spending $23 billion from 1995 levels. This was on top of a net $11 billion in previously approved fiscal 1995 spending which Congress rescinded the previous spring. Because of the two government shutdowns and the fact that the government was funded at fiscal 1995 levels through its first seven months, the fiscal 1996 budget deficit was projected at midyear to come in as low as $117 billion, nearly $47 billion less than the fiscal 1995 deficit and $83 billion less than Clinton had proposed. However, as this was written, no agreement had been reached on the overarching issue of balancing the budget over the longer term. The Clinton administration presented a budget on March 19, 1996, using optimistic OMB economic assumptions purporting to show the budget reaching balance in six years and surplus in the seventh year, but 60 percent of the proposed reductions in spending growth would be delayed until after the year 2000. Under more realistic CBO assumptions, the deficit would be a cumulative $300 billion more than the admin-

istration projected. On June 13, 1996, the Senate followed the House in passing a Republican-drafted 1997 budget resolution that called for balancing the budget in six years while providing a $122 billion tax cut. Once again, the administration and congressional Democrats derided it as "extremist" because of its proposed reductions in the rate of growth of Medicare and other domestic spending programs. While both Republicans and Democrats continued to talk about their desire for a balanced budget deal, the two sides remained far apart as the 1996 election drew nigh.

8. The Labor Department reported on March 8 that nonfarm payrolls had risen 705,000 (later revised to 631,000). It was the first of a series of strong economic numbers, accompanied by a rise in the price of oil to over $22 per barrel, that helped push the long bond yield above 7 percent. According to the Commerce Department's initial estimate, real GDP grew 2.8 percent in the first quarter. Second-quarter GDP growth was also expected to be near 3 percent, but at this writing, the Fed was expecting a return to noninflationary trend growth in the 2 to 2½ percent range, enabling it to avoid raising interest rates.

9. In his February 20, 1996, Humphrey-Hawkins testimony, Greenspan went further than he ever had in stressing that the Fed does not have a real growth ceiling and in allowing for the possibility that the economy might be able to grow faster than the presumed 2 to 2.5 percent. He said the Fed would "welcome" faster growth. He said productivity gains may increase the economy's growth potential, although he added, "We must be cautious in reaching conclusions that growth in productivity and hence of potential output has as yet risen. . . ." He said the Fed uses a notion of the economy's noninflationary growth potential only as a short-term policy guide, not as an absolute, long-term limit on growth. I asked Phillips on May 13, 1996, whether the high-profile attention the president and the CEA had given to the economy's ability to grow and the role of monetary policy had made Fed policymakers more self-conscious about growth or more inclined not to appear to be putting a ceiling on growth. "I don't think it directly affected the Fed," she responded. ". . . I don't think we've changed our modus operandi. I hope we're expressing it better."

10. His term as governor was no impediment to his tenure since it does not expire until January 31, 2006.

Index